ABOUT THE AUTHOR

Chris Barsanti is the author of *Filmology: A Movie-a-Day Guide to the Movies You Need to Know* (2010) and the *Eyes Wlde Open* annual film guide series. A member of New York Film Critics Online and the Online Film Critics Society, he is a regular film reviewer for *Film Journal International, PopMatters*, and *Film Racket*. He has also written for numerous other publlcations, including *The Barnes & Noble Review, The Chicago Tribune, Playboy, Publishers Weekly, The Millions, The Virginia Quarterly Review*, and *The Chicago Reader*. Barsanti earned his master's degree in journalism from Northwestern University and works in publishing. He cried the first time he saw *Star Trek II: The Wrath of Khan* and thinks anybody who didn't has a heart of stone. He resides in New York.

ALSO FROM VISIBLE INK PRESS

Alien Mysteries, Conspiracies and Cover-Ups
by Kevin D. Randle
ISBN: 978-1-57859-418-4

Conspiracies and Secret Societies: The Complete Dossier, 2nd edition
by Brad Steiger and Sherry Hansen Steiger
ISBN: 978-1-57859-368-2

The Government UFO Files: The Conspiracy of Cover-Up
by Kevin D. Randle
ISBN: 978-1-57859-477-1

Hidden Realms, Lost Civilizations, and Beings from Other Worlds
by Jerome Clark
ISBN: 978-1-57859-175-6

The Horror Show Guide: The Ultimate Frightfest of Movies
by Mike Mayo
ISBN: 978-1-57859-420-7

Real Aliens, Space Beings, and Creatures from Other Worlds
by Brad Steiger and Sherry Hansen Steiger
ISBN: 978-1-57859-333-0

Real Encounters, Different Dimensions, and Otherworldly Beings
by Brad Steiger and Sherry Hansen Steiger
ISBN: 978-1-57859-455-9

Real Ghosts, Restless Spirits, and Haunted Places, 2nd edition
by Brad Steiger
ISBN: 978-1-57859-401-6

Real Miracles, Divine Intervention, and Feats of Incredible Survival
by Brad Steiger and Sherry Hansen Steiger
ISBN: 978-1-57859-214-2

Real Monsters, Gruesome Critters, and Beasts from the Darkside
by Brad Steiger
ISBN: 978-1-57859-220-3

Real Vampires, Night Stalkers, and Creatures from the Darkside
by Brad Steiger
ISBN: 978-1-57859-255-5

Real Zombies, the Living Dead, and Creatures of the Apocalypse
by Brad Steiger
ISBN: 978-1-57859-296-8

The Superhero Book: The Ultimate Encyclopedia of Comic-Book Icons and Hollywood Heroes
by Gina Misiroglu
ISBN: 9781578593750

The Supervillain Book: The Evil Side of Comics and Hollywood
by Gina Misiroglu and Michael Eury
ISBN: 9781578591787

Unexplained! Strange Sightings, Incredible Occurrences, and Puzzling Physical Phenomena, 3rd edition
by Jerome Clark
ISBN: 978-1-57859-344-6

The Vampire Book: The Encyclopedia of the Undead, 3rd edition
by J. Gordon Melton, Ph.D.
ISBN: 978-1-57859-281-4

The Werewolf Book: The Encyclopedia of Shape-shifting Beings, 2nd edition
by Brad Steiger
ISBN: 978-1-57859-367-5

The Witch Book: The Encyclopedia of Witchcraft, Wicca, and Neo-paganism
by Raymond Buckland
ISBN: 978-1-57859-114-5

The Zombie Book: The Encyclopedia of the Living Dead
by Nick Redfern with Brad Steiger
ISBN: 978-1-57859-504-4

"Real Nightmares" E-Books by Brad Steiger

Real Nightmares: True and Truly Scary Unexplained Phenomena (Book 1)
Kindle ISBN: 978-1-57859-398-9
ePub ISBN: 978-1-57859-400-9
PDF ISBN: 978-1-57859-399-6

Real Nightmares: True Unexplained Phenomena and Tales of the Unknown (Book 2)
Kindle ISBN: 978-1-57859-402-3
ePub ISBN: 978-1-57859-403-0
PDF ISBN: 978-1-57859-404-7

Real Nightmares: Things That Go Bump in the Night (Book 3)
Kindle ISBN: 978-1-57859-405-4
ePub ISBN: 978-1-57859-406-1
PDF ISBN: 978-1-57859-407-8

Real Nightmares: Things That Prowl and Growl in the Night (Book 4)
Kindle ISBN: 978-1-57859-408-5
ePub ISBN: 978-1-57859-409-2
PDF ISBN: 978-1-57859-410-8

Real Nightmares: Fiends That Want Your Blood (Book 5)
Kindle ISBN: 978-1-57859-411-5
ePub ISBN: 978-1-57859-412-2
PDF ISBN: 978-1-57859-413-9

Real Nightmares: Unexpected Visitors and Unwanted Guests (Book 6)
Kindle ISBN: 978-1-57859-414-6
ePub ISBN: 978-1-57859-415-3
PDF ISBN: 978-1-57859-416-0

Real Nightmares: Dark and Deadly Demons (Book 7)
Kindle ISBN: 978-1-57859-436-8
ePub ISBN: 978-1-57859-435-1
PDF ISBN: 978-1-57859-434-4

Real Nightmares: Phantoms, Apparitions and Ghosts (Book 8)
Kindle ISBN: 978-1-57859-439-9
ePub ISBN: 978-1-57859-438-2
PDF ISBN: 978-1-57859-437-5

Real Nightmares: Alien Strangers and Foreign Worlds (Book 9)
Kindle ISBN: 978-1-57859-442-9
ePub ISBN: 978-1-57859-441-2
PDF ISBN: 978-1-57859-440-5

Real Nightmares: Ghastly and Grisly Spooks (Book 10)
Kindle ISBN: 978-1-57859-445-0
ePub ISBN: 978-1-57859-444-3
PDF ISBN: 978-1-57859-443-6

Real Nightmares: Secret Schemes and Conspiring Cabals (Book 11)
Kindle ISBN: 978-1-57859-448-1
ePub ISBN: 978-1-57859-447-4
PDF ISBN: 978-1-57859-446-7

Real Nightmares: Freaks, Fiends and Evil Spirits (Book 12)
Kindle ISBN: 978-1-57859-451-1
ePub ISBN: 978-1-57859-450-4
PDF ISBN: 978-1-57859-449-8

Please visit us at visibleinkpress.com.

THE SCI-FI MOVIE GUIDE

The Universe of Film from *Alien* to *Zardoz*

CHRIS BARSANTI

VISIBLE
INK
PRESS

Detroit

THE SCI-FI MOVIE GUIDE:
The Universe of Film from "Alien" to "Zardoz"

Visible Ink Press®
43311 Joy Rd., #414
Canton, MI 48187-2075

Visible Ink Press is a registered trademark of Visible Ink Press LLC.

Most Visible Ink Press books are available at special quantity discounts when purchased in bulk by corporations, organizations, or groups. Customized printings, special imprints, messages, and excerpts can be produced to meet your needs. For more information, contact Special Markets Director, Visible Ink Press, www.visibleink.com, or 734-667-3211.

Managing Editor: Kevin S. Hile
Art Director: Mary Claire Krzewinski
Typesetting: Marco Di Vita
Proofreaders: Larry Baker and Dorothy Scott
Indexer: Shoshana Hurwitz

Cover images: Kobal Picture Library images include: *Terminator, Blade Runner, Brazil, A Clockwork Orange, The Matrix, Star Wars: A New Hope, Godzilla, Tron, Metropolis, Close Encounters of the Third Kind, X-Men,* and *Avatar. The Day the Earth Stood Still* and *Forbidden Planet* images are in the public domain.

ISBN: 978-1-57859-503-7 (paperback)
ISBN: 978-1-57859-533-4 (pdf ebook)
ISBN: 978-1-57859-535-8 (Kindle ebook)
ISBN: 978-1-57859-534-1 (ePub ebook)

10 9 8 7 6 5 4 3 2 1

Library of Congress Cataloging-in-Publication Data

Barsanti, Chris.
   The science fiction movie guide : the universe of film from
Alien to Zardoz / by Chris Barsanti.
      pages cm
   Includes bibliographical references.
   ISBN 978-1-57859-503-7 (pbk. : alk. paper)
 1. Science fiction films—Catalogs. I. Title.
   PN1995.9.S26B275 2014
   016.79143'615—dc23   2014017822

CONTENTS

A *1*

Abbott and Costello Go to Mars ... Abbott and Costello Meet the Invisible Man ... The Abominable Dr. Phlbes ... Abraxas: Guardian of the Universe ... The Absent-Minded Professor ... The Abyss ... The Adjustment Bureau ... The Adventures of Buckaroo Banzai Across the Eighth Dimension ... The Adventures of Pluto Nash ... Aelita: Queen of Mars ... Aeon Flux ... After Earth ... Aftershock ... A.I. Artificial Intelligence .,. Akira ... Alien ... Alien³ ... Alien Contamination ... Alien Dead ... The Alien Factor ... Alien from L.A. ... Alien Nation ... Alien: Resurrection ... Aliens ... Alien vs. Predator: Requiem ... Alligator ... Alphaville ... Altered States ... The Amazing Colossal Man ... The Amazing Spider-Man ... The Amazing Transparent Man ... The Amphibian Man ... Android ... The Andromeda Strain ... The Angry Red Planet ... The Animatrix ... Another Earth ... The Ape Man ... Apollo 18 ... The Apple ... Appleseed ... Armageddon ... Around the World under the Sea ... The Arrival ... The Asphyx ... The Astounding She-Monster ... The Astronaut's Wife ... The Astro-Zombies ... Atlas Shrugged: Part I ... Atlas Shrugged: Part II ... The Atomic Brain ... The Atomic Submarine ... Attack of the 50 Foot Woman (1958) ... Attack of the 50 Ft. Woman (1993) ... Attack of the Killer Tomatoes ... Attack the Block ... The Aurora Encounter ... Avatar ... The Avengers ... AVP: Allen vs. Predator

B *31*

Babylon A.D. ... Back to the Future ... Back to the Future, Part 2 ... Back to the Future, Part 3 ... Bad Taste .,. The Bamboo Saucer ... Barbarella ... Barb Wire ... *batteries not included ... Battle Beneath the Earth ... Battle Beyond the Stars ... Battle Beyond the Sun ... Battlefield Earth ... Battle for Moon Station Dallos ... Battle for the Planet of the Apes ... Battle: Los Angeles ... Battle Royale ... Battleship ... The Beast from 20,000 Fathoms ... Beastmaster 2: Through the Portal of Time ... The Beast of Yucca Flats ... The Bed-Sitting Room ... Beginning of the End ... Beneath the Planet of the Apes ... Beyond the Stars ... Beyond the Time Barrier ... Bicentennial Man ... Biggles ... Bill & Ted's Bogus Journey ... Bill & Ted's Excellent Adventure ... The Birds ... The Black Hole ... Blade Runner ... Blindness ... The Blob (1958) ... The Blob (1988) ... The Blood of Heroes ... Blue Thunder ... Body Snatchers ... The Book of Eli ... Boom in the Moon ... Born in Flames ... The Borrower ... Bounty Killer ... The Box ... A Boy and His Dog ... The Boys from Brazil ... The Brain Eaters ... Brainstorm ... The Brain That Wouldn't Die ... Brazil ... The Bride of Frankenstein ... Bride of the Monster ... The Brides of Fu Manchu ... The Brood ... The Brother from Another Planet ... Buck Rogers Conquers the Universe ... Buck Rogers in the 25th Century ... Bug ... The Butterfly Effect

C............61

The Cabin in the Woods ... Capricorn One ... Captain America ... Captain America: The First Avenger ... Captain America: The Winter Soldier ... Carnosaur ... The Castle of Fu Manchu ... The Cat from Outer Space ... Cat-Women of the Moon ... The Cell ... Charly ... Cherry 2000 ... Children of Men ... Children of the Damned ... The China Syndrome ... Chopping Mall ... Chronicle ... The Chronicles of Riddick ... Chronopolis ... Circuitry Man ... City Limits ... City of Ember ... The City of Lost Children ... Class of 1999 ... Class of Nuke 'Em High ... A Clockwork Orange ... The Clonus Horror ... Close Encounters of the Third Kind ... Cloud Atlas ... Cloverfield ... Club Extinction ... Cocoon ... Cocoon: The Return ... Code 46 ... Cold Souls ... Colossus: The Forbin Project ... Communion ... Computer Chess ... The Computer Wore Tennis Shoes ... Coneheads ... Conquest of Space ... Conquest of the Planet of the Apes ... Contact ... Contagion ... The Cosmic Monsters ... Cosmopolis ... Cowboy Bebop: The Movie ... Cowboys & Aliens ... CQ ... The Crawling Eye ... The Crazies (1973) ... The Crazies (2010) ... The Creation of the Humanoids ... Creature ... Creature from the Black Lagoon ... The Creature Walks among Us ... Creepozoids ... Critters ... The Curse of Frankenstein ... Cyborg

D............89

Dagora, the Space Monster ... Daleks—Invasion Earth: 2150 A.D. ... Damnation Alley ... Danger: Diabolik ... Dark City ... The Darkest Hour ... Darkman ... Dark Skies ... Dark Star ... D.A.R.Y.L. ... The Day After ... The Day After Tomorrow ... Daybreakers ... The Day of the Triffids ... The Day the Earth Caught Fire ... The Day the Earth Stood Still (1951) ... The Day the Earth Stood Still (2008) ... The Day the World Ended ... Dead End Drive-In ... The Deadly Mantis ... Deadly Weapon ... Dead Weekend ... Death Race ... Death Race 2000 ... Death Sport ... Death Watch ... Deep Impact ... Deepstar Six ... DefCon 4 ... Déjà Vu ... Delicatessen ... Demolition Man ... Demon City Shinjuku ... Demon Seed ... Destination Moon ... Destroy All Monsters ... Destroy All Planets ... Devil Girl from Mars ... Die, Monster, Die! ... District 9 ... District 13 ... Divergent ... Doc Savage: The Man of Bronze ... Doctor Satan's Robot ... Doctor Who and the Daleks ... Doctor X ... Donnie Darko ... Donovan's Brain ... Doom ... Doomsday ... Dr. Cyclops ... Dreamcatcher ... Dreamscape ... Dredd ... Dr. Goldfoot and the Bikini Machine ... Dr.

Strangelove; or, How I Learned to Stop Worrying and Love the Bomb ... Dune ... Dust Devil

E............117

Earth Girls Are Easy ... Earth vs. the Flying Saucers ... Edward Scissorhands ... Electric Dreams ... The Electronic Monster ... The Element of Crime ... Elysium ... Embryo ... Empire of the Ants ... Ender's Game ... Enemy Mine ... Equilibrium ... Escape from L.A. ... Escape from New York ... Escape from Planet Earth ... Escape from Safehaven ... Escape from the Planet of the Apes ... E.T.: The Extra-Terrestrial ... Eternal Sunshine of the Spotless Mind ... Europa Report ... Event Horizon ... Eve of Destruction ... The Evil of Frankenstein ... Evolution ... eXistenZ ... Explorers

F............129

Face/Off ... The Face of Fu Manchu ... The Faculty ... Fahrenheit 451 ... Fail-Safe ... Fantastic Four ... Fantastic 4: Rise of the Silver Surfer ... Fantastic Planet ... Fantastic Voyage ... The Fifth Element ... Final ... Final Approach ... The Final Countdown ... The Final Cut ... Final Fantasy: The Spirits Within ... The Final Programme ... Fire in the Sky ... Fire Maidens of Outer Space ... First Man into Space ... First Men in the Moon ... First Spaceship on Venus ... Five ... Flash Gordon ... Flash Gordon Conquers the Universe ... Flash Gordon: Mars Attacks the World ... Flash Gordon: Rocketship ... Flatliners ... Flight of the Navigator ... Flight to Mars ... The Fly (1958) ... The Fly (1986) ... The Fly II ... The Flying Saucer ... The Food of the Gods ... Forbidden Planet ... Forever Young ... The Forgotten ... Fortress ... The Fountain ... 4:44 Last Day on Earth ... Frankenstein (1931) ... Frankenstein (1994) ... Frankenstein Meets the Space Monster ... Frankenstein's Army ... Frankenstein Unbound ... Freejack ... Frequency ... Frequently Asked Questions about Time Travel ... From Beyond ... From the Earth to the Moon ... Fugitive Alien ... Futureworld

G............153

Galaxis ... Galaxy of Terror ... Galaxy Quest ... Gamera, the Invincible ... Gamera vs. Barugon ... Gamera vs. Gaos ... Gamera vs. Guiron ... Gamera vs. Zigra ... Games of Survival ... The Gamma People ... Gas-S-S-S! ... Gattaca ... Ghidrah the Three-Headed Monster ... Ghost in the Shell ... Ghosts of Mars ... The Giant Claw ... The Gladiators ... Glen and Randa ... God Told Me To ... Godzilla ... Godzilla, King of the Monsters ... Godzilla 1985 ... Godzilla on Monster Is-

Contents

THE SCI-FI MOVIE GUIDE: The Universe of Film from "Alien" to "Zardoz"

ACKNOWLEDGMENTS

Books like this one can almost never be written alone. Wild praise is due to the stupendous work done by the VideoHound crew on their exuberantly enthusiastic 1997 edition, particularly their tenacity in hunting down rare prints and hard-to-find data. This edition stands on their collective shoulders.

Thanks are due to my diligent editor Kevin Hile and Visible Ink's intrepid captain, Roger Janecke, not to mention Mary Krzewinski for cover and page design and Marco Di Vita for typesetting.

And thanks, as always, to Marya.

PHOTO CREDITS

INTRODUCTION:
THE ART OF THE [IM]POSSIBLE

The first edition of this book came out in 1996 as *Videohound's Sci-Fi Experience: Your Quantum Guide to the Video Universe.* The many dedicated writers and researchers who contributed to that book dutifully scoured distribution catalogs and specialist shops for pretty much every science-fiction movie they could find, from the biggest blockbuster epic to the grottiest made-for-TV dud.

Before the Internet and its wealth of research sites really got going, books like this weren't just a great way to find the movies you wanted to watch, but also how to get them, whether by a mail-order catalog or specialty video store. Of course, after the mid-1990s came one technical revolution after another: the Web, DVDs-by-mail, file-sharing, YouTube, video on demand. Now, it's less a question of how to watch something than it is what to watch.

Independence Day was released the same year as our first edition; it just barely missed inclusion. That was also the year that science fiction arguably went mainstream. Before then, *Star Wars, Close Encounters of the Third Kind,* and other science-fiction films occasionally crossed over to a broader audience. But the genre still carried about it an odor of the dismissible leftover from the double-feature post-war years, when radioactive monsters stomped through cardboard cities and big-headed aliens kidnapped screaming starlets.

But after Will Smith beat back the alien hordes, something changed. Within a few years came *Contact, The Matrix, Men in Black, The Truman Show, The Fifth Element,* and *Gattaca.* By the 2000s, dystopias like *The Hunger Games* and alien/superhero franchises like *The Avengers* and *X-Men* ruled the multiplex with A-list stars, sometimes even receiving not-always-grudging critical respect. Out of the current list of 20 all-time box office hits, 12 of them are science fiction. Genre hasn't just infiltrated the mainstream, it's taken over.

Maybe this is because everyday life just feels more and more like science fiction. As the Internet, cellular technology, satellite imagery, and cloning moved from the incredible to the everyday, science fiction started to seem less fantastic. The title of Thomas Disch's prescient 1998 book summed it up perfectly: *The Dreams Our Stuff Is Made Of: How Science Fiction Conquered the World.*

In 1965, Susan Sontag wrote that science fiction films had nothing to do with science: "They are about disaster, which is one of the oldest subjects of art." Once the late-1990s revolution in computer-generated imagery (CGI) technology allowed filmmakers to impeccably render their apocalypse or dystopia or alien invasion, those visions started flooding onto screens for audiences ever more fascinated by the myriad ways humanity imagines destroying itself.

There is more to science-fiction film than destruction, of course. But what exactly is it? This heavily revised and fully updated guide to the universe of science-fiction films is, in part, an attempt to craft some kind of definition. Contra Sontag (who focused mostly on the B-movie side of things), science actually does have something to do with our calculations, even if it's not science that actually exists today. There are plenty of crossover fans who appreciate fantasy and science fiction; both deal in the art of the fantastic. But there is a reason why some science-fiction fans prefer the term "speculative fiction." Dragons and fairies are imaginative, not speculative. Films that speculate about what might happen as a result of this or that possible scientific advancement or (more often) mistake tended to make the cut.

Take zombie movies. At their core, these are really just monster tales. But many of those highlighted here have at least a germ of science-gone-wrong at their core, whether it's a manmade virus escaping from a lab (*28 Days Later ...*) or a satellite crashing to Earth and causing the dead to rise from their graves (*Night of the Living Dead*). Many of the films here, whether about zombies or re-animated super-soldiers, tend to bleed over into the old Frankenstein trope of flashing-light warnings about mortals who play God. It usually turns out badly for everybody involved.

There are also films included here that don't traffic in much science but are nevertheless heavy in historical speculation. Alternate-history films imagine what could have been. This usually entails a military counterfactual, like *It Can't Happen Here* (Nazis conquer England) or *Red Dawn* (Soviets and their allies conquer Middle America). These are the cinematic equivalent of Philip K. Dick's alternate-historical novel *The Man in the High Castle,* which dealt in no obviously science-fiction accoutrements but is still considered a classic of the genre.

Other films are more clearly science fiction. Your *Star Trek* and *Star Wars* space operas qualify automatically, as does nearly anything involving travel off the planet. Time travel counts as well (except for the time-travel romance genre), as do stories in which the world comes to an end. Also: aliens; the story might really just be about retirees learning to live again, but if aliens are involved, then *Cocoon* counts as science fiction for our purposes.

What about vampires? You wouldn't think they had anything to do with science fiction, but on occasion they do hail from outer space (so: *Lifeforce,* yes; *Interview with the Vampire,* no). Does highly advanced gadgetry alone make something science fiction? Probably not, which is why James Bond isn't included (with the exception of *Moonraker,* whose climax involves Space Marines, who don't quite exist yet). Superheroes? Yes and no. Batman no, as the gadgetry involved there is no more advanced than your average Bond film, but yes to Thor, given the amount of time he spends traveling to and battling on other planets.

Categorizing films into a specific genre is ultimately a fool's game. It's a judgment call for a genre that not everyone agrees on the exact parameters of but can come to a consensus on its general outlines. As novelist Ursula K. Le Guin remarked, "I don't think 'science fiction' is a very good name for it, but it's the name that we've got."

This updated edition contains almost a thousand movie entries, covering everything from *The Adventures of Buckaroo Banzai Across the 8th Dimension* to *Cloverfield, Invasion of the Saucer Men, Metropolis, THX 1138,* and *Zombieland.* In short, this book tries to cover just about everything that science-fiction film has to offer, from *The Terminator* to Tarkovsky. There is also an appendix on notable TV shows and miniseries like *The X-Files, Blake's 7,* and *Firefly.*

But what's here is by no means an exhaustive list. The bar for movie production seems to get lower with each passing year. The resulting flood of indies, straight-to-video/DVD movies, sequels, and sequels to sequels to sequels means that there are hundreds if not thousands more science-fiction films than could ever fit into a book the average person would be able to lift. So, all apologies: no *Cyborg 2.* Hopefully, you'll enjoy the highlights offered within these pages.

—Chris Barsanti

ABBOTT AND COSTELLO GO TO MARS

1953 (NR) 77m / D: Charles Lamont / **W:** John Grant / **C:** Bud Abbott, Lou Costello, Mari Blanchard, Robert Paige, Martha Hyer, Horace McMahon, Jack Kruschen, Anita Ekberg

But they don't. Loose-plotted slapstick finds the comedy duo as workmen accidentally launched aboard a rocket ship. First it lands near New Orleans during Mardi Gras, where A&C mistake marching mummers for monstrous Martians. Then they soar into space, hitting not Mars but Venus, where Miss Universe finalists play an Amazon race that hasn't seen a man in 400 years. Vintage f/x are surprisingly sharp, and the scriptwriters knew just enough about sci-fi to dump in the term "positronic brain" amid all the outdated buffoonery.

ABBOTT AND COSTELLO MEET THE INVISIBLE MAN

1951 (NR) 82m / D: Charles Lamont / **W:** Robert Lees / **C:** Bud Abbott, Lou Costello, Nancy Guild, Adele Jergens, Sheldon Leonard, William Frawley, Gavin Muir, Arthur Franz, Fred Rinaldo, John Grant

In one of their better comedies, Abbott and Costello play newly graduated detectives who take on the murder case of a boxer (Arthur Franz) accused of killing his manager. Using a serum that makes people invisible, the boxer helps Costello in a prizefight that will frame the real killers, who bumped off the manager because the boxer refused to throw a fight. An extra edge is added—this is one of the only Invisible Man features since the original (there were many) to make an issue of the drug's mind-altering properties. The combination of invisibility and gangsters leads to some truly bizarre sequences, as in the famous boxing match scene, in which Costello faces off against a big bruiser in the ring with some help from his unseen

Mari Blanchard plays the Martian Alura in 1953's *Abbott and Costello Go to Mars*.

friend. Good supporting cast of familiar faces adds to the fun. Decent f/x by some of the team that created those used in the original *Invisible Man* (1932).

THE ABOMINABLE DR. PHIBES

1971 (PG) 90m / **D:** Robert Fuest / **W:** James Whiton, William Goldstein / **C:** Vincent Price, Joseph Cotten, Hugh Griffith, Terry-Thomas, Virginia North, Susan Travers, Alex Scott, Caroline Munro

After being disfigured (and believed dead) in a freak car accident, a twisted genius decides that the members of a surgical team let his wife die and shall each perish by a different Biblical plague. Highly stylish, the murders all have a ceremonial feel to them. Though set in the 1920s, Phibes's equipment seems a bit ahead of its time—and where did he get a Frank Sinatra record? High camp balances gore with plenty of good humor, with the veteran cast of British character actors in top form. Caroline Munro appears only in photographs as the deceased wife, Victoria Regina (which was also the name of the hit play that made Vincent Price a star). Joseph Cotten, then in the midst of his 1970s-schlock phase, appears as one of the targets of Phibes's wrath. Followed in 1972 by *Dr. Phibes Rises Again*.

ABRAXAS: GUARDIAN OF THE UNIVERSE

1990 (R) 90m / **D:** Damien Lee / **W:** Damien Lee / **C:** Jesse Ventura, Sven Ole-Thorsen, Marjorie Bransfield, Michael Copeman, Francis Mitchell, Jerry Levitan

Cheapo Canadian production casts World Wrestling Federation vet Jesse "The Body" Ventura in the stiff title role, a space cop who lands on Earth to foil his evil ex-partner Secundas (Danish bodybuilder Sven-Ole Thorsen, who briefly hulked through Ventura-starrers *The Running Man* and *Predator* a few years earlier), who's inseminated a virgin with the "anti-life equation" that could destroy the universe. There's enough galactic gobbledygook to match *Robot Monster*, but a few camp touches (like James Belushi's cameo) indicate nobody should take it too seriously. Minimal f/x or gore; it's mainly two burly, gravel-voiced bruisers pummeling each other. Also available in an edited PG-13 version for those wanting less pummeling.

THE ABSENT-MINDED PROFESSOR

1961 (NR) 97m / **D:** Robert Stevenson / **W:** Bill Walsh / **C:** Fred MacMurray, Nancy Olson, Keenan Wynn, Tommy Kirk, Leon Ames, Ed Wynn

Classic dumb Disney fantasy of the era is still fun for kids and for adults who remember it with fondness. A professor (Fred MacMurray, at his easygoing best) accidentally invents an anti-gravity substance called flubber, causing inanimate objects and people to become airborne. Great sequence of the losing school basketball team taking advantage of flubber during a game, and, of course, the famous "flying flivver" Model T. Also available in a colorized version. Three Oscar nominations, including best black-and-white cinematography. Followed two years later by *Son of Flubber* and remade in 1997 as the Robin Williams vehicle *Flubber*; neither were nominated for much of anything.

THE ABYSS

1989 (PG-13) 140m / **D:** James Cameron / **W:** James Cameron / **C:** Ed Harris, Mary Elizabeth Mastrantonio, Todd Graff, Michael Biehn, John Bedford Lloyd, J. C. Quinn

With this underwater epic, James Cameron got away from the monsters and hardware populating his earlier work and went for a more emotional brand of sci-fi. It's an alternately claustrophobic nail-biter and sensuously beautiful vision as a team of divers investigates an American nuclear submarine stuck at the bottom of the ocean. Down below, mysterious and glowing watery aliens (like tropical fish that have swallowed Tiffany lamps) are making the situation even more confusing while on the surface World War III might be kicking off. Further tension-tighteners include dangerous nuclear warheads, an impending hurricane, and one insane diver. The finely tuned performances from Ed Harris, Mary Elizabeth Mastrantonio, and Cameron regular Michael Biehn do their best to overshadow the jaw-dropping f/x—groundbreaking for the time and still highly impressive as visual poetry today—and occasional script histrionics. The special edition runs 171 minutes and includes more of the U.S.-Soviet conflict taking

In between sci-fi smashes like *Terminator 2* and *Avatar,* James Cameron also directed the ambitious but less appreciated *The Abyss.*

place on the ocean's surface. Orson Scott Card (*Ender's Game*) wrote the novelization. Four Oscar nominations, won for best f/x.

THE ADJUSTMENT BUREAU

2011 (PG-13) 106m / D: George Nolfi / **W:** George Nolfi / **C:** Matt Damon, Emily Blunt, Michael Kelly, Anthony Mackie, John Slattery

An up-and-coming New York politician (Matt Damon), who can twist the electorate around his little finger, gets derailed on the cusp of victory by a keen, sassy dancer (Emily Blunt). That's when the mysterious guys in trim *Mad Men* suits and hats (including the dry and wry John Slattery from *Mad Men*) begin manipulating reality to keep the lovers apart. They come from an entity known as the Adjustment Bureau, which has bigger plans for Damon that his little romance could derail. The film has a lot of fun with wormhole-like passageways that allow the Bureau's chasers (and Damon, once he figures out the trick) to, say, open a door in midtown Manhattan and step out in Greenwich Village. Nolfi's sleek and cooly romantic take on the Philip K. Dick short story is one of the only adaptations of the master's work that has ever captured his playful side with such fidelity.

THE ADVENTURES OF BUCKAROO BANZAI ACROSS THE EIGHTH DIMENSION

1984 (PG) 100m / D: W. D. Richter / **W:** Earl Mac Rauch / **C:** Peter Weller, Ellen Barkin, Jeff Goldblum, Christopher Lloyd, John Lithgow, Lewis Smith, Rosalind Cash, Robert Ito, Pepe Serna, Vincent Schiavelli, Dan Hedaya, Yakov Smirnoff, Jamie Lee Curtis

After accidentally opening up a gateway to the eighth dimension, our (and everybody's) hero, Buckaroo Banzai (Peter Weller), must call on all of his talents in an interstellar battle for the world. Luckily, he is a multi-skilled genius-expert at everything. Race-car driver, top neurosurgeon, rock star, diplomat, comic-book hero, martial artist, scientist, last hope of the human race … these all describe Buckaroo. Teaming up with the good aliens that have come through the interdimensional wormhole, the Black Lectroids, Buckaroo and his rock 'n' roll commando squad/rock band (everybody should have one), The Hong Kong Cavaliers must go head-to-head against the evil Red Lectroids, whose leader inhabits the body of Dr. Lizardo (John Lithgow). Offbeat and nutty, campy and culty, this Pop Art masterpiece moves as fast as Buckaroo's jet-propelled Ford Fiesta. Ellen Barkin is great as sweetheart Penny Priddy and Weller has never been drier. The conclusion implies a sequel that was never delivered; probably for the best. Lightning doesn't strike twice, after all.

THE ADVENTURES OF PLUTO NASH

2002 (PG-13) 95m / D: Ron Underwood / **W:** Neil Cuthbert / **C:** Eddie Murphy, Randy Quaid, Rosario Dawson, Joe Pantoliano, Jay Mohr, Luis Guzman, James Rebhorn, Peter Doyle, Burt Young, Miguel A. Núñez, Pam Grier, John Cleese

Eddie Murphy plays Pluto Nash, a late-21st-century nightclub owner on the Moon who gets in trouble with some gangsters (yes, they still exist) and has to go on the run (yes, that still happens). "Bomb" doesn't quite begin to describe this epically expensive sci-fi comedy mess. There are cloned Eddie Murphys, chase scenes, and generally every plot contrivance from every on-the-run script of the previous century. It garnered more critical hate and audience apathy than just about anything else released that year or several more after. Director Ron Underwood should have known better, having handled both sci-fi (*Tremors*) and comedy (*City Slickers*) adeptly in the past. As for Murphy, it didn't slow him down a bit, sandwiched as it was between family friendly hits like 2001's *Shrek* and 2003's *Daddy Day Care*.

Comedian and actor Eddie Murphy starred in *The Adventures of Pluto Nash.*

AELITA: QUEEN OF MARS

1924 (NR) 104m / D: Yakov Protazanov / **W:** Fedor Ozep, Aleksey Fajko / **C:** Yulia Solntseva, Igor Illinski, Nikolai Batalov, Nikolai Tseretelli, Vera Orlova

Now we know how Mars became the Red Planet. The title has the stench of turkey about it, but wait; this silent is golden. Director Yakov Protazanov's influential epic concerns a Moscow engineer who, while awake, builds the new Russia, but asleep, dreams of life on Mars and the Martian queen, Aelita. In a machine of his own invention, he blasts off for Mars, where he eventually instigates a revolution amongst the imprisoned Martian slaves. A fascinating curio of early Soviet sci-fi, with impressive split-screen photography and eye-popping cubist sets. The costumes by Alexandra Exter influenced generations of designers. Based on the novel by Alexei Tolstoi. Some editions contain a piano score, and as with many silent classics, there are numerous edits of different lengths. AKA: *Aelita*; *Aelita: The Revolt of the Robots*.

The silent film *Aelita: Queen of Mars* was remembered more for its avant-garde costuming than its revolt-on-Mars plot.

AEON FLUX

2005 (PG-13) 93m / **D:** Karyn Kusama / **W:** Phil Hay, Matt Manfredi / **C:** Charlize Theron, Marton Csokas, Jonny Lee Miller, Sophie Okonedo, Frances McDormand, Pete Postlethwaite

*A*eon Flux was one of those odd 1990s fixtures on MTV, a surrealist animated series about an acrobatic female assassin in a dystopic future who spends half her time fighting for freedom and the other half twisted up with her lover/nemesis Trevor Goodchild. For Karyn Kusama's slightly more plotted live-action adaptation, the same basic dynamic held, with the ever bot-like Charlize Theron as Flux, waging war on the Orwellian police state (on orders from a curiously dreadlocked Frances McDormand) and looking fabulous doing it in a black bodysuit. Of course, in between the cartoon version and this one, *The Matrix* happened, as did *Equilibrium*, *Resident Evil*, and many other futuristic shoot-'em-ups with dead-eyed female protagonists in sleek outfits piling up two-and three-digit body counts.

AFTER EARTH

2013 (PG-13) 100m / **D:** M. Night Shyamalan / **W:** Gary Whitta, M. Night Shyamalan / **C:** Jaden Smith, Will Smith, Sophie Okonedo, Zoe Kravitz

THE SCI-FI MOVIE GUIDE: The Universe of Film from "Alien" to "Zardoz"

For all the warnings littered throughout this Smith family outer-space adventure, nobody thought to alert the audience about the metaphor overload to come. Set a thousand years in the future after humanity abandoned a pollution-ravaged Earth, the species is fighting off ravaging aliens called Ursas who hunt by smelling fear pheromones. An elite corps known as the Rangers—something of a Jedi/Vulcan hybrid—have learned to fight the Ursas by controlling their emotions. Ranger general Will Smith's not-quite-making-it recruit son Jaden Smith is provided a handy moment to prove himself when father and son crash-land on Earth, leaving dad critically injured. Little more than a dull vanity project, with director/co-writer M. Night Shyamalan showing little of the knack for spinning dread out of the thinnest material that's characterized even his weakest films. F/x are particularly unimpressive when it comes to Earth, where all the computer-generated animals have supposedly evolved to kill humans (even though mankind hasn't been around for centuries, but never mind). Notable for the controversy around its release due to charges of being thinly veiled Scientology propaganda.

AFTERSHOCK

1990 (R) 90m / D: Frank Harris / **W:** Michael Standing / **C:** Jay Roberts Jr., Elizabeth Kaitan, Chris Mitchum, Richard Lynch, John Saxon, Russ Tamblyn, Michael Berryman, Chris DeRose, Chuck Jeffreys

A beautiful alien bimbo beams down to Earth in the mistaken belief that there's intelligent life. Instead, civilization has collapsed, and between the usual *Road Warrior* punks and a repressive government, there are plenty of perils for this mysterious stranger and two kung-fu guys who appoint themselves her guardians. Silly action with a few political slogans thrown in for redeeming social value.

A.I. ARTIFICIAL INTELLIGENCE

2001 (PG-13) 146m / D: Steven Spielberg / **W:** Steven Spielberg / **C:** Haley Joel Osment, Frances O'Connor, Sam Robards, Jake Thomas, Jude Law, William Hurt, Ken Leung, Clark Gregg, Brendan Gleeson

It's possible that the great lost Stanley Kubrick movie is not his famously unrealized *Napoleon* but this one. Inspired by the Brian Aldiss story "Super-Toys Last All Summer Long," Kubrick tinkered for years with a futuristic *Pinocchio*-esque script about a mechanical boy pining for the love of a real mother. After Kubrick's death in 1999, Steven Spielberg—whose *Jurassic Park* had helped convince Kubrick that f/x could finally create his dystopic world of melted ice caps and drowned cities—took over the project that the two of them had been collaborating on for years. Spielberg's take is a heart-

One of sci-fi's most influential and optimistic directors, Steven Spielberg took a darker turn with *A.I. Artificial Intelligence.*

breaking picaresque journey through a grim and decaying world where robots seem more human than the humans they strive to emulate. The reek of dehumanization and pessimism is more pronounced here than in anything Spielberg had done since *Empire of the Sun*. It's still more sentimental, particularly with the tacked-on coda, than the cold-blooded Kubrick would have stood for (what wouldn't be?), but richly realized sci-fi tragedy of the first rank. Two Oscar nominations: music and f/x.

AKIRA

1988 (R) 124m / **D:** Katsuhiro Otomo / **W:** Katsuhiro Otomo, Izo Hashimoto

In the future megalopolis of Neo-Tokyo (the first Tokyo got wiped out a few decades earlier), secret government experiments on children with ESP go awry, resulting in a cataclysmic explosion. Akira, the most powerful of the children, is kept in cryogenic suspension under strict security. Some of the city's youth gang members, who may or may not be subjects of the experiment themselves, become involved with the various factions fighting to control the city. When Akira awakens, will he be their savior, or the agent of their destruction? Otomo started his massive, finely detailed manga novel in the early 1980s. It was a huge hit in Japan, while the pared-down but still epic-sized film helped open Western audiences to both anime and manga. Otomo's obsessive attention to detail shows in every frame—at one time, nearly every animation studio in southeast Asia worked on *Akira*. The work pays off with an exciting, impressive spectacle, although drastically paring down the print version's byzantine plot leaves the final third nearly incomprehensible. While conceptually it tends to wander at times, it still packs a punch with its awesome visuals. It's highly worth seeking out the subtitled version.

ALIEN

1979 (R) 116m / **D:** Ridley Scott / **W:** Dan O'Bannon / **C:** Tom Skerritt, Sigourney Weaver, Veronica Cartwright, Yaphet Kotto, Harry Dean Stanton, Ian Holm, John Hurt

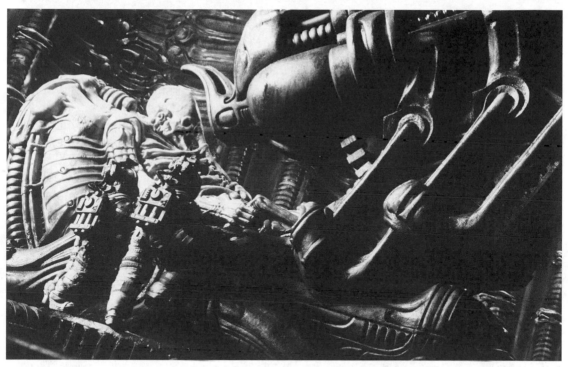

Set design based on the art of H. R. Giger lends an extra-creepy atmosphere to Ridley Scott's *Alien*.

Taut direction by Ridley Scott, stunning sets and f/x, and an excellent ensemble cast make this a suspenseful roller coaster ride in outer space. In the claustrophobic tradition of *The Thing*, an intergalactic freighter is invaded by an unstoppable, carnivorous, acid-spewing alien intent on picking off the crew one by one. Sigourney Weaver is exceptional as Ripley, the strong-willed survivor who goes toe to toe with the crew (who more resemble gruff intergalactic truckers than the bright-eyed astronauts of earlier sci-fi) and the alien. The gloomy industrial visual design creates a vivid sense of impending doom, enhanced further by the ominous Jerry Goldsmith score and the rarely seen, H. R. Giger-designed creature itself. Oscar-winning f/x include the classic alien "birth," as the creature springs from the chest of its first victim in one of writer Dan O'Bannon's more fruitful ideas (the ship's onboard computer is named "Mother" for those keen on digging into the film's redolent symbology). This scene was said to have movie-goers heading for the bathroom when the film was first released. Followed by *Aliens*, *Alien*[3], *Alien 4*, various offshoots where aliens battle Predators, ripoffs too numerous to count, and then Scott's 2012 return to the mythology: *Prometheus*. Possibly even more imitated than Scott's next great sci-fi film: *Blade Runner*. Two Oscar nominations; won for f/x.

ALIEN³

1992 (R) 135m / D: David Fincher / **W:** David Giler, Walter Hill, Larry Ferguson / **C:** Sigourney Weaver, Charles S. Dutton, Charles Dance, Paul McGann, Brian Glover, Ralph Brown, Danny Webb, Christopher John Fields, Holt McCallany, Lance Henriksen

This second *Alien* sequel picks up where the first film left off. Survivor Ripley crash-lands on a planet serving as a penal colony for sex offenders, whereupon her head is forcibly shaved (lice problem, apparently) and then has to fight to survive until a rescue ship can come. Fending off sexual advances from the prisoners, Ripley soon discovers this is actually the least of her problems. As fate (and sequel writers) would have it, Ripley wasn't the only survivor of the crash—an alien survived too, and has somehow implanted her with a gestating alien of her own, subverting her nascent sense of motherhood from the last film. This story attempts to recapture the original's disturbing claustrophobic tone by focusing more on character conflict and suspense than the unrelenting action of *Alien*. If it succeeds at all amidst the moody David Lynch-ian industrial design scheme, that's due to another soul-baring performance from Weaver. But the confused, dawdling story reflects the tortured years of development hell that preceded it. (One script by pioneering cyberpunk novelist William Gibson was entirely jettisoned; he later noted that just one detail of his remained: a prisoner with a barcode tattoo on the back of his neck.) Maligned at the time for being all dark flash with little substance, it nevertheless launched the career of one-time music video director David Fincher, who made a point of staying away from sci-fi later on. Some interesting subtext hints that Ripley's continued traumas are slicing away her sense of humanity; one scene has her talking out loud to the alien: "You've been in my life so long, I can't remember anything else." Oscar nomination for f/x.

> "Executed with a genuine affection for the genre, this is a fine film for fans of both regional and amateur film making."
>
> *The Alien Factor*

ALIEN CONTAMINATION

1981 (R) 90m / D: Luigi Cozzi / **W:** Luigi Cozzi / **C:** Ian McCulloch, Louise Monroe, Martin Mase, Siegfried Rauch, Lisa Hahn

Italian-made tale of two astronauts who return to Earth from an expedition to Mars carrying some deadly bacterial eggs. Controlled by a Martian intent on conquering the world, the eggs squirt a gloppy juice that makes people explode on contact. When more and more of the eggs appear, heroes Ian McCulloch and Louise Monroe trace them to a remote colony where a bigger, squishier alien is controlling humans to help it grow and harvest the eggs. A cheap and sloppy attempt to cash in on the success of *Alien*, with ideas cribbed from *Invasion of the Body Snatchers*. AKA: *Contamination*.

ALIEN DEAD

1980 (R) 74m / **D:** Fred Olen Ray / **W:** Fred Olen Ray, Martin Nicholas / **C:** Buster Crabbe, Linda Lewis, Ray Roberts

Meteorite lands on obnoxious teens, turning them into flesh-eating ghouls. Would you believe flying ace Eddie Rickenbacker is involved? Florida-lensed junk owns its place in history as the first commercially released feature from Z-movie factory Fred Olen Ray (*Hollywood Chainsaw Hookers*, et al.), supposedly shot for only $12,000. Guest star Buster Crabbe—one-time Flash Gordon—looks like he'd rather be somewhere else than this, his last screen appearance. Occasionally amusing dialogue: "She's deader than Mother's Day in an orphanage." AKA: *It Fell from the Sky*.

THE ALIEN FACTOR

1978 (PG) 82m / **D:** Don Dohler / **C:** Don Leifert, Tom Griffith, Mary Mertens, Dick Dyszel, George Stover

Another low-budget, crazed-critter-from-outer-space dispatch, this one features multiple aliens who have the misfortune of crash-landing near Baltimore. The grotesque extraterrestrials jolt a small town out of its sleepy state by wreaking havoc (except for the good alien, of course). Decent f/x for a low-budget cheapie, the cast also doubled as the crew. The main focus shifts to the intellectual problem of trying to separate the good alien from his identical evil cronies. Executed with a genuine affection for the genre, this is a fine film for fans of both regional and amateur film making. Worth a view, even if you're not, just to see Baltimorian George Stover wrasslin' with the alien. Director Don Dohler is known to some as the *third* best-known Baltimore filmmaker, after Barry Levinson and John Waters.

ALIEN FROM L.A.

1987 (PG) 87m / **D:** Albert Pyun / **W:** Albert Pyun, Debra Ricci, Regina Davis / **C:** Kathy Ireland, Thom Mathews, Don Michael Paul, Linda Kerridge, William R. Moses, Richard Haines

Limp comedy about a California girl (model Kathy Ireland) who unwittingly stumbles onto the ancient civilization of Atlantis while searching for her lost archaeologist father. She quickly becomes embroiled in a number of rather silly adventures. Much of the alleged humor revolves around the Atlanteans calling Ireland an "alien." Ireland makes an appealing heroine, but that's not enough to save this movie, which is weakly plotted, acted, and filmed, existing primarily to show off its star. Probably would have been more fun if it had been made in the 1970s.

ALIEN NATION

1988 (R) 89m / **D:** Graham Baker / **W:** Rockne S. O'Bannon / **C:** James Caan, Mandy Patinkin, Terence Stamp, Kevyn Major Howard, Peter Jason, Jeff Kober, Leslie Bevins

A few hundred thousand alien slaves in a hijacked saucer find sanctuary on "near-future" Earth and face the challenges of any immigrant minority. Some assimilate into American society, others dwell in the ghetto; most all are feared and resented. Mandy Patinkin plays an upscale "newcomer" (given a human name, à la Ellis Island) who becomes the first alien LAPD detective. He teams with surly, bigoted human cop James Caan to solve murders over an otherworldly narcotic. Transparently meaningful script uses sci-fi as a lens for examining contemporary racial conflicts and attitudes in an obvious, *Guess Who's Coming to Dinner?* way. Nothing wrong with that, but the filmmakers cuff the plot to every dumb action-buddy-cop cliché since *48 Hrs.*, and the mottle-headed aliens just aren't that interesting. One expects better from frequent James Cameron producer Gale Anne Hurd. The *Alien Nation* universe got a more detailed exploration in a subsequent short-lived TV series and small-screen sequels also on video.

Actress Sigourney Weaver played the tough-as-nails Ripley in the "Alien" film series.

ALIEN: RESURRECTION

1997 (R) 109m / **D:** Jean-Pierre Jeunet / **W:** Joss Whedon / **C:** Sigourney Weaver, Winona Ryder, Dominique Pinon, Ron Perlman, Gary Dourdan, Michael Wincott, Kim Flowers, Dan Hedaya, J. E. Freeman, Brad Dourif

Proving that corporations far in the future are just as rapacious as modern-day film studios, this fourth installment finds poor Ripley brought back to life two hundred years after the events of *Alien[3]* to serve as an incubator for infant aliens. When the ship that Ripley's on runs into a tramp freighter, we are introduced to a great ensemble cast who seem destined to end up in the acid-filled gut of one of the aliens Ripley's stoic countenance is starting to resemble. As crewmembers Johner and Call, the always reliable Ron Perlman gets some good and gruff one-liners, while a particularly waif-like Winona Ryder experiments with outer-space acting. Some powerful imaginations behind the camera, with *Delicatessen*'s Jean-Pierre Jeunet directing,

Joss Whedon penning the script, and Darius Khondji's cinematography giving the dark interiors a rich glow. Jeunet and Whedon's unique abilities aren't much on display, though, as the film turns into what the Space Marines from *Aliens* would have dismissively referred to as just another "bug hunt." A deleted alternate ending on the special edition DVD shows Ripley and Call pondering the dusty and devastated ruins of Paris; Ripley notes: "I'm a stranger here myself."

ALIENS

1986 (R) 137m / **D:** James Cameron / **W:** James Cameron / **C:** Sigourney Weaver, Carrie Henn, Michael Biehn, Paul Reiser, Lance Henriksen, Bill Paxton, Jenette Goldstein, William Hope, Al Matthews

Instead of the first film's "in space nobody can hear you scream" tagline, James Cameron's military-minded sequel goes for the gusto with "This time it's war." Cameron had just come off writing another simplistic, vengeful, and gun-crazy Reagan-era follow-up (*Rambo*) to a more nuanced and disaffected drama (*First Blood*), and so he was perfectly primed for sending the Space Marines after the acid-spewing alien of the first film. Setting up a pattern for films, books, and video games to follow, sole survivor Ripley is reawakened and sent back into space (ostensibly on a rescue mission to a colony Earth has lost contact with) by a military-industrial complex with ulterior motives. In arguably the finest example of tech noir sci-fi, Cameron—who basically invented the mini-genre with *The Terminator*—launches his platoon of hardened soldiers into a claustrophobic hive of darkened, alien-infested tunnels. Cameron company regulars like Lance Henriksen and Bill Paxton spike the white-knuckle proceedings with dark humor, while Ripley's adoption of an orphaned girl turns her into one of film history's most impressive warriors. So good that Cameron would use it to liberally rip himself off years later in *Avatar*. The 1992 special edition included 17 minutes of previously unseen footage. Rather incredibly nominated for seven Oscars, including best actress for Weaver; won for visual f/x and sound effects editing.

ALIEN VS. PREDATOR: REQUIEM

2007 (R) 94m / **D:** Colin Strause, Greg Strause / **W:** Shane Salerno / **C:** Reiko Aylesworth, Steven Pasquale, John Ortiz, Johnny Lewis, Ariel Gade, Kristen Hager, Sam Trammell

Where *AVP* brought aliens and predators to do battle at the South Pole while humans got messily caught in between, this dully mechanical installment does the same thing in an isolated Colorado town. A predator ship infested with face-hugging aliens crash-lands near town, establishing your standard horror-film template of "What was that?" and "Who's there?!" While night approaches and the town's population mysteriously declines, a mechanically constructed cast assembles for the usual running, shooting, and screaming in dark hallways. Shane Salerno's gleefully bloodthirsty script barely bothers to introduce characters before dispatching them as gruesomely as possible; a brief scene at an alien-infested hospital defies description. Years later, Salerno would write and direct the literary documentary *Salinger*, perhaps as penance for working on this.

ALLIGATOR

1980 (R) 94m / D: Lewis Teague / **W:** John Sayles / **C:** Robert Forster, Jack Carter, Henry Silva, Robin Riker, Dean Jagger, Michael V. Gazzo, Bart Braverman

Just when you thought it was safe to go back into the sewers, along comes Ramon, the urban legend that ate a city. Once a cute little alligator, he was flushed down the toilet and made a name for himself underneath Chicago. There, he ingests a dead lab animal chock full o' growth hormones and begins to swell at an amazing rate. No longer content with the Weight Watchers-approved human-a-day diet, Ramon begins to munch on everything and everyone in sight. So-so f/x and a thrown-in romance between the gator-chasin' cop and lovely lady scientist aside, the witty script by John Sayles and efficient direction by fellow John Corman veteran Lewis Teague (watch for the *Third Man* references in the sewer chases) makes for a pleasingly low-budget, eco-conscious, satiric chiller. A 1991 sequel, *Alligator II*, had nothing to do with the original.

ALPHAVILLE

1965 (NR) 100m / D: Jean-Luc Godard / **W:** Jean-Luc Godard / **C:** Eddie Constantine, Anna Karina, Akim Tamiroff, Howard Vernon, Laszlo Szabo

Stolid French actor Eddie Constantine was a B-movie bust in the States but a star in Paris, where he popularized on film the pulp hero Lemmy Caution, an American detective popularized in novels by British author Peter Cheyney. In this cheeky sci-fi noir comedy from Jean-Luc Godard, the trench-coated Caution arrives in the futuristic city of Alphaville to search for a defected scientist named von Braun. Contemporary Paris makes an eerie and yet comical stand-in for the conformist state run by a moralistic and dictatorial computer, Alpha 60. Godard's love for pulp film is almost more apparent here than in *Breathless*, though his later penchant for specious, tongue-in-cheek philosophizing is also already in evidence. The beautiful Anna Karina appears as von Braun's seductive daughter. Godard uses his non-budget to great satiric effect (Lemmy travels from one planet to the next by … getting in his car and driving down the road). Won the Golden Bear at the 1965 Berlin International Film Festival. AKA: *Alphaville, a Strange Case of Lemmy Caution*. Godard released an allegorical semi-sequel in 1991, *Germany Year 90 Nine Zero*, which featured Caution wandering a new post-historical Germany after the collapse of the Soviet Bloc.

ALTERED STATES

1980 (R) 103m / D: Ken Russell / **W:** Paddy Chayefsky / **C:** William Hurt, Blair Brown, Bob Balaban, Charles Haid, Dori Brenner, Drew Barrymore, Miguel Godreau

Probably everyone who's tried mind-altering substances has believed that the changes in personal perception can also change external reality. That's the idea behind Paddy Chayefsky's tale of a young scientist (William Hurt) who uses psychedelic drugs and sensory deprivation to go back to his evolutionary roots, as it were. Not surprisingly, his wife (Blair Brown) thinks it's a bad idea. Like all of director Ken Russell's best work, the ambitious but unfocused film has some wonderful moments within huge excesses. Hurt's climactic transformation into a nuclear mushroom man—or whatever—is truly nutty. Chayefsky eventually washed his hands of the project after artistic differences with the producers and is credited here as Sidney Aaron. Others who departed from the film include initial director William Penn and f/x genius John Dykstra (relieved ably by Bran Ferren). Drew Barrymore appears in her first feature film performance. Two Oscar nominations; best sound and best music.

THE AMAZING COLOSSAL MAN

1957 (NR) 79m / D: Bert I. Gordon / **W:** Mark Hanna, Bert I. Gordon / **C:** Glenn Langan, Cathy Downs, William Hudson, James Seay, Russ Bender, Lyn Osborn

Like nearly every other sci-fi film from the 1950s, here a monster is created by atomic radiation. However, where most similar films of this type were content to use giant insects or rats as the heavies, this one features a human monster. Gung-ho soldier Colonel Manning is exposed to massive doses of plutonium when an experiment backfires (literally) in his face. When his radiation burns heal practically overnight, the doctors figure something unusual is going on; their suspicions are confirmed when Manning begins growing ... and growing ... and growing.... The former good-guy shoots up to 70 feet and starts taking out his anger on a helpless Las Vegas. Can anything stop his murderous rampages? Maybe a really, really big hypodermic needle.... Cheesy effects are still better than average for this level of production. Climactic scene at the Boulder Dam has iconic status. Ultra-productive director Bert I. Gordon knocked out two other films this year alone.

THE AMAZING SPIDER-MAN

2012 (PG-13) 136m / D: Marc Webb / **W:** James Vanderbilt, Alvin Sargent, Steve Kloves / **C:** Andrew Garfield, Emma Stone, Rhys Ifans, Denis Leary, Martin Sheen, Sally Field, Irfan Khan, Campbell Scott, Embeth Davidtz

The studios' hunger for new comic-book product being so unsatiable in the 2010s, they only waited five years after Sam Raimi's last Spidey story to jumpstart the webslinger's adventures yet again. What the new series gains in this hero—the touchingly gawky Andrew Garfield being a much better fit than the confused-looking Tobey Maguire—it loses in just about every other department. Peter Parker's missing-parent issues, teen angst, and fateful bite by that pesky spider are all dutifully handled. But Marc Webb's direction is all over the place, muffing most of the big f/x action scenes where Spider-man does battle with The Lizard (Rhys Ifans) and failing to find that sense of escapist joy that Raimi labored so hard for. Bright spots include a saucy Emma Stone as Parker's crush and Denis Leary as her (gulp) cop dad.

THE AMAZING TRANSPARENT MAN

1960 (NR) 58m / D: Edgar G. Ulmer / **W:** Jack Lewis / **C:** Douglas Kennedy, Marguerite Chapman, James Griffith, Ivan Triesault

A mad scientist is forced to make a crook invisible in order to steal the radioactive materials he needs. A snaky crime boss has them both under his thumb. The crook decides to rob banks instead. Shot at the Texas State Fair in Dallas for that elusive futuristic look. For serious Edgar Ulmer fans only—don't expect another *Detour*. Aside from some exterior shots that emphasize the barren Texas plains, the direction is merely pedestrian, with little of Ulmer's usual visual magic. The invisibility transformation effects are great looking—instead of merely fading away, portions of the actor are wiped gradually. Made simultaneously with *Beyond the Time Barrier*; supposedly the two films only took a couple weeks total to make.

THE AMPHIBIAN MAN

1962 (NR) 96m / D: Vladimir Chebotaryov, Gennadi Kazansky / **W:** Akiba Golburt, Aleksei Kapler, Alexandr Ksenofontov / **C:** Vladimir Korenev, Anastasiya Vertinskaya, Mikhail Kozakov, Anatoliy Smiranin

What does a scientist do once he's created a young man with gills? Plunge him into the ocean to experience life and love, albeit underwater. Trouble is, the protagonist, who's come to be known as the Sea Devil, falls for a young pretty he's snatched from the jaws of death. Curious 1960s Soviet sci-fi romance.

Not one of director Edgar Ulmer's best efforts, *The Amazing Transparent Man* used the grounds of the Texas State Fair to try and achieve a futuristic look on a budget. Pictured left to right are: Douglas Kennedy, Ivan Triesault, and James Griffith.

ANDROID

1982 (PG) 80m / **D:** Aaron Lipstadt / **W:** James Reigle, Don Keith Opper / **C:** Aaron Lipstadt, Klaus Kinski, Don Keith Opper, Brie Howard

Humorous and offbeat sci-fi in which mad scientist Klaus Kinski (could he play any other kind?) needs a little help producing the now-illegal industrial robots that allow him to get by in the out-of-this-world. Enter human-wannabe Max 404, an android who wants to help, wants to be human, and thinks he's a mechanized Charlie Chaplin. When Max learns that he is about to be phased out and permanently retired, he takes matters into his own hands, including dealing with a trio of cosmic convicts that have invaded the research lab. Another must for fans of the mad-eyed Kinski (who raved on screens the same year in Werner Herzog's masterpiece *Fitzcarraldo*; apparently art films don't pay the bills), and Don Keith Opper isn't bad either.

THE ANDROMEDA STRAIN

1971 (G) 131m / **D:** Robert Wise / **W:** Nelson Gidding / **C:** Arthur Hill, David Wayne, James Olson, Kate Reid, Paula Kelly, George Mitchell

Based on a Michael Crichton novel, *The Andromeda Strain* poses a scenario in which people are dying from a mutating bacteria from outer space.

A satellite falls back to Earth carrying deadly bacteria that must be identified in time to save the population from extermination. A crack team of civilian scientists assemble at a secret underground laboratory to solve the crisis. Unfortunately, the bug keeps on mutating. Though highly dated technologically, the tension inherent in the best-selling Michael Crichton novel (he would return to this kind of tick-tock techno-thriller technique many times) is kept intact due to the precision-paced work of veteran sci-fi director Robert Wise (*The Day the Earth Stood Still*). Two Oscar nominations. Remade as a TV miniseries in 2008.

THE ANGRY RED PLANET

1959 (NR) 83m / **D:** Ib Melchior / **W:** Ib Melchior, Sid Pink / **C:** Gerald Mohr, Les Tremayne, Nora Hayden, Jack Kruschen

An unintentionally amusing sci-fi adventure about astronauts on Mars fighting off aliens and giant, ship-swallowing amoebas. Crew comes back infected by cancerous growths, and Nora Hayden must go through the whole story in flashbacks in order to save them. Filmed using bizarre "Cinemagic" process, which turns almost everything pink—it was originally meant to make the actors blend in better with painted backdrops, but it doesn't work very well. Wild effects have earned the film cult status. Romance is added as Jack Kruschen appears to fall in love with his sonic rifle. AKA: *Invasion of Mars*.

THE ANIMATRIX

2003 (PG-13) 102m / D: Peter Chung, Andrew R. Jones, Yoshiaki Kawajiri, Takeshi Koike, Mahiro Maeda, Kôji Morimoto, Shinichirô Watanabe / **W:** Andy Wachowski, Lana Wachowski, Yoshiaki Kawajiri, Kôji Morimoto, Shinichirô Watanabe, Peter Chung

After establishing that humanity's only hope lay in Keanu Reeves's kung-fu, the Wachowskis (like many sci-fi impresarios before them) decided to explore the backstory of the grim universe they'd created. This straight-to-DVD collection of nine anime shorts explores the world of the Matrix from a variety of angles. The most interesting of them is the "The Second Renaissance," which tells the story of the computer uprising that would ultimately enslave humanity. An uneven anthology but one whose vibrant storytelling stands in stark contrast to the Wachowskis' two embarrassing film sequels that hit theaters this same year.

ANOTHER EARTH

2011 (PG-13) 92m / D: Mike Cahill / **W:** Mike Cahill, Brit Marling / **C:** Brit Marling, William Mapother, Matthew-Lee Erlbach

Another in a spate of 2010s sci-fi films that used their other-worldly elements as poetical tools to illuminate powerful human dramas instead of serving as the whole reason for the story's existence. In this moody piece starring and co-written by Brit Marling (*Sound of My Voice*), she plays an MIT student entranced with the momentous announcement that a new planet has been discovered: It's an exact duplicate of Earth, and it's getting closer. Unfortunately, she's so obsessed with watching the planet that she drives into another car, killing a mother and child. Later, Marling tries to do penance by cleaning the house of the blind father and husband whose life she tore apart, only without telling him who she is. The quiet, nervy story plays out as the new Earth looms larger and larger in the sky, and attempts to contact it begins to hint at a disturbing truth. Potent stuff.

THE APE MAN

1943 (NR) 64m / D: William Beaudine / **W:** Barney A. Sarecky / **C:** Wallace Ford, Bela Lugosi

With the aid of a secret potion, a scientist (Bela Lugosi) turns himself into a murderous ape—as can occasionally happen to even the best-intentioned researchers. The only way to regain his human side is, of course, to ingest human spinal fluid. Donors are required; willingness to comply not

Louise Currie and Bela Lugosi starred in the campy *The Ape Man*.

necessary. Undoubtedly inspired by Lugosi rival Boris Karloff's 1940 film *The Ape*. AKA: *Lock Your Doors*.

APOLLO 18

2011 (PG-13) 86m / **D:** Gonzalo López-Gallego / **W:** Brian Miller / **C:** Warren Christie, Lloyd Owen, Ryan Robbins

The Blair Witch Project meets *Paranormal Activity* via *Capricorn One* in this thriller that tries to wring a few more jolts out of the found-footage genre. In 1973, the story goes, NASA launched a secret mission to the moon whose true purpose it kept secret from the astronauts. The conspiratorial gimmick is that the whole thing is purportedly composed of found footage kept locked away for all the years since by a paranoid government. Once a wrecked Russian spacecraft and some suspicious bloodstains are found, it becomes clear that the mission is likely to turn into one quite fatal step backward for at least part of humanity.

THE APPLE

1980 (PG) 90m / **D:** Menahem Golan / **W:** Menahem Golan / **C:** Catherine Mary Stewart, George Gilmour, Grace Kennedy, Allan Love, Joss Ackland, Vladek Sheybal, Ray Shell

What happens when schlock maestro Menahem Golan (*The Delta Force* and many, many lesser efforts) turns his hand to the nonsensical sci-fi rock opera? Acres of spandex, yards of cheese, and dance routines that you could imagine *Waiting for Guffman*'s Corky St. Clair putting a lot of heart and soul into a weekend of cocaine and binge-watching *Tommy*. The then-futuristic 1994-set story follows small-town bumpkin singers (Catherine Mary Stewart and George Gilmour) getting sucked in by devilish music executive Mr. Boogalow (the Peter Cushing-like Vladek Sheybal), who surrounds himself with suspiciously multicultural and polyamorous cohorts (the corrupted innocents are white, of course). Another confused tale of commerce corrupting art; very Faust meets Pink Floyd's *The Wall* meets *Rock and Rule*. The vision of lost innocents and maddened crowds of conformists prefigures the also little-known quasi-futuristic punk fable *Ladies and Gentlemen, the Fabulous Stains* (1982).

APPLESEED

2004 (R) 101m / **D:** Shinji Aramaki / **W:** Haruka Handa, Tsutomu Kamishiro

In this based-on-a-manga anime, a futuristic war rages, as per usual. Deunan, a legendary young soldier with even larger eyes than the other female characters, is plucked from the battlefield and brought to a glass palace of a utopian city called Olympus. Various factions are squabbling about the societal status of new partially cloned humans called Bioroids. Rebellion is fomenting. Meanwhile, Deunan tries to revive her relationship with a friend she thought was long dead. Things blow up at regular intervals, often for little reason. Nothing is ever quite explained, and the flat, slow-moving animation style makes the characters as expressive as balloons.

ARMAGEDDON

1998 (PG-13) 151m / **D:** Michael Bay / **W:** Jonathan Hensleigh, J. J. Abrams / **C:** Bruce Willis, Billy Bob Thornton, Ben Affleck, Liv Tyler, Will Patton, Steve Buscemi, William Fichtner, Owen Wilson, Michael Clarke Duncan, Peter Stormare, Keith David

An asteroid the size of Texas hurtles towards Earth. Humanity is threatened with extinction. What to do? Might we suggest sending oil-rigger Bruce Willis up into space to do battle with that damn rock? If he could be accompanied by a ragtag band of guys-being-guys scamps (Steve Buscemi and Michael Clarke Duncan among those in charge of providing color) who won't let the impending apocalypse keep them from frat-house antics, all the better. Michael Bay's spectacle is all fireworks all the time, whether it's a meteor shower smashing into Manhattan or the loud emoting of not-yet-a-star Ben Affleck. There's a riff on the astronaut-training sequence from *The Right Stuff* and a meant-to-be-comic bit with Peter Stormare as a crazed cosmonaut that defies description. This was demolishing theater sound systems the same summer as *Deep Impact* and *Godzilla*; strangely, it ended up with its own Criterion Collection edition. Even more strangely, it was nominated for four Oscars.

AROUND THE WORLD UNDER THE SEA

1965 (G) 111m / **D:** Andrew Marton / **W:** Arthur Weiss, Art Arthur / **C:** Lloyd Bridges, David McCallum, Shirley Eaton, Gary Merrill, Keenan Wynn, Brian Kelly

A bunch of men and one woman scientist plunge under the ocean in an experiment to predict earthquakes. They plant earthquake detectors along the ocean floor and discover the causes of tidal waves. They have men-woman battles. They see big sea critters.

THE ARRIVAL

1996 (PG-13) 115m / **D:** David Twohy / **W:** David Twohy / **C:** Charlie Sheen, Lindsay Crouse, Ron Silver, Richard Schiff, Teri Polo, Tony T. Johnson

1990s black-helicopter paranoia meets aliens-are-among-us suspense in this improbably successful effort from *Waterworld* scribe David Twohy. Charlie Sheen's obsessed radio astronomer brings evidence of a signal from another planet to Ron Silver, a sleazy NASA bureaucrat (there is no other kind in these movies) who promptly destroys said evidence. Sheen, sporting an array of goggle-like sunglasses but just one solitary wide-eyed expression, goes to Mexico to find proof that aliens are terraforming Earth to colonize it. Sweaty south-of-the-border stereotypes, an obnoxious street-urchin sidekick, and subpar action sequences junk up what could have been a halfway decent *X-Files* episode. A highly disliked sequel followed two years later, featuring none of the same actors or filmmakers.

THE ASPHYX

1972 (PG) 98m / **D:** Peter Newbrook / **W:** Brian Comport / **C:** Robert Stephens, Robert Powell, Jane Lapotaire, Alex Scott, Ralph Arliss, Fiona Walker, John Lawrence

Cleverish sci-fi/horror set in the 19th century, where doctor Robert Stephens uses the newly developed invention of photography to detect the Asphyx, an aura that supposedly surrounds a person just before death. The story goes that trapping one's Asphyx can provide the key to immortality, but it has to be done very carefully, or else…. The briefly glimpsed entity, a hideous puppet in double-exposure, testifies to the low budget of the proceedings; it's the script concepts and fine acting that give this moralistic occult tale its haunting impact. AKA: *Spirit of the Dead*.

THE ASTOUNDING SHE-MONSTER

1958 (NR) 60m / **D:** Ronnie Ashcroft / **W:** Frank Hall / **C:** Robert Clarke, Kenne Duncan, Marilyn Harvey, Jeanne Tatum, Shirley Kilpatrick, Ewing Miles Brown

A bad script and snail-paced plot are a good start for this fantastically titled film. Robert Clarke is a geologist wanting only to be left alone with his rocks and his dog who survives a brush with the kidnappers of a wealthy heiress only to happen upon an alien spacecraft that's crashed nearby. At the helm is a very tall, high-heeled femme alien fatale in an obligatory skintight space outfit and very scary eyebrows. Unfortunately for the men-folk, Miss Galaxy can kill with the slightest touch. With voiced-over narration to help explain the plot. For connoisseurs of truly bad movies; all others should approach with caution. Incredible as it may seem, was partially re-made by Fred Olen Ray in 1989 as *Alienator*. AKA: *Mysterious Invader*.

THE ASTRONAUT'S WIFE

1999 (R) 109m / **D:** Rand Ravich / **W:** Rand Ravich / **C:** Johnny Depp, Charlize Theron, Joe Morton, Clea DuVall, Donna Murphy, Nick Cassavetes

Woman-in-jeopardy story gets an unusual alien twist in this glossy dark thriller. Johnny Depp and Nick Cassavetes play space-shuttle astronauts who go out to repair a satellite, only to lose contact with ground control for a couple minutes. Everything seems fine at first when they return to Earth, only Depp's wife Charlize Theron (whose pixie haircut pointedly resembles Mia Farrow's from *Rosemary's Baby*, a clear influence) knows that something's amiss, that her husband *may not be her husband anymore*.

THE ASTRO-ZOMBIES

1967 (NR) 91m / **D:** Ted V. Mikels / **W:** Ted V. Mikels / **C:** Tura Satana, Wendell Corey, John Carradine, Tom Pace, Joan Patrick, Rafael Campos

Johnny Depp put his otherworldly style to good use in *The Astronaut's Wife*.

One of the schlockiest, most ineptly made, and yet compellingly mind-boggling films of all time. John Carradine plays a mad scientist who holes up in his basement lab and cranks out a series of skull-faced zombies who eat people's guts. Legendary cult-movie queen Tura Satana (*Faster Pussycat! Kill! Kill!*) stars as the leader of a cadre of foreign agents who try to stop the monsters. Cinematic weirdness of a very high order. This peculiar anti-masterpiece was co-written and co-produced by Wayne Rogers, who played Trapper John on *M*A*S*H*.

ATLAS SHRUGGED: PART I

2011 (PG-13) 97m / **D:** Paul Johansson / **W:** John Aglialoro, Brian Patrick O'Toole / **C:** Taylor Schilling, Michael O'Keefe, Grant Bowler, Matthew Marsden, Jon Polito

Much like *Battlefield Earth*, Ayn Rand's last novel was an overcooked and overlong summation of the author's favorite themes. Also like Hubbard's book, when Rand's was finally turned into a film, just about nobody except the acolytes (libertarian extremists, in this case) could be bothered to care. Rand's story is a free-market futuristic ghost story in which the bogeymen are the unionists and government bureaucrats trying to shackle the Aryan *ubermensch* capitalists like Dagny Taggart (Taylor Schilling) and Henry Rearden (Grant Bowler) fighting to get American business back on its feet. This socialistic nightmare is brought to a head by the mysterious business figure John Galt, who threatens to stop the world unless the meddling socialists get off his back. Here, greed isn't just good, it's compulsory.

ATLAS SHRUGGED: PART II

2012 (PG-13) 111m / **D:** John Putch / **W:** Duke Sandefur, Brian Patrick O'Toole / **C:** Samantha Mathis, Jason Beghe, Esai Morales, Patrick Fabian, Kim Rhodes

In the second installment of this planned trilogy, all the major roles were recast but the story continues to grind on. A collapsing America is being further driven into discord by the oppressively tax-and-regulation-crazy government. Meanwhile, stout-hearted businessmen and women fight for the right to make money. There's also some melodrama about a radical new limitless-energy type of engine and speeches about (economic) freedom. Appropriately, conservative talking heads like Sean Hannity have cameos. Revolutionary inspiration for *Forbes* readers, MBAs, and Tea Party types. AKA: *Atlas Shrugged II: The Strike*.

THE ATOMIC BRAIN

1964 (NR) 64m / **D:** Joseph Mascelli / **W:** Jack Pollexfen / **C:** Frank Gerstle, Erika Peters, Judy Bamber, Marjorie Eaton, Frank Fowler, Margie Fisco

An old woman hires a doctor to transplant her brain into the body of a beautiful young girl. Of the three who are abducted, two become homicidal zombies and the third starts to act catty when she's given a feline brain. Oh, and did we mention the hairy monster chained to a tether in the back yard? A serious contender to *Plan 9 from Outer Space*'s title of Worst Film Ever Made, this is a treasure trove of tripe: drunk, horny mad doctors; wheelchair-bound old biddies living in dilapidated gothic mansions; forbidden experiments with atomic power; mutations run amuck; and trampy Euro-dames (with atrocious fake accents). Add screamingly inept dialogue (by FOUR screenwriters!), a droning narrator, and feel your own brainpan go nuclear. A must-see for bad-brain movie devotees; makes a good cerebral double bill with *The Brain That Wouldn't Die*. Director Joseph Mascelli provided camera work for Ray Dennis Steckler's inexplicable *The Incredibly Strange Creatures Who Stopped Living and Became Mixed-Up Zombies!!?* the following year, as well as authoring a highly regarded book on cinematography. Co-producer/writer Jack Pollexfen is an old hand in the bad movie biz, having helmed the Lon Chaney Jr. electric-psycho flick *The Indestructible Man*. AKA: *Monstrosity*.

THE ATOMIC SUBMARINE

1959 (NR) 72m / **D:** Spencer Gordon Bennet / **W:** Orville H. Hampton / **C:** Arthur Franz, Dick Foran, Bob Steele, Brett Halsey, Joi Lansing, Paul Dubov, Tom Conway

Government agents battle alien invaders. The battle, however, is a bit out of the ordinary—it features an atomic-powered submarine clashing with an alien saucer and its monstrous crew underneath the Arctic ice floes. Despite some quarreling among crewmembers, our heroes find a way to win! Brawny cast resembles a B-movie version of a John Wayne feature, with Arthur Franz, Dick Foran, Bob Steele, and Brett Halsey competing to see who has the most granite jaw in the face of death. Sexbomb Joi Lansing, a pin-up favorite, provides inspiration for their struggles. The entire format was stolen a few years later by Irwin Allen for his silly feature and TV series *Voyage to the Bottom of the Sea*. A better-than-average 1950s sci-fi thriller, more imaginative than most.

ATTACK OF THE 50 FOOT WOMAN (1958)

1958 (NR) 65m / **D:** Nathan Juran / **W:** Mark Hanna / **C:** Allison Hayes, William Hudson, Roy Gordon, Yvette Vickers, George Douglas

The success of *The Incredible Shrinking Man* inspired this inevitable imitation. Allison Hayes stars as a woman recently released from an insane asylum, not the best time for her to tell police and her husband that she witnessed a flying saucer land in the desert. She is then zapped with a ray that

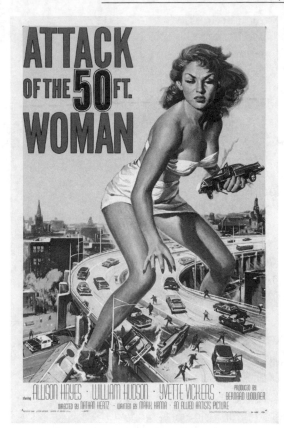

ATTACK
OF THE 50 FT.
WOMAN

ALLISON HAYES · WILLIAM HUDSON · YVETTE VICKERS   PRODUCED BY
BERNARD WOOLNER

DIRECTED BY NATHAN HERTZ · WRITTEN BY MARK HANNA · AN ALLIED ARTISTS PICTURE

Allison Hayes stars as a woman who might as well take advantage of her new colossal size by seeking revenge on her dirtbag husband.

transforms her into what the ads hyped as a bikini-clad "female colossus" with "a mountainous torso, skyscraper limbs, giant desires." Since hell hath no fury like a female colossus scorned, she tears up the town looking for her two-timing hubby. Written by Mark Hanna, who also penned the similarly themed *The Amazing Colossal Man*. Too bad no one thought to team those two up for a sequel. Originally released on a double bill with *War of the Satellites*. Later remade for cable starring Daryl Hannah; stick with Allison.

ATTACK OF THE 50 FT. WOMAN (1993)

1993 (R) 90m / D: Christopher Guest / **W:** Joseph Dougherty / **C:** Daryl Hannah, Daniel Baldwin, William Windom, Frances Fisher, Cristi Conaway, Paul Benedict, Lewis Arquette, Xander Berkeley, Hamilton Camp, Richard Edson, Victoria Haas, O'Neal Compton

Purposefully campy remake of the 1958 sci-fi cult classic that tries to expand on the original's subtle humor and feminist overtones. This made-for-TV version directed by improv comic genius Christopher Guest (*This Is Spinal Tap*) features the statuesque Daryl Hannah in the title role. As Nancy, Hannah's kept in a state of childish dependency by her domineering father (William Windom) and sleazy hubby (Daniel Baldwin). But after a close encounter of the enlarging kind with a flying saucer, Nancy finds that both her physique and self-esteem are steadily growing. After some initial trauma and humiliation, big Nancy decides it's payback time. If you've ever wanted to see Daryl Hannah trash a city, here's your chance. May not top the original, but it's colorful and amusing, and Hannah makes an attractive and sympathetic heroine.

ATTACK OF THE KILLER TOMATOES

1977 (PG) 83m / D: John DeBello / **W:** John DeBello, Costa Dillon / **C:** George Wilson, Jack Riley, Rock Peace, Eric Christmas, Sharon Taylor

"I know I'm going to miss her / A tomato ate my sister." Overripe low-budget spoof of low-budget horror and sci-fi films is a cult staple, but—much like many of the John Landis-style genre throwbacks of this time period—

it is hardly as entertaining as the movies it means to satirize. Some nice bits include the ominous prologue that references *The Birds*, a 1950s-style confrontation between the rampaging giant tomatoes (which appear to be just large red inflated trash bags) and the Army, and an unfortunate remark by an incognito human who has infiltrated the tomato forces: "Anybody have some ketchup?" Includes possibly the worst song ever recorded: "Puberty Love." Now available in a so-called "director's cut." Inexplicably followed by three direct-to-video sequels, one of which (1988's *Return of the Killer Tomatoes!*) starred a still-struggling George Clooney.

ATTACK THE BLOCK

2011 (R) 88m / **D:** Joe Cornish / **W:** Joe Cornish / **C:** John Boyega, Jodie Whittaker, Alex Esmail, Franz Drameh, Leeon Jones, Simon Howard, Luke Treadaway, Nick Frost

In most sci-fi movies, the racially mixed gang of South London teens who rob nurse Jodie Whittaker at the start of Joe Cornish's debut would be just a detail. But the filmmakers take the welcome tack of following those kids through a long night of battling the packs of ravenous, jet-black alien beasties descending on their 'hood. John Boyega makes a strong impression as the kids' leader, Moses, while Whittaker's slow realization that she must team up with her robbers to survive the night is nicely handled. The theme of children bravely facing down a deadly threat carries strong echoes of early Spielberg; fittingly, Cornish later co-wrote *The Adventures of Tintin* for the master.

THE AURORA ENCOUNTER

1985 (PG) 90m / **D:** Jim McCullough / **W:** Melody Brooke, Jim McCullough Jr. / **C:** Jack Elam, Mickey Hays, Peter Brown, Carol Bagdasarian, Dottie West, George "Spanky" McFarland

Small spaceman lands his flying jalopy in rural Texas around 1900, befriending Earth kids but panicking authorities (notably the villainous governor portrayed by one-time Little Rascal George "Spanky" McFarland). Warmhearted but hopelessly ragged cheapie claims to be based on a true story (aren't they all?), but even UFO buffs disbelieve that bit of regional folklore. The inspiration was clearly *E.T.* all the way. The alien is portrayed by Mickey Hays, a three-foot-tall Texas teenager who suffered from progeria, an extremely rare genetic disorder that caused rapid aging of the body and left him with bulbous eyes and a distended skull.

AVATAR

2009 (PG-13) 162m / **D:** James Cameron / **W:** James Cameron / **C:** Sam Worthington, Zoe Saldana, Sigourney Weaver, Stephen Lang, Michelle Rodriguez, Giovanni Ribisi, Joel David Moore, CCH Pounder, Wes Studi

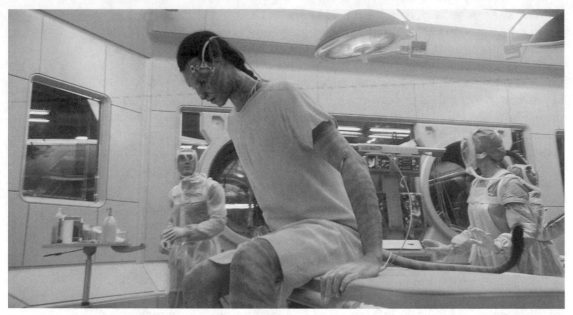

Sam Worthington plays a paraplegic marine who has his consciousness transferred into an alien in James Cameron's *Avatar*.

The first pure space opera to achieve real blockbuster status since *Star Wars*, James Cameron's groundbreaking movie was also the first to truly explore the possibilities of new 3D technology. In the year 2154, paraplegic ex-Marine Sam Worthington gets hired as a military contractor on the distant planet of Pandora. There, a massive and malevolent mining corporation is not-so-secretly plotting genocide against the native Na'vi aliens: 10-foot-tall, blue-skinned humanoids whose holistic and warrior ethos is meant to evoke that of Native American tribes. Worthington's conscience is torn after he goes undercover via a virtual-reality program that allows him to inhabit the consciousness of a Na'vi-like creature. It's both gorgeous spectacle and big-message movie, with billboard-sized anti-war and pro-environmental messages. Along the way, though, Cameron lifts liberally from all across the genre, particularly his own past (*Aliens*). After *Avatar*, big sci-fi movies hadn't just moved in from the fringe; they may well have *become* the mainstream. Nine nominations from overly impressed Oscar voters, including best picture; won for art direction, visual effects, and cinematography.

THE AVENGERS

2012 (PG-13) 143m / D: Joss Whedon / **W:** Joss Whedon / **C:** Robert Downey Jr., Chris Evans, Mark Ruffalo, Chris Hemsworth, Scarlett Johansson, Jeremy Renner, Tom Hiddleston, Clark Gregg, Cobie Smulders, Stellan Skarsgard, Samuel L. Jackson, Gwyneth Paltrow

Comic book movies didn't just come into their own with Joss Whedon's incomprehensibly successful brand of superhero adventures, they practically took over the business. Marvel had spent the previous several years building up their heroes like Thor, Captain America, Hulk, and Iron Man with individual blockbuster films before smashing them together in this serviceable romp about the good guys of S.H.I.E.L.D. defending Earth against some interdimensional bad dudes led by a scene-stealing Loki (Tom Hiddleston). All the better that S.H.I.E.L.D. gets to wage said fight from an aircraft carrier-sized airship that functions as essentially a gigantic floating boys' fort. Whedon plays to his strength with some flippant badinage between the various Avengers (Iron Man's sarcasm not playing well with either Captain America's earnestness or Thor's godly hubris) that almost keeps the whole mess from going totally off the rails—that, and Samuel L. Jackson's eyepatch. Oscar nomination for f/x.

AVP: ALIEN VS. PREDATOR

2004 (PG-13) 101m / **D:** Paul W. S. Anderson / **W:** Paul W. S. Anderson / **C:** Sanaa Lathan, Raoul Bova, Lance Henriksen, Ewen Bremner, Colin Salmon, Tommy Flanagan, Joseph Rye

After *Alien: Resurrection*, the suits at Fox weren't sure where to go with this hard-to-kill franchise. Letting well enough alone was clearly not an option. Paul W. S. Anderson's take broke the stalemate and though It's a thoroughly opportunistic and suspense-free exercise, it became the studio's most profitable film of the year. Efficient mash-up story set in the present day posits an ancient temple discovered under the Antarctic ice by series regulars the Weyland Corporation. The temple is seeded with frozen aliens that get hunted every century or so by the aliens from *Predator*. Research team led by ice-climber Sanaa Lathan and Mr. Weyland himself (Lance Henriksen, who played a Weyland Corporation android apparently designed after their dead boss centuries hence in the second and third films) gets in between the two murderous species and is made short work of. Cast is flat as a sheet of paper, directing is derivative, and creatures are revealed far too fast for any suspense to build up. That being said, the terrible script provides some laughs.

Babylon A.D.

2008 (PG-13) 90m / **D:** Mathieu Kassovitz / **W:** Mathieu Kassovitz, Eric Besnard / **C:** Vin Diesel, Michelle Yeoh, Mélanie Thierry, Gérard Depardieu, Charlotte Rampling, Mark Strong, Lambert Wilson

Grim action epic riddled with wasted potential has Vin Diesel as a former mercenary hired to shuttle innocent young Mélanie Thierry from her Russian convent to New York. Impressive early scenes show an uncomfortably recognizable succession of failed states riddled by terrorism. Turns more towards ridiculous action scenes (Diesel shooting down American border patrol drones from an airborne snowmobile, for instance) the closer it gets to the conclusion. Michelle Yeoh provides solid backup as Thierry's guardian, while Gérard Depardieu and Charlotte Rampling camp it up as Diesel's sleazy warlord employer and the vile head of a corporate New Age church. Reportedly marked by budget issues and studio interference, it disappeared quickly from theaters. Interesting for some of the futuristic detail but ultimately collapses under its own preposterousness.

Back to the Future

1985 (PG) 116m / **D:** Robert Zemeckis / **W:** Robert Zemeckis, Bob Gale / **C:** Michael J. Fox, Christopher Lloyd, Lea Thompson, Crispin Glover, Wendie Jo Sperber, Marc McClure, Thomas F. Wilson, James Tolkan, Casey Siemaszko, Billy Zane

When neighborhood mad scientist Doc Brown (Christopher Lloyd) constructs a time machine from a DeLorean sports car, his youthful companion Marty McFly (Michael J. Fox) accidentally transports himself to 1955. There, Marty inadvertently alters events leading up to his own birth and must do everything he can to bring his parents back together so he can be born

Christopher Lloyd (left) plays a brilliant scientist whose DeLorean time machine transports Michael J. Fox back to the 1950s in *Back to the Future.*

on schedule. At the same time, he has to elude the local bully, and he's still got to get back to his own time. Jokes are solid throughout, particularly the '50s-era Doc Brown refusing to believe there is a President Ronald Reagan in the future ("Then who's vice-president, Jerry Lewis?"), which is even better when you consider how much the Gipper liked referencing the movie in speeches. Zippy sci-fi comedy was an understandable smash hit due to the swift, humorous writing, '50s nostalgia, live-wire performances from Lloyd and also Crispin Glover as Marty's nerdish dad. (Zemeckis started shooting with a more angst-ridden Eric Stoltz in the Marty role but replaced him with the bright-eyed Fox after a few days.) Cameo from Huey Lewis, whose "Power of Love" theme song, a prime example of 1980s' synth-pop, was a huge hit. Followed by two sequels, a short-lived animated series, and some video games. Four Oscar nominations, including best original screenplay; won for f/x.

BACK TO THE FUTURE, PART 2

1989 (PG) 107m / **D:** Robert Zemeckis / **W:** Robert Zemeckis, Bob Gale / **C:** Michael J. Fox, Christopher Lloyd, Lea Thompson, Thomas F. Wilson, Elisabeth Shue, James Tolkan,

Casey Siemaszko, Jeffrey Weissman, Flea, Billy Zane, J. J. Cohen, Darlene Vogel, Jason Scott Lee, Crispin Glover, Ricky Dean Logan

Taking up exactly where the first film left off, this hit sequel has Doc Brown and Marty time-hopping into 2015 to save Marty's kids, then finding themselves returning to 1955 to retrieve a sports almanac that causes havoc for the McFly family. Clever editing allows for Marty Part 2 to see Marty Part 1 at the school dance. Most of the cast returns, although Crispin Glover appears only in cuts from the original and Elisabeth Shue steps in as girlfriend Jennifer. It's the rare satisfying sequel, albeit with a much darker tone, given the dystopic degeneracy (shades of the alternate Bedford Falls from *It's a Wonderful Life*) that Marty discovers in his future town. Zemeckis and Gale's script plays inventively with time-travel paradoxes, which become particularly tangled at this point in the series. Cliffhanger ending sets up *Part 3*, which was shot simultaneously with *Part 2*. Oscar nomination for f/x.

BACK TO THE FUTURE, PART 3

1990 (PG) 118m / **D:** Robert Zemeckis / **W:** Robert Zemeckis, Bob Gale / **C:** Michael J. Fox, Christopher Lloyd, Mary Steenburgen, Thomas F. Wilson, Lea Thompson, Elisabeth Shue

This third and final chapter of Robert Zemeckis's time-travel series picks up where *Part 2* climaxed. Stuck once again in 1955, Marty frantically searches for Doc Brown so he can return to 1985. Instead, he finds himself in the Wild West circa 1885, trying to save Doc's life and shepherd him through a love-affair with Mary Steenburgen. The plot is closely entwined with those of the earlier movies, so this is best viewed back-to-back with the first two films in order to best appreciate the clever weaving of apparently irreconcilable plot-elements. Nearly matches the original for nail-biting excitement and offers some snazzy new f/x. A superb conclusion to an excellent trilogy, even if it makes little sense that Marty's town of Hill Valley suddenly looks like it's in Monument Valley just because it's the 1800s.

Robert Zemeckis directed the "Back to the Future" films.

BAD TASTE

1988 (NR) 90m / **D:** Peter Jackson / **W:** Peter Jackson / **C:** Peter Jackson, Pete O'Herne, Mike Minett, Terry Potter, Craig Smith, Doug Wren, Dean Lawrie

Before Peter Jackson made the critically acclaimed gem *Heavenly Crea-tures*, before he took muppetry out of the kids' room (*Meet the Feebles*), before he got the government of New Zealand to fund his crowd-pleasing gore-comedy *Dead Alive*, and before he turned *The Lord of the Rings* into a blockbuster series, he wrote, directed, and starred in this sick little tale of alien fast-food manufacturers here on Earth, harvesting and processing hu-man munchies. The fate of the world lies in the hands (and chain saws) of a team of government-type guys trying to stop the rampant gobbling. As one would expect from early Jackson, the splatter is fast, funny, and extreme. From the head-cleaving-shovel beginning to the final-alien-chainsaw solution, this ultra-juicy horror-laughfest doesn't stop. The alien on the original VHS packaging came with a removable middle finger which video-store owners could choose to flip off or on.

THE BAMBOO SAUCER

1968 (G) 103m / **D:** Frank Telford / **W:** Frank Telford / **C:** Dan Duryea, John Ericson, Lois Nettleton, Nan Leslie

Roswell mania might give this relic some added interest, but only slightly. After buzzing the USA, a flying disk lands near a village in Maoist China and its (never seen) humanoids promptly perish from Earth germs. Russian and American scientists form an uneasy alliance to secretly investigate the craft. F/x and a space odyssey finale are ambitious for the era, but most of the narrative is talky and static, pushing a Cold War moral typical for the pe-riod: Soviets and Americans must learn brotherhood and cooperation—to crush the Red Chinese. Based on Gordon Fritz's novel *Flight of the Bamboo Saucer*. AKA: *Collision Course*.

BARBARELLA

1968 (PG) 98m / **D:** Roger Vadim / **W:** Terry Southern / **C:** Jane Fonda, John Phillip Law, David Hemmings, Marcel Marceau, Anita Pallenberg, Milo O'Shea

People change. Before Jane Fonda was a political activist or a serious ac-tress or a workout queen, she was, in the parlance of the times, a sex-kit-ten starlet. And what was once a boundary-challenging sci-fi romp now carries a tame PG rating. In actuality, this romp has never been anything more than a tongue-in-cheek comedy, and it has become more than a little dated. It's based on the popular French comic strip drawn by Jean-Claude Forest and brought to America in the pages of *Evergreen* magazine. The story has Fonda as a sexy bimbo who's sent by Earth's president in search of evil genius Duran Duran (Milo O'Shea), who has invented a new positronic ray weapon and is hiding out in a decadent city that has returned to a barbaric state of "neurotic irresponsibility." In order to complete her mission, she must face biting dolls, leather robots, a blind angel (John Phillip Law), the wickedly lesbianic Black Queen (Anita Pallenberg), a clumsy revolutionary (David Hemmings), and a living labyrinth, all while appearing in (and out of) many eccentric, sexy outfits. An attention-getting opening features Fonda in her famous zero-G strip tease. *Dr. Strangelove* author Terry Southern was responsible for most of the inanity but finds room for a few good lines perfectly suited for Fonda's robotic delivery: "What's that screaming? A good many dramatic things begin with screaming." AKA: *Barbarella, Queen of the Galaxy.*

BARB WIRE

1996 (R) 98m / D: David Hogan / **W:** Chuck Pfarrer, Ilene Chaiken / **C:** Pamela Anderson, Temuera Morrison, Victoria Rowell, Jack Noseworthy, Xander Berkeley, Steve Railsback

❝ Don't call me 'Babe'" is the catch phrase for this mid-1990s, post-*Tank Girl* semi-grrrl power futuristic action saga. Black-leather Barbie Pamela Anderson runs around the year 2017 in a bustier and heels beating

Jane Fonda is a space warrior who teams up with a winged alien played by John Phillip Law in the groovy 1968 sci-fi film *Barbarella.*

the holy tar out of clueless dudes who call her "Babe." Barb runs a nightclub in one of the last free cities in a civil war-racked America. It turns into a *Casablanca*-like scenario when some bad apples in suspiciously Nazi-esque uniforms try to shut down the party. Resolving said dispute involves many slow-motion scenes of Anderson high-kicking the villains. Everybody (including a very game Anderson) seems to be in on the joke. And really, what's not to like about a movie where a *Playboy* centerfold gets to take revenge on leering guys by planting a sharpened stiletto heel in their forehead?

*BATTERIES NOT INCLUDED

1987 (PG) 107m / D: Matthew Robbins / **W:** Matthew Robbins, Brad Bird, Brent Maddock, S. S. Wilson / **C:** Hume Cronyn, Jessica Tandy, Frank McRae, Michael Carmine, Elizabeth Peña, Dennis Boutsikaris

As an evil real estate developer schemes to demolish a New York tenement, the few remaining residents are aided in their struggle by small friendly flying saucers that have a talent for home improvement and crossing the deep void of space just to help out some nice old folks. Operating on *E.T./Cocoon* autopilot, Steven Spielberg produced this happy sci-fi reworking of the old elves-and-the-shoemaker fairy tale, with superb f/x from Industrial Light & Magic, awed stares from the human cast, and an overdose of schmaltz. Crusty Hume Cronyn is the only performer who doesn't get carried away by the cutes.

BATTLE BENEATH THE EARTH

1968 (NR) 91m / D: Montgomery Tully / **W:** Charles F. Vetter / **C:** Kerwin Mathews, Peter Arne, Viviane Ventura, Robert Ayres

The commies try to undermine democracy once again when American scientists discover a Chinese plot to invade the U.S. via a series of underground tunnels dug under the Pacific Ocean. Perhaps a tad jingoistic.

BATTLE BEYOND THE STARS

1980 (PG) 105m / D: Jimmy T. Murakami / **W:** John Sayles / **C:** Richard Thomas, Robert Vaughn, George Peppard, Sybil Danning, Sam Jaffe, John Saxon, Darlanne Fluegel

> **"The best parts include a sassy spaceship named Nell and Sybil Danning as a sexy Valkyrie in a minimal costume."**
>
> — *Battle Beyond the Stars*

This sci-fi comic book version of *The Magnificent Seven* appeals to the 10-year-old in all of us. And why not? It's a grand plot, and writer John Sayles does his usual playfully innovative work with the material. Richard Thomas is the callow youth who recruits a disreputable gang of adventurers to protect his backwater planet from marauding intergalactic outlaws. Robert Vaughn shows up to play exactly the same character as in *Magnificent Seven* and a pre-*A-Team* George Peppard is named simply Cowboy. The best parts include a sassy spaceship named Nell and Sybil Danning as a sexy Valkyrie in a minimal costume.

BATTLE BEYOND THE SUN

1963 (NR) 75m / D: Francis Ford Coppola / **W:** Nicholas Colbert, Edwin Palmer / **C:** Edd Perry, Arla Powell, Bruce Hunter, Andy Stewart

Francis Ford Coppola was just out of UCLA film school when he was hired as an assistant for $90 a week by Roger Corman. His first assignment was to Americanize (under the pseudonym "Thomas Colchart") a blatantly partisan Russian sci-fi adventure from 1959 called *Niebo Zowiet*. Coppola re-edited, wrote, and re-dubbed English dialogue. The story now takes place on a post-nuclear-war Earth that is divided into two countries, North and South Hemis. One of Coppola's most provocative inserts is a fight between two anatomically correct monsters, one male and the other female. Coppola would reshape another director's work without their input decades later with Walter Hill's *Supernova* in 2000.

BATTLEFIELD EARTH

2000 (PG-13) 118m / **D:** Roger Christian / **W:** Corey Mandell, J. D. Shapiro / **C:** John Travolta, Barry Pepper, Forest Whitaker, Kim Coates, Richard Tyson

Before creating the Church of Scientology, L. Ron Hubbard was a pulp writer of prodigious output who hobnobbed with the likes of Robert Heinlein. Many decades after starting his own religion, whose theology mixed self-help hints with generous lashings of space-opera backstory, Hubbard kept publishing fiction. His action-heavy tome of a bestseller was set on Earth centuries after the alien Psychlos knocked humanity back to *Planet of the Apes*-level primitivism. The rightfully savaged film version only makes the book's campy flaws more apparent. Barry Pepper plays upstanding human freedom fighter Jonnie Goodboy Tyler. John Travolta and Forest Whitaker appear under pounds of makeup and bad dreadlock wigs as not only the main nine-foot-tall Psychlo villains, but also the film's drillbit-shrill comic relief. The f/x wouldn't have passed muster fifteen years earlier, and Lucas collaborator Roger Christian's direction veers from dull to inept. Frequent high-scorer in all-time worst-film lists; an interesting development given how much of Hollywood is reportedly in thrall to Hubbard's Scientologists; one would imagine they could have called in more favors.

BATTLE FOR MOON STATION DALLOS

1986 (NR) 84m / **D:** Mamoru Oshii / **W:** Hisayuki Toriumi

Confusing but well-rendered cartoon feature from *Ghost in the Shell* director Mamoru Oshii about a rebellion waged on the moon by oppressed colonists against their heartless Earth masters. Surprisingly sober-minded (no comic-relief robots, cowboy sidekicks, or talking animals) and somewhat reminiscent of the works of popular Golden Age sci-fi authors like Robert Heinlein and Arthur C. Clarke, pic ends with too many unanswered questions; this was supposed to be chapter one of an ongoing saga, but viewer disinterest stifled any sequels. Despite its relative obscurity, this is notable as being the very first OVA (original video adaptation), a species of direct-to-video japanimation that became a booming marketplace for fantastic anime artists and enthusiasts—this one was just too ahead of its time. U.S. release is English-dubbed. AKA: *Dallos*.

BATTLE FOR THE PLANET OF THE APES

1973 (G) 96m / **D:** J. Lee Thompson / **W:** John W. Corrington, Joyce H. Corrington / **C:** Roddy McDowall, Lew Ayres, John Huston, Paul Williams, Claude Akins, Severn Darden, Natalie Trundy

*T*he *Guns of Navarone* director J. Lee Thompson shot this fifth and final film in the first *Apes* series as something of a straight war film. There's a framing device set in 2670 C.E. where a wise old orangutan (a resonant John Huston underneath the mask) is telling young chimps about Cornelius and Zira "descending upon Earth from Earth's own future to bring a savior, Caesar." The bulk of the film is a final prequel to the first installment, where we see how the ape revolt resulted in a devastating nuclear conflict. In the radioactive ruins, things get complicated, with mutants and gorillas making life miserable for peaceful apes. The inevitable result is all-out inter- and intra-species war, hampered in execution by this series' usual budget limitations. Shows how humans ultimately retreated to noncivilized ways and simian society broke into its ordered tiers (warlike gorillas, liberal chimps, and so on). Among the more curious actors playing apes are Claude Akins and 1970s soft rocker Paul Williams. A sign, perhaps, that this iteration of the ape saga had run out of juice.

BATTLE: LOS ANGELES

2011 (PG-13) 116m / D: Jonathan Liebesman / **W:** Christopher Bertolini / **C:** Aaron Eckhart, Michelle Rodriguez, Bridget Moynahan, Michael Peña

*T*he alien invasion trend really started taking off the year this by-the-numbers effort was released; this may have not been a positive devel-

Modern-day Los Angeles is attacked by hostile aliens and only outnumbered and outgunned heroic soldiers stand in their way in *Battle: Los Angeles.*

opment. Actioner has a solid premise: instead of taking the world-spanning view that most blockbusters go for, Christopher Bertolini's script zooms in on how one Marine platoon (led by sci-fi schlock veteran Aaron Eckhart) faces off against the extraterrestrial hordes after their spaceship-meteors blast into the ocean just off Los Angeles. The buildup is efficiently executed, with the various characters learning about the invasion through realistically depicted shaky news footage on cable news networks. But once the battle is joined, the script's severely limited imagination makes the second half of the film a real slog.

BATTLE ROYALE

2000 (NR) 114m / **D:** Kinji Fukasaku / **W:** Kinji Fukasaku / **C:** Takeshi Kitano, Tatsuya Fujiwara, Aki Maeda, Taro Yamamoto

A Japanese high school class on a bus trip is gassed unconscious and the students wake up to find themselves in a decrepit classroom on a deserted island. A stern teacher they once knew (the great, stone-faced Takeshi Kitano, providing the film's slim reed of dark humor) tells them that by government order, they have to take part in a three-day contest that ends when only one of the 42 is left alive. Concerned they're not listening, Kitano buries a knife in one girl's forehead. Each kid gets a randomly chosen weapon ranging from pot lid to assault rifle. The killing is fast and furious, with fighting patterns mirroring school-based cliques and romantic pairings. As unrealistic as the scenario is (*why* the Battle Royale act was passed, and what purpose it serves, is never addressed), writer/director Kinji Fukasaku relies less on credibly pulpy drama than on coincidence, cliché, and *deus ex machinas* galore. Poor sci-fi awash in a cynical mix of sentimentality and second-hand *Clockwork Orange*-isms, but plenty of bloodsoaked action here for those who like watching 14-year-olds in school uniforms bury axes in each other's heads. Based on a popular novel, *Battle Royale* spawned a sequel and a manga series, as well as, some would claim, *The Hunger Games*.

BATTLESHIP

2012 (PG-13) 131m / **D:** Peter Berg / **W:** Jon Hoeber, Erich Hoeber / **C:** Taylor Kitsch, Alexander Skarsgard, Rihanna, Brooklyn Decker, Tadanobu Asano, Hamish Linklater, Liam Neeson

A kind of miserable apogee of the 2000s' blockbuster mania was reached with this sodden and gargantuan mess of a battle royale based on the old board game. Herein, scientists make the silly mistake of trying to contact a recently discovered Earth-like planet. Result is a squadron of alien vessels plunging into the ocean near Hawaii just when an international naval exercise is going on. Wouldn't you know that the undisciplined scamp of a new sailor (Taylor Kitsch, who would have made for a great Tarzan once upon a time) is going to end up as humanity's last hope? For about five minutes, the last beleaguered destroyer uses a grid-like search pattern to find the aliens, just like in the game. After that, it's back to interspecies war. Director Peter Berg gamely tries to plug some humor into this grind, but otherwise it's just another alien-war story where f/x try to compensate for purpose. Pop star Rihanna shows up to battle aliens with a speedboat mounted with some kind of gatling gun, because it's just that kind of movie.

THE BEAST FROM 20,000 FATHOMS

1953 (NR) 80m / D: Eugène Lourié / **W:** Fred Freiberger, Louis Morheim / **C:** Paul Christian, Paula Raymond, Cecil Kellaway, Kenneth Tobey, Donald Woods, Lee Van Cleef, Steve Brodie, Mary Hill

One of the first prehistoric-monster-loosed-by-radiation movies of the 1950s, and still one of the best. When atomic testing defrosts a giant dinosaur in the Arctic, the hungry monster (the fictional "rhedosaurus") proceeds onwards to its former breeding grounds, now New York City. F/x genius Ray Harryhausen's creature isn't as detailed as some of his later work, but the film is still suspenseful, solidly constructed, and tons of fun to watch. Based loosely on the poetic Ray Bradbury story "The Fog Horn." Watch for a very young Lee Van Cleef.

BEASTMASTER 2: THROUGH THE PORTAL OF TIME

1991 (PG-13) 107m / D: Sylvio Tabet / **W:** R. J. Robertson, Jim Wynorski, Sylvio Tabet, Ken Hauser, Doug Miles / **C:** Marc Singer, Kari Wuhrer, Sarah Douglas, Wings Hauser, James Avery, Robert Fieldsteel, Arthur Malet, Robert Z'Dar, Michael Berryman

Unlike the first *Beastmaster* in 1982, in this vaguely sci-fi follow-up the laughs are intentional as Dar, the sword-swingin' and loincloth'd Beastmaster (Marc Singer) follows an evil monarch from their fantasy world through a dimensional gateway to modern-day L.A. Dar finds the shopping is better for both trendy clothes and weapons. It lacks the stupid charm of the first film (that's what happens when you get a different director), but this sequel is still fun for sword-and-sorcery fanatics. And there's a tiger!

THE BEAST OF YUCCA FLATS

1961 (NR) 53m / D: Coleman Francis / **W:** Coleman Francis / **C:** Tor Johnson, Douglas Mellor, Larry Aten, Barbara Francis, Conrad Brooks, Bing Stafford, Anthony Cardoza

Expecting a giant radioactive dinosaur? Try a radioactive Tor Johnson! In this unbelievably cheap, quasi-nuclear protest film, Tor plays a Russian scientist who's chased by communist agents into a testing area and is caught in an atomic blast. As a result, he turns into a club-wielding caveman—very like all the "monsters" Tor played in other movies. Droning voice-over narration was used instead of dialogue to keep costs down. Anyone who thinks pro wrestler-turned-actor Tor's roles in *Plan 9 from Outer Space* and *Bride of the Monster* were masterpieces of bad acting needs to check this dog out. Fellow Ed Wood crony Conrad Brooks shows up as a federal agent. Director/writer/actor Coleman Francis showed up in lots of B-westerns in the 1940s and '50s before ending up doing bit parts in movies for Russ Meyer and Ray Dennis Steckler.

Tor Johnson, already infamous for his bad acting in such dogs as *Plan 9 from Outer Space,* becomes the radioactive title character in 1961's *The Beast of Yucca Flats.*

THE BED-SITTING ROOM

1969 (NR) 90m / **D:** Richard Lester / **W:** Richard Lester / **C:** Rita Tushingham, Peter Cook, Dudley Moore, Spike Mulligan, Arthur Lowe, Marty Feldman, Ralph Richardson, Harry Secombe

A pre-Monty Python farce set in a post-apocalyptic England that looks to be nothing but a great junk heap following a "nuclear misunderstanding" that reduced the nation's population to just 20 people. Stocked with the cream of British comic talent, from Dudley Moore to Marty Feldman, playing various variations on post-traumatic crack-up. The last of Richard Lester's anarchic Mod-hippie skit-flicks (*How I Won the War*, *Petulia*) before he turned to more mainstream fare like *The Three Musketeers* and *Superman II*.

BEGINNING OF THE END

1957 (NR) 76m / **D:** Bert I. Gordon / **W:** Fred Freiberger, Lester Gorn / **C:** Peggie Castle, Peter Graves, Morris Ankrum, Richard Benedict, James Seay

From the opening shot of a couple necking in a convertible on lovers' lane to the tinny and overwrought musical score to the stock footage of soldiers and tanks, this is your archetypal 1950s big-bug B-movie. In short: Huge, radiation-spawned locusts attack Chicago. Peter Graves springs into action and saves the day. Easily the best giant grasshopper film ever made, it's good for giggles but little more. Graves (*It Conquered the World*), Morris Ankrum (*Earth vs. the Flying Saucers*), and even Peggie Castle (*Target Earth*)

Peggie Castle and Peter Graves starred in *Beginning of the End,* a B movie about giant grasshoppers. Who would have predicted it would all end this way?

were all veterans of cheap sci-fi battles against large animal domination. The ad campaign stressed the fact that the filmmakers used "real" grasshoppers in the movie, as opposed to that "phony" stop-motion stuff. Bert I. Gordon would move on to more oversized bugs with *The Spider,* followed by other BIG productions, similarly redolent with insect verisimilitude.

BENEATH THE PLANET OF THE APES

1969 (G) 95m / **D:** Ted Post / **W:** Mort Abrahams, Paul Dehn / **C:** Charlton Heston, James Franciscus, Kim Hunter, Maurice Evans, James Gregory, Natalie Trundy, Jeff Corey, Linda Harrison, Victor Buono

In this first sequel to the sci-fi classic, another 20th-century astronaut, Brent (James Franciscus), time-warps to the year 3995, looking for his lost colleague Taylor (Charlton Heston). Brent discovers Ape City, travels through the ruins of the post-apocalyptic New York subway system (looking not so different in the 40th century than in the late 1960s), and oh yes, discovers nuclear warhead-worshiping telepathic human mutants ("Glory be to the bomb and to his fallout"). Unfortunately, the militant apes above ground also discover their existence, leading to a violent confrontation. The sequel tries to maintain the allegorical bent of the original, including peace sit-ins and an anti-nuclear message, but falls short of the mark. However, the film's gonzo, borderline surreal quality deserves notice. Several members of the original cast are back, including Kim Hunter as Zira and Charlton Heston as Taylor. Roddy McDowall did not don the makeup for this one, but provided the voice for his character, Cornelius. Curiously rated G, given all the apocalyptic violence. A three-film prequel cycle would follow.

BEYOND THE STARS

1989 (PG) 88m / **D:** David Saperstein / **W:** David Saperstein / **C:** Martin Sheen, Christian Slater, Olivia d'Abo, F. Murray Abraham, Robert Foxworth, Sharon Stone

Christian Slater stars in this space family saga as a problem kid bent on an aerospace career, who befriends reclusive Apollo 11 astronaut Martin Sheen, still bitter over the NASA cover-up of a deadly accident on the moon. Weak drama with sci-fi overtones that come too little too late, though it's a novelty to see a movie so heavily promote the hobby of model rocketry. David Saperstein, the original author of *Cocoon*, wrote/directed from a script that turns to save-the-whales when it runs out of other messages. Interesting cast.

BEYOND THE TIME BARRIER

1960 (NR) 75m / **D:** Edgar G. Ulmer / **W:** Arthur C. Pierce / **C:** Robert Clarke, Darlene Tompkins, Arianne Arden, Vladimir Sokoloff

Air Force test pilot gets more than he bargained for when his high-speed plane carries him into the future. There he sees the ravages of an upcoming plague to which he must return. Subplot of a sterile population looking for viable reproductive partners prefigures *A Boy and His Dog*.

BICENTENNIAL MAN

1999 (PG) 132m / **D:** Chris Columbus / **W:** Nicholas Kazan / **C:** Robin Williams, Embeth Davidtz, Sam Neill, Oliver Platt, Kiersten Warren, Bradley Whitford

Fuzzy-minded wandering heartwarmer based on an Isaac Asimov robot story and novel about an android named Andrew (Robin Williams) bought by Sam Neill for household work, but ends up as the family's multi-generational companion. Eventually Andrew has to come to terms with his immortality and These. Strange. Emotions. Epic philosophical potential is smothered in sub-

In *Bicentennial Man*, Sam Neill played a father who buys his family a robot named Andrew as a household helper, inadvertently finding them a friend to span the ages.

par f/x, movie-star "aren't I cheeky?" smarm, and failure to explore broader impact of technology on society. View of the future is curiously *Jetsons*-ish. Oscar nomination for makeup.

BIGGLES

1986 (PG) 108m / **D:** John Hough / **W:** John Groves, Kent Walwin / **C:** Neil Dickson, Alex Hyde-White, Peter Cushing, Fiona Hutchison, Marcus Gilbert

Generations of English boys thrilled to W. E. Johns's tales of WWI flying ace Bigglesworth, his brave pal Algy, and their Snoopy-style dogfights with the Hun. But when this movie version finally emerged, the major influence was instead *Back to the Future*. Biggles is a modern guy—of all things, a bloody Yank—who abruptly materializes back in 1917 Europe and helps his "time twin" Biggles in a confrontation with an advanced German superweapon (which, surprisingly, isn't the cause of the time warp after all). Biggles purists will be outraged, but there are some spirited anachronisms and a proper tongue-in-cheek attitude. Beware the 1980s disco music. AKA: *Biggles: Adventures in Time*.

BILL & TED'S BOGUS JOURNEY

1991 (PG) 93m / **D:** Pete Hewitt / **W:** Chris Matheson, Edward Solomon / **C:** Keanu Reeves, Alex Winter, William Sadler, Joss Ackland, Pam Grier, George Carlin

A big-budget sequel to *Bill & Ted's Excellent Adventure* that features better f/x but not quite as much of the charm of the original. Slain by look-alike robot duplicates from the future, the titular airhead heroes pass through an impressively visualized heaven and hell before tricking Death into bringing them back for a second duel with their heinous terminators. Bill and Ted's duel with Death is definitely the high point of the film—an extended spoof on the chessboard match with Death in *The Seventh Seal*, here the long-haired duo play for their eternal souls via rounds of Twister and Battleship.

BILL & TED'S EXCELLENT ADVENTURE

1989 (PG) 90m / **D:** Stephen Herek / **W:** Chris Matheson, Edward Solomon / **C:** Keanu Reeves, Alex Winter, George Carlin, Bernie Casey

Apleasantly surprising magic-time travel diversion and something of a high-water mark in the up-and-way-down career of Keanu Reeves. When two amiable but intellectually challenged Valley Boys (Alex Winter and Reeves) find themselves in danger of failing their history final (whoa!), they're rescued by Rufus (George Carlin) and his time-traveling telephone booth (double-whoa!). It seems that Bill and Ted are destined to become the founders of a future utopia based on heavy metal music. This paradise will never come to pass if they fail their test, so Rufus has come back to give the proto-heroes a chance to brush up on history first-hand. Along the way they meet a host of historical figures and put every time-travel cliché through the wringer. Good-natured and surprisingly entertaining.

THE BIRDS

1963 (PG-13) 120m / **D:** Alfred Hitchcock / **W:** Evan Hunter / **C:** Rod Taylor, Tippi Hedren, Jessica Tandy, Veronica Cartwright, Suzanne Pleshette, Ethel Griffies, Charles McGraw, Ruth McDevitt

Hitchcock's borderline sci-fi chiller remains one of the best and most creative Man-versus-Nature shockers. Still wildly original in the way the plot slowly turns from a romantic soap opera—whole first hour details sophisticate Tippi Hedren venturing to a California island community to snare lawyer Rod Taylor, despite his disapproving mother—into an environmental

With his usual droll wit, director Alfred Hitchcock clowns around in a trailer for his film *The Birds*.

nightmare, with bloody, seemingly unmotivated bird attacks poking through the placid narrative until there's nothing else. Only Hitchcock can twist the harmless into the horrific while avoiding the ridiculous; for the deadly simplicity of its concept, this is perhaps the cinema's purest, most horrifying portrait of the apocalypse. While bluescreen f/x technology has improved considerably since this was made, Hitch's eye for camera placement and editing remains talon-sharp. Based on a short story by Daphne du Maurier; screenplay by Evan Hunter (AKA crime novelist Ed McBain), but also inspired by a real-life plague of birds that hit not far from Hitchcock's American home in Santa Cruz (an incident briefly mentioned in the dialogue). Oscar nomination for f/x.

THE BLACK HOLE

1979 (G) 97m / D: Gary Nelson / **W:** Jeb Rosebrook, Gerry Day / **C:** Maximilian Schell, Anthony Perkins, Ernest Borgnine, Yvette Mimieux, Joseph Bottoms, Robert Forster

What is mad scientist Maximilian Schell up to as his starship sits at the edge of a black hole? Lots of nasty robots and abominable dialogue provide the answers in this Disney space adventure. Throwback sci-fi recalls *Forbidden Planet* and even the studio's own *20,000 Leagues under the Sea*. Fine matte paintings by Peter Ellenshaw create a dark, mysterious atmosphere. Despite the glaring flaws in this glossy but creaky family vehicle, kids will probably enjoy the effects and the good "cute" robots. Overdue for a remake. Two Oscar nominations.

BLADE RUNNER

1982 (R) 117m / D: Ridley Scott / **W:** Hampton Fancher, David Peoples / **C:** Harrison Ford, Rutger Hauer, Sean Young, Daryl Hannah, M. Emmet Walsh, Edward James Olmos, Joe Turkel, Brion James, Joanna Cassidy

Like the best sci-fi, this one asks big questions and doesn't provide ready answers. In the case of this problematic but genre-redefining masterpiece, the question left hanging in the smoky air is: "What does it mean to be human?" In the year 2019, L.A. has been turned into a crowded megalopolis where flying cars float like blinking ghosts and billboard-cluttered skyscrapers tower into the rainy and neon-strobed mist over teeming streets. The retro-noir story has Harrison Ford playing Deckard, a private eye hired by his old police captain to hunt down some androids ("replicants" here, or "skin jobs" to the less enlightened) who have gone on a murderous rampage. The screenplay lifts its inspiration lightly from Philip K. Dick's novel *Do Androids Dream of Electric Sheep?*, turning the author's post-apocalyptic setting and theological musings into a metaphor of fallen humanity. Rutger

Hauer turns in a career-worthy performance as the lead replicant, quoting Blake and battling furiously for more life even as his manufacturer expiration date comes tragically nigh. The grandly foolish design scheme threatens at all points to overcome the admittedly weak screenplay, which compensated for its obliqueness in the original release by superimposing a faux world-weary narration from Deckard. While clarifying the plot (such as it was), the narration never quite gelled and was deleted from the numerous later director's cuts and special editions, which also got rid of the original's ridiculously tacked-on happy-ish conclusion and went with something more ambiguous. Later cuts also highlighted the unreliability of memory and the chillingly thin line separating cold-blooded humans from empathetic replicants. Numerous theories exploded later about whether Deckard himself was a replicant all along. Was trounced at the box office the year it came out by Spielberg's *E.T.* but has since proven to be a dystopic landmark. The future was never the same. Two Oscar nominations: art direction and set decoration.

In the dystopic landmark 1982 movie *Blade Runner,* the motto of the company that makes the androids called "replicants" is "more human than human."

BLINDNESS

2008 (R) 121m / **D:** Fernando Meirelles / **W:** Don McKellar / **C:** Julianne Moore, Mark Ruffalo, Alice Braga, Maury Chaykin, Danny Glover, Don McKellar, Gael García Bernal

In a generically modern anywhere city, a plague of blindness is rampaging. Amidst the amoeba-like spread of societal breakdown, a small group (carefully chosen for maximum racial diversity) bands together for survival in the hospital they've been isolated in. Fernando Meirelles's take on the José Saramago international best seller plays like a pale allegory for whatever calamity the audience might bring to the table. Smartly depicted mechanics of how the newly blind adjust to their surroundings: finding shelter, food, safety. Ensemble cast is smartly assembled, with Julianne Moore and Gael García Bernal (as a malevolent mini-warlord of the quarantine ward) being standouts. But the allegorical plot and washed-out cinematography make for a curiously bloodless affair.

THE BLOB (1958)

1958 (NR) 83m / D: Irvin S. Yeaworth Jr. / **W:** Theodore Simonson, Kate Phillips / **C:** Steve McQueen, Aneta Corsaut, Olin Howlin, Earl Rowe

Steve McQueen (shown here in 1959), got his first starring role in 1958's *The Blob*.

In his first starring role, Steve McQueen is a rebel with a cause: to save his small Pennsylvania town from a gelatinous invader from outer space. Naturally, the adults don't believe him, but they change their tune when this purple people eater engulfs a supermarket, a diner, and most memorably, a movie theater (where *Daughter of Horror* is playing). McQueen's girlfriend is played by Aneta Corsaut, who is best known as Helen Crump on *The Andy Griffith Show*. One of the most beloved monster movies of the 1950s (it was released the same year as *The Fly*). Producer Jack Harris later made *Mother Goose a Go Go* (or *The Unkissed Bride*) and the first 3D adult film, *Paradisio*, while McQueen went on to infinitely better things. Burt Bacharach co-wrote the awesomely swinging title tune "Beware of the Blob" ("it creeps, and leaps, and glides, and slides...."). Followed by Larry Hagman's 1972 direct-to-drive-in sequel, *Beware! The Blob* (or: *Son of Blob*), and a state-of-the-art remake in 1988.

THE BLOB (1988)

1988 (R) 92m / D: Chuck Russell / **W:** Frank Darabont, Chuck Russell / **C:** Kevin Dillon, Candy Clark, Joe Seneca, Shawnee Smith, Donovan Leitch, Jeffrey DeMunn, Del Close

The 1980s were a fertile breeding ground for remakes of such '50s sci-fi cult classics as *The Fly*, *The Thing*, *Invaders from Mars*, and *The Blob*. It is perhaps for sociologists to explain why, but the thumbnail explanation could have something to do with the '80s conservative backlash ... and after all, the Commies were still out there just like in the '50s, providing cause for all sorts of conspiratorial threat transference. Perhaps more to the point, f/x had gotten a lot better. In this do-over of the 1958 original, the massive glutinous monster is, at last, the star. It's now a meaner, more ravenous Blob. No longer content just to attack movie theater projectionists (as in the original), it also slurps dishwashers down the sink and engulfs phone booths. It's probably a sign of the times that the Blob is not an outer-space organism, but a product of the military gone bad. Unfortunately, a young Kevin Dillon is no young Steve McQueen. A very early effort from *The Walking Dead* and *The Shawshank Redemption* writer Frank Darabont. Beware Reverend Meeker (played by Chicago improv comedy giant Del Close), whose climactic warnings of the end of the world are given extra urgency by those remnants of the Blob he keeps in a jar....

THE BLOOD OF HEROES

1989 (R) 90m / **D:** David Peoples / **W:** David Peoples / **C:** Rutger Hauer, Joan Chen, Delroy Lindo, Vincent D'Onofrio, Anna Katarina

Post-apocalyptic blah-blah-blah detailing the adventures of a battered team of "juggers," warriors who challenge small village teams to a brutal sport (involving dogs' heads on sticks) that's a cross between jousting and football, only involving a dog's skull. Improbably A-list cast for this kind of mess. From the co-writer of *Blade Runner*. AKA: *The Salute of the Jugger*.

BLUE THUNDER

1983 (R) 110m / **D:** John Badham / **W:** Dan O'Bannon, Don Jakoby / **C:** Roy Scheider, Daniel Stern, Malcolm McDowell, Candy Clark, Warren Oates

Maverick LAPD helicopter pilots Roy Scheider and Daniel Stern test an experimental high-tech chopper that can see through walls, record a whisper, and destroy a city block. Cool! Unless you're considered an undesirable by the right-wing corporate ghouls who made the thing and will do anything to ensure security during the 1984 Olympics. Scheider's post-'Nam PTSD comes back to haunt him, particularly when he runs into a loathed figure from his wartime past (played by Malcolm McDowell with all appropriate villainy). Futuristic hardware qualifies this as sci-fi, otherwise it's standard-issue hard-to-believe 1980s tech thriller. The satisfying aerial combat scenes nearly crash with the much-rewritten script. Inspired a short-lived TV series and a (notably more popular) rival-network imitator, *Airwolf*. Chopper aficionados will note that the Blue Thunder, while often misidentified as an Apache craft, is actually a French-made Aerospatiale Gazelle with design modifications. Oscar nomination for editing.

> "Futuristic hardware qualifies this as sci-fi, otherwise it's standard-issue hard-to-believe 1980s tech thriller."
>
> *Blue Thunder*

BODY SNATCHERS

1993 (R) 87m / **D:** Abel Ferrara / **W:** Stuart Gordon, Dennis Paoli, Nicholas St. John / **C:** Gabrielle Anwar, Meg Tilly, Terry Kinney, Forest Whitaker, Billy Wirth, R. Lee Ermey

"They're out there. They're everywhere. They get you when you sleep, you hear?" The pod people are at it again, now set loose on the human race by *Bad Lieutenant* director Abel Ferrara, who's used to dealing with more energetically alienated characters. Ferrara's more gut-level horror show is set on an army base, a brilliant maneuver as the military's strict code of conduct provides perfect cover for the emotionless pods, not to mention a decent critique of the military mentality. The f/x, light years ahead of the 1956 and 1978 versions (entitled *Invasion of the Body Snatchers*) in which they were barely noticed, literally get under your skin. But after all these years, the paranoia of Jack Finney's original story is still palpable: "Where you gonna go?" asks pod-wife Meg Tilly. "Where you gonna run? Where you gonna hide? Nowhere. Because there is no one … like you … left."

THE BOOK OF ELI

2010 (R) 118m / D: Albert Hughes, Allen Hughes / **W:** Gary Whitta / **C:** Denzel Washington, Gary Oldman, Mila Kunis, Ray Stevenson, Jennifer Beals, Evan Jones, Joe Pingue, Frances de la Tour, Michael Gambon, Tom Waits

Denzel Washington roams the American desert in a dusty coat and sunglasses in this Hughes Brothers (*Menace II Society*) ode to the bullet-riddled post-apocalyptic action epics of yore. Less talkative than Clint Eastwood's Man with No Name but just as deadly (using shotguns, knives, martial arts; whatever it takes), the stoic Eli is on a mission to safely deliver a sacred book of powerful import to a secret location. This same book is desired by one Carnegie (Gary Oldman), the sadistic bossman of a nowhere town Eli has to fight his way through. Eli doesn't have a lot of trouble keeping his hide in one piece but still manages to pick up a couple of helpers (*That '70s Show*'s Mila Kunis as little girl lost and Tom Waits as … Tom Waits) along the way. Ridiculous but in an energetic sort of way, with a script that keeps a couple big secrets admirably close to its vest until the end.

BOOM IN THE MOON

1946 (NR) 90m / D: Jaime Salvador / **W:** Jaime Salvador, Victor Trivas / **C:** Buster Keaton, Ángel Garasa, Virginia Serret, Fernando Soto, Luis Barreiro

The great Buster Keaton fares poorly in this Mexican-produced sci-fi comedy where he ends up trapped on an experimental rocket that takes him to the moon. Poor production, with uneven direction and acting; understandably forgotten. Incredibly, this was Keaton's first starring role in over ten years. AKA: *A Modern Bluebeard*.

BORN IN FLAMES

1983 (NR) 80m / D: Lizzie Borden / **W:** Lizzie Borden / **C:** Honey, Adele Bertei, Jean Satterfield, Florynce Kennedy, Ed Bowes

In this lauded experimental fantasia set ten years after a much talked-about revolution has supposedly turned America into a paradise of a socialist democracy, the same old problems still fester: unemployment, racism, and sexism. On the streets of New York, underemployed men who resent the gains women have made take to rioting and rape. Feminist groups band together to fight for their rights and ultimately hijack the airwaves to broadcast their message of liberation. Lizzie Borden's debut film is something of a No Wave mess, blending faux-documentary sci-fi with stiff dialogue straight out of a boundary-pushing gender studies seminar. Still viable as a blast of pure radical feminist outrage, set against a rotting Manhattan and scored with atonal music that could have come straight from *Liquid Sky*.

THE BORROWER

1992 (R) 92m / **D:** John McNaughton / **W:** Mason Nage, Richard Fire / **C:** Rae Dawn Chong, Don Gordon, Antonio Fargas, Tom Towles

An exiled unstable mutant insect alien serial killer must switch heads with human beings regularly to survive. This colorful, garish gorefest has humor and attitude but never develops behind the basic gross-out situation. Director John McNaughton's follow-up to his cult hit debut *Henry, Portrait of a Serial Killer* (and sole attempt at sci-fi) fails to find the same balance between humor and horror.

BOUNTY KILLER

2013 (R) 93m / **D:** Henry Saine / **W:** Jason Dodson, Colin Ebeling, Henry Saine / **C:** Matthew Marsden, Kristanna Loken, Christian Pitre, Barak Hardley, Abraham Benrubi, Gary Busey, Beverly D'Angelo, Eve

Unlike most every other *Max Max* ripoff out there, this post-apocalyptic goof tries to keep its tongue firmly in cheek. It's the wisest approach for a story in which the remains of humanity have licensed so-called bounty killers to go after the corporate villains who started the world-annihilating wars that left civilization in a shambles. In the role that should have gone to Rose McGowan, Christian Pitre plays the people's favorite, Mary Death, while Matthew Marsden is her stubble-cheeked love-interest/competition, named Drifter. Fairly nonsensical throughout but gets off a couple decent gags, like Drifter's sycophantic "gun caddy" and the Mary Death-branded hand grenades.

THE BOX

2009 (PG-13) 115m / **D:** Richard Kelly / **W:** Richard Kelly / **C:** Cameron Diaz, James Marsden, Frank Langella, James Rebhorn, Holmes Osborne, Gillian Jacobs

In the Richard Matheson story "Button, Button," a mysterious man tells a poor couple that if they push the button in a box he leaves with them a

What would you do if you could have a million bucks, but the catch was that a stranger would have to die? That's the quandary in *The Box*.

stranger somewhere will die and they will win $200,000. Richard Kelly's fervid nightmare of a film takes Matheson's tight little moral quandary (filmed in 1986 as one of the better episodes in the first *Twilight Zone* revamp) as its starting point, ramping the reward up to $1 million, before going wildly off the rails with a 1970s-set story about aliens, the space program, and various secretive government agencies. There's also an impeccably ghoulish Frank Langella, who's not just given lines like "I work for those who control the lightning" but gets to say them through a gaping wound in his face. Not surprisingly, most of the source story's philosophical thrill goes out the window once Kelly's dark metaphysical fantasy takes over. An argument against Hollywood churning out nothing but safe and pandering pap; *somebody* said okay to giving the director of *Donnie Darko* tens of millions of dollars to make this fascinating oddity.

A BOY AND HIS DOG

1975 (R) 87m / **D:** L. Q. Jones / **W:** L. Q. Jones / **C:** Don Johnson, Susanne Benton, Jason Robards Jr., Charles McGraw, Alvy Moore

Curious piece of cult 1970s sci-fi comedy. In the post-holocaust world of 2014, Don Johnson plays Vic, a canny but ultimately dim-witted youth who treks across the barren wilderness foraging for food and women. In the clever role reversal that gave Harlan Ellison's award-winning novella such a kick, Vic's canine companion, Blood (a genetically enhanced breed who can communicate telepathically) is the more cultured and civilized of the two. Directed and adapted with witty panache by the great cowboy character actor L. Q. Jones, it goes slightly off the rails when the plot shifts underground to a creepy *Truman Show*-like society run by Jason Robards. Though Ellison has expressed "enormous appreciation" for Jones's adaptation, the legendarily contentious author disavows the controversial ending in which Johnson must choose between an ailing Blood and a woman trying to lure him to an underground society that desires his breeding potential. Suffice it to say the final pun is not for all tastes. Ellison reportedly raised money to re-dub the movie by hawking clippings from the editing room floor at sci-fi conventions, but Jones prevailed. Produced by Alvy Moore (best remembered as Hank Kimble on *Green Acres*). Blood was played by the late Tiger of *The Brady Bunch*. Tim McIntire supplies the voice.

THE BOYS FROM BRAZIL

1978 (R) 123m / D: Franklin J. Schaffner / **W:** Heywood Gould / **C:** Gregory Peck, James Mason, Laurence Olivier, Uta Hagen, Steve Guttenberg, Denholm Elliott, Lilli Palmer

Ira Levin's thriller is brought to the screen with Gregory Peck as an obsessed Nazi hell-bent on cloning a batch of little Adolfs, Laurence Olivier as a Jewish Nazi-hunter (two years after he played a Nazi war criminal in *Marathon Man*), and just a *slightly* ridiculous plot. With numerous "on-location" segments filmed around the world, the movie plays more as big-screen adventure than thought-provoking intrigue about the implications of a possible Fourth Reich. With the brood of young Hitlers needing the proper upbringing, a few murders are definitely called for, both as a plot device and to position the new youth corps into the right environment. Given the fairly trashy source material, not a bad movie at all, but with Olivier's acting, Heywood Gould's script, and another outstanding score by composer Jerry Goldsmith, the film could have been much, much more. Three Oscar nominations: editing, music, and Olivier for lead actor.

THE BRAIN EATERS

1958 (NR) 60m / D: Bruno VeSota / **W:** Gordon Urquhart / **C:** Ed Nelson, Alan Frost, Jack Hill, Joanna Lee, Jody Fair, Leonard Nimoy

A strange ship from inside the Earth invades a small town, and hairy monsters promptly attach themselves to people's necks in a daring bid to control the planet. The imaginative story compensates somewhat for the cheap f/x. Watch for a young Leonard Nimoy before he grew pointed ears. Robert Heinlein sued American International Pictures for $150,000, claiming that Gordon Urquhart's screenplay plagiarized liberally from his novel *The Puppet Masters*.

BRAINSTORM

1983 (PG) 106m / **D:** Douglas Trumbull / **W:** Robert Stitzel, Philip Frank Messina / **C:** Natalie Wood, Christopher Walken, Cliff Robertson, Louise Fletcher

Natalie Wood's last film is far from her best in terms of character or story but the inventive f/x and cinematography (not to mention one of the better James Horner scores) work hard to make up for it. Michael and Karen Brace (Christopher Walken and Wood) invent a device that can record dreams, thoughts, and fantasies, just like your home VCR, and allow other people to play them back. With their marriage on the rocks, Michael becomes obsessed with perfecting the head-trip machine. Things are going good until fellow scientist Lillian Reynolds (Louise Fletcher) wears the headset while suffering a fatal heart attack. The government, Michael, everybody, wants to see the tape, so for a bit it's a chase and then ... PLAYBACK. The effects really kick in as we get to see her final thoughts and her trip down the famous tunnel of near-death experiences, an idea further explored years later in Kathryn Bigelow's *Strange Days*. Something of a showcase for the f/x (director Douglas Trumbull had done similarly impressive things the previous year with *Blade Runner*), it's mostly remembered now for the fact that Wood died in controversial circumstances near the end of filming.

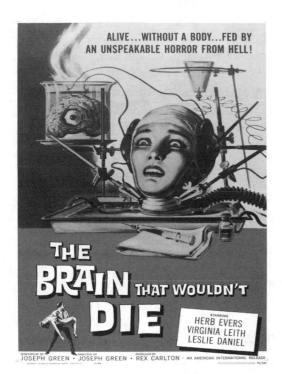

ALIVE...WITHOUT A BODY...FED BY AN UNSPEAKABLE HORROR FROM HELL!

THE BRAIN THAT WOULDN'T DIE

STARRING HERB EVERS VIRGINIA LEITH LESLIE DANIEL

JOSEPH GREEN • JOSEPH GREEN • REX CARLTON • AN AMERICAN INTERNATIONAL RELEASE

Like a decoration at a tacky haunted house, a living head without a body is the main gimmick in *The Brain That Wouldn't Die*.

THE BRAIN THAT WOULDN'T DIE

1963 (NR) 82m / **D:** Joseph Green / **W:** Joseph Green / **C:** Herb Evers, Virginia Leith, Adele Lamont

Another malevolent brain. Love is a many-splattered thing when a brilliant surgeon keeps the decapitated head of his fiancée alive after an auto accident while he searches for a suitably stacked body onto which to transplant the head. Absurd and satiric (head talks so much that Doc tapes her/its mouth shut), adding up to major entry in trash film genre. AKA: *The Head That Wouldn't Die*.

BRAZIL

1985 (R) 131m / D: Terry Gilliam / **W:** Terry Gilliam, Tom Stoppard, Charles McKeown / **C:** Jonathan Pryce, Robert De Niro, Michael Palin, Katherine Helmond, Kim Greist, Bob Hoskins, Ian Holm, Peter Vaughan, Ian Richardson, Jim Broadbent, Charles McKeown

Relentlessly nightmarish black comedy about an Everyman trying to survive in a paper-choked bureaucratic future society while fighting to find his dream girl. The aggressively bleak and surrealist screenplay mixes up *1984* with Kafka, Burgess, and Monty Python to create its alternate historical totalitarian world where dreams are not only impossible but dangerous. The immaculate art design is a jumbled-up mix of quasi-fascist art deco and prewar design (fedoras, Marlene Dietrich posters) with David Lynch-esque industrial clatter. The story follows petty bureaucrat Sam Lowry (Jonathan Pryce) who daydreams of flying through the clouds in Icarus armor and romancing his blonde-tressed goddess. In reality, he's a cog in the Orwellian Ministry of Information, which has just arrested and tortured to death an innocent man named Buttle because of a typo. When Lowry meets the intended arrestee Tuttle—Robert De Niro, in his greatest comic creation, as a renegade heating engineer, who thwarts the bureaucracy by ... fixing people's ducts without the proper paperwork—he starts fantasizing about rebellion and hunting down his dream girl. Although Gilliam (working from a screenplay written with ace playwright Tom Stoppard) is producing a grand dystopic fantasy here, the film's best moments are the comic/tragic satire of a naive everyman (Lowry) who is cluelessly bucking the system that only endangers everyone around him. Security state paranoia and lethally clumsy bureaucracy hold even more relevance decades later. Gilliam had a knock-down fight with Universal over the long-running time and bleak ending, detailed in Jack Mathews's book *The Battle of Brazil*. Both versions are available, as

Terry Gilliam's *Brazil* is like something George Orwell would have created if he had a black sense of humor.

well as the so-called "Love Conquers All" version, a nearly incomprehensible 94-minute studio edit that strains painfully hard for a happy ending. Two Oscar nominations: original screenplay and art direction.

THE BRIDE OF FRANKENSTEIN

1935 (NR) 75m / D: James Whale / W: William Hurlbut, John Balderston / C: Boris Karloff, Elsa Lanchester, Ernest Thesiger, Colin Clive, Una O'Connor, Valerie Hobson, Dwight Frye, E. E. Clive, O. P. Heggie, Gavin Gordon, Douglas Walton

The even-more classic sequel to the classic original. When his wife is kidnapped by his old associate Dr. Pretorious (Ernest Thesiger, in a highly amusing role), Dr. Frankenstein (Colin Clive) is forced to help build a mate for his monster. More humorous than the first, but also more pathetic, including the monster's famous but short-lived friendship with a blind hermit, who teaches the monster to speak. Boris Karloff's monster is once again touching and frightening at the same time. The unhappy, neurotic Clive disliked acting in horror films (director James Whale was also conflicted about the genre), which may have added to his tortured performances in them. Elsa Lanchester plays both the bride and Mary Shelley in the opening sequence. Una O'Connor contributes standout comedy relief. Features a spectacular score by Franz Waxman. Oscar nomination for best sound.

BRIDE OF THE MONSTER

1955 (NR) 70m / D: Edward D. Wood Jr. / W: Edward D. Wood Jr., Alex Gordon / C: Bela Lugosi, Tor Johnson, Loretta King, Tony McCoy, Dolores Fuller, Conrad Brooks, Harvey B. Dunn, Don Nagel, George Becwar, Paul Marco

> "... he delivers a remarkable performance, investing Wood's often laughable pulp dialogue with an undefinable style that's pure Lugosi."
>
> *Bride of the Monster*

This bargain-basement epic is a pretty good example of director Ed Wood's ability to cobble together a practically nonexistent budget and skimpy props into a memorable, if not exactly good, film. Bela Lugosi stars as the mad Dr. Vornoff, a scientist trying to create a race of "atomic supermen" in his laboratory. Bald muscle man Tor Johnson is "Lobo," one of his failed experiments. Vornoff captures intrepid girl reporter Loretta King, but she awakens Lobo's gentle side, and Vornoff gets a taste of his own atomic medicine. Lugosi's battle with a rubber octopus (a prop left over from *Wake of the Red Witch*) is now the stuff of legend, thanks to Tim Burton's affectionate tribute to *Ed Wood*, but it was actually a stuntman, not Lugosi, who braved the critter's lifeless tentacles. Bela was in his seventies when *Bride* was filmed and hardly up to a midnight splash in the swamp. Still, he delivers a remarkable performance, investing

Wood's often laughable pulp dialogue with an undefinable style that's pure Lugosi. It's not a great movie by any means, but Wood's desire to tell an exciting story and Lugosi's acting burn through the clichés and general ineptness. AKA: *Bride of the Atom*.

THE BRIDES OF FU MANCHU

1966 (NR) 94m / D: Don Sharp / **W:** Ernest Steward, Peter Welbeck / **C:** Christopher Lee, Tsai Chin, Douglas Wilmer, Howard Marion Crawford, Heinz Drache, Burt Kwouk, Marie Versini, Rupert Davies

Christopher Lee returns in this sequel to *The Face of Fu Manchu*. This time the supervillain turns up in North Africa, where he's gathered together twelve daughters of various world leaders. Needless to say, the young ladies aren't visiting Fu willingly, especially when the entertainment involves snake-pits and cat-fights. Scotland Yard-worthy Dennis Nayland Smith hotfoots it to the rescue once again, with the help of several colleagues and one of those blasted death rays. Doesn't pack quite the punch of *Face*, but it's still good fun, as long as you overlook the yellow-peril stereotypes.

THE BROOD

1979 (R) 92m / D: David Cronenberg / **W:** David Cronenberg / **C:** Samantha Eggar, Oliver Reed, Art Hindle

An emotionally disturbed woman (Samantha Eggar) falls under the influence of a mad doctor (Oliver Reed). Through his unorthodox treatments, her rage is made manifest in a brood of mutant children. The kids act out her violent emotional states, taking retribution on those who threaten their mother. Director David Cronenberg mixes the traditional mad scientist story with his trademark gross-out f/x, creating a disturbing melding of physical and psychological terror. The "birth" scene is one you won't be able to forget, even if you want to. Cronenberg's obsession with physical deformities continued with *Videodrome*, *The Fly*, *Dead Ringers*, and *Naked Lunch*.

THE BROTHER FROM ANOTHER PLANET

1984 (R) 109m / D: John Sayles / **W:** John Sayles / **C:** Joe Morton, Dee Dee Bridgewater, Ren Woods, Steve James, Maggie Renzi, David Strathairn, Tom Wright, Herbert Newsome, Leonard Jackson, John Sayles

Joe Morton stars as a mute and enigmatic black extraterrestrial recently arrived in Harlem. By all outward appearances he looks human, but he has hidden supernatural powers (repairing video machines with just the touch of his hand), not to mention clawed, three-toed feet. Like Chance the gardener in *Being There*, he has a profound effect on those he meets, because, like jazz singer Dee Dee Bridgewater tells him, "You could be anybody." (Later, she remarks, "You were great in bed last night, but you gonna have to do somethin' about those toenails.") Writer/director John Sayles goes for deadpan observational comedy rather than the tongue-in-cheek style he affects in other genre work. Sayles and stock company regular David Strathairn appear as alien bounty hunters.

BUCK ROGERS CONQUERS THE UNIVERSE

1939 (NR) 237m / **D:** Ford Beebe, Saul Goodkind / **C:** Buster Crabbe, Constance Moore, Jackie Moran

The character of Buck Rogers originated in the 1928 Philip Francis Nowlan novel *Armageddon 2419 A.D.*; Nowlan helped adapt it into the first sci-fi newspaper comic strip. Buck was also the first sci-fi story done in the modern super-hero space genre. Many of the "inventions" seen in this movie have actually come into existence—spaceships, ray guns (lasers), anti-gravity belts—a testament to Nolan's almost psychic farsightedness. The hero is played in this serial by the original Flash Gordon himself, Buster Crabbe. AKA: *Buck Rogers*.

BUCK ROGERS
IN THE 25TH CENTURY

1979 (PG) 90m / **D:** Daniel Haller / **W:** Glen A. Larson, Leslie Stevens / **C:** Gil Gerard, Pamela Hensley, Erin Gray, Henry Silva, Tim O'Connor, Joseph Wiseman

An American astronaut (Gil Gerard), preserved in space for 500 years, is brought back to life by a passing Draconian flagship. Outer-space adventures begin when he is accused of being a spy from Earth. There's a sexy princess, a good-girl heroine, and a very, very annoying little robot with voice provided by Mel Blanc. Based on the classic movie serial, this mildly diverting made-for-TV space opera (which was also given a brief theatrical release) is another example of the mad scramble in the late 1970s to cash in on the success of *Star Wars*. Producer Glen A. Larson launched a two-season series from this pilot, in between creating *Battlestar Galactica* and *Knight Rider*.

Gil Gerard starred in the title role for the very '70s-feeling *Buck Rogers in the 25th century*.

BUG

1975 (PG) 100m / **D:** Jeannot Szwarc / **W:** William Castle / **C:** Bradford Dillman, Joanna Miles, Richard Gilliland, Jamie Smith-Jackson, Alan Fudge, Jesse Vint, William Castle

The city of Riverside is threatened with destruction after a massive Earth tremor unleashes a mob of prehistoric cockroaches that set fires with their butts, attack cats and housewives, and are virtually impervious to Raid. A local biology teacher, not content to leave well enough alone, crosses the critters with the common kitchen-variety roach. The new and improved (and hungry) super-roaches proceed to drive the Riversiders buggy. Based on Thomas Page's novel *The Hephaestus Plague*, this fairly effective creepy-crawler was produced by William "Gimmick King" Castle, who was known in the 1950s for publicity stunts like wiring theater seats to administer mild electric shocks to audiences' bottoms. For *Bug*, Castle wanted to install windshield wiper-like devices under theater seats that would brush against the patrons' feet as the cockroaches crawled across the screen. This would have been a nice disco-era follow-up to Castle's previous gimmicks; unfortunately, the idea was squashed flat.

THE BUTTERFLY EFFECT

2004 (R) 113m / **D:** Eric Bress, J. Mackye Gruber / **W:** Eric Bress, J. Mackye Gruber / **C:** Ashton Kutcher, Amy Smart, Melora Walters, Ethan Suplee, Eric Stoltz

Subpar *Twilight Zone* takes on chaos theory, childhood trauma, and unintended consequences from the writing/directing team of the pop-Grand Guignol horror film *Final Destination 2*. Ashton Kutcher is a mopey guy who can't remember various blacked-out episodes from his childhood. When he discovers a way to travel back and relive those memories, side effects begin to multiply, à la Ray Bradbury's "A Sound of Thunder."

The Cabin in the Woods

2012 (R) 95m / **D:** Drew Goddard / **W:** Joss Whedon, Drew Goddard / **C:** Chris Hemsworth, Richard Jenkins, Bradley Whitford, Kristen Connolly, Anna Hutchison, Franz Kranz, Jesse Williams

Stop us if you've heard this one before: Band of hormone-reeking college students head off to a creepy cabin deep in the woods, ignoring more warning signs than are staked around the average nuclear test site, and proceed to get butchered in inventively savage fashion. The difference is that there's more than meets the eye in this cheeky send-up of slasher-film clichés. Joss Whedon and Drew Goddard's script, which mixes the former's penchant for knowing wit with the latter's knack for clever plotting, cuts between the cabin, where nubile young things venture slowly into darkened rooms, and a high-tech control room where a couple of bored engineers (Richard Jenkins and Bradley Whitford) are monitoring something that defies easy description. Suffice it to say that the apparent horror film twists more towards sci-fi. The blood-soaked battle royale at the conclusion, with its densely referential layerings of everything from J-horror to H. P. Lovecraft, is wonderfully canny having-it-both-ways genre satire.

Capricorn One

1978 (PG) 123m / **D:** Peter Hyams / **W:** Peter Hyams / **C:** Elliott Gould, James Brolin, Brenda Vaccaro, O. J. Simpson, Hal Holbrook, Sam Waterston, Karen Black, Telly Savalas

An Apollo-style mission to Mars stalls because Americans lack the brains to build a decent spacecraft. To ensure continued NASA funds, Hal Holbrook arranges a phony Martian landing for TV cameras in a remote desert soundstage. Once astronauts James Brolin, O. J. Simpson, and Sam Waterston learn that the scheme calls for their "heroic" demise to ensure silence, they try to escape. Remarkably, the smeared space agency cooperated in filming this intriguing but paper-thin conspiracy thriller, mixing a disaster-pic cast (Telly Savalas!) with Watergate-era cynicism at its peak (even the Congressional Medal of Honor earns an insult). There's a nice pair of menacing Unmarked Black Helicopters, but half the fun is spotting the mistakes in Peter Hyams's script. Nevertheless, there are many out there who take this fantasy as documentary fact. Stirring Jerry Goldsmith musical score.

CAPTAIN AMERICA

1989 (PG-13) 97m / **D:** Albert Pyun / **W:** Stephen Tolkin / **C:** Matt Salinger, Scott Paulin, Ronny Cox, Ned Beatty, Darren McGavin, Melinda Dillon

The Marvel Comics superhero got his own movie in time for his 50th anniversary, but this doesn't make the grade despite the ambitious plot. In 1941 a secret Axis serum turns polio-stricken Steve Rogers (Matt Salinger, actor son of author J. D. Salinger) into a superstrong superhero, but he's matched by the Nazis' own superfascist, the Red Skull. Their battle leaves

Captain America frozen in the Arctic for 40 years before he thaws to again confront his evil nemesis, now a typical gangster with a nuke. Though a fairly faithful transcription of the comic book's premise, what may have worked ages ago on paper now looks ridiculous. Low-budget production values—and clunky environmentalist themes—don't help. Kids may be amused; adults may note ruefully that this *Captain America* was made in Yugoslavia. Ace crime novelist Lawrence Block worked on the screenplay. Watch for Kolchak himself, Darren McGavin.

Chris Evans masters a blend of hunky hero and gee-whiz all-American joe in *Captain America: The First Avenger.*

CAPTAIN AMERICA: THE FIRST AVENGER

2011 (PG-13) 124m / **D:** Joe Johnston / **W:** Christopher Markus, Stephen McFeely / **C:** Chris Evans, Hayley Atwell, Sebastian Stan, Tommy Lee Jones, Hugo Weaving, Dominic Cooper, Richard Armitage, Stanley Tucci, Samuel L. Jackson, Toby Jones, Neal McDonough, Derek Luke

Instead of trying to grit up Jack Kirby and Joe Simon's all-American Avenger by modernizing him, Joe Johnston's two-fisted film keeps Steve Rogers where he belongs: as a hero so star-spangled he makes Eagle Scouts look like Commie infiltrators. This origin story shows Rogers as a sunken-chested army recruit who so desperately wants to fight for America in World War II that he joins an experiment that turns him into a supercharged fighting machine. Chris Evans plays Captain America with steely determination, while Tommy Lee Jones (as a cigar-chewing colonel) shows that he could have done a mean Patton. A devilish Hugo Weaving leads the Nazi opposition.

CAPTAIN AMERICA: THE WINTER SOLDIER

2014 (PG-13) 136m / **D:** Anthony Russo, Joe Russo / **W:** Christopher Markus, Stephen McFeely / **C:** Chris Evans, Scarlett Johansson, Samuel L. Jackson, Robert Redford, Sebastian Stan, Anthony Mackie, Cobie Smulders, Hayley Atwell, Toby Jones

The ever-expanding universe of Marvel superheroes takes on the moral ambiguities of the drone warfare age in a speedier-than-average, freshly minted vehicle for Chris Evan's bright-eyed boy scout appeal. In the aftermath of that assault on New York from *The Avengers*, S.H.I.E.L.D. takes a Bush administration approach to future threats, building a fleet of satellite-linked "heli-carriers" with the capacity to nearly simultaneously target and eliminate millions of people identified as threats. Steve Rogers isn't too crazy about that, growling to conflicted S.H.I.E.L.D. boss Nick Fury (Samuel L. Jackson) that it's like "holding a gun to everyone on Earth and calling it protection." Soon the Captain is facing down threats ranging from a secretive masked super-assassin known as the Winter Soldier to a suspiciously Rumsfeld-like Robert Redford, who convinces S.H.I.E.L.D. that Rogers is the real enemy. Doesn't know when to stop and any political ambiguities are quickly smashed aside in favor of more shootouts. But the scope is impressive, and occasional jabs of humor more than welcome. Scarlett Johansson smoulders as ex-KGB operative Natasha Romanoff. Anthony Mackie proves a fine fit as Rogers' sidekick, advising his Rip Van Winkle buddy to listen to Marvin Gaye's "Trouble Man" to understand everything that happened during the decades he was asleep.

CARNOSAUR

1993 (R) 82m / **D:** Adam Simon / **W:** Adam Simon / **C:** Diane Ladd, Raphael Sbarge, Jennifer Runyon, Harrison Page, Clint Howard, Ned Bellamy

Straight from the Corman trash dumpster (er, studio), this exploitative quickie about dinosaurs harkens back to 1950s-style monster epics. The title sequence—some really disgusting stuff apparently filmed in a real chicken processing plant—sets the tone for your basic mad-scientist plot with several environmental twists. Dr. Jane Tiptree (Diane Ladd), the mad scientist in question, has been up to nefarious doings out in the Nevada desert, something involving nasty but unseen critters that attack chickens. The film has a wicked sense of humor that gets consistently stronger and more crazed as it goes along; extra points for rare move of casting a woman as the mad scientist. Toward the end, it becomes downright Strangelovian. In true slap-dash Corman style, *Carnosaur* not only beat Spielberg's *Jurassic Park* to the theaters but also nodded to it by casting Ladd, mother of Spielberg's female lead (Laura Dern). Amazingly, this was actually based on a novel. Followed by two straight-to-video sequels.

THE CASTLE OF FU MANCHU

1968 (PG) 92m / **D:** Jess Franco / **W:** Peter Welbeck / **C:** Christopher Lee, Richard Greene, H. Marion Crawford, Tsai Chin, Gunther Stoll, Rosalba Neri, Maria Perschy

The final Christopher Lee Dr. Fu Manchu entry, directed by prolific sleaze-monger Jess Franco. This time, the evil Doc's plans for world domination involve a gadget that will put the earth into a deep freeze. To fine-tune this contraption, he enlists the help of a gifted scientist by abducting him. However, the helper/hostage has a bad ticker, so Fu must abduct a heart surgeon to save his life. Widely considered the weakest installment, it's a plodding drag. Apparently the producers had their own doubts about the film, as it was only released several years after completion. Only rabid Lee fans or those completing theses on unfortunate Asian stereotypes will find this one interesting. AKA: *Assignment: Istanbul*; *Sax Rohmer's The Castle of Fu Manchu*.

THE CAT FROM OUTER SPACE

1978 (G) 103m / **D:** Norman Tokar / **W:** Ted Key / **C:** Ken Berry, Sandy Duncan, Harry Morgan, Roddy McDowall, McLean Stevenson

Classic 1970s Disney live-action family fare. Released in theaters but more appropriate for TV. An extraterrestrial cat named Jake crashes his spaceship on Earth and leads a group of people on endless escapades. A cute idea combined with solid scripting and a cast of familiar faces, like Ken (*F-Troop*) Berry, Sandy Duncan as his girlfriend, and Roddy McDowall, who'd apparently gotten tired of monkeying around in the *Planet of the Apes* series.

CAT-WOMEN OF THE MOON

1953 (NR) 65m / **D:** Arthur Hilton / **W:** Roy Hamilton / **C:** Sonny Tufts, Victor Jory, Marie Windsor, Bill Phipps, Douglas Fowley, Carol Brewster, Suzanne Alexander, Susan Morrow

A team of scientists led by Sonny Tufts land on the moon and encounter a telepathic race of skimpily attired female chauvinists and a giant spider. An aggressively silly picture with romance, excitement, and plenty of unintentional laughs. Great cast of characters here. The "Hollywood Cover Girls" played various cat women. Tufts got his show biz start as an opera singer, then moved on to Broadway musicals (and was sued by showgirls in the 1950s for biting them on the thighs). Former Miss Utah Marie Windsor became a star playing bad girls. Director Arthur Hilton was a top editor (*The Killers*) before becoming a B-movie director. Remade (badly) in 1958 as *Missile to the Moon*. Features score by Elmer Bernstein two years before he'd get Oscar nominated for *The Man with the Golden Arm*. AKA: *Rocket to the Moon*.

THE CELL

2000 (R) 107m / **D:** Tarsem Singh / **W:** Mark Protosevich / **C:** Jennifer Lopez, Vince Vaughn, Vincent D'Onofrio, Dylan Baker, Marianne Jean-Baptiste, Pruitt Taylor Vince

A ticking-clock sci-fi dreamer that tried to breathe new life into the OCD serial killer-genre so played out by the end of the 1990s. Jennifer Lopez plays a particularly empathic social worker who's brought on board by the FBI to help them get information out of comatose serial killer Vincent D'Onofrio, whose latest victim will die unless located soon. Lopez accesses the killer's thoughts by way of a new device that allows two people to have an extended type of Vulcan mind meld. First-time director Tarsem Singh (later just plain old Tarsem) came out of music videos and it shows: Lopez's excursions into D'Onofrio's dark fairy-tale unconscious look like what Salvador Dali might have come up with were he hired to do a high-end perfume ad. Screenwriter Mark Protosevich was also a first-timer; he went on to write *I Am Legend* and *Thor*. Oscar nomination for makeup. Followed by a 2009 straight-to-DVD sequel.

CHARLY

1968 (PG) 103m / **D:** Ralph Nelson / **W:** Stirling Silliphant / **C:** Cliff Robertson, Claire Bloom, Lilia Skala, Leon Janney, Dick Van Patten, William Dwyer

C liff Robertson stars as Charly Gordon, a mentally disabled man who is the butt of cruel practical jokes. Experimental brain surgery transforms him into a genius. He turns the tables on his co-workers, lectures to scientists, and has an affair with his therapist (Claire Bloom). But his triumph is fleeting when he learns that he will soon regress. Some of director Ralph Nelson's stylistic flourishes date the film, but it is still a heartbreaker with the courage not to let audiences off the hook with a conventional happy ending. A labor of love for Robertson, who appeared in the original teleplay

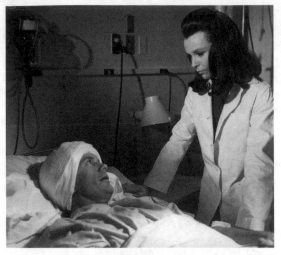

Charly is a touching story of a mentally impaired man (Cliff Robertson) who, through the talents of surgeon Claire Bloom, is given intelligence only to lose it again in an adaptation of *Flowers for Algernon* by Daniel Keyes.

based on Daniel Keyes's novel, *Flowers for Algernon*. He bought the film rights and reportedly spent seven years trying to bring it to the big screen. In a career footnote apropos to this book, Robertson was blacklisted in Hollywood for four years after reporting studio head David Begelman for forging his name on a check. Another sci-fi film, *Brainstorm*, marked his return to the screen. Robertson won an Oscar for this role.

CHERRY 2000

1988 (PG-13) 94m / **D:** Steve De Jarnatt / **W:** Michael Almereyda / **C:** Melanie Griffith, David Andrews, Ben Johnson, Tim Thomerson, Michael C. Gwynne, Brion James, Pamela Gidley, Harry Carey Jr.

It's 2017. Sam Treadwell has a quick one on the wet kitchen floor and short-circuits his Cherry 2000, a perfect, always-in-the-mood, man-made woman sex-toy robot. Missing his Cherry, Sam enlists the aid of female tracker E. Johnson (Melanie Griffith) and sets off for the treacherous "lawless zone" where replacement parts can still be found. As he beholds Johnson's way with snappy comebacks and rocket launchers, Sam ponders the advantages of a real flesh-and-blood woman. Does he want a woman who comes with instructions on which buttons to push, or one with her own emotions and thoughts … or maybe just an inflatable? An offbeat, occasionally funny, tongue-in-cheek 1980s goof. Score by Basil Poledouris and script by Michael Almereyda, who later wrote everything from *Twister* to the Ethan Hawke *Hamlet*.

CHILDREN OF MEN

2006 (R) 109m / **D:** Alfonso Cuarón / **W:** Alfonso Cuarón, Timothy J. Sexton, David Arata, Mark Fergus, Hawk Ostby / **C:** Clive Owen, Julianne Moore, Chiwetel Ejiofor, Michael Caine, Clare-Hope Ashitey, Danny Huston, Pam Ferris

In the year 2027, the world looks much like it did in the years immediately following 9/11, only much more so. Immigrants from collapsed nations are pouring across first world borders, terrorism and panic are in the air. At the start of this Alfonso Cuarón masterpiece, adapted from a P. D. James novel, people in a grimy and besieged London are despondently watching news of the murder of the world's youngest person, an eighteen-year-old who was the last person to have been born in almost two decades. Clive Owen is a government worker who gets kidnapped by an underground resistance (Julianne Moore and Chiwetel Ejiofor, among others) who want his help to get immigrant papers for young Clare-Hope Ashitey, who is somehow pregnant. Equal parts deft satire, chase film, and apocalyptic elegy, Cuarón's film is dense with foreboding but still cracklingly alive with gallows humor. The screenplay delves into post-9/11 anxieties like little else before or since, while Cuarón's impossibly long takes and intricately choreographed chases (including an epic battle in a refugee camp that caps the film) helped remake the way sci-fi film was conceived in the new millennium. Three Oscar nominations.

> **"The screenplay delves into post-9/11 anxieties like little else before or since...."**
> *Children of Men*

CHILDREN OF THE DAMNED

1963 (NR) 90m / **D:** Anton Leader / **W:** John Briley / **C:** Ian Hendry, Alan Badel, Barbara Ferris, Alfred Burke, Sheila Allen, Clive Powell, Frank Summerscales, Mahdu Mathen, Gerald Delsol, Roberta Rex, Franchesca Lee, Harold Goldblatt

In a living preview of what man will supposedly evolve into in a million years, six children are discovered, scattered around the world, with genius IQs, ray-gun eyes, and murderous dispositions. Two investigators round up the tykes for scientific examination, but before too long they manage to escape. The children hide out in a church, but alas, their destiny is to be destroyed in order to teach modern man a lesson. A fairly good sequel to the classic *Village of the Damned*, based loosely on the novel *The Midwich Cuckoos* by English sci-fi novelist John Wyndham. AKA: *Horror!*

THE CHINA SYNDROME

1979 (PG) 123m / **D:** James Bridges / **W:** Mike Gray, T. S. Cook, James Bridges / **C:** Jane Fonda, Jack Lemmon, Michael Douglas, Scott Brady, James Hampton, Peter Donat, Wilford Brimley, James Karen

Jack Lemmon is supervisor at a nuclear plant who uncovers evidence of an engineering flaw that could cause a devastating meltdown. When his bosses react with a ruthless cover-up, he takes drastic steps to get the proof to sympathetic TV journalists Jane Fonda and Michael Douglas. Solidly researched wire-taut thriller (done without ambient music) was considered sci-fi when it opened. Then the Three Mile Island accident occurred, and the script—which coincidentally compares the estimated lethal fallout zone to the size of Pennsylvania—seemed too prophetic for comfort. Note the on-screen thug tactics of the nuclear industry, and ponder that General Electric later bought NBC lock, stock, and news division. Produced by Douglas. Four Oscar nominations: art direction, screenplay, lead actor (Lemmon), and actress (Fonda).

CHOPPING MALL

1986 (R) 77m / **D:** Jim Wynorski / **W:** Steve Mitchell, Jim Wynorski / **C:** Kelli Maroney, Tony O'Dell, Suzee Slater, Russell Todd, Karrie Emerson

A freak electric storm unleashes killer security robots on a coed band of teens holding an after-hours slumber party inside the mall (where they can test out the mattresses, wink wink). The robots, created by Robert Short, carry most of the action, and they're pretty good; imagine R2D2 gone bad and you've got the idea. Otherwise this is trivial, low-grade stuff by Roger Corman alumni, laden with B-movie in-jokes (brief cameos by Paul Bartel and Mary Woronov reprise their characters from the cult comedy *Eating Raoul*), gore, and sleaze. AKA: *Killbots*. Shot at the Beverly Center mall, like so many other great Southland satires (*Scenes from a Mall, L.A. Story*).

CHRONICLE

2012 (PG-13) 84m / **D:** Josh Trank / **W:** Josh Trank, Max Landis / **C:** Dane DeHaan, Alex Russell, Michael B. Jordan, Michael Kelly, Ashley Hinshaw

A mismatched trio of Seattle teens find a big glowing, possibly alien whats-it, in a hole in the ground. After this unexplained encounter, they discover they can move objects with their minds (first Legos, later on … cars) and eventually fly. For star athlete Michael B. Jordan and philosophy-minded Alex Russell, their response can be boiled down to: Awesome! For the hollow-eyed and ever-videotaping loner Dane DeHaan, saddled with a dying mother and a violent alcoholic of a father, the gift of telekinesis becomes a route to empowerment. Director/co-writer Josh Trank's understated, faux-first-person style and emotional take on adolescent vulnerabilities bring a rare intimacy to what's basically a battling superhero story. The building-smashing climax can be best described as *Akira* in Seattle.

THE CHRONICLES OF RIDDICK

2004 (PG-13) 119m / **D:** David Twohy / **W:** David Twohy / **C:** Vin Diesel, Colm Feore, Thandie Newton, Judi Dench, Karl Urban, Alexa Davalos, Linus Roache, Keith David

An overstuffed space opera of the kind that just about never makes it to the big screen. David Twohy's sequel to the underrated *Pitch Black* ditches most of what made that film sing and slots into its place about two or three novels' worth of garbled back story. As the escaped prisoner Riddick, Vin Diesel stomps through the affair with all the subtlety of a headachey water buffalo. The idea is for Riddick, being a not-so-antihero behind that baleful goggled stare, to stop a genocidal race of death-worshipping aliens known as Necromangers from obliterating everything in their path. Although the plot is as bafflingly complex as the acting is one-note, credit is due to

Twohy for at least trying to keep this type of outer-space adventurism alive.

CHRONOPOLIS

1982 (NR) 70m / D: Piotr Kamler / **W:** Piotr Kamler

Stop-motion animated feature film (a five-year solo effort by Piotr Kamler in his home studio) about the placid, immortal citizens of Chronopolis—no relation to the namesake J. G. Ballard novel—who relieve the boredom of perpetual existence by creating time. Except for opening narration (French without subtitles—better have a translator on hand, Anglophones), it's a nonverbal spectacle of rhythmic fantastic imagery, visually impressive but too often merely repetitive and opaque.

CIRCUITRY MAN

1990 (R) 85m / D: Steven Lovy / **W:** Steven Lovy / **C:** Jim Metzler, Dana Wheeler-Nicholson, Lu Leonard, Vernon Wells, Barbara Alyn Woods, Dennis Christopher

Vin Diesel played a warrior out to stop the evil, destructive Necromangers in *The Chronicles of Riddick.*

In a stylishly bleak post-apocalyptic future that borrows freely from *Blade Runner*, *Mad Max*, and *Max Headroom*, people have been driven underground by pollution. A tough loner (Dana Wheeler-Nicholson) and an emotional robot (Jim Metzler) are on the run from a group of gonzo bad guys. Plughead (Vernon Wells) likes to experience other people's pain, and Yo-yo (Barbara Alyn Woods) is a tough-talking gangster. The main problems are a leaden pace and apparent ignorance of basic storytelling techniques. But the acting is above average, the characters are interesting, and beneath the gritty surface, there's a strange likable quality to the film. Followed by an unnecessary sequel.

CITY LIMITS

1984 (PG-13) 85m / D: Aaron Lipstadt / **W:** Don Opper / **C:** John Stockwell, Kim Cattrall, Darrell Larson, Rae Dawn Chong, Robby Benson, James Earl Jones, Jennifer Balgobin, John Diehl

Director Aaron Lipstadt's first film, *Android*, is a precious sleeper. This, his second film, has developed a less-welcome cult reputation after being given the *Mystery Science Theater 3000* treatment. In the not-so-distant future, a plague wiped out most adults, leaving the adolescents to form motorcycle-riding gangs to roam the landscape looking for food, gasoline, and comic books. Loner John Stockwell teams up with Rae Dawn Chong, John Diehl, and Darrell Larson (with an assist by James Earl Jones) to take on the sinister Sunya Corporation from violently wresting control of the city from the gangs. Robby Benson is Sunya's sinister boss. He spends most of the film glowering behind a desk and glancing at the red light blinking on his telephone. He is finally crushed when a betrayed gang leader rams his motorcycle into his desk. Good triumphs.

CITY OF EMBER

2008 (PG) 90m / **D:** Gil Kenan / **W:** Caroline Thompson / **C:** Saoirse Ronan, Harry Treadaway, Toby Jones, Bill Murray, Tim Robbins, Martin Landau, Marianne Jean-Baptiste, Mary Kay Place

Part-brilliant, mostly lazy adaptation of a young adult novel about an underground society built to keep humanity alive after some undetermined above-ground apocalypse. Two hundred years later, the city of Ember is a clattering place of jerry-rigged piping and frequent power outages where the crumbling streets are barely lit by a webbing of lamps. Saoirse Ronan does sprightly work as the fleet-footed city messenger who teams up with mechanically minded Harry Treadaway, who thinks he can fix the ailing generator that threatens to plunge them all into eternal darkness. A sly Bill Murray works wonders as the sinisterly small-minded mayor who's keeping secrets about the dangers facing the city and looking for a way to save his own skin. The city itself is well designed and feels fully lived-in, but the climax is far too interested in giving the kids an adventurous thrill and less about delving into possibilities inherent in this long-buried mini-society that's about to find out it's been lied to for many lifetimes.

THE CITY OF LOST CHILDREN

1995 (R) 111m / **D:** Jean-Marie Jeunet, Marc Caro / **W:** Jean-Marie Jeunet, Marc Caro, Gilles Adrien / **C:** Ron Perlman, Daniel Emilfork, Joseph Lucien, Judith Vittet, Dominique Pinon, Jean-Claude Dreyfus, Odile Mallet, Genevieve Brunet, Mireille Mossé

Fantastical, not-for-the-kiddies fairytale finds crazed inventor Krank (Daniel Emilfork) getting his evil one-eyed minions, the appropriately named "Cyclops," to kidnap local children so that he can steal their dreams (because Krank himself is incapable of dreaming). The latest victim is young Denree (Joseph Lucien), the adopted brother of sideshow strongman One (genre hero Ron Perlman), who single-mindedly pursues a way to get Denree back—aided by 9-year-old feral child Miette (Judith Vittet) and a band of orphan thieves. The visuals are striking in a steampunk Brothers Grimm way, including a bevy of mechanical flies and all-around sharp cinematography. Freaks galore with avant-garde designer Jean-Paul Gaultier in charge of costumes. AKA: *La Cité des Enfants Perdus*.

CLASS OF 1999

1990 (R) 98m / **D:** Mark L. Lester / **W:** C. Courtney Joyner / **C:** Bradley Gregg, Traci Lind, Malcolm McDowell, Stacy Keach, Patrick Kilpatrick, Pam Grier, John P. Ryan, Darren E. Burrows, Joshua Miller

Actually set in 1997, this loose follow-up to Mark L. Lester's non-sci-fi *Class of 1984* shows teen gangs now terrorizing the entire country. A desperate high school principal (Malcolm McDowell) reluctantly installs manlike robot instructors not fazed by homeroom punks. But the machines are actually surplus military 'droids (with rocket launchers in their arms), who go into full-combat mode at the flick of a spitball. Result is a violent, frankly amoral spectacle that makes vicious young thugs into heroes by default as they fight for their lives against their Terminator teachers. Undeniably exciting on a crude level. Class dismissed.

CLASS OF NUKE 'EM HIGH

1986 (R) 84m / **D:** Richard W. Haines, Lloyd Kaufman / **W:** Richard W. Haines, Mark Rudnitsky, Lloyd Kaufman, Stuart Strutin / **C:** Janelle Brady, Gilbert Brenton, Robert Prichard

Following its success in dealing with ecological issues in the *Toxic Avenger* series, Team Troma once again experiments with chemicals, with violent results. Jersey high school becomes a hotbed of mutants, punks, maniacs, and monsters after a nuclear spill occurs. Good teens Chrissy and Warren succumb, the school blows up, life goes on. It's a classic Troma production, meaning high camp, low budget, heavy gore, gross f/x, sexy babes. You were expecting *Sense and Sensibility*? Followed by many sequels and spin-offs of various worth. Known in France as *Atomic College*, which has a better ring to it.

A CLOCKWORK ORANGE

1971 (R) 137m / **D:** Stanley Kubrick / **W:** Stanley Kubrick / **C:** Malcolm McDowell, Patrick Magee, Adrienne Corri, Michael Bates, Warren Clarke, Aubrey Morris, James Marcus, Steven Berkoff, David Prowse, Miriam Karlin, John Clive, Carl Duering

Stanley Kubrick goes for the gut and the head in this cold, savage adaptation of the infamous Anthony Burgess novel. In Britain's grimy near future, sadistic young punk Alex (Malcolm McDowell, scalpel-funny and over-the-top throughout in a role originally meant for Mick Jagger), who loves

In a role originally intended for rocker Mick Jagger, Malcolm McDowell goes on sex and violence binges with his "droogies" in a bleak vision of the future.

music almost as much as he loves his violence, leads his gang of "droogs" on a nightly spree of rape and "ultra violence." After being caught he is the subject of a grim government experiment to eradicate his violent tendencies using behavior modification. Kubrick's none-too-subtle question is: Who's the real victim? Many sequences strum the kind of black-comic counterpoint that the likes of Quentin Tarantino would heavily traffic in years later, including a rape/beating conducted while assailant McDowell "kicks" out a version of "Singin' in the Rain." The "Nadsat" language Burgess created for the novel (he did the same for the prehistoric epic *Quest for Fire*) is heavily used throughout for a flowery and surreal feel, its quasi-Russian formulations mixed in with Cockney rhyming and teenybopper structures: "For in those care-free days, I and my so-called droogies wore our maskies, which were like real horror-show disguises." The jarring score is made up of both classical pieces and quavery electronic compositions by then-Walter now-Wendy Carlos (get a hold of the album featuring Carlos's renditions of the whole score for the best effect). Like many of the more thoughtful 1970s sci-fi films, no great sets were needed to depict the future, just some spiffed-up cars and strange outfits to complement the already bleak British architecture. Originally rated X, the film continues to be provocative years later. Influential, too: British punk band The Adicts were still dressing up like Alex and his droogs on stage for decades afterward. Notably does *not* include the Burgess novel's last chapter, excised from the American edition, in which Alex grows up and tires of the old ultra-violence. Oscar nominations for director, editing, adapted screenplay, and picture.

THE CLONUS HORROR

1979 90m / **D:** Robert S. Fiveson / **W:** Ron Smith, Bob Sullivan / **C:** Tim Donnelly, Keenan Wynn, Peter Graves, Dick Sargent, Paulette Breen

A scientist discovers a government plot, led by a sinister presidential candidate (perennial schlock sci-fi participant Peter Graves), to clone the population by freezing bodies alive and using their parts in surgery. AKA: *Parts: The Clonus Horror*. Director Robert S. Fiveson later sued the makers of *The Island*, claiming it too closely approximated his film's story.

CLOSE ENCOUNTERS OF THE THIRD KIND

1977 (PG) 152m / **D:** Steven Spielberg / **W:** Steven Spielberg / **C:** Richard Dreyfuss, Teri Garr, Melinda Dillon, François Truffaut, Bob Balaban, Cary Guffey, J. Patrick McNamara

Glorious sci-fi fantasy about how strangers from all over the world become involved in the attempts of benevolent aliens to contact Earthlings. Despite the (intentionally) mundane nature of the characters, this Spielberg epic is a stirring achievement. Studded with classic sequences; the ending is an exhilarating experience. Richard Dreyfuss and Melinda Dillon excel as new friends both bewildered by and obsessed with the alien presence, and French filmmaker François Truffaut is also strong as the stern, ultimately kind scientist. Departing from the common saucer design for extraterrestrial vehicles, the UFOs appear here as beautiful, multicolored light shows, swooping gracefully about the frame. Released the same year as *Star Wars: Episode IV—A New Hope*, the two hit films set new standards of f/x spectacle. While George Lucas's film was the bigger financial success, *Close Encounters* was arguably the more influential; it would be hard to imagine *The X-Files* without it. Steven Spielberg, claiming he was rushed to get the picture done for the release date, used his clout to engineer a "special edition" re-release in 1980, re-edited to his liking, that wasn't substantially different from the original. Screenplay is credited somewhat controversially to Spielberg, as numerous other writers (including Paul Schrader) contributed heavily to various drafts. Nine Oscar nominations; won for cinematography and sound effects editing.

Steven Spielberg's *Close Encounters of the Third Kind* remains one of the purest examples of an optimistic view of first contact.

CLOUD ATLAS

2012 (R) 172m / **D:** Tom Tykwer, Lana Wachowski, Andy Wachowski / **W:** Tom Tykwer, Lana Wachowski, Andy Wachowski / **C:** Tom Hanks, Halle Berry, Jim Broadbent, Hugo Weaving, Jim Sturgess, Doona Bae, Ben Whishaw, Keith David, James D'Arcy, Xun Zhou, Susan Sarandon, Hugh Grant

The Wachowskis turned a new page with this dizzyingly ambitious, omnibus take on David Mitchell's age-skipping novel that spins its actors through a linked chain of stories about oppression and revolution from the 1800s to the far future. The filmmakers' trademark cartoon overkill is mostly held in reserve—*Run Lola Run*'s Tom Tykwer took on directing duties for some segments—as the plotlets cycle through a cornucopia of settings from a slave plantation in the Pacific to conspiracy-haunted 1970s San Francisco to a dystopian flooded Korea to a barbaric post-apocalyptic future where cannibalism reigns to…. Everybody gets a chance to play multiple characters throughout the ages. Likeable types like Tom Hanks and Hugh Grant bloody themselves up as both villains and heroes while Hugo Weaving is stuck playing the bad guy each time, and Jim Broadbent delivers a great splashing dose of wry comedy. Densely layered and passionately delivered, even if many considered it something of a folly.

CLOVERFIELD

2008 (PG-13) 85m / **D:** Matt Reeves / **W:** Drew Goddard / **C:** Lizzy Caplan, Jessica Lucas, T. J. Miller, Michael Stahl-David, Mike Vogel, Odette Annable

The found-footage genre, mostly moribund since the one-off success of 1999's *The Blair Witch Project*, was kicked off again with this inventive, low-budget monster movie from the burgeoning J. J. Abrams factory. Director Matt Reeves and writer Drew Goddard put in their time on Abrams's tween-skewing shows like *Alias* and *Felicity* and it shows. The young and generically attractive but forgettably low-wattage cast gathers at a Manhattan loft to wish a buddy well on his move to Japan when disaster hits. It's a simple story: highly Godzilla-esque monster starts smashing up the city and everybody runs screaming. What gave the film its punch was a clever tease of an ad campaign; the blatantly manipulative 9/11 allusions; and its shaky-cam video being supposedly shot on the run by one of the party-goers and discovered later (à la *Blair Witch*) in the area "formerly known as Central Park." Nighttime setting, deliberately poor framing, and a judiciously less-is-more approach stretches the suspense far longer than it should have. The destruction of landmarks like a crowded Brooklyn Bridge and the Statue of Liberty (its severed head being thrown down the street like a giant bowling bowl) ultimately cause far more concern than the fate of any of the people.

CLUB EXTINCTION

1989 (R) 105m / **D:** Claude Chabrol / **W:** Sollace Mitchell / **C:** Alan Bates, Andrew McCarthy, Jennifer Beals, Jan Niklas, Hanns Zischler, Benoit Regent, Peter Fitz, Wolfgang Preiss, Isolde Barth

French filmmaker Claude Chabrol, best known for Hitchcocklan thrillers, pays tribute to vintage German movie ubergangster Dr. Mabuse (a sort of James Bond supervillain) in this arcane international coproduction, dumped straight into the American home-video market. Mystery tycoon Dr. Marsfeldt has an artificial heart powered by human suffering. Dwelling in his futuristic hideout beneath an industrial-music club, he employs both media idol Jennifer Beals and a New Age resort in a hypnotism scheme to drive Berlin citizens to commit mass suicide. His explanation: "I am the Wall." Loosely remade from Fritz Lang's 1922 silent, *Dr. Mabuse, the Gambler*. AKA: *Dr. M*.

COCOON

1985 (PG-13) 117m / **D:** Ron Howard / **W:** Tom Benedek / **C:** Wilford Brimley, Brian Dennehy, Steve Guttenberg, Don Ameche, Tahnee Welch, Jack Gilford, Hume Cronyn, Jessica Tandy, Gwen Verdon, Maureen Stapleton, Tyrone Power Jr., Barret Oliver, Linda Harrison, Herta Ware, Clint Howard

Humanist sci-fi fantasy in which Florida senior citizens discover a watery nest of dormant aliens (from Atlantis, natch) that serves effectively as a Fountain of Youth, restoring their health and vigor. Complications ensue when the cocoons' space cohorts return to check up on them. Warm-hearted and winning, even if the ooh'ing and ahh'ing f/x-crammed finale rips off *Close Encounters of the Third Kind* every which way. An Oscar winner for the visual whammies, but made memorable by screen greats Don Ameche, Wilford Brimley, Jack Gilford, Hume Cronyn, and Jessica Tandy. Based on David Saperstein's then-unpublished novel, which he followed with the literary sequel *Metamorphosis*, essentially unrelated to the inevitable Hollywood encore *Cocoon: The Return*. Ameche won the supporting actor Oscar.

COCOON: THE RETURN

1988 (PG) 116m / **D:** Daniel Petrie / **W:** Stephen McPherson / **C:** Don Ameche, Wilford Brimley, Steve Guttenberg, Maureen Stapleton, Hume Cronyn, Jessica Tandy, Gwen Verdon, Jack Gilford, Tahnee Welch, Courteney Cox, Brian Dennehy, Barret Oliver

"Cocoon: The Rerun," as old timers who left with aliens last time revisit Earth and basically go through the same stuff all over again. Filmmakers desperately push familiar emotional buttons in search of the fragile magic of Ron Howard's original. You may find yourself fast-forwarding to the f/x or away from the schmaltz. Good luck.

CODE 46

2003 (R) 93m / **D:** Michael Winterbottom / **W:** Frank Cottrell Boyce / **C:** Tim Robbins, Samantha Morton, Om Puri, Jeanne Balibar

In this atmospheric future-noir set in a *Gattaca*-like world divided between glossy high-rise cities and the desolate wastelands beyond, DNA is everything. People can't even have a child unless they are determined to have the right genetic mix. Tim Robbins is sent to investigate a forgery scheme that would allow people to move between the two zones. He falls in love with possible forger Samantha Morton (beguiling in her wide-eyed serenity as in *Minority Report*). This complicates matters. The story floats and drifts too widely to have much grip, but the film's jet-set urbanity and casual approach to invasive tech-

Ron Howard directed the first of the two *Cocoon* movies, which is about a group of seniors who find a fountain of youth thanks to the presence of an alien ship.

nology proved eerily omniscient at predicting how the modern world would look even a decade hence. Hard-to-pin-down director Michael Winterbottom eschewed big-budget sets by shooting in glittering metropolises like Shanghai and Dubai where the future seems to have already arrived.

COLD SOULS

2009 (PG-13) 101m / D: Sophie Barthes / **W:** Sophie Barthes / **C:** Paul Giamatti, Emily Watson, Dina Korzun, Lauren Ambrose, David Strathairn

Paul Giamatti plays himself in this surreal comedy about an actor (Paul Giamatti) who is having a hard time getting ready for a production of *Uncle Vanya*. Then he reads a *New Yorker* article about a company that will put your soul into cold storage. After getting his soul excised, though, Paul's life doesn't get better. Trying to get his soul back from the company and its slick functionary (David Strathairn) proves to be more complicated than he'd anticipated. Based on a dream that writer/director Sophie Barthes had about Woody Allen.

COLOSSUS: THE FORBIN PROJECT

1970 (R) 100m / D: Joseph Sargent / **W:** James Bridges / **C:** Eric Braeden, Susan Clark, Gordon Pinsent, William Schallert, Georg Stanford Brown

A massive computer designed to manage U.S. defense systems instead merges with its Soviet equal and proceeds to accomplish its prime purpose: to achieve world peace. It does this by the most logical means—world domination and elimination of former human bosses, if necessary. Wire-tight, suspenseful film seems at once dated yet timely—the chattering old computer equipment is used to put a mechanical face on Big Brother concepts, while touching on fears of technology out of control. Based on the novel by D. F. Jones, who also wrote two sequels. A cult item that served as a precursor to the *Terminator* series, in which a defense computer seeks world peace by attempting to extinguish the human race altogether. AKA: *The Forbin Project*.

COMMUNION

1989 (R) 103m / D: Philippe Mora / **W:** Whitley Strieber / **C:** Christopher Walken, Lindsay Crouse, Frances Sternhagen, Joel Carlson, Andreas Katsulas, Basil Hoffman, Terri Hanauer

A serious adaptation of the purportedly nonfiction best seller by genre novelist Whitley Strieber, about his supposed 1985 abduction by dwarf drones under the control of spindly, huge-eyed beings (a breed sometimes referred to by UFO hipsters as "Schwa"). Christopher Walken's twitchy

Quirky character actor Christopher Walken is cast as an equally oddball protagonist in *Communion*.

method acting backstops a story with dubious authenticity, to say the least. The film—produced and written by Strieber—is remarkably candid about the author's eccentricities, right down to the notorious episode in which Strieber claimed a vision of Mr. Peanut (replaced onscreen for copyright by a top-hatted toy robot). Philippe Mora's direction, full of strange juxtapositions and hallucination imagery, may be too loose to please all but the very curious and New Age types. Strieber, meanwhile, followed his book with two more vaporous accounts (*Breakthrough* and *Transformation*) and a Strieberesque novelization of the Roswell incident, *Majestic*.

COMPUTER CHESS

2013 (NR) 92m / D: Andrew Bujalski / **W:** Andrew Bujalski / **C:** Patrick Riester, Wiley Wiggins, Myles Paige, Gerald Peary, James Curry

Sometime in the early 1980s, a couple dozen pioneering programmers in the period's ill-fitting clothing gather at an anonymous chain hotel for their annual chess tournament. No humans play, just one team's software against the other. Rivalries brew in an atmosphere that's tense in an extremely nerdy way (lots of downcast eyes and hunched shoulders, no fist fights here), while around the fringes drugs are imbibed and philosophical debates rage over artificial intelligence and the apocalypse; reality starts to get a little screwy. Shades of Richard Linklater's headtrip sci-fi abounds; writer/director Andrew Bujalski shot this in Linklater's home of Austin, Texas. The smeary black-and-white video, mostly nonprofessional actors, and raw sound quality give it the feel of some documentary time capsule from a disappeared era.

THE COMPUTER WORE TENNIS SHOES

1969 (G) 87m / D: Robert Butler / **W:** Joseph L. McEveety / **C:** Kurt Russell, Cesar Romero, Joe Flynn, William Schallert, Alan Hewitt, Richard Bakalyan, Pat Harrington, Debbie Paine

Post-Walt live-action Disney comedy starring Kurt Russell as Dexter Riley, an underachieving college student who suddenly becomes a genius after the campus computer's memory bank is accidentally downloaded into his brain. Innocuous, inexplicable, and dated, but the expert cast keeps this online. Cesar Romero plays the local crime boss and the computer's original owner whose clandestine records wind up in Dexter's head. Joe Flynn (Captain Binghamton on *McHale's Navy*) is the fussbudget college dean and Dexter's nemesis. Pat Harrington (Schneider on *One Day at a Time*) hosts the TV quiz show on which Dexter appears. Followed by *Now You See Him, Now You Don't* and *The Strongest Man in the World*. This is precisely the kind of image Russell was trying to kill off when he signed up for *Escape from New York*.

CONEHEADS

1993 (PG) 86m / D: Steven Barron / **W:** Dan Aykroyd, Tom Davis, Bonnie Turner, Terry Turner / **C:** Dan Aykroyd, Jane Curtin, Laraine Newman, Jason Alexander, Michelle Burke, Chris Farley, Michael Richards, Lisa Jane Persky, Sinbad, Shishir Kurup, Michael McKean, Phil Hartman, David Spade, Dave Thomas, Jan Hooks, Chris Rock, Adam Sandler, Julia Sweeney, Danielle Aykroyd

Saturday Night Live skit inflated to feature-length. Boasts dozens of *SNL* regulars. Dan Aykroyd and Jane Curtin reprise their roles as Beldar and Prymaat, the alien couple with the bald peaked heads from the planet Remulak who are just trying to fit in on Earth. Laraine Newman, who created the role of teen-aged daughter Connie, appears as Beldar's sister, while Michelle Burke takes over as Connie (toddler Connie is Aykroyd's daughter, in her film debut). The jokes may be thin but, then again, it is based on an *SNL* skit many years past its prime.

CONQUEST OF SPACE

1955 (NR) 81m / D: Byron Haskin / **W:** James O'Hanlon / **C:** Walter Brooke, Eric Fleming, Mickey Shaughnessy, Phil Foster, William Redfield, William Hopper, Benson Fong, Ross Martin

Would you like a moon crater named after you? That honor was given to the late Chesley Bonestell for being this century's finest astronomical artist. His designs and constructions permeate this film—which is the only conceivable reason to see it. A space commander designs an orbital platform and helps build a moon rocket. When told the craft is to transport him, his son, and select crewmen to Mars instead, our leader looks into the Bible and, finding no mention of a Mars expedition, has a nervous breakdown (that Scripture mentions no space platform or moon flight either seems to elude him). Endure the melodrama for the stunning Bonestellian visuals; here is a Mars not as we found it but as it should have been. One scene should haunt you forever: the burial-at-space of the dead astronaut, encased in his space suit and floating off into the sun's zodiacal light. Inspired by Wernher von Braun's speculative nonfiction book *The Mars Project*.

CONQUEST OF THE PLANET OF THE APES

1972 (PG) 87m / **D:** J. Lee Thompson / **W:** Paul Dehn / **C:** Roddy McDowall, Don Murray, Ricardo Montalban, Natalie Trundy, Severn Darden, Hari Rhodes

This fourth *Apes* film picks up where 1971's *Escape* left off. After a disease brought from outer space kills all Earth's cats and dogs, humans begin to keep apes as house pets. Because of their intelligence and adaptability, these pets turn into ill-treated slaves governed by the Gestapo-like Ape Control. Caesar (Roddy McDowall) is the son of the super-intelligent time-traveling apes Cornelius (also previously played by McDowall) and Zira. Because of the threat he poses to the human race, Caesar was left hidden in the care of kind-hearted circus owner Armando (Ricardo Montalban) after his parents were killed. Soon Caesar discovers how his fellow apes are being treated and leads an armed revolt of the apes against their cruel human masters. The references to American slavery are overt, giving the story a powerful message. Still, the film is not heavy handed, and the story pulls viewers along. McDowall delivers a fine performance, especially difficult behind such heavy makeup. Director J. Lee Thompson does a good job handling the large riot scenes, which were reportedly based on footage of the Watts riots from a few years before.

CONTACT

1997 (PG) 150m / **D:** Robert Zemeckis / **W:** James V. Hart, Michael Goldenberg / **C:** Jodie Foster, Matthew McConaughey, James Woods, John Hurt, Tom Skerritt, William Fichtner, David Morse, Angela Bassett, Rob Lowe

Carl Sagan's novel about humanity's first contact with an alien intelligence is brought vividly to life in the sort of richly imagined mainstream speculative fiction that is just about never attempted, let alone delivered so wonderfully. Jodie Foster shines as Ellie, a researcher at SETI (Search for Extra-Terrestrial Intelligence) who finally discovers that somebody/thing is responding to the signals beaming out from her giant telescope array in Puerto Rico. The story from there, in which Ellie competes with government and private entities trying to derail or hijack her project to

In *Contact,* Jodie Foster is Ellie, a SETI researcher who is the first human to make contact with an extraterrestrial civilization.

establish contact, dives into a sharp-elbowed philosophical debate about the existence of God and man's place in the universe. The cast is strong, with John Hurt standing out in a small but key role as a Howard Hughes-esque billionaire with money to burn and a yen for humans to meet aliens. Possibly the most thoughtful mainstream film ever made about alien contact; the head to *Close Encounters of the Third Kind*'s heart. Had the bad luck to be released in the same year as *Titanic*, *Good Will Hunting*, and *L.A. Confidential*, so incredibly only garnered one Oscar nomination, for sound mixing.

CONTAGION

2011 (PG-13) 106m / D: Steven Soderbergh / **W:** Scott Z. Burns / **C:** Matt Damon, Marion Cotillard, Laurence Fishburne, Kate Winslet, Jude Law, Gwyneth Paltrow, Bryan Cranston

When businesswoman Gwyneth Paltrow dies after returning from a business trip to Hong Kong, a new kind of hyperfatal flu spreads across the planet like a forest fire, scything down all in its path. Instead of focusing on the panic and mayhem, however, Steven Soderbergh's drama is an anomaly in the disaster-movie genre: a procedural. Using one of the more reality-checked screenplays in sci-fi, the film shows how a committed network of CDC researchers work against the clock on a vaccine, while also showing how everyday people like Matt Damon's widowed dad have to make do In a society slowly shutting down. Jude Law is superbly vile as a conspiracy theorist hawking a fake cure. A welcome return to the mentality of sci-fi thrillers of old, where the analytical women and men of science were the true heroes.

THE COSMIC MONSTERS

1958 (NR) 75m / D: Gilbert Gunn / **W:** Joe Ambor, Paul Ryder / **C:** Forrest Tucker, Gaby André, Alec Mango, Hugh Latimer, Martin Benson

Scientist Forrest Tucker accidentally pops a hole in the ionosphere during a magnetism experiment. As a result, very huge, very unfriendly alien insects emerge to plague mankind. Can the intervention of a friendly alien save the world, or is mankind doomed to be bugged to death? Forrest made *The Crawling Eye* that same year, a much creepier tale of alien invasion. AKA: *The Strange World of Planet X*; *The Crawling Terror*.

COSMOPOLIS

2012 (R) 109m / D: David Cronenberg / **W:** David Cronenberg / **C:** Robert Pattinson, Sarah Gadon, Juliette Binoche, Samantha Morton, Kevin Durand, Paul Giamatti, Abdul Ayoola, Jay Baruchel, Mathieu Amalric

There's nothing *specifically* sci-fi about David Cronenberg's film of the Don DeLillo novel, but its mania for the bleeding-edge interconnected technological whirlwind feels like the future, even if it's just a slightly tweaked reality. Billionaire Robert Pattinson spends a day gliding through the streets of Manhattan, controlling a small nation's worth of wealth via intermediaries. As he surfs the churning waves of international finance, Pattinson is continually delayed on his metaphoric crosstown journey to get a haircut, whether by accommodating prostitute Juliette Binoche, the provocations of Occupy Wall Street-type protestors, or potential assassins. The Samuel-Beckett-meets-William-Gibson absurdist tone is not for every taste, but it captured something of the ruling class's post-crash panic, projecting a chaotic future all too close to reality.

COWBOY BEBOP: THE MOVIE

2001 (R) 116m / D: Shinichiro Watanabe / **W:** Marc Handler

Some versions of this film offshoot of the late-1990s anime series (which developed a cult following in the States via constant reruns on the Cartoon Network) carry the title "Knockin' on Heaven's Door," though any real connection to the song or Dylan himself can be hard to divine. A deadly pathogen gets released on Mars, heavily settled by the year 2071, and the ragtag bounty hunter crew on the ship *Bebop* are hired to track down the terrorist(s) responsible. The easy camaraderie on the ship is almost the equal of *Firefly* and the animation is superbly detailed throughout. Anachronisms abound, which befits the mood of the hero Spike, a laconic beanpole of an old-fashioned beatnik whose lazy demeanor masks a mean set of kung-fu skills. Most DVDs include both dubbed and subtitled tracks.

> "The easy camaraderie on the ship is almost the equal of *Firefly* and the animation is superbly detailed throughout."
>
> *Cowboy Bebop: The Movie*

COWBOYS & ALIENS

2011 (PG-13) 119m / D: Jon Favreau / **W:** Roberto Orci, Alex Kurtzman, Damon Lindelof, Mark Fergus, Hawk Ostby / **C:** Daniel Craig, Harrison Ford, Olivia Wilde, Sam Rockwell, Adam Beach, Paul Dano, Keith Carradine

The screenplay-by-committee story by a half-dozen credited writers (with surely a few more expensive off-the-radar script doctors contributing to the idea melee) is set in the 1870s Old West. One of those tiny dusty towns where the shopkeepers are meek and the local boss can have anybody killed at his whim is being threatened. Only this time, it's not rustlers or Apaches, but aliens who like to strafe the town and randomly abduct people for experiments. That's about where the creativity stops, as cold-eyed hero Daniel Craig, fitted with some alien bracelet that provides impressive firepower, helps the humans fight back. Like many of the more unimaginative big-budget sci-fi of recent years, this mess was produced under the aegis of

Stephen Spielberg. Olivia Wilde, Sam Rockwell, and Paul Dano fight for relevancy amid the explosions and chases, while Harrison Ford grumbles his way through as another of his reluctant heroes. Jon Favreau tries to leaven the ungainly story with his usual humor, but he would have been better served to just slash the budget to the bone and shoot a straight Western. Aliens and Apaches don't mix.

CQ

2001 (R) 88m / **D:** Roman Coppola / **W:** Roman Coppola / **C:** Jeremy Davies, Angela Lindvall, Élodie Bouchez, Gérard Depardieu, Giancarlo Giannini, Jason Schwartzman, Billy Zane

Francis Ford Coppola's son Roman's debut feature is a film-within-a-film comedy with fuzzy reality margins set in swinging Paris 1969. Wannabe auteur Jeremy Davies is working on a *Barbarella*-like sci-fi cheeseball disaster called *Dragonfly* that's set in 2001 and falling in love with the go-go-booted heroine. Meanwhile he's trying to get his own film made. Gérard Depardieu plays *Dragonfly*'s out-of-control director.

THE CRAWLING EYE

1958 (NR) 87m / **D:** Quentin Lawrence / **W:** Jimmy Sangster / **C:** Forrest Tucker, Laurence Payne, Janet Munro, Jennifer Jayne, Warren Mitchell

Quatermass-like sci-fi with Forrest Tucker as a UN science investigator visiting the Swiss town of Trollenberg, where a strange radioactive cloud hovers on a mountaintop. As the cloud descends and encloses the village, several climbers are discovered decapitated. Tucker teams up with two sisters, one of them a telepath (Janet Munro) who can communicate with aliens, which is very lucky because that darn cloud is chock-full of them. The ensuing battle provides plenty of tension, even though the effects are so-so at best, and the acting, at most, adequate. At least the aliens themselves don't disappoint with their huge Cyclopean-eyeball-tentacled-creaturoid good looks. Once again a low-budget film is directed and photographed with atmosphere to spare. Adapted by writer Jimmy Sangster from the BBC teleserial by Peter Kay. AKA: *The Trollenberg Terror*; *The Creature from Another World*.

THE CRAZIES (1973)

1973 (R) 103m / **D:** George A. Romero / **W:** George A. Romero, Paul McCollough / **C:** Lane Carroll, W.G. McMillan, Harold W. Jones, Lloyd Hollar, Lynn Lowry, Richard Liberty

When a small Pennsylvania town's water supply is contaminated with an experimental virus, the residents go on a chaotic, murderous rampage. The army is called in to quell the anarchy, and a small war breaks out. George A. Romero's second feature followed on the heels of his classic *Night of the*

Living Dead and features nary a zombie, though plenty of pointedly critical subtext is there. Unfortunately, though Romero proved once again it was possible to make an impressive film outside the Hollywood system, *The Crazies*'s overall impact was dulled by its muddled approach to its subject matter. The movie is still disturbing, but it hasn't aged well. Romero would go on to make better films, like 1978's vampire thriller *Martin*. AKA: *Code Name: Trixie*.

THE CRAZIES (2010)

2010 (R) 101m / **D:** Breck Eisner / **W:** Scott Kosar, Ray Wright / **C:** Timothy Olyphant, Radha Mitchell, Danielle Panabaker, Joe Anderson, Christie Lynn Smith, Brett Rickaby

Glossier, bigger-budget remake of the 1973 George Romero zombie-paranoia film that brings advances in camerawork and undead makeup, along with post-9/11 anxieties, to the party. Timothy Olyphant plays the sheriff of a small Iowa town whose residents start acting a mite antisocial (staggering around with shotguns, burning houses down) before going full-on zombie. Why's it happening? Well, that's a secret (hint: *it's the government*).

THE CREATION OF THE HUMANOIDS

1962 (NR) 84m / **D:** Wesley E. Barry / **W:** Jay Simms / **C:** Don Megowan, Frances McCann, Erica Elliot, Don Doolittle, Dudley Manlove

Set in a familiar post-holocaust future, this is a tale of humans outnumbered by androids and the resulting struggle for survival. Low budget and senseless, but at least it's slow as well. Andy Warhol was reported to love this film, specifically for how excruciatingly boring it was.

CREATURE

1985 (R) 97m / **D:** William Malone / **W:** William Malone, Alan Reed / **C:** Klaus Kinski, Stan Ivar, Wendy Schaal, Lyman Ward, Annette McCarthy, Diane Salinger

This low-budget *Alien* rip-off has at least one good thing going for it … Klaus Kinski. The rest of the nondescript cast should have taken some attitudinal hints from K. K. and relaxed, giving this lame material the nonchalant, tongue-in-cheek treatment it deserved. Captain Stan Ivar and crew are on Saturn's moon Titan, investigating a two-thousand-year-old alien life form that has been fatally anti-social to the previous spaceketeers. Not enough tension, and definitely not enough Kinski. AKA: *Titan Find*.

CREATURE FROM THE BLACK LAGOON

1954 (NR) 79m / **D:** Jack Arnold / **W:** Harry Essex, Arthur Ross / **C:** Richard Carlson, Julie Adams, Richard Denning, Antonio Moreno, Whit Bissell, Nestor Paiva, Ricou Browning, Ben Chapman

An anthropological expedition in the Amazon stumbles upon the Gill-Man, a prehistoric humanoid fish monster who supposedly represents a "missing link" between humans and ... well, fish. The scaled nasty takes a fancy to the fetching Julie Adams, a coed majoring in "science" (she has brains as well as beauty!), but the menfolk get all riled up (and occasionally bumped off by the monster). Originally filmed in 3D, this was one of the first movies to sport top-of-the-line underwater photography (the underwater scene where a bikini-clad beauty swims while the Gill-Man lurks unseen below was something of a prurient classic at the time) and remains one of the most enjoyable monster movies ever made. The Gill-Man, both utterly alien and strangely sympathetic, is an extraordinary creation. Joseph Gershenson's score became a late-night TV "Creature Features" standard. Based on a story by Maurice Zimm, the film spawned two sequels: *Revenge of the Creature* and *The Creature Walks among Us*.

The Creature from the Black Lagoon has become a classic monster movie; it also was a technical achievement in underwater photography.

THE CREATURE WALKS AMONG US

1956 (NR) 79m / **D:** John Sherwood / **W:** Arthur Ross / **C:** Jeff Morrow, Rex Reason, Leigh Snowden, Gregg Palmer, Ricou Browning, Don Megowan

The sequel to *Revenge of the Creature* has the much put-upon Gill-Man captured once more by scientists bent on "studying" him. During an accidental lab fire, the creature's gills are burned off and the science-boys undertake to save his life with surgery designed to turn him into an air-breather. Sadly, the (ex)Gill-Man remains a fish out of water, lurching around in dingy clothes and once again lusting after one of those faithless human floozies (Leigh Snowden). This final entry in the *Creature from the Black Lagoon* series has little of the original film's magic, but it's a weirdly compelling film in its own right. The altered monster is even more sympathetic here—his being forced to wear human clothes is an especially effective touch. Ricou Browning was back to perform the monster's underwater scenes; Don Megowan played the new and not necessarily improved creature. Also shot in 3D.

CREEPOZOIDS

1987 (R) 72m / **D:** David DeCoteau / **W:** David DeCoteau, Buford Hauser / **C:** Linnea Quigley, Ken Abraham, Michael Aranda, Richard Hawkins, Kim McKamy, Joi Wilson

In the near future, army deserters hiding out at an abandoned science complex are stalked by a slimy monster. Yet another *Alien* rip-off, substituting extreme, tasteless violence for the original's expert pacing and style. The one semi-effective element is a creepy monster baby, but that's not enough to save this waste of celluloid.

CRITTERS

1986 (PG-13) 86m / **D:** Stephen Herek / **W:** Don Opper, Stephen Herek, Dominic Muir / **C:** Dee Wallace-Stone, M. Emmet Walsh, Billy Green Bush, Scott Grimes, Nadine Van Der Velde, Terrence Mann, Billy Zane, Don Opper

One of the better *Gremlins* imitators. Hairy, fast-growing, faster-eating little alien "Krites" crash to Earth, with a pair of shape-shifting, blast-happy galactic bounty hunters right behind them. Both groups terrorize a farm family in a small Kansas community. Don Opper (*Android*) is especially fun as the local Barney Fife deputy. Smart and sarcastic sci-fi action that doesn't push the intrinsic gore to extremes, though the franchise has worn out its welcome with increasingly inferior sequels. Drolly subtitled Krite dialogue culminates in the devouring of an E.T. doll. Followed by three sequels, the second of which was co-written by *Pitch Black*'s David Twohy and the third of which featured a young Leonardo DiCaprio.

THE CURSE OF FRANKENSTEIN

1957 (NR) 83m / **D:** Terence Fisher / **W:** Jimmy Sangster / **C:** Peter Cushing, Christopher Lee, Hazel Court, Robert Urquhart, Valerie Gaunt, Noel Hood

What happens when England's Hammer Studios decides to take Mary Shelley's mad-scientist-makes-a-monster-and-boy-does-it-cause-trouble novel *Frankenstein* and give it some Technicolor juice? Pairing up Peter Cushing (as Baron Frankenstein) and Christopher Lee (as the monster) for the first time, Hammer created a scream-team that would last for decades. Also for the first time, the audience is treated to the surprisingly realistic stitched-up-body monster makeup by Jack Pierce (who also created the famous makeup for Universal's original Frankenstein monster). Just as before, the kinda-insane Baron gathers pieces of the freshly dead to assemble his experiment, with the one fatal flaw … a bad brain. Said brain, and a little disorientation, cause the dead-alive one to wreak havoc, spread destruction, and, of course, *kill*. When a gunshot takes off part of the creature's head in a swelter of blood, audiences—and censors—worldwide (except in Japan where they have always loved their violence) were aghast! Don't worry, you can take it. Worth it for the atmosphere alone.

CYBORG

1989 (R) 85m / **D:** Albert Pyun / **W:** Kitty Chalmers / **C:** Jean-Claude Van Damme, Deborah Richter, Vincent Klyn, Dayle Haddon, Alex Daniels, Rolf Muller

Plague reduces Earth to a deathly, dIrty, urban ruin patrolled by pumped-up punks. A lady cyborg transporting the disease cure must be protected by wandering avenger Jean-Claude Van Damme, in a non-plot full of caricatured creeps howling like animals and breaking each others' bones. If it all seems made up on the spot, it largely was; this was planned as a sequel to the He-Man movie *Masters of the Universe* but mutated into a surprisingly successful kickboxer apocalypse instead.

DAGORA, THE SPACE MONSTER

1965 (NR) 80m / D: Ishiro Honda / **W:** Shinichi Sekizawa / **C:** Yosuke Natsuki, Yôko Fujiyama, Akiko Wakabayashi, Hiroshi Koizumi

Gangsters with silly voices tangle with a giant, slimy, pulsating whatsit from space that eats diamonds. Meanwhile, a group of scientists with slightly less silly voices join together in a massive effort to destroy the critter. Far from the best Japanese monster movie, and the voices dubbed in for the U.S. version are particularly bad—coming from the grim-faced villains, they sound more like second-rate cartoon-characters. Nonetheless, the unusual blending of the gangster and monster genres makes it memorable. From *Godzilla* director Ishiro Honda. AKA: *Dagora; Space Monster Dagora*.

DALEKS—INVASION EARTH: 2150 A.D.

1966 (NR) 81m / D: Gordon Flemyng / **W:** Milton Subotsky / **C:** Peter Cushing, Bernard Cribbins, Ray Brooks, Andrew Keir, Jill Curzon, Roberta Tovey

A slightly more ambitious sequel to *Dr. Who and the Daleks*. Peter Cushing is back as the befuddled Doctor in a white wig, once again accidentally transported into the future to do battle with the exterminate-happy robotic mutants known as the Daleks. In this one the Daleks have taken over the Earth's population with mind control, and they plot to blow out the Earth's core and use the whole planet as a titanic spaceship. Slicker and more interesting than the first movie, it will still be a bit of a shock to U.S. fans used to the British TV series. AKA: *Invasion Earth 2150 A.D.*

Peter Cushing assumes the role of the British favorite Dr. Who in 1966's *Daleks—Invasion Earth: 2150* A.D.

DAMNATION ALLEY

1977 (PG) 87m / **D:** Jack Smight / **W:** Alan Sharp, Lukas Heller / **C:** George Peppard, Jan-Michael Vincent, Paul Winfield, Dominique Sanda, Jackie Earle Haley, Kip Niven

After a chilling World War III introduction, this post-apocalypse film slides downhill quickly. Several disposable characters, led by early 1980s TV stars George Peppard and Jan-Michael Vincent, set off across America in a huge armored survivalist RV in search of … Albany. They have a series of improbable adventures set against painfully cheap f/x, culminating in an ending so ridiculous it makes the rest of the film seem almost reasonable. Very poorly adapted from Roger Zelazny's fine novel.

DANGER: DIABOLIK

1968 (PG-13) 99m / **D:** Mario Bava / **W:** Mario Bava, Dino Maiuri, Adriano Barracio / **C:** John Phillip Law, Marisa Mell, Michel Piccoli, Terry-Thomas, Adolfo Celi

Supercool 1960s tongue-in-cheek thriller with loads of psychedelia, and a Bond-movie's worth of fast cars and mini skirts. But, unlike Bond, Diabolik is on the wrong side of the law. The title character even has an underground lair equipped with computers, an enormous rotating circular bed, and the coolest see-through showers ever. Diabolik (John Phillip Law) and his superbabe cohort (Marisa Mell) plan and execute one elaborate heist after another, each time managing to make government officials and the police look dumber and dumber. While the laughing gas press conference inspires as much confidence (and as many laughs) as most real-life briefings, something must be done to stop Diabolik. How about melting all the gold left in the treasury into one enormous twenty-ton bar that would be impossible for any supercriminal to steal … except? Italy's Mario Bava, best known for his atmospheric horror films, changes genres to this sci-fi-ish heist thriller with ease and even manages an explosive climax with a final image parodying his more horrific closings. Music by Ennio Morricone. AKA: *Diabolik*.

DARK CITY

1998 (R) 100m / **D:** Alex Proyas / **W:** Alex Proyas, Lem Dobbs, David S. Goyer / **C:** Rufus Sewell, William Hurt, Kiefer Sutherland, Jennifer Connelly, Richard O'Brien, Ian Richardson

German expressionism meets *Blade Runner* urban noir inside of a David Fincher-style music video in this kitchen-sink sci-fi fantasy dreamscape from the director of the landmark gothic comic action flick *The Crow*. The setting is a dystopic city that's less futuristic than it is completely unmoored from reality. Filled with jutting buildings and baroque chambers, the city is controlled by alien beings in trench coats and fedoras called the Strangers, who have powers over dreams and memory. Into this Kafka-light dream lands John Murdoch (Rufus Sewell, hunted-looking as always), who is on the run from the Strangers and the police, while looking for his missing beloved, a sultry singer played by Jennifer Connelly. Murdoch's chase provides a nifty reason for Proyas to explore the Escher angles of this dream-city, evoked by some truly inspired f/x that go more for beauty than sheer fanboy awesomeness. Watch for *The Rocky Horror Picture Show*'s Riff as one of the Strangers and a fantastically unhinged mad-scientist routine from Kiefer Sutherland. Poorly received on its first release, it was later championed by many diehard fans (including Roger Ebert, who called it his favorite movie of the year). The 2008 director's cut includes an extra 10 minutes or so of footage and does away with a much-maligned opening narration.

THE DARKEST HOUR

2011 (PG-13) 89m / **D:** Chris Gorak / **W:** Jon Spaihts / **C:** Emile Hirsch, Olivia Thirlby, Max Minghella, Rachael Taylor, Joel Kinnaman

Sam Raimi directed *Darkman* in which a heroic scientist uses synthetic skin as a disguise to go after criminals.

Russian blockbuster machine Timur Bekmambetov produced this foreign market-targeted epic about four American travelers in Moscow who are lucky enough to find shelter when clouds of mostly invisible, will-o'-the-wispish aliens start wreaking havoc. Eventually, the humans have to venture back out into the city's eerily emptied streets and figure out how to keep from getting vaporized by the energy-ravenous invaders and construct enough improvised weaponry to keep up a decent fight.

DARKMAN

1990 (R) 96m / **D:** Sam Raimi / **W:** Chuck Pfarrer, Daniel Goldin, Joshua Goldin, Sam Raimi, Ivan Raimi / **C:** Liam Neeson, Frances McDormand, Larry Drake, Colin Friels, Nelson Mashita, Jenny Agutter, Rafael H. Robledo

When he wasn't able to get the go-ahead to make a film of any established comic-book heroes, campy horror filmmaker Sam Raimi made up his own. Here, Raimi took the traditional gothic disfigured-man-seeks-revenge premise, mixed it with high-tech details, and turned the monster into a super-hero. Mild-mannered scientist Peyton Westlake (Liam Neeson), gruesomely burned and left for dead by gangsters, uses his invention of short-duration synthetic flesh to alter his charred visage and become Darkman, chameleon-like scourge of the criminal underworld. Kinetic camerawork, exquisite violence, and comic-book kitsch add up to a movie that's impossible to take seriously but enjoyable enough while it lasts. Westlake's girlfriend is played by Frances McDormand, in a role that Julia Roberts reportedly turned down for *Pretty Woman*. Music by Danny Elfman. Followed by two direct-to-video sequels that featured neither Raimi nor Neeson.

DARK SKIES

2013 (PG-13) 97m / **D:** Scott Stewart / **W:** Scott Stewart / **C:** Keri Russell, Josh Hamilton, Dakota Goyo, Kadan Rockett, J. K. Simmons

A post-*Paranormal Activity* home invasion haunter gets crossed with an alien invasion plot in this low-budget effort about a suburban family (Keri

Russell and Josh Hamilton play the beleaguered parents) who are haunted by mysterious, child-snatching beings. The filmmakers throw in possessions, spooky kids, and flocks of birds doing kamikaze dives into picture windows for good measure.

DARK STAR

1974 (G) 95m / **D:** John Carpenter / **W:** John Carpenter, Dan O'Bannon / **C:** Dan O'Bannon, Brian Narelle, Dre Pahich, Cal Kuniholm, Joe Saunders, Miles Watkins

John Carpenter's directorial debut is an innovative, no-budget, sci-fi stoner satire that's unlike just about anything made before or since. It focuses on a crew of unstable astronauts who have been drifting around the universe for years blowing up "unstable" planets. Needless to say, their definition of unstable is a little loose. During their journey, they battle an alien mascot who closely resembles a walking beach ball, as well as a "sensitive" and intelligent bombing device that starts to question the meaning of its existence. Faced with all these problems, the former captain is consulted—even though he's dead. Mercilessly lampoons the mysticism of *2001: A Space Odyssey* and prefigures everything from *Hitchhiker's Guide to the Galaxy* to *Alien* (co-writer Dan O'Bannon reworked some of the ideas into his script for the latter). Fun, weird, unpredictable, and ahead of its time.

D.A.R.Y.L.

1985 (PG) 100m / **D:** Simon Wincer / **W:** David Ambrose, Allan Scott, Jeffrey Ellis / **C:** Mary Beth Hurt, Michael McKean, Barret Oliver, Colleen Camp, Danny Corkill, Kathryn Walker, Josef Sommer

Boy found by the side of the road is too polite, too honest, and too smart. Taken in by a childless couple, Daryl is told by a kid pal the necessity of imperfection (if you don't want the grown-ups to bother you too much) and he becomes more like a real child. But he's actually a lost American military project ("Data Analyzing Robot Youth Lifeform"), a computer brain in a cloned body. Intriguing parental *Twilight Zone* situation, aimed at family audiences, concentrating on characterizations rather than f/x hardware. Doesn't quite hold up to the finale.

THE DAY AFTER

1983 (NR) 122m / **D:** Nicholas Meyer / **W:** Edward Hume / **C:** Jason Robards Jr., JoBeth Williams, John Lithgow, Steve Guttenberg

Powerfully made drama from *Star Trek II: The Wrath of Khan* director Nicholas Meyer, which graphically depicts the nuclear bombing of a Midwestern city and the after-effects on the survivors. A talented cast made the most of the topical and terrifying material. Originally made for broadcast TV, this film was the subject of enormous controversy when it aired in 1983. In the tradition of the best sci-fi horror films, it allowed a nation for whom nuclear war seemed a daily possibility to live out its worst nightmare, gathering huge ratings and vast media coverage in the process. Did for nuclear annihilation fears in the U.S. what *Threads* and *The War Game* did in England. Reportedly scared the daylights out of the always susceptible President Ronald Reagan and may even have influenced his nuclear-weapons policy.

THE DAY AFTER TOMORROW

2004 (PG-13) 124m / **D:** Roland Emmerich / **W:** Roland Emmerich, Jeffrey Nachmanoff / **C:** Dennis Quaid, Jake Gyllenhaal, Emmy Rossum, Dash Mihok, Jay O. Saunders, Sela Ward, Kenneth Walsh, Ian Holm, Perry King, Arjay Smith

The disaster movie done as confused Weather Channel extravaganza. Roland Emmerich, always looking for new ways to blow up various parts of America, does it this time via a plot wherein environmental damage is causing extreme and nearly instantaneous climate change. Emmerich's demolition derby doesn't have years to wait for sea levels to rise, it wants to wipe out New York with a monster tidal wave and then slam the Northeast with Arctic-style blizzards in a matter of days. Elsewhere, snow comes to India and American refugees flood into Mexico (ah, the irony). All of the computer-generated mayhem is keenly delivered, though in an overeager "can you top this?" manner that makes the human drama even more of a sideshow than it already is. Meanwhile, an indifferently gathered cast plays the same type of concerned politicians and scientists always on hand when the world is doomed ... or is it? Caused some discomfort at the time of its release with the anti-science crowd, as it acknowledges the reality of climate change—albeit in a way that would leave the average climatologist gasping with laughter.

DAYBREAKERS

2009 (R) 98m / **D:** Michael Spierig, Peter Spierig / **W:** Michael Spierig, Peter Spierig / **C:** Ethan Hawke, Willem Dafoe, Sam Neill, Claudia Karvan, Michael Dorman, Isabel Lucas, Vince Colosimo

By the year 2019, an outbreak of vampirism has turned almost everybody into night-haunting blood drinkers. People work and live to some extent just as before, albeit behind sun shutters and with less need for restaurants. Just one looming problem: the supply of humans, and thusly blood, is just about exhausted. Ethan Hawke is a morally tortured hematologist (he refuses to drink from humans) racing to create a blood substitute before his fellow undead begin starving and turning into skeletal bat-like homicidal furies. Australian writer/director team Michael and Peter Spierig have fun spinning out the logistics of a world of fully functioning vampires, splashing out moody dark-blue *Blade Runner*-esque sets and loading up on the quips ("life sucks … and then you don't die"). But once Hawke runs into the human resistance underground, led by Willem Dafoe sporting a giant crossbow and an ill-considered southern accent, comically inept action sequences take over. The rest of the flat cast is mostly Aussies trying out unconvincing American accents. The exception is Sam Neill, who delivers nicely in the role of the red-eyed vampire blood-corporation CEO who knows that the laws of supply and demand don't disappear just because everybody is now undead.

THE DAY OF THE TRIFFIDS

1962 (NR) 94m / D: Steve Sekely / **W:** Philip Yordan / **C:** Howard Keel, Janette Scott, Nicole Maurey, Kieron Moore, Mervyn Johns, Ian Wilson, Alison Leggatt, Janina Faye, John Tate, Arthur Gross, Ewan Roberts

The majority of Earth's population is blinded by a meteor shower. As if this isn't bad enough, it also causes plant spores to mutate into giant mobile carnivores. The plants look like big shaggy cornstalks, with poisonous whip-like tentacles. Our hero, Howard Keel, who managed to retain his sight, fights to survive in a hostile new world. Smartly done entry in the world apocalypse category, adapted from John Wyndham's classic novel. Remade twice for British TV as miniseries in 1981 and 2009.

THE DAY THE EARTH CAUGHT FIRE

1961 (NR) 95m / D: Val Guest / **W:** Val Guest, Wolf Mankowitz / **C:** Janet Munro, Edward Judd, Leo McKern, Michael Goodliffe, Bernard Braden

"World saved." "World doomed." Which headline will be correct after the Earth is knocked out of its orbit and hurtles toward the sun? Leo McKern stars as the gruff science reporter who discovers the catastrophe after investigating the sudden floods, cyclones, and mysterious mists that arise in the wake of simultaneous nuclear testing at the North and South Poles by the Americans and Russians. A literate script and played-for-realism news-

Meteors cause blindness in Earthlings and create mutant, carnivorous plants in 1962's *Day of the Triffids*.

room setting will keep you sweating as the world's powers unite to try and get the planet back on track. One of the better postwar world-annihilation stories.

THE DAY THE EARTH STOOD STILL (1951)

1951 (NR) 92m / D: Robert Wise / **W:** Edmund H. North / **C:** Michael Rennie, Patricia Neal, Hugh Marlowe, Sam Jaffe, Frances Bavier, Lock Martin, Billy Gray

The first big-budget sci-fi feature of the 1950s has aged gracefully. Michael Rennie stars as the alien Klaatu, who lands a flying saucer in the middle of Washington, D.C., to warn Earth's leaders that our planet faces obliteration should they not halt atomic testing. His stern invitation, backed up by his giant robot guardian Gort, to live in peace with "the other planets" is met with fear and hysteria. He escapes hospital confinement and takes a room in a boarding house among us. Patricia Neal co-stars as the woman with whom he entrusts his secret identity. The effects are a tad simple, but unlike so many sci-fi films of the period, they don't look cheap by over-

One of the all-time classics of sci-fi is the original *The Day the Earth Stood Still,* a 1951 film with a distinctly Cold War theme.

reaching their capabilities. Based on the Harry Bates story "Farewell to the Master," it has the power of an ancient parable, with the menacing sight of tanks and howitzers in the midst of Washington's monuments and memorials more frightening than any flying saucer. The moral guardian figures of Gort and Klaatu and their message of peace or else resonates particularly strongly with children; this is not a criticism. First-rate performances from all of the leads. One of Bernard Herrmann's better scores, using the spooky vibrato of the electronic theremin. Among the greatest sci-fi films of all time, well worth repeat looks.

THE DAY THE EARTH STOOD STILL (2008)

2008 (PG-13) 104m / D: Scott Derrickson / **W:** David Scarpa / **C:** Keanu Reeves, Jennifer Connelly, Kathy Bates, Jaden Smith, John Cleese, Jon Hamm, Kyle Chandler, James Hong

Supposedly, the reason to reinvent a classic film is that the filmmakers in question have something new to bring to the table. This is theoretically true in this instance, given that In 1951 there was no Keanu Reeves. For Scott Derrickson's noisy redo, the original's classic simplicity is balled up and tossed out like a bad first draft. A giant glowing sphere lands in Central Park and a creature comes out to greet the gathered Earthlings, only to get a bullet for its trouble. The alien later takes human form (Reeves) and then goes on the run with scientist Jennifer Connelly and her bratty stepson (Jaden Smith). These two become responsible for convincing Reeves, his giant killer robot buddy, and their unseen confederation of alien races *not* to destroy humanity before it makes Earth unlivable, life-sustaining planets being more rare than sentient beings. Any message about climate change is quickly lost and a last-minute race-against-the-apocalypse is underwhelming, to put it mildly. Civilization will likely survive the destruction of Giants Stadium.

THE DAY THE WORLD ENDED

1955 (NR) 79m / D: Roger Corman / **W:** Lou Rusoff / **C:** Paul Birch, Lori Nelson, Adele Jergens, Raymond Hatton, Paul Dubov, Richard Denning, Mike Connors

Exploitation guru Roger Corman's first sci-fi movie. Five survivors of a nuclear holocaust stumble onto a desert ranch house fortress owned by a survivalist (Paul Birch) and his daughter (Lori Nelson). Animosity quickly develops between the "good" survivors (Birch, Nelson, and wholesome Richard Denning) and the "bad" survivors—a tough-talking gangster (Mike "Mannix" Connors) and his moll (Adele Jergens). Eventually another survivor—this one disfigured and wasting away from radiation poisoning, stumbles into their refuge. The radiation is slowly changing him into something even less pleasant, and it seems he's got friends waiting in the hills around the house. The one monster we get to see isn't particularly convincing, and the heroes' 1950s-macho posturings will inspire more laughter than admiration from today's audiences. Still, the film holds up pretty well today and paved the way for countless other radiated monster epics during the '50s. Remade for cable in 2001 with Nastassja Kinski as part of Cinemax's "Creature Features" series.

DEAD END DRIVE-IN

1986 (R) 92m / **D:** Brian Trenchard-Smith / **W:** Peter Smalley / **C:** Ned Manning, Natalie McCurry, Peter Whitford

In a surreal, grim future a man is trapped at a drive-in-theater-cum-concentration-camp, where the government incarcerates undesirables. Fueled by an original concept and good acting, this dystopian Aussie New Wave drama has enough dark thrills to make it memorable. Cheap but stylish in the best way. Prime example of 1980s apocalypse-punk visuals; if you see a Mohawk or facial piercing, run!

THIS WAS THE DAY THAT ENGULFED THE WORLD IN TERROR!

THE DEADLY MANTIS

STARRING
CRAIG STEVENS · ALIX TALTON · WILLIAM HOPPER
with FLORENZ AMES · DONALD RANDOLPH DIRECTED BY NATHAN JURAN
SCREENPLAY BY MARTIN BERKELEY · PRODUCED BY WILLIAM ALLAND
A UNIVERSAL-INTERNATIONAL PICTURE

In yet another big-bug extravaganza from the 1950s, a giant praying mantis menaces New York City in *The Deadly Mantis*.

THE DEADLY MANTIS

1957 (NR) 79m / **D:** Nathan Juran / **W:** Martin Berkeley / **C:** Craig Stevens, William Hopper, Alix Talton, Pat Conway, Donald Randolph

After a training film-like opening explains the U.S. military's Distant Early Warning Line, that hardware tracks a giant prehistoric praying mantis released from an iceberg via volcanic eruption (hey, it could happen). Roaring like a bear, the insect bugs Washington, D.C., and New York City until humans fumigate. Typically silly 1950s sci-fi with *awful* comedy relief. AKA: *The Incredible Praying Mantis*.

DEADLY WEAPON

1988 (PG-13) 89m / **D:** Michael Miner / **W:** Michael Miner / **C:** Rodney Eastman, Gary Frank, Michael Horse, Ed Nelson, Kim Walker

Producer Charles Band raided his own *Laserblast* from 10 years earlier for this piece of nerdish wish fulfillment, when 15-year-old geek Rodney Eastman finds a secret anti-matter weapon conveniently fallen off a military transport. He uses the way-cool death ray to threaten bullies, parents, a preacher, and other nasty authority figures. You'll hardly like the kid any more than the grownups, even with the ultimately tragic script taking his side.

DEAD WEEKEND

1995 (R) 82m / **D:** Amos Poe / **W:** Joel Rose / **C:** Stephen Baldwin, David Rasche, Damian Jones, Alexis Arquette, Bai Ling

Alien is detected in town, so the government's psycho paramilitary riot squad clears out citizens and begins enthusiastically shooting whoever's left. Lucky soldier Stephen Baldwin has close encounters of the closest kind with the visitor, a hot space babe who needs sex to survive and regularly transforms into an entirely different, seductive woman. With no f/x worth mentioning, this airhead mixture of sleaze and would-be meaningful social commentary was a cable-only affair. Odd job from groundbreaking No Wave director Amos Poe, better known for his blank neo-punk films like *The Foreigner*.

DEATH RACE

2008 (R) 105m / **D:** Paul W.S. Anderson / **W:** Paul W.S. Anderson / **C:** Jason Statham, Joan Allen, Ian McShane, Tyrese Gibson, Natalie Martinez, Jason Clarke

Long, tiresome redo of the old Paul Bartel classic of some three decades prior, bereft (like most other big-budget cult-film overhauls) of the original's appealing low-budget anarchy. This tIme, the televised Death Race is a more controlled thing—not so much on the running down of pedestrians—in which convicts fight to the death in their supercharged *Mad Max* cars for the enjoyment of fickle, bloodthirsty audiences. Jason Statham is the heroic lead, while Joan Allen takes time off from making things of quality to play the ice-queen warden who organizes the races for maximum ratings-enhancing carnage. Ian McShane, in an apparent gravel-voiced competition with Statham to grind some entertainment out of the pallid screenplay, plays a downmarket Q, outfitting Statham's car with a cartoonish array of outlandish weaponry (smoke generators, gatling guns, flamethrowers, etc.). The vaguely dystopic setting is entirely ignored, used only as an excuse to stage vehicular gladiator contests. Almost impressive in its dullness. Supposedly once intended as a Tom Cruise vehicle.

DEATH RACE 2000

1975 (R) 80m / **D:** Paul Bartel / **W:** Charles B. Griffith, Robert Thom / **C:** David Carradine, Simone Griffeth, Sylvester Stallone, Mary Woronov, Roberta Collins

In the 21st century, a leather-suited David Carradine is the defending champion of the natIonally televised Transcontinental Death Race, in which participants score points for running over pedestrians. His challengers include

David Carradine starred in both *Death Race 2000* and its sequel, *Death Sport*.

Sylvester Stallone (just one year before *Rocky*) as Machine Gun Joe Viterbo, Mary Woronov as Calamity Jane, and Roberta Collins as Mathilda the Hun. Like some other 1970s sci-fi (*Rollerball*), it critiqued society's obsession with violent entertainment, only to revel in same. Influential cult item that made the reputation of director Paul Bartel. Based on the 1956 story by Ib Melchior. Remade in 2008.

DEATH SPORT

1978 (R) 83m / **D:** Henry Suso, Allan Arkush / **W:** Donald Stewart, Henry Suso / **C:** David Carradine, Claudia Jennings, Richard Lynch, William Smithers, Will Walker, David McLean, Jesse Vint

Roger Corman's shameless follow-up to *Death Race 2000* could have used more of that film's freewheeling spirit and black humor. David Carradine and former Playboy Playmate of the Year and legendary B-movie queen Claudia Jennings star as "Ranger Guides" being pursued across the post-nuclear wilderness by motorcycle-riding "Statesmen" who want them for gladiatorial contests. Oh, there are cannibal mutants as well. Plus: "destructocycles"! Jennings was killed in a car crash shortly after release. Much more interesting than the film are the accusations of rampant violence and drug use on the set that flew between Carradine and director Nicholas Niciphor (who for this film used the pseudonym Henry Suso).

DEATH WATCH

1980 (PG) 128m / **D:** Bertrand Tavernier / **W:** Bertrand Tavernier, David Rayfiel / **C:** Romy Schneider, Harvey Keitel, Harry Dean Stanton, Max von Sydow

Provocative drama that anticipated the tabloid talk shows of the future. In a future where science has banished disease and people die of old age, a terminal illness is big news. Romy Schneider stars as the doomed Katharine, courted by TV producer Harry Dean Stanton. He wants to give the morbid public what it wants—death—so he signs her to a contract allowing him to film her last days. When she flees, he hires Harvey Keitel to pursue her and gain her confidence. Keitel has had a miniature camera implanted in his brain which beams back to the station all that he sees. Brooding, thoughtful, and deliberately paced sci-fi from a filmmaker very new to the genre.

DEEP IMPACT

1998 (PG-13) 120m / D: Mimi Leder / **W:** Michael Tolkin, Bruce Joel Rubin / **C:** Robert Duvall, Téa Leoni, Morgan Freeman, Elijah Wood, Vanessa Redgrave

The most notable thing about this boldfaced issue/disaster/tearjerker event picture is that it was the less embarrassing of 1998's two "a comet is coming!" films. *Armageddon* turned the end of human life as we know it into a flag-waving belch of a Budweiser ad. But Mimi Leder's more hand-wringing take uses a tortured screenplay (half Big Ideas and half clumsy manipulation) to churn up histrionics of the kind familiar from Leder's work on *ER*. Head emoter is Téa Leoni, playing a reporter dealing with father issues who stumbles upon a government conspiracy. The powers that be don't want anybody to know that an E.L.E. (Extinction Level Event) is nearly due in the form of a massive comet, which *might* be stopped by a U.S.-Russian spacecraft going up there to nuke it. Tears are shed as everybody runs for cover. Morgan Freeman does yeoman's work as the grave-faced president trying to keep everyone from panicking before they die.

DEEPSTAR SIX

1989 (R) 97m / D: Sean S. Cunningham / **W:** Geof Miller, Lewis Abernathy / **C:** Taurean Blacque, Nancy Everhard, Greg Evigan, Miguel Ferrer, Matt McCoy, Nia Peeples, Cindy Pickett, Marius Weyers

While James Cameron's epic *The Abyss* was still in production, various cheapo filmmakers raced to have their own undersea sci-fi creature features in cinemas first. In this triumph of speed over quality, scientists in a submarine lab suffer a bad case of the crabs. Make that one crab: a giant, hungry crustacean out to avenge countless boiled lobster tails. Silly stuff shows its low budget when the monster surfaces, though there is a standout human performance by Miguel Ferrer.

DEF-CON 4

1985 (R) 85m / D: Digby Cook, Paul Donovan / **W:** Paul Donovan / **C:** Maury Chaykin, Kate Lynch, Tim Choate, Lenore Zann, Kevin King, John Walsch

Three astronauts watch helplessly as a nuclear holocaust devastates Earth below, then return to the planet's surface to try to start civilization again. In the way are the usual *Road Warrior* slimeballs (led by a young military brat), who don't want to give up their dominance. Canadian postnuke hijinks with streak of sadism unusually strong even for this genre.

THE SCI-FI MOVIE GUIDE: The Universe of Film from "Alien" to "Zardoz"

DÉJÀ VU

2006 (PG-13) 126m / **D:** Tony Scott / **W:** Bill Marsilii, Terry Rossio / **C:** Denzel Washington, Paula Patton, Jim Caviezel, Val Kilmer, Adam Goldberg

Standard-issue TV-style Jerry Bruckheimer procedural plays like *CSI Time Travel: New Orleans* meets *La Jetée*. After a terrorist bombing kills hundreds on a ferry, ATF agent Denzel Washington is assigned to investigate. Aiding his job is a secret government system that allows him to look into the past like it was a high-definition TV broadcast; only they can just see things from four days past. After far too much time spent watching the last days of one of the bombing's more attractive victims (Paula Patton), Washington tries to figure out a way he can do more than just watch the past unfold. There's a lot of talk about fate and destiny, and so plot holes in the essential illogic of the premise almost fade into insignificance. Would have been quite something if Christopher Nolan could have dreamed it up first.

DELICATESSEN

1992 (R) 95m / **D:** Jean-Marie Jeunet, Marc Caro / **W:** Gilles Adrien / **C:** Marie-Laure Dougnac, Dominique Pinon, Karin Viard, Jean-Claude Dreyfus, Ticky Holgado, Anne-Marie Pisani, Edith Ker, Patrick Paroux, Jean-Luc Caron

Set in post-apocalyptic 21st-century Paris, this hilarious debut from directors Jean-Marie Jeunot and Marc Caro focuses on the lives of the oddball tenants over a butcher shop. Although there is a famine on, the butcher shop is always stocked with fresh meat, and the building does seem to go through quite a few tenants.... Part comedy, part horror, part romance, this film is also a darkly joyful celebration of dialogue-free filmmaking that harkens back to the early French film pioneers. Watch for the scene involving a symphony of creaking bed springs, a squeaky bicycle pump, a cello, and clicking knitting needles. Shot almost entirely in browns and whites, you'll be hard pressed to find another film with such unique visuals. Terry Gilliam, a master of movie images himself, presented it worldwide. In French with English subtitles.

DEMOLITION MAN

1993 (R) 115m / **D:** Marco Brambilla / **W:** Daniel Waters, Robert Reneau, Peter M. Lenkov / **C:** Sylvester Stallone, Wesley Snipes, Sandra Bullock, Nigel Hawthorne, Benjamin Bratt, Bob Gunton, Glenn Shadix, Denis Leary

Sci-fi shoot-'em-up meets all the demands of the genre—lots of fights and macho posturing, gunfire and/or shattering glass at least every seven minutes, an explosion or two in between, car chases, and cartoon characterizations. As a cop and a criminal transported to a neutered near-future America where all kinds of behavior has been outlawed, a rock-faced Stallone plays straight man to a manic, dyed-blond Snipes. A pre-*Speed* Bullock is Stallone's uptight comic relief. To put it mildly, the film's team of writers plundered from everyone to throw this one together—most egregiously Vonnegut, Dick, and Wells—but still manage some occasionally witty jabs. Something of a 1990s cultural junk-yard (the jarring cameo by then-just-breaking-out comic Denis Leary, Snipes's Dennis Rod-man outfit, the knockoff John Woo fight choreography), but exuberant in its trashiness.

DEMON CITY SHINJUKU

1988 (PG-13) 82m / **D:** Yoshiaki Kawajiri / **W:** Kaori Okamura

Although best known for his Rocky and Rambo films, Sylvester Stalone has also starred in sci-fi shoot-'em-ups ranging from *Demolition Man* to *Judge Dredd*.

In the near future the evil Levlh Rah has cre-ated a "Demon City" surrounded by a moat in the heart of Tokyo, where he commands his army of thugs and monsters. Sayama Rama and the streetwise Kyoya venture into Shinjuku in search of Sayama's kidnapped father. They encounter the cynical Mephisto, an aging mys-tic whose strange healing powers may be able to help them. They'd better hurry—Levih Rah is scheduled to destroy the en-tire planet in just three days. An impressive example of Japanese animation. In Japanese with English subtitles. AKA: *Hell City, Shinjuku*; *Monster City*.

DEMON SEED

1977 (R) 97m / **D:** Donald Cammell / **W:** Robert Jaffe, Roger O. Hirson / **C:** Julie Christie, Fritz Weaver, Gerrit Graham, Berry Kroeger, Ron Hays, Lisa Lu

Early and rather infamously perverse entry in the computer-gone-nuts sub-genre, based on a Dean R. Koontz novel. The world's most sophisticated computer, Proteus IV, puts the moves on his creator's estranged wife (Julie Christie) when it takes over the running of her house. Directed by Donald Cammell, better remembered for the late-1960s Mick Jagger Satanism freakout *Performance*.

DESTINATION MOON

1950 (NR) 91m / **D:** Irving Pichel / **W:** Robert Heinlein, Rip Van Ronkel, James O'Hanlon / **C:** Warner Anderson, Tom Powers, Dick Wesson, Erin O'Brien Moore, John Archer, Ted Warde

American scientists and engineers finance their own moon rocket, despite government interference. No-nonsense story of man's first lunar voyage was so influential that it not only set the format for almost every space travel film for the next 15 years (for example, one crew member *must* be from Brooklyn), but it also probably gave NASA a few ideas. Contains Chesley Bonestell's famous astronomical artwork and a cartoon in which Woody Woodpecker helps explain how the mission will work to potential investors (and the audience). Co-scripted by libertarian sci-fi novelist Robert Heinlein. Two Oscar nominations; won for f/x.

DESTROY ALL MONSTERS

1968 (G) 88m / **D:** Ishiro Honda / **W:** Kaoru Mabuchi, Ishiro Honda, Akira Kubo, Jun Tazaki, Yoshio Tsuchiya, Kyoko Ai, Yukiko Kobayashi, Kenji Sahara, Andrew Hughes, Emi Ito, Yumi Ito

The ultimate Japanese monster bash! Aliens from the planet Kilaak take control of Godzilla and his monstrous colleagues, who've been incarcerated on a remote island so that they can repent for all the city-smashing they did. Various monsters are then dispatched to destroy different Earth cities (Godzilla is sent to New York, apparently to give Tokyo a rest). Adding insult to injury, the Kilaakians send three-headed Ghidrah in to take care of the loose ends. Can the planet possibly survive this madness? In addition to Godzilla, this classic piece of Toho destruction stars the son of Godzilla, Mothra, Rodan, Angilas, Varan, Baragon, Spigas, and others. If you're wondering why relative unknown Gorosaurus (from *King Kong Escapes*) is featured so prominently, the reason has to do with the condition of the monster suits, some of which were in bad shape and not vital enough to the plot to be rebuilt. Old Angilas (from *Godzilla Raids Again*) picked up some admirers with this film, as a result of his courage shown in the scrap with Ghidrah. This was director Ishiro Honda's second-to-last Godzilla pic, and the last really good one for nearly two decades. Dubbing is better than usual. Inspired a video game and an influential underground Detroit band. AKA: *Operation Monsterland*.

DESTROY ALL PLANETS

1968 (NR) 75m / **D:** Noriaki Yuasa / **W:** Fumi Takahashi / **C:** Peter Williams, Kojiro Hongo, Toru Takatsuka, Carl Crane, Michiko Yaegaki

Aliens whose spaceships turn into giant flying squids are attacking Earth. Once again Gamera, the flying, fire-breathing space-turtle, must bust his shell to save the day. He's assisted in his task by two rather annoying little boys with a miniature submarine. This lightweight effort was the fourth in the Gamera series and was padded out with a turtle soup of footage from the big guy's previous adventures. Anyone who thinks all heroic turtles are teenage ninjas should find this film very enlightening. AKA: *Gamela vs. Baius*.

DEVIL GIRL FROM MARS

1954 (NR) 76m / **D:** David MacDonald / **W:** John C. Mather, James Eastwood / **C:** Hugh McDermott, Hazel Court, Patricia Laffan, Peter Reynolds, Adrienne Corri, Joseph Tomelty, Sophie Stewart, John Laurie, Anthony Richmond

Sexy female from Mars, clad in a black vinyl skirt, arrives at a small Scottish inn with her very large, clumsy robot to announce that a Martian feminist revolution has occurred. But Mars needs men! The distaff aliens are in search of healthy Earth males for breeding purposes. Believe it or not, the red-blooded Earth males don't want to go and therein lies the rub. An enjoyably ridiculous space farce. Based on a stage play, the characters seem to be as equally concerned with their soap opera problems as they are with the Martian invasion and always take time for a cup of tea before planning their defenses. As one should.

DIE, MONSTER, DIE!

1965 (NR) 80m / **D:** Daniel Haller / **W:** Jerry Sohl / **C:** Boris Karloff, Nick Adams, Suzan Farmer, Patrick Magee

A young man (Nick Adams) visits his fiancée's family home, even though everyone in the neighboring village advises him against it. He finds that his prospective father-in-law is a reclusive, wheelchair-bound scientist (Boris Karloff) who's been fooling around with a radioactive meteorite in his laboratory. As a result, he's got a greenhouse full of mutant animals and his disfigured wife runs around the estate in a veil scaring people. Eventually, the meteorite gives Karloff back his ability to walk, but in the process it changes him into a glowing, metallic monster. Trade-offs. This adaptation of H. P. Lovecraft's classic "The Color Out of Space" is pretty pale compared to the horrific source material, but Karloff (in one of his last roles and beginning to look a bit peaked) still delivers a great performance, investing every line with quiet menace. AKA: *Monster of Terror*.

The king of horror flicks, Boris Karloff starred in *Die, Monster, Die!*, the heartwarming tale of a scientist who turns everyone around him, including himself, into radioactive monsters.

DISTRICT 9

2009 (R) 112m / **D:** Neil Blomkamp / **W:** Neil Blomkamp, Terri Tatchell / **C:** Sharlto Copley, David James, Vanessa Haywood, Mandla Gaduka, Kenneth Nkosi

An obvious allegory for the division of races in South Africa, *District 9* has hapless, marooned aliens being shoved into a filthy shantytown controlled by bureaucratic whites.

The era of cheap but impressive digital effects truly arrived with this skill-ful apartheid allegory disguised as a smash-'em-up, alien-chase movie. In a story that borrows liberally from both *Tetsuo* and *Alien Nation*, a city-sized spacecraft has been sitting above Johannesburg for years, its starving pas-sengers a miserable and beaten-down race bred for slave labor by other, as-yet unseen aliens. Since then, the seven-foot-tall crustacean-looking "prawns" have been trying to make do in Jo'burg's shantytowns, dealing with discrimination and deprivation like any other unwanted human ethnic group. Blomkamp's handheld aesthetic aims for newsreel authenticity, with mixed results. The plot is nothing terribly interesting, being mostly a series of shootouts as mendacious private security types fight to get a hold of an alien weapon that has biologically woven itself into the hand of a feckless South African bureaucrat (Sharlto Copley). He's been put in charge of clearing out the prawn settlement, using force if necessary; the comparisons between the rounding-up of aliens and battles of the apartheid era aren't difficult to divine and are arguably unnecessary. Tolkien film impresario and one-time cult oddity Peter Jackson produced. Four Oscar nominations, including (sur-prisingly) best picture and best adapted screenplay.

DISTRICT 13

2004 (R) 84m / D: Pierre Morel / **W:** Luc Besson, Bibi Naceri / **C:** Cyril Raffaelli, David Belle, Tony D'Amario, Bibi Naceri

Another programmatic pileup of punches, kicks, and explosions from Luc Besson's genre factory. In this one, John Carpenter's *Escape from New York* is reused in a near-future Paris, where the crime-ridden outer suburbs have been completely walled off, letting the gangs run things inside as they see fit. One of those incorruptible super-cops this sort of thing is made for infiltrates the feared District 13 to do battle with a vile drug lord *and* keep a nuclear warhead from annihilating the City of Light. Marketed to play off interest in the martial art of parkour, online videos of which were all the rage at the time. The film's fighters spend a lot of their time suspended in mid-air, leaping from great heights, running over speeding cars, and delivering punishing blows to their foes. Besson would later assign director Pierre Morel to more straightforward Parisian action exploitationers like *Taken* and *From Paris with Love*. AKA: *District B13*; *Banlieue 13*. A sequel, *District 13: Ultimatum*, followed in 2009.

DIVERGENT

2014 (PG-13) 139m / D: Neil Burger / **W:** Evan Daugherty, Vanessa Taylor / **C:** Shailene Woodley, Theo James, Kate Winslet, Miles Teller, Ashley Judd, Jai Courtney, Ray Stevenson, Joe Kravitz, Tony Goldwyn, Maggie Q, Mekhi Phifer

The school-clique dynamic of *Harry Potter* is crassly married with the post-apocalyptic teen melodrama of the *Hunger Games* in this sleepy adaptation of the first novel in Veronica Roth's young-adult series. In a half-ruined Chicago walled off from the wastelands (some unexplained war), society is divided into five factions that teenagers are allowed to sort themselves into by nature. The "faction before blood" ethos is very high school 101 meets Machiavelli, with Erudites as the brains, Candor as the truthtellers, and so on. None of it makes sense as a method of social control, but at least one can tell the factions apart by their distinctly silly costumes. Tris (an affectless Shailene Woodley) is born into selfless Abnegation (grey shifts, no jewelry) but chooses militaristic Dauntless (aggro tattoos, nightclub-athletic gear), even though she isn't sure *what* faction she is (a sign she could be a suspiciously non-conformist "Divergent"). Plus, there's a handsome drill instructor, who is both cruel and comforting to her; oh my! Egregiously saggy in structure and sloppily directed, the film trundles along at a dire pace that no amount of shootouts or bad teen-pop can balance out. Lazy, with little interest in this futuristic world beyond the emo-politicking. The energy-generating wind turbines barnacled on the skyscrapers make for a neat backdrop at least, as do the war games Tris plays on a ruined Navy Pier sticking into a dried-up Lake Michigan.

DOC SAVAGE: THE MAN OF BRONZE

1975 (G) 100m / D: Michael Anderson, Sr. / **W:** George Pal, Joe Morhaim / **C:** Ron Ely, Pamela Hensley, Paul Gleason, William Lucking, Paul Wexler

D r. Clark Savage Jr., and "The Amazing Five" fight a murderous villain who plans to take over the world. Based on the long series of pulp novels by Kenneth Robeson, the plotline loosely follows the initial entry *The Man of Bronze*, while incorporating several ideas from other stories. The curiously camp approach to the material is sure to disappoint Robeson fans of the pulp series. Fans of producer/co-writer George Pal may expect something more spectacular from the man behind the first *The War of the Worlds* and *The Time Machine*. Ron Ely, despite his years as Tarzan, serves as only a passable Doc. Many aspects of the series were later appropriated by the creators of *Superman*, *Batman*, and even *The Adventures of Buckaroo Banzai*.

DOCTOR SATAN'S ROBOT

1940 (NR) 100m / **D:** William Witney, John English / **W:** Franklyn Adreon, Ronald Davidson, Norman S. Hall, Joseph F. Poland, Sol Shor / **C:** Eduardo Ciannelli, Robert Wilcox, William Newell, Ella Neal

A rt is long and life is short, and if you haven't time to watch the 15-episode Republic serial *Mysterious Doctor Satan* in full-length video reissue, this feature condensation will do. Deranged Dr. Satan chews up the scenery as he cavorts with his metallic robot, and the superhero known as Copperhead (Robert Wilcox) makes his most sensational escape from an entrapped flaming coffin. Yes, that bit of business shows up again in the James Bond film *Diamonds Are Forever*, showing that good ideas for killing heroes are eternal.

DOCTOR WHO AND THE DALEKS

1965 (NR) 78m / **D:** Gordon Flemyng / **W:** Milton Subotsky / **C:** Peter Cushing, Roy Castle, Jennie Linden, Michael Coles, Roberta Tovey, Geoffrey Toone

A silly feature adapted from the perennial BBC series, with Peter Cushing playing the Doctor as an absent-minded old (human) inventor. The Doctor, his two granddaughters, and the older girl's boyfriend accidentally transport themselves to a barren planet inhabited by the Daleks, mutant creatures in protective robotic suits. The travelers must help the friendly, pacifistic Thals throw off the threat of Dalek tyranny. Obviously aimed at children, this is a good-natured but simple-minded film that will leave fans of the TV series disappointed or bewildered. Followed by the superior *Daleks—Invasion Earth 2150* A.D.

DOCTOR X

1932 (NR) 77m / **D:** Michael Curtiz / **W:** Robert Tasker, Earl Baldwin / **C:** Lionel Atwill, Fay Wray, Lee Tracy, Preston Foster

S omething weird is going on at Dr. Xavier's research labs—and murder is the least of it. A classic sci-fi horror oldie from journeyman director

Michael Curtiz (*Things to Come*), famous for its very early use of two-color Technicolor, as well as the spectacular sets designed by Anton Grot. Lee Tracy was an engaging personality in films of the time, but he grates on the nerves a bit here. Made a name for Lionel Atwill in horror films, not to mention some pre-Kong screams from Fay Wray. The who-done-it is easy to guess—but the how-done-it is a real mind blower. Referenced in the opening song from *The Rocky Horror Picture Show* ("Dr. X will build a creature").

DONNIE DARKO

2001 (R) 113m / **D:** Richard Kelly / **W:** Richard Kelly / **C:** Jake Gyllenhaal, Holmes Osborne, Maggie Gyllenhaal, Daveigh Chase, Mary McDonnell, James Duval, Arthur Taxier, Patrick Swayze, Jena Malone

A 1980s-set fever dream about a disturbed teen (Jake Gyllenhaal) who keeps seeing a giant talking rabbit that entices him to commit crimes. When an engine falls off a passing jet and destroys Donnie's bedroom, things start getting odd. Time travel gets its foot in, along with a New Wave soundtrack that feels more ghostly than nostalgic. Richard Kelly's intoxicatingly odd writing/directing debut marked him as something of a Jodorowsky for the

Jake Gyllenhaal (far left) is tormented by a giant rabbit that wants him to commit crimes in the surreal time-travel cult classic *Donnie Darko*.

new millennium. A critical darling that hit theaters just after 9/11, it features career-creating turns from both Gyllenhaals (Jake and Maggie, playing siblings), a queasy performance from Patrick Swayze as a motivational speaker, and James Duval (who's done this kind of thing before in Gregg Araki's shotgun-surreal teen sci-fi movies) underneath the rabbit suit. The 2004 director's cut includes about 20 minutes of extra footage for the legion of the dedicated. In the grand tradition of Hollywood never leaving well enough alone (see 2002's *American Psycho 2*, with Mila Kunis and, yes, William Shatner), an offshoot called *S. Darko* that Kelly had nothing to do with was released in 2009 to deafening disdain.

DONOVAN'S BRAIN

1953 (NR) 85m / **D:** Felix Feist / **W:** Hugh Brooke, Felix Feist / **C:** Lew Ayres, Gene Evans, Nancy Davis, Steve Brodie

Curt Siodmak's novel is the basis for this McCarthy-era brain-control thriller. Jerk millionaire W. H. Donovan is killed in a plane crash. So far, so good. Genius-type Patrick Cory (Lew Ayres) takes Donovan's brain and keeps it alive in his lab. Cory becomes obsessed with the brain ... or is it possessed? Gradually he is changed by the more and more powerful brain. No more Mister Nice Guy; in fact, he is doing the Jekyll/Hyde flip-flop, turning into the not-so-"Mellow Yellow" Donovan. Some of the subtleties of the book are gone, but overall a fine adaptation featuring future first lady Nancy Davis (Reagan).

DOOM

2005 (R) 100m / **D:** Andrzej Bartkowiak / **W:** Dave Callaham, Wesley Strick / **C:** Dwayne Johnson, Karl Urban, Rosamund Pike, Deobia Oparei, Ben Daniels, Yao Chin

Here's the idea behind this Marines-in-space yarn: A mysterious portal left behind by aliens has been discovered in the Nevada desert, leading to the Martian surface. Inquisitive humans follow said tunnel to the red planet. They set up one of those isolated research stations that never does well in films like this and discover some curiously humanoid remains. A distress signal goes out and in comes a squad of Marines led by pro wrestling's The Rock (Dwayne Johnson) to shoot every mutant monster they see. Based on a spectacularly popular first-person shooter video game, wouldn't you know. Poor reception even by fans of the game perhaps explains why so few other games of its like have been made into films.

DOOMSDAY

2008 (R) 105m / **D:** Neil Marshall / **W:** Neil Marshall / **C:** Rhona Mitra, Bob Hoskins, Alexander Siddig, Malcolm McDowell, David O'Hara

After a pandemic decimates the United Kingdom, the infected are walled off in Scotland behind a modern-day Hadrian's Wall and left to fend for themselves. In 2033, the sickness starts to spread again and authorities in London decide to send a team into the quarantine zone to find any survivors and hopefully a cure. Unfortunately for the team, what lies on the other side is a teeming cauldron of cannibalistic barbarians who have spent their time in isolation nurturing grudges against the larger society and perfecting their *Mad Max*-ian bondage couture (metal face masks, mohawks). Cult horror director Neil Marshall (*The Descent*) uses the scenario as an excuse to send one of his signature lean-muscled warrior heroines (Rhona Mitra) through the gates of hell and have fun with the occasional music cue (Siouxsie & the Banshees, Fine Young Cannibals).

DR. CYCLOPS

1940 (NR) 76m / D: Ernest B. Schoedsack / **W:** Tom Kilpatrick / **C:** Albert Dekker, Janice Logan, Victor Kilian, Thomas Coley, Charles Halton, Frank Yaconelli

Famous early Technicolor fantasia about a mad scientist miniaturizing a group of explorers who happen upon his jungle lab. Landmark f/x still hold up, while the slow-moving story takes on fairy-tale aspects. Albert Dekker makes for a fine mad scientist, his bald pate and thick glasses immediately recalling Erich von Stroheim. Ripped off in the 1970s by producers of the *Dr. Shrinker* television series. Oscar nomination for f/x.

DREAMCATCHER

2003 (R) 134m / D: Lawrence Kasdan / **W:** William Goldman, Lawrence Kasdan / **C:** Thomas Jane, Morgan Freeman, Damian Lewis, Jason Lee, Tom Sizemore, Timothy Olyphant, Donnie Wahlberg

Gastrointestinal sci-fi misfire based on a Stephen King novel that throws several bad ideas into a big-budget blender and watches it explode everywhere. Four lifelong buddies (Thomas Jane, Damian Lewis, Jason Lee, Timothy Olyphant) hole up in a mountain cabin for drinking, hunting, and bonding. Unfortunately, nearby there's a crashed spacecraft filled with shapeshifting aliens who like to infect human hosts before erupting out of their nether regions. This makes first contact something of a messy affair. Complicating matters is the trigger-happy black-ops unit led by a deranged Morgan Freeman doing a great Patton-versus-aliens routine; secretly stamping out alien incursions for a quarter-century does wear on a man. There's also a developmentally challenged child with magical powers, highly unnecessary flashbacks, and the irksome sight of a pos-

> "Gastrointestinal sci-fi misfire based on a Stephen King novel that throws several bad ideas into a big-budget blender and watches it explode everywhere."
>
> *Dreamcatcher*

sessed Lewis talking to himself in two different voices (the chipper British one is the alien). Oh, and the four buddies are telepathic. The wintry cinematography (courtesy of *The English Patient*'s John Seale) is incongruously gorgeous and Lawrence Kasdan, as usual, stocks the ensemble with non-showy but superb performers. If only it had mattered.

DREAMSCAPE

1984 (PG-13) 99m / D: Joseph Ruben / **W:** David Loughery, Chuck Russell, Joseph Ruben / **C:** Dennis Quaid, Max von Sydow, Christopher Plummer, Eddie Albert, Kate Capshaw, David Patrick Kelly, George Wendt, Jana Taylor

A doctor teaches a young psychic (Dennis Quaid) how to enter into other people's dreams in order to end their nightmares—but what if a rival psychic is causing those nightmares? The president of the United States (Eddie Albert) is the victim, suffering visions of nuclear holocaust designed to push him over the edge, and the hero enters the sleeping chief executive's dreams to try and undo the damage. Wild and remarkable premise peaks with a clash of mental titans within a White House bedroom silent except for the presidential snoring. Serviceable f/x include a stop-motion reptile man.

DREDD

2012 (R) 95m / D: Pete Travis / **W:** Alex Garland / **C:** Karl Urban, Olivia Thirlby, Lena Headey, Wood Harris, Langley Kirkwood, Junior Singo

A do-over adaptation that aimed to be more faithful to the cult British comic about all-powerful judge/jury/executioner "Judges" who fight to keep the peace in the overcrowded urban hell that is the future's Mega City One. Karl Urban's stubbled chin and grumble do all the acting required for the monosyllabic Judge Dredd, stuck with rookie partner and mutant psychic (a spunky Olivia Thirlby) as they fight to get a prisoner out of a 200-story highrise tower filled with bloodthirsty, heavily armed gang members. Novelist Alex Garland's screenplay is more dramatic scaffolding than anything else. Film dispenses with much of the backstory of the 1995 version but doesn't add much in its place except for more gleeful blood splattering as extras go down by the dozen. *Game of Thrones*' Lena Headey stands out as the scar-faced, feral gang leader Ma-Ma. Overall, slightly more true to the comic's loony, sociopathic humor, but that may not be a compliment.

DR. GOLDFOOT AND THE BIKINI MACHINE

1965 (NR) 88m / D: Norman Taurog / **W:** Robert Kaufman, Elwood Ullman / **C:** Vincent Price, Frankie Avalon, Dwayne Hickman, Annette Funicello, Susan Hart, Kay Elkhardt, Fred Clark, Deanna Lund, Deborah Walley, Harvey Lembeck

Vincent Price spoofs his image for the umpteenth time as a San Francisco mad scientist who uses gorgeous female robots to seduce the wealthy and powerful in a scheme to take over the world. Opposing him is Frankie Avalon as Secret Agent 00 ½; (later demoted to 00 ¼;). Harmlessly dumb drive-in fun from Roger Corman, with a great title sequence (theme song by the Supremes). Great cameos by Annette Funicello and fellow beach-movie cohort Harvey Lembeck. Italian-made sequel, *Dr. Goldfoot and the Girl Bombs*, is hard to find, possibly for good reason.

DR. STRANGELOVE; OR, HOW I LEARNED TO STOP WORRYING AND LOVE THE BOMB

1964 (PG) 95m / **D:** Stanley Kubrick / **W:** Terry Southern, Peter George, Stanley Kubrick / **C:** Peter Sellers, George C. Scott, Sterling Hayden, Keenan Wynn, Slim Pickens, James Earl Jones, Peter Bull

It's the end of the world as we know it in Stanley Kubrick's classic black comedy that remains undimmed by the collapse of the "evil empire." Sterling

Slim Pickens rides a nuclear bomb dropped by his B-52 in the apocalyptic Stanley Kubrick comedy *Dr. Strangelove*.

Hayden stars as cigar-chomping General Jack Ripper, who is so convinced of a Communist conspiracy to sap "our precious bodily fluids" via water fluoridation that he orders American bombers to attack Russia. George C. Scott is in his element as military hawk General Buck Turgidson, but it's Peter Sellers's show all the way. In a bravura triple role, he portrays the befuddled American president Merkin Muffley (a performance based on Adlai Stevenson), British officer Mandrake, and the wheelchair-bound former Nazi Dr. Strangelove. Aboard the plane racing obliviously toward its target are James Earl Jones and Slim Pickens as gung-ho pilot Major Kong. Keenan Wynn is Colonel "Bat" Guano, who has a memorable Coke machine encounter with "prevert" Sellers. Kubrick mixes the ripe and colorful satire of Terry Southern's screwball script with a highly realistic view of how such a scenario would happen; the combat scenes are indistinguishable from actual war footage. Not to be missed. Pickens riding down the bomb to oblivion is one of moviedom's most indelible images. Also notable as the last film in which Kubrick told a recognizable joke. Legend tells of an alternate ending Kubrick shot where the War Room erupts into a pie fight.

DUNE

1984 (PG-13) 137m / D: David Lynch **/ W:** David Lynch **/ C:** Kyle MacLachlan, Francesca Annis, José Ferrer, Max von Sydow, Jürgen Prochnow, Linda Hunt, Freddie Jones, Dean Stockwell, Virginia Madsen, Brad Dourif, Kenneth McMillan, Silvana Mangano, Jack Nance, Siân Phillips, Paul Smith, Richard Jordan, Everett McGill, Sean Young, Patrick Stewart, Sting

David Lynch adaptation of the first novel in Frank Herbert's epic sci-fi series features a strong cast, high-end f/x, and sweeping desert vistas. It is also saddled with a script that's highly muddled, even for fans of the novel. (The years it spent in development probably didn't help for story clarity.) Set in the year 10191, the story follows the political and religious intrigue between a group of noble houses fighting for control of the mind-enhancing drug spice, found only on the desert planet Arrakis (which also happens to be inhabited by giant worms). Paul (Lynch's stand-by guy Kyle MacLachlan), heir to House Atreides, leads the lowly but fierce desert-dwelling Freemen in revolt against the decadent Harkonnens, who have seized control of Arrakis and attempted to destroy House Atreides. Lynch's vision for Herbert's labyrinthine culture and mythos is impressively detailed amidst the littering of staple Lynch grotesquerie. Though far from perfect, the film strives to deliver intelligent sci-fi on an epic scale. An oiled-up, loinclothed, and knife-wielding Sting appears briefly. An extended version was disowned by Lynch, with directing credit going to the eponymous Alan Smithee. Stick with the original—just be sure to pay close attention (and reading the book sure couldn't hurt). Remade in 2000 as a TV miniseries; a length perhaps more appropriate for a book of this scope. Another miniseries, *Children of Dune*, followed in 2003.

DUST DEVIL

1992 (R) 87m / **D:** Richard Stanley / **W:** Richard Stanley / **C:** Robert John Burke, Chelsea Field, Zakes Mokae, Rufus Swart, John Matshikiza, William Hootkins, Marianne Sagebrecht

Three travelers find themselves in Africa's vast Namibia desert: a policeman (Zakes Mokae), a woman on the run (Chelsea Field), and her abusive husband. They all have the misfortune of meeting up with an evil spirit trapped in human form. This supernatural being, known as the "Dust Devil" (Robert Burke), must kill, stealing as many souls as he can, in order to re-enter the spiritual realm. Well-acted and highly stylized, this one puts some good quirky twists on the serial killer theme. Writer/director Richard Stanley (*Hardware*) saw the film mangled by a drastic studio editing job. There is a Stanley-approved director's cut that runs about twenty minutes longer.

EARTH GIRLS ARE EASY

1989 (PG) 100m / D: Julien Temple / **W:** Julie Brown, Charlie Coffey, Terrence McNally / **C:** Geena Davis, Jeff Goldblum, Charles Rocket, Julie Brown, Jim Carrey, Damon Wayans, Michael McKean, Angelyne, Larry Linville, Rick Overton

Sometimes hilarious sci-fi/musical with a New Wave twist, featuring bouncy shtick, Julie Brown's music, and a gleeful dismantling of modern culture. Valley girl Valerie (Geena Davis) is having a bad week: first she catches her fiancé with another woman, then she breaks a nail, then furry aliens land in her swimming pool. What more could go wrong? When the aliens are temporarily stranded, she decides to make amends by giving them a head-to-toe makeover with the help of her hairdresser, Julie "I Like 'em Big and Stupid" Brown. Devoid of their excessive hairiness, the handsome trio of fun-loving extraterrestrials (Jeff Goldblum, Jim Carrey, and Damon Wayons) set out to experience the Southern California lifestyle, with the help of surfer dude / pool cleaner Michael McKean. Stupid, stupid story that actually works, thanks to a colorful and energetic cast.

EARTH VS. THE FLYING SAUCERS

1956 (NR) 83m / D: Fred F. Sears / **W:** George Worthing Yates, Raymond T. Marcus / **C:** Hugh Marlowe, Joan Taylor, Donald Curtis, Morris Ankrum

"If it lands in our nation's capital uninvited, we don't meet it with tea and cookies." Hugh Marlowe, the jerk who turned in Klaatu in *The Day the Earth Stood Still*, plays a scientist who establishes contact with the survivors of a dying race of aliens looking to colonize our planet. The real star of this classic is, of course, f/x master Ray Harryhausen, whose peerless flying saucers crash into Washington, D.C.'s most treasured landmarks. AKA: *Invasion of the Flying Saucers*.

EDWARD SCISSORHANDS

1990 (PG-13) 105m / D: Tim Burton **/ W:** Caroline Thompson, Tim Burton **/ C:** Johnny Depp, Winona Ryder, Dianne Wiest, Vincent Price, Anthony Michael Hall, Alan Arkin, Kathy Baker, Conchata Ferrell, Caroline Aaron, Dick Anthony Williams, Robert Oliveri, John Davidson

Ever felt like you hurt those you try to help? Edward's (Johnny Depp) a young man created by a loony scientist (Vincent Price, in one of his last roles), who dies before he can attach hands to his boy-creature. Then the boy is rescued from his lonely existence outside of suburbia by an ingratiating Avon lady. With scissors in place of hands, gothic-looking Edward has more trouble fitting into suburbia than would most new kids on the block, and he struggles with being different and lonely in a cardboard-cutout world. Also, his love for Winona Ryder is complicated by those sharp metal fingers of his. However predictable the Hollywood-prefab denouement, this is a visually captivating fairy tale full of splash and color that downplays the mad scientist angle in favor of Pop Art styling and an old-fashioned love story. Director Tim Burton created the character of the Inventor specifically for his idol, Price. Oscar nominated for makeup, though sadly not for Danny Elfman's grand, romantic score.

ELECTRIC DREAMS

1984 (PG) 95m / D: Steve Barron **/ W:** Rusty Lemorande **/ C:** Lenny Von Dohlen, Virginia Madsen, Maxwell Caulfield, Bud Cort, Koo Stark

Despite its terminally cute ending, this "fairy tale for computers" manages to generate a mild paranoid buzz for anyone who has ever been on the down side of a mainframe. Lenny Von Dohlen stars as Miles, an architect whose life is gradually taken over by Edgar, his home computer which (don't ask) develops feelings of its own and tries to sabotage Miles' budding romance with Madeline, his cello-playing upstairs neighbor (Virginia Madsen). Edgar is no HAL or even Joshua (*WarGames*), but he/it is still more interesting than his bland B-movie co-stars. This is thanks to the voice of Bud Cort, who makes this newly plugged-in being both menacing (he cancels Miles's credit cards and rigs his apartment's security system) and sympathetic (he woos Madeline with a poem composed of words gleaned from TV commercials). Steve Barron was among the first generation of music video directors (Michael Jackson's "Billie Jean") who brought the MTV aesthetic to the big screen. He later moved on to such immortal fare as *Teenage Mutant Ninja Turtles: The Movie* and *The Coneheads*. Writer Rusty Lemorande is best unremembered as the co-writer of *Captain Eo*, Coppola and Lucas's 3D Michael Jackson short that played for years as part of a ride at Epcot Center.

THE ELECTRONIC MONSTER

1958 (NR) 72m / **D:** Montgomery Tully / **W:** Charles Eric Maine, J. MacLaren-Ross / **C:** Rod Cameron, Mary Murphy, Meredith Edwards, Peter Illing

Insurance claims investigator Rod Cameron looks into the death of a Hollywood starlet and discovers an exclusive therapy center dedicated to hypnotism. At the facility, people vacation for weeks in morgue-like body drawers, while an evil doctor uses an electronic device to control the sleeper's dreams and actions. Eerie, but falls victim to static handling and dull acting that wastes the premise's potential. Intriguingly, it is one of the first films to explore the possibilities of brainwashing and mind control. AKA: *Escapement*; *The Electric Monster*.

THE ELEMENT OF CRIME

1984 (NR) 104m / **D:** Lars von Trier / **W:** Niels Vørsel / **C:** Michael Elphick, Esmond Knight, Jerold Wells, Meme Lei, Astrid Henning-Jensen, Preben Leerdorff-Rye, Gotha Andersen

In a monochromatic, post-holocaust future, a detective tracks down a serial killer of young girls. Starkly Hitchcockian, with a heavily self-conscious noir overlay. Made in Denmark but with English dialogue, this minor festival favorite features an impressive directional debut from Lars von Trier, who would go on to make a scandalous name for himself with horror films like *The Kingdom* and art house boundary-pushers like *Dancer in the Dark*, *Nymphomaniac*, and *Antichrist*. Filmed in Sepiatone.

ELYSIUM

2013 (R) 109m / **D:** Neill Blomkamp / **W:** Neill Blomkamp / **C:** Matt Damon, Jodie Foster, Sharlto Copley, Alice Braga, Diego Luna, Wagner Moura, William Fichtner

In the 22nd century, Earth looks like one dull-brown, overpopulated, and polluted favela. The one percent has left for their penthouse in the sky: Elysium, a lush green paradisiacal Ringworld-like space station with near-magical health facilities. Matt Damon's Max is an Earthbound ex-con with a terminal dose of radiation poisoning who makes a deal with a

Actor Matt Damon stands in front of a poster for 2013's *Elysium*.

refugee smuggler to get up there; the plan involves soldering him into a metal exo-skeleton and turning his brain into a hard drive. Jodie Foster's quasi-fascist Elysium security chief and her bug-crazy mercenary henchman Sharlto Copley have other ideas. Writer/director Neill Blomkamp (*District 9*) finds some fascinating parallels here with the modern refugee crisis (Earth-dwellers risking all on banged-up shuttles to make it to a better life in Elysium evoking Africans who die on rickety boats crossing the Mediterranean today), but gets overexcited with all the battle-tech that keeps blowing apart his sets and actors in the final third. Still, superb, cannily deployed f/x and ambitious script make for smarter than average sci-fi blockbuster.

EMBRYO

1976 (PG) 108m / **D:** Ralph Nelson / **W:** Anita Doohan, Jack W. Thomas / **C:** Rock Hudson, Barbara Carrera, Diane Ladd, Roddy McDowall, Anne Schedeen, John Elerick

Rock Hudson looks uncomfortable here as a scientist who salvages a human fetus, treating it with genetic serum that creates a fully mature, intelligent, beautiful test-tube woman (Barbara Carrera) in a matter of days. After her "birth," things look upbeat for the happy couple—until those pesky side effects. An average sci-fi drama in the *Frankenstein* mold (not to mention Germany's Alraune tales of lab-created femme fatales), this plods along predictably until a finale that's truly shocking and ghastly compared with the blandness that preceded it. AKA: *Created to Kill*.

EMPIRE OF THE ANTS

1977 (PG) 90m / **D:** Bert I. Gordon / **W:** Bert I. Gordon / **C:** Joan Collins, Robert Lansing, John David Carson, Albert Salmi, Jacqueline Scott, Robert Pine

A group of enormous, nuclear, unfriendly ants stalk a real estate dealer and prospective buyers of undeveloped oceanfront property. The humans (including a pre-*Dynasty* Joan Collins) flee down a river in boats, only to reach the safety of a neighboring town. Or do they? The 1970s' fashions will make you think you happened upon a very odd episode of *The Love Boat*. Story originated by master sci-fi storyteller H. G. Wells, but for marquee value only. Good fun for fans of inept cinema that occasionally slips into mind-bending surrealism.

ENDER'S GAME

2013 (PG-13) 114m / **D:** Gavin Hood / **W:** Gavin Hood / **C:** Asa Butterfield, Harrison Ford, Ben Kingsley, Hailee Steinfeld, Abigail Breslin, Viola Davis

Splashy f/x but muted drama in this staid adaptation of Orson Scott Card's novel. Decades after narrowly besting an invading alien armada, humanity has sent an armada of its own to assault the alien home world. Ender Wiggin

(Asa Butterfield) is one of the most promising kids in the military's training program. Harrison Ford plays the steely eyed colonel doing his best to burn any trace of weakness out of the kids, particularly the preternaturally gifted but socially outcast Ender. He advances steadily in the training program's mock battles, gaining allies and trying to ignore the strange dreams he keeps having. By the time training comes to an end, the film switches from Hogwarts-in-space fantasy school drama—like J. K. Rowling's dueling houses, Card's 1985 novel featured rival student teams with iconic names, like Salamander and Dragon—to heart-rending moral dilemma. Most of what works here comes straight from Card's sturdy plot and Butterfield's affecting mix of vulnerability, cool calculation, and tactical viciousness. Hood's direction is efficient enough, particularly in the marshalling of the bigger f/x scenes whose audience-pleasing splashiness still doesn't overwhelm the characters. But his screenplay is strictly lowest-common denominator when it comes to parsing Ender's strategic thinking (it's too easy in this film to remember that Ender is just a preteen; his successes seem too preordained) and the ethical nightmare he is ultimately trapped in.

Well known for his roles in the "Star Wars" and "Indiana Jones" franchises, Harrison Ford plays a colonel who tries to toughen up a teenager enough to attack an alien race in *Ender's Game*.

ENEMY MINE

1985 (PG-13) 108m / **D:** Wolfgang Petersen / **W:** Edward Khmara / **C:** Dennis Quaid, Louis Gossett Jr., Brion James, Richard Marcus, Lance Kerwin, Carolyn McCormick, Bumper Robinson

Moralistic tale in which two pilots from warring planets—one an Earthling, the other an asexual reptilian "Drac"—crash-land on a barren planet and must work together to survive. Friendship born of the two being at heart soldiers of a very similar kind. The occasionally heavy-handed messaging never slows down the compelling story. Plus, Louis Gossett Jr. makes one of the most effectively "alien" aliens ever seen on screen. His Drac purrs, hisses, and warbles in a language that seems more feline than reptilian; it's fascinating, a bit scary, and mercifully (considering what many aliens were like in this decade) not the least bit cutesy. Efficiently directed by *Das Boot*'s Wolfgang Petersen just after his first Hollywood film, 1984's family fantasy *The NeverEnding Story*. Fast-moving space opera with a thoughtful meditation on cooperation and friendship.

EQUILIBRIUM

2002 (R) 107m / **D:** Kurt Wimmer / **W:** Kurt Wimmer / **C:** Christian Bale, Taye Diggs, Emily Watson, Sean Bean, Angus Macfadyen, William Fichtner

After barely surviving World War III, humanity arrives at a solution to end war: drug the entire populace, make everyone wear monochromatic clothing, outlaw emotions, and enforce the "peace" with highly trained warrior "clerics" who can do two things: Intuit when a person is feeling emotion, and dodge every bullet fired at them while never *ever* missing. Pre-Batman Christian Bale plays a top cleric who's undergoing a Montag-ish crisis of conscience that has him secretly weeping to an outlawed Bach concerto and teaming up with the rebels (there's *always* a rebel underground). Kurt Wimmer's laughably over-the-top cult bulletfest has some good ideas in it, even if they're all cribbed from *1984* and *Fahrenheit 451*, and its smart usage of Nazi-era Berlin architecture evokes the Vulcan Fascist future. But the absurdly one-sided nature of Bale's every fight scene gets old fast, and Wimmer's mania for slo-mo gunplay makes *The Matrix* look measured in comparison.

ESCAPE FROM L.A.

1996 (R) 101m / **D:** John Carpenter / **W:** John Carpenter, Debra Hill, Kurt Russell / **C:** Kurt Russell, Steve Buscemi, Peter Fonda, Cliff Robertson, Valeria Golino, Stacy Keach, Pam Grier, Bruce Campbell, Georges Corraface

Apparently tired of everybody else ripping him off (see every other low-budget sci-fi film from the 1980s), Carpenter decided to go back to the well and see whether Snake Plissken (Kurt Russell) had anything left in him. He doesn't, as this overconfident and self-impressed sequel to *Escape from New York* shows. The story has just about all the earlier film's elements: major city turned into walled-off prison; presidential kidnapping (this time it's the chief executive's daughter who's gone missing); sterling roll call of character actors (Steve Buscemi and Bruce Campbell among the legion of worthies); and a minority villain (Latin American revolutionary instead of black gang boss this time). The ingredients are all here for a good time, but Carpenter doesn't do much to mix them all together, relying instead of lightly

> "The ingredients are all here for a good time, but Carpenter doesn't do much to mix them all together...."
>
> *Escape from L.A.*

poking fun at exploitative sci-fi trash while not bringing any new ideas. The sort of thing that Quentin Tarantino could have had a blast with.

ESCAPE FROM NEW YORK

1981 (R) 99m / **D:** John Carpenter / **W:** John Carpenter, Nick Castle / **C:** Kurt Russell, Lee Van Cleef, Ernest Borgnine, Donald Pleasence, Isaac Hayes, Adrienne Barbeau, Harry Dean Stanton, Season Hubley

Once you accept the premise—that Manhattan, one of the most expensive pieces of real estate on the planet, would be turned into a big jail circa 1997—you've got one of the best sci-fi shoot-'em-ups ever done. In fact, director John Carpenter established the formula of grimy future cityscapes roamed by dangerous punks that so many others would copy in the 1980s and '90s. When convicts hold the president (Donald Pleasance) hostage, disgraced war hero turned eyepatch'd criminal Snake Plissken (a stoic Kurt Russell putting his Disney movie past behind him) unwillingly attempts an impossible rescue mission. He's got 24 hours to get the chief executive back safe and sound or that bomb that Lee Van Cleef implanted in his body goes off. The cast is perfection, particularly Harry Dean Stanton and Ernest Borgnine as a couple of the prisoners helping Snake out. Largely shot in downtown St. Louis because Manhattan didn't look quite rundown enough. Followed by *Escape from L.A.* 15 years later.

ESCAPE FROM PLANET EARTH

1972 (NR) 91m / **D:** Harry Hope, Lee Sholem / **W:** Stuart J. Byrne / **C:** Grant Williams, Bobby Van, Ruta Lee, Henry Wilcoxon, Mala Powers, Casey Kasem, Mike Farrell, Harry Hope

As Red Chinese blow up Earth (probably with a bicycle pump; such is the budget), a co-ed crew of astronauts rocket toward an uncertain future in deep space. Soon petty rivalries and claustrophobia take their toll. Lousy f/x take their own toll on a quaint cast—dig song-and-dance man Bobby Van as a hep-cat survivor—and the abrupt ending came about because the clueless production ran out of money. Later, doubles in spacesuits were posed for a quickie epilogue. Not to be confused with 2013 animated film of the same name. AKA: *The Doomsday Machine*.

ESCAPE FROM SAFEHAVEN

1989 (R) 87m / **D:** Brian Thomas Jones, James McCalmont / **W:** Brian Thomas Jones, James McCalmont / **C:** Rick Gianasi, Mollie O'Mara, John Wittenbauer, Roy MacArthur, William Beckwith

Give the makers of this cheapie Z-movie something for having the chutzpah to set their *Mad Max* variant almost entirely within the budget-friendly confines of one crummy apartment building. Brutal slimeballs rule a mad, sadistic world in the post-apocalyptic future. A family pays dearly to enter a supposedly crime-free community but learns it's just a protection racket run by yet another freakish street gang. Violent retribution ensues.

ESCAPE FROM THE PLANET OF THE APES

1971 (G) 98m / **D:** Don Taylor / **W:** Paul Dehn / **C:** Roddy McDowall, Kim Hunter, Sal Mineo, Ricardo Montalban, William Windom, Bradford Dillman, Natalie Trundy, Eric Braeden

Reprising their roles as intelligent, English-speaking apes from a future Earth society, Roddy McDowall and Kim Hunter flee their world before it's destroyed and travel back in time to present-day America. In L.A. they become the subjects of a relentless search by the fearful population, much like humans Charlton Heston and James Franciscus were targeted for experimentation and destruction in simian society in the earlier *Planet of the Apes* and *Beneath the Planet of the Apes*. Plays more to "fish out of water" comedy, with some heavily overt messages delivered throughout. One of the cheapest-looking of the series, and less interesting; though it does set the stage for some of the time travel paradoxes in the two sequels to follow.

The blockbuster hit *E.T.: The Extra-Terrestrial* is a heartwarming tale about a boy who befriends a marooned alien.

THE SCI-FI MOVIE GUIDE: The Universe of Film from "Alien" to "Zardoz"

E.T.: THE EXTRA-TERRESTRIAL

1982 (PG) 115m / D: Steven Spielberg / **W:** Melissa Mathison / **C:** Henry Thomas, Dee Wallace Stone, Drew Barrymore, Robert MacNaughton, Peter Coyote, C. Thomas Howell, Sean Frye, K. C. Martel

Steven Spielberg's exquisite enchantment, one of the most popular films in history, portrays a limpid-eyed alien stranded on Earth and his special bonding relationship with the young children who find and try to conceal him from grown-up authorities. A tear-jerking, modern fairy tale replete with warmth, humor, and sheer wonder, this was conceived as a second chapter for "Night Skies," a much-discussed but never-filmed thriller about close encounters of a very unfriendly kind. That was scrapped (though elements of it would show up both here and in *Close Encounters of the Third Kind*), and E.T. went into production under the smokescreen title "A Boy's Life." An immediate smash and cultural phenomenon, it held the first-place spot as the highest-grossing movie of all time ... until a later Spielberg hit replaced it—*Jurassic Park*. Spielberg declared he would never sequelize this, but an authorized follow-up did appear in print, *E.T.—The Storybook of the Green Planet*, by William Kotzwinkle. Debra Winger contributed to the throaty voice of E.T.; script by Harrison Ford's then-wife, *The Black Stallion* screenwriter Melissa Mathison. A 20th anniversary edition includes new scenes where E.T. and Elliot are taking a bath together and (somewhat controversially) agents chasing them were digitally altered to replace their guns with walkie-talkies. Nine Oscar nominations, won four, including for John Williams's score.

ETERNAL SUNSHINE OF THE SPOTLESS MIND

2004 (R) 108m / D: Michel Gondry / **W:** Charlie Kaufman / **C:** Jim Carrey, Kate Winslet, Elijah Wood, Mark Ruffalo, David Cross, Kirsten Dunst, Tom Wilkinson, Jane Adams

Whimsical, heartbreaking, mindtwisting sci-fi of the best kind, where the tech is all very workaday and the special effects are used only sparingly and never to distract. Charlie Kaufman's story follows a lovelorn man (Jim Carrey) who discovers that his ex-girlfriend (Kate Winslet) underwent a procedure to have memories of him removed from her consciousness and then decides to do the same himself. Only once the thing is done (via a clearly incredible technology that's deglamorized by being housed in an ordinary doctor's office; one of many nice Philip K. Dick-ian touches), it proves less than perfect: she keeps popping back up. The mixture of Michel Gondry's playful techniques and Kaufman's deeply heartsick moodiness makes for something of a masterpiece and maybe the single greatest sci-fi achievement of the 2000s. A film that rewards repeated viewings, though perhaps not on Valentine's Day. Two Oscar nominations; won for best original screenplay.

EUROPA REPORT

2013 (PG-13) 90m / **D:** Sebastián Cordero / **W:** Philip Gelatt / **C:** Christian Camargo, Embeth Davidtz, Anamaria Marinca, Michael Nyqvist, Daniel Wu, Karolina Wydra, Sharlto Copley, Dan Fogler, Isiah Whitlock Jr.

Tired of national space agencies not doing anything about getting astronauts out there to explore the galaxy, a private company does it itself, sending a multinational crew to look for life in the frozen seas of Europa, one of Jupiter's largest moons. A few months in, mission control loses communication. Sebástian Cordero's spare and imaginatively creepy story is constructed almost entirely from surveillance camera footage inside the ship during its voyage, with some interview scenes spliced in to give it the spine of a faux documentary assembled after the fact. The acting is nothing to write home about and the f/x occasionally chintzy, but Cordero's superbly claustrophobic found-footage slow build manages to create both terror and a genuine sense of wonder at the mysteries of the universe.

EVENT HORIZON

1997 (R) 96m / **D:** Paul W. S. Anderson / **W:** Philip Eisner / **C:** Laurence Fishburne, Sam Neill, Kathleen Quinlan, Joely Richardson, Richard T. Jones

A particularly bloody and moody entry in the outer-space haunted-house field, directed with panache by Paul W. S. Anderson, the Brit wunderkind then fresh off the success of his *Mortal Kombat* video game adaptation. In the 25th century, a rescue ship is sent to find out what happened to the *Event Horizon*, a vessel with an experimental faster-than-light drive that went missing years earlier and just reappeared off Neptune. Once the rescue crew boards the *Event Horizon*, and is eventually stranded there, they discover that the ship returned from the beyond with something ... *evil*. What happens next is something like cross-pollinating the individual psychological horrors of *Solaris* with the gory hauntings of *The Haunting* and *The Shining*; and then adding another few hundred gallons of blood and gore. Still quite effectively unsettling, even if Anderson frequently goes overboard and doesn't use the sci-fi setting for much more than an excuse to abandon his characters millions of miles from help.

> "Anderson frequently goes overboard and doesn't use the sci-fi setting for much more than an excuse to abandon his characters...."
>
> *Event Horizon*

EVE OF DESTRUCTION

1991 (R) 101m / **D:** Duncan Gibbins / **W:** Duncan Gibbins / **C:** Gregory Hines, Renée Soutendijk, Kevin McCarthy, Ross Malinger

Hell knows no fury like a cutting-edge android-girl on the warpath. Modeled after her creator, Dr. Eve Simmons, Eve VII has android-babe good looks and a raging nuclear capability. Wouldn't you know, something goes haywire during her trial run, and debutante Eve turns into a PMS nightmare machine, blasting all the good Doctor's previous beaux. That's where military agent Gregory Hines comes in, though you wonder why. Dutch actress Renée Soutendijk does well playing the dual Eves in her first American film.

THE EVIL OF FRANKENSTEIN

1964 (NR) 84m / **D:** Freddie Francis / **W:** John Elder / **C:** Peter Cushing, Duncan Lamont, Peter Woodthorpe, Sandor Eles, Kiwi Kingston, Katy Wild

Peter Cushing returns as Baron Frankenstein in the third Frankenstein film from Hammer. Not dead (just chilling), the monster-man is found by the mad doctor, who decides that even a cold monster is better than no monster. Back in the lab, the Baron puts the beast on defrost. Unfortunately, the ice-ing on the cake is that being frozen alive made the monster-brain dormant. Enter a supposedly mystical and definitely sleazy hypnotist who is able to make contact and control the monster … and knows how to use him to the best advantage. Director Freddie Francis supplies enough atmosphere but has to work with a predictable script. The monster make-up Is very reminiscent of the classic Universal films. Preceded by *Revenge of Frankenstein* and followed by *Frankenstein Created Woman*.

EVOLUTION

2001 (PG-13) 101m / **D:** Ivan Reitman / **W:** / **C:** David Duchovny, Julianne Moore, Orlando Jones, Seann William Scott, Ted Levine, Ethan Suplee, Dan Aykroyd

Ghostbusters' Ivan Reitman goes back to the monster/comedy well with this send up of the kind of 1950s B-movies where big beasts run amok in the desert and it's up to a few intrepid scientists to do what the army can't. A meteor crashes on Earth, delivering mischievous organisms that cause the local fauna to get dangerously large and frisky. David Duchovny plays off his *X-Files* persona at the head of a cast (Orlando Jones and Dan Aykroyd in particular) whose subtle timing does what it can against a script that's written as broad as a *Three Stooges* short. Lots of cameos from great comic actors like Ty Burrell and Sarah Silverman who would later hit it big.

EXISTENZ

1999 (R) 97m / **D:** David Cronenberg / **W:** David Cronenberg / **C:** Jennifer Jason Leigh, Jude Law, Ian Holm, Willem Dafoe, Don McKellar, Callum Keith Rennie, Christopher Eccleston, Sarah Polley

Cronenberg's last real body-horror film is more of a comedy than anything else he's done, and a surprisingly successful one at that (he being more associated with suppurating flesh wounds than ha-ha). It's set in some near-future world where the population appears fully devoted to the making, marketing, and enjoying of virtual-reality games. Jennifer Jason Leigh plays a legendary game designer on the run from pro-reality terrorists, with gaming virgin Jude Law at her side. In between spinning viewers through layered and line-blurring realities, Cronenberg plays up the sexual aspects of the technology, with organically grown "meta-flesh gamepods" whose umbilical-like cords plug directly into a person's spinal column via a fleshy "bioport." The organic tech extends to pistols that look like a collection of old chicken bones and shoot human teeth. Leigh and Law play it all for comedy, a fact that would have been appreciated by Philip K. Dick, a big inspiration here and who Cronenberg gives a nod to with a fast food joint called Perky Pat's.

EXPLORERS

1985 (PG) 107m / **D:** Joe Dante / **W:** Eric Luke / **C:** Ethan Hawke, River Phoenix, Jason Presson, Amanda Peterson, Mary Kay Place, Dick Miller, Robert Picardo, Dana Ivey, Meshach Taylor, Brooke Bundy

What if, in the middle of *E.T.*, Spielberg's classic alien suddenly took off his mask and revealed ... Mork from Ork? That's more or less what happens to this delicate, promising sci-fi tale that takes a galactic detour into gonzo comedy. In a reworking of *This Island Earth*, three boys are prompted by mysterious dreams to build a circuit that turns a scrapped carnival ride into a real spaceship (a tad crude; the control console is an Apple IIC). Zooming into space, the heroes discover who invited them, and that's where the picture either charms or falls apart, take your choice. Recommended for kid viewers who may better appreciate/forgive the punchline. First starring roles for both Ethan Hawke and River Phoenix. Creature f/x by Rob Bottin and brisk direction from Joe Dante.

FACE/OFF

1997 (R) 138m / **D:** John Woo / **W:** Mike Werb, Michael Colleary / **C:** John Travolta, Nicolas Cage, Joan Allen, Alessandro Nivola, Gina Gershon, Dominique Swain, Nick Cassavetes, Harve Presnell, Colm Feore, CCH Pounder, Robert Wisdom, Margaret Cho

Mike Werb and Michael Colleary's script started out as more straight futuristic action, but once Hong Kong director John Woo came on board, the action shifted to the present-day with some sci-fi overtones. The result is just as absurd as many purportedly realistic action films, only with glorious lashings of camp. John Travolta, in the height of his post-*Pulp Fiction* glow, plays FBI agent Sean Archer, who's obsessively hunting down depraved terrorist-for-hire Castor Troy, played by Nicolas Cage in full eye-popping mania. Convoluted plotting has Archer surgically switching faces with a comatose Troy to go undercover, only to have the tables turned on him when Troy wakes up, has Archer's face put on him and himself goes undercover inside the FBI. The balletic shootouts are some of Woo's best-choreographed since *Hard Boiled* and the complications arising from each man taking over the other's life are played out for their full dark comic potential. As Castor's little brother Pollux (one of the Greek mythological elements scattered in the script), a sniveling Alessandro Nivola shows that he would have made an amazing Renfield for some production of *Dracula*.

THE FACE OF FU MANCHU

1965 (NR) 96m / **D:** Don Sharp / **W:** Peter Welbeck / **C:** Christopher Lee, Nigel Green, James Robertson Justice, H. Marion Crawford, Tsai Chin, Walter Rilla

Christopher Lee plays novelist Sax Rohmer's nefarious Chinese arch-villain Fu Manchu, holed up in England in a secret laboratory under the

Thames. With the help of his daughter and an imprisoned German scientist, Fu is after a deadly gas that will allow him to take over the world. It's the very proper Sir Nayland Smith to the rescue, along with enough dynamite to blow the Fu-ster's hiding place sky high. Will goodness prevail? Or will Fu triumph? This highly silly but enjoyable sci-fi mystery was the first of Lee's Fu Manchu films (and the first film with the character since a 1940 movie serial), followed in 1966 by *The Brides of Fu Manchu*.

THE FACULTY

1998 (R) 104m / **D:** Robert Rodriguez / **W:** Kevin Williamson / **C:** Jordana Brewster, Clea DuVall, Laura Harris, Josh Hartnett, Shawn Hatosy, Salma Hayek, Famke Janssen, Piper Laurie, Christopher McDonald, Bebe Neuwirth, Robert Patrick, Usher Raymond, Jon Stewart, Elijah Wood

The factory for slick, tongue-in-cheek teen flicks that the Weinsteins had going in the 1990s at Dimension Films reached a kind of apotheosis with this sci-fi/horror/comedy that posits a high school where the teachers aren't just *acting* like they're from another planet, they actually *are* aliens. All the elements come together, with crisp direction from a pre-*Spy Kids* Robert Rodriguez, an efficiently suspenseful and funny script from Kevin Williamson (in between writing *Scream* movies for Dimension), and self-mocking performances from Robert Patrick and Usher. Josh Hartnett got his break here playing a prematurely wizened drug dealer.

FAHRENHEIT 451

1966 (NR) 112m / **D:** François Truffaut / **W:** François Truffaut, Jean-Louis Richard / **C:** Oskar Werner, Julie Christie, Cyril Cusack, Anton Diffring, Jeremy Spenser

French auteur François Truffaut adapts Ray Bradbury's classic novel about an oppressive future where books are burned. Firemen are responsible for eliminating all books by burning them—Fahrenheit 451 is the temperature at which paper begins to burn. Recollections of firemen putting out fires have become ancient myths. The story follows Montag, a fireman, content and unquestioning in his work, until he meets a book-loving subversive played by Julie Christie (who also plays Montag's pill-popping, TV-addicted wife).

Cyril Cusack (left) and Oskar Werner are "firemen" whose job it is to burn books in *Fahrenheit 451,* a film based on the book by Ray Bradbury.

Montag begins to question the morality of his actions and actually begins to read the books he is supposed to burn. Enthralled by the words of Dickens, Montag too becomes a rebel from the police state. Though heavy handed in its portrayal of a society where free thought has been outlawed, the film succeeds in capturing the essence of the novel, if not Bradbury's poetic subtleties. A haunting ending helps make up for slow going early on. Oskar Werner gives a solid performance as the hero who begins to question the system, and Cyril Cusack is splendid as his evil boss. Bernard Herrmann provides the highly dramatic score while future director provocateur Nicolas Roeg is behind the camera. This was Truffaut's first color and only English-language film.

FAIL-SAFE

1964 (NR) 111m / **D:** Sidney Lumet / **W:** Walter Bernstein / **C:** Henry Fonda, Dan O'Herlihy, Walter Matthau, Larry Hagman, Fritz Weaver, Frank Overton

A nail-biting nuclear-age nightmare, in which American planes have been erroneously sent to nuke Moscow with no way to recall them. This straight-faced flipside to *Dr. Strangelove* has absolutely no comic relief and is high-tension all the way through. The all-star cast impels the drama as the heads of the Russian and U.S. governments try to end the crisis as time runs out. A stolid Henry Fonda is impressive as the U.S. president forced to offer an eye for an eye. Fine black-and-white cinematography and an intelligent script top off this great adaptation of the Eugene Burdick/Harvey Wheeler novel. Remade in very straightforward fashion in 2000 as a live black-and-white film for CBS starring George Clooney and Richard Dreyfuss and directed by Stephen Frears.

FANTASTIC FOUR

2005 (PG-13) 106m / **D:** Tim Story / **W:** Mark Frost, Michael France / **C:** Ioan Gruffudd, Michael Chiklis, Chris Evans, Jessica Alba, Julian McMahon, Hamish Linklater, Kerry Washington

After being hit by a cloud of space debris/energy/whatever, several researchers return from their space station to earth to find themselves wielding strange new powers. Dr. Victor von Doom (Julian McMahon) starts using his for evil; and can you blame him, with that name? The other four band together to fight for good under new names that mirror their abilities— the ultra-stretchy Mister Fantastic (Ioan Gruffudd), Invisible Woman (Jessica Alba), fiery Human Torch (Chris Evans), and Hulk-like Thing (Michael Chiklis)—which means battling their old buddy Doom and saving the occasional stray innocent. Adaptation of the old Marvel comics was a hit in the *Spider-*

man mold, its good-natured and family friendly demeanor stood in contrast to the gloomier comic-book sagas to follow.

FANTASTIC 4: RISE OF THE SILVER SURFER

2007 (PG) 92m / **D:** Tim Story / **W:** Don Payne, Mark Frost / **C:** Ioan Gruffudd, Michael Chiklis, Chris Evans, Jessica Alba, Julian McMahon, Hamish Linklater, Kerry Washington, Andre Braugher, Laurence Fishburne

More trouble for the Fantastic Four when the Silver Surfer (voiced by Laurence Fishburne) shows up and appears to be leaving devastation everywhere on Earth that his weird alien self and that ultra-powerful surfboard pass through. The stakes are higher this time out than the Four's first outing (destruction of the world and a massively malevolent cosmic entity known as Galactus) but Tim Story keeps the emphasis on relationships and lightly handled comedy. Watch for nerd-comic Brian Posehn as the minister at the (interrupted) wedding between Mister Fantastic and the Invisible Woman. Just four years later, Chris Evans would create a major rift in Marvel comics-movie continuity by appearing as Captain America.

FANTASTIC PLANET

1973 (PG) 68m / **D:** René Laloux / **W:** Roland Topor, René Laloux

A critically acclaimed, animated French sci-fi epic based on the drawings of Roland Topor. A race of small humanoids is enslaved and exploited by a race of telepathic blue giants on a savage planet. The film follows one of the small creatures on a quest to unite his people and win them equality with their captors. This film has a haunting, alien quality that makes it stand out even today; there's little dialogue, and the backgrounds and character designs are delicate with a dreamlike strangeness. Full of inventive, startling images: the hero is in one scene forced to fight another of his race with vicious, snapping reptiles strapped to their chests. The blue giants, with their staring, emotionless faces, are particularly haunting. The story, however, is humanistic and gently satirical. A memorable, eerie film that'll stay with you for some time.

FANTASTIC VOYAGE

1966 (PG) 100m / **D:** Richard Fleischer / **W:** Harry Kleiner / **C:** Stephen Boyd, Edmond O'Brien, Raquel Welch, Arthur Kennedy, Donald Pleasence, Arthur O'Connell, William Redfield, James Brolin

An important scientist, rescued from behind the Iron Curtain, is wounded by enemy agents. A tiny clot within his brain means that traditional surgery is impossible. After being shrunk to microscopic size, a medical team uses

A medical team and their craft are shrunk down in size and injected into an important scientist's body to treat a tiny blood clot in the 1966 film *Fantastic Voyage*.

a hi-tech submarine to journey inside his body where members find themselves threatened by the patient's natural defenses, as well as a sabotaging spy who has made his way aboard. Action-filled drama efficiently delivered by journeyman director Richard Fleischer and award-winning f/x. The weird "inner space" settings depicting a microbes'-eye-view of the human body sometimes recall Jules Verne films, especially *Journey to the Center of the Earth*. The performances are generally bland—except for Donald Pleasence, who gives us one of his trademark twitchy, nervous characterizations. Later adapted into a Saturday morning cartoon series. Five Oscar nominations, won for f/x and art direction. AKA: *Microscopia*; *Strange Journey*.

THE FIFTH ELEMENT

1997 (PG-13) 126m / **D:** Luc Besson / **W:** Luc Besson, Robert Mark Kamen / **C:** Bruce Willis, Gary Oldman, Ian Holm, Milla Jovovich, Chris Tucker, Luke Perry, Brion James, Tommy Lister

Manic, bullet-pocked, 23rd-century sci-fi actioner that throws a perfectly dry Bruce Willis into a *Heavy Metal*-inspired story about alien beauty

Milla Jovovich (mostly wordless and nearly naked throughout) whose powers can save or destroy the planet. Gary Oldman is the head baddie, chewing all the scenery in sight that a bug-eyed Chris Tucker (in a crazed drag queen caricature that might have been inspired by Ray Shell's similarly over-the-top performance in 1980's *The Apple*) has left ungnawed. Unlike most turgid space operas, the pace is unrelenting, the story bafflingly silly, the body count staggering, and the f/x nothing less than glorious. It underperformed in the United States, but did just fine abroad, where the illogical plotting and mood shifts proved less of a problem. This established a formula seized on afterward by much less imaginative Hollywood films, which found they could often underdeliver on story as long as the action and f/x were big and obvious enough to play abroad. Highly insane adventure, in the best way. One Oscar nomination.

FINAL

2001 (R) 111m / **D:** Campbell Scott / **W:** Bruce McIntosh / **C:** Denis Leary, Hope Davis, J. C. MacKenzie, Jim Gaffigan

Comic Denis Leary is credible as a hospital patient who wakes up from a coma convinced that he's been the subject of a government cryogenic/organ-harvesting program. Hints of a post-apocalyptic reality hover around the edges as Leary's psychiatrist (Hope Davis) tries to unravel what if anything is true in his rantings, which seem to come straight from the notebooks of Philip K. Dick. Efficiently bottled-up direction heightens the drama of this play-like chamber piece. An early example of dirt-cheap, imaginative digital filmmaking that arrived a few years before its time.

FINAL APPROACH

1991 (R) 100m / **D:** Eric Steven Stahl / **W:** Eric Steven Stahl, Gerald Laurence / **C:** James B. Sikking, Hector Elizondo, Madolyn Smith, Kevin McCarthy, Cameo Kneuer, Wayne Duvall

U.S. Air Force stealth pilot Jason Halsey (James B. Sikking) crashes in the desert and awakens in the office of ominous psychiatrist Dio Gottlieb (Hector Elizondo). Remembering nothing of his past, and not even recognizing his own face, Halsey begins to work with Gottlieb while the commander of the covert stealth operation, General Geller (Kevin McCarthy), tries to debrief him on the crash. Although the video packaging suggests that this might be an aerial shoot-'em-up, it's really a well-acted, fairly intense drama with plenty of plot twists. Scenes of the SR-71, the spy plane that could fly so fast and high that it was nearly impossible to shoot down, are pretty incredible, and the computer display effects give the feel of being in the cockpit. Notable as the first film made with a totally digital soundtrack, and claims over 18,000 digital sound effects.

THE FINAL COUNTDOWN

1980 (PG) 92m / **D:** Don Taylor / **W:** Thomas Hunter, David Ambrose, Gerry Davis, Peter Powell / **C:** Kirk Douglas, Martin Sheen, Katharine Ross, James Farentino, Charles Durning, Ron O'Neal

On December 7, 1980, the nuclear carrier USS *Nimitz* is caught in a time warp and transported back in time to Pearl Harbor, December 7, 1941, just hours before the Japanese bombing attack that crippled the U.S. and propelled the country into WWII. The commanders are faced with the ultimate decision—leave history intact or stop the incident and maybe the war itself. Making the decision are the captain (Kirk Douglas), his first mate (James Farentino), and a civilian observer (Martin Sheen). The real star of the movie is the *Nimitz* itself; the footage

> **"Excellent cinematography and a surprise ending wrap things up nicely."**
> *The Final Countdown*

taken aboard it offered a look at the magnitude of power available and adds to the realistic feel of the film. Excellent cinematography and a surprise ending wrap things up nicely. Future schlock merchant Lloyd Kaufman was an associate producer here; a rare detour into good taste.

THE FINAL CUT

2004 (PG-13) 95m / **D:** Omar Nalm / **W:** Omar Naim / **C:** Robin Williams, Jim Caviezel, Mira Sorvino, Genevieve Buechner, Stephanie Romanov

In the future, people have so-called "Zoe implant" chips put in them at birth that record everything they see. In this sci-fi mystery, Robin Williams (going for a similar blank, stalkerish affect that he used in 2002's *One Hour Photo*) plays the mild-mannered editor whose job it is to take the life's worth of downloaded memories from the deceased and edit it into a cohesive work for the funeral. Unsurprisingly, Williams's serene life gets thrown into turmoil when he's faced with a life memory that he will be particularly hard-pressed to turn into something positive. Slightly ahead-of-its-time thriller.

FINAL FANTASY: THE SPIRITS WITHIN

2001 (PG-13) 106m / **D:** Hironobu Sakaguchi, Motonori Sakakibara / **W:** Al Reinert, Jeff Vintar

Final Fantasy is a sprawling video game universe that started in 1987 and spawned straight-to-video movies, TV series, manga, radio dramas, novels, and this moribund feature. In 2065, Earth is your basic grey and skeleton-littered wasteland haunted by invisible aliens called "phantoms." Some humans live on in gleaming "barrier cities." Salvation might be found in the dreams of Dr. Akin Ross, but dangers lurk in the struggle between her two surrogate father figures: the ingenious Dr. Sid and the warmongering Gen.

Hein. Lots of dialogue about spirits and "bio-etheric lasers" paired with scenes of hulking armored soldiers blasting phantoms to smithereens. The first near-photorealistic computer-animated film, it took four years and north of $100 million to create this tiresome non-adventure whose stiff dialogue isn't helped by the all-star voice cast (Donald Sutherland, James Woods). Most interesting for the hypnotically swirling, individually animated hairs on Ross's head.

THE FINAL PROGRAMME

1973 (R) 85m / **D:** Robert Fuest / **W:** Robert Fuest / **C:** Hugh Griffith, Harry Andrews, Jon Finch, Jenny Runacre, Sterling Hayden, Patrick Magee, Sarah Douglas

In this futuristic story, a man must rescue his sister—and the world—from their brother, who holds a microfilmed plan for global domination. Meanwhile, he must shield himself from the advances of a bisexual computer programmer who wants to make him father to a new, all-purpose human being. Based on the Michael Moorcock "Jerry Cornelius" stories, the film has gained a cult following. AKA: *The Last Days of Man on Earth*.

FIRE IN THE SKY

1993 (PG-13) 98m / **D:** Robert Lieberman / **W:** Tracy Torme / **C:** D. B. Sweeney, Robert Patrick, Craig Sheffer, Peter Berg, James Garner, Henry Thomas, Kathleen Wilhoite, Bradley Gregg, Noble Willingham

The mysterious disappearance of logger D. B. Sweeney sparks a criminal investigation of his drinking buddies. Then Sweeney returns, telling a frightening story of alien abduction. Though everyone in town doubts his story, viewers won't, since the alleged aliens have already made an appearance, shifting the focus to Sweeney and friends as he tries to convince skeptics that his trauma is genuine. Sweeney is sympathetic and believable as the abductee, as is Robert Patrick as the unjustly accused friend. James Garner is great as the incredulous hard-nosed investigator. Still, the movie does a better job of making viewers feel sorry for everyone than turning them into believers. A weekly episode of *The X-Files* is better than this. Spooky and captivating scenes of the alien abduction and alien experiments are some of the few bright spots. Based on a story claimed to be true.

FIRE MAIDENS OF OUTER SPACE

1956 (NR) 80m / **D:** Cy Roth / **W:** Cy Roth / **C:** Anthony Dexter, Susan Shaw, Paul Carpenter, Harry Fowler, Jacqueline Curtiss, Sydney Tafler, Maya Koumani, Jan Holden, Kim Parker, Owen Barry, Ian Struthers ire maidens prove the space opera code that dictates all alien women be in desperate need of human male company. Astronauts on an expedition to Jupiter's thirteenth moon discover the lost civilization of Atlantis, which, as luck would have it, is inhabited only by women (except for one busy old man). An unexplained beast man prowls around looking to carry off fire maidens (can you blame him?). What with *Cat Women on the Moon*, *Queen of Outer Space*, *Abbott & Costello Go to Mars*, *Invasion of the Star Creatures*, and *Missile to the Moon*, one might get the impression that outer space was swarming with scantily clad beauty queens. Was this part of a secret government plot to recruit volunteers for the space program?

FIRST MAN INTO SPACE

1959 (NR) 78m / D: Robert Day / **W:** John C. Cooper, Lance Z. Hargreaves / **C:** Marshall Thompson, Marla Landi, Bill Edwards, Robert Ayres, Bill Nagy, Carl Jaffe

An astronaut returns to Earth covered with a crust of strange space dust and with an organism feeding inside him. The alien needs human blood to survive and starts killing in order to get it. Prototypical "astronaut turns into monster" plotline sets down the plodding formula used for years afterward (see *Monster A Go-Go* and *Incredible Melting Man* for more of the same) until the climax, which creates a great deal of sympathy for the helpless man within the monster. May have served as partial inspiration for Marvel Comics' Fantastic Four series. Rushed into production by MGM in order to capitalize on public interest in the U.S.-Soviet space race. AKA: *Satellite of Blood*.

FIRST MEN IN THE MOON

1964 (NR) 103m / D: Nathan Juran / **W:** Nigel Kneale, Jan Read / **C:** Martha Hyer, Edward Judd, Lionel Jeffries, Erik Chitty, Peter Finch, Miles Malleson

A fun, f/x-laden adaptation of the H. G. Wells novel about an Edwardian civilian spacecraft visiting the moon and the creatures found there. Wells's vision of space travel has a unique twist—the vehicle is a globe covered with an anti-gravity substance, controlled by a shutter system. The explorers hang in webbed hammocks for protection during the rough landing, stretching credibility even beyond the light tone of the film, and they quickly discover a breathable atmosphere below the Moon's surface. However, the insectoid "sellenites" inhabiting the lunar caverns are genuinely unsettling. Lionel Jeffries's performance as the outlandish inventor is an easy scene stealer—at times too much so. F/x by Ray Harryhausen. Peter Finch makes a brief appearance.

> "Lionel Jeffries's performance as the outlandish inventor is an easy scene stealer—at times too much so."
>
> *First Men in the Moon*

FIRST SPACESHIP ON VENUS

1960 (NR) 78m / **D:** Kurt Maetzig / **W:** Jan Fethke, Wolfgang Kohlhaase, Günther Reisch, Günther Rücker, Alexander Stenbock-Fermor / **C:** Yoko Tani, Oldrich Lukes, Ignacy Machowski, Julius Ongewe, Michail Postnikow, Kurt Rackelmann, Gunther Simon, Tang-Hua-Ta, Lucyna Winnicka

Eight international scientists set foot on Venus, but what they find is as downbeat as it was a decade earlier on Mars in *Rocketship X-M*, which showed structures of a dead civilization standing silent as blind Martians staggered about. The cause: atomic war, but here the nukes have also done in the natives; the only identifiable life form is a gray organic ooze that spurts out with such menacing force that the entire Earth expedition retreats and goes home. Pic is worth one viewing just to drink in the bizarre architecture of the Venusian ruins. It's like being caught in an Yves Tanguy painting: elongated, twisted, curvy shapes cast forth by alien minds who knew different laws of time and space. Antinuke sci-fi effort was made with German and Polish backing and originally released at 130 minutes. Based on the Stanislaw Lem novel *The Astronauts*.

FIVE

1951 (NR) 93m / **D:** Arch Oboler / **W:** James Weldon Johnson / **C:** William Phipps, Susan Douglas, James Anderson, Charles Lampkin, Earl Lee

This difficult-to-find film is an allegorical exercise in which Susan Douglas plays perhaps the last woman left alive after the apocalypse who must figure out how to deal with the four male survivors she bands together with, not to mention her pregnancy and missing and presumed dead husband. Tensions flare as one of the men, a white supremacist (James Anderson), is antagonistic towards the black member of their group (Charles Lampkin), and signs of radiation poisoning begin to spread. Coming just two years after the Soviets tested their first atomic bomb and released the same year as *The Day the Earth Stood Still*, *Five* is considered the first American film to deal with the consequences of an atomic or nuclear conflict. Filmed mostly at director Arch Oboler's Frank Lloyd Wright-designed house in Malibu. Oboler had something of a thing for the apocalypse, having previously written the play *Night of the Auk*, about astronauts who discover on their return to Earth that World War III has broken out in their absence. The following year, Oboler produced *Bwana Devil*, in which British railway workers get eaten by Kenyan lions … in 3D.

FLASH GORDON

1980 (PG) 111m / **D:** Mike Hodges / **W:** Lorenzo Semple Jr. / **C:** Sam J. Jones, Melody Anderson, Chaim Topol, Max von Sydow, Ornella Muti, Timothy Dalton, Brian Blessed

Acampy, updated version of the classic adventures of the blonde, space-faring hero. The bones of the story are the same: Flash and his gal-pal Dale Arden are forced by nutty Dr. Zarkov (Chaim Topol from *Fiddler on the Roof*) to accompany him on a mission to far-off planet Mongo. It seems Mongo's head bad-guy, one Ming the Merciless, is threatening to destroy the Earth, and they Must Stop Him. Sam J. Jones makes a pretty unconvincing Flash, but if you can overlook his leaden performance, this is fast moving, cheerfully sleazy fun. Max von Sydow does a fine job of rehashing Charles Middleton's classic performance as Ming and Brian Blessed is great as Vultan, the blowhard king of the hawkmen. Queen did the soundtrack; why not? Apparently George Lucas had lobbied for the rights years earlier and when he couldn't get them, he went ahead and made his own space opera.

FLASH GORDON CONQUERS THE UNIVERSE

1940 (NR) 240m / D: Ford Beebe, Ray Taylor / **W:** George Plympton / **C:** Buster Crabbe, Carol Hughes, Charles Middleton, Frank Shannon

Third and last "Flash Gordon" serial works well as both a 12-chapter play and a feature-length condensation (both have the same title). Ming the Merciless of Mongo is dusting the Earth with toxic spores, the Purple Death. Naturally, Flash, Dale Arden, and Dr. Zarkov visit Mongo to frustrate the Emperor; assisting them are the running characters Prince Barin of Arboria and Aura, Ming's daughter who is now married to Barin. Considered by serial authorities as the weakest of the three "Flash" serials, it's nonetheless the most elegant looking. Filmmakers had the sense to copy the medieval-styled clothing and set designs predominant in Alex Raymond's source comic strip. In the concluding chapter Flash unleashes an out-of-control rocketship against Ming's castle battlement, which was actually part of the set for Universal's 1939 *Tower of London*. Whence came the title of this serial? Ming, in his egotistical blindness, calls himself "The Universe," and because Flash so thoroughly quells him at the conclusion, Flash is entitled, according to Dr. Zarkov, to say that he has conquered the universe. AKA: *Purple Death from Outer Space*.

FLASH GORDON: MARS ATTACKS THE WORLD

1938 (NR) 87m / D: Robert F. "Bob" Hill, Ford Beebe / **W:** Ray Trampe / **C:** Buster Crabbe, Jean Rogers, Charles Middleton

This feature condensation of the second *Flash Gordon* serial was supposed to take place on Mongo, but all the characters and the locale switched to Mars after Orson Welles's famed *War of the Worlds* Halloween broadcast of 1938. So Azura, Queen of the Blue Caverns on Mongo in the

From left to right, Frank Shannon, Buster Crabbe, Carol Hughes, and Roland Drew are dressed like Robin Hood's Merry Men (as they were in the original comic strip) in *Flash Gordon Conquers the Universe*.

Alex Raymond comic strip, became Azura, Queen of Mars. And so on. Plot concerns Ming the Merciless, planet-hopping, aiming a death ray at Earth in revenge for what Flash did to him in the first serial. Mongo's Prince Barin of Arboria also drops in to help his old friend Flash, and there are some put-upon Martian citizens called the Clay People to lend a muddy hand. Note their eerie language, actually just English played backwards. Overall, this serial is not as good as the first *Flash Gordon* but is worth a look. AKA: *The Deadly Rays from Mars*; *Flash Gordon's Trip to Mars*.

FLASH GORDON: ROCKETSHIP

1936 (NR) 97m / D: Frederick Stephani / **W:** George Plympton / **C:** Buster Crabbe, Jean Rogers, Frank Shannon, Charles Middleton, Priscilla Lawson, Jack Lipson

Re-edited from the original *Flash Gordon* serial in which Flash and company must prevent the planet Mongo from colliding with Earth. Its ruler, Ming the

Merciless (impeccably played by Charles Middleton), is hurling his world into Earth's orbit to crush all terrestrial life, but the human adventurers, united with rebel citizens of Mongo, stop his despotic schemes. Buster Crabbe is a perfectly heroic Flash, Frank Shannon his brainy scientist sidekick Hans Zarkov, and Jean Rogers a demure blonde Dale Arden. She turned into a brunette in the succeeding serial, more accurate to the classic Alex Raymond comics (which this otherwise follows with great fidelity). Yes, much was cut out in this condensation, but the smooth story progression will amaze you, as will the production values; this is considered the most expensive serial ever lensed. Condensed feature version has something the original serial lacks, Franz Waxman's stirring music, excerpted from *The Bride of Frankenstein*. AKA: *Spaceship to the Unknown*; *Perils from Planet Mongo*; *Space Soldiers*; *Atomic Rocketship*.

FLATLINERS

1990 (R) 111m / **D:** Joel Schumacher / **W:** Peter Filardi / **C:** Kiefer Sutherland, Julia Roberts, William Baldwin, Oliver Platt, Kevin Bacon, Kimberly Scott, Joshua Rudoy

High-tech gothic spooker with attractive young cast. A group of medical students begin after-hours experimentation with death, taking turns being "killed" and brought back to life with CPR techniques. Some start to see frightening visions afterwards—is a part of them still connected to the afterlife? Plot is weak, but visuals are striking and spooky. The briefly engaged Julia Roberts and Klefer Sutherland create an energy that makes it worth watching. Oscar nomination for sound effects editing.

FLIGHT OF THE NAVIGATOR

1986 (PG) 90m / **D:** Randal Kleiser / **W:** Michael Burton, Matt MacManus / **C:** Joey Cramer, Veronica Cartwright, Cliff DeYoung, Sarah Jessica Parker, Matt Adler, Howard Hesseman

A 12-year-old comes back from a walk in the woods to learn that eight years have passed for his family and the rest of the world. Meanwhile NASA finds a parked UFO nearby but can't open it. The bewildered boy is the key and has an incredible adventure in time and space. Disney sci-fi starts with a genuine sense of mystery and wonder, later largely abandoned in favor of comedy as Paul Reubens, in his Pee Wee Herman character, provides the voice of the alien intelligence. Good fun nonetheless.

FLIGHT TO MARS

1951 (NR) 72m / **D:** Lesley Selander / **W:** Arthur Strawn / **C:** Cameron Mitchell, Marguerite Chapman, Arthur Franz, Virginia Huston, John Litel, Richard Gaines

Interplanetary explorers crash-land on Mars and find an advanced underground society that looks and acts just like humans, except they've never heard of uranium. Mars leaders help fix the rocket, while secretly scheming to copy its atom-powered design for an invasion fleet. Notable as the first color movie of this genre (two-strip Technicolor), it's still static and uninvolving—Flash Gordon with no flash. Turn down your TV brightness and this talky opus could pass for a vintage radio play. Nice touch: Marguerite Chapman plays a Martian maiden named Alita, in reference to the 1924 expressionist Soviet fantasy *Aelita, Queen of Mars*.

THE FLY (1958)

1958 (NR) 94m / **D:** Kurt Neumann / **W:** James Clavell / **C:** Vincent Price, David Hedison, Herbert Marshall, Patricia Owens

> "[R]umor has it Vincent Price and Herbert Marshall had to stifle giggles while shooting the notorious "Help me … help meeeeeee!" climax."
>
> *The Fly*

The original sci-fi tale about hapless scientist David Hedison, experimenting with teleportation, who accidentally gets anatomically mixed with a housefly. Now, how to tell the wife? No matter how repellently fascinating the premise, an earnest, wordy script (by *Shogun* novelist James Clavell) that stays true to George Langelaan's short story and direction better suited to domestic-crisis drama lend this a campy air even the actors couldn't ignore—rumor has it Vincent Price and Herbert Marshall had to stifle giggles while shooting the notorious "Help me … help meeeeeee!" climax. Required viewing nonetheless.

THE FLY (1986)

1986 (R) 96m / **D:** David Cronenberg / **W:** David Cronenberg, Charles Edward Pogue / **C:** Jeff Goldblum, Geena Davis, John Getz, Joy Boushel

David Cronenberg's remake of the 1958 classic turns into one of his ultimate body-horror studies. Jeff Goldblum is pitch-perfect as the eccentric scientist Seth Brundle, whose genes and molecules are intermixed with those of a housefly via his experimental teleportation device. As he begins to change, Seth at first becomes stronger, more agile, and virile as hell. But girlfriend Geena Davis watches in horror as genetic mutation kicks into high gear and Seth's body literally begins to fall apart. Cronenberg sets things up with some lighthearted humor during the degeneration, only to lead into one of the more brutally emotional conclusions ever put on film. A thoughtful, sensitive, and ultimately shocking horror film whose amazing, grotesque f/x by Chris Walas won an Oscar.

THE FLY II

1989 (R) 105m / **D:** Chris Walas / **W:** Mick Garris, Jim Wheat, Ken Wheat, Frank Darabont / **C:** Eric Stoltz, Daphne Zuniga, Lee Richardson, John Getz, Harley Cross lthough inferior to Cronenberg's opus, this sequel continues the study of the decay of the flesh and how it affects the mental and emotional as well as the physical. Martin (Eric Stoltz), son of fly/man Seth Brundle, achieves full genius maturity in five years. Machiavellian industrialist Anton Bartok (Lee Richardson) cares about his ward about as much as he cares for his other experimental animals, but the sheltered Martin loves him as a father. Computer operator Beth (Daphne Zuniga) awakens Martin's human desires and makes him long for a life outside the confines of his laboratory. Continuing his father's work to perfect the teleportation device, Martin's insect genes (note title of film) begin to transform him into a powerful lf pathetic son-of fly/man. Like father like son. Director Chris Walas originally handled f/x for the 1986 *The Fly*.

THE FLYING SAUCER

1950 (NR) 69m / **D:** Mikel Conrad / **W:** Mikel Conrad / **C:** Mikel Conrad, Pat Garrison, Hantz von Teuffen

.S. and Russian scientists clash over their search for a huge flying saucer that is hidden under a glacier. The first movie to deal with flying saucers.

THE FOOD OF THE GODS

1976 (PG) 88m / **D:** Bert I. Gordon / **W:** Bert I. Gordon / **C:** Marjoe Gortner, Pamela Franklin, Ralph Meeker, Ida Lupino, Jon Cypher, Belinda Balaski

husband and wife on a secluded island discover some bubbling, seething stuff oozing out of their property. When fed to animals, the unappetizing glop creates giant offspring. The pious couple think this is the Lord's way of ending world hunger, since it makes for some mighty big chickens. Inevitably, though, some less pleasant critters get hold of it and as a result the wife, a couple of young folks, and a corrupt businessman are trapped on the island by a platoon of giant rats and wasps. This updated version of the H. G. Wells novel was a 1970s comeback for '50s giant-radioactive-monster auteur Bert I. Gordon. The performances are nothing special—in fact, they're lousy. But the film does have some surprisingly effective visual moments; the giant rats (regular-sized vermin swarming over model cars) look much better than you'd have any reason to suspect. On the other hand, the giant fake rooster-head that attacks the hero is pretty lame.

FORBIDDEN PLANET

1956 (NR) 98m / **D:** Fred M. Wilcox / **W:** Cyril Hume / **C:** Walter Pidgeon, Anne Francis, Leslie Nielsen, Warren Stevens, Jack Kelly, Richard Anderson, Earl Holliman, George Wallace

M·G·M PRESENTS

FORBIDDEN PLANET

AMAZING!

STARRING WALTER PIDGEON · ANNE FRANCIS · LESLIE NIELSEN

WITH WARREN STEVENS AND INTRODUCING ROBBY, THE ROBOT SCREEN PLAY BY CYRIL HUME PHOTOGRAPHED IN EASTMAN COLOR

DIRECTED BY FRED McLEOD WILCOX · NICHOLAS NAYFACK IN CINEMASCOPE AND COLOR

A METRO·GOLDWYN·MAYER PICTURE

Otherwise a classic, 1956's *Forbidden Planet* also introduced the world to Robby the Robot, a dubious distinction.

"Prepare your minds for a new scale of scientific values, gentlemen." MGM's first foray into the genre is must-see sci-fi. Following Disney's lead in the wake of the success of *20,000 Leagues under the Sea*, the studio lavished its considerable resources on this adventure that was loosely based on William Shakespeare's *The Tempest*. In the 23rd century, Leslie Nielsen leads an expedition to Altair-4 to discover the fate of a previous mission to colonize the planet. They are warned away by Morbius (Walter Pidgeon), who claims to be the only survivor and states that he needs no help and cannot be responsible for the consequences if Nielsen and company land. Turns out Morbius, who lives in automated luxury, is not alone. He has a beautiful daughter (Anne Francis) who greets the visitors with, "What beautiful men!" They are tended to by Robby the Robot (the film's breakout star, he would pop up later in various films and TV shows). More malevolent is the Monster from the Id, a beast unwittingly summoned from Morbius's subconscious after his daughter hooks up with Nielsen. Thoughtful and smartly put together, this is arguably the best sci-fi film of the 1950s. Eerie soundtrack of "electronic tonalities." Oscar nominated for f/x.

FOREVER YOUNG

1992 (PG) 102m / D: Steve Miner / **W:** J. J. Abrams / **C:** Mel Gibson, Jamie Lee Curtis, Elijah Wood, Isabel Glasser, George Wendt, Joe Morton, Nicolas Surovy, David Marshall Grant, Art LaFleur

When test pilot Mel Gibson's girlfriend is hit by a car and goes into a coma, he volunteers to be cryogenically frozen for one year. Slight problem—he's left frozen for fifty years, until being accidentally thawed out by a couple of kids. Predictable, designed to be a tearjerker, though it serves mostly as a star vehicle for Gibson, who bumbles with 1990s technology, finds his true love, and escapes from government heavies. Through all the schmaltz, the relationship Gibson develops with the young Elijah Wood turns out to be the most authentic part of the film. Early genre effort from *Lost*'s J. J. Abrams.

THE FORGOTTEN

2004 (PG-13) 91m / D: Joseph Ruben / **W:** Gerald Di Pego / **C:** Julianne Moore, Dominic West, Gary Sinise, Linus Roache, Anthony Edwards, Alfre Woodard, Jessica Hecht

Julianne Moore scrapes through dreary days as a bereaved mother who can't get over the death of her child in a plane crash. Therapist Gary Sinise and husband Anthony Edwards are understanding, until she accuses them of trying to erase evidence of her son. Then they start telling her she never *had* a son. Then the NSA shows up, and it seems like something in the sky is watching her.... Riddle-wrapped ghost-memory story starts with smartly played psychological mystery and beautifully fall-tinged Brooklyn locations, not to mention a wire-tight Dominic West as an alcoholic dad with the same memories as Moore. But a hack-ish script and powerfully underwhelming conclusion do this one in. There's an extended version available with an alternate ending which is not much of an improvement.

FORTRESS

1992 (R) 95m / D: Stuart Gordon / **W:** Steve Feinberg, Troy Neighbors, Terry Curtis Fox / **C:** Christopher Lambert, Kurtwood Smith, Loryn Locklin, Lincoln Kilpatrick

Once again, future dystopias frown on people having sex at will. When Christopher Lambert and Loryn Locklin are caught trying to have an illegal second child, they are shipped to the Fortress, a miles-deep underground desert prison, run by a huge corporation with designs on the yet-to-be-born child. Act up in this slammer and you'll get a jolt on the "intestinator," a device implanted in each new prisoner allowing instantaneous and excruciating indigestible pain. Act up too often and face instant laser disembowelment, as one would expect from the director of *Re-Animator*. The sick fantasies of the cyber-warden (frequent hardass Kurtwood Smith) add to the merriment of this good-but-could-be-better, depressing-but-not-as-much-as-*Soylent Green* depiction of our wonderful future.

THE FOUNTAIN

2006 (PG-13) 96m / D: Darren Aronofsky / **W:** Darren Aronofsky / **C:** Hugh Jackman, Rachel Weisz, Ellen Burstyn, Mark Margolis, Stephen McHattie, Sean Patrick Thomas

Long-gestating epic from *Pi* dazzler Darren Aronofsky about three couples in different eras—conquistador and his queen, modern-day doctor and his cancer-sickened wife, and a futuristic traveler looking for his lost love—all played by the same people (Hugh Jackman and Rachel Weisz). Ideas about time, immortality, love, death, and eternity get thrown into the mix and ultimately ground into vaguely New Age muck centering around the idea of a tree of life. Visually dazzling throughout, particularly the futuristic scenes with an ancient tree drifting elegantly through space. Booed by most, cheered by a few die-hards who await the director's cut that seems inevitable.

4:44 LAST DAY ON EARTH

2011 (R) 82m / **D:** Abel Ferrara / **W:** Abel Ferrara / **C:** Willem Dafoe, Shanyn Leigh, Natasha Lyonne, Anita Pallenberg

Since *everyone* else was making an end-of-the-world movie in the 2010s, crusty New York filmmaker Abel Ferrara decided to give his own spin on the apocalypse. Like Don McKellar's *Last Night* and Lars von Trier's *Melancholia*, though, Ferrara's version is less about the why and more about how people spend their last hours. In this instance, the end times are due because of environmental collapse; the reckoning will happen at exactly 4:44 in the morning. In the meantime, we follow a painter (Shanyn Leigh) and an actor (Willem Dafoe) spending their last hours together in her apartment on the Lower East Side. When the apocalypse comes, it appears that people may well kill time beforehand by just arguing and eating takeout like any other night.

FRANKENSTEIN (1931)

1931 (NR) 71m / **D:** James Whale / **W:** Francis Edward Faragoh, Garrett Fort, John Balderston, Robert Florey / **C:** Boris Karloff, Colin Clive, Mae Clarke, John Boles, Dwight Frye, Edward Van Sloan, Frederick Kerr, Lionel Belmore

The definitive expressionistic Gothic horror film classic. Adapted from the Mary Shelley novel about Dr. Henry Frankenstein (Colin Clive), the mad scientist who creates life from death. He accidentally installs a criminal brain, making for a terrifying, yet strangely sympathetic monster. Great performances by Clive as the ultimate mad doctor and Boris Karloff as the tragically unfinished creation, which made him a monster star. Several powerful scenes, excised from the original version (including one in which the monster accidentally drowns a little girl, thinking that she'll float), were later restored. Generated too many sequels to count, almost none of which hold a candle to the original.

FRANKENSTEIN (1994)

1994 (R) 123m / **D:** Kenneth Branagh / **W:** Steph Lady, Frank Darabont / **C:** Robert De Niro, Kenneth Branagh, Tom Hulce, Helena Bonham Carter, Aidan Quinn, Ian Holm, Richard Briers, John Cleese

At the height of one of Hollywood's periodic manias for classic novel adaptations, Shakespearean vet Kenneth Branagh came up with this blood-and-

Of all the early Frankenstein's monster movies, the 1931 version with Boris Karloff conveyed the greatest sense of tragedy.

guts take on the 1818 Mary Shelley novel, a foundational sci-fi text. The idea here was to take the tragic story of scientific hubris and reinvention back to the source material and away from the bad joke which the old Universal films (and Mel Brooks) had turned it into. Robert De Niro (before he started taking any role offered him) gives his all as the new man made of sewed-together corpses, while Branagh revels as the arrogant doctor who thinks he can challenge the laws of nature. Layers on the mood and agony quite effectively. Sure to be redone again, but this was a good start toward reconnecting with Shelley's intentions. (A 2011 stage production by *Sunshine* director Danny Boyle starring Benedict Cumberbatch and Jonny Lee Miller was an even more visceral take.) Oscar nomination for best makeup. AKA: *Mary Shelley's Frankenstein*.

FRANKENSTEIN MEETS THE SPACE MONSTER

1965 (NR) 80m / D: Robert Gaffney / **W:** George Garret / **C:** James Karen, Nancy Marshall, Marilyn Hanold, David Kerman, Robert Reilly, Lou Cutell

Proclaimed by its writers—English professors at the University of Virginia—as the worst sci-fi/horror movie ever made, this wonder actually lives up (or down, as the case may be) to its billing. When a human-looking NASA android goes berserk after crash-landing in Puerto Rico, James Karen and Nancy Marshall are sent to track it down, but they instead run across weird-looking aliens intent on kidnapping poolside go-go girls for breeding purposes. They fix up their android buddy enough to try to stop the invaders, but the aliens counter-attack with their watchdog space monster, Mull. It was once shown at a drive-in with the reels out of order and no one noticed, or at least no one bothered to honk a horn. Required viewing for alternative aficionados. AKA: *Mars Invades Puerto Rico*; *Frankenstein Meets the Spacemen*; *Duel of the Space Monsters*.

FRANKENSTEIN'S ARMY

2013 (R) 84m / **D:** Richard Raaphorst / **W:** Chris Mitchell / **C:** Karel Roden, Joshua Sasse, Robert Gwilym, Alexander Mercury, Luke Newberry

It's 1945 and some Red Army troops are advancing through German territory when they come across a research lab where those ever-inventive Nazis have been using Victor Frankenstein's methods to sew together bits of soldiers (dead or not) and turn them into reanimated super-soldiers with knives for hands. Much running, screaming, and bloody ick follows. The idea here is that it's all found footage captured by a Russian cameraman; but then why is it in color? Also, how do the Nazis figure a few lurching cyborgs will turn the tide against, say, several dozen divisions of Soviet tanks? Questions aren't answered, blood is spilled.

The King of the B Movies, Roger Corman had not directed in 19 years when he returned to movies with *Frankenstein Unbound* in 1990.

FRANKENSTEIN UNBOUND

1990 (R) 86m / **D:** Roger Corman / **W:** Roger Corman, F. X. Feeney / **C:** John Hurt, Raul Julia, Bridget Fonda, Jason Patric, Michael Hutchence, Catherine Rabett, Nick Brimble, Catherine Corman, Mickey Knox

It took Roger Corman 19 years to decide to make a comeback, and he did it Corman-style, completing the shooting in seven weeks, co-writing the screenplay, and making a better-than-B "B" movie. It's 2031 and Dr. Joseph Buchanan is about to perfect the ultimate humanitarian weapon. No splattering, no charring, just instantaneous, implosionary vaporization. Quite thoughtful, really. Unfortunately, the experiment ruptures the time continuum and lands the Doc in Geneva, 1817. Upside is he gets to rub elbows with poet Percy Shelley, Lord Byron, future *Frankenstein* author Mary Shelley, and fellow scientist Victor Frankenstein (Raul Julia), whose own experiment has also gone haywire. In trying to create life, Victor has constructed a monster who kills Victor's six-year-old brother. Promising to cut out the murdering in exchange for love, the monster bullies the bad doctor into making him a mate. The monster is a surprisingly touching sort of brute and the climatic, apocalyptic time trip is sure to grab you. The atmosphere is striking, the effects are fun, the actors have fun, and the plot twists fly. Based on a novel by Brian Aldiss. AKA: *Roger Corman's Frankenstein Unbound*.

FREEJACK

1992 (R) 110m / **D:** Geoff Murphy / **W:** Dan Gilroy, Ronald Shusett, Steven Pressfield / **C:** Emilio Estevez, Mick Jagger, Rene Russo, Anthony Hopkins, Jonathan Banks, David Johansen, Amanda Plummer, Grand Bush, Frankie Faison, Esai Morales, John Shea

There is a $15 million bounty on Emilio Estevez's head, placed not by outraged *Men at Work* viewers, but by a tycoon who wants to achieve immortality by transplanting his deranged mind into Estevez's body. The year is 2009, when such "psychic surgery" is possible. Except that in the polluted future, uncontaminated host bodies are scarce. So scientists reach back to 1991, snatching race car driver Alex Furlong (Estevez) just before a fatal crash. Furlong escapes and the chase is on. Mick Jagger, as the chief bounty-hunting "bone-jacker," chose an ill-fated vehicle with which to return to the screen after two decades. Rene Russo also stars as the woman Alex left behind, but who 18 years later (she hasn't aged a bit) works for the very corporation hunting him down. A post-Hannibal Lecter Anthony Hopkins lends his freshly minted Oscar stature to the brief role of the tycoon who wants Estevez's body. Amanda Plummer gives another characteristically quirky performance as a groin-kneeing nun. Geoff Murphy also directed the sci-fi classic *This Quiet Earth*. Adapted from Robert Sheckley's more highly regarded novel, *Immortality Inc.*

FREQUENCY

2000 (PG-13) 118m / **D:** Gregory Hoblit / **W:** Toby Emmerich / **C:** Dennis Quaid, Jim Caviezel, Shawn Doyle, Elizabeth Mitchell, Andre Braugher, Noah Emmerich

New York cop Jim Caviezel starts fooling around with his dead father's old ham radio set only to end up being able to communicate, via the disruption of solar flares, 30 years back in time to when his firefighter dad was still alive. The two of them catch up on all the things they never said, and they get right to figuring out how to use this thing to set various things right, maybe solve some crimes. Hugely successful for its mix of dramatically convenient time-travel and three-handkerchief father-son bonding.

FREQUENTLY ASKED QUESTIONS ABOUT TIME TRAVEL

2009 (NR) 83m / **D:** Gareth Carrivick / **W:** Jamie Mathieson / **C:** Chris O'Dowd, Marc Wootton, Dean Lennox Kelly, Anna Faris

Lower-budget addition to the self-referential Brit sci-fi geekery of Edgar Wright and Simon Pegg has three friends in a pub who run into a young woman who claims to be a traveler from the future (Anna Faris). Before they know it, they're locked into a nest of time-travel paradoxes that quickly spin out of control.

FROM BEYOND

1986 (R) 90m / **D:** Stuart Gordon / **W:** Dennis Paoli, Brian Yuzna / **C:** Jeffrey Combs, Barbara Crampton, Ted Sorel, Ken Foree, Carolyn Purdy-Gordon, Bunny Summers, Bruce McGuire

A gruesome, tongue-in-cheek modern gothic based on a story by H. P. Lovecraft that goes way beyond its source material with highly original, occasionally shocking f/x. Two scientists discover a way to tap into another dimension by fooling around with a vibrating whatchamacallit that stimulates the human pineal gland. One of them turns into a rather amazing monster. Another guy is devoured by bees, and gigantic worm-like beasties turn up in the basement. Hero Jeffrey Combs must battle his transformed colleague, who in addition to a grotesque new body now has an unpleasant array of super-powers. From the makers of *Re-Animator*, and just as funny and unpredictable.

FROM THE EARTH TO THE MOON

1958 (NR) 100m / **D:** Byron Haskin / **W:** Robert Blees, James Leicester / **C:** George Sanders, Joseph Cotten, Debra Paget, Don Dubbins, Patric Knowles, Morris Ankrum

Is this trip really necessary? George Sanders and Joseph Cotten launch themselves (as well as Debra Paget) on the title voyage. Despite a top-flight cast, this never gets off the ground. Jules Verne has been served better on the screen with *The War of the Worlds*, Disney's *20,000 Leagues under the Sea*, *The Fabulous World of Jules Verne*, and *First Men in the Moon*. Not to be confused with the 1998 moon program documentary of the same name.

FUGITIVE ALIEN

1986 (NR) 103m / **D:** Kiyosumi Kuzakawa, Minoru Kanaya / **W:** Bunzou Wakatsuki, Hiroyasu Yamaura, Hideyoshi Nagasaka, Toyohiro Andô / **C:** Tatsuya Azuma, Miyuki Tanigawa, Joe Shishido, Choei Takahashi, Akihiko Hirata

Alien invaders from Valnastar and Earth forces battle it out. Ken, an enemy soldier with superhuman strength, deserts and becomes a hero for the home team. Dubbed and re-edited from Japanese, this is a condensation of part of a TV series from Tsuburaya Studios called Sutaurufu ("Starwolf"). As a result, the plot is rushed, episodic, and confusing. Joe Shishido, the chipmunk-cheeked star of flashy gangster films in the 1960s, turns up as hard-drinking Captain Joe. Followed by *Star Force: Fugitive Alien 2*.

FUTUREWORLD

1976 (PG) 107m / **D:** Richard T. Heffron / **W:** Mayo Simon, George Schenck / **C:** Peter Fonda, Blythe Danner, Arthur Hill, Yul Brynner, Stuart Margolin, John P. Ryan

In this inevitable yet at least competent sequel to Michael Crichton's *Westworld*, two reporters, one cynical and one enthusiastic, cover the grand reopening of the Delos theme park, closed since the disaster chronicled in the first film. The super-expensive park offers visitors experiences in different worlds, populated by robots who meet guests' every need. The exclusive park draws guests from the highest echelon of society who somehow can't imagine that the same problems could erupt again. Once again, however, Delos is the center of trouble as its head scientist and chief executive are up to no good. Convincing performances from Blythe Danner and Peter Fonda as the reporters and an intriguing premise help overcome the predictability of the story. Yul Brynner makes a cameo appearance as his memorable Gunslinger character from *Westworld*. Includes footage shot at NASA locations.

GALAXIS

1995 (R) 91m / **D:** William Mesa / **W:** Nick Davis / **C:** Brigitte Nielsen, Richard Moll, Craig Fairbrass

In a *Star Wars* opening, space tyrant Kila (Richard Moll) wipes out a planetful of rebels and seizes their magic crystal. A second crystal is hidden on present-day Earth and Kyla time-warps here after it. The physically impressive Brigitte Nielsen stars as alien freedom fighter Ladera, who beams down to battle the hammy villain. Derivative and joyless, it's an example of what happens when an f/x expert (William Mesa, who worked on Sam Raimi's *Army of Darkness*) turns director and gives visuals top priority.

GALAXY OF TERROR

1981 (R) 85m / **D:** B. D. Clark / **W:** Mark Siegler, B. D. Clark / **C:** Erin Moran, Edward Albert, Ray Walston, Grace Zabriskie, Sid Haig, Zalman King

Astronauts sent to rescue a stranded spaceship find themselves with a new mission: find the hidden alien leader in a mysterious pyramid (which contains a gauntlet of weird death traps) before they all get killed by vicious aliens. Big first: Erin Moran (Joanie on *Happy Days*) explodes. The entertaining cast also includes Sid Haig. Inferior Corman-produced *Alien* imitation still manages to shock and displays generous gore and nudity. Actor Zalman King later became a producer/director churning out piles of glossy soft-core like *Red Shoe Diaries*. Followed by *Forbidden World*. AKA: *Mindwarp: An Infinity of Terror*; *Planet of Horrors*.

Tim Allen (of TV's *Home Improvement* fame) plays a has-been sci-fi television series actor who is mistaken for the real thing by a dying alien race that need help from him and his crew of fellow actors.

GALAXY QUEST

1999 (PG) 102m / **D:** Dean Parisot / **W:** Robert Gordon, David Howard / **C:** Tim Allen, Sigourney Weaver, Alan Rickman, Tony Shalhoub, Sam Rockwell, Daryl Mitchell, Enrico Colantoni

The washed-up stars of a long-cancelled *Star Trek*-esque TV show (Tim Allen, Sigourney Weaver, Alan Rickman, Tony Shalhoub, Daryl Mitchell, all splendid) dutifully make the spirit-crushing rounds of store openings and fan conventions, signing autographs and shamefacedly fanning the cooled embers of their minor fame. They're so used to fans dressing up like aliens from the show that they don't realize one especially adoring band are *actually* aliens. Unfortunately, these aliens—who are being driven to extinction by another, quite nastier race—have been watching *Galaxy Quest* as well and think it's a documentary about a heroic crew who will help save them. Rickman's self-hating one-time Shakespearean is awesomely dour while Sam Rockwell is superb as the one-episode no-name actor who's terrified he's going to end up getting killed just like he was on the show. An uncommon sci-fi comedy that delivers in both genres.

GAMERA, THE INVINCIBLE

1966 (NR) 86m / D: Noriaki Yuasa / **W:** Fumi Takahashi / **C:** Eiji Funakoshi, Harumi Kiri-tachi, Junichiro Yamashiko, Yoshiro Uchida, Brian Donlevy, Albert Dekker, Diane Findlay, John Baragrey, Dick O'Neill, Yoshiro Kitahara

Fun Japanese monster movie that was Daiei Studio's answer to *Godzilla*. Gamera, a monstrous prehistoric turtle with huge tusks, is released from his arctic tomb by an ill-timed atomic explosion. Able to breathe fire and fly (presumably a side-effect of that pesky ol' radiation), the Shelled Wonder zooms around destroying things and generally causing panic. The first and probably the best of the *Gamera* series, this one is in black and white and portrays the mighty turtle as a villain. A turtle-obsessed little boy named Kenny, however, foreshadows Gamera's later transformation into "Friend to Children Everywhere." Like *Godzilla*, the American theatrical version of *Gamera* was altered to include added scenes featuring Anglo actors—in this case, Brian Donlevy and Albert Dekker as U.S. military men. This version has almost completely disappeared in favor of the current, more straightforward incarnation. After this initial outing, director Noriaki Yuasa stepped down to concentrate on only the f/x. The giant turtle returned for seven silly sequels full of juvenile hijinks aimed at children, before returning for a surprisingly good semi-remake in 1985. Dubbed in English. AKA: *Gamera*; *Gammera*.

GAMERA VS. BARUGON

1966 (NR) 101m / D: Shigeo Tanaka / **W:** Fumi Takahashi / **C:** Kojiro Hongo, Kyoko Enami, Akira Natsuki, Koji Fujiyama, Ichirô Sugai

The monstrous turtle returns to Earth after being freed from his outer-space prison by a passing meteor and battles with 130-foot lizard Barugon, who comes equipped with a rainbow-melting ray and a freeze gas-shooting tongue. This strange beast hatched from an egg smuggled to Japan from New Guinea and has been raising hell ever since. Tokyo and Osaka get melted and/or frozen in the process. This first sequel to *Gamera, the Invincible* is not quite as goofy as those that came later, and the battle scenes even achieve a sort of wacky grandeur. This Barugon is not to be confused with the monster Baragon, featured in Toho's *Frankenstein Conquers the World*. Star Kojiro Hongo returned for two more *Gamera* films. AKA: *Gamera Strikes Again*; *The War of the Monsters*.

GAMERA VS. GAOS

1967 (NR) 87m / D: Noriaki Yuasa / **W:** Nisan Takahashi / **C:** Kojiro Hongo, Kichijiro Ueda, Naoyuki Abe, Reiko Kasahara ow fully the good guy just a year after his film debut, giant flying turtle Gamera slugs it out with a bloodthirsty bat-like critter named Gaos, who has been gobbling up folks. Gaos is also able to generate ultra-powerful sound waves from his throat in the form of a cutting beam, which neatly slices a few vehicles in half. With Gamera recovering from injuries sustained from his first clash with Gaos, heroic scientists come up with an outrageous idea. Hundreds of gallons of blood are used to lure Gaos atop a revolving tower restaurant, in the hope that the beast will become too dizzy to escape until dawn, when the sunlight will destroy him. Aimless subplot about road construction and a young boy serves as filler. AKA: *The Return of the Giant Monsters*; *Gamera vs. Gyaos*; *Boyichi and the Supermonster*.

GAMERA VS. GUIRON

1969 (NR) 80m / **D:** Noriaki Yuasa / **W:** Nisan Takahashi / **C:** Nobuhiro Kashima, Christopher Murphy, Miyuki Akiyama, Yuko Hamada, Eiji Funakoshi

exy, leotard-clad aliens take two boys on a ride to a distant planet. They have fun playing with hi-tech equipment, until they find out the aliens really want to eat their brains. They call on the monster Gamera—who is Friend to All Children, lest we forget—to come rescue them, but the alien headquarters is guarded by the evil, cleaver-headed monster Guiron. Meanwhile, little sister tries to tell disbelieving adults about the abduction. List most kaiju films, this one has been released in multiple English-dubbed versions; in one of the more commonly available ones, the kooky alien girls have Southern accents, and in one scene we get to see Guiron slice up guest star Gaos like a sausage. Intentionally funny monster mind-twister. AKA: *Attack of the Monsters*.

GAMERA VS. ZIGRA

1971 (NR) 91m / **D:** Noriaki Yuasa / **W:** Nisan Takahashi / **C:** Reiko Kasahara, Mikiko Tsubouchi, Koji Fujiyama, Arlene Zoellner, Gloria Zoellner, Isamu Saeki, Yasushi Sakagami

amera the flying turtle visits Sea World to battle a cheap, shoddy-looking monster and hand out some cheap morality. Alien Zigrans try to wrest Earth from the hands of polluting humans. The alien monster Zigra nearly kills the staunch turtle, but some of his human friends revive him that he may defend Earth once more. A particularly tired episode in this series, as the producers padded out running time with stock footage from earlier films. Probably the only novelty is that Zigra can talk. AKA: *Gamera vs. the Deep Sea Monster Zigra*.

GAMES OF SURVIVAL

1989 (NR) 85m / **D:** Armand Gazarian / **W:** Lindsay Norgard / **C:** Nikki Hill, Cindy Coatman, Roosevelt Miller Jr.

A giant turtle named Gamera that flies like a spinning, jet-propelled top is one of the more imaginative creations of the Japanese monster movie genre.

Amusement-hungry masters of the planet Xenon teleport seven of the galaxy's most brutal warriors to an unsuspecting Earth to fight barbarian blood matches over a ball. The token good alien gets help from Los Angeleans against these non-American gladiators. Amateurish, badly photographed excuse for stunts and stupid dialogue.

THE GAMMA PEOPLE

1956 (NR) 76m / D: John Gilling / **W:** John Gilling, John Gossage / **C:** Walter Rilla, Paul Douglas, Eva Bartok

Cold War sci-fi in which two Eastern European journalists stumble into the obscure socialist state of Gudavia, where no-goodnik doctor uses gamma rays to turn kids into fanatical geniuses or adults into brainless zombies. Bland relic has very weak *Village of the Damned* vibes; they should have given the radioactive kids a crack at the script.

GAS-S-S-S!

1970 (R) 79m / D: Roger Corman **/ W:** George Armitage **/ C:** Bob Corff, Elaine Giftos, Bud Cort, Talia Shire, Ben Vereen, Cindy Williams

Depending on your point of view, this kitchen-sink apocalyptic comedy from Roger Corman was either his honest attempt to wrestle with the societal chaos of the late 1960s or a crass stab at jumping on the countercultural bandwagon (dig the special appearance by Country Joe and the Fish) via his American International Pictures outfit. Either way, the backdrop owes something to 1968's *Wild in the Streets*, with its nerve gas that turns everyone over the age of 25 into an instantly feeble oldster. Rambling structure follows a road trip that some hippies take from Dallas to find a friendly commune in New Mexico. Screenwriter George Armitage, who later specialized in comic crime stories like *Miami Blues*, shows up as Billy the Kid himself. AKA: *Gas! Or It Became Necessary to Destroy the World in Order to Save It*.

GATTACA

1997 (PG-13) 106m / D: Andrew Niccol **/ W:** Andrew Niccol **/ C:** Ethan Hawke, Uma Thurman, Jude Law, Alan Arkin, Loren Dean, Gore Vidal, Xander Berkeley, Elias Koteas, Maya Rudolph, Blair Underwood

Overly slick but purposeful sci-fi about the price of perfection. First-time writer/director Andrew Niccol posits a near-future where genetic advancements have made those with less-desirable DNA strands into a permanent underclass of undesirables, or "In-Valids." Ethan Hawke, blocked from advancement for being an In-Valid, colludes with the genetically perfect Jude Law (his American film debut) to climb the corporate ladder. Things get complicated: there's a murder, and Alan Arkin comes to investigate. Look for a grave and wooden Gore Vidal in a small role. The ideas are laid out there in obvious (Hawke's character's last name is Freeman) but occasionally provocative ways, such as one scene where a doctor guilts an expecting couple into genetically modifying their unborn baby: "We have enough imperfection built in already." Niccol's screenplay for *The Truman Show*, another suspicious look at a too-perfect society, would hit screens the following year. Oscar win for art direction.

GHIDRAH THE THREE-HEADED MONSTER

1965 (NR) 85m / D: Ishiro Honda **/ W:** Shinichi Sekizawa **/ C:** Akiko Wakabayashi, Yosuke Natsuki, Yuriko Hoshi, Hiroshi Koizumi, Takashi Shimura, Emi Ito, Yumi Ito, Kenji Sahara, Eiji Okada

This fun all-star monster fight is a more-or-less direct sequel to *Godzilla vs. Mothra*. When a three-headed monster from outer space threatens the world, hapless humans are forced to appeal to the (comparatively) friendly Mothra, Rodan, and Godzilla. Mothra's tiny priestesses are back (guests on a TV talk-show, no less). Ghidrah makes for an impressive monster, materializing out of a flaming meteorite. It's rock'em-sock'em giant monster action as poor Tokyo once again is threatened with the trampling of a lifetime. 1966 U.S. version was heavily re-edited, damaging continuity. Most viewers will likely be able to puzzle their way through. AKA: *Ghidora, the Three-Headed Monster*; *Ghidrah*; *The Greatest Battle on Earth*; *The Biggest Fight on Earth*; *Monster of Monsters*.

GHOST IN THE SHELL

1995 (NR) 82m / **D:** Mamoru Oshii / **W:** Kazunori Ito

Densely layered futuristic cyberpunk anime action that draws heavily in design from *Blade Runner* and in concept from *Neuromancer*, almost all for the good. A cyborg policewoman tries to hunt down a villainous computer intelligence known only as The Puppet Master, who has the power to inhabit both people and machines. The intricately designed tech noir atmosphere is extremely world-weary, and the script veers too much toward exposition-heavy monologues. But this remains one of the smarter and more forward-looking sci-fi films of the decade. Among the first anime designed explicitly to appeal to fans outside of the Japanese as well, and it shows. Based on a manga series, the film spawned a sequel nine years later and a couple offshoot series.

GHOSTS OF MARS

2001 (R) 98m / **D:** John Carpenter / **W:** Larry Sulkis, John Carpenter / **C:** Natasha Henstridge, Ice Cube, Pam Grier, Jason Statham, Clea DuVall

In 2176, Mars is being colonized, but it's taking awhile. Causing bigger problems is the recent discovery of a tunnel that unleashed Martian spirits that possess humans and turn them into rabid killers. So when supercop Natasha Henstridge leads a squad to a mining camp that's been overrun with these Red Planet zombies, she's got her work cut out for her. Disliked by John Carpenter fans for the chintzy f/x. At least it features Ice Cube as a character named Desolation Williams and an interesting twist on Martian human society of the future: It's matriarchal. A genre-bender from the increasingly unreliable Carpenter that marked his last sci-fi effort and the last time he worked with this many name performers

THE GIANT CLAW

1957 (NR) 76m / **D:** Fred F. Sears / **W:** Samuel Newman, Paul Gangelin / **C:** Jeff Morrow, Mara Corday, Morris Ankrum, Louis D. Merrill, Edgar Barrier, Robert Shayne, Morgan Jones, Clark Howat

A mix of science fiction and ghost story, *Ghosts of Mars* has colonists being possessed by Martian spirits.

Hilarious giant-monster flick with a buzzard-like bird that arrives from outer space to hatch an egg. It's surrounded by an anti-matter shield that makes it radar-invisible and prevents conventional weapons from doing any damage. The big bird will wreak a little havoc, and have a lot of fun before the inevitable down-in-flameless plunge, which will probably save the world for a little while longer. Scientist Mara Corday was *Playboy*'s Miss October, 1958. Goofy, goofy, goofy.

THE GLADIATORS

1970 (NR) 102m / **D:** Peter Watkins / **W:** Nicholas Gosling, Peter Watkins / **C:** Arthur Pentelow, Frederick Danner

In the near future, televised gladiatorial bouts known as Peace Games are designed to subdue man's violent tendencies until a computer makes a fatal error. A pre-*Hunger Games*, *Running Man*, and *Battle Royale* effort from *The War Game* director Peter Watkins, again using a faux-documentary approach to chilling effect. AKA: *The Peace Game*; *Gladiatorerna*.

GLEN AND RANDA

1971 (X) 94m / **D:** Jim McBride / **W:** Rudy Wurlitzer, Jim McBride / **C:** Steven Curry, Shelley Plimpton

Twenty years after a nuclear holocaust, two teenagers living with an isolated tribe strike out to explore the outside world after seeing images of a city in old comic books. Early Jim McBride film, before the hired-gun success of *The Big Easy*. Playfully trippy hippie script was worked on by Rudy Wurlitzer (*Two-Lane Blacktop*). Rated X for all that Flower Power nudity.

GOD TOLD ME TO

1976 (R) 89m / **D:** Larry Cohen / **W:** Larry Cohen / **C:** Tony Lo Blanco, Deborah Raffin, Sylvia Sidney, Sandy Dennis, Richard Lynch, Andy Kaufman

When this Larry Cohen-directed opus hit the screens, many TV stations refused to run the original trailer, fearing its nature too offensive. Religious New York cop (Tony Lo Bianco) is investigating a series of grisly murders. In each case when the murderers are questioned for their motives, they simply state "God told me to." Lo Bianco quickly becomes embroiled in the occult, finding his belief systems challenged by a "religious" cult composed of not-so-ordinary worshipers and a not-so-traditional "god." One of Cohen's subversive best. AKA: *Demon*.

GODZILLA

1998 (PG-13) 139m / **D:** Roland Emmerich / **W:** Dean Devlin, Roland Emmerich / **C:** Matthew Broderick, Jean Reno, Maria Pitillo, Hank Azaria, Kevin Dunn, Michael Lerner, Harry Shearer

After the solidly rah-rah military sci-fi duo of *Stargate* and *Independence Day*, Roland Emmerich decided to try somebody else's genre and the results weren't pretty. Figuring that Hollywood had never done a full-on, real-budget kaiju film where Godzilla gets to smash an American instead of a Japanese city. Like a latter-day Irwin Allen, Emmerich threw a murderer's row of random talent into the mix (Matthew Broderick as a curious scientist, Jean Reno as a shadowy French spy, and so on) and then spent every dime possible on making a Statue of Liberty-sized Godzilla look as scary as possible. The resulting demolition of large swaths of Manhattan doesn't quite work on any level, though a later scene in which Godzilla lays eggs in Madison Square Garden has an appealingly gonzo weirdness to it. Another American reboot followed in 2014.

GODZILLA, KING OF THE MONSTERS

1954 (NR) 80m / **D:** Ishiro Honda, Terry Morse / **W:** Takeo Murata, Ishiro Honda / **C:** Takashi Shimura, Raymond Burr, Akira Takarada, Akihiko Hirata, Momoko Kochi, Sachio Sakai

Monstrous prehistoric reptile emerges from the depths to terrorize Tokyo after being awakened by atomic testing (humanity never learning the lessons of previous awakenings). Godzilla is finally foiled by means of a heroic scientist's "oxygen destroyer," though as we all know, he would survive to

The monster Godzilla has become an icon of sorts in Japan. This statue of the beast is located at a plaza by the Hibiya Chanter Building in Tokyo, and there is another statue at Toho Studios.

menace Japan again and again. Raymond Burr scenes added in the 1956 American version (directed by Terry Morse), where he serves as a narrator telling the monster's tale in flashbacks. In addition, the scenes in which the scientist sacrifices himself to destroy Godzilla with his invention were downplayed in the U.S. release. Unlike many of the later sequels, the original Godzilla was a grim, serious movie that helped give voice to the world's collective fears about nuclear weapons. Significantly, it was one of the first post-WWII Japanese films to break through commercially in the U.S. Followed by 21(!) sequels to date. AKA: *Godzilla*; *Gojira*.

GODZILLA 1985

1985 (PG) 87m / D: Koji Hashimoto, Robert J. Kizer / **W:** Hidekazu Nagahara, Lisa Tomei / **C:** Keiju Kobayashi, Ken Tanaka, Raymond Burr, Yasuko Sawaguchi, Shin Takuma

Latter-day sequel released to coincide with the 30th anniversary of the original *Godzilla, King of the Monsters*. The Great Green One is awakened from underwater slumber by trolling nuclear submarines. The giant monster's newly acquired appetite for nuclear energy inadvertently precipitates an international incident. Raymond Burr is called in yet again to help mediate the conflict, being the only living American witness to Godzilla's destructive 1955 outburst. Sadly, the film doesn't quite make it; it's talky and lacks the original's monstrous urgency.

GODZILLA ON MONSTER ISLAND

1972 (PG) 89m / D: Jun Fukuda / **W:** Shinichi Sekizawa / **C:** Hiroshi Ichikawa, Tomoko Umeda, Yuriko Hishimi, Minoru Takashima, Zan Fujita, Kunio Murai, Toshiaki Nishizawa

Aliens conduct their nefarious schemes from the cover of Godzilla Tower in the World Children's Land amusement park—the nerve. When discovered by an unemployed cartoonist and his friends, aliens summon the giant three-headed dragon Ghidrah (last seen taking a beating in *Destroy All Monsters*) and giant cyborg space monster Gigan to destroy Earth. Godzilla and Angilas defend humanity from the invaders, perhaps to make up for all the times they smashed up Tokyo. Though perhaps not the very worst of the *Godzilla* series, this one's not a big favorite even among fans. The script is a disjointed mess and the f/x are either poorly executed or lifted from other films. An embarrassing highlight comes when Godzilla and Anguiras actually speak to each other—the original Japanese version wasn't much better, having the monsters' growls translated within little cartoon speech balloons. AKA: *Godzilla vs. Gigan*.

GODZILLA RAIDS AGAIN

1955 (NR) 78m / **D:** Motoyoshi Oda / **W:** Takeo Murata / **C:** Hiroshi Koizumi, Setsuko Wakayama, Minoru Chiaki

Warner Bros. had a problem securing rights to Godzilla's name and opted to release this theatrically using a monster pseudonym ("Gigantis"), doing some heavy editing while they're at it. In this first *Godzilla* sequel of the original series, a second Godzilla appears to cause trouble, while another monster—the spiny Anguiras—also appears to threaten mankind. They battle to the death while trashing Osaka. Although the monster scenes are fun, with Godzilla facing off against another creature for the first time, too much of the story centers around a fishing industry troubled by the behemoths. Cheapo f/x but the climax shows a lot of imagination. The American version was released four years later. AKA: *Gigantis, the Fire Monster*; *Godzilla's Counter Attack*.

GODZILLA'S REVENGE

1969 (G) 70m / **D:** Ishiro Honda / **W:** Shinichi Sekizawa / **C:** Kenji Sahara, Tomonori Yazaki, Machiko Naka, Sachio Sakai, Chotaro Togin, Yoshibumi Tajima

Not really a monster movie at all, but actually a strange juvenile drama. A young boy having problems with school, family, and local bullies dreams of going to Monster Island to learn from Minya, son of the boy's hero, Godzilla, who is having similar problems. Using the monster's lessons in real life, the boy captures some bandits and beats up the tough kid who's been bothering him (and even gets the girl). The scenes depicting the boy's bleak urban environment, as well as the harsh lessons he must learn in order to survive there, are surprisingly grim—somewhat at odds with the fantasy-filled adventure as intended. Shamelessly recycles footage from *Godzilla vs. the Sea Monster* and *Son of Godzilla* for battle scenes. Certainly the oddest *Godzilla* of all.

> **"Certainly the oddest**
> **Godzilla of all."**
>
> *Godzilla's Revenge*

GODZILLA VS. BIOLLANTE

1989 (PG) 104m / **D:** Kazuki Ohmori / **W:** Kazuki Ohmori / **C:** Koji Takahashi, Yoshiko Tanaka, Megumi Odaka, Kunihiko Mitamura

In this sequel to *Godzilla 1985*, Doctor Surigama's secret plant formula could free the industrialized world from oil dependency. He also runs his pet Godzilla experiment from the same laboratory. When terrorist thieves attempt to steal the plant formula, a petri dish mixup unleashes Biollante, a titanic rose-monster. Yes, rose-monster. As if a gigantic rosebush wasn't enough, Godzilla soon arrives to do some more Tokyo sight-seeing. The world's only hope may lie in the tendrils of Biollante itself. May come as a surprise to long-time fans of the *Godzilla* series since it's visually lush, with a moody and even poetic sensibility featuring a truly unforgettable monster. First appearance by psychic girl Miki Saegusa (Megumi Odaka), who became a series regular. The same team returned in 1991 for the even-better *Godzilla vs. King Ghidorah*.

GODZILLA VS. MECHAGODZILLA

1974 (G) 80m / **D:** Jun Fukuda / **W:** Jun Fukuda, Hiroyasu Yamamura / **C:** Masaaki Daimon, Kazuya Aoyama, Reiko Tajima, Hiroshi Koizumi, Akihiko Hirata, Kenji Sahara

Godzilla appears once again to ravage the Japanese countryside. Nothing new about that—until he beats up on his ol' pal Angilas. Then, a second Godzilla shows up to battle the first! The first monster's skin is torn away to reveal a robot version of Godzilla, which is under the control of evil apes from the black hole nebula (swiping an idea from the then-popular *Planet of the Apes* series). The apes don't seem like much of a threat—instead of just marching in to take over, they needed to enlist an Earth scientist to build Mechagodzilla. Why do they disguise the robot as Godzilla? Why do they disguise themselves as humans? Since Mechagodzilla is such a match for Godzilla, why not build two robots just to be sure? Enjoy the fireworks, as the giant monsters wage war across a crumbling cityscape. Originally released by AIP as *Godzilla vs. the Bionic Monster* in an attempt to cash in on *The Six Million Dollar Man* television series, the prints and ad campaign had to be quickly altered when a lawsuit was threatened. Remade for digital era in 2002. AKA: *Godzilla vs. the Bionic Monster*.

GODZILLA VS. MEGALON

1973 (G) 80m / **D:** Jun Fukuda / **W:** Jun Fukuda, Shinichi Sekizawa / **C:** Katsuhiko Sasaki, Hiroyuki Kawase, Yutaka Hayashi, Robert Dunham, Kotaro Tomita

Godzilla is once again a good guy in this outing, considered by many one of the series' worst. This time, the villainous "Seatopians" unleash two giant monsters to conquer the world: Megalon, a giant cockroach with drills for arms, and Gigan, a flying metal creature with a buzz-saw in its stomach. Fortunately, cyborg hero Jet Jaguar (sort of a low-rent Ultraman) is on hand to slug it out side by side with Tokyo's ultimate defender. Oh yes, and there's also an annoying little boy to round things out. Filled with clumsily used stock footage and laughable dialogue, this film was obviously aimed at children. A low mark in monster history. Adding insult to injury, NBC cut out half the footage and aired it in 1977 with campy segments hosted by John Belushi in a shoddy Godzilla costume.

GODZILLA VS. MONSTER ZERO

1965 (G) 93m / **D:** Ishiro Honda / **W:** Shinichi Sekizawa / **C:** Akira Takarada, Nick Adams, Kumi Mizuno, Jun Tazaki, Akira Kubo, Keiko Sawai

Novel *Godzilla* adventure with the big guy and Rodan in outer space. Suspicious denizens of Planet X (who wear some truly suspicious goggles) require the help of Godzilla and Rodan to rid themselves of the menacing "Monster Zero." Earth agrees to "lend" the Xians the monsters (they're transported through space in giant, levitating bubbles). Turns out that "Monster Zero" is none other than Godzilla's old foe Ghidrah, the three-headed superdragon. Will Godzilla and Rodan defeat Ghidrah? Will the men from Planet X help Earth in return for the favor, or is this just one big, fat double cross? Despite the shaky logic of the plot, this direct sequel to *Ghidrah the Three-Headed Monster* remains one of the more entertaining of Toho's kaiju films. The addition of Nick Adams as the hipster astronaut (at the suggestion of producer Henry Saperstein) provides as much amusement from his daddy-o dialogue and manner as it does the intended Anglo identification. Released in the U.S. In 1970 on a twin bill with *War of the Gargantuas*. AKA: *Monster Zero*; *Battle of the Astros*; *Invasion of the Astro-Monsters*; *Invasion of the Astros*; *Invasion of Planet X*.

GODZILLA VS. THE SEA MONSTER

1966 (PG) 80m / **D:** Jun Fukuda / **W:** Shinichi Sekizawa / **C:** Akira Takarada, Toru Watanabe, Hideo Sunazuka, Kumi Mizuno, Jun Tazaki

A young man and his friends steal aboard a sailboat, hoping to use it to find his brother, who was lost at sea. The "owner" of the boat turns out to be a thief, who happened to be hiding out on board. They all end up on an island guarded by a gigantic monster crustacean. The island is also the secret headquarters of a group of criminals bent on world domination. In a desperate gamble for survival, the new arrivals decide to awaken Godzilla, found sleeping in a cave, and the monster mayhem begins. This engaging adventure was originally planned as a *King Kong* film, but Toho Studios substituted Godzilla when rights to the big ape proved too expensive. The first of a trio of cost-cutting *Godzilla* adventures set on South Pacific islands,

Godzilla has appeared in over two dozen movies and has fought everything from King Kong to an android version of himself.

where no miniature cities were required. Alas, no cities to stomp into oblivion. Also the first *Godzilla* film for director Jun Fukuda, who would go on to helm four others, although none would turn out quite as well as this one. AKA: *Ebirah, Terror of the Deep*; *Big Duel in the North Sea*.

GODZILLA VS. THE SMOG MONSTER

1971 (PG) 87m / **D:** Yoshimitsu Banno / **W:** Kaoru Mabuchi, Yoshimitsu Banno / **C:** Akira Yamauchi, Hiroyuki Kawase, Toshie Kimura

Godzilla battles a creature borne of pollution, an ever-growing sludge blob named Hedora. Godzilla fans expecting another apocalyptic sci-fi adventure of mythical proportions may be disappointed. Avant-garde director Yoshimitsu Banno tried to take this *Godzilla* film further into surrealism, with mixed results. Some scenes are illustrated with animated children's drawings. Japanese teenagers marshal their dancing talents to combat the threat amid the hypnotic swirl of disco lighting. Great opening song: "Save the Earth." Hedora is seen flying over crowds of people as they drop in their tracks, dead from poison gas—and yet, at one point, the monster spares a little kitten. Just plain odd, but in the best way. The anti-pollution message is strident in keeping with the original's fear of atomic testing. AKA: *Godzilla vs. Hedora*.

GORATH

1962 (NR) 83m / **D:** Ishiro Honda / **W:** Takeshi Kimura / **C:** Ryo Ikebe, Akihiko Hirata, Jun Tazaki, Yumi Shirakawa, Takashi Shimura, Kumi Mizuno

A collapsed star is on a collision course with Earth. Top scientists of 1979 cooperate internationally to construct huge nuclear jet engines in the Antarctic to literally shove Earth out of Gorath's path. Imaginative details (à la Immanuel Velikovsky, who wrote the 1950 bestseller *Worlds in Collision*) show disasters spawned by Gorath's gravity, like the sucking away of Saturn's rings. Because Toho Studios specialized in giant monster movies, a last-minute cast addition was "Magma," a prehistoric walrus awakened by the heat. He was cut from the U.S. release—no great loss—but the re-edits and clumsy dubbing (half the actors speak with distinct pipes of voiceover artist Paul Frees) lend a tacky feel to this elaborate space-disaster drama.

GORGO

1961 (NR) 78m / **D:** Eugene Lourie / **W:** John Loring, Daniel Hyatt / **C:** Bill Travers, William Sylvester, Vincent Winter, Bruce Seton, Christopher Rhodes, Joseph O'Conor

An undersea explosion off the coast of Ireland brings to the surface a prehistoric sea monster, which is captured and brought to a London circus. All seems well, until scientists learn that Gorgo is but an infant. Its irate (and much larger) mother appears looking for her baby, creating havoc in her wake. Though London had been used as a setting for monster rampages before (director Eugene Lourie had done so just two years before in *The Giant Behemoth*), never has the destruction been quite as spectacular—although the monsters are portrayed by stiff costumes, the miniatures and matte work are impressive. Commonly mistaken by critics as the only monster movie where "the monster wins"—giant movie monsters seem to get away with their rampages quite often, even as far back as 1925's *The Lost World*.

GRAND TOUR: DISASTER IN TIME

1992 (PG-13) 98m / **D:** David N. Twohy / **W:** David N. Twohy / **C:** Jeff Daniels, Ariana Richards, Emilia Crow, Jim Haynie, Nicholas Guest, Marilyn Lightstone, George Murdock

"Grand, simply grand." The aliens visiting Jeff Daniels's midwestern inn are among the most terrifying ever put on film. They have no superpowers. They do not wish to rule our planet. Worse, they are tourists so bored with their perfect world that they have become disaster junkies, time-traveling to catch such cataclysmic events as the 1906 San Francisco earthquake, the *Hindenberg* crash, and the eruption of Mt. St. Helens. Starts off slow, but things pick up after Daniels is given some friendly words of advice: "Leave. Today. Take your family and do not come back until you're absolutely certain it is safe." David Twohy went on to direct *The Arrival*. AKA: *Timescape*.

GRAVITY

2013 (PG-13) 90m / **D:** Alfonso Cuarón / **W:** Alfonso Cuarón, Jonas Cuarón / **C:** Sandra Bullock, George Clooney

Alfonso Cuarón took seven years after *Children of Men* to make another feature, but it was worth it. This alternately quiet and nerve-shredding story is an atmospheric frightener in which two astronauts, rookie Sandra Bullock and cocky veteran George Clooney, fight to survive after debris from an exploded satellite destroys their space shuttle. What happens after is an exercise in the deadly physics of isolation. At 400 miles above the

In *Gravity*, Sandra Bullock is the last surviving crew member of her mission when the space shuttle is hit by debris from an exploded satellite.

earth's surface, there is no sound but the ominous score and Bullock's panicked breathing. When a satellite disintegrates before their eyes, the quietness of the disaster and Cuarón's long takes are more panic-inducing than the most drum-pounding Michael Bay music and smash edits. The technical realism makes it not *quite* sci-fi but adventurous enough in scope and gorgeously imaginative in its Kubrickian display of cold beauty that it deserves inclusion regardless. Ed Harris voices Mission Control in a respectful nod to *Apollo 13*. Ten Oscar nominations and seven wins, including for best directing and f/x.

GREEN LANTERN

2011 (PG-13) 114m / D: Martin Campbell / **W:** Greg Berlanti, Michael Green, Marc Guggenheim, Michael Goldenberg / **C:** Ryan Reynolds, Blake Lively, Peter Sarsgaard, Mark Strong, Tim Robbins

Slipping in between *Iron Man* and *Batman* sequels during the 2010s' comic-book movie binge, this unloved adaptation of DC's Green Lantern character tries to take things in a less Earth-bound direction. Fighter jockey Ryan Reynolds is busy being a top gun (crashing planes, getting girls) when a crash-landed alien hands him a magical green ring and tells him he's been chosen to be one of the Green Lantern Corps, who defend the Galaxy. Specifically, he needs to defend Earth against the evil entity Parallax and villainous scientist Peter Sarsgaard. Any bets on whether he rises to the challenge? Mega budget is blown on the f/x depicting the other alien Green Lanterns—not to mention the "yellow power of fear."

THE SCI-FI MOVIE GUIDE: The Universe of Film from "Alien" to "Zardoz"

GREMLINS

1984 (PG) 106m / **D:** Joe Dante / **W:** Chris Columbus / **C:** Zach Galligan, Phoebe Cates, Hoyt Axton, Polly Holliday, Frances Lee McCain, Keye Luke, Dick Miller, Corey Feldman, Judge Reinhold, Glynn Turman

An appealing comedy/horror tale about fuzzy gnomes who turn into murderous goblins, delivered with an unexpectedly satiric edge. Produced by Steven Spielberg, at a time when he was backing kid-targeted hit after hit. A fumbling gadget salesman named Rand Peltzer (Hoyt Axton) is looking for something really special to get his son Billy for Christmas. He finds it in a dingy little store run by a wise Chinese shopkeeper. The shopkeeper is reluctant to sell him the adorable, bulgy-eyed, furry, lisping, sweet-natured, not-at-all-revolting "mogwai." He eventually relents, but not before laying down the three commandments of mogwai ownership: "Don't expose him to bright light, don't get him wet, and don't ever, *ever* feed him after midnight." Naturally, those rules are all quickly broken and the result is a gang of nasty, reptilian gremlins who tear up the town on Christmas Eve. The film is a wild, good-natured romp, but there's a decidedly dark side to its humor that might make it less appropriate for kids than the PG rating would suggest. Some might prefer the sequel's lighter laughs.

GREMLINS 2: THE NEW BATCH

1990 (PG-13) 107m / **D:** Joe Dante / **W:** Charles Haas / **C:** Phoebe Cates, Christopher Lee, John Glover, Zach Galligan, Robert Prosky, Richard Picardo

Lightning strikes twice in this sequel that manages to repeat the premise of the original on a bigger canvas. Here, director Joe Dante presents a less violent but far campier tale of critters on the rampage. This time the gremlins take Manhattan, getting into a research lab housed in a skyscraper; disaster results as the little monsters get everywhere. The film pays cracked tribute to classics like *The Wizard of Oz* and musical extravaganzas of the past (the gremlins' version of "New York, New York" is not to be missed). Tony Randall is splendid as the voice of "the Brain," a gremlin inadvertently given super intelligence, while the likes of Christopher Lee and John Glover gloriously ham it up.

THE GROUNDSTAR CONSPIRACY

1972 (PG) 103m / **D:** Lamont Johnson / **W:** Douglas Heyes / **C:** George Peppard, Michael Sarrazin, Christine Belford, Cliff Potts, James Olson, Tim O'Connor, James McEachin, Alan Oppenheimer

Spy thriller with sci-fi twist very loosely based on L. P. Davies's novel *The Alien*. After an explosion kills all but one space project scientist, George

Peppard is sent to investigate suspicions of a cover-up. Meanwhile, the surviving scientist (Michael Sarrazin) suffers from disfigurement and amnesia. He pursues his identity while Peppard accuses him of being a spy. Splendid direction by Lamont Johnson. Sarrazin's best role.

THE GUYVER

1991 (PG-13) 88m / **D:** Steve Wang, Screaming Mad George / **W:** Jon Purdy / **C:** Mark Hamill, Vivian Wu, David Gale, Jeffrey Combs, Michael Berryman, Jack Armstrong, Jimmie Walker

Wimp college student is transformed into a chitinous superhero thanks to his discovery of an organic alien battle suit, the "Guyver," and helps CIA agent Mark Hamill keep the device from falling into the claws of Zoanoids, evil mutants guiding the evolution of mankind. Based on a popular Japanese comic book (and resulting cartoons), this rather predictable series of creature wrestling matches has its roots in Ultraman, Infra-Man, and other futuristic good guys who combat guest-starring monstrosities. Co-director and legendary f/x artist Screaming Mad George endows each Zoanoid with a different grotesque look, and thus the whole thing feels like an excuse for the collectible trading cards. Incredibly, there is a director's cut. AKA: *Mutronics*. A direct-to-video sequel *sans* Hamill followed in 1994.

H

HACKERS

1995 (PG-13) 105m / D: Iain Softley / **W:** Rafael Moreu / **C:** Jonny Lee Miller, Angelina Jolie, Fisher Stevens, Lorraine Bracco, Jesse Bradford, Wendell Pierce, Alberta Watson, Laurence Mason, Renoly Santiago, Matthew Lillard, Penn Jillette

Teenage computer hackers break into the wrong system in this desperately hip and calculated attempt to cash in on the then-burgeoning Internet. When Dade (Jonny Lee Miller) breaks into the computer system at Ellingson Oil, he becomes the perfect scapegoat for the industrial espionage being conducted by corporate security chief Fisher Stevens. The underground hackers band together in an effort to clear their good names and buy better hardware. Unfortunately, without the techno gadgets, the plot is mundane. Miller and Angelina Jolie (her first starring role) generate a good amount of chemistry between them, but Stevens is about as scary as a kitten with a ball of yarn. Director Iain Softley (*K-Pax*), despite taking drastic liberties with the technology, does a good job with the visuals, taking viewers inside the minds of the hackers, rather than just watching geeks type. A snappy techno soundtrack adds spice to this otherwise flavorless faux-cyberpunk thriller. Look for magician Penn Jillette (of Penn & Teller) in a small role.

THE HANDMAID'S TALE

1990 (R) 109m / D: Volker Schlöndorff / **W:** Harold Pinter / **C:** Natasha Richardson, Robert Duvall, Faye Dunaway, Aidan Quinn, Elizabeth McGovern, Victoria Tennant, Blanche Baker, Traci Lind

Set in "the recent future" when "a country went wrong," this fundamentally sterile adaptation of Margaret Atwood's best-selling novel still manages to be chilling thanks to its perennially relevant premise. Militant Old

Testament fundamentalists seize control of the United States and establish a theocratic police state renamed Gilead. Smoking, drinking, and sex are officially outlawed. Abortion is punishable by hanging. An ecological disaster has left most of the population infertile. The women who can still reproduce are packed off for indoctrination before they are assigned to the homes of infertile couples as surrogate "handmaids." Natasha Richardson stars as a fertile woman whose escape attempt lands her in the home of Robert Duvall and his increasingly resentful wife, Faye Dunaway, who, in a ceremony inspired by the Old Testament, is present in bed while her husband tries to conceive with Richardson. Elizabeth McGovern energizes her scenes as a "gender-traitor," who recruits Richardson to join the rebels and assassinate the Commander.

THE HAPPENING

2008 (R) 91m / **D:** M. Night Shyamalan / **W:** M. Night Shyamalan / **C:** Mark Wahlberg, Zooey Deschanel, John Leguizamo, Ashlyn Sanchez, Betty Buckley, Spencer Breslin

For his first R-rated film, M. Night Shyamalan used a real phenomenon then just starting (the rapid die-off of bee colonies) as a springboard to a Hitchcockian exercise in invisible fear. Members of a small family go on a run

> "Shyamalan's usual mastery of the dreadful quiet and slow-building fright is stretched here to its breaking point....
>
> *The Happening*

when an atmospheric disturbance seems to sweep through people in Central Park, causing them to wander around in confusion and then kill themselves. (Thus, the R-rating, unusual for Shyamalan.) There's little in the way of cataclysmic crowd scenes or urban destruction so beloved of the modern disaster film. In fact, Shyamalan's quieter, character-centric approach presages some of the smaller-budget, more personal apocalypse films that would follow years later. Shyamalan's usual mastery of the dreadful quiet and slow-building fright is stretched here to its breaking point by a premise that begins as one of those universally terrifying sci-fi tropes (the planet suddenly going insane as revenge on wicked humanity) but gets awfully thin the longer it's played out.

HARDWARE

1990 (R) 94m / **D:** Richard Stanley / **W:** Richard Stanley / **C:** Dylan McDermott, Stacey Travis, John Lynch, William Hootkins

Post-apocalyptic ragpicker gives artist Stacey Travis some robot remains he collected (ours is not to ask why). The skeletal 'droid she reassembles turns out to be a government-spawned population controller programmed to destroy warm bodies—though looks more like a heavy metal drummer, thanks to Simon Boswell's delirious music-video camerawork. With more attitude than originality (and some carnage excised to avoid an X rating), this holds one's attention only briefly. Due to a plagiarism lawsuit, the tape now carries a tacked-on end credit attributing the story to *SHOK!*, a piece in the cult comic book *2000 A.D.* Iggy Pop is heard in voiceover only as DJ Angry Bob, while former Sex Pistol John Lydon performs the theme song. Motorhead's grizzled Lemmy appears as a cabbie. Most notable for the industrial soundtrack.

HAVE ROCKET WILL TRAVEL

1959 (NR) 76m / D: David Lowell Rich / **W:** Raphael Hayes / **C:** Moe Howard, Larry Fine, Joe DeRIta, Anna-Lisa, Jerome Cowan, Bob Colbert

Three janitors of dubious expertise (named Moe, Larry, and Curly Joe) help a scientist who is about to lose her job if she can't send a rocket to Venus. They accidentally initiate the launch while still onboard and introduce their brand of slapstick to a whole new planet. While on Venus (which looks a lot more like Colorado), the boys encounter a unicorn who speaks archaic English, a giant spider, and clones of themselves. This feature-length film gave the Stooges' lagging careers a jump-start and led to five more movies, including *The Three Stooges Go Around the World in a Daze* and *The Three Stooges Meet Hercules* (!).

THE HEAD

1959 (NR) 97m / D: Victor Trivas / **W:** Victor Trivas / **C:** Horst Frank, Michel Simon, Paul Dahlke, Karin Kernke, Helmut Schmid, Christiane Maybach, Dieter Eppler

Mad scientist (whose lab-enhanced genius has driven out all conscience) keeps the head of an old surgeon alive when the guy's heart fails. The unhappy cranium reluctantly assists the villain in his personal project to transfer the head of a hunchbacked nurse to the body of a beautiful stripper. Moody cinematography and production design is reminiscent of German Expressionism from the great days of silent cinema, but it doesn't quite help. Lurid, tacky cheapie.

HEARTBEEPS

1981 (PG) 79m / D: Allan Arkush / **W:** John Hill / **C:** Andy Kaufman, Bernadette Peters, Randy Quaid, Kenneth McMillan, Christopher Guest, Melanie Mayron, Jack Carter

In a 1995 very different from what we experienced, two domestic robot-servants fall in love and run off together. This weird sci-fi romance from director Alan Arkush (*Rock 'n' Roll High School*, *Heroes*) isn't without its charms, and Andy Kaufman and Bernadette Peters tackle their robotic parts gamely enough. Comedy pitched between the surreal and juvenile,

Kinky space opera with a hard rock sound track combined to create the animated cult favorite *Heavy Metal*.

while the f/x are on the level of an early *Dr. Who* episode. A few loose screws too many. Oscar nomination for makeup.

HEAVY METAL

1981 (R) 90m / D: Gerald Potterton / **W:** Dan Goldberg, Len Baum / **C:** Rodger Bumpass, Jackie Burroughs

Midnight movie-staple anthology of animated tales loosely derived from the "adult comics" mag of the same name. The stories are all vaguely connected by the presence of a malevolent green globe that somehow represents Ultimate Evil. Best of the tales is the John Carter of Mars-esque "Den," in which a teenage boy is thrown across space and time into the body of a mighty warrior; he's thrust into an ages-old fight between religious cults, rescues bare-breasted babes, and has a general, all-around good time. Occasionally impressive animation, but highly dependent on one's tolerance for T&A, forced drug humor, and a discordant soundtrack that runs the gamut of 1970s lameness and brilliance (Devo to Nazareth). SCTV's John Candy and Eugene Levy provided some of the voices. Based on original art and stories by Richard Corben, Angus McKie, Dan O'Bannon, Thomas Warkentin, and Berni Wrightson. Very, very *heavy*.

HEAVY METAL 2000

2000 (R) 88m / D: Michael Coldeway, Michel Lemire / **W:** Kevin Eastman

Sequel of sorts to the earlier cult animated anthology, this one follows just one story (busty warrior woman battles evil pirate after he kills most of her family) and has a soundtrack of 1990s aggro-metal. By the time this came out, the landscape of cult films had changed so much, fans of the first barely noticed; that, or they had gone sober. AKA: *Heavy Metal F.A.K.K.2.*

HELLBOY

2004 (PG-13) 122m / D: Guillermo del Toro / **W:** Guillermo del Toro / **C:** Ron Perlman, John Hurt, Selma Blair, Rupert Evans, Karel Roden, Jeffrey Tambor, Doug Jones

Guillermo del Toro's energetic take on Mike Mignola's Lovecraftian comic-book series about a good-hearted demon who was conjured up as a baby in a Nazi occult ceremony but who later went to work for the forces of good has a few things going for it. Most importantly, a gravely sarcastic Ron Perlman underneath slabs of red latex as the grumpy, cigar-smoking Hellboy himself. Also, the set decoration has the same kind of baroque appeal as delf Toro's Spanish-language films like *Pan's Labyrinth*. The story is much as one would expect, with the forces of darkness and various Nazis trying to take over the world and only Hellboy and his employers, the Bureau of Paranormal Research and Defense, able to stop them. But Perlman's deadpan and the welcome presence of John Hurt as his kindly benefactor turn this into a better-than-average comic-book smash-'em-up.

HELLBOY II: THE GOLDEN ARMY

2008 (PG-13) 120m / **D:** Guillermo del Toro / **W:** Guillermo del Toro / **C:** Ron Perlman, Selma Blair, Doug Jones, Luke Goss, John Alexander, James Dodd, Seth MacFarlane, Jeffrey Tambor

Too many times to the well hurt this sequel to Guillermo del Toro's first *Hellboy* film. The cast remains appealing, in particular Doug Jones as Hellboy's fey butler-esque sidekick; imagine Jeeves as a fish-like humanoid with blue skin and web-like hands. This time, the threat to the world comes from an underground kingdom of elves and fairies, who signed a treaty with humans a long time ago, which humans reneged on by overbuilding. A vengeful elvish prince wants to unleash his people's indestructible mechanical Golden Army; Hellboy and his giant rock fist stand in his way. The creature feature designs are nothing less than splendid, with five movies' worth of nightmarish and yet gorgeous beasties packing every frame of certain scenes. But the Babylonian excess doesn't make up for a rote feeling to the apocalypse-is-nigh story. Oscar nomination for makeup.

HELL COMES TO FROGTOWN

1987 (R) 88m / **D:** Donald G. Jackson, Robert J. Kizer / **W:** Randall Frakes / **C:** Roddy Piper, Sandahl Bergman, Rory Calhoun, Cec Verrell

When you're running with the *Mad Max* ripoff pack, you need gimmicks to stand out, and this one sure has a few. In post-nuclear holocaust land, hostile mutant frog people abduct precious, fertile human women. Sam Hell (thesp'd by "Rowdy" Roddy Piper, of pro wrestling and *They Live* fame), being one of the few fertile males left, is a government-sanctioned stud and must rescue the ladies to impregnate them. Fitfully fun sci-fi spoof has some good frog getups despite the extreme low-budget. Filmmaker Donald G. Jackson also did postnuke cheapie *Roller Blade*, as well as an unfortunate *Frogtown* sequel.

HER

2013 (R) 120m / D: Spike Jonze / **W:** Spike Jonze / **C:** Joaquin Phoenix, Scarlett Johansson, Amy Adams, Rooney Mara, Olivia Wilde, Matt Letscher

The near-future is an Apple commercial in this gauzy, soft-filter, highly color-coordinated pseudo-parable about lonely divorced Theodore (Joaquin Phoenix), who turns to a new service promising a personalized operating system and gets more than he'd bargained for. The OS turns out to be a chipper and flirty personality (voiced by Scarlett Johansson) that names itself Samantha and seems to already know him better than he knows himself. As Theodore and Samantha's relationship goes quickly from surprised friendship to actual romance, he's ecstatic, thinking he's found a soul mate. In contrast, interactions with actual humans (ex-wife Rooney Mara, best friend Amy Adams, blind date Olivia Wilde) can't quite compare, since after all they're not programmed to fulfill his every need. The not-quite-real look of the film is like walking through an ultra-hip design agency, all bright primary colors and the reassuringly soft hum of personalized technology. Furthering the futuristic dissonance is the setting: technically Los Angeles, but much of it was shot in Shanghai. But while Jonze pushes the boundaries of the human-technological relationship further and more convincingly than most modern sci-fi—scenes where people start integrating their OS's into life as just another friend or lover are startlingly plausible, particularly for anybody who's lost an acquaintance to the lure of a smartphone—the film never truly grapples with the darker side of its proposition. Five Oscar nominations; won for best original screenplay.

> "The not-quite-real look of the film is like walking through an ultra-hip design agency...."
>
> *Her*

HERCULES AGAINST THE MOON MEN

1965 (NR) 88m / D: Giacomo Gentilomo / **W:** Arpad De Riso, Nino Scolaro, Angelo Sangermano, Giacomo Gentilomo / **C:** Alan Steel, Jany Clair, Anna Maria Polani, Nando Tamberlani

One of the more visually striking of the many 1960s bargain-basement *Hercules* movies. The big guy is summoned to an isolated kingdom in the shadow of the Mountain of Death, wherein live a race of beings from the moon, brought to Earth by a prehistoric meteorite. The moon-men themselves are groovy-looking humanoids made of jagged rock and led by a really tall guy with an impressive metallic skull-mask. They promise the kingdom's evil queen immortality in return for a human sacrifice every year. Young lovers are separated, oppressed peasants plot revolution, and time is drawing near to revive the moon-men's dead queen Selena. Can Herc triumph? Not even fun to make fun of.

HERCULES IN NEW YORK

1970 (G) 93m / D: Arthur Seidelman / **W:** Aubrey Wisberg / **C:** Arnold Schwarzenegger, Arnold Stang, Deborah Loomis, James Karen, Ernest Graves

Arnold Schwarzenegger's motion-picture debut, wherein he plays the muscle-bound son of Zeus. In a sort of mythological precursor to *The Terminator*, Hercules is transported through time by his deity dad to 20th-century Manhattan. Schwarzenegger (his voice is dubbed in the original, but the future governor of California redid the dialogue himself in later releases) and his geeky friend Arnold Stang have all kinds of fun in the Big Apple, including driving a chariot up Broadway. Wouldn't you, if you had the chance? Eventually the muscle-bound future star becomes a professional wrestling superstar. Two hundred and fifty pounds of highly stupid, lighthearted fun. AKA: *Hercules: The Movie*; *Hercules Goes Bananas*.

THE HIDDEN

1987 (R) 98m / D: Jack Sholder / **W:** Bob Hunt / **C:** Kyle MacLachlan, Michael Nouri, Clu Gulager, Ed O'Ross, Claudia Christian, Clarence Felder, Richard Brooks, William Boyett

Seasoned cop Michael Nouri and a benign alien posing as an FBI agent (Kyle MacLachlan, working that blank affect that served him so well in David Lynch films at the time) team up to track down and destroy a hyperviolent alien life-form that lives for fast cars and loud rock music and survives by invading the bodies of humans, causing them to go on murderous rampages. Overly derivative 1980s *Terminator/Robocop* sci-fi action material about indestructible beings in human shape, but decent sense of humor, high-velocity action, and credible performances later earned a substantial cult following. MacLachlan bowed out of the inevitable and unworthy 1994 sequel.

THE HIDEOUS SUN DEMON

1959 (NR) 75m / D: Robert Clarke / **W:** E. S. Seeley Jr. / **C:** Robert Clarke, Patricia Manning, Nan Peterson

A physicist exposed to radiation must stay out of sunlight or he will turn into a scaly, lizard-like creature. Commonly lumped in with most other 1950s radioactive monster pictures, but stands slightly apart for being a kind of allegory for alcoholism. Star/director Robert Clarke hides from the sun all day, but stays out all night in saloons, eventually alienating his friends as the monster within him takes control. The scene of the maddened Clarke eating a rat was excised from most TV prints, but was later restored,

In *Highlander* Sean Connery and Christopher Lambert are immortals who are fated to kill all other immortals until only one is left to inherit their combined power.

thus ensuring viewers will appreciate the film-maker's complete artistic vision. AKA: *Blood on His Lips; Terror from the Sun*.

HIGHLANDER

1986 (R) 110m / **D:** Russell Mulcahy / **W:** Gregory Widen, Peter Bellwood, Larry Ferguson / **C:** Christopher Lambert, Sean Connery, Clancy Brown, Roxanne Hart, Beatie Edney, Alan North, Sheila Gish, Jon Polito

Action-fantasy about "immortals," a race of people occasionally born to regular humans who must meet in battle down through the centuries, decapitating each other—the only way to kill one—until the last survivor inherits their accumulated power. Christopher Lambert is 16th-century Scotsman Connor MacLeod, whose feud with an equally ageless foe ultimately comes to blows in modern Manhattan. Sean Connery makes a memorably wry appearance as MacLeod's mentor, but the real energy comes from spectacular swordfights and death scenes, plus a glam-rock lyricism thanks to musical inserts by Queen. A cult fave for Russell Mulcahy's flashy visual style, this spawned weak sequels (which more or less jettisoned the already loose logic of the original) and inspired both animated and live-action TV spinoffs.

HIGHLANDER II: THE QUICKENING

1991 (R) 90m / **D:** Russell Mulcahy / **W:** Peter Bellwood / **C:** Christopher Lambert, Sean Connery, Virginia Madsen, Michael Ironside, John C. McGinley

Even Christopher Lambert disowned this second chapter in the saga of Connor MacLeod, which tries retroactively to explain everything that happened in the first movie in a sci-fi context. Now we learn that immortals are political exiles from the planet Zeist, whose psycho tyrant (Michael Ironside), not satisfied to let MacLeod die old in the year 2024, sends flying porcupine men to Earth to restore the Highlander to youth so they can kill him. As long as that's clear. There's a sense the filmmakers were seriously drunk when they made this; in any case, Connery looks like he's having fun. Visual f/x are extremely iffy. A so-called "Renegade Director's Cut" is available at 108 minutes.

HIGHLANDER: ENDGAME

2000 (R) 87m / **D:** Douglas Aarniokoski / **W:** Joel Soisson / **C:** Christopher Lambert, Adrian Paul, Bruce Payne, Lisa Barbuscia, Donnie Yen

The third *Highlander* sequel finds Connor MacLeod (Christopher Lambert) starting to get a little long in the tooth for an immortal. This entering finds MacLeod waging a centuries-long war (which the previous films didn't bother mentioning) against another immortal (Bruce Payne), who's not playing by the rules of There Can Be Only One. Connor gets a sidekick, his old clansman Duncan MacLeod, who starred in the *Highlander* TV series.

HIGHLANDER: THE FINAL DIMENSION

1994 (PG-13) 99m / **D:** Andrew Morahan / **W:** Paul Ohl / **C:** Christopher Lambert, Mario Van Peebles, Deborah Kara Unger, Mako

Pointedly ignores what went on in the second *Highlander* but can't claim much of an improvement. Immortal Connor MacLeod (Christopher Lambert) battles sadistic master illusionist Kane (Mario Van Peebles, hamming it up laughably amid all the computer-generated f/x), who seeks to rule the world. MacLeod returns to his old Scottish stomping grounds to prepare for battle, giving armchair tourists something to look at, anyway. Original theatrical release was PG-13 and 94 minutes; the director's cut has been re-edited and footage added. AKA: *Highlander 3: The Magician*; *Highlander 3: The Sorcerer*.

THE HITCHHIKER'S GUIDE TO THE GALAXY

2005 (PG-13) 109m / **D:** Garth Jennings / **W:** Douglas Adams, Karey Kirkpatrick / **C:** Martin Freeman, Mos Def, Sam Rockwell, Zooey Deschanel, John Malkovich, Bill Nighy, Helen Mirren, Alan Rickman

In development since practically the moment Douglas Adams started publishing his brilliantly mordant sci-fi comedy novels in 1979, *The Hitchhiker's Guide to the Galaxy* was almost destined not to work. The limited audience for its dry Brit-wit story—in which hapless Arthur Dent catches a ride on a spaceship just before Earth gets demolished to make way for an interstellar bypass and travels the galaxy with a band of squabbling misfits—was always going to run up against the broader studio demands that come into play when expensive f/x are involved. Casting couldn't have been more on-point, particularly Martin Freeman as Dent and Alan Rickman's gloomy voicing of "paranoid android" Marvin. But the patchwork screenplay doesn't cohere and the straining effort to find the right comic tone amidst Adams's more existential queries only works in fits and starts. If only they could have hung on a few more years until *Shaun of the Dead* was a hit, then Simon Pegg and Edgar Wright could have taken a run at it.

H-MAN

1959 (NR) 79m / D: Ishiro Honda / **W:** Takeshi Kimura / **C:** Koreya Senda, Kenji Sahara, Yumi Shirakawa, Akihiko Hirata, Mitsuru Sato

Police are stumped when a gangster disappears in the middle of a busy Tokyo street, leaving only his clothes. While they investigate, more people disappear in the same fashion. A young scientist doing research into the effects of radioactivity comes forth with an incredible theory: the victims are being dissolved by formerly human creatures turned into protoplasmic monsters by exposure to H-bomb radiation. His theory turns out to be true, and the sewers beneath the city are soon infested with the oozing, ghostly monsters. Genuinely creepy f/x highlight this mixture of two commonly underrated genres of Japanese cinema—sci-fi and gangster dramas. Though Ishiro Honda was famous for his giant monster sagas (*Godzilla*, among others), he was also adept at these less-epic chillers.

HOLLOW MAN

2000 (R) 112m / D: Paul Verhoeven / **W:** Andrew W. Marlowe / **C:** Kevin Bacon, Elisabeth Shue, Josh Brolin, Kim Dickens, Greg Grunberg, Joey Slotnik, Mary Randle, William Devane

Paul Verhoeven ended his Hollywood run with this ugly and unimaginative twist on H. G. Wells's *Invisible Man*. Kevin Bacon is a Pentagon researcher working on a serum that can turn creatures invisible once it's injected. Once Bacon shoots it into himself, he becomes infatuated with the potential power inherent in being unseen. In not much time at all, he has descended to sexual predator and killer. Not much to see here.

HONEY, I BLEW UP THE KID

1992 (PG) 89m / D: Randal Kleiser / **W:** Thom Eberhardt, Peter Elbling, Garry Goodrow / **C:** Rick Moranis, Marcia Strassman, Robert Oliveri, Daniel Shalikar, Joshua Shalikar, Lloyd Bridges, John Shea, Keri Russell, Gregory Sierra, Julia Sweeney, Kenneth Tobey

Rick Moranis returns as Wayne Szalinski, the screwball inventor who shrunk his kids in the first *Honey, I....* misadventure. It's a *Son of Flubber* for the 1990s, with better f/x. Cherubic twins Daniel and Joshua Shalikar steal their scenes as Wayne's toddler who he accidentally blew up to 150 feet tall. A third *Honey* has been produced for the direct-to-video market.

HONEY, I SHRUNK THE KIDS

1989 (G) 101m / D: Joe Johnston, Rob Minkoff / **W:** Ed Naha, Tom Schulman, Stuart Gordon / **C:** Rick Moranis, Matt Frewer, Marcia Strassman, Kristine Sutherland, Thomas Wilson Brown, Jared Rushton, Amy O'Neill, Robert Oliveri

Rick Moranis is a goofy scientist who accidentally shrinks his own children down to insect size in *Honey, I Shrunk the Kids.*

Popular Disney fantasy about a suburban inventor (Rick Moranis), who acts like the son of Fred MacMurray's character in *The Absent-Minded Professor*. His shrinking device accidentally reduces his kids to a quarter-inch tall, and he subsequently throws them out with the garbage. Now they must journey back to the house through the jungle that was once the back lawn, overcoming the dangers of insects, sprinklers, and the like. A fine comic script that takes things in stride, plus outstanding effects make this one worthwhile. Matt Frewer steals scenes as Moranis's annoying neighbor.

HORROR PLANET

1980 (R) 93m / **D:** Norman J. Warren / **W:** Nick Maley, Gloria Maley / **C:** Robin Clarke, Jennifer Ashley, Stephanie Beacham, Judy Geeson, Steven Grives, Victoria Tennant, Barry Houghton

Cheapie takeoff on *Alien*. In the catacombs of a dead planet, a female member of an Earth research team meets one of the not-quite-extinct natives, who impregnates her. Now endowed with superhuman strength, the mother-to-be goes on a crazed cannibal rampage among her former comrades. Monster-happy viewers must wait until the grisly end to get a clear look at the alien creatures. Graphic and sensationalistic waste. AKA: *Inseminoid*.

THE HOST (2006)

2006 (R) 119m / **D:** Joon-ho Bong / **W:** Joon-ho Bong, Won-jun Ha, Chul-hyun Baek / **C:** Kang-ho Song, Hee-bong Byun, Hae-il Park, Doona Bae, Ah-sung Ko

South Korea's long, complicated relationship with the U.S. military gets a tough examination in this fanged monster metaphor. Years after an American military researcher dumps hundreds of bottles of formaldehyde into Seoul's Han River, a ravenous amphibious beast erupts from the river and runs amok in a crowded park. The battle to contain the creature takes a more personal twist when it runs off with a young girl and her father must fight to get her back. Hard-to-pin-down filmmaker Joon-ho Bong directs with speed and humor but not without forgetting the human element or the political and environmental issues lurking in the background.

THE HOST (2013)

2013 (PG-13) 125m / **D:** Andrew Niccol / **W:** Andrew Niccol / **C:** Saoirse Ronan, Diane Kruger, William Hurt, Jake Abel, Max Irons

Based on one of Stephenie Meyers's young-adult novels that *doesn't* feature vampires or werewolves, this bright and sparkly but nearly drama-free story takes place years after glowing, parasitic aliens have occupied the bodies of most of humanity. They're benign, in that old *Invasion of the Body Snatchers* way, where aliens want to make humanity more peaceful but end up stealing their souls. Saoirse Ronan plays a young woman on the run whose body is taken over, but not completely, so that most of the movie is spent with her alien host arguing with the persistent human voice in its head. Diane Kruger is the alien "seeker" who's curiously obsessed with hunting down the last stragglers. Like Andrew Niccol's other films, the gleaming and minimalist design scheme is *Architecture Digest*-worthy (one visual gag shows a color-coordinated IKEA-like alien store simply called "STORE"). This cool mood clashes poorly with the forced attempt at a *Twilight*-ish love triangle between Ronan and two perfectly colorless, mussed-hair hunks.

HOT TUB TIME MACHINE

2010 (R) 101m / **D:** Steve Pink / **W:** Josh Heald, Sean Anders, John Morris / **C:** John Cusack, Craig Robinson, Rob Corddry, Clark Duke, Lizzy Caplan, Chevy Chase

The microscopically small mini-genre of time-travel comedies received a credible addition with this effort, which starts off with disappointed-with-life Rob Corddry trying to kill himself in the car while listening to Mötley Crüe. His buddies John Cusack and Craig Robinson try an intervention, which just turns out to be a boozing weekend at an old skiing chalet. Things go sideways once mysterious handyman Chevy Chase turns their hot tub into a time machine that will allow them each to go back to the 1980s and fix what went wrong with their lives. Avoids *Wedding Singer*-level overkill on the pop-culture references and delivers some halfway decent jokes, along with a near-complete lack of interest in any of the deeper ramifications of travelling in time.

HOWARD THE DUCK

1986 (PG) 111m / **D:** Willard Huyck / **W:** Willard Huyck, Gloria Katz / **C:** Lea Thompson, Jeffrey Jones, Tim Robbins

A megabucks megaflop from Lucasfilm, an adaptation of the short-lived, cult Marvel Comics superhero spoof. Alien from a parallel world where everything is ducky, literally, accidentally beams to Earth (technically Cleveland, badly portrayed by Marin County, California). First half has Howard trying to fit into human society, amid lame sex and drug jokes. When those fowl gags run dry, the filmmakers give him space demons to fight in a climactic f/x barrage. The hero's creature costume looks stiff and lifeless enough to be a decoy. Nobody escapes unscathed.

HOW I LIVE NOW

2013 (R) 101m / **D:** Kevin Macdonald / **W:** Jeremy Brock, Tony Grisoni, Penelope Skinner / **C:** Saoirse Ronan, George MacKay, Tom Holland, Harley Bird, Danny McEvoy, Anna Chancellor

Jangled and jittery internal monologues of teenage alienation riff through this adaptation of Meg Rosoff's award-winning novel about an American teenager sent to live with her step-cousins in the British countryside just as a continent-wide war is about to break out. Saorise Ronan, playing the alienating teen in question with all the slit-eyed brio she brought to her junior-assassin role in *Hanna*, is surprised to find herself falling in love with the hunkier of her step-cousins when a nuclear blast obliterates much of London and sends clouds of snow-like ash raining down on their house. The rest of the film is a bruising, millennial take on what happens when modern warfare (guerrilla ambuscades, civilian massacres) comes to a once-civilized nation and children are left to scramble for survival. Ties up a touch too tidily at the end, but director Kevin Macdonald (*One Day in September*) neatly balances the romantic subtext (love might conquer all) and beautifully idyllic setting with the darker verisimilitude you'd expect from a documentary filmmaker.

HULK

2003 (PG-13) 138m / D: Ang Lee / **W:** John Turman, Michael France, James Schamus /
C: Eric Bana, Jennifer Connelly, Sam Elliott, Josh Lucas, Nick Nolte

In his seeming effort to embrace each film genre at least once, Ang Lee—best known for award-winning fare like *Crouching Tiger, Hidden Dragon* and *Sense and Sensibility*—made news when it was announced he was going to be responsible for the first big-screen reboot of *The Incredible Hulk*. This was years before Christopher Nolan made superhero stories a more critically respectable field. Although the film that resulted wasn't quite smash-'em-up enough to please the fanboys and too much a lavishly operatic comic-book origin story to interest Lee's usual constituency, it was impressive for how serious it took Bruce Banner's transformation into the enraged beast. There are some real emotions at work under the surface here, mostly thanks to Eric Bana's underrated acting. Nick Nolte turns in one of his most cragged performances as the Hulk's father.

THE HUNGER GAMES

2012 (PG-13) 142m / D: Gary Ross / **W:** Gary Ross, Suzanne Collins, Billy Ray / **C:** Jennifer Lawrence, Woody Harrelson, Liam Hemsworth, Josh Hutcherson, Wes Bentley, Stanley Tucci, Elizabeth Banks, Lenny Kravitz

Suzanne Collins's futuristic trilogy gets a respectable film kickoff with this broadly appealing adaptation that introduces Jennifer Lawrence as Katniss Everdeen. A teenage girl from a poor, Appalachian-like village is chosen in a lottery to take part in a televised gladiatorial contest known as the Hunger Games. Being young-adult fiction of the *Twilight* era, Katniss must contend not just with saving her own skin but navigating the tricky shoals of competing romantic interests. Everything here, from the old Latinate place names to the orgiastic luxury of the capital city and the population's distracted eagerness for entertainment amidst growing political unrest, is meant to evoke the Roman Empire's tradition of bread and circuses. From Lawrence's righteous bravery to the solid pros who pop up throughout (Stanley Tucci and Donald Sutherland), it's excellently cast. The details of this future society are never convincingly evoked, however, a failing of the books that this film failed to rectify.

THE HUNGER GAMES: CATCHING FIRE

2013 (PG-13) 146m / D: Francis Lawrence / **W:** Simon Beaufoy, Michael Arndt / **C:** Jennifer Lawrence, Liam Hemsworth, Josh Hutcherson, Woody Harrelson, Elizabeth Banks, Donald Sutherland, Stanley Tucci, Lenny Kravitz, Philip Seymour Hoffman, Jeffrey Wright, Willow Shields

A more assured second entry in the young-adult dystopia series that mashes up classic archetypal mythmaking (the strong warrioress, the

Jennifer Lawrence plays a teenager fighting for her life in savage gladiator contests geared to entertain the wealthy in *The Hunger Games.*

pure-hearted knight) with a more modern kind of mythmaking (TV's *Survivor* made a life-and-death struggle). The poor Districts, forced each year to send randomly selected young people to the capital's games, are growing restive. Katniss (Jennifer Lawrence) plays a risky game of pretending to be a lovestruck TV star while not-so-secretly inspiring the brewing revolution. Francis Lawrence (*I Am Legend*) spends less time on the games themselves than on contrasting the Roman decadence of the capital with the districts' grinding poverty (there's even an absurd feast where one of the professed drinks is like a vomitorium in the glass) and on the dictatorial president's (Donald Sutherland) gamesmanship with Katniss.

I Am Legend

2007 (PG-13) 101m / **D:** Francis Lawrence / **W:** Mark Protosevich, Akiva Goldsman / **C:** Will Smith, Alice Braga, Charlie Tahan, Salli Richardson-Whitfield

For this third go-round of Richard Matheson's novel (1964's *The Last Man on Earth* and 1971's *The Omega Man* preceded), the action has been moved from Los Angeles to New York and a whole extra layer of backstory grafted onto it. Will Smith is the last man on earth, a military researcher who is apparently immune to the plague that wiped out humanity and turned the survivors into vampire-like monsters. He scrapes by in his fortress-like Manhattan townhome, trying to use his blood to create an antidote and generally trying not to go insane from loneliness. Though we get tiny glimpses of the plague's spread, an impressive amount of the film just follows Smith as he traipses through the emptied-out city, renting videos from a store where he's dressed up mannequins to talk to and dodging the shadowy corners where vampires lurk. Not perfect by any means, but its emphasis on a mournful sadness is rare in this kind of blockbuster. Likely much better than the long-planned Ridley Scott version that never came off. That one would have had Arnold Schwarzenegger, after all.

I Am Number Four

2011 (PG-13) 109m / **D:** D. J. Caruso / **W:** Alfred Gough, Miles Millar, Marti Noxon / **C:** Alex Pettyfer, Timothy Olyphant, Teresa Palmer, Dianna Agron, Callan McAuliffe, Kevin Durand

Glossy, ridiculous Michael Bay-produced adaptation of the young adult novel introduces extraterrestrials who can shoot blue rays out of their hands into the usual dystopian/vampire mix. Alex Pettyfer plays the telekinetically powered alien with the pretty-boy looks using an Ohio high school as cover while hiding out from alien bounty hunters looking to eliminate all nine of his kind. For complicated reasons that *might* make sense to those who have read the novel, they can only be killed in order; three are already dead. D. J. Caruso's direction has more punch than most pallid YA-lit productions, but the chase-chase-chase plotting and by-the-numbers romancing between Pettyfer and *Glee* star Dianna Agron grinds things to a halt in short order. Sidenote: source novel was co-written by James Frey, who prior to this was best known for his discredited addiction memoir *A Million Little Pieces*.

ICE PIRATES

1984 (PG) 91m / **D:** Stewart Raffill / **W:** Stewart Raffill / **C:** Robert Urich, Mary Crosby, Michael D. Roberts, John Matuszak, Anjelica Huston, Ron Perlman, John Carradine, Robert Symonds

> "Time warping finale may have taken things too far—then again maybe not."
>
> *Ice Pirates*

Space pirates in the far future steal blocks of ice to fill the needs of a thirsty galaxy. With its cast of goofy characters and crazy situations, this is nearly the *Airplane* of space operas. Time warping finale may have taken things too far—then again maybe not. Much funnier than *Spaceballs*. Director Stewart Raffill may have peaked in 1984, making this film and the surprisingly charming *The Philadelphia Experiment*.

IDAHO TRANSFER

1973 (PG) 90m / **D:** Peter Fonda / **W:** Thomas Matthiesen / **C:** Keith Carradine, Kelley Bohanan

Director Peter Fonda's sober-sided cautionary tale is about time travel, government repression, and ecological disaster. Made on a minuscule budget with modest effects and a mostly non-professional cast. Before Fonda arrives at a leaden downbeat ending, he presents the future as a post-apocalyptic camping trip taken by obnoxious teens to Idaho in the year 2044. (By the way, the last words of the film, "Esto Perpetua," are the state motto of Idaho: "May she endure forever.") Keith Carradine's first screen appearance. AKA: *Deranged*.

IDIOCRACY

2006 (R) 84m / **D:** Mike Judge / **W:** Mike Judge, Etan Cohen / **C:** Luke Wilson, Maya Rudolph, Dax Shepard, Terry Crews

Averager-than-average soldier Luke Wilson wakes up in the 26th century, victim of a cryofreeze experiment gone wrong. In the intervening years, over-fertile morons have continued the world's slide into boorish degeneracy, and Wilson now qualifies as a certified genius. Along with fellow 21st-century refugee Maya Rudolph, Wilson must navigate a landscape of trash heaps and trash culture (a popular TV show is nothing but a man being hit in the crotch) in which politics is more like a pro wrestling match (Congress is now called the House of Representin'). The president (Terry Crews) is a cross between Hulk Hogan and Bootsie Collins, and he is shocked as any of his people to realize that Wilson is right: maybe they *shouldn't* be irrigating crops with a popular sports drink. There's some irony in this infuriated screed against the lowering of standards coming from the creator of *Beavis and Butthead*, but its real problem is just not being funny enough. Still unfairly abandoned by the studio, which didn't know what to to do with such an uncommonly angry piece of work.

THE ILLUSTRATED MAN

1969 (PG) 103m / D: Jack Smight / **W:** Howard B. Kreitsek / **C:** Rod Steiger, Claire Bloom, Robert Drivas, Don Dubbins, Tim Weldon, Christine Matchett, Jason Evers

Ambitious but limited attempt at dramatizing Ray Bradbury's landmark short-story anthology. Young drifter meets obsessed wanderer Rod Steiger, searching for a mystery woman (Claire Bloom, at the time Steiger's wife) who, before dematerializing, tattooed him head to foot. Uncanny tattoo designs inspire three narratives with the same three actors: "The Veldt" concerns a children's holographic-type playroom that becomes all too real; "The Long Rains," probably the most effective of the lot, details astronauts on Venus struggling to survive the planet's eternal downpour that makes it a true *Waterworld*; "The Last Night of the World" botches a Bradbury mood piece about, well, the last night of the world. The skin-art framing story tries too hard to be weird. Conversely, the short segments aren't halfway weird or imaginative enough.

I MARRIED A MONSTER FROM OUTER SPACE

1958 (NR) 78m / D: Gene Fowler Jr. / **W:** Louis Vittes / **C:** Tom Tryon, Gloria Talbott, Maxie "Slapsie" Rosenbloom, Mary Treen, Ty Hardin, Ken Lynch, John Eldredge, Valerie Allen

Vintage thriller about a race of monstrous aliens who try to conquer Earth by turning themselves into duplicates of human beings. One of them marries Gloria Talbott. The poor woman soon learns the horrible truth (on their wedding night, no less), but nobody will believe that her good-looking, clean-cut hubby is really a thing from another world. Ignore the hokey title; this is a highly effective 1950s sci-fi creeper with truly frightening monsters. Newlyweds, however, should approach with caution.

IMPOSTOR

2001 (R) 95m / D: Gary Fleder / **W:** Scott Rosenberg, Caroline Case, Ehren Kruger, David Twohy / **C:** Gary Sinise, Madeleine Stowe, Vincent D'Onofrio, Tony Shalhoub, Mekhi Phifer, Gary Dourdan, Lindsay Crouse, Elizabeth Pena

In a vaguely totalitarian 2079, Gary Sinise (flat, as ever) is a happily married scientist who gets arrested one morning and charged by government agent Vincent D'Onofrio (cranking up the camp) with being a cyborg sent to infiltrate Earth by the aliens humanity is at war with. Futuristic Hitchcock wrong-man chase ensues, amidst much "is-he-or-isn't-he" dramatics. This very free adaptation of Philip K. Dick's story "The Impostor" was supposed to be just one entry in a three-part sci-fi anthology but was then expanded to feature length so it could stand on its own. The final product, which mixes generic '90s action-flick stylistics with canned sci-fi tropes (bland faux-utopian architecture, grimy but good-hearted rebels), shows that decision to have been a curious one. Released in theaters as PG-13 but most versions available now are R-rated with cuts restored.

INCEPTION

2010 (PG-13) 148m / **D:** Christopher Nolan / **W:** Christopher Nolan / **C:** Leonardo DiCaprio, Joseph Gordon-Levitt, Ellen Page, Tom Hardy, Ken Watanabe, Dileep Rao, Cillian Murphy, Tom Berenger, Marion Cotillard, Michael Caine

For his cool-headed but trippy corporate espionage sci-fi thriller, Christopher Nolan broke almost every rule in the Hollywood playbook and still came away with a runaway success that was also a critical darling. Leonardo DiCaprio (on break from Scorsese pics just as Nolan was taking a breather from *Batman*) plays a so-called extraction specialist, whose dangerous but lucrative job is stealing business secrets from people while they dream. While DiCaprio assembles a best-of-the-best team for an awesome last gig,

Dreams within dreams within dreams form the complicated labyrinth that must be navigated by corporate espionage specialists in the thriller *Inception*.

implanting an idea, ghosts of the past keep looming. Nolan toys with multiple layers of consciousness here, making interlocking realities as malleable as toy blocks; the scenes where the film reassembles an entire city into an M. C. Escher-like foldable puzzle is truly gasp-inducing. Sometimes baffling and occasionally overlong, but highly worth the journey. Eight Oscar nominations, including best picture; won four.

THE INCREDIBLE HULK

2008 (PG-13) 112m / **D:** Louis Leterrier / **W:** Zak Penn / **C:** Edward Norton, Liv Tyler, Tim Roth, William Hurt, Tim Blake Nelson, Ty Burrell

The problem with the Incredible Hulk as a film character—as this second reboot in five years shows—is that his origin story is very nearly the most interesting thing about him. Once Bruce Banner is fully locked into his Hulk persona, there's not as much left to build an entire film around; short appearances in ensembles like *The Avengers* work better. That being said, Louis Leterrier's version is certainly speedier and more action-oriented than Ang Lee's more psychologically attuned portrait. Edward Norton makes a superbly schizophrenic Banner and William Hurt nicely handles the role of the general who wants to capture the Hulk's transformative abilities in order to create super-soldiers. But the chases and destruction quickly overwhelm what there is of a story. Hulk smash.

THE INCREDIBLES

2004 (PG) 115m / **D:** Brad Bird / **W:** Brad Bird

The Pixar brilliance streak was still going strong when Brad Bird (*The Iron Giant*) delivered this galloping animated adventure about superhero married couple Elastigirl and Mr. Incredible (voiced by Holly Hunter and Craig T. Nelson), who put their superpowers aside and hide out in suburbia to raise their kids. Then, just when the kids have hit maximum precociousness, a message lures them to a remote island, where Bondian villainy, henchmen, and world-ending plots lurk. The comic sensibility is a tart mix of *Simpsons* and a family friendly *Austin Powers*, while the head-snapping action and elaborate techno-gimmickry is like some spy fiction junkie's dream. This being Pixar, he layers in some emotive family moments that hit the mark, even for being a touch programmatic. Four Oscar nominations; won two, including best animated film.

THE INCREDIBLE SHRINKING MAN

1957 (NR) 81m / **D:** Jack Arnold / **W:** Richard Matheson / **C:** Grant Williams, Randy Stuart, April Kent, Paul Langton, Raymond Bailey, William Schallert

A FASCINATING ADVENTURE INTO THE UNKNOWN!

THE INCREDIBLE

SHRINKING MAN

A UNIVERSAL INTERNATIONAL PICTURE STARRING

GRANT WILLIAMS · RANDY STUART

with APRIL KENT · PAUL LANGTON · RAYMOND BAILEY

DIRECTED BY JACK ARNOLD · SCREENPLAY BY RICHARD MATHESON · PRODUCED BY ALBERT ZUGSMITH

One of the best sci-fi achievements of its time, *The Incredible Shrinking Man* brings a philosophical edge to a gimmicky premise.

By any standard, a sci-fi masterpiece. Adapted by Richard Matheson from his smartly non-gimmicky novel, the film is a philosophical thriller about Robert Scott Carey (Grant Williams) who is exposed to a radioactive mist and begins to slowly shrink. Why? That's not really the question. Each new size means that everyday objects take on sinister meaning, and he must fight for his life in an increasingly hostile, absurd environment. If some of the effects are dated, few sci-fi films contain more psychological truths, particularly in regard to men and matters of size. Surreal, suspenseful allegory also has a serious intellectual dimension that's almost never seen in American popular movies. It's also endowed with the tension usually reserved for Hitchcock films. Williams, a familiar figure in sci-fi films of the era, was never more effective.

THE INCREDIBLE SHRINKING WOMAN

1981 (PG) 89m / D: Joel Schumacher / **W:** Jane Wagner / **C:** Lily Tomlin, Charles Grodin, Ned Beatty, Henry Gibson, Elizabeth Wilson

Good-natured spoof of *The Incredible Shrinking Man*, with some inoffensive social satire. Various environmental toxins combine to slowly shrink homemaker Lily Tomlin down to doll-house size. Everyday chores suddenly become "big" challenges, and just as she starts getting comfortable with her new size, she's snatched by a cabal of scientists who want to similarly down-size (er, right-size?) the rest of the world. Suddenly the tiny Tomlin must become a hero. The cuteness starts shrinking a bit itself toward the end, but Tomlin is charming, and the satire still works today. That's makeup wizard Rick Baker making a cameo in the gorilla suit, by the way.

INDEPENDENCE DAY

1996 (PG-13) 145m / D: Roland Emmerich / **W:** Dean Devlin, Roland Emmerich / **C:** Will Smith, Jeff Goldblum, Bill Pullman, Mary McDonnell, Judd Hirsch, Robert Loggia, Randy Quaid

The post-*Star Wars* sci-fi summer spectacular was truly invented on July 4, 1996, when *Stargate*'s Roland Emmerich threw a vast alien horde at fighter jockey Will Smith and made it seem a foregone conclusion that Smith would wipe the board with them. Junkyard script has the American government, reeling from a surprise invasion, regrouping in the desert at Area 51 where it just so happens the Pentagon's been sitting on a spaceship for a few decades. (When President Bill Pullman asks how it's all been funded without him knowing, Judd Hirsch snaps, "You don't think they actually spend $20,000 on a hammer, $30,000 on a toilet seat, do you?") The final counterattack involves Smith delivering a computer virus to the alien mothership. Relentless ad campaign focused on a money shot of the aliens vaporizing the White House. Managed to not be the stupidest blockbuster of the summer only for coming out the same year as Michael Bay's cretinous *The Rock*. Two Oscar nominations; won for best sound.

INDIANA JONES AND THE KINGDOM OF THE CRYSTAL SKULL

2008 (PG-13) 122m / **D:** Steven Spielberg / **W:** David Koepp / **C:** Harrison Ford, Shia LaBeouf, Cate Blanchett, Karen Allen, John Hurt, Jim Broadbent

Coming almost twenty years after *Indiana Jones and the Last Crusade* laid the capstone on Spielberg and Lucas's Saturday matinee archaeological adventure series, Harrison Ford puts the dusty hat back on for one more ride into the unknown. Now, instead of battling Nazis, Ford is up against scheming Commies; cue Cate Blanchett in full Soviet vixen-dominatrix mode, sporting a killer Natasha accent. The first half works like a dream, with all the chaotic zip and grin that can happen when Ford and Spielberg are firing on all cylinders. Unfortunately, once the adventure heads into the jungles of South America and the sci-fi-ish elements are revealed (spoiler: the crystal skull everybody's hunting for *isn't from this planet*), David Koepp's script turns into straight nonsense.

INFRA-MAN

1976 (PG) 92m / **D:** Shan Hua / **W:** Peter Fernandez / **C:** Li Hsiu-hsien, Wang Hsieh, Yuan Man-tzu, Terry Liu, Tsen Shu-yi, Huang Chien-lung, Lu Sheng

The *Mighty Morphin Power Rangers* TV show, with its cheesy monsters and hyper-kinetic fight sequences, owes a lot to this classic, outrageous Hong Kong production. Ancient Princess Dragon Mom unleashes an incredible array of creatures (including Octopus Man and Beetle Man) on the Earth. She wreaks such apocalyptic havoc that a scientist is forced to tell the world's leaders, "This situation is so bad that it is the worst that has ever been." It's Infra-Man, a bionic superhero, to the rescue. Tremendous fun cheese, with non-stop martial arts action and priceless English-dubbed dialogue ("Drop the Earthling to her doom"). It's "infratastic." AKA: *The Super Infra-man*; *The Infra Superman*.

INNERSPACE

1987 (PG) 120m / **D:** Joe Dante / **W:** Jeffrey Boam, Chip Proser / **C:** Dennis Quaid, Martin Short, Meg Ryan, Kevin McCarthy, Fiona Lewis, Henry Gibson, Robert Picardo, John Hora, Wendy Schaal, Orson Bean, Chuck Jones, William Schallert, Dick Miller

A space pilot (Dennis Quaid) is miniaturized for an experimental journey through the body of a lab rabbit (à la Fantastic Voyage) and is accidentally injected into a nebbishy supermarket clerk (Martin Short), and together they nab some bad guys and get the girl. Although Short's brand of physical slapstick gets a little tiresome, he and the exasperated Quaid make an effective, unusual comedy team. The Oscar-winning f/x support some funny moments, including a scene in which Short manages to off a miniature villain by getting an upset stomach. Meg Ryan supplies the slightly confused romantic interest.

INTERZONE

1988 (R) 97m / **D:** Deran Sarafian / **W:** Clyde Anderson, Deran Sarafian / **C:** Bruce Abbott

A heroic adventurer battles mutant punks in a post-apocalyptic world to keep the unsullied "Interzone" region free from despoiling. Despite the title, there's no connection to William S. Burroughs or *Naked Lunch*. Too bad; anything could have helped.

IN THE AFTERMATH: ANGELS NEVER SLEEP

1987 (NR) 85m / **D:** Carl Colpaert / **W:** Carl Colpaert, Mamoru Oshii / **C:** Tony Markes, Rainbow Dolan

Trippy, post-*Heavy Metal* mix of Japanese gothic album-cover animation and cheap live-action fight scenes in a post-nuclear wasteland has some interesting ideas floating around but is too embarrassingly chintzy to count for much. AKA: *In the Aftermath*.

IN TIME

2011 (PG-13) 109m / **D:** Andrew Niccol / **W:** Andrew Niccol / **C:** Justin Timberlake, Amanda Seyfried, Cillian Murphy, Olivia Wilde, Vincent Kartheiser, Alex Pettyfer, Johnny Galecki

An artfully done future imagineering whereby a seemingly dream-come-true advance (everybody stops aging at 25) comes with a hell of a catch (at 25, forearm-displayed digital clocks start at one year and count down to death). The erasure of visible aging makes for some tricky sight gags like a man's mother-in-law, wife, and daughter all looking the same age. All transactions are time-based; buying a cup of coffee takes three minutes off your life and criminals can rob time just by twisting your arm. Justin Timberlake lives in a ghetto where nobody can afford more than a few days at a time. Chance encounter with a suicidal rich man nets Timberlake a century of life; he heads into the wealthier "time zones" (it's a pun-littered film) to exact revenge on a cruel system. Vincent Kartheiser is a baby-faced Methusaleh easily separated from his ill-gotten gains, whose fetching daughter (Amanda Seyfried) is all too happy to help out Timberlake. The two make a sharp-dressed pair of Robin Hood time-robbers, with bloodhound "Timekeeper" Cillian Murphy on their trail. The romantic cuteness falls flat fast but writer/director Andrew Niccol's brisk pacing and inventive humor make for a lively surprise.

INTRUDERS

1992 (NR) 162m / D: Dan Curtis / **W:** Barry Oringer, Tracy Torme / **C:** Richard Crenna, Mare Winningham, Susan Blakely, Ben Vereen, Steven Berkoff, Daphne Ashbrook

In a future world posited, it is not money but life itself that can be saved and spent like currency. Two heroes played by Justin Timberlake and Amanda Seyfried decide to take down the corrupt establishment in *In Time*.

Follows the story of three people who have unexplained lapses of time in their lives which they eventually believe are connected to visits by aliens. The three are brought together by a skeptical psychiatrist. The aliens are your typical bugged-eyed, white-faced spooks but part of the film remains genuinely unsettling.

INVADERS FROM MARS (1953)

1953 (NR) 78m / D: William Cameron Menzies / **W:** Richard Blake / **C:** Helena Carter, Arthur Franz, Jimmy Hunt, Leif Erickson, Hillary Brooke, Morris Ankrum

Famous but dated classic sci-fi fave from the underrated director of *Things to Come* and the 1940 color fantasy *The Thief of Baghdad* about a little boy who sees a flying saucer bury itself behind his house. He can't convince grown ups, though, and parents and playmates are systematically brainwashed by the green meanies. Though the cheapo budget shows (note the balloons bobbing on the walls of the Martians' glass cave stronghold), this can be enjoyed both as a basic juvie adventure and on a deeper level, as the camera and production design conveys a child's-eye-view of grown-up society—dominant, threatening, and sometimes hostile as any space invader. Nightmarish, in its way, and ground-zero for many later fantasies of alien abduction. Originally released in 3D.

INVADERS FROM MARS (1986)

1986 (PG) 102m / **D:** Tobe Hooper / **W:** Dan O'Bannon, Don Jakoby / **C:** Hunter Carson, Karen Black, Louise Fletcher, Laraine Newman, Timothy Bottoms, Bud Cort, James Karen

Adequate but pointless remake of Menzies' 1953 semi-classic about a body-snatching Martian invasion perceived only by one young boy and a sympathetic school nurse (played by mother and son Karen Black and Hunter Carson). Jimmy Hunt, child star of the first movie, cameos here as an adult cop, and even the fishbowl-headed 1953 Martian leader prop can be glimpsed in the background of his big scene. Otherwise Stan Winston's colorful creature f/x are the main attractions.

INVASION

1966 (NR) 82m / **D:** Alan Bridges / **W:** Roger Marshall / **C:** Edward Judd, Yoko Tani, Valerie Gearon, Lyndon Brook, Tsai Chin, Barrie Ingham

A hospital opens its doors to an accident victim, and his attractive female visitors don't seem sympathetic to the idea of a long hospital stay. Turns out he's an escaped alien prisoner, and the alien babes, intent on intergalactic extradition, place a force field around the hospital and demand his return. Early effort from director Alan Bridges, who later did *The Shooting Party*. Interesting, creepy, atmospheric, with fantastic cinematography.

THE INVASION

2007 (PG-13) 99m / **D:** Oliver Hirschbiegel / **W:** David Kajganich / **C:** Nicole Kidman, Daniel Craig, Jeremy Northam, Jeffrey Wright, Jackson Bond, Veronica Cartwright

Yet another variation on Jack Finney's *The Body Snatchers*—this one has a crashed space shuttle spreading the don't-sleep-or-they'll-take-you-over alien spores across America. By the time psychiatrist Nicole Kidman and doctor friend Daniel Craig realize what's happening, half of Washington, D.C., is walking around like robots and asking the uninfected why won't they just go to sleep and join the collective hive-mind, after which there will be world peace. The first English-language film for German director Oliver Hirschbiegel (*Downfall*) was one of those negative-buzz disasters, with rumors about last-minute rewrites and reshoots (by an uncredited James McTeigue and Andy and Lana Wachowskis) helping squelch its chances. The film that resulted has that hacked-apart feeling, with abrupt shifts in mood and continuity lapses. But while no masterpiece, the early scenes of the alien takeover have a rare, subtle creepiness. It's also a fairly nettlesome and bleak view of modern society—there's a lot of ironic comparison of the aliens' glassy inhumanity to the pills Kidman prescribes, and a constant media backdrop of the wartime slaughters that the aliens promise to stop. Unlike most stories of conformity-demanding alien takeovers, here it's not immediately apparent that it would be such a horrible thing.

INVASION OF THE BEE GIRLS

1973 (R) 85m / D: Denis Sanders / **W:** Nicholas Meyer / **C:** Victoria Vetri, Anitra Ford, Cliff Osmond, Wright King, Ben Hammer

Early in their television career, critics Gene Siskel and Roger Ebert declared this to be one of their favorite "guilty pleasures" and its reputation was set. Add in the presence of Playmate Victoria Vetri, who has a dedicated following of her own, Anitra "Big Bird Cage" Ford, and a gloriously wacky plot involving the "Queen Bee" and her conquests, and you've got prime camp fun. The murky audio sounds as if it were coming from a drive-in speaker, which ideally is the best way to experience this compellingly quirky and perversely comic thriller. Written by *Star Trek II: The Wrath of Khan* director Nicholas Meyer. AKA: *Graveyard Tramps*.

INVASION OF THE BODY SNATCHERS (1956)

1956 (NR) 80m / D: Don Siegel / **W:** Sam Peckinpah, Daniel Mainwaring / **C:** Kevin McCarthy, Dana Wynter, Carolyn Jones, King Donovan, Donald Siegel, Larry Gates, Jean Willes, Whit Bissell

Based on Jack Finney's novel, the definitive take on 1950s American paranoia and conformity is still one of the most frightening sci-fi movies ever made, a chilling exercise in nightmare dislocation. The infamous "pod people" are just like you and me ... only they're not. Everything about the film works right from the small town setting of Santa Mira to the flawless acting and the tight script. Director Don Siegel's solid craftsmanship was seldom applied to a better story. Yes, that's *Wild Bunch* director Sam Peckinpah as the meter reader in the cellar. He also worked on the screenplay. Remade many times, usually not for the better.

INVASION OF THE BODY SNATCHERS (1978)

1978 (PG) 115m / D: Philip Kaufman / **W:** W. D. Richter / **C:** Donald Sutherland, Brooke Adams, Veronica Cartwright, Leonard Nimoy, Jeff Goldblum, Kevin McCarthy, Art Hindle

The subtlety of Donald Siegel's original gives way to gaudy f/x and self-consciously artsy camera work from director Philip Kaufman. The film is indulgently overlong, too, though it certainly has some shocking moments. In the leads, Donald Sutherland and Brooke Adams are excellent, and they get solid support from Leonard Nimoy and Jeff Goldblum. The change in setting from small town to big city (San Francisco) provides more complications and striking visuals, but it doesn't really add to the atmosphere of dread created in the first film. Siegel himself pops by for a quick cameo as a cabbie.

INVASION OF THE SAUCER MEN

1957 (NR) 69m / **D:** Edward L. Cahn / **W:** Robert J. Gurney Jr., Al Martin / **C:** Steven Terrell, Gloria Castillo, Frank Gorshin, Lyn Osborn, Ed Nelson, Angelo Rossitto

Frank Gorshin (*Batman*'s Riddler) plays the town drunk in this kinda slow sci-fi comedy about bulbous-headed long-fingered aliens who are hassling teenagers at the local lovers' lane. Suspected of murder, the teenagers must convince the authorities that said aliens can multiply and take over the world. Designer Paul Blaisdell's aliens are the best part, but the atmosphere is great considering the budget. Remade with John Ashley and more gore as *The Eye Creatures* in 1965.

THE SCIENCE-MONSTER WHO WOULD DESTROY THE WORLD!

M·G·M PRESENTS *The Invisible Boy*

STARRING
RICHARD EYER · PHILIP ABBOTT · DIANE BREWSTER

WITH HAROLD J. STONE ROBERT H. HARRIS AND ROBBY THE ROBOT

BASED ON THE STORY BY EDMUND COOPER A PAN PRODUCTION

SCREEN PLAY BY CYRIL HUME DIRECTED BY HERMAN HOFFMAN · NICHOLAS NAYFACK

PRODUCED BY

Robby the Robot from *Forbidden Planet* makes another appearance in 1957's *The Invisible Boy*.

THE INVISIBLE BOY

1957 (G) 89m / **D:** Herman Hoffman / **W:** Cyril Hume / **C:** Richard Eyer, Diane Brewster, Philip Abbott, Harold J. Stone, Robert Harris

A mathematically challenged little boy ("Three? Seventeen? Forty four? A hundred?" he responds to his father's quizzing him on how many 24ths there are in one quarter) is a disappointment to his father, keeper of the super-computer at the Stoneman Mathematical Institute. Dad takes the problem to the massive computer ("He's ten and can't even play a decent game of chess."); said computer hypnotizes ten-year-old Timmy and teaches him the ins and outs of the game, so Timmy subsequently sandbags Dad at chess and wrangles a wish—he wants to play with Robby (*Forbidden Planet*) the Robot. Timmy quickly finds many uses for his newfound friend, including ordering the Robot to build him the biggest kite ever—which Timmy climbs upon for a flight above the trees. When Mom objects to this play, Timmy complains to Robby: "I wish there was some way she couldn't see me when I was having fun." And the fun really begins when Robby makes it so. Timmy plays childish pranks on the adults (giggling while his parents smooch in bed, giving himself away) and whacking "that nasty Sidney," a bigger boy who'd socked Timmy. The whole adventure turns devious when the super-computer uses Robby for evil purposes, with Timmy as a hostage. Charming boy-and-his-robot story with amusing dialogue and campy 1950s computer plot; anything with Robby in it has to be a winner. Based on a story by Edmund Cooper.

INVISIBLE INVADERS

1959 (NR) 67m / **D:** Edward L. Cahn / **W:** Samuel Newman / **C:** John Agar, Robert Hutton, Hal Torey, Jean Byron, Philip Tonge, John Carradine

Short, cheap, and silly aliens-try-to-take-over-the-Earth movie. This time they're moonmen who use the bodies of dead Earthlings (ugh) to attack the living until John Agar can save the day. He and Robert Hutton seem so bored with this script one can hardly pick them out among the zombies. John Carradine has a brief role as a formerly dead scientist. Though this film's lack of vision wasted the idea, ten years later George Romero would pick up their fumble and run it in for a touchdown with his *Night of the Living Dead*.

THE INVISIBLE MAN

1933 (NR) 71m / **D:** James Whale / **W:** R. C. Sherriff / **C:** Claude Rains, Gloria Stuart, Dudley Digges, William Harrigan, Una O'Connor, E. E. Clive, Dwight Frye

The vintage horror-fest based on H. G. Wells's novella about a scientist whose formula for invisibility slowly drives him insane. His mind definitely wandering, he plans to use his recipe to rule the world. Claude Rains's first role; though his body doesn't appear until the final scene, his voice characterization is magnificent. The visual detail is excellent, setting standards that are imitated because they are difficult to surpass; with f/x by John P. Fulton.

THE INVISIBLE MAN RETURNS

1940 (NR) 81m / **D:** Joe May / **W:** Lester Cole, Curt Siodmak / **C:** Cedric Hardwicke, Vincent Price, John Sutton, Nan Grey

Vincent Price stars as the original invisible man's brother. Using the same invisibility formula, Price tries to clear himself after being charged with murder. He reappears at the worst times, and you gotta love that floating gun. Fun sequel to 1933's classic *The Invisible Man*.

THE INVISIBLE RAY

1936 (NR) 82m / **D:** Lambert Hillyer / **W:** John Colton / **C:** Boris Karloff, Bela Lugosi, Frances Drake, Frank Lawton, Beulah Bondi, Walter Kingsford

For a change, this horror film features Bela Lugosi as the hero, fighting Boris Karloff, a scientist who locates a meteor that contains a powerful substance. Karloff is poisoned and becomes a murdering megalomaniac. Watching Karloff and Lugosi interact, and the great f/x—including a hot scene where a scientist bursts into flames—helps you ignore a hokey script.

THE INVISIBLE WOMAN

1940 (NR) 73m / D: Edward Sutherland / **W:** Robert Lees, Fred Rinaldo, Gertrude Purcell / **C:** John Barrymore, Virginia Bruce, John Howard, Charlie Ruggles, Oscar Homolka, Margaret Hamilton, Donald MacBride, Edward Brophy, Shemp Howard, Charles Lane, Thurston Hall

Above-average comedy about zany professor John Barrymore discovering the secret of invisibility and making luscious model Virginia Bruce transparent. Great cast makes this a very likeable movie. Based on a story by Curt Siodmak and Joe May, the same team that wrote *The Invisible Man Returns*.

I, ROBOT

2004 (PG-13) 115m / D: Alex Proyas / **W:** Jeff Vintar, Akiva Goldsman / **C:** Will Smith, Bridget Moynahan, Alan Tudyk, James Cromwell, Bruce Greenwood, Chi McBride, Shia LaBeouf

In Chicago, circa 2035, seemingly everybody has a robot helper and drives cars on autopilot. Except gloomy homicide detective Will Smith, who's resolutely analog and hates everything to do with robotics. So when he looks into the suspicious suicide of a researcher and uncovers evidence of a dangerous conspiracy in the new model androids coming off the assembly line, nobody believes him. Script takes almost nothing from the Isaac Asimov short stories except the concept of the three laws of robotics ("A robot must never harm a human being or, through inaction, allow any harm to come to a human," etc.). Interesting ideas about sentience and free will get buried in a generic rogue cop story. Gleaming, overly CGI'd effort feels about as robotic as Smith's legions of co-stars; too bad they ignored the script that Harlan Ellison finished in 1978 that Asimov himself liked so much that he serialized it years later in his namesake magazine. Watch for future Spielberg protégé and *Transformers* star Shia LaBeouf as an annoying teenager.

THE IRON GIANT

1999 (PG) 86m / D: Brad Bird / **W:** Tim McCanlies

Brad Bird's thoughtfully dark animated take on poet Ted Hughes's novel about a lonely boy who discovers a huge robot who has fallen from space. Eventually he needs to protect his new buddy from the Army, who see only a threat to be annihilated. The Spielbergian touch is that the boy makes friends with the clanking giant. The non-Spielbergian elements are just about everything else, from the evocatively handled Cold War paranoia of the smalltown 1950s setting to the classically sci-fi anti-militarist message and the heartwrenching conclusion. A pre-*Pitch Black* Vin Diesel voiced the robot, while Harry Connick Jr. provides deft comic relief as the town's resident beatnik. Horribly mishandled by the studio on its release, it was belatedly and correctly recognized as a classic.

IRON MAN

2008 (PG-13) 126m / **D:** Jon Favreau / **W:** Mark Fergus, Hawk Ostby, Art Marcum, Matt Holloway / **C:** Robert Downey Jr., Terrence Howard, Jeff Bridges, Gwyneth Paltrow, Leslie Bibb, Shaun Toub, Faran Tahir, Clark Gregg

Never one of the biggest comic-book stars, Iron Man nevertheless helped create the near-unstoppable machine that was the Marvel film franchise, and it's mostly due to a newly cleaned-up Robert Downey Jr. His Tony Stark is a billionaire playboy and arms merchant who smashes up race cars and beds models when not designing hyper-complex weapons systems; like Bruce Wayne without the emotional baggage. Stark gets a cold slap of reality when he's captured by the Taliban and only escapes by MacGyvering an armored suit. Back in his California pad, he announces that his company is out of the guns and bombs business and starts perfecting his super-powered flying suit and the gadget that's keeping his shrapnel-laced heart going. Of course, there's a baddie (Jeff Bridges) who doesn't want Stark to wave the peace flag just yet. There's a couple light satirical slaps here at the military-industrial complex but mostly this is light-hearted tech-heavy superhero action. Favreau directs with a gleeful zip. He keeps the action scenes clipped and impressive and essentially hands the reins to Downey, whose dry sarcasm is far and away the best thing about the film. Gwyneth Paltrow makes an unexpected appearance as Stark's would-be girlfriend, and Clark Gregg pops up in the first of his *Avengers* series cameos as S.H.I.E.L.D.'s Agent Coulson. Two Oscar nominations.

IRON MAN 2

2010 (PG-13) 124m / **D:** Jon Favreau / **W:** Justin Theroux / **C:** Robert Downey Jr., Gwyneth Paltrow, Don Cheadle, Scarlett Johansson, Sam Rockwell, Mickey Rourke, John Slattery, Samuel L. Jackson, Clark Gregg

Robert Downey Jr. is a wealthy weapons manufacturer who becomes a superhero by designing a flying supersuit in *Iron Man.*

Highly superior sequel scripted by actor Justin Theroux takes up where the first *Iron Man* left off. Robert Downey Jr.'s Tony Stark is trying to do the right thing for humanity while simultaneously keeping his flying armored suit technology out of greedy hands. Don Cheadle assumes the duties of Stark's straight-man sidekick Lt. Col. Rodney Rhodes, while future *Avengers* stars Samuel L. Jackson and Scarlett Johansson get cameos as S.H.I.E.L.D. operatives who really, *really* want Stark on their side. Mickey Rourke plays the grizzled villain with impressive panache. Again, Downey steals the show as easily as John Dillinger emptied bank vaults. The film works much better as a comedy with occasional gadget-tastic action scenes than a straight superhero movie. One Oscar nomination for f/x.

IRON MAN 3

2013 (PG-13) 130m / **D:** Shane Black / **W:** Shane Black, Drew Pearce / **C:** Robert Downey Jr., Gwyneth Paltrow, Don Cheadle, Guy Pearce, Rebecca Hall, Ben Kingsley, Jon Favreau

Things get darker in Iron Man's third outing, which sees the once flippant superhero undergoing some variant of PTSD following the nerve-shattering combat of *The Avengers*. This leaves him particularly vulnerable to back decision-making when a new threat in the form of international super-terrorist The Mandarin (Ben Kingsley) starts ripping his life and industry to shreds. The switchup in tone—courtesy of director Shane Black, whose sardonic humor once made action blockbusters like *Lethal Weapon* semi-bearable—brings a bite to some of the comedy and even creates the possibility that Downey's Tony Stark could be developing into something more complex than a Happy Meal giveaway. But no worry, the metal-man suits come out in force for an f/x-heavy battle-royale conclusion that destroys everything in its path. Oscar nomination for f/x.

IRON SKY

2012 (R) 93m / **D:** Timo Vuorensola / **W:** Michael Kalesniko, Timo Vuorensola / **C:** Julia Dietze, Christopher Kirby, Götz Otto, Udo Kier, Peta Sergeant, Stephanie Paul

The idea here is that the Third Reich wasn't entirely defeated in 1945, but they didn't decamp to South America to clone the Führer. Nope, the Nazis have been hiding out on the dark side of the moon (yes, the moon) and waiting for the right moment to launch a new blitzkrieg on an unsuspecting world. Sci-fi action comedy with a high tongue-in-cheek factor. (Sample dialogue: "Invasion? Y'all must be trippin'.") Fairly high-level f/x, considering. Ever-reliable Z-movie actor Udo Kier is here as Adolf Hitler, while Stephanie Paul plays a Sarah Palin-like American president. From the Finnish makers of the *Star Wreck* parody video series.

THE ISLAND

2005 (PG-13) 136m / D: Michael Bay / **W:** Caspian Tredwell-Owen, Alex Kurtzman, Roberto Orci / **C:** Ewan McGregor, Scarlett Johansson, Djimon Hounsou, Sean Bean, Steve Buscemi, Michael Clarke Duncan, Ethan Phillips, Brian Stepanek

Lincoln Six Echo (Ewan McGregor) and Jordan Two Delta (Scarlett Johansson) have got it made in their futuristic underground residence. Along with hundreds of others in matching white jumpsuits, they are kept safe from a contaminated outside world that they will one day repopulate. To no viewers' surprise, the truth is much uglier and more prosaic (their home is less shelter than farm). Michael Bay's first collaboration with producer Steven Spielberg (their *Transformers* series started a couple years later) is surprisingly patient in building drama for the first hour or so; but once the movie bursts into the light, it turns into another long chase with subliterate dialogue. Caspian Tredwell-Owen's thoughtful script was reportedly hacked apart by Bay and his *Transformers* scripters Alex Kurtzman and Roberto Orci to emphasize action; result is neither fish nor fowl. Gorgeously shot, though, with top-notch sets and a strong supporting cast.

THE ISLAND OF DR. MOREAU (1977)

1977 (PG) 99m / D: Don Taylor / **W:** John Herman Shaner, Al Ramus / **C:** Burt Lancaster, Michael York, Nigel Davenport, Barbara Carrera, Richard Basehart, Nick Cravat

Burt Lancaster is Dr. Moreau, a scientist who has isolated himself on a Pacific island in order to continue his chromosome research. He can transform animals into near-humans and humans into animals. He imprisons Michael York and nearly turns him into an animal. Barbara Carrera is a panther converted into a woman. The beast-man makeup is more impressive here than in the 1932 original, but the final product is too slick. Another wrong-headed and regrettable adaptation of a classic H. G. Wells novel.

> "The beast-man makeup is more impressive here than in the 1932 original, but the final product is too slick."
>
> *The Island of Dr. Moreau (1977)*

THE ISLAND OF DR. MOREAU (1996)

1996 (PG-13) 96m / D: John Frankenheimer / **W:** Richard Stanley, Ron Hutchinson / **C:** David Thewlis, Val Kilmer, Marlon Brando, Fairuza Balk, Ron Perlman

In this everything-went-wrong redo of the H. G. Wells novel, plane-crash survivor David Thewlis gets rescued at sea by Val Kilmer and taken to the titular island of unholy experiments. There, he discovers Dr. Moreau (Marlon Brando) in a disturbing variety of muumuus playing the piano, jabbering in that raspy whisper of his, and occasionally doing human-animal gene-splicing experiments when he gets bored. Thewlis finds that the island is populated by the none-too-happy and barely civilized feral results of the good doctor's work. It doesn't take much for them to throw off the shackles of Moreau's rule and good, old-fashioned hybrid-versus-human combat is joined in paradise. Thewlis and Kilmer turn in nervy work amidst the rubble of a laughable exercise in over-budgeted and under-thought 1990s sci-fi horror pretending at significance, while Brando is just everything that's terrible about late-period Brando. John Frankenheimer came on board a few days into shooting after the original director was fired, but the trainwreck was already unavoidable.

ISLAND OF LOST SOULS

1932 (NR) 71m / **D:** Erle C. Kenton / **W:** Philip Wylie, Waldemar Young / **C:** Charles Laughton, Bela Lugosi, Richard Arlen, Leila Hyams, Kathleen Burke, Stanley Fields, Robert F. (Bob) Kortman, Arthur Hohl

A horrifying, highly effective adaptation of H. G. Wells's *The Island of Dr. Moreau*, initially banned in parts of the U.S. because of its disturbing content. Charles Laughton is a mad scientist on a remote tropical island, obsessed with making men out of jungle animals through extensive, painful surgery. The jungle is full of Laughton's half-finished experiments, all of whom are kept in line by a rigid code of behavior ("the Law") and threats of a return to the laboratory where they were created (the aptly named "House of Pain"). When a shipwreck survivor is stranded on the island, Laughton plots to mate him with Lota, a young woman who was originally a panther. The film is as unsettling today as it was in the 1930s. Kathleen Burke beat out more than 60,000 young women in a nationwide search to play Lota the Panther Woman; she won the role with her "feline" looks. Bela Lugosi has a small but unforgettable role as the Sayer of the Law. Alan Ladd, Randolph Scott, Buster Crabbe appear in cameos. Two inferior adaptations followed.

ISLAND OF TERROR

1966 (NR) 90m / **D:** Terence Fisher / **W:** Alan Ramsen, Edward Andrew Mann / **C:** Peter Cushing, Edward Judd, Carole Gray, Sam Kydd, Niall MacGinnis, Eddie Byrne

First-rate chiller about a British island overrun by single-celled creatures with protective shells that suck the bones out of their living prey with slimy tentacles. Good performances and interesting twists make for prickles up the spine. Another British sci-fi feature in the tried-and-true tradition of the Quatermass series: a remote community is slowly overrun by a creeping terror from beyond, while a tough scientist is called in to battle it. Terence Fisher is better known for his Hammer horror films (*Horror of Dracula*, *Curse of Frankenstein*, *The Mummy*, etc.), but he also could deliver solid sci-fi when called upon. AKA: *Night of the Silicates*; *The Creepers*.

ISLAND OF THE BURNING DOOMED

1967 (NR) 94m / D: Terence Fisher / **W:** Ronald Liles, Jane Baker, Pip Baker / **C:** Christopher Lee, Peter Cushing, Patrick Allen, Sarah Lawson, Jane Merrow

Director Terence Fisher's atmospheric style usually worked for his Hammer Studio gothic horror films, but when it comes to this attempt at sci-fi, a little more punch was needed. Based on the John Lymington novel *Night of the Big Heat*, this story concerns an alien protoplasm that takes over a British island and somehow causes a bizarre winter heatwave intense enough to burn most of the inhabitants to death. Peter Cushing and Christopher Lee (as usual, the film's saving graces) survive to do battle with the egg-like blobacious creatures who are desperate for any heat source. AKA: *Island of the Burning Damned*; *Night of the Big Heat*.

IT CAME FROM BENEATH THE SEA

1955 (NR) 80m / D: Robert Gordon / **W:** George Worthing Yates, Hal Smith / **C:** Kenneth Tobey, Faith Domergue, Ian Keith, Donald Curtis, Dean Maddox

A giant octopus arises from the depths of the sea to scour San Francisco for human food. Ray Harryhausen f/x are special, but more suspense is generated by the unusual soap-opera triangle among the three leads than by any plans to deal with the menacing behemoth. Harryhausen's inventive scenery has the creature's tentacles invade the city streets like serpents, and the sight of the octopus breaking apart the Golden Gate bridge is especially inspired. All this with only five tentacles, which is all the budget would allow. Kenneth Tobey's affable charm was used to better effect battling *The Thing from Another World*, but beautiful Faith Domergue fared less well in *This Island Earth*.

IT CAME FROM OUTER SPACE

1953 (NR) 81m / D: Jack Arnold / **W:** Harry Essex / **C:** Richard Carlson, Barbara Rush, Charles Drake, Russell Johnson, Morey Amsterdam, Joseph Sawyer

Non-humanoid aliens crash in the Arizona desert and take the form of captured local residents to repair their spacecraft and get away before Earth authorities move in. Good performances and outstanding direction by genre specialist Jack Arnold enhances an unusually sympathetic portrayal—for the time period—of cosmic visitors (compare this with *Invaders from Mars* that same year), not

Barbara Rush and Richard Carlson starred in *It Came from Outer Space,* a somewhat sympathetic portrayal of aliens who have crash landed on Earth.

to mention what some saw as an anti-McCarthyite subtext. Based on the story "The Meteor" by Ray Bradbury, though Hollywood vet Harry Essex (*The Creature from the Black Lagoon*) insisted he rather than Bradbury authored the shooting script. Originally filmed in 3D.

IT CONQUERED THE WORLD

1956 (NR) 68m / **D:** Roger Corman / **W:** Charles B. Griffith, Lou Rusoff / **C:** Peter Graves, Beverly Garland, Lee Van Cleef, Sally Fraser, Russ Bender, Jonathan Haze, Dick Miller, Karen Kadler, Paul Blaisdell

Eccentric scientist Lee Van Cleef makes radio contact with a dying race of intelligent creatures on Venus. By the time he finds out that their plans are less than benevolent, it's too late, and only his buddy Peter Graves can stop the resulting invasion. The largely immobile (and goofy looking) Venusian invader hides out in a cave giving birth to creepy bat-like creatures, which fly to their specified human targets and implant stingers in the backs of their necks, bringing them under telepathic control. Shares many attributes of *Invasion of the Body Snatchers* (released several months earlier), but with all the subtlety removed for the target drive-in crowd. Much like the work of Ed Wood during the same years, Corman's early vintage zero-budget exploitation pictures are just as hilariously bad, but with a knowing, intellectual subtext. This one's hip-deep in anti-fascist rhetoric. Graves brings the message home with a huge thud by making a closing speech. Remade for television as *Zontar, the Thing from Venus*.

IT HAPPENED HERE

1965 (NR) 93m / **D:** Andrew Mollo, Kevin Brownlow / **W:** Andrew Mollo, Kevin Brownlow / **C:** Pauline Murray, Sebastian Shaw, Fiona Leland, Honor Fearson

Filmed over 10 years on a tiny budget, this scrappy, thoughtful alternate-history war film imagines England several years after being conquered by the Wehrmacht in 1940. Rich with detail: German soldiers in full kit rush onto an Underground train filled with commuters, while Jews are cordoned off by barbed wire into a London ghetto. What there is of a plot follows small-town nurse Pauline Murray, who signs up with the local British Nazi party offshoot after partisans kill many of her neighbors. She tries to keep out of politics but like quicksand, the immoral imperatives of working for the occupation—first loyalty oaths and eventually euthanizing people deemed useless by the Nazis—keep dragging her further into the muck. Dramatically thin but convincing look at how easily middle-of-the-road attitudes can be translated into collaboration. Mostly available in poor transfers with muddy sound and visuals that don't help clarify an already sketchy storyline.

IT'S ALIVE

1974 (PG) 91m / D: Larry Cohen / **W:** Larry Cohen / **C:** John P. Ryan, Sharon Farrell, Andrew Duggan, Guy Stockwell, James Dixon, Michael Ansara

A memorable cult film about a mutant baby born to a normal Los Angeles couple. The clawed, fanged infant wreaks havoc in the delivery room, then escapes from the hospital and goes on a bloodthirsty, murderous rampage. In one grimly amusing scene, Junior goes after a milk-truck. The concept is ingenious, the gore kept at a minimum, and the monster all the more effective for being rarely glimpsed. This nasty little gem was followed by two sequels, all to be avoided by prospective parents.

IT! THE TERROR FROM BEYOND SPACE

1958 (NR) 68m / D: Edward L. Cahn / **W:** Jerome Bixby / **C:** Marshall Thompson, Shawn Smith, Kim Spalding, Ann Doran, Dabbs Greer, Paul Langton, Ray Corrigan, Robert Bice

Sole survivor of a Mars expedition is arrested for the mass slaughter of his colleagues. As he protests his innocence, the real culprit, a big, hungry Martian, stows away aboard the Earth-bound rocket and begins killing crew members en route. An obvious inspiration for *Alien*, though suspense here is even more claustrophobic, as the brute pounds its way through hatch after hatch, backing the desperate survivors up into the nose cone. Jerome Bixby's commendably sober script ends with the warning "Another name for Mars is Death!," and Paul Blaisdell contributed a fearsome lizard man costume. Tape includes the original theatrical trailer ("See IT! Don't miss IT!"). AKA: *It! The Vampire from Beyond Space.*

I WAS A ZOMBIE FOR THE F.B.I.

1982 (NR) 105m / D: Maurice Penczner / **W:** Maurice Penczner / **C:** James Raspberry, Larry Raspberry, John Gillick, Christina Wellford, Anthony Isbell, Laurence Hall, Rick Crowe

Aliens who look just like old-fashioned gangsters land near Pleasantville, USA, and make a deal with a couple of human criminals to rule the world. Their extraterrestrial super-science hypnotizes victims "clinically in what is known as a zomboid state," while just-the-facts-ma'am federal agents combat the un-American menace and their badly animated reptile monster. Black-and-white production by Memphis State University students is a dry, deadpan recreation of McCarthy-era sci-fi quickies, so close to the real thing that the mirth turns to tedium under an interminable running time. Still, some kind of achievement.

Jason X

2001 (R) 91m / **D:** James Isaac / **W:** Todd Farmer / **C:** Kane Hodder, Jeff Geddis, Lexa Doig, Chuck Campbell, Jonathan Potts, Peter Mensah, Lisa Ryder, David Cronenberg

Having apparently run out of people to kill on Earth, Jason of *Friday the 13th* infamy is thawed out hundreds of years in the future to kill people on a spaceship in a variety of exciting and blood-spurting ways. Director James Isaac did some f/x work for David Cronenberg on *eXistenz*; Cronenberg pops up here in a cameo.

La Jetée

1964 (NR) 28m / **D:** Chris Marker / **W:** Chris Marker / **C:** Davos Hanich, Hélène Chatelain

One of the greatest film shorts of all time, filled with more mystery and dread than most feature-length films. Told almost completely through still photographs and narration, this post-WWIII tale takes place in a future Paris where survivors now live in subterranean vaults. Repeating image of a woman's face and a childhood experience at an airport provide impetus for time travel through memory projection. Director Chris Marker, also a novelist and photographer, makes use of all his talents and delivers a unique, spellbinding photo-novel-movie whose dense philosophical paradox gives you a punch right in the cerebellum. Later served as the inspiration for Terry Gilliam's sci-fi plague thriller *12 Monkeys*.

John Carter

2012 (PG-13) 132m / **D:** Andrew Stanton / **W:** Andrew Stanton, Mark Andrews, Michael Chabon / **C:** Taylor Kitsch, Lynn Collins, Samantha Morton, Willem Dafoe, Thomas Haden Church, Mark Strong, Ciarán Hinds, Dominic West

By the time Hollywood got around to making a movie out of Edgar Rice Burroughs's sci-fi adventure series, which first appeared in 1912, the books had inspired so many writers and filmmakers (everyone from Lucas to Bradbury) that the ideas couldn't help but feel second-hand. Sharp-cheekboned Taylor Kitsch plays the titular Civil War veteran who is mysteriously transported to Mars, where he discovers warring tribes of 12-foot aliens as well as weak gravity that grants him superhero-like powers. Much leaping about and swinging of swords follows, when Carter isn't romancing the beautiful Martian princess Dejah Thoris (Lynn Collins), who in true 21st-century fashion is much more willing to scrap with the guys than Burroughs had her. The mixture of old and new technologies (swords and spears intermingling with rifles and hovercraft) is convincingly depicted. Veteran Pixar director Andrew Stanton is on less sure ground in his first live-action outing than he was with more unified-seeming work like *WALL-E*. An occasionally rambunctious piece of pulp that might have succeeded had Disney not dumped hundreds of millions of dollars, and thusly far too many expectations, into it. Novelist Michael Chabon—who years earlier had come close to having his own Burroughs-influenced film, *The Martian Agent*, made—contributed to the screenplay.

JOHN DIES AT THE END

2012 (R) 99m / D: Don Coscarelli / **W:** Don Coscarelli / **C:** Chase Williamson, Rob Mayes, Paul Giamatti, Clancy Brown, Glynn Turman, Doug Jones

In this reality-bending tongue-in-cheeker from Don Coscarelli (*Phantasm*), there's an insanely addictive new drug on the street called Soy Sauce that people have been taking, even though it provides psychic powers, sends them into parallel dimensions, and unleashes all kinds of hellspawn. Things get complicated for Dave (Chase Williamson) and John (Rob Mayes), the two slacker guys at the center of the film. Journalist Paul Giamatti (also a producer) interviews Dave, the one who's *not* supposed to die at the end, in a Chinese restaurant and tries to make sense of things. Based on a cult Web serial and later novel by David Wong.

JOHNNY MNEMONIC

1995 (R) 98m / D: Robert Longo / **W:** William Gibson / **C:** Keanu Reeves, Dina Meyer, Ice-T, Takeshi Kitano, Dolph Lundgren, Henry Rollins, Udo Kier, Barbara Sukowa, Denis Akiyama

Sleepy sci-fi thriller based on a screenplay by cyberpunk godfather William Gibson (author of cult favorite *Neuromancer*) and directed by artist Robert Longo (in his first film). Keanu Reeves plays a high-tech courier of the future, whose brain has been technologically enhanced, allowing him to carry a huge amount of computer information in his head. Only problem is, he can only store the information for a limited amount of time before his brain turns to mush (even in the future they can't fix that). Johnny takes one last mission to earn enough money to restore memories he gave up for added cyber storage. Of course, things go badly as Johnny is hunted by the Japanese Yakuza and various other unsavory characters who want his head (literally). Johnny is aided by an implant-enhanced bodyguard (Dina Meyer), a group of underground hackers called the LoTeks (dig the neo-Luddite subtext), and a former doctor (Henry Rollins) trying to cure a technology-induced plague. Keanu gives an even more dead-pan performance than usual, perhaps because he is missing part of his brain. Look for an almost-unrecognizable Dolph Lundgren as the Preacher.

JUBILEE

1978 (NR) 106m / **D:** Derek Jarman / **W:** Derek Jarman / **C:** Jenny Runacre, Nell Campbell, Toyah Wilcox, Jordan, Hermine Demoriane, Ian Charleson, Karl Johnson, Jayne County, Richard O'Brien, Adam Ant

Before he starred in the "Matrix" films, Keanu Reeves played a high-tech courier in *Johnny Mnemonic.*

Anarchic revolutionary skit show has Queen Elizabeth I time-traveling from the 16th century to a futuristic London populated by bored, homicidal punks. This being Derek Jarman, what there is of a story is interrupted by bluntly satirical avant-absurdist performance pieces. The acting is stiff as a board, much like what you'd expect from a poorly considered video art installation. Bleak atmospherics keenly evoke the embittered British underground mood of the time. Nice touches include nods to *The Rocky Horror Picture Show* in a couple scenes, also the casting of Richard O'Brien as one of the Queen's courtiers and Nell Campbell as one of the more murderous gutter punks. Scattershot rummaging through classical tropes and nihilist futurism suggests *Fellini Satyricon* meets *A Clockwork Orange*.

JUDGE DREDD

1995 (R) 96m / **D:** Danny Cannon / **W:** Steven E. de Souza, Michael De Luca, William Wisher / **C:** Sylvester Stallone, Armand Assante, Diane Lane, Rob Schneider, Joan Chen, Jürgen Prochnow, Max von Sydow

An overblown but serviceable film version of the famous cult comic *2000 AD* that retains some but not all of the chaotic spirit of the British strip. Sylvester Stallone even looks the square-jawed part, and once you get over his slurring of Dredd's most noted line—"I am the law!"—he isn't quite so bad. Dredd is framed for murder by ex-judge/arch-criminal Rico (Armand Assante), who loves to kill and knows some dark, Dredded family secret. Banished from Mega City One with nothing but would-be comic relief in the unctuous form of Rob Schneider, Dredd has to face inbred mutants in the wasteland while trying to clear his name. Add to this lady judge Diane Lane, an opening aerial tour of Mega City One that tries to one up *Blade Runner*, a high-altitude motorcycle chase, dialogue delivered with an acting-be-damned attitude, and you've got a solid piece of dystopian celluloid.

JUMPER

2008 (PG-13) 88m / D: Doug Liman / **W:** Jim Uhls, David S. Goyer, Simon Kinberg / **C:** Hayden Christensen, Samuel L. Jackson, Rachel Bilson, Jamie Bell, Diane Lane

Young adult-styled sci-fi fantasy adventure in which a permanently pained-looking Hayden Christensen discovers he can teleport himself anywhere. Fun opener in which he zips around the world for a few years living the high life (teleportation making bank-robbing a cinch) whips by too quickly before a murderous, white-haired Samuel L. Jackson shows up on his trail. Apparently, "Paladins" (that's Jackson) are an ancient cult of religious extremists who hate "Jumpers" (Christensen) because, well, they just do. That's about it for plot. Rachel Bilson is Christensen's pallid love interest and Jamie Bell a cynical, cocky jumper who has things a little more worked out: "Paladins kill Jumpers. I kill Paladins. Class dismissed."

JURASSIC PARK

1993 (PG-13) 127m / D: Steven Spielberg / **W:** David Koepp, Michael Crichton / **C:** Sam Neill, Laura Dern, Jeff Goldblum, Richard Attenborough, Bob Peck, Martin Ferrero, B. D. Wong, Joseph Mazzello, Ariana Richards, Samuel L. Jackson, Wayne Knight

Michael Crichton's Frankenstein genetic engineering thriller translates well (but not entirely faithfully) to the big screen due to its main attraction: realistic, rampaging dinosaurs. Rich industrialist Richard Attenborough plans to open a theme park on a remote island whose attraction is genetically cloned dinosaurs hatched from prehistoric DNA. Just when Attenborough brings some visitors over for a preview visit, the dinosaurs escape from their pens, smarter and less predictable than expected, and quickly change the vibe from Disneyland to Tokyo in a *Godzilla* movie. Though Crichton recycles plot elements from his other work and Steven Spielberg is working

When scientists discover how to create real-live dinosaurs, they naturally decide to turn the idea into a tourist trap in *Jurassic Park.* If only they had stuck with the herbivores....

in a strictly B-movie idiom, the movie is still tremendously entertaining. The characters are the typical mix of scientists (Laura Dern, Sam Neill, Jeff Goldblum), who argue about the implications of man playing God (Goldblum's speeches about chaos theory introduced it to a mass audience), and the millionaire's grandchildren, initially awestruck by the creatures that quickly try to eat them. The real stars are the dinos themselves, a convincing mix of computer imagery and models that marked the true beginning of modern f/x. Suspenseful popcorn matinee that's just a touch too violent for the small children who are bound to be most interested in it. Oscars for sound effects editing, f/x, and sound.

JURASSIC PARK III

2001 (PG-13) 92m / D: Joe Johnston / **W:** Peter Buchman, Alexander Payne, Jim Taylor / **C:** Sam Neill, William H. Macy, Téa Leoni, Alessandro Nivola, Trevor Morgan, Michael Jeter, John Diehl

So why would a third outing for Michael Crichton's genetically reborn dinosaurs be necessary? Clearly because the first two films never got around to dealing with flying dinosaurs like pteranodons. Steven Spielberg hands over the reins to f/x journeyman Joe Johnston (*Jumanji*) for this cashing-in sequel wherein researcher Sam Neill is convinced to go back to Site

B (the island from *The Lost World*) in order to help William H. Macy and Téa Leoni rescue their lost child; apparently he needs the money. Things go south in a hurry, only unfortunately this time there's no cheery-doomy chaos-theory carping from Jeff Goldblum to leaven things out. New dino-threats include the spinosaurus and deadly flocks of pteranodons, whose fog-shrouded prehistoric cage makes for one of the series' most memorable images. The pacing is swift, almost manic. But while the lack of are-we-playing-God theorizing speeds things up, it also turns the film into something of a mechanical theme-park ride. *Election* filmmakers Alexander Payne and Jim Taylor worked on the script.

KABOOM

2010 (NR) 86m / D: Gregg Araki / **W:** Gregg Araki / **C:** Thomas Dekker, Haley Bennett, Roxane Mesquida, Chris Zylka, Nicole LaLiberte, Juno Temple

After detouring briefly into creative maturity with *Mysterious Skin* (2004), Gregg Araki returns to the stylistic security blanket of earlier work like *The Doom Generation* (1995), where nubile young things are thrown into a blender of frenetic sex and non-sequitur violence. The arbitrary setting is a college where polyamorously confused and dazed-looking student Thomas Dekker is stuck between his lust for a blonde surfer named Thor and confusing advice from his bitchy girlfriends. There's also a nest of dark conspiracies and disturbing dreams about aliens messing with his head. Fast, cheap, and junky.

KAMIKAZE 1989

1983 (NR) 90m / D: Wolf Gremm / **W:** Wolf Gremm, Robert Katz / **C:** Rainer Werner Fassbinder, Günther Kaufman, Boy Gobert

German director Rainer Werner Fassbinder has the lead role (his last) in this offbeat futuristic story of a police lieutenant in Berlin, circa 1989, who investigates a puzzling series of bombings. Fassbinder's leopard-print suit makes an impression. In German with English subtitles. AKA: *Kamikaze '89*.

KILLERS FROM SPACE

1954 (NR) 80m / D: W. Lee Wilder / **W:** William Raynor / **C:** Peter Graves, Barbara Bestar, James Seay, Frank Gerstle, Steve Pendleton, John Merrick

Big-eyed men from beyond Earth bring scientist Peter Graves back to life and force him to assist them with their evil plan for world domination.

Some atmospheric photography makes this almost worthwhile as an entry in the newborn genre of early 1950s sci-fi noir. But some incredibly shoddy f/x involving enlarged shots of bugs and lizards, along with a lethargic pace, put this one deep in the trash barrel. The same year W. Lee Wilder made this cheapie and *The Snow Creature*, his brother Billy was making *Sabrina*.

KING KONG VS. GODZILLA

1963 (NR) 105m / **D:** Ishiro Honda / **W:** Shinichi Sekizawa / **C:** Tadao Takashima, Mie Hama, Kenji Sahara, Akihiko Hirata, Michael Keith

An entrepreneur captures a giant ape on a South Pacific island, names him King Kong (after the classic movie, of course), and plans to bring him back to Japan to star on the TV show he sponsors. Unfortunately, the beast escapes. Meanwhile, Godzilla breaks out of an iceberg and begins another campaign of destruction. The government figures that if they get the two monsters to fight, maybe they'll finish each other off. Or destroy the world. Either way: Fight! Humankind can only stand by and watch in impotent horror as the two mightiest monsters slug it out. For Godzilla's third appearance, Toho went for a more whimsical atmosphere, spicing their outlandish story with doses of satire. Godzilla appears positively nasty and looking for trouble—while the Kong costume is, sadly, rather shoddy looking, and the actor inside fails to act like an ape. For the U.S. version, Universal altered the film drastically, deleting and rearranging scenes while adding bland sequences from the viewpoint of a TV anchor desk. Even Akira Ifukube's powerful score was thrown out in favor of stock library music. In any case, *King Kong vs. Godzilla* became a monster hit at the box office all over the world and is still a mighty entertaining monster mash.

KING OF THE ROCKETMEN

1949 (NR) 156m / **D:** Fred Brannon / **W:** Royal Cole, William Lively, Sol Shor / **C:** Tristram Coffin, Mae Clarke, I. Stanford Jolley

Mystery villain Dr. Vulcan is knocking off eminent scientists, so researcher Jeff King (Tristam Coffin, a mustachioed actor often seen in bad-guy roles) fights back in disguise, using a newly invented jet backpack and metal mask to become the flying hero Rocket Man. Twelve-chapter Republic serial created the simple but way-cool Rocket Man costume later reused in non-sequel serials *Radar Men from the Moon* and *Zombies of the Stratosphere*, and, of course, inspired *The Rocketeer*. Action is lively, if a bit on the low-budget side (Dr. Vulcan's lavish death-ray mayhem is actually composed of clips from the vintage disaster flick *Deluge*), but flying scenes, done using a mannequin on cables, are pretty good for the era. Later released as a feature titled *Lost Planet Airmen*.

KISS ME DEADLY

1955 (NR) 105m / **D:** Robert Aldrich / **W:** A. I. Bezzerides / **C:** Ralph Meeker, Albert Dekker, Paul Stewart, Wesley Addy, Cloris Leachman, Strother Martin, Marjorie Bennett, Jack Elam

Robert Aldrich's adaptation of Mickey Spillane's private-eye tale takes pulp literature high concept and adds a sci-fi twist. Ralph Meeker, as Mike Hammer, is a self-interested, rough-and-tumble all-American dick (detective, that is). When a woman to whom he happened to give a ride is found murdered, he follows the mystery straight into a nuclear conspiracy. Aldrich, with tongue deftly in cheek, styles a message through the medium; topsy turvy camerawork and rat-a-tat-tat pacing tell volumes about Hammer, the world he orbits, and that special 1950s brand of paranoia. Now a cult fave, it's considered to be the American grandaddy to French New Wave. The crisp black-and-white cinematography by Ernest Laszlo (*Inherit the Wind*, *Judgment at Nuremberg*) shows a lost Los Angeles destined for the wrecking ball. The original, slightly less apocalyptic, ending was restored in the '90s.

A sci-fi element is introduced into a Mickey Spillane detective story in 1955's cult fave *Kiss Me Deadly*.

KNOWING

2009 (PG-13) 121m / **D:** Alex Proyas / **W:** Ryne Douglas Pearson, Juliet Snowden, Stiles White / **C:** Nicolas Cage, Chandler Canterbury, Rose Byrne, Lara Robinson, Phil Beckman, Nadia Townsend

Nicolas Cage plays an MIT astrophysics professor (stay with us, here) who can easily boil his thoughts on causation down to "shit just happens." Then his son's school opens up a time capsule filled with letters written by students about what the future will bring. The letter his son gets is covered in numbers, which Cage soon realizes all correspond to the dates of horrendous accidents from the past as well as the all-too-near future. As veterans of time-travel scenarios know all too well, having the knowledge of a future or past event doesn't give somebody the ability to stop it. So knowledge provides him no comfort. Those shadowy figures lurking in director Alex

Proyas's many dark shadows don't help, either. Photographed in rich but gloomy tones and about as sonorous as you can imagine, this quasi-mystical sci-fi curiosity offers occasionally intriguing metaphysical, philosophical, and religious debate about determinism versus randomness against a convincingly haunted, apocalyptic backdrop.

K-PAX

2001 (PG-13) 120m / D: Iain Softley / **W:** Charles Leavitt / **C:** Kevin Spacey, Jeff Bridges, Mary McCormack, Alfre Woodard, David Patrick Kelly

Wearing the same vague smirk of superiority that's sustained him through much of his career, Kevin Spacey shows up in this soft-minded spiritual allegory as a mental patient who calls himself Prot and claims to be an alien from "about 1,000 of your light years away." Jeff Bridges plays the initially skeptical but increasingly credulous therapist assigned to Prot, who is soon getting his fellow inmates excited about the possibility of beaming away to his home planet. Director Iain Softley (*Hackers*) turns in a glossy, rote piece of sci-fi-dusted, is-he-or-isn't-he Hollywood guff that has about as much to do with actual mental illness as *The Terminator* has to do with the physics of time travel.

KRONOS

1957 (NR) / 78m / D: Kurt Neumann / **W:** Lawrence Louis Goldman / **C:** Jeff Morrow, Barbara Lawrence, John Emery, George O'Hanlon, Morris Ankrum

Energy-hungry aliens send an "accumulator"—a giant robot resembling a piston—to drain the Earth of all power sources. Scientists and their computer SUSIE (Synchro Unifying Sinometric Integrating Equitensor) sweat out a solution. Offbeat space-invader saga is hopelessly hobbled by a low budget; whenever Kronos is on the move it turns into a cartoon so obviously hand-drawn that Wile E. Coyote could order it from Acme to use on the Roadrunner.

KRULL

1983 (PG) 121m / D: Peter Yates / **W:** Stanford Sherman / **C:** Ken Marshall, Lysette Anthony, Freddie Jones, Francesca Annis, Liam Neeson, Alun Armstrong

Though set on the distant world of Krull, filled with fantasy creatures of myth and magic, there's a labored sense of familiarity all over this costly dud, in which a Kong-sized invader called the Beast lands his starship/fortress in a peaceful kingdom and sends hordes of insectoid stormtroopers to ravage the land. Handsome prince embarks on a quest to find the Glaive (a sort of buzzsaw-boomerang weapon) and joins with Merrie Men types to save his Beastnapped bride. Actors unfortunately treat this material like Shakespeare; in truth, it's yet another pompous 1980s try at the Ultimate Fairy Tale, never mind that one had already been done in 1977—*Star Wars*. F/x by Derek Meddings (*Batman*).

THE LAND OF THE DEAD

2005 (R) 93m / D: George A. Romero / **W:** George A. Romero / **C:** John Leguizamo, Asia Argento, Simon Baker, Dennis Hopper, Eugene Clark, Robert Joy

Almost four decades after starting the zombie genre, George Romero returned to it with this bigger budgeted futuristic take that finds the undead showing something they tend not to in these movies: organizational skills. Granted, their strategizing against the humans—who are mostly holed up now in a Trump-esque luxury high-rise while their hired guns scour the ruined city around them for supplies—isn't something that would make Rommel jealous. Nevertheless, the notion of a zombie leader (Eugene Clark) puts a new spin on things. This being Romero, though, human greed and in-fighting causes almost as much damage as the undead themselves. Featuring John Leguizamo as one of the hired guns who yearns for a better life, Asia Argento (family friend of Romero) as fishnet-clad warrior babe, and Dennis Hopper as the sleazy suit profiting off the apocalypse.

LASERBLAST

1978 (PG) 87m / D: Michael Rae / **W:** Franne Schacht, Frank Ray Perilli / **C:** Kim Milford, Cheryl Smith, Keenan Wynn, Roddy McDowall

Prolific low-budget producer Charles Band first gained genre attention (little of it positive) with this drive-in hybrid of *Carrie* and *Close Encounters* in which an abused wimp gets revenge when he finds a powerful laser gun dropped by dinosaur-like aliens. The more our antihero wields the death ray, the more mutated he becomes, though his tiny-budget rampage mainly zaps just an empty street, a few parked cars, a mailbox, and a crudely handmade billboard for *Star Wars* (take *that*, Lucas!). Lamentable stop-motion f/x by David Allen. Later remade as *Deadly Weapon*.

THE LAST BATTLE

1984 (R) 93m / D: Luc Besson / **W:** Luc Besson, Pierre Jolivet / **C:** Pierre Jolivet, Fritz Wepper, Jean Bouise, Jean Reno

For his debut feature, French action auteur Luc Besson created a strikingly conceived black-and-white nightmare world of deserts, ruins, and bleached wreckage, with no dialogue (possible explanation: poison gas has burned out everyone's vocal cords) and weird weather phenomena. The "Man," a spear-

> "For his debut feature, French action auteur Luc Besson created a strikingly conceived black-and-white nightmare world...."
>
> *The Last Battle*

carrying every barbarian, tires of life in the parched wastelands and pilots his homebuilt aircraft to a devastated city where he befriends a doctor (who does caveman-style paintings on the walls) and fights a running duel with relentless brute Reno. Good luck puzzling through some of the grunting mime "dialogue," and the ending feels like a bit of a cheat. The movie is a glimpse at what lies beyond the fall of civilization, but it will stick in your mind a lot longer than all those other low-octane *Road Warrior* wannabes. AKA: *The Final Combat*.

THE LAST CHASE

1981 (PG) 106m / D: Martyn Burke / **W:** Christopher Crowe, Martyn Burke / **C:** Lee Majors, Burgess Meredith, Chris Makepeace, Alexandra Stewart

Famed race car driver becomes a vocal dissenter against the sterile and oppressive society of the near future. Keen-minded viewers of this fast-paced piece of camp may note the possibility that driving fast cars with abandon *could* serve as a metaphor for freedom. Made for television. Screenplay written by Christopher Crowe under the pseudonym C. R. O'Christopher.

LAST DAYS OF PLANET EARTH

1974 (NR) 88m / D: Toshio Masuda / **W:** Toshio Yasumi, Yoshimitsu Banno / **C:** Tetsuro Tamba, So Yamamura, Takashi Shimura

More interesting as societal symptom than entertainment, this Japanese doomsday movie focuses on scientists and their families who witness a build-up of pollution responsible for giant mutant slugs, marauding bats, freak weather conditions, birth defects, and other environmental calamities. Positively gleeful in describing how bad things could possibly get, it inserts footage from previous Toho disaster classics like *The Last War* and *The Submersion of Japan*, then abandons pretense of narrative to become a documentary about the prophecies of Nostradamus. Join our doomsday cult, listen to our leader, be saved. Dubbed in English. AKA: *Prophecies of Nostradamus*; *Catastrophe 1999*.

THE LAST DAYS ON MARS

2013 (PG-13) 98m / D: Ruairi Robinson / **W:** Clive Dawson / **C:** Liev Schreiber, Olivia Williams, Romola Garai, Elias Koteas, Johnny Harris, Goran Kostić, Tom Cullen, Yusra Warsama

Another entry in the increasingly popular Don't Venture Out There subgenre about astronauts who go exploring and get very, very dead for their troubles. A grim, acting-his-heart-out Liev Schreiber is the standout here in a crack ensemble cast playing a crew of researchers coming to the frustrating end of a fruitless six-month research mission on Mars. The performers get the first half-hour or so to create real characters and dramatic tension before one dramatic convenience too many and one superlatively foolish crew member brings a zombie bacteria into the equation. Superbly acted but ultimately generic off-Earth sci-fi horror.

THE LAST MAN ON EARTH

1964 (NR) 86m / **D:** Ubaldo Ragona, Sidney Salkow / **W:** Richard Matheson, William F. Leicester / **C:** Vincent Price, Franca Bettoia, Giacomo "Jack" Rossi-Stuart, Emma Danieli

Richard Matheson's compelling novel *I Am Legend* has been the uncredited inspiration for many zombie/plague/end-of-the-world films, but this was the first credited adaptation. Vincent Price plays The Last Man on Earth, lone survivor of a plague that first kills, and then zombifies its victims. On one of his daytime zombie hunts, Price comes across a group who, through injections, are not as zombied-out as the rest of the neighbors, but still have a bit of the ol' pasty face and resent his total aliveness. Poorly done repetitive violence and a hero who is pretty much too tired to go on. Matheson himself was so dissatisfied with the project that he used the fictitious name Logan Swanson for his co-scripting credit.

LAST NIGHT

1998 (R) 95m / **D:** Don McKellar / **W:** Don McKellar / **C:** Don McKellar, Sandra Oh, Roberta Maxwell, Robin Gammell, Sarah Polley, Genevieve Bujold

It's never made clear why, but everyone knows that the world is going to come to an end at exactly midnight. Don McKellar's multi-character study follows several people as they negotiate the last few hours of their life on earth. People talk, reveal, vent, revel, destroy, and mope while the sun steadfastly refuses to set. The whole thing is heavy with music; a radio station counting down the 500 best songs of all time and a climactic scene set to Pete Seeger's rendition of "Guantanamera." Something of a Canadian allstars show, with Sarah Polley and Genevieve Bujold showing up, along with a cameo from David Cronenberg as a utility company employee.

THE LAST STARFIGHTER

1984 (PG) 100m / **D:** Nick Castle / **W:** Jonathan Betuel / **C:** Lance Guest, Robert Preston, Barbara Bosson, Dan O'Herlihy, Catherine Mary Stewart, Cameron Dye, Kimberly Ross, Wil Wheaton, Norman Snow

The outer-space scenes in this warm-hearted adventure aren't nearly as interesting as the Starlight Starbright Trailer Court where the beginning is set. As a young man whose talent at video games turns him into the title character (making this the last word in nerd wish-fulfilments), Lance Guest is an engaging hero. The film is almost stolen by veteran character actors Robert Preston and Dan O'Herlihy, even though his face is completely hidden behind a lizard mask.

LAST WAR

1968 (NR) 79m / **D:** Shue Matsubayashi / **W:** Takeshi Kimura / **C:** Frankie Sakai, Nobuko Otowa, Akira Takarada, Yuriko Hoshi, Yumi Shirakawa

After World War III, continued tensions between the United States and Russia trigger Armageddon. Made by Toho Studios in 1961 during a period in which several films were made dealing with global destruction via atomic weapons, but not released in the U.S. (directly to TV) until 1968. The difference in this one is in its viewpoint from the unique perspective of the only country (so far) to have actually been a victim of nuclear warfare. As such, it's a sad tale of helpless victims resigned to destruction, as things continue to get worse around the globe. Awfully depressing stuff, enlivened only by the spectacle of Eiji Tsuburaya's masterful f/x work. The U.S. distributor tacked on the familiar song "It's a Small World" and an excerpt from President John Kennedy's anti-arms race speech in an attempt to Americanize the production. Often confused with the rarely seen and reportedly similar *The Final War*, produced by Toei the year before.

> "... it's a sad tale of helpless victims resigned to destruction ...."
>
> *Last War*

THE LAST WOMAN ON EARTH

1961 (NR) 71m / **D:** Roger Corman / **W:** Robert Towne / **C:** Antony Carbone, Edward Wain, Betsy Jones-Moreland

Two men vie for the affections of the sole surviving woman after a vague and unexplained disaster of vast proportions. Robert Towne, credited here under the pseudonym Edward Wain, wrote the script (his first screenwriting effort). You might want to watch this if it were the last movie on earth, although Corman fans will probably love it.

LATHE OF HEAVEN

1980 (NR) 120m / **D:** David Loxton / **W:** Diane English / **C:** Bruce Davison, Kevin Conway, Margaret Avery

In a near-future world, young George Orr visits a psychologist complaining that his dreams can alter and mold the real world. The ambitious shrink tries hypnosis to use the awesome superpower on a grand scale and cure mankind's many ills. Unfortunately, Orr's dreams have disastrous consequences—a demand for peace between all nations is realized via alien invasion—and much-redreamt reality, not to mention the plot, starts to fall apart. Promoted as the first made-for-TV movie done by public television, this adaptation of Ursula K. Le Guin's novel gets points for striving to be a highly cerebral affair (in an era when the commercial networks, not to mention major studios, mainly brainstormed over how to best rip off *Star Wars*). Suffers from an opaque finale, not helped by a PBS-level budget, but maintains a strong cult of admirers even though it can be notoriously difficult to find.

THE LAWLESS LAND

1988 (R) 81m / **D:** Jon Hess / **W:** Tony Cinciripini, Larry Leahy / **C:** Leon, Xander Berkeley, Nick Corri, Amanda Peterson

Post-holocaust America is ruled by a tyrant. Two young lovers who can't take it anymore try to escape his despotic rule, with a punk bounty-hunter in pursuit. Minimal sci-fi elements in this Roger Corman chase flick (shot in Chile), executed in the belief that a cattle skull mounted on the grill of a car is all you need to enter *Mad Max* territory.

THE LAWNMOWER MAN

1992 (R) 108m / **D:** Brett Leonard / **W:** Brett Leonard, Gimel Everett / **C:** Jeff Fahey, Pierce Brosnan, Jenny Wright, Mark Bringelson, Geoffrey Lewis, Jeremy Slate, Dean Norris

Scientist Pierce Brosnan uses a dim-witted gardener named Jobe (Jeff Fahey, in a fright wig) to test his virtual-reality computer techniques for enhancing intelligence. He's able to increase Jobe's mental powers beyond human measure, and not necessarily for the better, as the simple groundsman becomes a wrathful superbeing. So minimally based on a non-sci-fi short story by Stephen King that the author successfully sued to remove his precious name from the credits. Instead this is the premise of *Charly* crossbred with tired *Frankenstein* clichés and pumped up with trendy computer graphics f/x (including a memorable cybersex scene). Available in an unrated version with additional footage.

LAWNMOWER MAN 2: JOBE'S WAR

1995 (PG-13) 93m / **D:** Farhad Mann / **W:** Farhad Mann / **C:** Patrick Bergin, Matt Frewer, Austin O'Brien, Kevin Conway, Ely Pouget, Camille Cooper

Since just about everything and everyone had been blown up at the end of the first film, this one's less a sequel than a cinematic videogame. As such, it's a good sci-fi adventure for teen audiences with a quick pace and whiz-bang computer effects. In all other respects, it's not nearly as interesting as the original. Corporate baddie Walker (Kevin Conway) enlists Jobe to (what else?) take over the world using virtual reality. To the rescue

Sean Connery plays Allan Quartermain in *The League of Extraordinary Gentlemen*.

come one burned-out computer expert (Patrick Bergin) and a group of VR-addicted kids living in an abandoned subway. Technobabble abounds but nothing interesting ever happens. AKA: *Lawnmover Man 2: Beyond Cyberspace*.

THE LEAGUE OF EXTRAORDINARY GENTLEMEN

2003 (PG-13) 110m / **D:** Stephen Norrington / **W:** James Dale Robinson / **C:** Sean Connery, Naseeruddin Shah, Peta Wilson, Tony Curran, Stuart Townsend, Shane West, Jason Flemyng, Richard Roxburgh, David Hemmings

In 1899, Europe is lurching towards world war, terrorized by bandits with high-tech weaponry. The British Crown calls on adventurer Allan Quartermain (Sean Connery, still in fine fettle) to assemble a team to uncover the evil mastermind behind it all. Like its leader, the league is composed of literary characters made real: Captain Nemo, the Invisible Man, Dr. Jekyll, Tom Sawyer, Dorian Gray, and Mina Harker from *Dracula*. It's faithful to the plot of the first part of Alan Moore's inventive comic series, but *Blade* director Stephen Norrington surgically removes almost everything that made the original story special and replaces it with endless shootouts and overenthusiastic, underwhelming f/x (though the reimagining of the *Nautilus* as a gilded undersea palace is impressive). Doesn't do much of anything to reimagine a history where literary figures walk the Earth, though the addition of Gray is a nice touch and the introduction of Nemo's mysterious first mate makes for a halfway decent gag: "Call me Ishmael." Good loud fun at the start but gets lazy fast, particularly when compared to Moore's playfully layered alternate literary history.

LEFT BEHIND: THE MOVIE

2000 (PG-13) 96m / **D:** Vic Sarin / **W:** Alan McElroy, Paul Lalonde, Joe Goodman / **C:** Kirk Cameron, Brad Johnson, Janaya Stephens

The first of three movies based on Tim LaHaye and Jerry B. Jenkins' astoundingly successful series of Christian evangelical novels about what happens after millions of people suddenly disappear as part of the biblically prophesied Rapture. Various minions of Satan are at loose in the land and it's up to some good believers to stop them. Spoiler alert: the United Nations Secretary-General is the Antichrist.

LEVIATHAN

1989 (R) 98m / D: George P. Cosmatos / **W:** David Peoples, Jeb Stuart / **C:** Peter Weller, Ernie Hudson, Hector Elizondo, Amanda Pays, Richard Crenna, Daniel Stern, Lisa Eilbacher, Michael Carmine, Meg Foster

A motley crew of ocean-floor miners unwarily open a scuttled Soviet sub and are exposed to a failed genetic experiment that turns humans into insatiable, regenerating fish-creatures. Inspired by *The Abyss* but ripped off from *Alien*, this one sinks instead of swims, leaving a good cast all wet. Toothy monster f/x by Stan Winston.

LIFEFORCE

1985 (R) 100m / D: Tobe Hooper / **W:** Dan O'Bannon, Don Jakoby / **C:** Steve Railsback, Peter Firth, Frank Finlay, Patrick Stewart, Michael Gothard, Nicholas Ball, Aubrey Morris, Nancy Paul, Mathilda May, John Hallam

The most common complaint about this Tobe Hooper effort used to be that it moved too fast. The recent release of the European cut solves that problem (if it was one) by delivering 20 more minutes of story. Everything you'd ever want in a sci-fi/horror film is here. Halley's comet, the space shuttle, a gigantic spaceship, exploding bodies, apocalyptic zombie mob scenes, oversized batlike creatures, weird sex featuring Mathilda May showing herself off in her first film, and Steve "Manson" Railsback ranting and raving as only he can. May and two pals are brought to Earth from a ship found following a comet. Things take a nasty turn when the three are found to be soul-draining vampires, channeling their goodies back up to the vessel which has now parked itself in orbit around Earth and has unfolded a gigantic umbrella as a collector. Railsback, having gotten very close to May on the shuttle trip, finds himself psychically linked to her and is hot on her trail as she moves from body to body, spreading her plague of soulless zombies across Great Britain. *The Next Generation*'s Patrick Stewart appears as an asylum's head shrink in one of the niftiest effects scenes involving an incredibly tense "conversation." Score by Henry Mancini ends with quirky march during the credits and is exhilarating on its own; the longer and more explicit international edit features the complete Mancini score. Script by Dan O'Bannon was originally titled *They Bite*.

> "Everything you'd ever want in a sci-fi/horror film is here."
>
> *Lifeforce*

LIGHT YEARS

1988 (PG) 83m / **D:** René Laloux / **W:** René Laloux, Raphael Cluzel / V: Glenn Close, Jennifer Grey, Christopher Plummer, Penn Jillette, John Shea, David Johansen, Bridget Fonda, Paul Shaffer, Terrence Mann, Teller

Garish animated fantasy epic about an idyllic land suddenly beset by evil mutations and death rays. Based on the novel *Robots Against Gondohar* by Jean-Pierre Andrevon. Isaac Asimov worked on the script for the American adaptation, which was "directed" by indie producer Harvey Weinstein (who has a long history of chopping up foreign works for the domestic audience) and featured voice work by Glenn Close, Penn and Teller, and Christopher Plummer. AKA: *Gandahar*

LILO & STITCH

2002 (PG) 85m / **D:** Dean DeBlois, Chris Sanders / **W:** Dean DeBlois, Chris Sanders

A neat little surprise from Disney, whose animation in the post-*Little Mermaid* era has flipped back and forth between fairy-tale musicals and Pixar extravaganzas. Stitch is a rambunctious little monster of an alien bred for destruction and later exiled to a prison planet who ends up escaping to Earth. There, he's befriended by Lilo, a lonely young Hawaiian girl. The animation is gorgeously realized, and the relatedly non-idyllic family situation and Elvis songs on the soundtrack are just icing on the cake for non-Disney fans. Best sci-fi wrinkle: aliens are using Earth as a protected wildlife preserve to help rebuild the supposedly endangered mosquito population. Oscar nomination for best animated feature.

LIQUID SKY

1983 (R) 112m / **D:** Slava Tsukerman / **W:** Anne Carlisle / **C:** Anne Carlisle, Paula Sheppard, Bob Brady, Susan Doukas, Otto von Wernherr

Androgynous bisexual model (Anne Carlisle) living in Manhattan attracts a miniature UFO, which lands atop her penthouse. Its tiny, invisible occupant is in search of the chemical high it can only get by killing her sex partners in the throes of ecstasy, and a weird symbiotic relationship develops. Viewers either adore or despise this talky, one-of-a-kind weirdness directed by Russian expatriate Slava Tsukerman. Either way, the film succeeds in bringing its seedy early 1980s punk environment to life. Title is slang for heroin.

LOBSTER MAN FROM MARS

1989 (PG) 84m / **D:** Stanley Sheff / **W:** Bob Greenberg / **C:** Tony Curtis, Deborah Foreman, Patrick Macnee, Tommy Sledge, Billy Barty, Phil Proctor, Anthony Hickox

When a rich movie producer (Tony Curtis) learns from his accountant that he must produce a flop as a tax writeoff, he buys and promotes the titular homemade sci-fi movie from a young Ed Wood type. The film takes up most of the narrative, a cross between Corman's *It Conquered the World*, *Robot Monster*, and other notorious turkeys, about an invading lobster man, a screaming damsel, and a metaphor-spouting detective (stand-up comic Tommy Sledge). Not strictly a sci-fi film (and not too original either, having borrowed the premise of Mel Brooks's *The Producers*), but enough knowing spoofs of the genre warrant its inclusion here. Narration by radio's Dr. Demento.

LOCKOUT

2012 (PG-13) 95m / D: James Mather, Stephen Saint Leger / **W:** Stephen Saint Leger, James Mather, Luc Besson / **D:** Guy Pearce, Maggie Grace, Vincent Regan, Joseph Gilgun, Lennie James, Peter Stormare

Another sloppy *Escape from New York* clone from the Luc Besson action-factory. Set in outer space with a minimum of imagination, at least it keeps things brief. It's the year 2079, and Guy Pearce is the Snake Plissken secret operative who's framed for a murder but gets One Last Chance to clear his name: Hop the next space shuttle up to an orbiting supermax prison and rescue the president's daughter (Maggie Grace, who honed her blonde-in-danger chops In Besson's *Taken*) from the rioting maniacs who took her hostage. The cynicism is painted-on and the f/x vary from the competent to the laughable (one chase scene looks like it was put together by some teenager on his PC back in 1995). But an energized Pearce delivers his character's smartass lines ("I'm being beaten up by a guy called *Rupert*?") with an impressively cocky ease that makes some of the nonsense fly past a little quicker.

LOGAN'S RUN

1976 (PG) 120m / D: Michael Anderson Sr. / **W:** David Zelag Goodman / **C:** Michael York, Jenny Agutter, Richard Jordan, Roscoe Lee Browne, Farrah Fawcett, Peter Ustinov, Camilla Carr, Ann Ford

In the 23rd century, a hedonistic society exists in a huge bubble and people are only allowed to live to the age of 30, at which point they are expected to participate in ritual public suicide. Michael York plays a "Sandman," a sort of cop assigned to track down and assassinate "Runners"— those who try to escape and live past 30. The central government sends him on a mission to track down a rumored Runner enclave beyond the city and turn him into a Runner himself to do so. Intriguing concepts and great futuristic sets prevail here, but the plot tends to wander all over the place. The f/x, thought impressive at the time, were made instantly obsolete with the

In *Logan's Run,* a seemingly idyllic future world has one catch to it: everyone is put to death when they reach the age of 30.

release of *Star Wars* the following year. Roscoe Lee Browne provides the voice of a rather clumsy looking robot named Box, while Peter Ustinov shows up late in the game as the oldest man in the world. Based on the novel by William Nolan and George Clayton Johnson.

LOOKER

1981 (PG) 94m / **D:** Michael Crichton / **W:** Michael Crichton / **C:** Albert Finney, James Coburn, Susan Dey, Leigh Taylor-Young, Dorian Harewood, Darryl Hickman

Models being digitized for computer-generated TV commercials are systematically murdered. Albert Finney (looking understandably confused) plays their Beverly Hills plastic surgeon, who investigates and discovers a subliminal-ad conspiracy. Though subject matter was ahead of its time, a half-baked plot by the normally reliable Michael Crichton ultimately makes no sense and offers only mild distractions through semi-satirical potshots at the media, virtual reality, and mind control. Title refers to "Light Ocular Oriented Kinetic Energetic Responsers." And the occasional bimbo.

LOOPER

2012 (R) 119m / **D:** Rian Johnson / **W:** Rian Johnson / **C:** Joseph Gordon-Levitt, Bruce Willis, Emily Blunt, Paul Dano, Noah Segan, Piper Perabo, Jeff Daniels

One of the only time-travel films that doesn't even bother with the present day. The baseline date of Rian Johnson's thoughtful yet action-packed head-twister is 2044, when hired guns ("loopers") are paid to eliminate people deemed troublesome by the mob, who shoots them back in time from thirty years *further* in the future. Joseph Gordon-Levitt plays a looper whose life gets real complicated after finding himself looking down the barrel of a gun at his older self (Bruce Willis). The solution to his problem involves more paradoxes than an advanced quantum physics seminar. It plays with some noir elements here and there (the 2044 gangsters dress like mobsters of a century earlier, aping old movies) and there's a Stephen King-ian twist later on involving a telekinetic kid. But for the most part this is inventive, fully realized sci-fi of the highest order from a writer-director who not only appreciates the genre but is committed to pushing its limits.

THE LOST CONTINENT

1951 (NR) 82m / **D:** Sam Newfield / **W:** Richard H. Landau / **C:** Cesar Romero, Hillary Brooke, Chick Chandler, John Hoyt, Acquanetta, Sid Melton, Whit Bissell, Hugh Beaumont

An expedition searching for a lost rocket on a jungle island discovers dinosaurs and other extinct creatures. Are you ready for this? The dinosaurs are animated cartoons, the hero is Cesar Romero, and the director previously did the classic "all-midget western" *The Terror of Tiny Town*. A cast of dependable faces from 1950s sci-fi rounds things out. Not precisely a "must-see," the movie's sheer audacity makes it worth a look.

LOST IN SPACE

1998 (PG-13) 130m / **D:** Stephen Hopkins / **W:** Akiva Goldsman / **C:** William Hurt, Mimi Rogers, Heather Graham, Lacey Chabert, Jack Johnson, Gary Oldman, Matt LeBlanc

Fine, none-too-exciting example of 1990s big-studio tentpole strategizing: take a favorite old TV show with family friendly name-

William Hurt played a scientist who takes his family on a danger-filled ride to another planet in the big-budget, no-substance *Lost in Space*.

recognition potential, pump it full of f/x to bring in the teenagers, and stock the big and noisy concoction with enough popular TV stars and Oscar-nominated thespians to broadly appeal. Researcher William Hurt insists on bringing his family along (and thus continually putting them in harm's way) when he leads a mission to a nearby planet that he hopes can be colonized by everyone who wants to flee a dangerously polluted Earth. Gary Oldman plays the not-so-secretly evil Dr. Zachary Smith ("evil knows evil"), while puffed-chest crewman Matt LeBlanc makes goo-goo eyes at Hurt's daughter, Heather Graham. Director Stephen Hopkins (*Predator 2*) and writer Akiva Goldsman (*Batman Forever*) here prove their extreme comfort with check-cashing event-movie emptiness.

THE LOST WORLD: JURASSIC PARK

1997 (PG-13) 127m / **D:** Steven Spielberg / **W:** David Koepp / **C:** Jeff Goldblum, Julianne Moore, Pete Postlethwaite, Arliss Howard, Richard Attenborough, Vince Vaughn, Vanessa Lee Chester, Richard Schiff, Peter Stormare

Since either studio bookkeepers must have demanded it ("how hard can it be? Find some more dinosaurs") or he just really had a fun time on the first one. Steven Spielberg delivered this sequel to *Jurassic Park* in between more serious historical fare like *Schindler's List* and *Saving Private Ryan*. The story isn't precisely original: turns out there's *another* island where genetically engineered dinosaurs are being raised. Added to the mix of earnest, joke-cracking researchers who go there to explore and study are a band of mercenaries looking to grab themselves a few dinos to bring back to the mainland and display, King Kong-style. Needless to say, things don't go as planned. The dino-mayhem is impressively choreographed throughout, particularly in one rampaging homage to *Hatari!*, though the family dynamics become tiresome fast. Indie vets like Vince Vaughn, Pete Postlethwaite, and Peter Stormare bring some snap to the ensemble scenes. A returning Jeff Goldblum gets the one undeniably genius line from David Koepp's so-so screenplay: "Taking dinosaurs off this island is the worst idea in the long, sad history of bad ideas." Oscar nomination for f/x.

MAC AND ME

1988 (PG) 94m / **D:** Stewart Raffill / **W:** Stewart Raffill / **C:** Christine Ebersole, Jonathan Ward, Katrina Caspary, Lauren Stanley, Jade Calegory

Heavy backing by McDonalds created a merchandising opportunity that turns into a subplot-for-subplot ripoff of *E.T.* Here a whole family of Chaplinesque aliens are hauled to Earth by a Mars probe. "Mac," the smallest, escapes government captivity and befriends a handicapped boy. Apparently feeling he had nothing to lose critic-wise, director Stewart Raffill (of *Wilderness Family* fame) takes the plot into directions that Steven Spielberg wouldn't have dared; dig that wild final scene. Might please younger kids, and could even break down the resistance of adult viewers. Maybe.

MAD MAX

1980 (R) 93m / **D:** George Miller / **W:** James McCausland, George Miller / **C:** Mel Gibson, Joanne Samuel, Hugh Keays-Byrne, Steve Bisley, Tim Burns, Roger Ward

First entry in the futuristic supercharged George Miller-directed series featuring Mel Gibson as a fresh-faced cop whose life will be as devastated as the society around him. Leather-punk rebel bikers have nothing better to do than roam the Australian countryside, chasing and being chased by police guarding the remnants of civilization. (One of its better touches is never spelling out exactly *what* has caused order to break down; it was possibly inspired by the guerrilla warfare that resulted in the outback during 1970s gas shortages.) When his best-buddy cop is killed, Max calls it quits and takes off cross country with the family. But boozin', brawlin', brain-bustin' punks with really fast vehicles are hard to lose, and tragedy results. Max gases up one of the cops' last muscle cars and spends the rest of the film

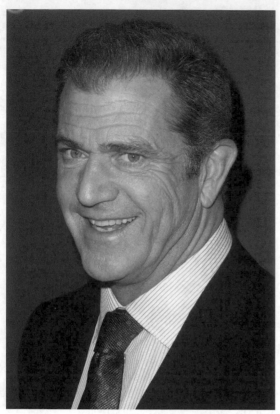

Mel Gibson starred in the "Mad Max" films, which are set in a future Australia after an unknown event has caused the collapse of society.

in vicious, to-the-death chases. The American release originally had dubbed dialogue (Aussie-accented English being seen as nearly a foreign language) though the original voices were replaced in later releases. Smart, muscular, exploitation action that inspired dozens, if not hundreds, of unimaginative knockoffs. Followed by two sequels.

MAD MAX 2: THE ROAD WARRIOR

1982 (R) 95m / D: George Miller / **W:** George Miller / **C:** Mel Gibson, Bruce Spence, Emil Minty, Vernon Wells

Futuristic sci-fi western that's one of the only sequels to surpass the original on sheer intensity. Sometime after the events of *Mad Max*, Max (Mel Gibson) has become a wanderer of the desert outback, scavenging for fuel and living off canned dog food. A narrated prologue tells the story of the war that destroyed civilization and the chaos that followed ("on the roads, it was a white-line nightmare"), establishing Max as more of a tragic hero. Our "burnt-out, desolate man" falls in with an outpost of oil-drilling survivors fighting off savage punk bikers and agrees to help them fight their way to the coast. Superb cinematography and thrilling chase choreography makes for a pulse-racing classic with thrillingly epic overtones, though a quasi-Wagnerian *ubermensch* subtext takes some of the fun away. Became one of the 1980s' most influential movies; unfortunately 99 percent of those inspired filmmakers made unwatchable and derivative dreck featuring variations on mohawk'd villains and scruffy heroic loners. AKA: *The Road Warrior.*

MAD MAX: BEYOND THUNDERDOME

1985 (PG-13) 107m / D: George Miller, George Ogilvie / **W:** George Miller, Terry Hayes / **C:** Mel Gibson, Tina Turner, Helen Buday, Frank Thring Jr., Bruce Spence, Robert Grubb, Angelo Rossitto, Angry Anderson, George Spartels, Rod Zuanic

Sequel to *The Road Warrior* has Max (Mel Gibson) drifting into the squalid methane-fueled Bartertown (pig slop abounds) ruled by the heavy-metal desert queen Auntie Entity (Tina Turner, using her strutting stage persona for full effect). Disputes are settled in the Thunderdome, gladiator style ("Two men enter. One man leaves"), and Max is tossed in there with an iron-clad behemoth. Spears, maces, spikes, and even chainsaws are all used while the opponents are tethered from the top of the Thunderdome. George Miller and Gibson reportedly wanted a "much more human story" and not a "reworking of *The Road Warrior*." Therefore, dumped-in-the-desert, Max is rescued by a band of feral orphans who have survived the dimly remembered nuclear holocaust and believe that Max is their prophesized savior (they call him Captain Walker, in homage to Russell Hoban's post-apocalyptic novel *Riddley Walker*). Broad expansion of the series' first two entries aims for both a more epic and intimate feel, as Max faces the possibility of a life revolving around something besides wandering, revenge, and pain.

MAKING CONTACT

1986 (PG) 83m / **D:** Roland Emmerich / **W:** Hans J. Haller, Thomas Lechner, Roland Emmerich / **C:** Joshua Morrell, Eva Kryll

Oddball German production is one long tribute/ripoff of the imagery of George Lucas and Steven Spielberg. Joey (pic's original title), a sci-fi obsessed small boy with a pet R2D2 robot, is assailed by poltergeists—something to do wlth hls deceased father and a malevolent ventriloquist's dummy. Can his souvenir Jedi window curtains save him? How about his *E.T.* drinking glass? Harmless but obnoxiously unoriginal, this celluloid fan letter is a telling footnote in the career of Roland Emmerich, who finally reached Hollywood and helmed genre blockbusters like *Stargate*, *2012*, and *Independence Day*.

MAKING MR. RIGHT

1986 (PG-13) 95m / **D:** Susan Seidelman / **W:** Laurie Frank, Floyd Byars / **C:** John Malkovich, Ann Magnuson, Glenne Headly, Ben Masters, Laurie Metcalf, Polly Bergen, Hart Bochner, Polly Draper, Susan Anton

Despite an inspired performance from Ann Magnuson as an "image consultant," Susan Seidelman's off-beat satire never quite lives up to its promise. John Malkovich plays the dual role of a scientist and his innocent robot creation. The unbalanced film begins as *Splash* with the sexes reversed, wanders into social satire for a time, and almost becomes a bedroom farce before it sputters to an unconvincing conclusion.

THE MANHATTAN PROJECT

1985 (PG-13) 112m / **D:** Marshall Brickman / **W:** Marshall Brickman, Thomas Baum / **C:** John Lithgow, Christopher Collet, Cynthia Nixon, Jill Eikenberry, John Mahoney, Sully Boyer, Richard Council, Robert Schenkkan, Paul Austin

For a science fair, a high-school genius builds a functional nuclear bomb, complete with plutonium swiped from a government lab, and a manhunt (or kidhunt) begins. John Lithgow is excellent as a flippant weapons scientist who belatedly realizes the destructive power held by a mere boy—and, by extension, anyone with nukes. Teen technothriller has a splendid concept (far better than *My Science Project*), but after raising viewer expectations it is disarmed by way too many plot implausibilities. Director Marshall Brickman co-wrote Woody Allen's similarly titled but ever-so-unrelated *Manhattan*. AKA: *Manhattan Project: The Deadly Game.*

MAN OF STEEL

2013 (PG-13) 143m / **D:** Zack Snyder / **W:** David S. Goyer / **C:** Henry Cavill, Amy Adams, Russell Crowe, Michael Shannon, Diane Lane, Kevin Costner, Laurence Fishburne, Christopher Meloni, Richard Schiff

Zack Snyder's relaunch of the *Superman* franchise might have had more going for it than Bryan Singer's meeker 2006 effort, but the end result is far less entertaining or necessary. The hack-by-numbers script gives us Kal-El's (Henry Cavill) origin story on Krypton in full detail while relegating his Earth childhood as Clark Kent to a few scattered flashbacks. While the f/x and acting (particularly from Kevin Costner and Russell Crowe, as Kal-El's human and alien fathers) are mostly top-drawer, the story is straight superhero drudgery, with none of the chipper humility that Christopher Reeve brought to the original series. Having skipped Superman's evolution from Kal-El into Clark Kent, there is little drama when the evil General Zod (Michael Shannon) starts laying waste to Earth and Kent has to stop hiding his alien origins in order to save mankind. The climactic Zod-Superman fight scene feels long enough to be its own movie.

THE MAN WHO FELL TO EARTH

1976 (R) 118m / **D:** Nicolas Roeg / **W:** Paul Mayersberg / **C:** David Bowie, Candy Clark, Rip Torn, Buck Henry, Bernie Casey

Enigmatic, visionary cult pic about a man from another planet (David Bowie, in a bit of typecasting) who ventures to Earth in hopes of finding water to save his drought-stricken planet. Instead he becomes a successful American inventor and businessman, discovering the human vices of booze, sex, TV, and apathy. Full of eccentric performances and off-key moments that seem to portend non-linear timelines and parallel universes. Based on the relatively straightforward Walter Tevis novel, but with an apparent influence from Robert Heinlein's *Stranger in a Strange Land* (an oft-discussed and oft-aborted film project itself). Also available in a considerably improved restored version at 138 minutes. Remade for TV in 1987.

A man from another world—played by rocker David Bowie—travels to Earth in search of water and instead gets caught up in our world's vices.

MAROONED

1969 (G) 134m / D: John Sturges / **W:** Mayo Simon / **C:** Gregory Peck, David Janssen, Richard Crenna, James Franciscus, Gene Hackman, Lee Grant

Three-man team of American astronauts are stranded in orbit 200 miles above Earth when their ship engines fail, but it's a deadly 200 miles if Yankee ingenuity cannot launch a rescue mission in time. Try desperately to care in this overlong film when James Franciscus looks out a spaceport at a rather fetching painting of Mother Earth and announces "So beautiful … so beautiful" in a quavering voice as his oxygen fails. Three Oscar nominations, won for f/x.

MARS ATTACKS!

1996 (PG-13) 106m / D: Tim Burton / **W:** Jonathan Gems / **C:** Jack Nicholson, Glenn Close, Annette Bening, Pierce Brosnan, Danny DeVito, Martin Short, Sarah Jessica Parker, Michael J. Fox, Rod Steiger, Tom Jones, Lukas Haas, Natalie Portman, Jim Brown, Lisa Marie

After the success of 1994's affectionate biopic *Ed Wood*, Tim Burton decided to go the camp sci-fi route himself. He ginned up this star-heavy monstrosity out of a controversial series of 1962 trading cards about a Martian invasion that were banned for their violent and sexual content. In Burton's more good-natured version, short aliens with giant brains encased in glass helmets land on Earth (in Ed Wood-ian circular flying saucers) and commence zapping every human they see. If Burton had tried something like this earlier in his career, during the *Pee-wee* and *Beetlejuice* years, it probably would have had the right satiric zip. But given the oversized budget, scattered script, and all the stars making strained comic cameos (though Pierce Brosnan gets great mileage from tweaking the humorless 1950s scientist cliché), the tone is hard to sustain. A shameful waste, given Burton's clearly encyclopedic knowledge and loving understanding of the genre. Jack Nicholson, working hard to carry the comedy here, gets the one decent line while making a national address: "I want the people to know that they still have two out of three branches of government working, and *that ain't bad.*"

MARS NEEDS WOMEN

1966 (NR) 80m / **D:** Larry Buchanan / **W:** Larry Buchanan / **C:** Tommy Kirk, Yvonne Craig, Byron Lord, Roger Ready, Warren Hammack

From the director of *Zontar, the Thing from Venus* comes one of the classic golden turkeys of all time. Former Disney kid Tommy Kirk virtually reprises his character from *Pajama Party* as Dop, the leader of a Martian advance team looking for Earth women with whom to repopulate their planet. Yvonne Craig, best known as Batgirl, stars as Pulitzer Prize-winner Dr. Marjorie Bolen, our foremost expert on extraterrestrial reproduction. A Martian fashion tip: they "abandoned neckties 50 years ago as foolish vanity."

THE MASK OF FU MANCHU

1932 (NR) 68m / **D:** Charles Brabin, Charles Vidor / **W:** Irene Kuhn, Edgar Allan Woolf / **C:** Boris Karloff, Lewis Stone, Karen Morley, Charles Starrett, Myrna Loy, Jean Hersholt, Lawrence Grant, David Torrence

The original, and many feel the best, *Fu Manchu* movie. The evil Dr. Fu (played here by Boris Karloff) and his equally evil daughter (Myrna Loy) set out to capture the scimitar and golden mask of Genghis Khan. With them (and the help of a somewhat more up-to-date death ray) they will be able to destroy the white race and rule the world. Although Scotland Yard detective Nayland Smith tries his best to stop them, the pair get the treasures and several prisoners in their evil clutches. Tortures follow. Can Fu be stopped before he carries out his evil plans? Can the world be made safe for the white race? Even though its portrayal of Asians seems offensive today, this is still an exciting, creepy movie with killer performances by Karloff and Loy, but one has to wade through cringe-worthy Asian stereotypes to enjoy them.

MASTER OF THE WORLD

1961 (NR) 95m / **D:** William Witney / **W:** Richard Matheson / **C:** Vincent Price, Charles Bronson, Henry Hull

This charming aerial version of *20,000 Leagues under the Sea* is actually based on two Jules Verne novels, *Clipper of the Clouds* (known in America as *Robur the Conqueror*), and *Master of the World*. Vincent Price plays Robur, a fanatical-but-genius-type 19th-century inventor who flies his incredible fortress, the Albatross, around the world, attacking only men and weapons of war, unless someone else gets in the way. Charles Bronson, who began his career in Price's horror classic *House of Wax*, is the government agent trying to stop the moral(?) killing. American International spent a lot (for them, at least) on this one and it shows. Richard Matheson's entertaining screenplay cohesively merges the two novels and Lex Baxter's score is everything adventure music should be.

MASTERS OF THE UNIVERSE

1987 (PG) 109m / **D:** Gary Goddard / **W:** David Odell, Stephen Tolkin / **C:** Dolph Lundgren, Frank Langella, Billy Barty, Courteney Cox, Meg Foster

A big-budget live-action version of the sci-fi fantasy cartoon character's adventures, with Viking-esque warrior He-Man (Dolph Lundgren) battling the evil Skeletor (Frank Langella) for the sake of the universe. As their war rages on a distant planet, a cosmic gate is opened up that allows the whole motley crew of masked and muscled strongmen to show up in California and keep on fighting there amidst a strange backdrop. Remember, this was based on a cartoon that was based on a line of toys.

THE MATRIX

1999 (R) 136m / **D:** Andy Wachowski, Lana Wachowski / **W:** Andy Wachowski, Lana Wachowski / **C:** Keanu Reeves, Laurence Fishburne, Carrie-Anne Moss, Hugo Weaving, Joe Pantoliano, Gloria Foster

Take Plato's allegory of the cave, add postmodernist theories about simulated reality and some sub-Marxist critique of consumer culture, throw into a shaker with the entire *Star Wars* oeuvre and about a dozen gravity-defying kung fu flicks, garnish with a quasi-fascist fashion sense, and you have some sense of what *The Matrix* is like. Keanu Reeves is programmer Neo, who is shown by hacker Morpheus (played by Laurence Fishburne as the coolest man in cinematic history) that Neo's life is only a simulation. Although humans

Notable for its then-groundbreaking f/x, *The Matrix* posited that reality was, in fact, a computer simulation created by sentient machines who have conquered and enslaved humanity.

think they're living their lives, in fact aliens conquered Earth years before and humanity is now enslaved in giant pod-farms that harvest their body's electrical energy; their minds kept happily unaware by a vast computer simulation everyone thinks of as reality. Morpheus and his catsuit-wearing sidekick Trinity (Carrie-Anne Moss) drag Neo into a rebel conspiracy that wants to smash the simulation and free humanity. The aliens' chief computer avatar enforcer Agent Smith (Hugo Weaving) is dead-set on stopping them. Writer/directors Andy and Lana Wachowski throw a lot of ideas at viewers here but keep it all well within the boundaries of a Joel Silver-produced action movie. The shootouts and hand-to-hand combat are hyperactively choreographed, and lovingly captured via the filmmakers' then-revolutionary "bullet-time" ultra-slo-mo technique. A true game-changer for both sci-fi and action film, but not necessarily for the better. The slick sense of rebellious superiority in which Neo is equated with some kind of Jesus-savior and most of humanity is seen as thoughtless sheep leaves a bad taste. Spawned numerous pop-philosophical treaties and scads of conspiracy theories; most of the latter swirled around the idea that the Matrix *is real*. Pop philosopher Slavoj Zizek wrote about having the "unique opportunity of sitting close to the ideal spectator of the film— namely, an idiot." Won four technical Oscars, deservedly.

THE MATRIX RELOADED

2003 (R) 138m / D: Andy Wachowski, Lana Wachowski / **W:** Andy Wachowski, Lana Wachowski / **C:** Keanu Reeves, Laurence Fishburne, Carrie-Anne Moss, Hugo Weaving, Jada Pinkett Smith, Gloria Foster, Nona Gaye, Harry Lennix, Harold Perrineau, Monica Bellucci

With the first *Matrix*, the Wachowskis showed how far they could push the envelope. That film had little interest in restraint, except in terms of a color palette (green and black, maybe the occasional grey). For the first of the two sequels that came right on top of each other four years later, the series tripled down on everything that had made the original film so fascinating and killed it in the process. The story is a straight continuation from before, with the revolution continuing against the alien overlords, who are trying to destroy the humans' underground stronghold of Zion. All the combat (and there's a *lot* of it) still takes place in the virtual-reality space of the Matrix, where gravity doesn't matter and new combat training can be instantly downloaded like a software upgrade. With his Prada-sleek robes and un-flappable surfer-zen cool, Keanu Reeves's Neo is even more the kung-fu Je-sus this time out, clobbering dozens of enemies simultaneously without catching his breath. It's all more of the same: Morpheus is given new grandil-oquent speeches to proclaim, and Agent Smith has gained the ability to repli-cate himself. Somewhat worthy of note for being the rare sci-fi action film with an ethnically diverse cast. The endless Zion-set rave scene, intercut with Neo and Trinity having sex, is rightly beloved by appreciators of camp.

THE MATRIX REVOLUTIONS

2003 (R) 129m / **D:** Andy Wachowski, Lana Wachowski / **W:** Andy Wachowski, Lana Wa-chowski / **C:** Keanu Reeves, Laurence Fishburne, Carrie-Anne Moss, Hugo Weaving, Jada Pinkett Smith, Monica Bellucci, Harry Lennix, Nathaniel Lees, Mary Alice

The curse of the trilogy makes for a grim ending to the Wachowskis' sci-fi adventure, which has essentially turned into a war film for its conclu-sion. Leaving barely a breath between the end of *Reloaded* and the start of *Revolutions*, the human city of Zion is threatened with an annihilating assault by the aliens' army of slithering metallic beasts. Everybody races to hold down the fort, while Neo goes off to get some tarot-card advice from the Or-acle (played here by Mary Alice, replacing the late Gloria Foster). Nothing here that couldn't have been edited together with *Reloaded*. Then there would have been just one disappointing sequel, instead of two.

MAXIMUM OVERDRIVE

1986 (R) 97m / **D:** Stephen King / **W:** Stephen King / **C:** Emilio Estevez, Pat Hingle, Laura Harrington, Yeardley Smith

In Stephen King's short story "Trucks," vehicles start taking on minds of their own; it ends with a man enslaved at a gas station, fueling up an end-less line of angry, thirsty big rigs. In this feature-length expansion, what could have been a neat little *Twilight Zone* becomes an excuse for King himself (in the director's seat) to play Roger Corman. The results aren't pretty. Emilio Estevez leads a gaggle of humans trapped at a truck stop by the homicidal rigs. Torqued-up soundtrack by AC/DC might be the high point; either that or the scene where a vending machine (*with a mind of its own!*) guns a man in the crotch with soda cans.

MEET DAVE

2008 (PG) 90m / **D:** Brian Robbins / **W:** Rob Greenberg, Bill Corbett / **C:** Eddie Murphy, Elizabeth Banks, Gabrielle Union, Scott Caan, Ed Helms, Kevin Hart

Having not thoroughly scoured the lowest regions of PG-rated comedy, Eddie Murphy does one of his multiple-role full-spectrum performances in this fish-out-of-water story of an alien space captain who has arrived on Earth to steal the ocean's water. Here's the catch: his spaceship looks like Eddie Murphy (or "Dave"). Inside Dave is where his crew members (Ed Helms, Gabrielle Union) can be found, if anybody cares to look for them.

MEET THE HOLLOWHEADS

1989 (PG-13) 89m / **D:** Tom Burman / **W:** Tom Burman / **C:** John Glover, Nancy Mette, Richard Portnow, Matt Shakman, Juliette Lewis, Anne Ramsey

Futuristic sitcom-style family have Dad's boss over for dinner in hopes of securing that promotion that he so richly deserves. Slicing off a chunk of some prime-tentacle from the kitchen's living food supply, Mom cooks up a sickly gourmet delight, but the guest of honor has something else in mind. Juliette Lewis starts to show her one-sided acting talents as the dysfunctional daughter. Trying to be one of those entertainingly weird alternative-world grossout comedies, it almost succeeds, but most of the cast seems a little uncomfortable, and the whole thing has been done better (*The Dark Backward* for example).

MEGAFORCE

1982 (PG) 99m / **D:** Hal Needham / **W:** James Whittaker, Albert S. Ruddy, Hal Needham, Andre Morgan / **C:** Barry Bostwick, Persis Khambatta, Edward Mulhare, Henry Silva, Michael Beck, Ralph Wilcox

Famously terrible futuristic thriller directed by stuntman Hal Needham follows the adventures of the military task force, Megaforce, on its mission to save a small democratic nation from attack. Lotsa cool cars that shoot missiles! Barry Bostwick leads the attack in an awesomely glittery disco jumpsuit.

MELANCHOLIA

2011 (R) 130m / **D:** Lars von Trier / **W:** Lars von Trier / **C:** Kirsten Dunst, Charlotte Gainsbourg, Kiefer Sutherland, Alexander Skarsgard, Brady Corbet, Charlotte Rampling, John Hurt, Stellan Skarsgard, Udo Kier

Given the apocalypti that were all the rage in the 2000s and 2010s, it was a matter of time before even Lars von Trier got in on the act. This misanthropic dark fantasy starts off as a minor-key romantic satire as an expensive wedding on a grand estate starts to go south as the bride (Kirsten Dunst) drowns in helpless gloom. Meanwhile, a new planet named Melancholia has just been discovered. Apparently it was hiding on the other side of the sun and now has a new orbit that will bring it crashing into Earth sometime soon. Von Trier's view of humanity remains stuck at the snide-adolescent level. Nevertheless, he's an artist with the camera. Some memorable images here of Earth's gloriously operatic end, many redolent with his typical Grimms-ian fatalism.

MEMOIRS OF AN INVISIBLE MAN

1992 (PG-13) 99m / **D:** John Carpenter / **W:** Robert Collector / **C:** Chevy Chase, Daryl Hannah, Sam Neill, Michael McKean, Stephen Tobolowsky, Jim Norton, Patricia Heaton, Rosalind Chao

Nick Halloway (Chevy Chase), a slick and shallow stock analyst, is rendered invisible by a freak accident. When he is pursued by a CIA agent/hit man who wants to exploit him, Nick turns for help to Alice (Daryl Hannah), a documentary filmmaker he has just met. Naturally, they fall in love along the way. There are some effective sight gags, but the hardworking cast can't overcome pitfalls in the script, which indecisively meanders between comedy and thrills. Lacks the focus of John Carpenter's earlier horror films but still an impressive attempt to stretch into new, less easily defined territory.

MEN IN BLACK

1997 (PG-13) 98m / **D:** Barry Sonnenfeld / **W:** Ed Solomon / **C:** Tommy Lee Jones, Will Smith, Linda Fiorentino, Vincent D'Onofrio, Rip Torn, Tony Shahloub

Will Smith went right from nearly single-handedly destroying the alien menace in *Independence Day* to letting himself play comic relief to a cracklingly dry Tommy Lee Jones in this unusually spry blockbuster sci-fi comedy. Smith is the newest recruit of the MiB agency, tasked with protecting Earth not just from aliens, but from any knowledge of them; thusly the "deneuralizer," a cool mind-eraser flash-gadget they use on passersby. There's a low-key cop-plot in which Smith and Jones need to stop evil alien Vincent D'Onofrio from wreaking more havoc than usual. But mostly the film is about Smith getting easy laughs at the stone-faced Jones' expense and pinpointing the ways that aliens hide out in that most obvious place to not be noticed: New York. Also, since summertime movies demanded it, lots of aliens getting zapped by the MiB's giant shiny rayguns. The design scheme is straight-1960s finger-snapping cool, from the natty black suits and Ray-Bans to the space-age architecture, and the script is one-liner heavy ("human thought is so primitive it's looked upon as an infectious disease in some of the better galaxies"). Director Barry Sonnenfeld started out as a cinematographer for early Coen Brothers comedies like *Raising Arizona* and it shows here in his penchant for smash zooms and mugging comedy. Three Oscar nominations, won for Rick Baker's makeup.

Will Smith (left) is taught by Tommy Lee Jones how to protect the world from alien threats in the droll 1997 sci-fi comedy *Men in Black.*

MEN IN BLACK II

2002 (PG-13) 88m / D: Barry Sonnenfeld / **W:** Robert Gordon, Barry Fanaro / **C:** Tommy Lee Jones, Will Smith, Lara Flynn Boyle, Johnny Knoxville, Rosario Dawson, Rip Torn, Patrick Warburton, Tony Shahloub

More gross-out aliens-among-us subterfuge and expensively silly f/x in one of the more obvious sequels out there. The story has Tommy Lee Jones's MiB agent having been deneuralized and forgotten his alien-fighting past; now, he works at the post office. Meanwhile, there are aliens for Will Smith to track down. Again, the deadpan cop-buddy rapport between Smith and Jones is the highlight of this messy and blessedly short exercise in revenue-grubbing. The charm, though, doesn't go quite as far the second time around.

MEN IN BLACK III

2012 (PG-13) 106m / D: Barry Sonnenfeld / **W:** Etan Cohen / **C:** Will Smith, Tommy Lee Jones, Josh Brolin, Jemaine Clement, Emma Thompson, Michael Stuhlbarg

Nearly a decade on, Barry Sonnenfeld waited until he had a decent enough story to make it worthwhile to get his agents back into their mod suits. This time out, Agent J (Will Smith) is getting annoyed with Agent K's (Tommy Lee Jones) particularly ornery reticence about his past, only to find out that an alien supervillain recently escaped from maximum security on the moon has figured out how to travel back in time to kill Jones and ensure he is never arrested. J hops back to 1969 and has to convince young K (Josh Brolin, doing an uncanny Jones impersonation) that he's from the future. Layers emotion with humor quite neatly and keeps up Sonnenfeld's penchant for bright Pop décor and camp. Doesn't have as much fun as it could with the ease of aliens hiding out in the 1960s, though there's a nice bit at Andy Warhol's Factory where it's revealed the silver-haired one is actually a man in black undercover. Michael Stuhlbarg stands out as a tender-hearted oracle who can see all time paths and dimensions simultaneously.

MESA OF LOST WOMEN

1952 (NR) 70m / **D:** Herbert Tevos, Ron Ormond / **W:** Herbert Tevos / **C:** Jackie Coogan, Richard Travis, Allan Nixon, Mary Hill, Robert Knapp, Tandra Quinn, Lyle Talbot, Katherine Victor, Angelo Rossitto

A madder-than-usual mad scientist (played by *Addams Family* regular Jackie "Uncle Fester" Coogan) cloisters himself on a remote Mexican mesa. Here he creates a giant tarantula and a brave new race of vicious women with long fingernails … and that's pretty much it. This is one of those "bad" films that's SO bad it can't even properly be called a B picture; a "wanna-B" is more like it. Trailers for the film showed one of the "Lost Women" glowering with psychotic sultriness at the camera, while a voice asks the puzzling question "Have you ever been kissed by a woman like this"? AKA: *Lost Women*; *Lost Women of Zarpa*.

METALSTORM: THE DESTRUCTION OF JARED SYN

1983 (PG) 84m / **D:** Charles Band / **W:** Alan J. Adler / **C:** Jeffrey Byron, Mike Preston, Tim Thomerson, Kelly Preston, Richard Moll

The last time we saw Lemuria it was a legendary continent between Australia and Africa, populated by creatures of myth and Ray Harryhausen's Sinbad. Well, it didn't do the Atlantean sink thing, it became a stark desert island planet, controlled by the evil intergalactic magician Jared Syn. Syn and his army of Cyclops have created deadly forbidden zones, killing and enslaving for the purpose of sacrifice to their life-giving crystal. Enter Dogen, a peacekeeping ranger, who enlists the aid of Rhodes (Tim Thomerson—*Trancers*'s Jack Deth) and the ex-enemy cyclopean warlord Hurok (Richard Moll). Strange combination of sorcery and space jockeys is actually quite entertaining with more than adequate f/x. Sacrifice-wanna-be Dhyanais is played by Kelly Preston in her first billed role.

METEOR

1979 (PG) 107m / **D:** Ronald Neame / **W:** Stanley Mann, Edmund H. North / **C:** Sean Connery, Natalie Wood, Karl Malden, Brian Keith, Martin Landau, Trevor Howard, Henry Fonda, Joseph Campanella, Richard Dysart

American and Soviet scientists attempt to save the Earth from a fast-approaching barrage of meteors from space (with their big daddy on its way) in this disaster dud. Destruction ravages parts of Hong Kong, the Big Apple, and other areas of the world, allowing producer Irwin Allen to incorporate scenes from other movies. Big-name actors do their professional best, but they all seem rather embarrassed by the big flooding of New York climax, which was included for no other reason than to get them personally involved in the crisis. Good for a laugh, and for a few nice effects scenes. Oscar nominated for sound.

THE METEOR MAN

1993 (PG) 100m / **D:** Robert Townsend / **W:** Robert Townsend / **C:** Robert Townsend, Robert Guillaume, Marla Gibbs, James Earl Jones, Frank Gorshin

Robert Townsend is a school teacher who becomes a reluctant superhero after being socked in the gut by a meteor. As "Meteor Man," Townsend—who also wrote and directed this family friendly goof—flies only four feet off the ground (he's afraid of heights) and wears costumes fashioned for him by his mother. An excellent, good-natured satire on superhero movies with a strong pro-community message. James Earl Jones has what may be the most unusual role of his career as Townsend's eccentric neighbor (who's constantly changing his hairstyle). Includes some fine cameos by Sinbad, Luther Vandross, LaWanda Page, and Bill Cosby as a wise street person.

METEOR MONSTER

1957 (NR) 73m / **D:** Jacques Marquette / **W:** Ray Buffum / **C:** Anne Gwynne, Stuart Wade, Gloria Castillo, Chuck Courtney

A young boy is hit by a meteor and grows up to be a raving, hair-covered maniac. His mom tries to keep him a secret but has little success. One of those movies that feels like it was built purely around budget. Since Western sets and costumes were available, they made it a Western. Even though the "monster" is just a big ugly guy with mental problems, they threw in a meteor and sold it as sci-fi, which was hot at the box office at the time. Director Jacques Marquette was better known as a cinematographer, notably for Roger Corman's *A Bucket of Blood*. Probably the last leading role for Anne Gwynne, a familiar face in Universal horror films of the 1940s. She was last seen in a small role in 1970's *Adam at 6 A.M.* AKA: *Teenage Monster*.

METROPOLIS

1927 (NR) 115m / D: Fritz Lang / **W:** Fritz Lang, Thea von Harbou / **C:** Brigitte Helm, Alfred Abel, Gustav Froehlich, Rudolf Klein-Rogge, Fritz Rasp, Heinrich George

Classic meditation on technology and mass mentality, about the mechanized society of 2000 A.D. where workers are trudging drones on constant duty underground, as upper classes dwell in splendor and decadence on the surface. Then the son of an elite leader falls for a prominent worker chick. Disapproving dad commissions an evil android duplicate of the girl to incite the workers into doomed revolt. Part fairy tale, part allegory of Capital and Labor, so politically simplistic it had admirers simultaneously in the Reichstag and the Kremlin; all inspired by German director Fritz Lang's awestruck first sight of Manhattan by night. Outstanding set designs, colossal crowd shots, and still-striking f/x made this innovative and influential, though the silent-mime style of acting badly dates the material. True landmark of the genre, and gener-

Released in 1927, Fritz Lang's *Metropolis* featured groundbreaking special effects and a relevant story about social oppression.

ally held to be the first sci-fi screen epic. Certainly set a trend by nearly ruining the German UFA studios, who spent about six million marks on its cost. Foreign export re-edits and the loss of the original negative in WWII means that various versions circulate widely. The 1984 re-release features some color tinting, partial reconstructions of long-lost sequences, sound effects, and a controversial rock score with songs by Pat Benatar, Bonnie Tyler, Giorgio Moroder, and Queen. A special treat for completists: a little-known, recently republished novelization by Lang's then-wife and screenwriter Thea von Harbou fills in the gaps between title-cards. About a half-hour's worth of long-unseen footage was discovered in Buenos Aires in 2008; the so-called *Complete Metropolis* was exhibited in 2010 in a restored, 148-minute version.

MIDNIGHT MOVIE MASSACRE

1988 (NR) 86m / D: Larry Jacobs, Mark Stock / **W:** Roger Branit, John Chadwell, David Houston, Larry Jacobs, Mark Stock, Wade Williams / **C:** Robert Clarke, Ann Robinson

Retro splatterama has really gross alien land outside a movie theater in 1956, and the movie patrons try to terminate it with extreme prejudice.

MILLENNIUM

1989 (PG-13) 108m / D: Michael Anderson Sr. / **W:** John Varley / **C:** Kris Kristofferson, Cheryl Ladd, Daniel J. Travanti, Lloyd Bochner, Robert Joy, Brent Carver, Maury Chaykin, David McIlwraith, Al Waxman

A Federal Aviation Agency investigator finds temporal anomalies at plane crashes and is haunted by mystery woman Cheryl Ladd. It seems that 1,000 years from now Earth's people are sterile and rotting. To keep humanity alive they send time-travel squads back to yank fresh, untainted people off doomed airliners, thus skirting apocalyptic time paradoxes—until Kris Kristofferson and Daniel J. Travanti begin putting the pieces together. John Varley's source novel (an expansion of his superior short story "Air Raid") was so frazzled it required a cameo by God to sort things out. This Canadian adaptation has no such luck and warps unsteadily between the serious premise and mere camp (much of the latter provided by a sarcastic robot). Good f/x.

MIMIC

1997 (R) 105m / D: Guillermo del Toro / **W:** Matthew Robbins, Guillermo del Toro / **C:** Mira Sorvino, Charles S. Dutton, Jeremy Northam, Alexander Goodwin, Giancarlo Giannini, Josh Brolin, F. Murray Abraham

For his first Hollywood outing, Guillermo del Toro was hired for this creature feature that was originally planned as another short in the same sci-fi anthology film that also eventually sprouted *Impostor*. The story is set in a future New York where children are being cut down by a terrible disease. Researchers Mira Sorvino and Jeremy Northam find out it's carried by cockroaches, so they breed a new roach called the Judas Breed that kills the disease, only to escape into the sewers where they evolve into subterranean predators that can imitate their prey. The scientists and one grumpy cop (Charles S. Dutton) go underground to hunt down the bugs. The studio took the film away from del Toro and added new material; the resulting work was seen as a disappointingly generic sci-fi horror film from a promising talent. Del Toro's director's cut, which reinstates some deleted material and removes the second-unit scenes shot without him, was released in 2011. Followed by two video-only sequels.

MINDWARP

1991 (R) 91m / D: Steve Barnett / **W:** Henry Dominick / **C:** Marta Alicia, Bruce Campbell, Angus Scrimm, Elizabeth Kent, Mary Becker, Wendy Sandow, Gene McGarr

When Judy (Marta Alicia) rebels against the Sysop and goes offline from the "The Happiness System" (brought to us by Infinisynth), she actually uses the line "There's no place like home" when she teams up with Stover (Bruce Campbell) to battle the mutant monsters (who all look like the Toxic Avenger but with a lot less imagination) of the outside world. Campbell plays the straight hero he consistently spoofs in all of his better parts (*Thou Shalt Not Kill ... Except*, *Army of Darkness*, *Evil Dead 1* and *2*); it's hard to watch him try to be serious. Not to be confused with 1972's *Mind Warp*.

MINORITY REPORT

2002 (PG-13) 145m / D: Steven Spielberg / **W:** Scott Frank, Jon Cohen / **C:** Tom Cruise, Samantha Morton, Max von Sydow, Colin Farrell, Tim Blake Nelson, Steve Harris, Neal McDonough

Like most movies sprouted from a Philip K. Dick short story, this one has to go pretty far afield from the source material to create a workable feature-length story. But in reworking the story's plot about a political coup into a murder mystery, Scott Frank and Jon Cohen's script doesn't just pad the material, it opens up the possibilities in as thrilling a manner as anything since *Blade Runner*. Tom Cruise plays a cop heading up the Pre-Crime department in 2054 Washington, D.C. (Incredibly, given Steven Spielberg's long career, this was his first police procedural.) He uses a trio of people called "Pre-cogs" who can pick up people's thoughts to pinpoint and arrest would-be killers before they actually commit their planned crime. The plot itself, in which Cruise is framed for a pre-crime, is little more than an excuse for Spielberg to stage dizzingly vertiginous chase scenes through a glassy Googleplex of microrobotics and laser-focused target-marketing that seems less impossible every day. Questions are posed about free will and society that the film doesn't pretend can be tied up in a pat or reassuring manner. Visually brighter than just about any other Dick adaptation, but dark enough in what it says about the inevitable loss of agency in an ever-more linked-in world. Oscar nomination for sound editing.

Tom Cruise plays a cop in a future world where crimes can be predicted before they happen in *Minority Report*.

MISSILE TO THE MOON

1959 (NR) 78m / D: Richard Cunha / **W:** H. E. Barrie, Vincent Fotre / **C:** Gary Clarke, Cathy Downs, K. T. Stevens, Laurie Mitchell, Michael Whalen, Nina Bara, Richard Travis, Tommy Cook, Marjorie Hellen

First expedition to the moon encounters not acres of dead rock but a race of gorgeous women in lingerie and high heels. Take one cheap, silly sci-fi groaner, then remove the name stars and the 3D effects, and there you have it—a bad but entertaining remake of *Cat Women of the Moon*, featuring a bevy of beauty contest winners from New Hampshire to Yugoslavia. Cast is not quite as accomplished as the original's. Gary Clarke (who took over Michael Landon's Teenage Werewolf role in *How to Make a Monster*) is pretty good, but he's no Sonny Tufts. Laurie Mitchell no doubt put this on her résumé right next to *Queen of Outer Space*. Cathy Downs was also in *The Amazing Colossal Man* and *She Creature*. K. T. Stevens was the daughter of famed comedy director Sam Wood. Tommy Cook was in Arch Oboler's *Strange Holiday* and played Little Beaver in the "Red Ryder" series. Director Richard Cunha churned out this quickie to fill out a bill with *Frankenstein's Daughter*.

MISSION MARS

1967 (NR) 95m / D: Nicholas Webster / **W:** Michael St. Clair / **C:** Darren McGavin, Nick Adams, George DeVries

American astronauts Darren McGavin and Nick Adams, on a mission to the red planet, discover the bodies of two cosmonauts floating in space. After landing on the planet's surface, they find a third cosmonaut, this one in a state of suspended animation. While putting the viewer to sleep, they proceed to revive the third cosmonaut and have at it with the sinister alien force responsible for all the trouble.

MISSION TO MARS

2000 (PG) 114m / D: Brian De Palma / **W:** Jim Thomas, John Thomas, Graham Yost / **C:** Gary Sinise, Tim Robbins, Don Cheadle, Connie Nielsen, Jerry O'Connell

Just one of 2000's two Mars movies, Brian De Palma's was likely the better, not least because it doesn't feature Val Kilmer. A manned mission to the red planet goes haywire, so in the grand sci-fi tradition, another batch of resourceful astronauts is sent to find out what happened. In short, they are quickly put in peril, and once they discover what happened to the original mission, things get mysterious. Although De Palma handles the danger-danger scenes ("We're losing air pressure!") with cool precision, he is also able to convey a true sense of awe and wonder once the mysteries of Mars start to be revealed. Much of the film is board-stiff, though, in the classic manner of

1950s space-mission groaners, only at least this one substitutes Gary Sinise for the likes of Leslie Nielsen; not a bad trade, all things considered.

THE MIST

2007 (R) 126m / **D:** Frank Darabont / **W:** Frank Darabont / **C:** Thomas Jane, Andre Braugher, Marcia Gay Harden, Laurie Holden, Toby Jones, William Sadler, Jeffrey DeMunn, Frances Sternhagen

After a powerful storm in one of those small Maine towns that are always getting ripped to shreds in Stephen King stories (like the novella this film is based on) sends him looking for supplies, artist Thomas Jane is trapped inside a supermarket with his son while a terrifying mist encircles them. Everybody's too frightened to leave, even those who don't believe the mounting evidence that the mist contains nightmarish beasts. Rumors fly and factions form while suspicions grow about the mist's connection to mysterious goings-on at a nearby Army base. Jane tries to find allies amid the rapidly shrinking numbers of the rational; everybody else is too busy looking for scapegoats and following the rantings of a Christian fanatic (a fully uncorked Marcia Gay Harden). As in his *Walking Dead* zombie series, writer/director Frank Darabont is less concerned with harum-scarum than he is with how bands of people coalesce and fall apart *in extremis*. Highly unsettling claustrophobic horror with a sci-fi backdrop and understated, nearly existential tone. The bottled-up tension becomes nearly unbearable long before the gripping, tragic conclusion.

MISTRESS OF THE WORLD

1959 (NR) 107m / **D:** William Dieterle / **W:** Jo Eisinger, Harald G. Petersson / **C:** Martha Hyer, Micheline Presle, Gino Cervi, Lino Ventura, Sabu, Wolfgang Preiss

A scientist, aided by Swedish Intelligence agent Ventura, works to protect his gravity-altering invention from Chinese agents. Partly based on a German serial from the silent film era, but not up to director William Dieterle's usual fare. A must-see for Lino Ventura fans and Dr. Mabuse mavens.

MODERN PROBLEMS

1981 (PG) 93m / **D:** Ken Shapiro / **W:** Ken Shapiro, Tom Sherohman, Arthur Sellers / **C:** Chevy Chase, Patti D'Arbanville, Mary Kay Place, Brian Doyle-Murray, Nell Carter, Dabney Coleman

Chevy Chase gets splashed with nuclear waste and develops some rather tasteless telekinetic powers, including the ability to vacuum up cocaine through his nostrils like a Hoover. Ah, the magic that was Hollywood in the early 1980s. Slapstick takeoff on psy-pics like *The Fury* and *Scanners* was done with a fine comic cast at low points in their personal lives, and their distraction shows in this unsuccessful fission trip.

THE MOLE PEOPLE

1956 (NR) 78m / **D:** Virgil W. Vogel / **W:** László Görög / **C:** John Agar, Cynthia Patrick, Hugh Beaumont, Alan Napier, Nestor Paiva, Phil Chambers

Atrocious creature feature finds two archeologists accidentally discovering an underground civilization of albinos who shun all forms of light. They've also enslaved the local populace of half-human, half-mole creatures who decide to help the good guys escape by rising up in a revolt against their evil masters. When the weapon of choice is a flashlight, you know not to expect much.

MOM AND DAD SAVE THE WORLD

1992 (PG) 87m / **D:** Greg Beeman / **W:** Chris Matheson, Ed Solomon / **C:** Teri Garr, Jeffrey Jones, Jon Lovitz, Eric Idle, Wallace Shawn, Dwier Brown, Kathy Ireland, Thalmus Rasulala

Scientists uncover an underground civilization ruled by evil albinos who oppress a species that is half mole/half human in *The Mole People*.

Planet Spengo, populated entirely by idiots, plans to destroy Earth. But nasty King Tod spies an average suburban housewife, Marge Nelson (Teri Garr), through his telescope and falls in love. He teleports Mr. and Mrs. Nelson to Spengo and postpones death-raying their world until he can marry Mom and dispose of Dad. Highlights are the goofy playpen sets, mixing vintage *Flash Gordon* style with *Romper Room*. Lowlight is the misuse of a gifted cast in an attempt to do a picture that's so dumb it's funny, but only gets the dumb aspect correct. *Very* young viewers *might* be amused.

THE MONITORS

1969 (PG) 92m / D: Jack Shea / **W:** Myron J. Gold / **C:** Guy Stockwell, Susan Oliver, Avery Schreiber, Sherry Jackson, Shepperd Strudwick, Keenan Wynn, Ed Begley, Larry Storch

In the late 1960s, Chicago's groundbreaking Second City improv comedy troupe decided to try its hands at making a movie. It partnered with Bell & Howell, a Skokie-based camera equipment company trying to generate interest in Chicago as a filmmaking destination, and optioned a Keith Laumer novel about some very nice-seeming but pushy and hall monitor-like aliens in black bowler hats who just want humans to *behave* already. Their rules chafe, however, and humans fight back in this rough-and-ready, goofy, highly late-1960s comic parable. Look for cameos from everyone from Alan Arkin and Peter Boyle to Senator Everett McKinley Dirksen. Nice wide-angle cinematography from the great Vilmos Zsigmond (*The Deer Hunter*, *McCabe & Mrs. Miller*).

THE MONOLITH MONSTERS

1957 (NR) 76m / D: John Sherwood / **W:** Norman Jolley, Robert M. Fresco / **C:** Grant Williams, Lola Albright, Les Tremayne, Trevor Bardette

Despite the title and goofy premise (killer rocks), this is one of the more enjoyable 1950s B-movies. A meteor, described by the orotund narrator as "another strange calling card from the limitless reaches of space," is the source. Geologist Grant Williams discovers strange crystals that absorb silicon from people and objects, killing the humans and

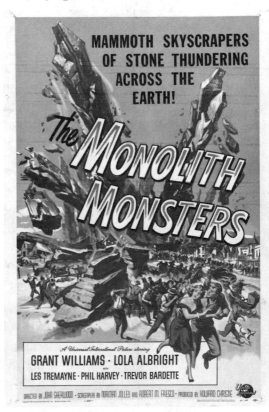

Killer rocks attack Earth in 1957's campy *The Monolith Monsters*.

growing to towering heights in the process. The plot is inventive enough that the film stays reasonably fun.

MONSTER A GO-GO!

1965 (NR) 70m / D: Herschell Gordon Lewis / **W:** Norman Jolley, Robert M. Fresco / **C:** Phil Morton, June Travis, Bill Rebane, Sheldon Seymour

A team of go-go dancers battle a ten-foot monster from outer space who's actually a mutated astronaut. Cool! Herschell Gordon Lewis, director of *Blood Feast* and other timeless trash/gore movies, acquired this pile of footage (then titled *Terror at Halfday*) in an unfinished state, threw in a couple of new scenes, and released it as a co-feature with his hillbilly epic *Moonshine Mountain*. That may seem like an unlikely combo, but hey, monsters and hillbilly music were a big draw in the 1960s (see Lee Frost's 1961 girly/monster epic *House on Bare Mountain* for a perfect example). The fellow who played the Frankenstein-looking monster was a genuine giant. Too bad he couldn't dance.

MONSTER FROM THE OCEAN FLOOR

1954 (NR) 66m / D: Wyott Ordung / **W:** William Danch / **C:** Wyott Ordung, Anne Kimbell, Stuart Wade, Jonathan Haze, Dick Pinner, Jack Hayes

Roger Corman's first production was shot in six days for $12,000. The comely Anne Kimbell stars as a tourist vacationing in a Mexican village that is being terrorized by an octopus-type sea monster (actually, a puppet shot from behind a cloudy fishtank—but no matter, you don't get to see it until the end of the movie). Stuart Wade costars as a marine biologist who dismisses the monster talk as superstition, until he is forced to go mano-a-monster in his mini-sub. Director Wyott Ordung also appears in the film and later wrote the immortal *Robot Monster*. Making his film debut is Jonathan Haze, who was discovered pumping gas on Santa Monica Boulevard and became a part of Corman's ensemble. His finest hour is, of course, *The Little Shop of Horrors*. AKA: *It Stalked the Ocean Floor*; *Monster Maker*.

MONSTERS

2010 (R) 94m / D: Gareth Edwards / **W:** Gareth Edwards / **C:** Scoot McNairy, Whitney Able

Smart, if limited, example of adventurously thoughtful no-budget sci-fi. Several years before the events of the film begin, a NASA probe contaminated with alien spores crash-landed in Mexico. Those spores reacted to the local flora and fauna in … interesting ways. Much of Mexico has been turned into a quarantine zone to keep the beasts at bay. Since this is a monster movie, stupid protagonists are required. Enter an American photographer trying to get a shot of one of the creatures. He is forced by his boss to get the old man's flighty daughter back to safety. A few logically challenged decisions later, the two are trying to make it through the quarantine zone to America. Afflicted as it is with a by-the-numbers script and nonsensical plotting, this is still an occasionally remarkable odyssey into the heart of a strange wilderness where, left to their own devices, the alien creatures aren't just threatening to humans but radically rewiring an entire ecosystem. The climax at a massive containment wall along the Rio Grande tries to work as both an ironic comment on the era's immigration debate and exploration of the possibilities inherent in setting massive, Lovecraftian creatures loose in densely populated areas. Writer/director and f/x whiz Gareth Edwards was tapped to direct the 2014 reboot of *Godzilla*.

Moon

2009 (R) 97m / D: Duncan Jones / **W:** Nathan Parker / **C:** Sam Rockwell, Kevin Spacey, Dominique McElligott, Kaya Scodelario

The closest thing that sci-fi cinema in the new millennium has come to revisiting some of the 1970s quieter futuristic stories. Sam Rockwell plays an outer-space maintenance man in astronaut gear who might be starting to crack up after too much time on his own. He works on a station that mines Helium-3 on the Moon, which produces clean energy back on Earth. The only person he has to talk to is the station computer, voiced with a kindly lilt by Kevin Spacey. There's also some plants whom he's given names to (shades of Bruce Dern). His sanity comes close to snapping when, after nearly getting killed in an accident, he wakes up next to a man who looks like a younger version of himself. Most viewers will have figured out the secret long before Rockwell, but that won't spoil any of the film's sad, wistful greatness. Director Duncan Jones had solid tech and outer-space credentials, being a former camera operator for Tony Scott and the son of David Bowie.

Moon 44

1990 (R) 102m / D: Roland Emmerich / **W:** Dean Heyde, Oliver Eberle / **C:** Malcolm McDowell, Lisa Eichhorn, Michael Paré, Stephen Geoffreys, Roscoe Lee Browne, Brian Thompson, Dean Devlin, Mechmed Yilmaz, Leon Rippy

One of German filmmaker Roland Emmerich's Hollywood-style B movies before he had a mainstream commercial hit with *Stargate*. Filching largely from *Outland*, it's mediocre mayhem about cop Michael Paré going undercover as a cosmic convict. His mission: thwart corporate marauders planning to attack a giant space prison that doubles as a mining colony. Some impressive f/x are largely lost on the small screen.

MOON PILOT

1962 (NR) 98m / **D:** James Neilson / **W:** Maurice Tombragel / **C:** Tom Tryon, Brian Keith, Edmond O'Brien, Dany Saval, Tommy Kirk, Bob Sweeney, Kent Smith

First astronaut scheduled to orbit the moon is followed prior to the launch by an enticing mystery woman. She turns out to be a (French-accented?) alien from the planet Beta Lyrae, who's only trying to be helpful. But government security forces panic and chase them both. Outdated, frankly dull comedy from Walt Disney productions, more of a romantic farce than sci-fi. No f/x whatsoever.

MOONRAKER

1979 (PG) 126m / **D:** Lewis Gilbert / **W:** Christopher Wood / **C:** Roger Moore, Lois Chiles, Michael Lonsdale, Richard Kiel, Corinne Clery, Bernard Lee, Desmond Llewelyn, Lois Maxwell

Never ones to miss an obvious trend, the producers of James Bond decided not to think too hard about why 007 would go to space but how quickly can they get him up there? After all, a little thing called *Star Wars* had

Roger Moore (at right) is 007 and Lois Chiles (at left) is his current love interest. Together, they battle baddies like metal-mouthed Richard Kiel (center) both at home and in *Moonraker*.

scrambled everything everybody thought they knew about movies, and even this already-venerable series couldn't take anything for granted. There's a bored megalomaniac trying to destroy the world (Michael Lonsdale) and a comely CIA agent named Holly Goodhead for Bond to get cozy with. Jet-setting, immaturely prurient, gadget-happy business as usual (the scene in Venice where the gondola turns into a hovercraft is a nice touch). It's all just buildup to another showdown at the villain's lair, this time instead of being underground it's a space station. So: Space Marines, attack! The impressive f/x were Oscar-nominated, as were *The Black Hole* and *Star Trek: The Motion Picture* (this was a strong year for sci-fi), but they all lost out to *Alien*.

MOONTRAP

1989 (R) 92m / **D:** Robert Dyke / **W:** Tex Ragsdale / **C:** Walter Koenig, Bruce Campbell, Leigh Lombardi, Robert Kurcz, John J. Saunders, Revis Graham, Tom Case

USS *Enterprise* icon Walter Koenig, reputedly the member of the Classic Trek cast most seriously into sci-fi, takes a rare lead role here as an Apollo astronaut who returns to the moon to investigate evidence of ancient alien habitations. He and comrade Bruce Campbell find a killer race of evolving, self-replicating robots with Earth next on their agenda. Made-in-Detroit feature has ambitions far beyond its low budget.

MOSQUITO

1995 (R) 92m / **D:** Gary Jones / **W:** Gary Jones, Steve Hodge, Tom Chaney / **C:** Gunnar Hansen, Ron Asheton, Steve Dixon, Rachel Loiselle, Tim Loveface

An alien spaceship crash-lands on earth and a hungry mosquito snacks on one of the dead pilots. The extraterrestrial blood transforms the annoying insects into turkey-sized monsters able and very willing to suck their victims dry. A bunch of misfits do battle with the killer bugs at an isolated campground. Not what you'd call a good film, *Mosquito* does manage to deliver some laughs and a storyline that feels more like an homage to old monsters than a blatant rip-off.

MOTHRA

1961 (NR) 101m / **D:** Ishiro Honda, Lee Kresel / **W:** Shinichi Sekizawa / **C:** Frankie Sakai, Hiroshi Koizumi, Kyoko Kagawa, Yumi Ito, Emi Ito

Classic Japanese monster shenanigans about an enraged giant caterpillar that invades Tokyo while searching for the Alilenas, a pair of tiny twin princesses who've been kidnapped by an evil nightclub owner in the pursuit of big profits. After tiring of crushing buildings and wreaking incidental havoc, the enormous creepy-crawler zips up into a cocoon and emerges as

Mothra, a moth distinguished by both its size and bad attitude. Mothra and the wee babes make appearances in a number of later *Godzilla* epics. The Alilenas were played by Emi and Yumi Ito, who had a singing career in Japan as "the Peanuts." One of the best of the 1960s Japanese giant monster epics, a colorful, fast-moving fantasy with an unforgettable monster.

Mothra vs. Godzilla

1964 (NR) 88m / **D:** Ishiro Honda / **W:** Shinichi Sekizawa / **C:** Akira Takarada, Yuriko Hoshi, Hiroshi Koizumi, Emi Ito, Yumi Ito

A gigantic egg washes ashore in Japan via a hurricane. Despite warnings from a pair of tiny girls (the fairy priestesses of Mothra from the earlier movies), a wealthy industrialist plans to build an amusement park around it. Before too long, however, Godzilla shows up, hungry to do some city-mashin'. The fairies convince Mothra to come to Tokyo's aid. Though the huge flying critter fares badly against the Big G, two junior Mothras hatch from the giant egg in the nick of time and join the fray. The first *Godzilla* film where he went up against other beasts, with highly sequel-worthy results; wonderful entertainment for monster-fans. Except for a sequence added at the request of American International, in which Godzilla is attacked by U.S. Navy missiles, the U.S. version is nearly the same as the original, and the dubbing was done decently. AKA: *Godzilla vs. the Thing*; *Godzilla vs. the Giant Moth*; *Godzilla Fights the Giant Moth*; *Godzilla vs. Mothra*; *Godzilla Fights the Giant Moth*.

Muppets from Space

1999 (G) 87m / **D:** Tim Hill / **W:** Jerry Juhl, Joseph Mazzarino, Ken Kaufman

A going-through-the-motions effort from the Jim Henson crew that displays little of the whimsicality or big song-and-dance numbers of the first few *Muppets* films. Turns out that Gonzo is in fact an alien and soon his fellow Gonzoians will be coming back to Earth, forcing a choice between his friends and his kin. Underwhelming.

Mutant on the Bounty

1989 (PG-13) 93m / **D:** Robert Torrance / **W:** Martin Lopez / **C:** John Roarke, Deborah Benson, John Furey, Victoria Catlin, John Fleck, Kyle T. Heffner

Jazz musician, lost in space as a beam of light for 23 years, is materialized aboard a spaceship alive but with a face that looks like he's been "bobbing for French fries." As if that's not enough (and it isn't), the motley crew then must fight a couple of thugs who are trying to steal a vial of serum. Good f/x go to waste in a galactic spoof whose biggest laugh is the pun in the title.

MY FAVORITE MARTIAN

1999 (PG) 94m / **D:** Donald Petrie / **W:** Sherri Stoner, Deanna Oliver / **C:** Christopher Lloyd, Jeff Daniels, Elizabeth Hurley, Daryl Hannah, Wallace Shawn, Christine Ebersole, Michael Lerner, Ray Walston

The ransacking of "beloved" old TV properties was starting to slow down when Disney got its hands on feature-izing this mostly forgotten comedy series from the early 1960s; they'd already gotten to *Flipper*. Christopher Lloyd bugs his eyes out as best he can to play the Martian who crash-lands on Earth and ends up living with TV news guy Jeff Daniels. The original series star Ray Walston appears in a small role and Wallace Shawn is a government suit eager to chase down the missing alien.

MY STEPMOTHER IS AN ALIEN

1988 (PG-13) 108m / **D:** Richard Benjamin / **W:** Herschel Weingrod, Timothy Harris, Jonathan Reynolds / **C:** Dan Aykroyd, Kim Basinger, Jon Lovitz, Alyson Hannigan, Joseph Maher, Seth Green, Wesley Mann, Adrian Sparks, Juliette Lewis, Tanya Fenmore

Eccentric physicist Steve Mills (Dan Aykroyd) sends a beam out to a galaxy far, far away and gets a visit from the beautiful and sexy (although from some angles she does look like Mick Jagger) Celeste (Kim Basinger). Fortunately for the plot, and the ensuing slapstick comedy, this gorgeous blonde is an alien with a mission: seduce the recently widowed Steve and get the details of his experiments that could save her planet. Despite her rather odd (and sometimes funny) habits, romance commences, love and marriage follow. Celeste's fellow alien on the mission comes off as a living Felix-the-Cattish bag and supplies some great comic moments—the kissing scene is a classic. Jon Lovitz is fun as the pervert-playboy brother. Fast forward through the Jimmy Durante imitations. Otherwise it's good fluff.

Kim Bassinger played an alien out to seduce the widowed Dan Aykroyd in *My Stepmother Is an Alien*.

THE MYSTERIANS

1958 (NR) 85m / **D:** Ishiro Honda / **W:** Takeshi Kimura / **C:** Kenji Sahara, Yumi Shirakawa, Takashi Shimura

Caped aliens land their saucers on Earth and release the giant death-ray-shooting robot bird Mogella, hoping to find some fresh tail to replenish their race after the home planet was destroyed by a nuclear explosion. Even though alien, this "big monster" was also a result of the misuse of nuclear power (the aliens only need to be here because of the nuclear disaster), so once again Japan is portrayed as the victim. Directed by Ishiro Honda, who also directed the original *Godzilla*, with music supplied by the Japanese classical composer Akira Ifukube. AKA: *Earth Defense Forces*.

MYSTERIOUS ISLAND

1961 (NR) 101m / **D:** Cy Endfield / **W:** Daniel Ullman, John Prebble, Crane Wilbur / **C:** Michael Craig, Joan Greenwood, Michael Callan, Gary Merrill, Herbert Lom, Beth Rogan, Percy Herbert, Dan Jackson, Nigel Green

Solid and often-overlooked adventure combines the talents of three proven crowd-pleasers—author Jules Verne, f/x pioneer Ray Harryhausen, and composer Bernard Herrmann—each at the top of his game. The story continues the saga of Captain Nemo and concerns escaped Civil War prisoners who fly a balloon to a remote island filled with wondrous giant beasts and a new surprise around every corner. One of stop-motion animation's finest hours.

MYSTERIOUS SKIN

2004 (R) 105m / **D:** Gregg Araki / **W:** Gregg Araki / **C:** Joseph Gordon-Levitt, Brady Corbet, Elisabeth Shue, Michelle Trachtenberg, Bill Sage, Mary Lynn Rajskub

The sci-fi contained in this dark, masterful character study might be completely notional, but it pervades the story like a thick cloud nonetheless. Gregg Araki's potent story involves a couple of boys growing up in small-town Kansas who are both sexually abused by their baseball coach. The two deal with the memory of abuse in different ways: Neil (Joseph Gordon-Levitt) turns to the self-destruction playbook of petty crimes and hustling while Brian (Brady Corbet) blocks out the memory and dreams of disturbing alien abductions, possibly as a coping mechanism. Araki shows a previously unseen ability to deliver emotionally resonant drama, while also portraying the abuse itself and its legacy with a forthright, horrific honesty. One of the decade's unsung greats.

MYSTERY SCIENCE THEATER 3000: THE MOVIE

1996 (PG-13) 73m / **D:** Jim Mallon / **W:** Mike Nelson, Trace Beaulieu, Jim Mallon, Kevin Murphy, Mary Jo Pehl, Paul Chaplin, Bridget Jones / **C:** Mike Nelson, Trace Beaulieu, Jim Mallon, Kevin Murphy

For their one feature-film outing, the *MST3K* crew chose a classic slab of alien-invasion bunk: 1955's *This Island Earth*. In deference to this being something to watch in theaters, the writers concoct a more robust skein of interstitial light comedy to explain to newbies why Mike Nelson and his robot companions are stuck on the *Satellite of Love* and forced to watch terrible movies. The result isn't exactly successful, or funny. Things improve once the trio settles into their seats to watch the movie, in which giant-brained aliens try to steal Earth's uranium. The wisecracks come faster than in the small-screen version, and more of them land successfully, even if the references are typically oblique (in one scene showing a range of mountains, one of them cracks, "Aww, there's soccer teams *everywhere*").

THE NAVIGATOR

1988 (PG) 90m / D: Vincent Ward / **W:** Geoff Chapple, Kelly Lyons, Vincent Ward / **C:** Bruce Lyons, Chris Haywood, Hamish McFarlane, Marshall Napier

A beautiful little time-travel gem from New Zealand, whose film industry produced a few sci-fi think pieces back before it became an animation factory for Middle-earth. The story begins in the 14th century, where the people of a small English village are terrified by the Black Death that is laying waste to the country. Following the curious visions of young Hamish McFarlane, who imagines digging a tunnel through the center of the Earth to a magical city, the villagers do just that—and emerge in 20th-century New Zealand. Visionary filmmaker Vincent Ward doesn't ruin his exquisitely shot piece by trying to explain what happened; we're in pure fever-dream country here. Debut film for Ward, who was involved in the early production of *Alien³* (the prisoners' shabby monk-like aura in that film seems straight from Ward) and went on to create a few other gorgeously foolish fantasies like *What Dreams May Come* and *Map of the Human Heart*. Nominated for the Cannes Film Festival's Palme d'Or. AKA: *The Navigator: An Odyssey Across Time*; *The Navigator: A Medieval Odyssey*.

THE NAVY VS. THE NIGHT MONSTERS

1966 (NR) 87m / D: Michael Hoey / **W:** Michael Hoey / **C:** Mamie Van Doren, Anthony Eisley, Pamela Mason, Bobby Van, Russ Bender, Walter Sande

When Antarctic plant specimens collected by the Navy turn out to be horrible, acid-secreting monsters out to take over the world, blonde bombshell Mamie Van Doren and her pals have to come to the rescue. Most of the action takes place in a South Pole military base that looks remarkably like southern California. Far too many dated, tiresome jokes about the rigors of Navy life. Supposedly based on a novel by classic sci-fi writer Murray Leinster. Cinematography by the great Stanley Cortez (*The Magnificent Ambersons*). AKA: *The Night Crawlers*.

NEMESIS

1993 (R) 95m / **D:** Albert Pyun / **W:** Rebecca Charles / **C:** Olivier Gruner, Tim Thomerson, Cary-Hiroyuki Tagawa, Merle Kennedy, Yuji Okumoto, Marjorie Monaghan, Nicholas Guest, Vincent Klyn, Deborah Shelton, Brion James

Kung-fu cyborgs clash in the post-nuke future in this cyberpunk tribute to John Woo. Olivier Gruner plays a human crime fighter (mostly composed of mechanical replacement parts) in a world overrun with terrorists, sexy gangsters, and android cops intent on conquering their own creators. The confusing script plugs Gruner into gory fight gymnastics in exotic locations, with far more visual style than attempts at logic. Decent f/x despite the obviously negligible budget. Inevitable sequel followed in 1995.

NEON CITY

1991 (R) 99m / **D:** Monte Markham / **W:** Jeff Begun, Buck Finch, Monte Markham, Gus Peters / **C:** Michael Ironside, Vanity, Lyle Alzado, Valerie Wildman, Nick Klar, Juliet Landau, Arsenio "Sonny" Trinidad, Richard Sanders

There's an old critical saw that sci-fi movies merely reinvent the Western. While frequently inaccurate, that definitely applies to the likes of this Canadian post-apocalypse actioner clearly patterned after John Ford's *Stagecoach*. Eight travelers in an armored transport truck seek safety from the Earth's toxic environment, circa 2053, via an overland trek to the title settlement. Mutants and highway bandits take the place of the traditional marauding Indians.

NEO-TOKYO

1987 (NR) 50m / **D:** Rintaro, Yoshiaki Kawajiri, Katsuhiro Otomo / **W:** Rintaro, Yoshiaki Kawajiri, Katsuhiro Otomo

Three adventurous Japanese animated shorts. In "The Order to Stop Construction" (by *Akira* filmmaker Katsuhiro Otomo), an anal-retentive bureaucrat is sent to inspect an automated mining city in a remote jungle, only to be imprisoned by the resident robots who generate something of an existential crisis. "Labyrinth" follows a young girl and her pet cat into a strange wonderland, and "The Running Man" is a startling tale of a futuristic racer. All visually stunning, but "The Order to Stop Construction," with its wry satire, is probably the most readily accessible.

The Nest

1988 (R) 89m / D: Terence H. Winkless / **W:** Robert King / **C:** Robert Lansing, Lisa Lan-glois, Franc Luz, Terri Treas, Stephen Davies, Diana Bellamy, Nancy Morgan

After an experiment goes Terribly Wrong, killer mutant cockroaches take over a small New England resort island. That's the plot. Gets funnier and grosser as it goes along. Stars Robert Lansing, who previously showed his insectoid-acting abilities in *Empire of the Ants*.

Neutron and the Black Mask

1961 (NR) 86m / D: Frederick Curiel / **W:** Alfredo Ruanova / **C:** Wolf Ruvinskis, Julio Alemán, Armando Silvestre, Rosa Arenas, Claudio Brook

Only the first of several Mexican-made adventures featuring the wrestling superhero with the lightning-bolt mask. Many were hastily dubbed into English and sold to American TV stations in the 1960s to delight a small but determined cluster of fans. This time out, Neutron needs to save the world from the evil, world-threatening, neutron bomb-wielding Dr. Caronte. In the sequels that followed, Neutron faced down zombies and killer robots, but nothing the masked hero couldn't handle.

Never Let Me Go

2010 (R) 103m / D: Mark Romanek / **W:** Alex Garland / **C:** Keira Knightley, Carey Mulli-gan, Andrew Garfield, Charlotte Rampling, Sally Hawkins

One of the great, most underrated sci-fi films about what it means to be human. In this alternate history, unspecified "medical breakthroughs" in the early 1950s resulted in an incredible lengthening of the human lifes-pan. Cut to the mid-80s, where three best friends (Keira Knightley, Carey Mul-ligan, Andrew Garfield) are playing out a sub rosa love triangle at a board-ing school with mysterious origins. The story only hints for a long time about what separates these three and their fellow students from other people. Once the secret is made clear, the implications are morally shattering. Mark Romanek's take on the Kazuo Ishiguro novel (from a screenplay by *Sunshine* and *28 Days Later ...* writer Alex Garland) is cool to the touch but the emo-tive performances ground the scenario in a tragic humanity.

New Rose Hotel

1998 (R) 93m / D: Abel Ferrara / **W:** Abel Ferrara / **C:** Christopher Walken, Willem Dafoe, Asia Argento, Yoshitaka Amano, Annabella Sciorra, John Lurie

Normally, when a crusty old New York gutter punk like Abel Ferrara ventures into sci-fi (*Body Snatchers*, *4:44 Last Night on Earth*), the results might be nonsensical but at least he's swinging for the fences. This pallid adaptation of the classic William Gibson short story is just plain nonsensical. The Japan-set near-future story is about a brilliant researcher (Yoshitaka Amano) who's working for one corporation but a couple operatives (Christopher Walken, Willem Dafoe) are trying to steal him for another corporation; Asia Argento, bringing her best feral sex kitten look, is the honey trap. It's a quick, tough-minded story in Gibson's best sci-fi noir vein. But Ferrara's baffling edits and glacier-like pacing suggest a project that was never quite visualized before shooting began. Vies with *Johnny Mnemonic* for worst Gibson adaptation; this one gains a few extra points just for having Walken being Walken ("You're *dead*, in case you didn't know it. You just don't have the sense to lie down").

NEXT

2007 (PG-13) 96m / D: Lee Tamahori / **W:** Gary Goldman, Jonathan Hensleigh, Paul Bern-baum / **C:** Nicolas Cage, Julianne Moore, Jessica Biel, Thomas Kretschmann

In the Philip K. Dick story "The Golden Man," a gold-skinned mutant who can see the future is hunted down by government agents wanting to har-ness that power. This adaptation arm-twists that story into a generic loose-nuke thriller. Nicolas Cage (occasional evidence to the contrary, *not* a mu-tant) plays a Las Vegas magician with limited, *Choose Your Own Adventure*-ish pre-cog abilities. He can see a couple minutes into the future, just long enough to clean up at poker. Or try different pickup lines on blonde co-star Jessica Biel. In a dramatically convenient twist, Cage can see farther ahead when Biel is involved. They get roped into helping the FBI (led by Julianne Moore) stop a terrorist nuke from taking out Los Angeles. Before it's over, Moore's apparently human rights-averse Feds strap Cage into a chair for some *Clockwork Orange*-style forced fortune telling. Some Heisenberg Un-certainty Principle ideas with possibilities get left behind in favor of another cops-vs.-baddies shootout in a warehouse.

NIGHTFLYERS

1987 (R) 88m / D: T. C. Blake / **W:** Robert Jaffe / **C:** Michael Praed, Michael Des Barres, Catherine Mary Stewart, John Standing, Lisa Blount, Glenn Withrow, James Avery, Helene Udy

A deep-space horror mistake through and through, from its strained prem-ise about a half-baked search for an extraterrestrial entity to the sets that make a spaceship look like a living room from the pages of *Architectural Di-gest*. Colored light and haze hide the limited f/x. Adapted by Robert Jaffe, of *Demon Seed* infamy, from an early novella by *Game of Thrones* author George R. R. Martin. The original director, Fritz Kiersch, was replaced by Robert Collector, here using the pseudonym T. C. Blake.

NIGHT OF THE BLOOD BEAST

1958 (NR) 65m / D: Bernard L. Kowalski / **W:** Martin Varno / **C:** Michael Emmet, Angela Greene, John Baer, Ed Nelson

Astronaut comes back from space only to find that he's been impregnated by an alien creature, and a mass of extraterrestrial larvae is growing within him. Worse, his parental instincts are kicking in. Creepy venereal horror, decades before David Cronenberg and *Alien*. The lack of a budget becomes most apparent when the rubber monster waddles out of Bronson Canyon cave and handily defeats a solid B-movie premise. AKA: *Creature from Galaxy 27*.

NIGHT OF THE COMET

1984 (PG-13) 90m / D: Thom Eberhardt / **W:** Thom Eberhardt / **C:** Catherine Mary Stewart, Kelli Maroney, Robert Beltran, Geoffrey Lewis, Mary Woronov, Sharon Farrell, Michael Bowen

After surviving the explosion of a deadly comet, two California girls discover that they are the last people on Earth. What to do? Go shopping, of course! Their end-of-the-world mall spree starts to pall, though, when the zombies show up as well as some creepy government types who also managed to survive. Luckily, Daddy taught the girls how to shoot machine guns. Curiously cheery post-nuke Valley Girl comedy has a conspicuously 1980s bright-minded sensibility to it. Director Thom Eberhardt started out in award-winning social-issue documentaries before moving on to light-hearted narratives like this one.

NIGHT OF THE CREEPS

1986 (R) 89m / D: Fred Dekker / **W:** Fred Dekker / **C:** Jason Lively, Jill Whitlow, Tom Atkins, Steve Marshall

Alien meanies crash-land on Earth in 1958 and assume the form of parasitic slugs. The man they infect is cryogenically frozen, then thawed out thirty years later on the campus of Corman (as in Roger) University, where he staggers about as a moldering zombie, spreading the living-dead contagion throughout the town. Good-looking B-movie satire plays around with every schlock-horror cliché there is, yet manages to avoid the sleaze factor itself. Contains numerous nods to B-movie folks, including cameos by such regulars as Dick Miller. Director Fred Dekker's first film.

NIGHT OF THE LIVING DEAD

1968 (NR) 96m / D: George A. Romero / **W:** John A. Russo, George A. Romero / **C:** Judith O'Dea, Duane Jones, Karl Hardman, Russell Streiner, Keith Wayne, Judith Ridley, Kyra Schon

George A. Romero directed the quintessential modern zombie movie, *Night of the Living Dead.*

There might have been other movies, particularly in the pre-war horror days, that played around with zombies. But those were less reanimated corpses in the starving-for-brains understanding than they were victims of some wicked voodoo dark magic. George A. Romero's still-unsettling chiller can be understood as Film Number One in the modern zombie canon. A sister and brother are visiting their father's gravesite when a man staggers toward them and viciously kills the brother. She flees to a farmhouse, where she finds a half-dozen other people hiding out from the flesh-eaters scouring the land for food. A news report suggests that radiation from a satellite has caused the dead to rise. Soon, they're clawing at the doors and windows. The simple survival scenario becomes trickier as the humans in the farmhouse fracture and bicker. Romero's allusions reach all the way from *Paradise Lost* to lynchings. It's a pared-down exercise in gut-churning horror whose success not only opened up the American film market to all manner of grindhouse grisliness but also tried to introduce a more thoughtful subtext to all the mayhem; the latter being something most of Romero's imitators never bothered with. To paraphrase Terry Pratchett talking about Tolkien's influence on fantasy, all other zombie films simply rearrange the furniture in Romero's attic. Followed by numerous sequels, only one of which (2005's *Land of the Dead*) had any sci-fi elements. Added to the Library of Congress' National Film Registry in 1999.

9

2009 (PG-13) 79m / D: Shane Acker / **W:** Pamela Pettler

Tim Burton produced this action-packed animated fantasy, and it's not too hard to see his influence in the grimy landscapes and big-eyed little creatures trying to make sense of it. The heroes are small stitched-doll robots fighting to survive in the post-apocalyptic ruins years after an intelligent machine designed by a dictator to fight his enemies decided in Skynet fashion to simply exterminate all of humanity. The nine dolls, each signified by a number stitched into their fabric, were created to fight the machine but their inventor

As producer of 9, Tim Burton leaves his mark on the feature-length version of an 11-minute Shane Acker short about doll-robots in a post-apocalyptic world.

died before they could go to work. Animator Shane Acker stretches his beloved 11-minute short film well past its dramatic possibilities, padding the story with industrial steampunk spectacle. Initially beautiful, ultimately tedious.

1984

1984 (R) 117m / D: Michael Radford / **W:** Michael Radford / **C:** John Hurt, Richard Burton, Suzanna Hamilton, Cyril Cusack, Gregory Fisher, Andrew Wilde, Rupert Baderman

A timely and impressive adaptation of George Orwell's dystopic novel. This version differs from the overly simplistic and cautionary 1954 film in its fine casting and production design. John Hurt delivers an excellent performance as Winston Smith, a government official in an ultra-totalitarian future whose illegal love affair inspires him to defy the crushing inhumanity of his world. Richard Burton appears in his last feature film performance as O'Brien, Smith's cold-blooded interrogator. Filmed in a very grey London by future Coen brothers cinematographer Roger Deakins, it skillfully visualizes our time's most central prophetic nightmare. Unforgettably bleak and hauntingly beautiful.

No Escape

1994 (R) 118m / D: Martin Campbell / **W:** Joel Gross / **C:** Ray Liotta, Lance Henriksen, Stuart Wilson, Kevin Dillon, Kevin J. O'Connor, Michael Lerner, Ernie Hudson, Ian McNeice, Jack Shepherd nother dreadful prison-of-the-future story. In 2022, Captain Robbins (Ray Liotta) has been banished (unjustly, of course) to a prison-colony island called Absalom by a sadistic prison warden (Michael Lerner). The island, which looks more like it should be inhabited by Ewoks than the world's most dangerous criminals, is without walls and guards, leaving the prisoners free to kill each other. Robbins discovers a relatively peaceful community of prisoners known as the Insiders, led by The Father (Lance Henriksen). The Insiders help each other and build a sort of medieval community. They are predictably plagued by some bad guys who live on the other side of the island and are called … the Outsiders. This cross between *Lord of the Flies* and *Escape from New York* becomes a redundant series of clashes between the good guys and bad guys (can you guess which is which?) and fruitless attempts to escape. Smartly done action sequences are no substitute for an empty story. Adapted from Richard Herley's novel *The Penal Colony*.

NON-STOP NEW YORK

1937 (NR) 71m / **D:** Robert Stevenson / **W:** J. O. C. Orton, Roland Pertwee, Curt Siodmak / **C:** Anna Lee, John Loder, Francis L. Sullivan, Frank Cellier

ystery tale with interesting twist. A wealthy woman can give an alibi for a murder suspect, but no one will listen, and she is subsequently framed. Pays homage to Hitchcock with its photography and humor. Quick and charming. Nod to sci-fi comes in the marvel of a setting: a luxury aerial cruise ship that is likely how people of the 1930s thought they would be traveling by the year 1960 or so.

NOT OF THIS EARTH

1988 (R) 92m / **D:** Jim Wynorski / **W:** Jim Wynorski, R. J. Robertson / **C:** Traci Lords, Arthur Roberts, Lenny Juliano, Rebecca Perle, Ace Mask, Roger Lodge

im Wynorski's remake of Roger Corman's 1957 original has virtually everything that a B-movie fan could ask for: zippy plot, cheesy f/x, and oodles of gratuitous nudity. Vampire from the planet Davonna is on Earth to send blood to the folks back home. Traci Lords is the nurse who unwittingly helps him by providing transfusions. But before long, she and her policeman beau realize that something untoward is going on down in the basement. Why is there smoke coming from the furnace when the temperature is close to 100 outside? Is someone getting rid of the remains of an unlucky door-to-door vacuum cleaner salesman?

NOWHERE

1997 (R) 82m / **D:** Gregg Araki / **W:** Gregg Araki / **C:** James Duval, Rachel True, Nathan Bexton, Chiara Mastroianni, Debi Mazar, Kathleen Robertson, Jordan Ladd, Christina Applegate

Indie cinema's one-time *enfant terrible* Gregg Araki caps off his "Teen Apocalypse" trilogy with this overloaded garbage can of pop culture debris. There are about a dozen bratty teenage Los Angelenos here who hang out at the coffee shop and blankly emote like they're on an acid-tripped "very special episode" of *Beverly Hills 90210*—albeit one with bisexual affairs and drawers full of kink. (Araki plays up the subversive, John Waters mood by casting the likes of Traci Lords and a batch of squeaky-clean sitcom kids and bright young stars like Heather Graham looking to slum.) Everybody is so busy trying to bed one another and work out their sexual orientation issues that they barely notice the alien who occasionally stops by to vaporize unwary adolescents. The slick colors and lushly atmospheric soundtrack (Chemical Brothers, Hole, Catherine Wheel, Radiohead) only partially make up for the amateurish narrative.

THE NUTTY PROFESSOR (1963)

1963 (NR) 107m / D: Jerry Lewis / **W:** Bill Richmond, Jerry Lewis / **C:** Jerry Lewis, Stella Stevens, Howard Morris, Kathleen Freeman, Del Moore

Mild-mannered (but nutty) chemistry professor creates a potion that turns him into a suave, debonair, playboy type. Jerry Lewis has repeatedly denied the slick character is a parody of his one-time buddy Dean Martin, but the evidence is quite strong. Easily Lewis's best film, with many great bits of comedy and substantial contributions from the supporting cast. Remade with Eddie Murphy in 1996 with many more bodily functions.

THE NUTTY PROFESSOR (1996)

1996 (PG-13) 95m / D: Tom Shadyac / **W:** David Sheffield, Barry W. Blaustein, Tom Shadyac, Steve Oedekerk / **C:** Eddie Murphy, Jada Pinkett Smith, James Coburn, Larry Miller, Dave Chappelle

Ancient Jekyll and Hyde premise meets 1990s gross-out comedy with grim results. Perhaps as a sign of changing social mores, in this remake, the professor doesn't want to be *cool*, he wants to be *thin*. In any case, the professor (Eddie Murphy) wants to ask out Jada Pinkett Smith and turning into the trim, polished Buddy Love by way of a special potion is the only way to do it. Murphy plays both parts, as well as every single member of his family during some grotesque, theoretically comic dinners. Rick Baker won the Oscar for makeup.

OBLIVION (1994)

1994 (PG-13) 94m / **D:** Sam Irvin / **W:** Peter David / **C:** Richard Joseph Paul, Andrew Divoff, Jackie Swanson, Meg Foster, Isaac Hayes, Julie Newmar, Carel Struycken, George Takei

It's cowboys versus aliens in this Charles Band production. Not the first sci-fi western by a long shot, but pretty much the only one that doesn't take itself seriously. On a frontier planet, the sheriff of Oblivion Is murdered by outlaws led by reptilian desperado Redeye. The lawman's peace-loving son (genetically unable to do violence, unless it's convenient to the script) reluctantly returns to the settlement to face the bad guys. Pic has fun with the clichés instead of merely slouching through them, and a droll gallery of characters includes *Star Trek*'s George Takei as a drunken doctor, Carel Struycken as a giant psychic undertaker, and Julie Newmar spoofing her Catwoman persona as the overtly feline town madame. Like other Full Moon productions, this was shot back-to-back with its own sequel, *Backlash*.

OBLIVION (2013)

2013 (PG-13) 124m / **D:** Joseph Kosinski / **W:** Karl Gajdusek, Michael deBruyn / **C:** Tom Cruise, Morgan Freeman, Olga Kurylenko, Andrea Riseborough, Melissa Leo

In the year 2077, Earth isn't looking so hot. A few decades back, aliens called Scavengers blew apart the moon and invaded; humanity won a pyrrhic victory using nukes that devastated the planet. Tom Cruise and Andrea Riseborough are the only ones left: Cruise roams the desertified surface fixing drones that fight left-behind aliens and helping extract the planet's remaining resources for the human colony on the moon of Titan. *Or are they?* Joseph Kosinski's visuals are gorgeously epic and refreshingly light-drenched for the post-apocalyptic genre; shooting in Iceland's black sands

Tom Cruise believes himself one of just a few surviving Earthlings after a war against alien invaders, but he's surprised that the world is not what he thinks in 2013's *Oblivion*.

gives everything a peculiar beauty. But Cruise's hyperkinetic energy is a bad fit for an ultimately mournful story. Intriguing premise but without much ability to create believable characters. Too derivative to warrant much attention.

THE OMEGA MAN

1971 (PG) 98m / **D:** Boris Sagal / **W:** John William Corrington, Joyce H. Corrington / **C:** Charlton Heston, Anthony Zerbe, Rosalind Cash, Paul Koslo

Very loose take on Richard Matheson's *I Am Legend* that substitutes action for existential drama. In post-plague Los Angeles, scientist Charlton Heston is immune to the effects of a biologically engineered plague and battles those survivors who aren't—an army of albino victims who've formed a crazed religious Luddite cult bent on destroying what's left of the world. Heston's darkly comic portrayal of a lone man slowing losing it was adopted wholesale by Will Smith for the 2007 film version. Strong suspense with considerable violence, despite the PG rating. Heston's pairing with black co-star Rosalind Cash was one of the first on-screen interracial romances.

THE ONE

2001 (PG-13) 87m / **D:** James Wong / **W:** Glen Morgan, James Wong / **C:** Jet Li, Carla Gugino, Delroy Lindo, Jason Statham

After cranking out a few great *X-Files* episodes, longtime TV writer James Wong switched over to the horror side of things (starting the *Final Destination* series, for one). Given what happened with his f/x-heavy, martial-arts multiverse extravaganza, that might be a good thing. In the world of the film, there are 124 parallel universes. Villain Jet Li is running from one of them to the next, killing off each of his parallel selves and becoming more powerful each time he does so. Ultimate goal, of course, to be *The One*. It's like a more self-hating version of *Highlander*. Delroy Lindo and Jason Statham play agents from the Multiverse Bureau of Investigation (well, what would you call it, Galactipol?) who are trying to track Li down. Initially great fight choreography is ultimately ruined by overuse of so-so f/x.

ON THE BEACH (1959)

1959 (NR) 135m / D: Stanley Kramer / **W:** John Paxton / **C:** Gregory Peck, Anthony Perkins, Donna Anderson, Ava Gardner, Fred Astaire, Guy Doleman

The good news from the near future: Australia escaped getting hit in a worldwide nuclear war that took out the northern hemisphere. The bad news: there's a monster cloud of radiation heading Down Under and once it arrives, everybody's going to die. Stanley Kramer's anti-war drama, based on the best seller by Nevil Shute, is a dramatically stiff and scientifically inaccurate but sadly thoughtful look at how those waiting for the end pass their final days. Fred Astaire is strong in his first dramatic role. One of the first films to be heavily advertised as an Important Event by a Hollywood studio (rightfully worried at the reception a film would receive in which all of the characters are doomed from the start). It paid off big at the box office. Oscar nominations for editing, music.

ON THE BEACH (2000)

2000 (NR) 195m / D: Russell Mulcahy / **W:** David Williamson, Bill Kerby / **C:** Armand Assante, Rachel Ward, Bryan Brown, Jacqueline McKenzie, Grant Bowler

Three-parter adaptation for Australian TV of Nevil Shute's anti-war novel about Aussie civilians and the crew of an American submarine passing their last days on the beach before a cloud of nuclear radiation kills all of them. Substitutes Armand Assante and Rachel Ward for Gregory Peck and Ava Gardner; perhaps not the strongest trade.

ON THE COMET

1968 (NR) 76m / D: Karel Zeman / **W:** Karel Zeman, Jan Procházka / **C:** Emil Horváth Jr., Magda Vásáryková, Frantisek Filipovský

Lesser-known sci-fi fantasy by Jules Verne brought to life by Czech animator Karel Zeman. Wandering planetoid brushes past 19th-century Earth and takes part of the Mediterranean coast with it. Drifting through the solar system, assorted Europeans, Arabs, dinosaurs (?), soldiers, lovers, and scalawags realize their old nationalist squabbles are pointless now that they're completely alone, and there are some satirical jabs at human nature. Zeman's signature animation whimsies—combining live-action, stop-motion, and life-size cutouts—put the viewer in a storybook universe where anything seems possible. Not the easiest to locate, but a real treasure if you do. Dubbed in English. AKA: *Hector Servadac's Ark*.

OUTBREAK

1994 (R) 128m / **D:** Wolfgang Petersen / **W:** Laurence Dworet, Robert Roy Pool / **C:** Dustin Hoffman, Rene Russo, Morgan Freeman, Donald Sutherland, Cuba Gooding Jr., Kevin Spacey, Patrick Dempsey, Zakes Mokae

Animal smuggler Patrick Dempsey sneaks a rare African monkey into the U.S., not knowing it carries a deadly virus. The plague begins to spread through a California suburb, requiring the help of military disease-expert Dustin Hoffman and his ex-wife Rene Russo, a Centers for Disease Control scientist. They search for an antidote as the virus continues to mutate, and they uncover a secret government plot to exterminate the victims to prevent the spread of the disease. Despite scientific pretensions, the film ends with the traditional chase scene. Morgan Freeman and Donald Sutherland give solid performances as military higher-ups at odds with each other. Theoretically based on two nonfiction books—Richard Preston's *The Hot Zone* and Laurie Garrett's *The Coming Plague*—which it mined for scary plague details.

OUTLAND

1981 (R) 109m / **D:** Peter Hyams / **W:** Peter Hyams / **C:** Sean Connery, Peter Boyle, Frances Sternhagen, James B. Sikking, Kika Markham, Clarke Peters

On Io, a volcanic moon of Jupiter, miners begin suffering from spells of insanity (stepping out into the vacuum without their suits, for your viewing pleasure). Sean Connery plays the mining colony's lone federal marshal whose murder investigation makes him a target for the bad guys. Nice blue-collar feel to the down-and-dirty industrial tech, which put it at odds with much sci-fi of the period. Essentially *High Noon* in space, with some of Peter Hyams's typically poor science, so-so f/x, and some spectacular exits for the villains. Sired its own blatant imitator, *Moon 44*.

OUTLANDER

2008 (R) 115m / **D:** Howard McCain / **W:** Dirk Blackman, Howard McCain / **C:** Jim Caviezel, Sophia Myles, Jack Huston, John Hurt, Cliff Saunders, Patrick Stevenson, Aidan Devine, Ron Perlman

*B*eowulf meets *Enemy Mine* and somehow doesn't result in a complete train wreck. An intergalactic soldier who looks awfully human (Jim Caviezel) crash-lands in 8th century Norway—apparently Earth was an "abandoned seed colony"—where he is suspected by the local Vikings of working with a rival clan. Once it turns out that Caviezel's ship carried with it a reptilian monster that moves at light speed and has a nearly impregnable hide, everybody bands together to fight the mythic beast. Yet another story where Caviezel plays the self-sacrificing stoic while others look on in awe. John Hurt carries all of his scenes as the local chieftain, while Ron Perlman swings a giant mace with the best of them. Sophia Myles is the red-haired swordmaiden whose heart goes aflutter everytime the "Outlander" strides past. Drags on a quarter-hour past its expiration date, but energetically delivered and superbly shot.

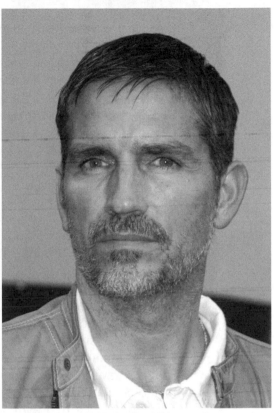

A strange mix of Middle Age Vikings, aliens, and monsters (with Jim Caviezel as the alien) gives audiences a thrill ride in 2008's *Outlander.*

OUT THERE

1995 (PG-13) 98m / D: Sam Irvin / **W:** Thomas Strelich, Alison Nigh / **C:** Bill Campbell, Wendy Schaal, Julie Brown, David Rasche, Paul Dooley, Bill Cobbs, Bobcat Goldthwait, Rod Steiger, June Lockhart, Jill St. John, Carel Struycken, Billy Bob Thornton, P. J. Soles

*U*nemployed photojournalist buys obsolete camera at a yard sale and discovers the 25-year-old film shows pictures of a flying saucer encounter and abduction by aliens. Attempts to verify the photos plunges him into an underground of crackpots, Hollywood has-beens, tabloid reporters, and insane conspiracies. Gag topics in this cable-made farce touch on such arcane matters as the Ada computer compiler, Nixon's hidden heroism, and *THX-1138*, but during the film shoot there must have been a humor-dampening field switched on; amazingly little of it is funny despite the promising cast.

OVERDRAWN AT THE MEMORY BANK

1983 (NR) 84m / D: Douglas Williams / **W:** Corinne Jacker / **C:** Raul Julia, Linda Griffiths

*S*hot-on-tape cerebral sci-fi was done for public television and remains one of the better (and least-known) screen translations of cyberpunk. Complicated setup finds a nonconformist in the sterile future separated from his body due to a bureaucratic snafu. For safekeeping, his mind is stored inside the giant HX368 Novicorp computer that more or less runs the world. Inside the computer he manipulates virtual reality to simulate his favorite movie *Casablanca* and tries to access software controls to the outside to work some serious mischief. Raul Julia plays both the hacker hero and Humphrey Bogart, and the whole thing is a fun lark even if you're scratching your head by the end. Based on a short story by John Varley.

PACIFIC RIM

2013 (R) 132m / D: Guillermo del Toro / **W:** Travis Beacham, Guillermo del Toro / **C:** Charlie Hunnam, Idris Elba, Rinko Kikuchi, Charlie Day, Burn Gorman, Max Martini, Robert Kazinsky, Clifton Collins Jr., Ron Perlman

Coastal cities around the Pacific take it on the chin when hammer-headed beasties the size of supertankers crawl out of an interdimensional gash in the ocean floor and start rampagin'. Humanity fights back with Jaegers, giant robot war machines each controlled by two pilots with cybernetically meshed minds. But the beasts (actually called kaiju, in case viewers didn't get director Guillermo del Toro's nod to the great Toho monster movies) keep getting bigger, and so the few remaining Jaegers have to make one last heroic push to save the planet. As the Jaegar force commander, Idris Elba commands everything he surveys with a lean dominance that even invests lines like "Today we are *cancelling* the apocalypse!" with a certain gravity. The f/x battles are epic throughout; no clumsy actors in rubber suits stumbling through cardboard city sets here. Del Toro's knack for broad comedy keeps the pacing brisk even when the wooden dialogue (another nod to classic kaiju films?) threatens to drag everything to a stop.

PANDORUM

2009 (R) 108m / D: Christian Alvart / **W:** Travis Milloy / **C:** Dennis Quaid, Ben Foster, Cam Gigandet, Antje Traue, Cung Lee, Eddie Rouse, Norman Reedus

Another entry in the monsters-on-board genre that fell into comparative disuse in the 2000s. Ben Foster and Dennis Quaid are two crew members on a massive spaceship who wake up in their deep-sleep pods with only vague memories as to what they're doing out there, and no clue what happened to the tens of thousands of other passengers. Eventually they find other passengers, as well as the kind of monsters who like to jump out at people who walk slowly down dimly lit spaceship passageways. Paul W. S. Anderson produced in between his *Resident Evil* duties.

PANIC IN THE YEAR ZERO!

1962 (NR) 92m / D: Ray Milland / **W:** Jay Simms, John Morton / **C:** Ray Milland, Jean Hagen, Frankie Avalon, Mary Mitchell, Joan Freeman, Richard Garland, Rex Holman

Ray Milland doubled as actor/director on this one, generally considered to be the best of his five efforts. Milland and family luck out (?) after an urge for a fishing trip saves them from getting nuked in Los Angeles. Continuing out into the wilderness for safety, the family finds a survivalist's dream come true in an every-man-for-himself world. An intriguing plot and very competent cast (even Frankie Avalon does the job) make this an above average 1960s end-of-the-world thriller. AKA: *End of the World*.

PAPRIKA

2006 (R) 90m / D: Satoshi Kon / **W:** Seishi Minakami, Satoshi Kon

"I think so" is the answer given here to one character's frantic question, "Is this *really* the real world?" Tricky head-trip mystery pushes boundaries of modern anime, long trapped in a cycle of big robots and ingénues with fluttery eyelashes. Psychiatric researchers invent a device that lets them not only watch and alter patients' dreams as though they were a DVD but to actually enter them. Naturally, the device is stolen by somebody with mischievous intentions and the llnes between reality and dreamtime get shredded fast. Director Satoshi Kon smartly skips past the technical how of this breakthrough and jumps right into *Inception*-like consciousness games, adding playful fillips like the titular dream-avatar (a red-haired pixie who is part ghostly seductress and part dreamworld guide) and a recurring dream of a chaotic carnival parade with apocalyptic overtones. Kon's story gets a little bogged down at times in rambling, what-does-it-all-mean conversation (à la *Ghost in the Shell*). But his creation of a world sinkholed with waking nightmares and technology-tweaked fantasies is something else.

PAUL

2011 (R) 104m / D: Greg Mottola / **W:** Simon Pegg, Nick Frost / **C:** Simon Pegg, Nick Frost, Seth Rogen, Jeffrey Tambor, John Carroll Lynch, Kristen Wiig, Jason Bateman, Jane Lynch, Sigourney Weaver

Simon Pegg and Nick Frost brought their immature-fanboy schtick to American film with this road-trip action comedy about two comic geeks (Pegg and Frost) who have been friends far too long and are taking an RV pilgrimage to Area 51 when they run into an actual alien (voiced by Seth Rogen). Lots of nods to alien conspiracies like Project Blue Book and the Black Mailbox ("one of the coolest things I've ever seen") mixed in with road-trip tropes like getting chased by rednecks. The humor is defiantly R-rated in a

In the fanboy ode *Paul*, a friendly alien escapes Area 51 with the help of two dorky tourists in an RV.

Judd Apatow way (probe jokes galore), but the premise—wisecracking alien becomes nerds' new best friend while they have adventures—is straight out of the 1980s. Genre references abound, including Sigourney Weaver getting her big line from *Aliens* thrown back in her face.

PAYCHECK

2003 (PG-13) 119m / **D:** John Woo / **W:** Dean Georgaris / **C:** Ben Affleck, Aaron Eckhart, Uma Thurman, Paul Giamatti, Colm Feore, Joe Morton, Michael C. Hall

John Woo spent about 10 years making movies in Hollywood, the last being this efficient but strangely anodyne adaptation of the Philip K. Dick story about an engineer (Ben Affleck) whose memory is erased after working on a secret project. Once the FBI gets on his tail, it's classic wrong-man territory, with Affleck puzzling out why his pre-erasure self left him such a motley assortment of clues. Although the film is nominally set in the future, Woo downplays its sci-fi elements as he did in *Face/Off* in favor of more straightforward action scenarios that critically lack the over-the-top brio of his earlier work, not to mention his previous fascination with doubling and identity, which should have meshed perfectly with Dick's preoccupation with same. A true paycheck performance from all involved.

THE PEOPLE

1971 (NR) 74m / **D:** John Korty / **W:** James M. Miller / **C:** Kim Darby, Dan O'Herlihy, Diane Varsi, William Shatner

A young teacher takes a job in a small town and finds out that her students have telepathic powers and other strange qualities. Adapted from a series of novels by Zenna Henderson. Good atmosphere, especially for a TV movie. Produced by Francis Ford Coppola, with music by his father Carmine.

THE PEOPLE VS. GEORGE LUCAS

2010 (NR) 93m / **D:** Alexandre O. Philippe / **W:** Alexandre O. Philippe

Yes, it *does* matter whether Han Solo shoots first in that cantina scene in the original *Star Wars*, damnit. It's easy to dismiss most of the hyperventilating in this multifaceted and highly entertaining documentary about fans' critique of George Lucas's later career as just the carping of over-indulged nerds who expect too much from their pop-culture heroes. But dig past the convention cosplay footage and manic micro interpretations of *Star Wars* universe arcana and you'll discover a nuanced argument about the ownership of cultural artifacts and the integrity of authorship. The primary grumble of most of the fans interviewed here is not *just* that Lucas's second trilogy of films was miserably uninspired. More to the point, they are enraged at his reediting the original trilogy to either add f/x shots he couldn't do the first time around or tweaking certain scenes (Han shooting first) and *then* ensuring that that was the only version available. The disgruntled meme repeated here of "George Lucas raped my childhood" goes a mite too far, but the film does raise interesting questions about who actually owns *Star Wars*, Lucas or his fans? *Room 237* for the lightsaber set.

THE PEOPLE WHO OWN THE DARK

1975 (R) 87m / **D:** León Klimovsky / **W:** Armando de Ossorio / **C:** Paul Naschy, Tony Kendall, Maria Perschy, Terry Kemper, Tom Weyland, Anita Brock, Paul Mackey

A group of wealthy men and a coterie of call girls are having an orgy in the basement of an old home when a nuclear war breaks out. Everyone outside is blinded by the blast but some survivors manage to make their way to the house where they try to attack the inhabitants. Don't bother.

PERFECT SENSE

2011 (R) 92m / **D:** David Mackenzie / **W:** Kim Fupz Aakeson / **C:** Ewan McGregor, Eva Green, Lauren Tempany, Connie Nielsen, Denis Lawson, Stephen Dillane

Emotive sci-fi romance in the vein of *Blindness* that posits a fast-spreading plague that systematically robs people of their senses (smell, then taste, hearing, and so on). Ewan McGregor and Eva Green play a chef and scientist in Glasgow who fall in love just before the plague starts and their budding romance plays out as global chaos mounts and their senses deteriorate. Kim Fupz Aakeson's thoughtful script finds numerous clever wrinkles to show humanity adjusting to each new onslaught (i.e., when taste goes, restaurants focus on tactile qualities like crunch and heat). The plot's slightly precious conceit is more than balanced by pitch-perfect timing, heartbreak performances, and a sense of the tragic that eludes most apocalypse tales. As the film inexorably builds to its logical conclusion, the threat of a final fade to black becomes almost unbearable.

THE PHANTOM EMPIRE

1935 (NR) 245m / D: B. Reeves Eason, Otto Brower / **W:** Wallace MacDonald, Gerald Geraghty / **C:** Gene Autry, Frankie Darro, Betsy King Ross, Smiley Burnette

So you think you've seen it all with computer-generated dinosaurs and liquid-metal Terminators? Bah! No true fan should turn down a chance to watch truly one of the weirdest of the vintage serials. Bad guys want to force singing cowboy Gene Autry off his ranch so they can mine a secret radium depot. Meanwhile 25,000 feet underground is the "Scientific City" of Murania, an advanced and ancient civilization driven beneath the surface by glaciers. They want to avoid discovery, so they dispatch oxygen-masked 'Thunder Riders' to the surface to ward off nosy cowboys. Autry is framed for murder, beaten up, slain, and resurrected throughout the 12 episodes; but no matter what happens he always gets back to a microphone, often with the help of his kiddie fan club, in time to croon another number for his radio program. Dig the cheesy robots in their metal stetsons and the Muranian production design. Studio publicity of the era claimed that the writer dreamt up the plot while doped with anesthesia in a dentist's chair (thus classifying it as a "head" movie 30 years before *2001*). Influences include the hollow-Earth theories of assorted crackpot authors. The script lifts lines from such far-flung sources as Shakespeare's *Henry V* and *Ripley's Believe It or Not*. Also available in an edited theatrical version at 80 minutes. AKA: *Radio Ranch*.

> "The plot's slightly precious conceit is more than balanced by pitch-perfect timing, heartbreak performances, and a sense of the tragic that eludes most apocalypse tales."
>
> *Perfect Sense*

PHASE 4

1974 (PG) 84m / D: Saul Bass / **W:** Mayo Simon / **C:** Nigel Davenport, Michael Murphy, Lynne Frederick, Alan Gifford, Helen Horton, Robert Henderson

Sole directorial effort from Saul Bass (eminent screen title designer who also claimed to have helped Hitchcock bring off the shower scene in *Psycho*) is a bizarre, visionary chiller of common ants suddenly endowed by extraterrestrial force with mass-intelligence. After the ants conquer a patch of Arizona countryside, scientists in a high-tech domed lab try to destroy the environmental menace. The humans have pesticides, grenades, and their own fierce cunning. The ants have adaptive mutation, Archimedean engineering talents, and *their* own fierce cunning. It's not a fair fight.... The six-legged thespians turn in a remarkable performance, and half the pic occurs from their minute point of view. Inspired by *2001: A Space Odyssey*, Bass planned a cosmic f/x sequence at the end that had to be scrapped for budget reasons; thus the finale seems truncated. Offbeat genre effort deserving more attention.

PHENOMENON

1996 (PG) 123m / **D:** Jon Turteltaub / **W:** Gerald Di Pego / **C:** John Travolta, Kyra Sedgwick, Robert Duvall, Forest Whitaker

Magical-extraterrestrial story about small-town car mechanic John Travolta who gets zapped by a light one night and wakes up with extraordinary powers, à la *Flowers for Algernon*. After this possible UFO encounter, he reads books as quickly as if they were greeting cards, learns new languages in a matter of minutes, and is even capable of predicting earthquakes. Whole town is duly astonished. Reflected a superbeing mini-trend in Travolta's career, released the same year as *Michael*, where he played an actual archangel.

THE PHILADELPHIA EXPERIMENT

1984 (PG) 101m / **D:** Stewart Raffill / **W:** William Gray, Michael Janover / **C:** Michael Paré, Nancy Allen, Eric Christmas, Bobby Di Cicco, Michael Currie, Louise Latham

According to legend, in 1943, the U.S. destroyer *Eldridge* was involved in a WWII experiment to make its radar invisible. In this fictional take on that maybe-true story, not only did the *Eldridge* disappear from the radar screens, it completely vanished. Two sailors from the vessel reappear in the year 1984 and as they try to figure out where they are, one of them has trouble holding it all (his molecules, that is) together and vanishes. The other (Michael Paré) is captured by the military, escapes, finds romance and an old friend or two, and discovers that they are trying to duplicate the 1943 experiment in 1984. All this leads to trouble with his molecules, the discovery of a rip in the very fabric of time, and the revealing of the horrible consequences of the first experiment. Nancy Allen plays Allison Hayes (a tribute to the actress who played 1958's *Attack of the 50 Foot Woman*), who energetically tries to help the sailors adjust to their new home. Based on the book by William I. Moore and Charles Berlitz. A pet project of John Carpenter, who didn't direct but became executive producer. Redone as a TV movie in 2012.

PHILADELPHIA EXPERIMENT II

1993 (PG-13) 98m / **D:** Stephen Cornwell / **W:** Kevin Rock, Nick Paine / **C:** Brad Johnson, Gerrit Graham, Marjean Holden, James Greene, Geoffrey Blake, John Christian Graas, Cyril O'Reilly

David Herdeg, the surviving time-transplanted sailor from the original *Philadelphia Experiment*, is alive and well in 1993 until he begins to experience the same molecular displacement that had destroyed his fellow tar ten years ago. In a nearby top-secret military lab, a mad scientist (Gerritt Graham) is conducting another experiment. Unknown to everyone, the goal of this experiment is to transport a stealth fighter back to 1943 in order to bomb Washington, D.C., thus ensuring Germany's victory in WWII. Seems said mad scientist's dad (also Graham) was a cohort of Adolf's, and his son wants to fertilize his Nazi roots. Consequently, Herdeg (Brad Johnson) must risk life and molecular stabilization to travel back to 1943, prevent the bombing, thusly saving his son, the world, life, liberty, justice for all, and all those sorts of good-type things.

Pɪ

1998 (R) 84m / **D:** Darren Aronofsky / **W:** Darren Aronofsky / **C:** Sean Gullette, Mark Margolis, Ben Shenkman, Pamela Hart, Stephen Pearlman

Few of the films that came clawing out of the indie scene in the 1990s were about ideas. Limited resources pushed most indie filmmakers to relationship stories; dialogue being cheap to shoot. Darren Aronofsky's migraine-starting numerological debut is a grainy black-and-white idea factory that buzzes like a feedback loop, implanting theory seeds with almost every scene. Obsessed nerd and narrator Sean Gullette leaves in a techno-bunker of a New York apartment, where he tinkers and tweaks computer stock-picking. Things turn toward the surreal when his computer gives him a random 216-digit number. Later, he gets clued by a rabbi into Talmudic theories where a number is assigned to each letter of the alphabet. As Gullette becomes convinced that the 216-digit number is some kind of correspondence from God, he is approached by a Wall Street firm that wants his stock-picking program, bad. Aronofsky jangles and jumbles the film's structure (aided by Clint Mansell's fractured electronica score) almost as much as he did with his follow-up *Requiem for a Dream*, creating just enough paranoid confusion to raise the possibility that Gullette *isn't* completely crazy. Like *Primer*, Aronofsky works on the limits of the real to create the impossible.

Pɪᴛᴄʜ Bʟᴀᴄᴋ

2000 (R) 109m / **D:** David Twohy / **W:** David Twohy, Jim Wheat, Ken Wheat / **C:** Vin Diesel, Cole Hauser, Radha Mitchell, Keith David, Lewis Fitz-Gerald

Vin Diesel took his big step up from being a bit-player with this tough-minded actioner about a ship that crash-lands on an alien planet, forcing the crew to figure out how they're going to survive. One problem is Riddick (Diesel), a prisoner with a violent past who seems to have the moral capacity of a cockroach. The other is that the planet they're on is full of vicious creepy-crawlies that only come out at night. Advantage Riddick: he has surgically improved eyes that let him see in the dark; thusly those goggles so prominently featured in the advertising. Although it's a potential train wreck of a premise, writer/director Twohy keeps the pacing wire-tight throughout in a manner that he didn't manage with a more sluggish effort like *The Arrival*. A couple of the characters, particularly Radha Mitchell's pilot and Keith David's conflicted imam, play nicely against stereotype, and Diesel makes for an engagingly complex anti-hero. Tough-minded pulp sci-fi that lost much of its appeal when Twohy took Riddick's character and ran with it in subsequent sequels: *The Chronicles of Riddick* (2004) and the imaginatively titled *Riddick* (2013).

PLANETA BUR

1962 (NR) 78m / D: Pavel Klushantsev / **W:** Pavel Klushantsev, Alexander Kazantsev / **C:** Vladimir Temelianov, Gennadi Vernov, Kyunna Ignatova, Georgi Zhonov

Classic Soviet sci-fi about a space exploration team landing on Venus whereupon they are threatened by volcanic eruptions, hostile plant life, monstrous animals, and other dangers. Although there are some silly moments, some good plot twists and acting make up for them. The robot "John" they take with them could easily rival *Forbidden Planet*'s Robby in personality—his final scene of self-sacrifice is truly touching. In Russian with English subtitles. Much footage from this was reused by American International and turned into *Voyage to the Prehistoric Planet* (1965). AKA: *Cosmonauts on Venus*; *Storm Planet*; *Planet of Storms*.

PLANET OF BLOOD

1966 (NR) 81m / D: Curtis Harrington / **W:** Curtis Harrington / **C:** John Saxon, Basil Rathbone, Judi Meredith, Dennis Hopper, Florence Marly, Forrest J. Ackerman

Space opera about an alien vampire (Florence Marly) discovered by a rescue team in a derelict spaceship on Mars. If you've ever seen the Soviet film *Niebo Zowiet*, don't be surprised if some scenes look familiar; the script was written around f/x segments cut from that film. Surprisingly effective nonetheless; director Curtis Harrington wrings suspense within the limited confines of the low-budget sets, and Marly (*Sealed Verdict*) makes for a sexy/creepy monster. Yet another inspiration for *Alien*. Basil Rathbone is mainly seen standing around mission control barking orders via radio. Harrington and Dennis Hopper had collaborated previously on the atmospheric *Night Tide* (1963). AKA: *Queen of Blood*.

PLANET OF THE APES (1968)

1968 (G) 112m / D: Franklin J. Schaffner / **W:** Rod Serling, Michael G. Wilson / **C:** Charlton Heston, Roddy McDowall, Kim Hunter, Maurice Evans, Linda Harrison, James Whitmore, James Daly

Astronaut Charlton Heston crash-lands on a planet in the future (3978 C.E.) where apes are masters and humans are merely brute animals. Heston delivers one of his more plausible performances, and superb ape makeup creates realistic pseudo-simians of Roddy McDowall, Kim Hunter, Maurice Evans, James Whitmore, and James Daly. Rod Serling co-wrote the screenplay—adapted from Pierre Boulle's highly ironic novel *Monkey Planet*—which is slightly reminiscent of the *Twilight Zone* episode in which astronauts end up inhabitants in an alien zoo. Superior sci-fi with sociological implications ranging from the civil rights struggle to the Scopes evolution trial. Followed by many sequels of wildly varying quality, including *Beneath ...*, *Escape from ...*, *Conquest of ...*, and *Battle for ...*, Tim Burton's 2001 remake, and two television series. Two Oscar nominations (costume design and Jerry Goldsmith's primeval score) and one honorary award for John Chambers's ape makeup job.

PLANET OF THE APES (2001)

2001 (PG-13) 119m / D: Tim Burton / **W:** William Broyles Jr., Lawrence Konner, Mark Rosenthal / **C:** Mark Wahlberg, Tim Roth, Helena Bonham Carter, Michael Clarke Duncan, Paul Giamatti, Cary Hiroyuki-Tagawa

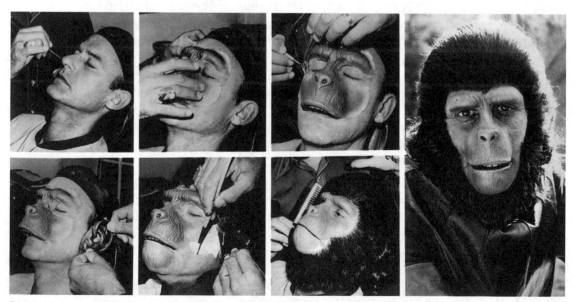

Roddy McDowall gets turned into an ape for 1968's *Planet of the Apes,* which spawned so many sequels it practically created its own mini-genre.

The original *Planet of the Apes* was not a classic. The acting was stony and many of the shots cheap-looking; it felt like an overextended *Twilight Zone* episode at times, which in many ways it was. But compared to Tim Burton's purposeless remake, it stands tall. Mark Wahlberg's astronaut is sucked into a wormhole of sorts and crash-lands on a planet millennia in the future. He discovers that primates rule the place, having enslaved humans who are on the verge of revolt. As in the more underwritten Burton films like *Alice in Wonderland*, it all builds to a big, highly anti-climactic showdown without developing much story along the way. Any of the original's satirical elements are here completely defanged and even a hinted cross-species romance between Wahlberg and chimpanzee Helena Bonham Carter is strangely lacking in bite. Since it's Burton, the whole thing looks smashing. But by the time it gets around to the twisteroo ending (which is more convoluted than in the original), the whole thing feels like a cynical exercise rather than boundary-pushing sci-fi. Reactions were mixed, to put it mildly, convincing the studio to forgo a sequel and instead start over again with 2011's *Rise of the Planet of the Apes*.

PLANET OF THE VAMPIRES

1965 (NR) 86m / D: Mario Bava / **W:** Mario Bava, Callisto Cosulich, Antonio Roman / **C:** Barry Sullivan, Norma Bengell, Ángel Aranda, Evi Marandi, Fernando Villena

Atmospheric, low-budget, sci-fi horror at its best. Dan O'Bannon has admitted that this Mario Bava gem was one of his main influences while writing *Alien*; many other outer-space horror filmmakers owe a debt as well. Responding to a SOS from the planet Aura, the spaceship *Argos* crash-lands on a set previously used for an Italian sword-and-sandal not-quite epic. The landscape is loaded with other wrecked space hulks, including the SOSer. A hologram of the ship's commander confirms that all the crew went mad and butchered each other. Faced with new murders and disappearances, the captain of the *Argos* (Barry Sullivan) finds he is dealing with dastardly mind-possessing space vampires. To make matters worse, the minds of all the dead astronauts can also be controlled, leading to an outer space zombie revival in which the newly resurrected shed their cellophane shrouds in Bavaesque style and flair. AKA: *Terror in Space*; *Space Mutants*; *The Demon Planet*.

PLANET TERROR

2007 (NR) 105m / D: Robert Rodriguez / **W:** Robert Rodriguez / **C:** Rose McGowan, Freddy Rodriguez, Josh Brolin, Marley Shelton, Jeff Fahey, Michael Biehn, Bruce Willis, Naveen Andrews

One half of the *Grindhouse* experiment in drive-in retro pulp was Quentin Tarantino's *Death Proof*, about Kurt Russell and one cool car. This was the other half, a loose and gag-filled homage to 1980s, John Carpenter-style, anything-goes, shoot-'em-up gross-out humor destined for late-night cable rotation. A small town is infected by the release of a zombie-creating weaponized virus by some entrepreneurial soldiers led by Bruce Willis. Leading the fight against the undead hordes are ex-soldier Wray (Freddy Rodriguez) and his ex-girlfriend, go-go dancer Cherry Darling (Rose McGowan). Rodriguez pays professorial attention to getting the jagged angles and gag edits just right for that exploitation look; even if the stylized grainy film stock is of an earlier time period than he's spoofing. While a high point certainly arrives after McGowan's zombie-infected leg is amputated and Wray slaps an assault rifle in there as replacement (don't ask how she pulls the trigger), there's gems aplenty here. Several decent gags amid the bloodletting (bodily fluids regularly explode out of bodies here by the gallon). Faced with a hospital full of infected flesh-eaters, doctor Josh Brolin is asked "What do you think?" by a colleague. "Self-preservation comes to mind" is his eminently logical reply.

So bad it's hysterical to watch, the Ed Wood film *Plan 9 from Outer Space* was a very sad way for actor Bela Lugosi to end his career.

PLAN 9 FROM OUTER SPACE

1956 (NR) 78m / D: Edward D. Wood Jr. / **W:** Edward D. Wood Jr. / **C:** Bela Lugosi, Tor Johnson, Lyle Talbot, Vampira, Gregory Walcott, Duke Moore, Tom Keene

Everything you've heard about this movie is true. Bela Lugosi died a few days after production on this film began. Wood supplemented the few minutes of footage he had by substituting a stand-in (a chiropractor noticeably taller than Lugosi) to walk through the film with a cape over his face. The story deals with resurrected corpses, aliens, a weapon called Solobonite, and a woman named Vampira. The sets are pitiful (cardboard gravestones, shower curtain cockpit, Cadillac hubcaps for UFOs) and the dialogue stupefying. Tell your friends. AKA: *Grave Robbers from Outer Space.*

PLUGHEAD REWIRED: CIRCUITRY MAN 2

1994 (R) 97m / D: Steven Lovy, Robert Lovy / **W:** Steven Lovy, Robert Lovy / **C:** Vernon Wells, Deborah Shelton, Jim Metzler, Dennis Christopher, Nicholas Worth, Traci Lords

About half as good as the original. It tells essentially the same futuristic story about a romantic robot (Jim Metzler), a tough woman (Deborah Shelton), and the villainous Plughead (Vernon Wells), who lives to share other people's pain and terror directly. It shares most of the first film's strengths and weaknesses, too, but has a stronger emphasis on comedy, much of it broad and hammy, with two supporting characters whose appearance and shtick could have come straight from the mad scientists on *Mystery Science Theater 3000*. Recommended for fans of the original only. AKA: *Circuitry Man 2*.

THE POSTMAN

1997 (R) 177m / **D:** Kevin Costner / **W:** Eric Roth, Brian Helgeland / **C:** Kevin Costner, Will Patton, Larenz Tate, Olivia Williams, James Russo, Daniel von Bargen, Scott Bairstow, Giovanni Ribisi, Brian Anthony Wilson, Tom Petty

Coming just a couple years after *Waterworld*, Kevin Costner's *other* post-apocalyptic epic manages to combine the soaring landscapes of *Dances with Wolves* with the bright-eyed enthusing of *Field of Dreams*. Costner plays your basic wanderer of the wasteland, only less fell-eyed warrior and more Bob Hope-ish comic coward. A tossed-off scheme to get some grub by pretending to be a mail carrier from a restored U.S. government goes too far, and soon everyone is thrusting letters at him, keen for civilization to return. Engagingly goofy humor and Frank Capra-esque optimism (David Brin wrote the source novel in response to the post-apoc fiction he thought welcomed the devastation instead of mourning it) get lost in the unforgivably bloated runtime and Costner's smarm. Will Patton is incongruously cast as a neo-Nazi militia warlord and Tom Petty shows up as ... Tom Petty, rock star and indomitable plague survivor ("I was once [famous], sorta").

PRAYER OF THE ROLLERBOYS

1991 (R) 94m / **D:** Rick King / **W:** W. Peter Iliff / **C:** Corey Haim, Patricia Arquette, Christopher Collet, Julius W. Harris, J. C. Quinn, Jake Dengel, Devin Clark, Mark Pellegrino, Morgan Weisser

Violent, futuristic, funky action as Corey Haim infiltrates a criminal militia of syncopated roller-blading neo-Nazi youth (references to *The Turner Diaries* abound) with plans for nationwide domination via narco-terrorism. Yes, you read that correctly. Though routinely plotted and predictable, it's got plenty of bitchin' slo-mo rollerblading action and a wry vision of tomorrow's shattered America—broke, drug-soaked, homeless, foreign owned; even sharper when you realize this is a Japanese-American co-production. No apparent relation to the "rollerboy" gangs of William S. Burroughs' erotic head-trip novel *The Wild Boys*.

A space alien goes on a hunting expedition—for well-muscled humans led by Arnold Schwarzenegger—in the sci-fi shoot-'em-up *Predator*.

PREDATOR

1987 (R) 107m / D: John McTiernan / **W:** Jim Thomas, John Thomas / **C:** Arnold Schwarzenegger, Jesse Ventura, Sonny Landham, Bill Duke, Elpidia Carrillo, Carl Weathers, R. G. Armstrong, Richard Chaves, Shane Black, Kevin Peter Hall

Arnie leads a team of overmuscled Special Forces types (just look at those gleaming muscles!) into the Central American jungle to rescue hostages. The human baddies don't put up much resistance, but that invisible-at-will dreadlocked alien on a hunting expedition is more of a problem. In no time at all, the Predator is picking off the Americans in various gruesome ways. Soon it's just Arnold and the Predator locked in deadly combat. Solid supporting cast plays it with tongues planted just slightly in the cheek. One of the better big-gun 1980s actioners. Breakthrough film for John McTiernan, who directed *Die Hard* the next year and thusly cemented his place in the testosterone movie hall of fame. Followed by a sequel and numerous offshoots.

PREDATOR 2

1990 (R) 105m / D: Stephen Hopkins / **W:** John Thomas, Jim Thomas / **C:** Danny Glover, Gary Busey, Ruben Blades, Maria Conchita Alonso, Bill Paxton, Robert Davi, Adam Baldwin, Kent McCord, Morton Downey Jr.

Badass cop Danny Glover takes time away from battling drug dealers to deal with the malicious extraterrestrial who exterminated Arnold's band of commandos in the original. Shifting the scene from the Central American jungle to near-future L.A. would seem like a good idea, urban jungle and all. The Predator does have a good time leaping down from skyscrapers Batman-style and snatching up gangsters and cops alike. The sprawling and surprisingly diverse (for its time) cast bring a lot of pop to the running and gunning, and the twist ending is clever enough. But the plotting is ludicrous in that *Die Hard / Lethal Weapon* clone manner so common at the time. The straining humor fails pretty consistently, despite sweating efforts from shouters Bill Paxton, Gary Busey, and then-famous tabloid-TV star Morton Downey, Jr.

PREDATORS

2010 (R) 107m / **D:** Nimrod Antal / **W:** Alex Litvak, Michael Finch / **C:** Adrien Brody, Laurence Fishburne, Topher Grace, Alice Braga, Walton Goggins, Oleg Taktarov, Danny Trejo

Robert Rodriguez produced and wrote an early version of the script for this sharp, funny series return to "Most Dangerous Game" territory that (thankfully) ignores the *AVP* offshoot and *Predators 2*. Adrien Brody plays a mercenary who finds himself falling out of the sky into a jungle along with several other people. None of them know each other, and the jungle doesn't look like anything on Earth. Turns out, they're all killers of some kind (soldier, mercenary, Yakuza, etc.). They've been snatched from Earth and transported to this place to provide at least somewhat challenging prey to some Predators (who must be among the most phenomenally bored aliens ever to be seen on screen, if they spend *this* much time finding new ways to hunt humans). Strong casting, particularly a cold-eyed Brody and smartass geek Topher Grace as the one guy who doesn't appear to be a killer, complements the punchy story, which tries to return a sense of drama to the long-cheapened series. Watch for Laurence Fishburne in a great cameo that playfully tweaks his teenage role in *Apocalypse Now*.

PRIEST

2011 (PG-13) 87m / **D:** Scott Stewart / **W:** Cory Goodman / **C:** Paul Bettany, Cam Gigandet, Maggie Q, Karl Urban, Brad Dourif, Christopher Plummer

Alternate-historical *Blade Runner* vampire-slaying with an extra dose of the funereal. In this grim world, humans and vampires have been warring for centuries. Humans are now stuck mostly inside sprawling half-medieval and half-futuristic walled cities under the control of a definitely pre-Vatican II Catholic Church. The land outside is your basic irradiated wasteland that looks good on screen but doesn't make much sense (where do all the humans grow their food?). Paul Bettany is a former member of the elite warrior "priests" trained to hunt vampires; only he's caught in a crisis of faith when bloodsuckers (whom the church claims have been made extinct) make off with his niece. Super slo-mo schismatic battling follows between Bettany, the other priests sent to stop him, and priestess Maggie Q, who just wants to help. Karl Urban is his usual dull growling self as the priest-gone-bad whom they have to battle. Film gains points for finding a new way to spin bloodsuckers; loses many many more by ransacking factory-line B-movies for every cliché possible.

PRIMER

2004 (PG-13) 77m / **D:** Shane Carruth / **W:** Shane Carruth / **C:** Shane Carruth, David Sullivan, Casey Gooden, Anand Upadhyaya, Carrie Crawford

Elliptical garage-hacker sci-fi that spins a web so dense it's almost impenetrable. But what can be glimpsed through writer/director/star Shane Carruth's stubbornly obscurationist shards of story is one of those glimmering kernels of possibility that will fascinate lovers of alternate universes and time-travel paradoxes and absolutely alienate almost everybody else. As far as can be determined, a pair of engineers have been working on an invention in one of their garages. Along the way, they accidentally discover that they may have created a time travel machine. Little of this is seen. Most of Carruth's film involves watching over the men's shoulders as they talk in fragments that are always hinting at some great undiscovered possibility but never quite spell it out. The last third is a rabbit-hole of multiplying realities and dopplegangers that has engaged numerous web-fans to parse with Talmudic intensity. Shot for no money on a wing and a prayer, Carruth's film has a sharp but dreamlike look to it, the exurbia setting of tract homes and big-box stores both alluringly beautiful and alienating. Potentially not worth the trouble for those opposed to repeat viewings.

PROGRAMMED TO KILL

1986 (R) 91m / **D:** Allan Holzman / **W:** Robert Short / **C:** Robert Ginty, Sandahl Bergman, James Booth, Louise Caire Clark, Paul Walker

A beautiful terrorist is killed by the CIA and transformed on the operating table into a cyborg assassin, to infiltrate and slay her former comrades. She does, but vestigial memories compel the bionic babe to turn against her creators with equal fury. Sandahl Bergman goes the *Terminator* career route in imitation of her leading man from *Conan the Barbarian*. Action and violence galore, but ultimately average. Very early appearance by *Fast and the Furious*'s Paul Walker. AKA: *Retaliator*.

PROJECT A-KO

1986 (NR) 86m / **D:** Katsuhiko Nishijima / **W:** Tomoko Kawasaki, Yuji Moriyama, Katsuhiko Nishijima

Futuristic Japanese animated feature, which is intended for adults, concerns teenagers with strange powers, an alien spaceship, and lots of action. Seventeen year-old A-ko possesses superhuman strength and a ditzy sidekick, C-ko. B-ko, the spoiled and rich daughter of a business tycoon, decides to fight A-ko for C-ko's companionship. Meanwhile, an alien spaceship is headed toward Earth with unknown intentions. Somehow, everything ties together—watch and see how. In Japanese with English subtitles.

PROJECT MOON BASE

1953 (NR) 64m / **D:** Richard Talmadge / **W:** Robert Heinlein, Jack Seaman / **C:** Donna Martell, Hayden Rourke

Espionage runs rampant on a spaceship headed by a female officer. Eventually the ship is stranded on the moon. Actually filmed for a television series titled *Ring Around the Moon*. A cold-war sexist relic; not surprising given the co-screenwriting credit from Robert Heinlein.

PROJECT X

1987 (PG) 107m / **D:** Jonathan Kaplan / **W:** Stanley Weiser, Lawrence Lasker / **C:** Matthew Broderick, Helen Hunt, William Sadler, Johnny Ray McGhee, Jonathan Stark, Robln Gammell, Stephen Lang, Jean Smart, Dick Miller

Bemused Air Force pilot Matthew Broderick gets a strange assignment—training lab chimpanzees to pilot planes in a computerized flight simulator. He grows close to the appealing apes and is shocked to learn the true, cruel purpose of the experiments. High-tech tale falls somewhere between sci-fi drama and animal-rights fable, but some scenes possess a true sense of wonder. Great performances by the primates, somewhat soured by persistent allegations by activists of real-life animal abuse on the set.

PROMETHEUS

2012 (R) 124m / **D:** Ridley Scott / **W:** Jon Spaihts, Damon Lindelof / **C:** Noomi Rapace, Michael Fassbender, Charlize Theron, Idris Elba, Guy Pearce, Logan Marshall-Green, Sean Harris, Rafe Spall

Ridley Scott's return to the outer-space and inner-body horror show that made his career strains mightily to return the series to its gloomier and moodier origins. But despite skirting right past the *AVP*-style dreck that followed the last Ripley entry (1997's *Alien: Resurrection*), it all still feels like much ado about the same old. Jon Spaihts and Damon Lindelof's reductive script circles back to 2093, just a few years before the *Nostromo* crew discovered their first face-hugger, and puts another batch of fools and hardy survivors in harm's way. The massive research ship *Prometheus* lands on an alien planet looking for clues to humanity's origins recently uncovered by archaeologists back on Earth. As keeps happening in this series, they discover an ancient spacecraft that they realize far too late is full of hostile lifeforms.

Ridley Scott returned to the director's chair he first sat in for *Alien* to oversee the filming of the prequel *Prometheus*.

The ensemble cast makes for a better set of alien-bait than previous films; you occasionally care whether some characters, like the religious scientist played by Noomi Rapace or Michael Fassbender's gentle, *Lawrence of Arabia*-obsessed android, survive the ordeal. But the script opens up too many fascinating tangents about faith and the origins of intelligent life only to summarily hack them off with more of the usual run-and-scream. There's even a tilt toward zombie-esque horror that feels far too cynical. Far, far too many trips back to this gruesome well. Oscar nomination for its sleek and non-showy f/x; lost out to the splashy fantasy *Life of Pi*.

PULSE

1988 (PG-13) 90m / D: Paul Golding / **W:** Paul Golding / **C:** Cliff De Young, Roxanne Hart, Joey Lawrence, Charles Tyner, Dennis Redfield, Robert Romanus, Myron Healey

Fear of technology pervades this low-voltage thriller in which electricity goes awry, causing common appliances and other household devices to supercharge, malfunction, and threaten their owners. Genre fans who enjoy the sight of glowing circuits and melting insulation should find plenty to enjoy.

THE PUPPET MASTERS

1994 (R) 109m / D: Stuart Orme / **W:** Terry Rossio, David S. Goyer, Ted Elliott / **C:** Donald Sutherland, Eric Thal, Julie Warner, Keith David, Will Patton, Richard Belzer, Yaphet Kotto

Government official Donald Sutherland discovers aliens are taking over the bodies of humans, and if he doesn't find a way to stop the parasites they'll soon rule the Earth. The parasites are sufficiently yucky but in the main this is a mediocre adaptation with a good but wasted cast. Filmmakers are fairly faithful to Robert Heinlein's 1951 novel, but they missed its atmosphere of pervading paranoia, leaving the film reminiscent of but not measuring up to the likes of the 1956 *Invasion of the Body Snatchers* or even a really good episode of *The X-Files*. AKA: *Robert A. Heinlein's The Puppet Masters*.

THE PURGE

2013 (R) 90m / D: James DeMonaco / **W:** James DeMonaco / **C:** Ethan Hawke, Lena Headey, Max Burkholder, Adelaide Kane, Edwin Hodge, Rhys Wakefield, Tony Oller, Arija Bareikis, Tom Yi, Chris Mulkey, Tisha French

Shirley Jackson by way of the Tea Party. In 2022, America has a smashing way to fix the once-soaring crime rate and cratering economy: One night a year, *every* crime is legal. The Visigothian "purge" purportedly helps unleash the beast within, but might be an excuse to eliminate those too poor to defend themselves. The normalcy of it all is what's most frightening, with talk-radio callers blithely chirping about their murderous plans and neighborhoods filled with the sound of people sharpening weapons. A none-too-subtle allegory plays out as a gated-suburban family (Ethan Hawke playing the status-grubbing dad) finds their perfectly secured bunker threatened when their son lets in a bleeding, homeless black man being chased by a Nazi Youth-like squad of preppies looking to execute the "homeless pig." The fascinating morality play scenario shifts more generically horror once defenses are breached. Clever, up to a point.

THE PURPLE MONSTER STRIKES

1945 (NR) 209m / **D:** Spencer Bennet, Fred C. Brannon / **W:** Royal Cole, Albert DeMond, Basil Dickey, Lynn Perkins, Joseph Poland, Barney Sarecky / **C:** Dennis Moore, Linda Stirling, Roy Barcroft

The first and best of Republic's three Martian-invasion chapter plays is the last of the studio's great movie serials. The red planet's emissary, a humanoid in a purple-colored scaly suit and played by cowboy star Roy Barcroft, comes to Earth to kill the human inventor of a reusable rocketship. If he can get back home with the technology, we will soon have a Mars invasion fleet in our backyard. The Purple Monster is also able to reanimate and possess the corpse of the late inventor (shades of *Invasion of the Body Snatchers* a decade ahead of time) but pops out for fistfights with a heroic lawyer attempting to foil him throughout the 15 cliffhanger episodes. These choreographed punchouts, so beloved by serial buffs, are the last good ones Republic would ever film.

PURPLE PEOPLE EATER

1988 (PG) 91m / **D:** Linda Shayne / **W:** Linda Shayne / **C:** Ned Beatty, Shelley Winters, Neil Patrick Harris, Kareem Abdul-Jabbar, Little Richard, Chubby Checker, Peggy Lipton

The alien of the title lands on Earth to mix it up with young girls and rock 'n' roll. Based on the song of the same name, whose performer, Sheb Wooley, appears in the film, as do classic rock performers like Chubby Checker and Little Richard. Harmlessly stupid "fun" for the whole family.

QUARANTINE

1989 (R) 92m / **D:** Charles Wilkinson / **W:** Charles Wilkinson / **C:** Beatrice Boepple, Garwln Sanford, Jerry Wasserman, Charles Wilkinson

"Declare war on bacteria!" is one of the slogans used during an ill-defined plague epidemic, during which a power-mad senator (Jerry Wasserman, a look-alike for Roy Cohn) seizes control of the government and holds HUAC-style hearings to determine which citizens are "healthy" and which get forcibly ejected into the lawless quarantine zones. This overlooked Orwellian sci-fi from Canada is part AIDS metaphor, part McCarthyism satire. Not all of it works, and some is downright looney, but this takes a fresh approach to oft-bungled material.

QUATERMASS AND THE PIT

1968 (NR) 180m / **D:** Roy Ward Baker / **W:** Nigel Kneale / **C:** André Morell, Cec Linder, James Donald, Barbara Shelley, Julian Glover

While constructing a new subway, British workers unearth a Martian spaceship and insect-like alien remains. Professor Quatermass is called in, and through a telepathic link, is able to learn the history of the craft, the Martians, and mankind itself. Writer Nigel Kneale supplies speculation of the third, fourth, and occult kind, even having the dear professor refer to the Marians as "satanic." The alien influence starts having an effect on the good people of London, who begin rioting in the streets; soon the whole city is erupting in fire and chaos. May have a little too much plot for the allotted time, but this is a fine example of gripping storytelling and grand-concept fllmmaking done on a sparse budget. Released in the U.S. as *Five Million Miles to Earth*.

QUATERMASS CONCLUSION

1979 (NR) 105m / **D:** Piers Haggard / **W:** Nigel Kneale / **C:** John Mills, Simon Mac-Corkindale, Barbara Kellerman, Margaret Tyzack

Elderly and eccentric Professor Bernard Quatermass is called out of retirement when a death ray from outer space begins to zap youths around the world. Adding to the problems, the superpowers aren't so super anymore and anarchy has taken over the streets, and it appears that Armageddon is just around the corner. A poorly produced, and only slightly better acted, edited-down version of the BBC miniseries broadcast the same year, the story is still enthralling and as entertaining and thought-provoking as the other *Quatermass* films.

THE QUATERMASS EXPERIMENT

1955 (NR) 78m / **D:** Val Guest / **W:** Richard H. Landau, Val Guest / **C:** Brian Donlevy, Margia Dean, Jack Warner, Richard Wordsworth

Preceding *The Blob* by two years, this excellent British production is the story of an astronaut who returns to earth unknowingly carrying an alien infestation that causes him to mutate into an ever-growing, giant-tentacled blob-like creature. Features the first big-screen appearance of the BBC's TV hero Dr. Bernard Quatermass (played with pushy perfection by Brian Donlevy). A tense adaptation by director Val Guest and co-screenwriter Richard Landau. Not as bleak or quite as good as the 1957 sequel, but still a well-acted, well-written, sci-fi classic. AKA: *The Creeping Unknown*.

QUATERMASS 2

1957 (NR) 84m / **D:** Val Guest / **W:** Val Guest, Nigel Kneale / **C:** Brian Donlevy, John Longden, Sidney James, Bryan Forbes, William Franklyn, Vera Day, John Van Eyssen, Michael Ripper, Michael Balfour, Tom Chatto, Percy Herbert

Second film based on Nigel Kneale's critically acclaimed 1953 BBC series. British egghead Professor Quatermass is sent to investigate some abnormalities in a rural area. Soldiers and government officials in the area are behaving like brainwashed zombies. Meteorites are far too plentiful and tend to erupt and injure when approached. A large "food" processing plant has been set up with too much security for the professor's liking. When a friend is covered by, eaten away by, and killed by the food, the professor knows what must be done. Extremely well-scripted Hammer horror also contains sharp commentary on the dangers of authoritarianism. Preceded by *The Quatermass Experiment* and followed by *Quatermass and the Pit*. AKA: *Enemy from Space*.

QUEEN OF OUTER SPACE

1958 (NR) 80m / D: Edward L. Bernds / **W:** Charles Beaumont / **C:** Zsa Zsa Gabor, Eric Fleming, Laurie Mitchell, Paul Birch, Barbara Darrow, Dave Willcock, Lisa Davis, Patrick Waltz, Marilyn Buferd, Marjorie Durant, Lynn Cartwright, Gerry Gaylor

Notorious male-chauvinist sci-fi cheapie set in 1985, by which time space travel will have of course become a reality. Space cadet guys crash on Venus and find it ruled by "dolls," such as a beautiful masked queen who has wicked plans in store for mankind. Starts out slow, but then the unintentional laughs keep coming as the cast plays the hyperdumb material straight—famed scribe Ben Hecht allegedly intended his script outline (rewritten by Charles Beaumont) as satire, but maybe that's just an excuse. Most of the women were recruited from beauty pageants, as in *Abbott & Costello Go to Mars*. Don't be surprised if you've seen the sets and costumes before, either; they were borrowed from *Forbidden Planet* and others.

THE QUIET EARTH

1985 (R) 91m / D: Geoff Murphy / **W:** Bruno Lawrence, Sam Pillsbury, Bill Baer / **C:** Bruno Lawrence, Alison Routledge, Peter Smith

Zac Hobson (Bruno Lawrence, the Gérard Depardieu of New Zealand films) awakens one morning to find himself seemingly alone in the world. This part of the film is best, as he desperately searches for survivors, sets up housekeeping in a mansion, and enjoys the run of the city before beginning to go a bit mad. Then, recalling *The World, The Flesh, and the Devil*, he finds two survivors: a woman and a Maori tribesman. Predictable sexual tensions erupt before Lawrence turns to the more pressing issue of trying to restore the damage wrought by a government experiment that disrupted space and time. A multidimensional story that builds to a haunting, enigmatic finish. Director Geoff Murphy later directed *Freejack* to much less acclaim.

> "A multidimensional story that builds to a haunting, enigmatic finish."
>
> *The Quiet Earth*

QUINTET

1979 (R) 118m / D: Robert Altman / **W:** Lionel Chetwynd, Patricia Resnick, Robert Altman, Frank Barhydt / **C:** Paul Newman, Bibi Andersson, Fernando Rey, Vittorio Gassman, David Langton, Nina Van Pallandt, Brigitte Fossey

Many consider this atypical Robert Altman sci-fi effort one of the unpredictable director's worst films, but it definitely has an indefinable something. Setting is a nuke-inspired second Ice Age, where Paul Newman and wife Brigitte Fossey wander into the last known city. There, peasant-garbed inhabitants, having given up hope for tomorrow, play an assassination game called Quintet, which Newman learns quickly. Curious frozen production design and heavy symbolism (like ubiquitous carrion black dogs) make this tough sledding, but the hypnotic musical score and general aura of fatalism set it apart from more conventional apocalyptic fare. Main complaint is a buildup to an action climax that just doesn't happen; not an uncommon occurrence with Altman.

RADIOACTIVE DREAMS

1986 (R) 94m / **D:** Albert Pyun / **W:** Albert Pyun / **C:** John Stockwell, Michael Dudikoff, Lisa Blount, George Kennedy, Don Murray, Michelle Little

Surreal, practically senseless fantasy wherein two men, trapped in a bomb shelter for 15 years with nothing to read but mystery novels, emerge as detectives into a post-holocaust world looking for adventure. John Stockwell plays Philip Chandler and Michael Dudokoff plays Marlowe Hammer (get it?).

RADIO FREE ALBEMUTH

2010 (NR) 116m / **D:** John Alan Simon / **W:** John Alan Simon / **C:** Jonathan Scarfe, Shea Whigham, Katheryn Winnick, Alanis Morissette, Hanna Hall

This low-low-budget adaptation of Philip K. Dick's posthumously released novel is a classic example of why the author's later work proved so much less accessible to filmmakers than his short stories from the 1950s and '60s. Instead of purloined identities or human-masquerading androids, the pseudo-futuristic story features a Dickian author and his best friend, a record-store worker who's starting to receive strange visions of himself in some alternate universe. His dreams lead him to a singer (played not unconvincingly by Alanis Morissette), with whom he plans to work on a new song whose subliminal lyrics will convince the people of America to rebel against their fascist, McCarthyite president. The story is straight out of Dick's later Valis period, when his schizoid theological visions were spinning out of control. Writer/director John Alan Simon never quite figures out how to portray what's happening without making everything look like a cheaply rendered acid trip.

REAL STEEL

2011 (PG-13) 127m / **D:** Shawn Levy / **W:** Josh Gatins / **C:** Hugh Jackman, Dakota Goyo, Evangeline Lilly, Anthony Mackie, Kevin Durand, Hope Davis, James Rebhorn

Long-in-development feature version of Richard Matheson's 1956 short story "Steel" (already made into a *Twilight Zone* in 1964), which posited a near future where people watch giant robots box, instead of humans. Hugh Jackman is the down-on-his-luck ex-boxer who makes a sketchy living as the ringman/programmer on the fighting-bot circuit. Dakota Goyo is his estranged, plucky son who convinces him to train a skinny old sparring bot as a prize fighter. Evangeline Lilly is the tomboy with the heart of gold waiting in the wings. Kevin Durand is the mean rival who Jackman just can't wait to beat. And so it goes. Dad and son's hopes for a brighter future get tied up in their spunky new avatar, who still might have something to show the world. Needless to say, it's all quite a lot lighter and more family friendly than Matheson's original, not to mention easily a half-hour longer than necessary. Steven Spielberg produced, which could also be why the battling bots bear more than a slight resemblance to the Transformers. Oscar nomination for f/x.

RE-ANIMATOR

1984 (R) 86m / D: Stuart Gordon / **W:** Stuart Gordon, Dennis Paoli, William J. Norris / **C:** Jeffrey Combs, Bruce Abbott, Barbara Crampton, David Gale, Robert Sampson

Based on H. P. Lovecraft's serial novella, this grisly Gothic deals with a medical student (Jeffrey Combs) who re-animates the dead and finds that, strangely enough, unexpected consequences result. Later became a black-humor cult classic for its numerous excesses and terrific acting. The famous "head" scene is the horror/sci-fi equivalent to the campfire scene in *Blazing Saddles*. Director Stuart Gordon was a Chicago theater director before directing this entertaining gorefest; Combs has become a familiar character actor specializing in psychosis; and Barbara Crampton became something of a scream queen. Available in "R" and un-rated versions, plus a special remastered "10th Anniversary" edition containing extra footage and commentary by director and cast. For true fans, it's required viewing; far and away the best of the three. Followed by two sequels: 1990's *Bride of Re-Animator* and 2003's *Beyond Re-Animator*.

REBEL STORM

1989 (R) 99m / D: Francis Schaeffer / **W:** William Fay, Gary Rosen / **C:** Zach Galligan, Wayne Crawford, June Chadwick, Rod McCary, John Rhys-Davies, Elizabeth Kiefer

A group of freedom fighters teams up to rescue America from the totalitarian rulers, and fundamentalist religion runs the place in 2099 C.E. AKA: *Rising Storm*.

RED DAWN

1984 (PG-13) 114m / D: John Milius / **W:** John Milius, Kevin Reynolds / **C:** Patrick Swayze, C. Thomas Howell, Lea Thompson, Charlie Sheen, Jennifer Grey, Harry Dean Stanton, Ron O'Neal, Powers Boothe

The *ne plus ultra* of Reagan-era anti-Commie fervor, sporting an *Outsiders*-long list of up-and-coming fresh-faced stars playing *mujahideen* in Colorado. This gonzo alternate history posits a near future where the Soviet bloc, desperate after crop shortfalls, launches a surprise attack on the United States. Soviet, Cuban, and Nicaraguan paratroopers take key passes in the Rocky Mountains, while surgical nuke strikes incapacitate the command structure, and the main invasion force attacks from Mexico and Alaska. Caught in the middle are the plucky teens of Calumet, Colorado, who form a guerrilla resistance whose battle cry comes from their high school football team: "Wolverines!" Highly enjoyable nonsense in which AK-47-and RPG-wielding Brat Packers like C. Thomas Howell and Charlie Sheen easily take out whole detachments of Spetsnaz commandos. *Apocalypse Now* writer John Milius indulges a whole host of red-state fantasies here, not the least of which is the scene where a paratrooper pulls a gun from a dead American's hand after the camera meaningfully lingers on an NRA bumper sticker. Crisp directing and an eye for striking framing—the opening shot of soldiers parachuting down outside the high school while confused students look on, is one of the decade's more redolent images—keeps the film from overheating on its own ridiculousness. Great supporting work from Harry Dean Stanton and *Superfly* himself, Ron O'Neal.

Action hero star Val Kilmer starred in a less-than-thrilling trip to Mars in *Red Planet*.

RED PLANET

2000 (PG-13) 106m / **D:** Antony Hoffman / **W:** Jonathan Lemkin, Chuck Pfarrer / **C:** Val Kilmer, Carrie-Anne Moss, Tom Sizemore, Benjamin Bratt, Simon Baker, Terence Stamp

Once again, it's the near-future and Earth has been so crudded up by pollution that humanity is looking for another planet to settle on and start polluting. A project to terraform Mars has gone haywire and a team of astronauts is sent to investigate. Of course, things go wrong en route, and when the astronauts land, malfunctions proliferate. It all turns into an engineering puzzle, with the crew needing to figure out how to survive with limited equipment in a harsh environment where their robot assistant is starting to act a little … funny. Less broad in appeal than 2000's other red planet movie, *Mission to Mars*, the cast and directing in this film are strictly functional, with a new-millennium budget being about all that separates this at times from space-mission movies of a half-century earlier; they even use the cheap old trick of presenting an alien landscape by shooting in the desert through a colored gel. No great surprises here. Strictly for the hard sci-fi crowd.

RED PLANET MARS

1952 (NR) 87m / **D:** Harry Horner / **W:** Anthony Veiller, John Balderston / **C:** Peter Graves, Andrea King, Marvin Miller, Herbert Berghof, House Peters Jr., Vince Barnett, Morris Ankrum, Walter Sande

"The Sermon on the Mount … on Mars!" The ads promised "out of this world excitement and suspense," but this adaptation of the play *Red Planet* is mostly limited to two laboratory sets. Peter Graves stars as a scientist who picks up radio transmissions from a utopian Mars that plunge our planet into economic and spiritual chaos, especially when later messages appear to be coming from God. Herbert Berghof co-stars as an ex-Nazi (in cahoots with the Russians) who is causing all the static. Not what one would call *good*, *per se*, but you've definitely never seen anything like it.

REIGN OF FIRE

2002 (PG-13) 101m / **D:** Rob Bowman / **W:** Gregg Chabot, Kevin Peterka, Matt Greenberg / **C:** Christian Bale, Matthew McConaughey, Izabella Scorupco, Gerard Butler

Hints of *Quatermass and the Pit* in this bottom-drawer story about how people tunneling underneath London in the future discovered a dormant dragon, which proceeded to come to the surface, wipe out everything it saw with its napalm-like breath, and started to breed prodigiously. Christian Bale and Matthew McConaughey play the grubby alpha males leading the fight in 2020, battling of course almost as much with each other as they do their legions of winged foes. What they call "high concept" in some parts of Hollywood.

REMOTE CONTROL

1988 (R) 88m / **D:** Jeff Lieberman / **W:** Jeff Lieberman / **C:** Kevin Dillon, Deborah Goodrich, Christopher Wynne, Jennifer Tilly

A circulating videotape of a 1950's sci-fi flick is turning people into murderous zombies, thanks to some entrepreneurial aliens. Off-the-wall, but performed by young actors with gusto.

REPO MAN

1984 (R) 92m / **D:** Alex Cox / **W:** Alex Cox / **C:** Harry Dean Stanton, Emilio Estevez, Tracey Walter, Olivia Barash, Sy Richardson, Del Zamora, Eddie Velez, Miguel Sandoval

Scuffed-up, barely hanging together sci-fi comedy is one of the 1980s' more standout indies. Government agents are hunting down a mad physicist who's driving around with a neutron bomb in the trunk of his 1964 Chevy Malibu. Meanwhile, grizzled repo man Harry Dean Stanton is teaching the new kid, barely reformed punk Emilio Estevez, the "repo code," while also hunting the Malibu. The story's an ambling thing, allowing writer/director Alex Cox to string together little Dadaist vignettes of life on the edge in a sunbleached and scuzzy, Reagan-era Los Angeles. Stanton is a font of speed-frazzled commandments ("I don't want no Commies in my car ... *no Christians either!*") and embittered gravitas. Eventually, aliens get thrown into the mix, along with gun-toting punks, fascist feds, Scientology riffs, and dunderheaded koans ("the more you drive, the less intelligent you are"). Sterling soundtrack of Southern California punk (Black Flag, Suicidal Tendencies) and atmospheric surf instrumentals.

Repo Men

2010 (R) 111m / D: Miguel Sapochnik / **W:** Eric Garcia, Garrett Lerner / **C:** Jude Law, Forest Whitaker, Alice Braga, Liev Schreiber, Carice van Houton

Yet *another* movie about a future where organ transplants are plentiful but the company that does them has a vicious way with repossessions. Jude Law and Forest Whitaker play a manic best-buddy pair of repo men who collect by finding delinquents, stunning them, and then slicing out the mechanical organ they no longer own. A moral dilemma presents itself when Law has to get a transplant of his own that's hard to afford. There's a woman for him to help out, of course (Alice Braga) and a big fight scene at the end, though sadly no musical numbers. Glimmers of satiric potential are drowned by relentless cheap second-hand cynicism and casual violence that treats essentially every human being—except a few of the stars—as livestock for the slaughterhouse.

Repo! The Genetic Opera

2008 (R) 98m / D: Darren Lynn Bousman / **W:** Darren Smith, Terrance Zdunich / **C:** Alexa Vega, Paul Sorvino, Anthony Head, Sarah Brightman, Paris Hilton

Adolescent futuristic freak show goth rock opera (based on a live musical that had something of a cult following) about a sheltered teenager (Alexa Vega) with a rare disease and a protective father with a dark secret. An epidemic of organ failure has left humanity beholden to the monopolistic GeneCo firm, which has a nasty habit of repossessing transplanted body parts by force when payments are in arrears. Said repossessions are captured in gut-splattering glory by director Darren Lynn Bousman, known for several *Saw* sequels. The "What am I doing here?" cast includes Paul Sorvino as Gene-Co's villainous patriarch and Paris Hilton as one of many plastic surgery victims, not to mention an uncredited Joan Jett playing guitar in a dream sequence. Wallpaper score and oppressive sadism that wants to be wit. Sci-fi horror for the Slipknot and Rammstein crowd.

REPTILICUS

1962 (NR) 90m / D: Sidney Pink / **W:** Sidney Pink, Ib Melchior / **C:** Carl Ossosen, Ann Smyrner, Mimi Heinrich, Poul Wildaker, Asbjørn Andersen, Marla Bregens

A monster that looks like a puppet from the old TV show *Kukla, Fran and Ollie* makes *Reptilicus* a laughable addition to the monster movie genre.

Laughable attempt to get Denmark into the *Godzilla* business. Nordic miners find the skeleton of a previously unclassified dinosaur with its tail section frozen and intact. The beast's defrosted flesh regenerates into a vast acid-spitting serpent that looks like the dragon of medieval folklore but moves like a puppet from the *Kukla, Fran and Ollie* show. Oh, and we get some travelogues of Copenhagen and the song "Tivoli Nights." Reptilicus later justified his limp existence by reappearing in recurrent gag clips on the Monkees' TV show, and reports from Denmark hint that the film at least briefly was considered wonderfully bad in the tradition of *The Rocky Horror Picture Show*, with revival-house audiences echoing the lame dialogue back at the screen.

RESIDENT EVIL

2002 (R) 100m / D: Paul W. S. Anderson / **W:** Paul W. S. Anderson / **C:** Milla Jovovich, Michelle Rodriguez, Eric Mabius, James Purefoy, Martin Crewes

In the near future, most consumer products are made by the aptly named Umbrella Corporation, which gets most of its profits through weaponized genetic research (meaning, it's one *evil* corporation). One of its special viruses runs rampant in an underground research lab called the Hive, which locks itself down. Commando team accompanied by confused amnesiac Alice (Milla Jovovich) enters the Hive and discovers employees have now become bloodthirsty zombies. Fortunately, they can be shot, so: bang, bang. Former model Jovovich shows impressive fashion sense, killing zombies while sporting a tight red spaghetti strap number and high boots. Lewis Carroll references abound (computer system is called the Red Queen), but mostly this is just another Paul W. S. Anderson effort where heavily armed people get messily slaughtered in a maze. The most successful film franchise ever based on a video game, for whatever that's worth.

RESIDENT EVIL: AFTERLIFE

2010 (R) 97m / D: Paul W. S. Anderson / **W:** Paul W. S. Anderson / **C:** Milla Jovovich, Ali Larter, Kim Coates, Shawn Roberts, Sergio Peris-Mencheta, Spencer Locke, Boris Kodjoe, Wentworth Miller

Series mentor Paul W. S. Anderson (he directed the first film, wrote all of them, and married his star) returns to the director's chair for this 3-D effort, along with series regular Ali Larter. The worldwide zombie infection has resulted in humanity trying to regroup in Alaska. Meanwhile, Milla Jovovich spends most of her time stuck in a prison filled with ... can you guess?

RESIDENT EVIL: APOCALYPSE

2004 (R) 94m / D: Alexander Witt / **W:** Paul W.S. Anderson / **C:** Milla Jovovich, Sienna Guillory, Oded Fehr, Thomas Kretschmann, Jared Harris, Sandrine Holt, Raz Adoti, Mike Epps

Second *Resident Evil* shows what happens when the Umbrella Corporation opens up the zombie virus-filled underground Hive research lab from the first film. Answer: Zombies take over the city unluckily located above the Hive. Milla Jovovich is back as Alice the gun-toting fetish object, and this time she has some similarly scantily clad female friends to help (Sienna Guillory, Sandrine Holt) blast their way out of the city before it gets nuked.

RESIDENT EVIL: EXTINCTION

2007 (R) 94m / D: Russell Mulcahy / **W:** Paul W. S. Anderson / **C:** Milla Jovovich, Oded Fehr, Ali Larter, Iain Glen, Ashanti, Christopher Egan, Mike Epps

With the third film in the series, genetically modified zombie-killer Milla Jovovich is now stuck in the desert with some other survivors (including singer Ashanti), allowing *Highlander* director Russell Mulcahy to stage plenty of CGI monster mayhem amidst a sand-smothered Las Vegas.

RESIDENT EVIL: RETRIBUTION

2012 (R) 96m / D: Paul W. S. Anderson / **W:** Paul W. S. Anderson / **C:** Milla Jovovich, Michelle Rodriguez, Sienna Guillory, Kevin Durand, Colin Salmon

Fifth time out, undead-battling superheroine Milla Jovovich (who has clones now, by the way) is stuck inside the headquarters of her old bosses, the Umbrella Corporation, whose supercomputer, the Red Queen, doesn't really want to let her leave alive. Lots of slo-mo blazing-gun riffs on *The Matrix* and virtual reality battle mazes. Several characters from earlier iterations (Michelle Rodriguez, Sienna Guillory) return for the fun.

THE RESURRECTION OF ZACHARY WHEELER

1971 (G) 100m / **D:** Bob Wynn / **W:** Jay Simms, Tom Rolf / **C:** Angie Dickinson, Bradford Dillman, Leslie Nielsen, Jack Carter, James Daly

Interesting curio in which a presidential candidate, severely injured in a car crash, is deemed worthy for lifesaving organ transplants at a mysterious clinic in New Mexico. Leslie Nielsen is fun as the nervy reporter who snoops around and discovers the surgeons' secret: grotesque "somas," genetically blank clones whose organs are fully compatible with recipients. A somewhat open ending lets viewers ponder the morality of it all.

Milla Jovovich fights an endless array of monsters in the *Resident Evil* franchise, which is based on a popular video game and shows it.

THE RETURN

1980 (PG) 91m / **D:** Greydon Clark / **W:** Ken Wheat, Jim Wheat, Curtis Burch / **C:** Cybill Shepherd, Raymond Burr, Jan-Michael Vincent, Martin Landau, Vincent Schiavelli, Zachary Vincent, Farah Bunch, Neville Brand, Susan Kiger

Jan-Michael Vincent and Cybill Shepherd meet as adults and discover that they had both, as children, been visited by aliens who had given technology to a cattle-mutilating prospector. A mess with no idea of what sort of film it wants to be. AKA: *The Alien's Return*.

THE RETURN OF CAPTAIN INVINCIBLE

1983 (PG) 90m / **D:** Philippe Mora / **W:** Steven E. de Souza, Andrew Gaty / **C:** Alan Arkin, Christopher Lee, Kate Fitzpatrick, Bill Hunter, Graham Kennedy, Michael Pate, Hayes Gordon, Max Phipps, Noel Ferrier

Beloved wartime superguy Captain Invincible (Alan Arkin) was subpoenaed before a McCarthyite panel and blacklisted for wearing a red-colored cape and flying without a license. Now the president decides America needs its hero again and puts the now-derelict "Legend in Leotards" through alcohol rehab and superpower retraining. Australian spoof from the writer of *48 Hrs.* and *The Running Man* has great premise, let down too often by slipshod storytelling and weak f/x. Gains altitude with its outlandish musical numbers, some of them written by the *Rocky Horror* team of Richard Hartley and Richard O'Brien. A singing Christopher Lee plays archvillain Mr. Midnight with lordly gusto. AKA: *Legend in Leotards*.

THE RETURN OF SWAMP THING

1989 (PG-13) 88m / **D:** Jim Wynorski / **W:** Neil Cuthbert, Grant Morris / **C:** Louis Jourdan, Heather Locklear, Sarah Douglas, Dick Durock

DC Comics creature rises again out of the muck to fight mutants and evil scientists. Tongue-in-cheek, and nothing at all like the literate, ecologically oriented comic from which it was derived.

Revenge of the Creature is the sequel to *Creature from the Black Lagoon*. In this one, the Gill-man escapes after being put on display at a Florida marine park.

RETURN OF THE FLY

1959 (NR) 80m / **D:** Edward Bernds / **W:** Edward Bernds / **C:** Vincent Price, Brett Halsey, John Sutton, Dan Seymour, David Frankham

Slightly lame sequel to 1958's classic *The Fly* finds Vincent Price reprising his role as the brother of the first film's doomed inventor. Better take this one as an almost-comedy, especially once you get a load of the much larger fly head designed for the Fly's son Philippe (Brett Halsey) to wear. This time around it's the meddling assistant David Frankham who screws things up, causing the teleported one to become part-man part-fly. Can't manage to maintain continuity, and despite Price, lacks the charm of the original. The next sequel, *The Curse of the Fly*, had to wait to 1965 to be made.

REVENGE OF THE CREATURE

1955 (NR) 82m / **D:** Jack Arnold / **W:** Martin Berkeley / **C:** John Agar, Lori Nelson, John Bromfield, Robert Williams, Nestor Paiva, Clint Eastwood

Follow-up to *The Creature from the Black Lagoon* in which the monstrous Gill-man is captured in his Amazon habitat and taken to a Florida marine park. He is put on display for visitors and cheerfully subjected by John Agar to experiments involving an electric prod. Growing restless in his captive surroundings, the creature breaks free and makes for the ocean. His escape is only a cover for his true intentions, however, which involve stalking and kidnapping pretty grad student Lori Nelson. Rather weak sequel, originally shot in 3-D and based on a story by William Alland, includes screen debut of Clint Eastwood as a lab technician. Between exciting moments, we're treated to endless billing and cooing by Agar and Nelson, and time-killing footage of marine park attractions like "Flippy, the Educated Porpoise."

RIDDICK

2013 (R) 119m / D: David Twohy / **W:** David Twohy / **C:** Vin Diesel, Karl Urban, Katee Sackhoff, Jordi Mollà, Bokeem Woodbine

The third *Riddick* film is a back-to-basics entry that puts the gravel-voiced convict (Vin Diesel) back in his favorite habitat: Marooned on a planet filled with deadly creatures who can help him take out the teams of bounty hunters that are after him. Twist: one team wants him dead, the other alive. Highly testosteroned sci-fi action.

RIDERS OF THE STORM

1988 (R) 92m / D: Maurice Phillips / **W:** Scott Roberts / **C:** Dennis Hopper, Michael J. Pollard, Eugene Lipinski, James Aubrey, Nigel Pegram

A motley crew of Vietnam vets runs a covert TV broadcasting station from an in-flight B-29, jamming America's legitimate airwaves. Plenty of rockin' classics on the soundtrack, from Hendrix to Derek and the Dominos. Interesting premise with highly boring result. AKA: *The American Way*.

RISE OF THE PLANET OF THE APES

2011 (PG-13) 105m / D: Rupert Wyatt / **W:** Rich Jaffa, Amanda Silver / **C:** Andy Serkis, James Franco, Freida Pinto, John Lithgow, Brian Cox, Tom Felton

In *this* reboot of the perennial sci-fi concept about primates taking over Earth after humans blew their chance, we're in prequel territory. James Franco and Freida Pinto are the impossibly attractive researchers who start noticing strange things about the apes in their charge. Turns out Franco's been feeding one of them an anti-Alzheimer's drug that he's developing to save his addled father (John Lithgow). His bad luck that that increasingly sentient ape, Cesar (Andy Serkis under the CGI, outdoing his Gollum), turns out to have more in common with Che Guevara than Koko. It's revolution as the apes discover the joys of smashing up downtown San Francisco and generally sticking it to the humans. Much better in theory than execution, though still brings much more to the table than Tim Burton's shallow remake. Watch for Brian Cox as the sleazy head of a down-at-heel ape sanctuary.

THE ROAD

2009 (R) 111m / **D:** John Hillcoat / **W:** Joe Penhall / **C:** Viggo Mortensen, Charlize Theron, Kodi Smit-McPhee, Robert Duvall, Michael K. Williams

A father and son trudge through the wasteland remaining after some form of natural disaster—one or just an accumulation of climate-changing sins—has ground civilization to dust. Like the Pulitzer Prize-winning Cormac McCarthy novel it's deftly adapted from, the story is less about just plain survival than it is about surviving with your soul intact. The barriers faced on their quixotic journey to a faraway sea are many; not starving in a land where seemingly nothing can grow anymore, for one, and avoiding wolfpacks of cannibalistic scavengers, for another. Viggo Mortensen's father is hollowed-out and held together with spit and tape, while the son (Kodi Smit-McPhee) is more a diamond in the rough. The boy might not remember what life was like before the destruction, but instead of being some new breed of savage, he's the sensitive spirit who keeps his father from losing all hope. Robert Duvall, Charlize Theron, and Michael K. Williams appear memorably in small roles as varied manifestations of bleak fear. Director John Hillcoat hews to an uncompromising vision that doesn't cop out with grafted-on backstory or *Mad Max*-style action scenes.

ROBINSON CRUSOE ON MARS

1964 (NR) 109m / **D:** Byron Haskin / **W:** Ib Melchior, John C. Higgins / **C:** Adam West, Vic Lundin, Paul Mantee

When the orbital ship Mars Gravity Probe 1 is forced to make an emergency landing on the planet's surface, Commander Draper (Paul Mantee) faces the immediate problems of limited supplies of air, water, and food. "Hard" science purists will be put off by the unrealistic nature of the solutions he discovers, but this quirky adaptation of Daniel Defoe's novel is more about loneliness anyway. To create a believable alien world, director Byron Haskin (who worked with George Pal on *The War of the Worlds*) imaginatively combined sets and models with well-chosen Death Valley locations. Frequently campy, but fun and crisply shot in Techniscope.

ROBOCOP (1987)

1987 (R) 103m / **D:** Paul Verhoeven / **W:** Michael Miner, Edward Neumeier / **C:** Peter Weller, Nancy Allen, Ronny Cox, Kurtwood Smith, Ray Wise, Miguel Ferrer, Dan O'Herlihy, Robert DoQui, Felton Perry, Paul McCrane, Del Zamora etroit cop Peter Weller is killed in action and is then used as the donor for the face and brain of a crime-fighting cyborg. Trouble begins when RoboCop starts remembering his life as a human and discovers corruption within the giant corporation that created him. Paul Verhoeven neatly snaps together a superhero action narrative (all those bad guys whose bullets bounce harmlessly off the armored cyborg) with a bleakly cynical view of the future (catastrophes sprightly described by happy-talk newscaster Leeza Gibbons). There's also an undercurrent of an acid satire on urban privatization and corporate values that's become more relevant in later years given the setting, as well as an underlying sadness about the dehumanized, strangely forlorn main character, which Weller (usually a fairly robotic performer anyway) conveys with a minimum of expression—or flesh, for that matter. Terrific f/x include Rob Bottin's cyborg suit and the slick stop-motion animation by Phil Tippett that brings to life Robocop's deadliest (but dumbest) nemesis, Enforcement Droid 209. Ferocious violence nearly earned this an X-rating; copies of Verhoeven's original cut are sought by collectors. Inspired two sequels and a short-lived TV series, all progressively less interesting, as well as a 2014 remake.

RoboCop 2

1990 (R) 117m / **D:** Irvin Kershner / **W:** Walon Green, Frank Miller / **C:** Peter Weller, Nancy Allen, Belinda Bauer, Dan O'Herlihy, Tom Noonan, Gabriel Damon, Galyn Gorg, Felton Perry, Patricia Charbonneau

Even more cynical and violent sequel to the 1987 original. New addictive drug "Nuke" has made streets of future Detroit worse than ever. RoboCop's corporate owners, dissatisfied with his performance and vulnerabilities during a police strike, replace him with a stronger cyborg powered by the brain of a psycho pusher/addict/cult leader (after a series of other unwilling donors gruesomely self-destruct). RoboCop 2 goes berserk, of course, and the metal beings fight an epic battle, in between enough subplots for three movies. Comic-book elements predominate in a story concocted by graphic novelist Frank Miller (*Batman: The Dark Knight Returns*) and kinetically directed by Irvin Kershner (*The Em-*

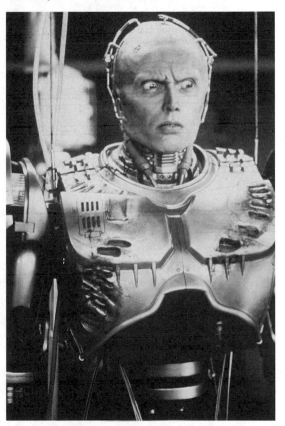

Peter Weller starred as the police officer brought back to life as a cyborg enforcer of the future in the first two *RoboCop* movies.

pire Strikes Back). Emphasis on bitter sarcasm and graphic savagery comes at the expense of the original's muted but vital emotion quotient.

ROBOCOP 3

1993 (PG-13) 104m / D: Fred Dekker / **W:** Fred Dekker, Frank Miller / **C:** Robert Burke, Nancy Allen, John Castle, CCH Pounder, Bruce Locke, Rip Torn, Remi Ryan, Felton Perry

Second *RoboCop* sequel sat on the studio shelf before belated release in 1993. RoboCop's new Japanese owners plan to build an ultra-modern city in place of the decrepit 21st-century Detroit, but first must evict thousands of residents. The rebel cyborg (now played by Robert Burke) joins with common citizens to protect their homes, befriending a tiny waif/computer hacker for maximum kid appeal. There's an agile robot Ninja warrior to do battle with the surprisingly slow-moving hero. It all makes for an apt if (even then) dated metaphor for sleek Japanese cars replacing America's lumbering gas-guzzlers, but the plot and action are cheap-looking and rehashed.

ROBOCOP (2014)

2014 (PG-13) 117m / D: Jose Padilha / **W:** Joshua Zetumer / **C:** Joel Kinnaman, Gary Oldman, Michael Keaton, Abbie Cornish, Michael K. Williams, Jennifer Ehle, Jay Baruchal, Arianne Jean-Baptiste, Samuel L. Jackson

The point at which satire devolves to mere comedy is perfectly illustrated in Jose Padilha's bloodless (in more ways than one) remake of Paul Verhoeven's anarchic original. The near-future Detroit setting is ostensibly the same, as are the heartless corporate villains who want to use the body of one good but horribly injured cop (Joel Kinnaman) as guinea pig for their lucrative new urban pacification cyborg. In imitation of the first film's skewering of TV junk culture, there's even a Bill O'Reilly-like talkshow in which Samuel L. Jackson shouts down anybody who doesn't toe the military industrial complex party line. The set up leaves ample room to take on everything from militarization of the police to urban blight to drone warfare mission creep (i.e., what happens when those robots delivering supposedly surgical strikes on insurgents overseas start getting used on American streets). But the satirical edge is sanded down, the plot a non-starter, and the disturbingly blood-free action scenes reduced to something like a first-person shooter game. Even a top-notch cast and a director like Padilha with a strong background in bloody urban melodrama (solid Brazilian action films and documentaries like *Elite Squad* and *Bus 174*) can't do much with this robotic reboot.

ROBOT & FRANK

2012 (PG-13) 89m / D: Jake Schreier / **W:** Christopher D. Ford / **C:** Frank Langella, Peter Sarsgaard, Susan Sarandon, Liv Tyler, James Marsden, Jeremy Sisto

Genial geriatric buddy comedy in which irascible old-timer Frank (Frank Langella) agrees to his son's demand that he take on a robot helper as tradeoff for not going to a retirement home. The faceless and nameless robot (voiced with flat affect by Peter Sarsgaard, who still invests the role with a thin spirituality) then becomes accessory to Frank's schemes for not getting bored in old age, not to mention an easier friend for him to handle than actual humans. Since Frank was a pretty good second-story man in his day, having fun means using the robot to help him bust into places, particularly the home of an obnoxious yuppie whose foundation is turning the local library into some digital age "reimagined" nonsense. Affecting character study with small-scale but pointed sci-fi examination of people's automatic anthropomorphizing of their inventions. Despite all Frank's initial resistance to his new helper, it's ultimately the robot itself who has to remind him that it's only a machine.

> "Affecting character study with small-scale but pointed sci-fi examination of people's automatic anthropomorphizing of their inventions."
>
> *Robot & Frank*

ROBOT CARNIVAL

1987 (NR) 90m / D: Atsuko Fukushima, Katsuhiro Otomo, Hiroyuki Kitazume, Mao Lamdo, Hidetoshi Ohmori, Kouji Morimoto, Yasuomi Umetsu, Hiroyuki Kitakubo, Takashi Nakamura

Anthology of eight Japanese animated shorts, each revolving around the theme of artificial life. Many are without dialogue, and most are lyrical evocations of emotion, like "Presence," the tale of an aging inventor haunted by the android girl he created. In the improbable but beautifully animated "Cloud," a little robot-boy trudges through a shifting cloudscape of romantic images. "Starlight Dancer" is a charming love-story featuring two girls, a futuristic amusement park, and a lovesick robot. "Deprive" is a straightforward sci-fi vignette, and "Nightmare" echoes Disney's version of "The Legend of Sleepy Hollow" as a city-dweller is pursued by mechanized monsters. "Franken's Gears" explores the Frankenstein legend with unexpected results, and "A Tale of Two Robots" is a delightful satirical fantasy about a group of young people frantically battling a crazed inventor's monster robot in 18th-century Japan. Those looking for straightforward action should look elsewhere, but there are wonderful things here.

ROBOT JOX

1990 (PG) 84m / D: Stuart Gordon / **W:** Joe Haldeman / **C:** Gary Graham, Anne-Marie Johnson, Paul Koslo, Robert Sampson, Danny Kamekona, Hilary Mason, Michael Alldredge

In the future, wars between East and West are eliminated, but Cold War competition thrives thanks to officiated gladiator duels between titanic robots, each one piloted by a single human operator. Will brotherhood and goodness prevail? Semi-meaningful, semi-ludicrous sci-fi (with uneven quality f/x by David Allen), this hijacked hardware concepts from the role-playing game *Battletech*, the Japanese sagas *Robotech* and *Gundam*, and others; toy-conscious viewers will also note the fighting machines' suspicious similarity to popular playthings like Transformers and Gobots. Better perhaps than those respective cartoon features, but considering that the script is by award-winning sci-fi novelist Joe Haldeman (*The Forever War*), this must be classed as a disappointment.

ROBOT MONSTER

1953 (NR) 62m / D: Phil Tucker / **W:** Wyott Ordung / **C:** George Nader, Claudia Barrett, Gregory Moffett, Selena Royle, George Barrows, John Mylong

Legendary golden turkey that gives *Plan 9 from Outer Space* a run as the worst movie of all time. The last six people on Earth—a professor, his wife and daughter, assistant, and two children—make their stand against Ro-Man, a ridiculous alien outfitted in a gorilla suit, topped by a deep sea diver's helmet. Ro-Man is instructed by his ruler, the Great One, to kill the Earthlings, but he is conflicted: "To be like the hu-man. To laugh. Feel. Want. Why are these things not in the plan?" Shot in four days for less than $20,000. Director Phil Tucker went on to direct *Dance Hall Racket*, starring Lenny Bruce, and *Cape Canaveral Monsters*. Music is by the venerable Elmer Bernstein, who went on to score *To Kill a Mockingbird*, *The Great Escape*, and, yes, *Cat Women of the Moon*. AKA: *Monsters from the Moon*.

ROBOTS

2005 (PG-13) 91m / D: Chris Wedge, Carlos Saldanha / **W:** David Lindsay-Abaire, Lowell Ganz, Babaloo Mandel, Robin Williams

Family friendly animated comedy from the makers of *Ice Age* set in a world entirely populated by robots. Find-your-dream storyline follows eager Rodney Copperbottom (voice by Ewan McGregor) traveling from his birthplace of Rivet City to Robot City to impress an industrialist with his inventions. Gorgeous, bright animation and the chaotic clanking whiz-bang of Rube Goldberg machinery looks like something from an earlier era. Pulitzer Prize-winning playwright David Lindsay-Abaire (*Rabbit Hole*) had a hand in the screenplay.

ROCK & RULE

1983 (PG) 85m / D: Clive A. Smith / **W:** Peter Sauder, John Halfpenny

Ambitious animated film that tries to rise above a hackneyed storyline and never makes it. After a nuclear war has wiped out humanity, a new race of beings descended from rats and dogs takes over. Problem is, they look

Brightly colored, retro-looking robots are featured in the family friendly animated film *Robots*.

and act for the most part exactly like humans, only with shaggier hair, so ... why? Mok, "legendary super rocker" and quasi-dictator who bridges the swagger of Mick Jagger with the thin-skinned ambition of Stalin, wants to conjure up a demon that will grant him control of this brave new world. However, Mok finds he needs a perfect voice to complete the summoning spell. He attempts to seduce Angel, a singer in a struggling rock band, into helping him fulfill his evil purpose. Mok spirits Angel away to "Nuke York," and her friends rush to her rescue; will they be too late? Dark animation comes straight from the Ralph Bakshi school. The film pushes its rock soundtrack hard since there isn't much to grasp onto here; solid songs are provided by Deborah Harry, Cheap Trick, Lou Reed, and Iggy Pop. This was Canadian studio Nelvana's last feature; possibly for the best.

ROCKET ATTACK U.S.A.

1958 (NR) 68m / **D:** Barry Mahon / **C:** Monica Davis, John McKay, Dan Kern, Edward Czerniuk, Art Metrano

Antiquated and ridiculous tale of Sputnik-era nuclear warfare, with Russia's first strike blowing up New York City and environs. Mercifully short, with time for a little romance. Everything about this movie is so bad it's good for a laugh. AKA: *Five Minutes to Zero*.

THE SCI-FI MOVIE GUIDE: The Universe of Film from "Alien" to "Zardoz"

THE ROCKETEER

1991 (PG) 109m / **D:** Joe Johnston / **W:** Danny Bilson, Paul De Meo / **C:** Bill Campbell, Jennifer Connelly, Alan Arkin, Timothy Dalton, Paul Sorvino, Melora Hardin, Tiny Ron, Terry O'Quinn, Ed Lauter, James Handy

Bill Campbell plays a 1930s stunt pilot who stumbles upon a prototype jet-backpack sought after by the nasty Nazis. Donning the secret weapon and a custom-made mask, he becomes a flying superhero, in the spirit of prewar matinee serials. Breezy, family entertainment with stupendous f/x and tons of Hollywood references, like a great villain (Timothy Dalton) clearly based on Errol Flynn, and a Rondo Hatton lump-a-like (the not-so-tiny Tiny Ron with accents by makeup king Rick Baker). Campbell's All-American girlfriend is played by Jennifer Connelly, obviously chosen for her resemblance to pin-up queen Bettie Page. Lighthearted fun.

ROCKETSHIP X-M

1950 (NR) 77m / **D:** Kurt Neumann / **W:** Kurt Neumann / **C:** Lloyd Bridges, Osa Massen, John Emery, Hugh O'Brian, Noah Beery Jr.

Cheaply produced and rushed into theaters to beat out George Pal's much-touted *Destination Moon,* this vintage tale depicts a pioneering lunar mission that goes awry thanks to a pencil-and-paper navigational error and lands instead on Mars, where the Earth explorers discover the portentous remnants of a human-like society destroyed by atomic war. Static and melodramatic, but worthy as a historic curio. Considered the first American movie that took space travel seriously, if not entirely accurately—astronaut garb seems to consist of street clothes or bomber jackets. Scenes on Martian terrain (actually Death Valley, a good guess at the real thing) were tinted red. Some versions carry additional f/x footage lensed much later, with long-shot doubles for the actors. Script was actually written by the blacklisted Dalton Trumbo. AKA: *Expedition Moon.*

ROCK N' ROLL COWBOYS

1992 (R) 83m / **D:** Rob Stewart / **W:** David Young / **C:** Peter Phelps, David Franklin, John Doyle

A humble roadie wants to become a rock and roll star. A Mephistophelian character (there's always one of 'em in stories about naive rockers) promises him the opportunity with an instrument that taps directly into the brain to transform thought into music. The Psychotronic Alpha Sampler is actually an evil mind-control device, but clear minds were evidently in short supply when this malfunctioning Australian satire with scattered music-videos came together. More cyberbunk than cyberpunk.

THE ROCKY HORROR PICTURE SHOW

1975 (R) 105m / D: Jim Sharman / **W:** Jim Sharman, Richard O'Brien / **C:** Tim Curry, Susan Sarandon, Barry Bostwick, Meatloaf, Little Nell, Richard O'Brien

Campy, vampy, and anything but subtle, the mother of all midnight movies can't help but lose something when screened in private and not with an audience shouting back at the screen. The hook-heavy glam-rock score for this kinky, tongue-in-cheek musical is loud and energetic, with lyrics playing wittily off conventions of the B-grade sci-fi and horror flicks it's celebrating and lampooning. (The opening number, "Science Fiction Double Feature," is a veritable roll call of the greats: "Michael Rennie was ill the day the earth stood still ... Claude Rains was the invisible man.") Origins as an underground cult theater oddity in early 1970s London result in a fairly nonsensical, episodic story. Barry Bostwick and Susan Sarandon play the innocent hero and heroine sucked into the sexual vortex of the castle-dwelling, high heels-and-fishnet-wearing "sweet transvestite" alien Dr. Frank-N-Furter (Tim Curry). Curry wrings every drop of cocked-eyebrow humor from the role—and there's a lot to wring, showing how a talented stage performer can take a

The underground classic *Rocky Horror Picture Show* was an ode to Golden Age sci-fi done as sexually transgressive, glam-rock opera.

film and make it beg for mercy. Followed by the even more surreal, but non-sci-fi *Shock Treatment*.

RODAN

1957 (NR) 74m / **D:** Ishiro Honda / **W:** Takeshi Kimura, Takeo Murata / **C:** Kenji Sahara, Yumi Shirakawa, Akihiko Hirata, Akio Kobori

Gigantic pterodactyl Rodan is awakened from his slumbers in a mineshaft by ill-considered H-bomb tests. He breakfasts on some gigantic mutant grubs (good) and then flies around destroying things (bad ... very bad). After a while the monster is joined by a mate, and then the fun (and havoc) begins in earnest. Rodan, who would appear in several later monster epics, seems less than impressive in his solo debut. Japanese monster-maniacs will enjoy it, but the uninitiated might want to stick with the better *Godzilla* movies. AKA: *Radon*; *Radon the Flying Monster*.

ROLLERBALL (1975)

1975 (R) 123m / **D:** Norman Jewison / **W:** William Harrison / **C:** James Caan, John Houseman, Maud Adams, Moses Gunn, Ralph Richardson, John Beck

James Caan plays a troubled jock in the near-future who is starting to question his role as an athlete in the future's most popular sport of Rollerball (an ultraviolent game supposed to function as a bread-and-circuses giveaway to the masses). Though this message film from Norman Jewison (*In the Heat of the Night*) was meant as a critique of violent sports and the public's reaction to them in a totalitarian society, it undercuts that message with its own visceral thrills. Word has it that during breaks in the filming, the crew actually played a version of the game on the sets. Flashy, shocking, sometimes exhilarating.

ROLLERBALL (2002)

2002 (R) 98m / **D:** John McTiernan / **W:** Larry Ferguson, John Pogue / **C:** Chris Klein, Jean Reno, LL Cool J, Rebecca Romijn-Stamos, Naveen Andrews

Extreme-sports remake of Norman Jewison's 1975 message film follows a trio of athletes (Chris Klein, LL Cool J, Rebecca Romijn-Stamos) who are the best in their chosen sport of Rollerball: like roller derby only with motorcycles and pro-wrestling theatrics; also, occasionally the odd person dies, to the delight of the audience at home. Jean Reno is the sleazy boss who doesn't mind the occasional corpse if it juices ratings. Long in development, very briefly in theaters.

ROLLER BLADE

1985 (NR) 88m / **D:** Donald G. Jackson / **W:** Donald G. Jackson, Randall Frakes / **C:** Suzanne Solari, Jeff Hutchinson, Shaun Michelle

In a post-holocaust world where the slogan "skate or die" is taken quite literally, a sexy sect of Amazonian nuns on in-line rollerskates worships a "have a nice day" happy face and battles forces of evil (a masked-wrestler type with a gnomelike puppet pal fixed to his hand) using martial arts, mysticism, communal bathing, and hockey sticks. Cheapjack filmed-on-video mutation must truly be seen to be believed. Initially good for a few laughs, but once you realize the no-brainer dialogue and schlock production values aren't going to improve, the bizarre novelty turns into an irritant very quickly. Sequellized in *Roller Blade Warriors*; not surprisingly, filmmaker Donald Jackson also wrought *Hell Comes to Frogtown*.

RUNAWAY

1984 (PG-13) 100m / **D:** Michael Crichton / **W:** Michael Crichton / **C:** Tom Selleck, Cynthia Rhodes, Gene Simmons, Stan Shaw, Kirstie Alley, Joey Cramer, G. W. Bailey

Less-than-top-drawer Michael Crichton effort is a formula near-future thriller with a cop (Tom Selleck) and his new partner (Cynthia Rhodes) tracking down out-of-control robots and being chased by same. Definitely not another *Blade Runner*. Features KISS's Gene Simmons as the villain. Well photographed by veteran John Alonzo with some nice mechanical and visual f/x.

THE RUNNING MAN

1987 (R) 101m / **D:** Paul Michael Glaser / **W:** Steven E. de Souza / **C:** Arnold Schwarzenegger, Richard Dawson, Maria Conchita Alonso, Yaphet Kotto, Mick Fleetwood, Dweezil Zappa, Jesse Ventura

An f/x-laden adaptation of the Stephen King novel (published under his Richard Bachman pseudonym) about a futuristic television game show in which convicts are given a chance for pardon—all they have to do is survive an ongoing battle with specially trained assassins in the bombed-out sections of Los Angeles. Arnold Schwarzenegger is suitably grim, and couch potatoes will enjoy seeing longtime game show host and ex-*Hogan's Hero* Richard Dawson in a major role. Film makes a vague stab at *Rollerball*-esque satire (casting pro wrestler Jesse Ventura as a game show contestant named Captain Fireball) but loses much of the novel's bite in its drive to create a lowest-common-denominator action flick. If you're wondering what most straight-to-DVD low-grade sci-fi actioners would like to be if they had a budget, this is it.

S1mOne

2002 (PG-13) 117m / **D:** Andrew Niccol / **W:** Andrew Niccol / **C:** Al Pacino, Catherine Keener, Elias Koteas, Rachel Roberts, Evan Rachel Wood, Winona Ryder

Andrew Niccol continues his exploration of how artificiality impacts humanity in the technological future-now with this semi-satire about the limits of creative control. A failing director (Al Pacino) discovers a great idea for his new project: "synthespians," or completely computer-generated performers who don't pout or talk back, like the moody star of his last, canceled film (Winona Ryder, playing off her tabloid issues). Pacino shoots an entire movie without its star, inserting the synthespian (a gorgeous blonde who always does exactly what he says) later on without telling anybody she's a fake. As his star's popularity skyrockets, Pacino becomes increasingly unable to admit the truth about his success. Synthespian S1mOne is played by former model Rachel Roberts, Niccol's wife.

THE SACRIFICE

1986 (PG) 142m / **D:** Andrei Tarkovsky / **W:** Andrei Tarkovsky / **C:** Erland Josephson, Susan Fleetwood, Allan Edwall, Guderun Gisladóttir, Sven Wollter, Valérie Mairesse, Filippa Franzén

A writer living in isolation in Sweden has finished explaining to his young son the problems with the modern world (the decay of belief and purpose seem to be at issue) when an uncomfortable family gathering is broken up by the sound of jets roaring overhead. The TV flickers on briefly to deliver vague bulletins of worry about what appears to be the advent of World War III before going dark. After that, the writer spins further into despair before realizing, in a moment that's either spiritual revelation or psychotic break, that a curious sacrifice must be made in order to save the world. When Andrei Tarkovsky made this film, he was in exile from the Soviet Union. His final, apocalyptic statement came via the theologically questing spirit of Ingmar Bergman. (Tarkovsky used Bergman's cinematographer Sven Nyquist and frequent star Erland Josephson, not to mention shooting on the island of Faro, where Bergman lived and often filmed.) It's a spare and elegant film on entropy and the futility of intellectualism, though not without its empty patches.

SAMSON IN THE WAX MUSEUM

1963 (NR) 92m / **D:** Alfonso Corona Blake / **W:** Fernando Galiana, Julio Porter / **C:** Santo, Claudio Brook, Rubén Rojo, Norma Mora, Roxana Bellini, José Luis Jiménez

Silver-masked Mexican wrestling hero Santo (called Samson in the U.S. version) does battle with a mad scientist who has discovered a way to make wax monsters (including a not-very-convincing Frankenstein creature) come to life. Not one of the best Santos, but still good fun for old and new fans. Viva Santo! AKA: *Santo in the Wax Museum*.

Even children can't take *Santa Clause Conquers the Martians* seriously, but that's okay. Silly holiday fun.

SANTA CLAUS CONQUERS THE MARTIANS

1964 (NR) 80m / **D:** Nicholas Webster / **W:** Glenville Mareth / **C:** John Call, Pia Zadora, Leonard Hicks, Vincent Beck, Victor Stiles, Donna Conforti, Bill McCutcheon

A Martian spaceship comes to Earth and kidnaps Santa Claus and two children. Martian kids, it seems, are jealous that Earth tykes have Christmas. One of those low-budget holiday items that raked in the cash year after year at holiday matinees. Not able to be taken seriously even by children, there are a few touches of intentional satire aimed at parents. Features then-child star Pia Zadora. AKA: *Santa Claus Defeats the Aliens*.

SATURN 3

1980 (R) 88m / **D:** Stanley Donen / **W:** Martin Amis / **C:** Farrah Fawcett, Kirk Douglas, Harvey Keitel, Ed Bishop

Funnier than *Spaceballs*, but this is no joke. Stanley Donen—yes, director of *Singin' in the Rain* and *An American in Paris* Stanley Donen—helmed this nearly incomprehensible black hole of a movie set on the Planet of Cheap Special Effects. Farrah Fawcett and Kirk Douglas are operating an experimental space station and are visited by Harvey Keitel, whose voice has been dubbed to make him sound like George Sanders. Farrah is easily upstaged by Hector, Keitel's killer robot, which develops the hots for her. Amazingly, acclaimed novelist Martin Amis supplied the screenplay early in his career. Everyone involved did a good job afterward of pretending this never happened.

A SCANNER DARKLY

2006 (R) 100m / D: Richard Linklater / **W:** Richard Linklater / **C:** Keanu Reeves, Robert Downey Jr., Woody Harrelson, Winona Ryder, Rory Cochrane

Keanu Reeves spies on himself in Richard Linklater's pitch-perfect animated take on Philip K. Dick's novel. America's future here is a toxic, entrapping slurry of technology, the surveillance state, and consciousness-fraying drugs. Reeves plays Bob Arctor, a drug dealer who also works undercover for the cops and is having some schizoid personality issues. He wears a "scramble suit" that cycles through thousands of identities every second (looking like everybody he looks like nobody), making it psychologically easier to spy on himself. His friends (the murderously funny trio of Robert Downey Jr., Woody Harrelson, and Rory Cochrane) are all strung out on Bob's newest product, Substance D, which doesn't help Reeves's sanity. Dick's twist ending is the sort of thing that keeps frightened addicts up all day and all night. The setting is a quasi-futuristic America that feels suspiciously like 1970s California tract-home flatlands jangled with a little dope-fiend paranoia. Linklater's rotoscoping animation technique—in which the actors are filmed and then animators draw on top of their moments—gives the film a watery and slightly unmoored quality, as though everything was on the verge of washing away. The best and most faithfully adapted Philip K. Dick story out there.

SCANNERS

1981 (R) 102m / D: David Cronenberg / **W:** David Cronenberg / **C:** Stephen Lack, Jennifer O'Neill, Patrick McGoohan, Lawrence Dane, Michael Ironside

"Ephemerol," a sedative administered to pregnant women in the 1940s, has sired a generation of so-called Scanners, mutant telepaths pushed toward madness by their own lethal brain waves. Scanner Michael Ironside harbors Hitlerian aspirations for his band of psychic gangsters and goes about eliminating any opposition. David Cronenberg's sketchy script (inspired by the real-life birth-defect epidemic caused by Thalidomide) got attention, for good or ill, from Dick Smith's trendsetting, gruesome makeup f/x—most notoriously, a man's head exploded apart by telekinesis. Carnage aside, it's a creepy freak-out, low on characterization but with a perpetually pulsing Howard Shore soundtrack that may drive some viewers out of their own skulls. Followed by a few non-Cronenberg straight-to-video sequels and offshoots.

SCOTT PILGRIM VS. THE WORLD

2010 (PG-13) 112m / **D:** Edgar Wright / **W:** Michael Bacall, Edgar Wright / **C:** Michael Cera, Mary Elizabeth Winstead, Kieran Culkin, Jason Schwartzman, Alison Pill, Ellen Wong, Anna Kendrick, Chris Evans

Six volumes of Bryan Lee O'Malley's goofy graphic novel get boiled down into Edgar Wright's just-as-goofy film. It's an awesomely entertaining distillation of geek culture and insecurities spun through a larger-than-life mythological quest, all of it with tongue stuck firmly in cheek. Michael Cera (because, who else?) is Scott Pilgrim, quivery-voiced and doe-eyed Canadian youngster who's not even getting over his last bad relationship when a new girl swoops (literally) into his life and doesn't just take it over but very nearly ends it. Pilgrim's Helen of Troy is Ramona Flowers (Mary Elizabeth Winstead), an adorably tough pixie whose hair goes through a rainbow's worth of Manic Panic colors and whose secret is this: For Pilgrim to win her heart, he must

Scott Pilgrim vs. the World is like watching a video game in which hit points and power-ups are prominently displayed as the hero battles foes.

do battle with all of her seven ex-boyfriends. The exuberant fight scenes are crafted like a video game, with level-ups and extra points. Wright's bone-deep understanding of geek outsider culture and psychology, from the obsession with games and unattainable romantic ideals to even Pilgrim's fuzz-rock band Sex-Bob-Omb, ensures that the jokey stylistics never overwhelm the core of what is actually a sweet story. Captain America himself, Chris Evans, plays the square-jawed action star Pilgrim must defeat, and Kieran Culkin is memorably louche as Pilgrim's ever-so-bored gay roommate.

SCREAM AND SCREAM AGAIN

1970 (PG) 95m / D: Gordon Hessler / **W:** Christopher Wicking / **C:** Vincent Price, Christopher Lee, Peter Cushing, Judy Huxtable, Alfred Marks, Anthony Newlands, Uta Levka, Judi Bloom, Yutte Stensgaard

Vincent Price is a sinister doctor who tries to create a super race of people devoid of emotions. Peter Cushing is the mastermind behind the plot. Christopher Lee is the agent investigating a series of murders. Three great horror stars, a psychedelic disco, great 1960s fashions; it's all here.

SCREAMERS

1995 (R) 108m / D: Christopher Duguay / **W:** Dan O'Bannon, Miguel Tejada-Flores / **C:** Peter Weller, Roy Dupuis, Jennifer Rubin, Andy Lauer

In the Philip K. Dick story "Second Variety," trench-bound grunts fight an endless extension of the Cold War on Earth while being menaced by an ever-evolving brand of quick, burrowing, homicidal mini-droids with razor-sharp blades. In this grungy-looking adaptation, the action is transplanted to another planet and the fighting is going on between some miners and management. But the problem is still the same: the screamers are starting to reproduce themselves and are learning how to imitate the look of humans. Peter Weller leads the dwindling band of grim-faced humans fighting for their survival. Dan O'Bannon of *Alien* fame worked on the screenplay.

SECONDS

1966 (R) 106m / D: John Frankenheimer / **W:** Lewis John Carlino / **C:** Rock Hudson, John Randolph, Salome Jens, Frances Reid, Khigh Dhiegh, Wesley Addy

The third and most chilling of John Fankenheimer's so-called "paranoia" trilogy (preceded by 1962's *The Manchurian Candidate* and 1964's *Seven Days in May*). This sounds like a role-reversal caper of the kind that became so popular in the 1980s but is really an existential horror story with a sci-fi twist. Wealthy but depressed middle-aged banker Arthur Hamilton (black-listed TV actor John Randolph), looking for a fresh start, turns to a secretive company that promises to give him a new life. With advanced plastic surgery and a lot of social engineering (they fake his death, give him a new identity), he reemerges into the world as Rock Hudson, a handsome painter who lives in a Malibu beach bungalow. Originally Frankenheimer wanted Laurence Olivier to play both parts, and Olivier was thrilled with the idea, but the studio insisted on a Rock Hudson type. The bandages are barely off, though, before Frankenheimer—with an able assist from James Wong Howe's expressionist camerawork and Jerry Goldsmith's funereal score—starts twisting the screws. Hamilton realizes far too late that not only can a new face and identity not cure his ennui, but that it's too late to turn back. Corrosive, multi-layered satire on all levels of mid-1960s American society, from the East Coast corporate rat race to West Coast therapy fads and the consumerist insecurities that unite them all, that also operates perfectly well as a riveting sci-fi noir.

THE SECRET OF THE TELEGIAN

1961 (NR) 85m / D: Jun Fukuda / **W:** Shinichi Sekizawa / **C:** Koji Tsurata, Yumi Shirakawa, Akihiko Hirata, Tadao Nakamura, Seizaburo Kawazu

A rare Japanese curiosity about a soldier who uses a teleportation device to avenge himself on fellow soldiers who tried to kill him. Oddly subdued and disturbing for 1960s Japanese sci-fi, especially considering that it came from the same folks that made the *Godzilla* series. The last of Toho's "transformation" movies, preceded by *The H Man* (1958) and *The Human Vapor* (1960). AKA: *The Telegian*.

SEEKING A FRIEND FOR THE END OF THE WORLD

2012 (R) 101m / D: Lorene Scafaria / **W:** Lorene Scafaria / **C:** Steve Carell, Keira Knightley, Adam Brody, Derek Luke, Martin Sheen

Schmuck-gets-the-girl comedy reconfigured for the end times; aka the rom-com take on Don McKellar's *Last Night*. Writer/director Lorene Scafaria brings a sitcom-light touch to her story about a personality-free milquetoast guy (Steve Carell) whose wife freaks out and leaves him after news gets out that an asteroid is going to be annihilating the planet in a few days' time. His sweater-vest world gets interrupted by Keira Knightley's music-obsessed, pot-smoking disaster of a neighbor. While Scafaria peppers the early stretches with some decently barbed humor (the DJ who chirpily promises his listeners not just the "End of Days" countdown but a steady stream of "*all* your classic rock favorites"), the film quickly transitions into another dreary and would-be wacky road-trip comedy that runs out of gas well before the apocalypse.

SERENITY

2005 (PG-13) 119m / **D:** Joss Whedon / **W:** Joss Whedon / **C:** Nathan Fillion, Gina Torres, Chiwetel Ejiofor, Summer Glau, Adam Baldwin, Morena Baccarin, Alan Tudyk, Jewel Staite

Three years after Fox pulled the plug on the first season of Joss Whedon's space western series *Firefly*, an outpouring of fan-love convinced Universal to pony up the money for this standalone feature outing that tries to tie up all the plot strands left dangling at cancellation. A quick opener gets everyone up to speed: 500 years in the future a motley crew of lovable criminals zips around the fringes of the galaxy doing some light piracy to pay the bills. Unfortunately, they have a mysterious young woman on board with extraordinary powers that the Empire ... er, Alliance ... wants back. There's also the cannibalistic barbarians the Reavers to deal with. All in a day's work for the *Serenity*'s captain, Nathan Fillion, a loveably sarcastic lug who's been nurturing a core of wounded idealism since fighting on the los-

Joss Whedon directed *Serenity,* a film designed to provide some closure to fans of the space western *Firefly* television series.

ing side of an anti-Alliance rebellion some years back. Fillion's deadpan cockiness is about the best thing to be seen on movie screens since Bogart. While Whedon's dialogue and character interplay is as richly involving as anything on the show, his inexperience as director shows up in too many poorly staged fights and generic desert "alien planet" settings. Still, a richly rewarding space adventure that doesn't stint on the comedy.

THE SHADOW

1994 (PG-13) 112m / **D:** Russell Mulcahy / **W:** David Koepp / **C:** Alec Baldwin, John Lone, Penelope Ann Miller, Peter Boyle, Ian McKellen, Tim Curry, Jonathan Winters

Highly stylized big-screen version of Orson Welles's old 1930s pulp matinee series and radio show. Billionaire playboy Lamont Cranston (Alec Baldwin) is a master of illusion and defender of justice thanks to his alter ego and his secret network of operatives. Aided by companion Margo Lane (Penelope Ann Miller), the Shadow battles super-criminal Shiwan Khan (John Lone), the deadliest descendant of Genghis Khan, now trying to build an atomic bomb. Elaborate f/x and retro art deco styling provide icing on the cake for those in the mood for a journey back to the radio past or a quick superhero fix. Bad scripting reveals the Shadow's origin from the beginning, ruining the opportunity for suspense and mystery, but this is still a fun, glossy adaptation. Plenty of wry humor, but surprisingly, none of it comes from Jonathan Winters, who plays his police chief role straight.

SHAUN OF THE DEAD

2004 (R) 99m / **D:** Edgar Wright / **W:** Simon Pegg, Edgar Wright / **C:** Simon Pegg, Nick Frost, Kate Ashfield, Lucy Davis, Dylan Moran, Nicola Cunningham, Bill Nighy

Suppose there was a zombie apocalypse and nobody noticed? That's the canny conceit behind Edgar Wright and Simon Pegg's genius slacker comedy, which came just a couple years after *28 Days Later ...* and helped ensure the genre would remain undead for some time. Co-writer Pegg is a going-nowhere electronics store clerk whose girlfriend is sick of just hanging out at the pub with him and his even-more-of-a-slacker best friend Nick Frost. Wright's long tracking shots follow Pegg in the well-worn grooves of his routine, not noticing in the background signs of zombie infestation from a downed satellite. The film's almost a third done before the first flesh-eater makes a grab for Pegg and Frost, who realize it's best to keep a shovel and cricket bat at hand for zombie-killing. It's then up to Pegg to rescue his girlfriend, her annoying flatmates, and his oblivious stepdad and mum (who notes about the odd people trying to break into her house, "they were a little *bitey*"); where else to hide out at but the pub? The zombies are extremely old-fashioned, moving slow and sludgy as in the *Thriller* video, which makes for easy head-whacking fun. Call-outs to other genre films are seeded throughout, along with some tart satire on the zombie-like nature of modern culture. Landmark horror comedy with an emphasis on the latter.

SHE DEMONS

1958 (NR) 68m / **D:** Richard Cunha / **W:** Richard Cunha, H. E. Barrie / **C:** Irish McCalla, Tod Griffin, Victor Sen Yung, Rudolph Anders, Tod Andrews

> "So-bad-it's-good non-sense at its finest."
>
> *She Demons*

A truly unique experience. A pleasure craft loaded with babes crashes into a remote island controlled by a mad ex-Nazi scientist with a really hokey accent. Instead of doing the sensible thing and establishing a private harem, Herr Doktor transforms the lovelies into rubber-faced monsters (who from the neck down remain perfectly normal). Everyone's favorite 1950s TV jungle heroine, Irish "Sheena, Queen of the Jungle" McCalla, turns up with Tod Griffin to confront the villains amid luxuriously phony sets. So-bad-it's-good nonsense at its finest.

SHOPPING

1994 (R) 87m / **D:** Paul W. S. Anderson / **W:** Paul W. S. Anderson / **C:** Sadie Frost, Jude Law, Jonathan Pryce, Sean Bean, Marianne Faithfull, Sean Pertwee

Jude Law is a street punk in some dreary northern British city of the quasi-future who gets out of prison and starts right back into "shopping," which for him and fellow Brit Packer Sadie Frost means ramming cars through store windows and making off with everything they can carry. This is perhaps a fine example of a sublimated sex drive; but who are we to say? The cops and local gangsters get wise to what they're doing and the race is on to see whether Law and Frost get stopped before they can carry off their biggest shopping excursion at a fortified shopping mall. Shades of *Streets of Fire*. Caused some *Clockwork Orange*-ish controversy for steering gullible youth in the wrong direction and was banned from some English cinemas. A calling card to Hollywood for Law and Paul W. S. Anderson, the latter who would later be hired on as a reliable hack for the churning out of big-screen gore-fare for Xbox addicts who wanted to give their thumbs a rest.

SHORT CIRCUIT

1986 (PG) 98m / **D:** John Badham / **W:** S. S. Wilson, Brent Maddock / **C:** Steve Guttenberg, Ally Sheedy, Austin Pendleton, Fisher Stevens, Brian McNamara, G. W. Bailey

Advanced robot designed for the military is hit by lightning and begins to think for itself. The vaguely humanoid tin man is taken in by a spacey animal lover (who initially mistakes her visitor for an alien first contact and exults "I always knew they would pick me!"), then hides from meanies at the weapons lab who want their hardware back. Asimovlan themes about the nature and rights of artificial sentient life forms are embedded in the screenplay, but such deep thoughts are buried under tons of slapstick gags and short-attention-span chase scenes.

SHORT CIRCUIT 2

1988 (PG) 95m / **D:** Kenneth Johnson / **W:** S.S. Wilson, Brent Maddock / **C:** Fisher Stevens, Cynthia Gibb, Michael McKean, Jack Weston, David Hemblen

Sequel to the adorable-robot-outwits-bad-guys tale is aimed strictly at the small fry but counts as an improvement, with better pacing and wittier whimsy. The cheerful metal hero, Number Five, arrives in the city to visit old friends, draws the attention of a greedy toy merchant and a gang of jewel thieves. Downside is you'll probably need to see the first *Short Circuit* to fully appreciate how comparatively cute and painless this one is.

SHREDDER ORPHEUS

1989 (NR) 93m / **D:** Robert McGinley / **W:** Robert McGinley / **C:** Jesse Bernstein, Robert McGinley, Vera McCaughan, Megan Murphy, Carlo Scandiuzzi

Your chance to witness Greek mythology updated/mangled in a post-apocalyptic setting with skateboard-thrash culture sensibilities. Armed with a mind-altering "lyre-axe guitar" that Jimi Hendrix secretly developed, future rocker Orpheus skateboards through hell (actually its closest equivalent, a cable-TV network) to rescue his zombified wife from the Gray Zone underworld. Cluttered with pop-culture parodies, slogans, gratuitous pavement surfing, and miscellaneous oddities, this holds the attention for about 40 minutes until it just runs out of plot and tries unsuccessfully to coast along on Attitude.

SIGNS

2002 (PG-13) 120m / **D:** M. Night Shyamalan / **W:** M. Night Shyamalan / **C:** Mel Gibson, Joaquin Phoenix, Rory Culkin, Abigail Breslin, Cherry Jones, Patricia Kalember, Jose L. Rodriguez

M. Night Shyamalan was still coasting easily on the success of 1999's ghostly smash *The Sixth Sense* when he released this allegorical story about crop circles and faith. Reportedly the first major film to go into production after 9/11, it's an unabashedly Spielbergian paean to wonder and inchoate fears. One-time movie star Mel Gibson suffers mightily here as an ex-priest (not Catholic, one assumes) with a tragic past working a farm with his children and brother (Joaquin Phoenix) in beautifully shot rural Pennsylvania. When crop circles start appearing in ornate patterns worldwide, it seems like a sign of something monumental approaching. Then mysterious things start moving around in his fields and inching closer to their farmhouse…. The lack of a satisfying payoff after all the wire-tight buildup (beginning here to be a Shyamalan trademark) is a problem, but not a fatal one, given how expertly he plays the tension and mystery leading up to that point.

SILENT RUNNING

1971 (G) 90m / **D:** Douglas Trumbull / **W:** Michael Cimino, Deric Washburn, Steven Bochco / **C:** Bruce Dern, Cliff Potts, Ron Rifkin

Astronauts of a future overtechnologized Earth grudgingly care for the last remaining wilderness environments, sent into orbit for eventual reforestation. When authorities instead order the project scrapped and the vegetation destroyed, nature-loving Bruce Dern mutinies and pilots his dome-enclosed woodland into the safety of deep space. Douglas Trumbull's directorial debut; he created f/x for *2001*, but this small-budget, more

THE SCI-FI MOVIE GUIDE: The Universe of Film from "Alien" to "Zardoz"

moralistic effort (filmed largely aboard a disused aircraft carrier) is clearly an eco-product of the 1960s, with a Joan Baez theme ballad and heavy-handed tree-hugging. If you can slog through the sentimentality, there's a haunting closer that one commentator called the most powerful image in modern sci-fi cinema. The film's three waddling robots—Huey, Dewey, and Louie—can be seen as the inspiration for R2D2 and his cutesy brethren.

SIX-STRING SAMURAI

1998 (PG-13) 91m / **D:** Lance Mungia / **W:** Jeffrey Falcon, Lance Mungia / **C:** Jeffrey Falcon, Justin McGuire, Stephane Gauger

In *this* 1960s America, Russia won a short-lived nuclear war a few years before. The city of "Lost" Vegas is all that's left of America. Now that Vegas's king, Elvis, has died, the call has gone out for new guitar-slingers to compete to be the new rockin' head of state. Buddy (Jeffrey Falcon), a guitar-pickin', kung-fu-fightin' badass with Buddy Holly glasses and a Clint Eastwood rasp is heading to Ve-

Dewey from *Silent Running* was added to the Robot Hall of Fame at the Carnegie Science Center in Pittsburgh in 2010.

gas. Two problems: he's got a mostly mute kid tagging along making him feel bad, and Death himself is on the move, taking out the competition with extreme prejudice. It's your basic post-apocalyptic spaghetti western where the conceptualizing seemed to stop at imagining the poster. That being said, one has to appreciate the big showdown where Buddy and his sword lay waste to a couple hundred Red Army soldiers. One asks their general, "Why don't they just shoot him?" "We haven't had bullets since 1957" is the answer. The raucous rockabilly and surf guitar soundtrack (by the Red Elvises) is *echt* 1990s indie-film-dork stuff.

THE 6TH DAY

2000 (PG-13) 123m / **D:** Roger Spottiswoode / **W:** Cormac Wibberley, Marianne Wibberley / **C:** Arnold Schwarzenegger, Michael Rapaport, Tony Goldwyn, Michael Rooker

Jumbled cloning thriller that seemingly wants to blend *Gattaca* and *Total Recall* manages to misplay its comedy *and* tragedy in almost equal amounts. The setting is the near future ("sooner than you think," the portentous opening credits note), but a future so, so speculative that the XFL is still a going concern. Human cloning is possible though outlawed, while genetic technology is widely used otherwise; a strained vein of "gee, what'll they think of next?" innovations include nacho-flavored bananas, resurrected pets, and lifelike "Simpal" dolls. Arnold Schwarzenegger, doing a worse job than usual of playing human, gets cloned against his will and sucked into a conspiracy led by evil mastermind Michael Rooker, who can just resurrect his New Wave gunsels via "blanks" at the cloning lab whenever they get killed. It's a neat trick, but seems mostly there to give Arnold the chance to grump, "Doesn't anybody stay dead anymore?"

SKY CAPTAIN AND THE WORLD OF TOMORROW

2004 (PG) 106m / **D:** Kerry Conran / **W:** Kerry Conran / **C:** Gwyneth Paltrow, Jude Law, Angelina Jolie, Giovanni Ribisi, Michael Gambon, Bai Ling

More *objet d'art* than film, this was one of those expensive follies that occasionally suckers studio heads into opening up the checkbook for no better reason than it looks cool. Kerry Conran's idiosyncratic creation is something of an Art Deco phantasmagoria, all *Metropolis* skylines, slashing beams of white light, gleaming chrome surfaces, and soft amber hues. In this Manhattan, it's 1939 and nobody's heard of the Nazis. Giant robots are kidnapping scientists and occasionally smashing up the city. Intrepid reporter Gwyneth Paltrow (no, not the best fit) thinks she has a lead on the robot story, but needs fighter jockey Jude Law to help her out. Adding some fizz to the proceedings is Angelina Jolie, as Law's smouldering, eyepatched ex (no mean pilot herself). It might be overdone CGI without much of a story, but there's such a genuinely gee-whiz quality to everything that it's hard not to cut Conran a little slack. In a perfect world, there would now be an entire series: *Sky Captain and the Red Menace*, *Sky Captain vs. the Venusians*, and so on.

> "... there's such a genuinely gee-whiz quality to everything that it's hard not to cut Conran a little slack."
>
> *Sky Captain and the World of Tomorrow*

SKYLINE

2010 (PG-13) 94m / **D:** Colin Strause, Greg Strause / **W:** Joshua Cordes, Liam O'Donnell / **C:** Eric Balfour, Scottie Thompson, Donald Faison, Britanny Daniel, David Zayas

Eric Balfour and pregnant girlfriend Scottie Thompson arrive in Los Angeles to visit his old buddy Donald Faison, who throws a party for the occasion. The next morning's hangover, though, is nothing compared to the shafts of blue light pouring down from the heavens. Seems that alien spacecraft are hanging in the skies over Southland and hovering up all the hypnotized Los Angelenos drawn to their light beams. The Strause brothers—whose only previous feature effort was 2007's abysmal *Aliens vs. Pred-*

ator: *Requiem*—are primarily f/x guys. In this instance, they were nearly sued by the studio behind the bigger-budgeted and similarly themed *Battle: Los Angeles*, which the Strauses worked on and which hit theaters several months later. In the end, neither film was remembered fondly.

SLAUGHTERHOUSE-FIVE

1972 (R) 104m / D: George Roy Hill / **W:** Stephen Geller / **C:** Michael Sacks, Valerie Perrine, Ron Leibman, Eugene Roche, Perry King, Sharon Gans, Roberts Blossom

Fine adaptation of Kurt Vonnegut's challenging breakthrough novel about World War II and time-travel has never managed to find an audience. Perhaps Vonnegut's quizzical pessimism (based in large part on his experiences during the war) and director George Roy Hill's straightforward approach to it simply don't mesh for viewers. The story trips back and forth across time and space—never losing its intelligent humor—from the savage Allied firebombing of Dresden (which Vonnegut, as a POW, barely survived) to hero Billy Pilgrim's (Michael Sacks) imprisonment with B-movie queen Montana Wildhack (Valerie Perrine) by extraterrestrials. Considerable philosophizing occurs in between, and expectations continually upended, as Billy has become "unstuck in time." So it goes. Hill directed this more adventurous effort in between crowd-pleasers *Butch Cassidy and the Sundance Kid* (1969) and *The Sting* (1973). Nominated for Palme d'Or and won jury prize at Cannes Film Festival.

SLEEP DEALER

2008 (PG-13) 90m / D: Alex Rivera / **W:** Alex Rivera / **C:** Luis Fernando Peña, Leonor Varela, Jacob Vargas, Tenoch Huerta, Metztli Adamina, José Concepción Macías

Tiny-budgeted Mexican satirical sci-fi thinker about tech-obsessed Luis Fernando Peña, who lives in a small Oaxaca town where the only source of water is a reservoir run by an American corporation. After listening in on drone pilot transmissions (drone strikes are televised as a popular reality show), he is targeted as a potential "aqua terrorist." He escapes to Tijuana and has cybernetic "nodes" implanted in his body so that he can jack straight into networked virtual reality systems that allow him and thousands of others to work jobs in America at a distance. As a supervisor notes sardonically, this "gives the U.S. what it always wanted: all the work without the workers." Small-bore and sleepily-paced but fascinating in concept.

SLEEPER

1973 (PG) 88m / D: Woody Allen / **W:** Marshall Brickman, Woody Allen / **C:** Woody Allen, Diane Keaton, John Beck, Howard Cosell, Mary Gregory, Don Keefer

THE SCI-FI MOVIE GUIDE: The Universe of Film from "Alien" to "Zardoz"

" I can't believe you haven't had sex in 200 years." "204 if you count my marriage." In the early 1970s, Woody Allen saw the future, and it was a place where tobacco, fat, and hot fudge are the healthiest things for you, and watching Howard Cosell is considered cruel and unusual punishment. Allen's most ambitious film from his early period is as much homage to silent comedy as it is sci-fi. Allen portrays Greenwich Village health food store owner Miles Monroe, who goes to the hospital with a peptic ulcer and is cryogenically frozen. He wakes up "in a Bird's-Eye wrapper" in the year 2173, where he immediately finds himself on the ten most wanted list. Diane Keaton costars as ditzy would-be poetess Luna, whom he is forced to take hostage. Great gags involve jet-pack suits, giant vegetables, stereotypically gay and Jewish tailor robots, and a malfunctioning Orgasmatron. Diane gets to do her Marlon Brando imitation. The rebel fight song ("Rebels are we / Born to be free …") was first heard in Allen's *Bananas*. The Dixieland soundtrack features Woody wailing on clarinet.

SLIPSTREAM

1989 (PG-13) 92m / **D:** Steven Lisberger / **W:** Tony Kayden / **C:** Mark Hamill, Bill Paxton, Bob Peck, Eleanor David, Kitty Aldridge, Robbie Coltrane, F. Murray Abraham

H andsomely made sci-fi is set in a future where an ecological disaster has destroyed society as we know it. Mark Hamill is an ill-tempered cop who

Best known for his role as Luke Skywalker in the "Star Wars" films, Mark Hamill also starred in 1989's *Slipstream*.

flies a wild-looking plane. He and partner Kitty Aldridge capture poetry-spouting murderer Bob Peck, but before they can bring him to justice, he's kidnapped by dim-witted bounty hunter Bill Paxton. The chase is on. Unfortunately, the chase is filled with holes. At first that doesn't matter because director Steven Lisberger captured some stunning aerial footage and much of the Turkish landscape is exotic and fascinating. Whenever the action moves to ground level, though, it falters in a welter of amateurish dialogue. Then Ben Kingsley shows up in a cameo and everyone begins to talk in fortune-cookie aphorisms meant to pass for wisdom.

SLITHER

2006 (R) 95m / **D:** James Gunn / **W:** James Gunn / **C:** Nathan Fillion, Michael Rooker, Elizabeth Banks, Gregg Henry, Tania Saulnier, Jenna Fischer

"What's gotten into you?" was the ad tag line for this creepy-crawler about a meteorite that smashes into a small town and promptly results in a profusion of slimy slugs who love nothing more than burrowing into and … well, things get icky. The mood is wall-to-wall comic gross-out, with gallons of goo, exploding body parts, and oh-dear-god reactions from the in-the-know cast. Writer/director James Gunn started out in the wink-wink Troma factory (*Tromeo and Juliet*) before detouring into the *Scooby-Doo* films.

THE SNOW CREATURE

1954 (NR) 69m / D: W. Lee Wilder / **W:** Myles Wilder / **C:** Paul Langton, Leslie Denison

Very bad monster epic that strains credibility frame by frame. Stupid troop of explorers bring back a snow creature from the Himalayas. Critter escapes in Los Angeles and terrorizes all in its path before blending in with club crowd. Occasionally, depending upon camera angle, light, and viewer mood, monster appears to be something other than guy in bad suit sweating. Directed by Billy Wilder's brother; another argument against genetic consistency.

SOLARBABIES

1986 (PG-13) 95m / D: Alan Johnson / **W:** Walon Green, D. A. Metrov / **C:** Richard Jordan, Sarah Douglas, Charles Durning, Lukas Haas, Jami Gertz, Jason Patric

Rollerskating kids in a drought-stricken future vie for a mysterious power that will replenish the Earth's water. Shades of every sci-fi movie you've ever seen, from *Mad Max* to even *The Ice Pirates*, plus the added bonus of preposterous costumes and plenty of laughs that don't actually appear to be intentional. Little about this movie makes sense, given that it was co-authored by the writer of *The Wild Bunch* and directed by a guy better known for choreographing Broadway musicals.

SOLAR CRISIS

1992 (PG-13) 111m / D: Richard Sarafian / **W:** Joe Gannon, Crispan Bolt / **C:** Tim Matheson, Charlton Heston, Peter Boyle, Annabel Schofield, Jack Palance

In 2050 the sun begins throwing off giant solar flares that turn the Earth extra-crispy. A space team is sent to divert the heat waves, but the mission falls prey to corporate sabotage. Eye-popping f/x highlight this futuristic disaster pic, an international co-production with a jumble of plot tangents that testify to reworking and re-editing that likely compelled director Richard Sarafian to use the standard industry pseudonym of "Allen Smithee" in the credits. Note the talking bomb (voiced by Paul Williams), a bit borrowed from the much cheaper and better-regarded *Dark Star*. Based on a novel by Takeshi Kawata.

SOLARIS (1972)

1972 (PG) 167m / **D:** Andrei Tarkovsky / **W:** Andrei Tarkovsky, Fridrikh Gorenshtein / **C:** Donatas Banionis, Natalya Bondarchuk

In the Soviet film industry's attempt to eclipse *2001: A Space Odyssey* in terms of cerebral sci-fi, they somehow managed to bring on a director even *less* interested in providing audience thrills than Stanley Kubrick. One's response to the original Russian-language *Solaris* is generally predicated on one's tolerance for Andrei Tarkovsky's epically slow and thoughtful dream spaces. Adapted from a classic and frequently imitated Stanislaw Lem novel, it depicts a dilapidated space lab orbiting the planet Solaris, whose ocean, a vast fluid "brain," materializes the stir-crazy cosmonauts' obsessions—usually morose ex-girlfriends. Nearly plotless, with minimal f/x, but Tarkovsky's ghostly sadness—which imagines the past as almost a physical thing, which loses no potency simply for being over with—inhabits every frame with a poetic melancholy. Alternately maddening and fascinating.

SOLARIS (2002)

2002 (PG-13) 99m / **D:** Steven Soderbergh / **W:** Steven Soderbergh / **C:** George Clooney, Natascha McElhone, Viola Davis, Jeremy Davies, Ulrich Tukur, Morgan Rusler

Another journey back to the haunted space station of Stanislaw Lem's novel, memorably explored in Andrei Tarkovsky's original 1972 film. A funereal George Clooney plays the psychiatrist sent to the station orbiting and studying a distant planet after it's reported two of the astronauts there have died. Studying the emotive magnetism exerted by the planet below, he realizes things are happening that shouldn't be. In particular, thoughts are manifested, frequently the ones nobody *wants* to see. In a twist on the physician-heal-thyself dictum, Natascha McElhone shows up as Clooney's wife—who killed herself some time earlier. Although nobody would pick Steven Soderbergh as a filmmaker with much of a

Steven Soderbergh's remake of *Solaris* was an emotional ghost story about an astronaut meeting his dead wife in a space station orbiting a mysterious alien planet.

heartbeat, in this shorter, sharper remake he burns away some of the lugubri-ousness swaddling of Tarkovsky's adaptation to uncover the primal human fears (loneliness, abandonment, regret) at the root of this beautifully sad love story.

SOLDIER

1998 (R) 99m / D: Paul W. S. Anderson / **W:** David Webb Peoples / **C:** Kurt Russell, Jason Scott Lee, Jason Isaacs, Connie Nielsen, Sean Pertwee, Gary Busey

Attempt at a more meaningful *Universal Soldier*-type tale about a program that tries to create "perfect" (i.e., emotionless robotic drone) soldiers out of ordinary humans. Stone-faced Kurt Russell plays Todd 3465, trained from birth to the ways of bloodthirsty combat. After surviving numerous conflicts—one of the better moments shows Todd and his fellow soldiers sitting on their bunks, just waiting for the next war—he's faced with a new threat: geneti-cally bred super-soldiers faster and stronger than his old breed. Left for dead, Todd is dumped onto a garbage planet where he just so happens to come across a plucky and big-hearted band of refugees to take him in. When his old nemesis Caine 607 (Jason Scott Lee) comes looking to use those refugees as target practice, Todd puts his deadly skills to use for good. David Webb Peoples's script has the hint of an epic story about redemption at its core, but Paul W. S. Anderson's comically inept direction—which not only ig-nores the story's emotional theme but also blew a for-the-time massive budget on inexcusably hokey f/x—hides that potential more than burnish-ing it. Russell utters maybe 100 words throughout.

SOLO

1996 (PG-13) 94m / D: Norberto Barba / **W:** David L. Corley / **C:** Mario Van Peebles, William Sadler, Barry Corbin, Demian Bichir

In this post-*Terminator*, pre-*Universal Soldier* action flick, Mario Van Peebles plays Solo, a cyborg soldier created by the U.S. to go enforce Manifest Des-tiny in Central America. Like any good-hearted cyborg, he rebels against his masters and decides *not* to kill the innocents when the mission, and his bloodthirsty commanders, calls for it. Early appearance by Adrien Brody as Solo's inventor.

SON OF BLOB

1971 (PG) 87m / D: Larry Hagman / **W:** Anthony Harris, Jack Woods / **C:** Robert Walker Jr., Godfrey Cambridge, Carol Lynley, Shelley Berman, Larry Hagman, Burgess Meredith, Gerrit Graham, Dick Van Patten, Gwynne Gilford

A post-*Jeannie*, pre-*Dallas* Larry Hagman directed this exercise in zaniness. A scientist brings a piece of frozen blob home from the North Pole; his wife accidentally revives the dormant gray mass. It begins a rampage of terror by digesting nearly everyone within its reach, including Shelley Berman and Burgess Meredith. One poor guy drinks a blob cocktail and then it ... well, sort of drinks him. From the inside out. Sequels to classics of *The Blob*'s stature don't usually work, but this one is great fun. AKA: *Beware! The Blob*.

SON OF FLUBBER

1963 (G) 100m / **D:** Robert Stevenson / **W:** Bill Walsh, Don DaGradi / **C:** Fred MacMurray, Nancy Olson, Tommy Kirk, Leon Ames, Joanna Moore, Keenan Wynn, Charlie Ruggles, Paul Lynde, Ed Wynn

Fred MacMurray reprises his role from *The Absent-Minded Professor* as a silly scientist with a goofy invention in *Son of Flubber*.

Enjoyable sequel to *The Absent-Minded Professor* finds Fred MacMurray still toying with his prodigious invention Flubber, now in a convenient gaseous form. "Flubbergas" causes those who inhale it to float away (which comes in handy during the town's big football game). Fred also monkeys with a weather-changing device and has assorted other problems. Classic family Disney wackiness, with appearances by Ed Wynn and Paul Lynde.

SON OF FRANKENSTEIN

1939 (NR) 99m / **D:** Rowland V. Lee / **W:** Willis Cooper / **C:** Basil Rathbone, Bela Lugosi, Boris Karloff, Lionel Atwill, Josephine Hutchinson, Donnie Dunagan, Emma Dunn, Edgar Norton, Lawrence Grant, Lionel Belmore

After a reissue double feature of *Frankenstein* and *Dracula* in 1938 became a surprise knockout hit, Universal decided to start making horror movies once again. This is the second sequel (after *The Bride of Frankenstein*) to the 1931 classic. The good doctor's skeptical son (Basil Rathbone, in a fine bombastic performance) returns to the family manse and becomes obsessed with his father's work and with reviving the creature, giving us a peek at the Monster's physiology in the process. Full of memorable characters and brooding ambience. Boris Karloff's last appearance as the Monster, but Bela Lugosi's characterization of Ygor, the broken-necked friend of the Monster, steals the show. Originally, Ygor was barely supposed to be in the movie, but director Rowland Lee—who'd thrown out the original script and was making things up as he went along—did Bela a favor by substantially expanding his part.

SON OF GODZILLA

1966 (PG) 86m / **D:** Jun Fukuda / **W:** Shinichi Sekizawa, Kazue Shiba / **C:** Akira Kubo, Beverly Maeda, Tadao Takashima, Akihiko Hirata, Kenji Sahara

The second of Godzilla's "south seas" pictures (after *Godzilla vs. the Sea Monster*), this one concerns the adventures of a group of scientists trying to control weather conditions on a tropical island. Their lives are threatened when their experiments hatch the title infant, drawing the unwelcome attention of the adult monster and some gigantic insects as well. It's refreshing to see Godzilla marching among the waving palms instead of smashing cities, and no doubt less expensive for the producers. While Godzilla and his young ward (dubbed "Minya" in Japan) look awful in this entry, and the juvenile aspect of the baby's antics are slightly annoying, this is nevertheless a solidly paced and plotted sci-fi adventure. Minya would return to tug at our heartstrings in *Destroy All Monsters* and *Godzilla's Revenge* before retiring from the screen forever.

SOUND OF MY VOICE

2011 (R) 85m / **D:** Zal Batmanglij / **W:** Zal Batmanglij, Brit Marling / **C:** Christopher Denham, Nicole Vicius, Brit Marling, Richard Wharton

Ominous without being portentous, Zal Batmanglij's crisp mystery is like some top-secret, incomplete dossier that was somehow turned into a film. Would-be investigative filmmaker Christopher Denham and his girlfriend Nicole Vicius pretend to join a cult in the Valley in order to film what's going on. After penetrating the NSA-esque levels of security, they meet the cult's focal point of adoration: Brit Marling, a spookily enticing figure who shrouds herself in robes and the fantastical story that she has come from the future with a message of warning. Not surprisingly, much of her message comes straight out of the Cult 101 handbook for breaking down followers' individuality and turning them into obedient robots. The infiltrators not only begin to break down under Marling's quiet but demanding methods, but start to suspect that she might be telling the truth. Goes a little too far in leaving viewers hanging, but Batmanglij's spooky level of control creates a powerfully chilling and disorienting experience. *The Conversation* by way of *Primer*.

> "Batmanglij's spooky level of control creates a powerfully chilling and disorienting experience."
> *Sound of My Voice*

A SOUND OF THUNDER

2005 (PG-13) 110m / **D:** Peter Hyams / **W:** Thomas Dean Donnelly, Joshua Oppenheimer, Gregory Poirier / **C:** Edward Burns, Ben Kingsley, Catherine McCormack, Jemima Rooper, August Zirner, Corey Johnson aughably inept take on the classic time-travel short story about the dangers of meddling with the past helps, if nothing else, to prove the dictum that it is nearly impossible to create anything watchable out of Ray Bradbury's fiction. In 2055 Chicago, your standard greedy-stupid corporation takes huge fees from bored rich guys to zip them back in time to hunt dinosaurs. Shock-haired baddie Ben Kingsley takes things too far, space-time continuum gets duly screwed with, and it's up to handsome scientist pair Edward Burns and Catherine McCormack to set things right. The sub-*Jurassic Park* dino-battles that follow are about as dull as it gets. Surprisingly cheap f/x for a new-millennium, big-studio effort; more believable future-city scenes can be seen on *Mystery Science Theater 3000* re-runs. But then, if nobody was worried about the writing or directing, why spend money or time on making it look professional?

SOURCE CODE

2011 (PG-13) 93m / **D:** Duncan Jones / **W:** Ben Ripley / **C:** Jake Gyllenhaal, Michelle Monaghan, Vera Farmiga, Jeffrey Wright, Michael Arden

nother tightly boxed story of tweaked realities from *Moon* auteur Duncan Jones. Ben Ripley's script seems initially more a boilerplate post-9/11 security thriller, with war vet Jake Gyllenhaal—who has memories of crashing a helicopter in Afghanistan—waking up in a Chicago commuter train just minutes before it is destroyed by a bomb. What happens after is something of a *Groundhog Day* scenario for the age of terror. After "dying" the first time, Gyllenhaal wakes up in a pod where he's being given instructions by Vera Farmiga about what to do *when he goes back*. Time and again, Gyllenhaal is returned to the same moment on the train eight minutes before the explosion, trying to discover who the bomber before he and everybody else dies … again. Meanwhile he's getting romantic vibes from Michelle Monaghan and increasingly dire orders from the military intelligence types pushing his already-fried consciousness (wasn't I *dead?*) well past the breaking point. It's a thriller, so most of the story's existentialist concerns are ultimately shuttled aside for plot exigency, but not without conjuring up a crackerjack mystery with a nightmarish and Beckett-like fatalistic backdrop.

SOUTHLAND TALES

2006 (R) 145m / **D:** Richard Kelly / **W:** Richard Kelly / **C:** Dwayne Johnson, Sarah Michelle Gellar, Mandy Moore, Seann William Scott, Jon Lovitz, Justin Timberlake

udaciously surrealist idea-dump about a near-future Los Angeles that's under the thumb of crackpot corporate conservatives and about to explode. There's a lot of unimpeded guff rushing through Richard Kelly's follow-up to *Donnie Darko*, and a menagerie of tangled plots to boot. The cast is a Gregg Araki-esque team of pop stars trying to play against type. Dwayne Johnson and his lover Sarah Michelle Gellar are trying to get a movie made about the end of the world, though Johnson is suffering from amnesia and doesn't remember he already has a wife, whose family just so happens to be running the government's Orwellian identity program (much more fantastical in the mid-2000s than now). Meanwhile, Marxist revolutionary cells are popping up all over the Southland and everything rumbles toward catastrophe. The flashback-riddled story is narrated by troubled Fallujah vet Justin Timberlake and spiked with the occasional musical interlude (Pixies, the Killers). Overambitious mess, riddled with inflections of borderline genius, that still manages to highlight just how rigid in comparison most sci-fi film became in the 2000s.

Soylent Green

1973 (PG) 95m / D: Richard Fleischer / **W:** Stanley R. Greenberg / **C:** Charlton Heston, Leigh Taylor-Young, Chuck Connors, Joseph Cotten, Edward G. Robinson, Brock Peters

The future is ... no future. That's the message behind this relentlessly dark film lifted above being just a downbeat shocker by excellent performances, including Edward G. Robinson in his final role, and an inventively grim satire on urban overcrowding. In the year 2022, New York City is jammed with 40 million people (mostly unemployed), suicide is not only legal—it's encouraged, jam is $150 a jar, and crowd control is done with bulldozers. The most common (and only affordable) food for the masses is the green wafer, Soylent. Policeman Thorn (Chuck Heston) is a worn-out, hard-nosed cop assigned to the murder of a Soylent Company exec. Tab (Chuck Connors) is one of those cleaner types for the company, getting rid of loose ends, one of which is Thorn. Their fight at the apartment is a doozy. Thorn's researcher (Robinson) remembers when there were trees, vegetables, democracy, and real sunshine. His operatic demise is the "pretty" part of this film. Based on Harry Harrison's novel *Make Room! Make Room!*

Spaceballs

1987 (PG) 96m / D: Mel Brooks / **W:** Ronny Graham, Thomas Meehan, Mel Brooks / **C:** Mel Brooks, Rick Moranis, John Candy, Bill Pullman, Daphne Zuniga, Dick Van Patten, John Hurt, George Wyner, Lorene Yarnell, Sal Viscuso, Stephen Tobolowsky, Michael Winslow, Dom DeLuise

The force was not with Mel Brooks, whose spoof of the George Lucas franchise felt light years too late. But why ask for the moon when you have such stars as Rick Moranis as the petulant geek Dark Helmet, John Candy as Barf, who is half-dog/half-man ("I'm my own best friend"), Dom DeLuise

Mel Brooks' *Star Wars* spoof, *Spaceballs,* features the doglike Bark (instead of a Wookie), a gelatinous Pizza the Hut, and a tiny, nerdy version of Darth Vader (Dark Helmet) played by Rick Moranis.

as the voice of Pizza the Hut, and Brooks, revising his 2,000-Year-Old Man character as the sage Yogurt, whose motto is "May the Schwartz be with you." Chiding the vast *Star Wars* merchandising empire is about as biting as the satire gets. John Hurt busts a gut reprising his role from *Alien*. Incredibly, it became one of Brooks's most successful films. Followed up by a short-lived animated series in 2008.

SPACED INVADERS

1990 (PG) 100m / D: Patrick Read Johnson / **W:** Patrick Read Johnson, Scott Lawrence Alexander / **C:** Douglas Barr, Royal Dano, Ariana Richards, J. J. Anderson, Gregg Berger

Ship full of little green Martians is en route to an alien war but mistakenly lands in rural Illinois (they overhear a rebroadcast of Orson Welles's "War of the Worlds" and assume the target has changed). It's Halloween, and the bumbling would-be conquerors are mistaken for trick-or-treaters. Earth children know the truth: "They're not bad, just stupid." The same can be said for the satire's loud and repetitive bathroom humor.

SPACEHUNTER: ADVENTURES IN THE FORBIDDEN ZONE

1983 (PG) 90m / D: Lamont Johnson / **W:** David Preston, Edith Rey, Daniel Goldberg, Len Blum / **C:** Peter Strauss, Molly Ringwald, Michael Ironside, Ernie Hudson, Andrea Marcovicci

If the jokes were better, this could pass as a comedy. Galactic bounty hunter agrees to rescue three damsels held captive by a cyborg on a bizarre rubble-strewn world. Peter Strauss tries, but he ain't no Harrison Ford, and Molly Ringwald won't give Chewbacca much serious competition either. Interesting costumes and set design in this no-brainer, which on video loses its novelty of being lensed in 3-D.

SPACE JAM

1996 (PG) 88m / D: Joe Pytka / **W:** Leo Benvenuti, Steve Rudnick, Timothy Harris, Herschel Weingrod / **C:** Michael Jordan, Wayne Knight, Theresa Randle, Bill Murray

Warner Bros. branding reboot exercise mixed with a little post-*Who Framed Roger Rabbit?* wink-winkery. Bugs Bunny and the gang have a problem: the only way they can avoid getting sent to staff a sad-sack amusement park on a distant planet is by winning a bet placed by the ever-wiley Bugs: We'll beat you in basketball. Only the aliens have a roster full of 1990s' NBA ringers (Charles Barkley and the like). Clearly, the only solution is for Bugs et al. to kidnap Michael Jordan—then still just about at his peak of perfection—into their alternate Looney Tunes universe and use him to win the big game. Mix of live-action and 3-D animation was catnip for audiences at the time; who wouldn't like watching animated aliens dunk basketballs while the occasional human makes goggle eyes at the green-screen chaos?

> "Mix of live-action and 3-D animation was catnip for audiences at the time...."
>
> *Space Jam*

SPACESHIP

1981 (PG) 88m / D: Bruce Kimmel / **W:** Bruce Kimmel / **C:** Cindy Williams, Bruce Kimmel, Leslie Nielsen, Gerrit Graham, Patrick Macnee, Ron Kurowski

Attempted *Airplane*-style sci-fi spoof that only works in fits and starts. A pre-*Naked Gun* Leslie Nielsen commands a spacecraft that picks up an alien that looks like a load of glop with a single Cyclopean eye-stalk on top—wouldn't you know it starts eating the crew. F/x are flagrantly cheap, and then there are those song-and-dance numbers and excerpts from Japanese monster movies edited in. AKA: *The Creature Wasn't Nice*; *Naked Space*.

SPACE TRUCKERS

1996 (PG-13) 95m / **D:** Stuart Gordon / **W:** Ted Mann / **C:** Dennis Hopper, Debi Mazar, Stephen Dorff, Charles Dance, George Wendt

So, it's 2196 and humanity has figured out interstellar space travel. The joke, though, is that freight still needs to get hauled from one planet to the next by guys with bad attitudes wearing baseball hats. Trucker Dennis Hopper discovers that his cargo hold is full of killer robots, which is no good. So it's up to him, Stephen Dorff, and a frequently partially disrobed Debi Mazar to save Earth. The look is about one cut above the average Roger Corman monstrosity. Curiously non-R-rated given the director (*Re-Animator*'s Stuart Gordon).

SPECIES

1995 (R) 108m / **D:** Roger Donaldson / **W:** Dennis Feldman / **C:** Ben Kingsley, Michael Madsen, Alfred Molina, Forest Whitaker, Marg Helgenberger, Natasha Henstridge

If the outline for a crackerjack episode of *The X-Files* fell into the wrong hands, the result might have been this crazed chase adventure. At heart, it's B-grade sci-fi pumped up with a smart cast, gobs of gore, and lots of morphing effects. The plot revolves around a hot-to-trot blonde babe (model Natasha Henstridge in her debut) who's also a murderous shape-shifting alien monster. Ben Kingsley leads the team that's trying to kill outer-space succubus before, well, world domination and whatnot. Lots of laughs, sometimes even intended, and some undeniably enjoyable cheap thrills. Followed by three sequels where much the same happens.

SPEED RACER

2008 (PG) 135m / **D:** Andy Wachowski, Lana Wachowski / **W:** Andy Wachowski, Lana Wachowski / **C:** Emile Hirsch, Susan Sarandon, John Goodman, Christina Ricci, Matthew Fox, Roger Allam

After the cyber-grime of the *Matrix* trilogy, the Wachowskis detoured into sci-fi fantasy with this mega-budget, mega-fun, psychedelic live-action (sort of) expansion of the 1960s-era Tatsuo Yoshida anime about a spunky young race-car driver. Speed Racer (Emile Hirsch) tries to exorcise the racing death of his older brother by, well, driving really fast. There's conniving aplenty, courtesy of villainous corporations who want to subsume the Racer into their vile schemes. But the sheer, overpowering goodness of Speed, his pixie-bright girlfriend Christina Ricci (dolled up here like a character from *Sailor Moon*), and chipper parents John Goodman and Susan Sarandon simply cannot be defeated. The Wachowskis splash neon-bright colors everywhere in a look that's so Pop it is practically *avant garde*; it's as though a candy store exploded all over downtown Tokyo. The race scenes are patently fake but nevertheless thrilling, with Speed's Mach 5 deploying a Swiss Army knife-level of gadgets to defeat the corporate stooges trying to beat him in the demolition derbies that take up much of the film's (admittedly padded) running time. Moral: Cheaters never prosper!

SPHERE

1998 (PG-13) 134m / D: Barry Levinson / **W:** Kurt Wimmer, Stephen Hauser, Paul Attanasio / **C:** Dustin Hoffman, Sharon Stone, Samuel L. Jackson, Peter Coyote, Liev Schreiber, Queen Latifah

Another Michael Crichton novel gets the blockbuster treatment in hopes of scaring up a *Jurassic Park*-sized hit. But Barry Levinson's characterless direction and the grab-bag of ill-matching stars don't do wonders for a story that would be tricky for the best team to pull off. A spaceship is discovered nestled in a few hundred years' growth of coral at the bottom of the Pacific, and a team of U.S. Navy specialists dive down to check it out. The big reveal comes early: it's not an alien spaceship, it's an American one from a few decades in the future that got sucked through time and deposited at the bottom of the ocean. After that, a malevolent presence makes itself known and the intrepid explorers scramble to survive.

SPIDER-MAN

2002 (PG-13) 121m / D: Sam Raimi / **W:** David Koepp / **C:** Tobey Maguire, Willem Dafoe, Kirsten Dunst, James Franco, Cliff Robertson, Rosemary Harris, J. K. Simmons

The modern comic-book movie truly took flight with something of a "woo-hoo!" with the first Tobey Maguire Spider-Man. 2000's *X-Men* made it clear that the genre could appeal to more than fanboys, but this was the one that showed comics could again appeal to everybody and their mother. In a sharp about-face, Sam (*Evil Dead*) Raimi piloted this webslinger origin story to mainstream success by zeroing in on the goony and gawky adolescent appeal of nerdy young orphan Peter Parker (Tobey Maguire), who seems fated to never quite get the right girl or right career when he's bitten by a radioactive spider and given arachnid powers (incredible strength, leaping abilities, shooting sticky webs). After having a good time using his webs to zip around Manhattan skyscrapers like some supernatural gymnast, tragedy strikes his family and reminds Parker that his powers come with great responsibility. Just in time for him to test those powers, Willem Dafoe turns himself into supervillain the Green Goblin and starts tearing up the city. The action scenes are swift and gleefully vertiginous, Raimi's typically goony humor infectious as ever, and Parker's romancing of Mary Jane (Kirsten Dunst) touching

Kirsten Dunst gives Spidey (Toby Maguire) a topsy-turvy kiss in 2002's *Spider-Man*.

through and through. Coming just a year after 9/11, the film's full embrace of New York served as a kind of balm. Oscar nominations for sound and f/x.

SPIDER-MAN 2

2004 (PG-13) 127m / D: Sam Raimi / **W:** Alvin Sargent / **C:** Tobey Maguire, Kirsten Dunst, Alfred Molina, Rosemary Harris, J. K. Simmons, Donna Murphy

A sequel that takes the story in darker, more emotive directions without losing the flash and vim of the original. Peter Parker is in the doldrums, having lost his pizza delivery job (Bruce Wayne never had to worry about thirty minutes or less), failing in college, and on the verge of losing Mary Jane to another guy. Also, the Green Goblin's son (James Franco) is spinning into evil villain psychosis while Dr. Octopus (Alfred Molina)—who suffered the fate of many comic-book scientists in letting his experiment run out of control, leaving him with four swerving metallic tentacles snaking out of his back—is starting a one-man crime wave. The climactic showdown might show signs of blockbuster series bloat but it's still an impressively adult sci-fi adventure that maintains its sense of wonder. Novelist Michael Chabon, whose *Ad-*

ventures of Kavalier and Clay told the story of the comic industry's early years, contributed to the screenplay. Three Oscar nominations; won for f/x.

SPIDER-MAN 3

2007 (PG-13) 139m / **D:** Sam Raimi / **W:** Ivan Raimi, Sam Raimi, Alvin Sargent / **C:** Tobey Maguire, Kirsten Dunst, James Franco, Thomas Haden Church, Topher Grace, Bryce Dallas Howard, Rosemary Harris, J. K. Simmons, James Cromwell

The Raimi Spidey series started showing the spackle in its cracks with his third and final installment. The need to come up with new villains who have met unlikely transformations reached its nadir with the introduction of Sandman (Thomas Haden Church), who was turned into a shape-shifting sand creature after falling into a particle accelerator. Otherwise, Green Goblin Jr. is still on Spidey's case, and some kind of alien goo lands in Central Park and starts turning Parker into a darker version of himself (evil Spidey!). Repetitive and dramatically random. Still, nice scene with Parker and Mary Jane hanging out under the stars … on a giant spiderweb slung between two trees.

SPLICE

2009 (R) 104m / **D:** Vincenzo Natali / **W:** Vincenzo Natali / **C:** Adrien Brody, Sarah Polley, Delphine Chaneac, Brandon McGibbon

It's Alive for the Dolly era. Researchers Adrien Brody and Sarah Polley are pushing the boundaries with what's (at that point, at least) acceptable in mixing human DNA with their own hybridized animal clone. They end up with a full-on whatsit in their care, which they take into hiding once the bosses get suspicious about what's going on in the lab. The part-human, part-amphibian Dren (Delphine Chaneac) grows up as a sleek, bulbous-headed young woman with the leaping abilities of a primate, a needle-topped whip of a tail, and handsome eyes just too big and too far apart to be quite human. Brody is appropriately terrified and wants to get rid of Dren. Polley develops stubborn parental sensations mixed with "they just don't understand" paranoia familiar to anyone who's seen or read *Frankenstein*. Some deft, underplayed humor gives way eventually to increasingly preposterous and curiously sexual cross-species ick. Polley and Brody carry much of the film, particularly Brody, an arthouse guy who by this point had become a reliably wry presence in above-average genre flicks. Just don't watch what Dren does to her cat when she's upset.

SPLIT

1990 (NR) 85m / **D:** Chris Shaw / **W:** Chris Shaw/ **C:** John Flynn, Timothy Dwight, Chris Shaw, Joan Bechtel

A vagrant named Starker changes his identity repeatedly to elude detection by the all-seeing "Company Director," who in the course of the narrative replaces his body with cybernetic components and ends up looking like the Silver Surfer. Surreal tale lends itself to various interpretations, but debuting director Chris Shaw keeps things moving and mildly satirical in tone. Cult discovery still awaits.

SPLIT SECOND

1992 (R) 91m / **D:** Tony Maylam / **W:** Gary Scott Thompson / **C:** Rutger Hauer, Kim Cattrall, Neil Duncan, Michael J. Pollard, Alun Armstrong, Pete Postlethwaite, Ian Dury, Roberta Eaton

Rutger Hauer is a cop tracking down a vicious alien serial killer in London in the year 2008. The monster rips out the hearts of his victims and then eats them ritualistically in this blood-soaked thriller wannabe. Hauer gives a listless performance, and overall the action is quite dull. As a bonus, the Moody Blues' "Nights in White Satin" plays at the most inappropriate times.

SPUTNIK

1961 (NR) 80m / **D:** Jean Dréville / **W:** Noël-Noël, Jacques Grello, Robert Rocca / **C:** Noël-Noël, Mischa Auer, Denise Grey, Jean-Paul Belmondo

Charming, if dated, family film in which a Frenchman, amnesiac after a car crash, comes up against Russian scientists, space-bound dogs, and weightlessnes. Another fine performance from Mischa Auer. Dubbed. AKA: *A Dog, a Mouse, and a Sputnik.*

STALKER

1979 (NR) 160m / **D:** Andrei Tarkovsky / **W:** Arkadiy Strugatskiy, Boris Strugatskiy / **C:** Alexander Kaidanovsky, Nikolai Grinko, Anatoli Solonitzin, Alice Freindlikh

A meteorite, crashing to Earth, creates a wasteland area known as the Zone, which is forbidden to anyone except special guides called Stalkers. Three Stalkers enter the region searching for its center, which contains a room that supposedly reveals one's fantasies. Filming in both color and black-and-white, *Solaris* director Andrei Tarkovsky creates a suspenseful, kaleidoscopic atmosphere that will enrapture fans of minimalist speculative film. In Russian with English subtitles.

STARCHASER: THE LEGEND OF ORIN

1985 (PG) 107m / **D:** Steven Hahn / **W:** Jeffrey Scott

This exciting, family oriented sci-fi animated feature was released on theater screens in dizzying 3-D. That factor is gone on home viewing but the roller coaster sensation still lingers in its *Star Wars*-plundered plot about a young boy recruited by a Han Solo-type space pilot (whose cigar and unshaven jowls give him a villainous appearance). His instructions see the boy through tests of bravery and courage to eliminate a nasty horde of malevolent robots planning to crush all organic sentient life in the universe.

STAR CRASH

1978 (PG) 92m / D: Lewis Coates / **W:** Lewis Coates / **C:** Caroline Munro, Marjoe Gortner, Christopher Plummer, David Hasselhoff, Robert Tessier, Joe Spinell, Nadia Cassini, Judd Hamilton

Spaghetti space opera from the director of *Hercules* that followed closely on the heels of *Star Wars*. A trio of adventurers (a woman, a man, and a robot) are sent by space-emperor Christopher Plummer to square off against interstellar bad-guy Joe Spinell with wits and high-tech (for the time) wizardry. Highly cheesy but pulled off with a style and flair way beyond its limited budget. The sultry Caroline Munro, as always, makes for an appealing heroine. Early David Hasselhoff appearance. AKA: *Stella Star.*

STARGATE

1994 (PG-13) 119m / D: Roland Emmerich / **W:** Dean Devlin, Roland Emmerich / **C:** Kurt Russell, James Spader, Jaye Davidson, Viveca Lindfors, Alexis Cruz, Leon Rippy, John Diehl, Erick Avari, Mili Avital

In this deMille/Spielbergian space adventure, a U.S. military probe of a ring-shaped ancient Egyptian artifact sends he-man colonel Kurt Russell and geeky Egyptologist James Spader into a parallel universe. There they meet the pyramids' builders, who are enslaved by an evil despot (*The Crying Game*'s Jaye Davidson), posing as a sun god. Ambitious premise gets an A for effort, but the plot jumbles biblical epic panoramas and "Oh Wow!" f/x with otherworldly mysticism and needless emotional hang-ups. Spader's shaggy scholar is neurotically fun and Russell's jarhead a bore, but at least Davidson's vampy villain provides some surprises. The mix proved to be a smash with audiences, paving the way for four (at last count) spinoff TV series, not to mention novels, comics, and straight-to-DVD sequels.

STARMAN

1984 (PG) 115m / D: John Carpenter / **W:** Bruce A. Evans, Raynold Gideon / **C:** Jeff Bridges, Karen Allen, Charles Martin Smith, Richard Jaeckel, Robert Phalen

After an alien from an advanced civilization lands in Wisconsin, he hides beneath the guise of a grieving young widow's recently deceased husband. Later, the Jeff Bridges-looking Starman makes her drive him across country to rendezvous with his spacecraft so he can return home. Not the

James Spader is an Egyptologist who travels through a trans-dimensional portal to a world very much like ancient Egypt in *Stargate*.

E.T. rip-off you'd expect, this is a well-acted, interesting twist on the *Stranger in a Strange Land* theme. Karen Allen is lovely and earthy in her worthy follow-up to *Raiders of the Lost Ark*, while Bridges received an Oscar nomination. A solidly done sci-fi story that was also director John Carpenter's most mainstream success.

STAR QUEST

1994 (R) 95m / **D:** Rick Jacobson / **W:** Mark Evan Schwartz / **C:** Steven Bauer, Emma Samms, Alan Rachins, Brenda Bakke, Ming-Na Wen, Gregory McKinney, Cliff DeYoung

Competently told space tale has a good cast and a nice O. Henry ending. In an opening lifted straight from *Planet of the Apes*, astronauts en route to the planet Trion in the year 2035 are awakened from hibernation to find that their captain is dead and someone is after them. As their numbers dwindle, the crew faces that eternal sci-fi query: Which of us is the robot? The tale moves right along with good effects, sets, and characters with some depth to go along with their goofy accents. AKA: *Terminal Voyage*.

STARSHIP

1987 (PG) 91m / **D:** Roger Christian / **W:** Roger Christian, Matthew Jacobs / **C:** John Tarrant, Cassandra Webb, Donogh Rees, Deep Roy, Ralph Cotterill

No-frills *Star Wars* ripoff about human slaves trying to escape a planet run by evil robots. British sci-fi has a surface veneer of cool f/x but absolutely nothing underneath—no sense of fun, wonder, or whatever. Director Roger Christian was art director on *Alien* but you would never know it. AKA: *Lorca and the Outlaws*; *2084*.

STARSHIP INVASIONS

1977 (PG) 89m / **D:** Edward Hunt / **W:** Edward Hunt / **C:** Christopher Lee, Robert Vaughn, Daniel Pilon, Helen Shaver, Henry Ramer, Victoria (Vicki) Johnson

Christopher Lee leads a group of bad aliens seeking to take over the Earth. He's thwarted by UFO expert Robert Vaughn, who is aided by a group of good aliens. Cheesy f/x have this one looking like a bad 1940s sci-fi serial.

STARSHIP TROOPERS

1997 (R) 129m / **D:** Paul Verhoeven / **W:** Edward Neumeier / **C:** Casper Van Dien, Dina Meyer, Denise Richards, Jake Busey, Neil Patrick Harris, Clancy Brown, Seth Gilliam, Patrick Muldoon, Michael Ironside, Rue McClanahan

Paul Verhoeven reteamed with *Robocop* writer Edward Neumeier for this adaptation of Robert Heinlein's hugely influential novel about an all-out future war against an alien race. Needless to say, this mega-budget adaptation slices out Heinlein's philosophizing about militarism and democracy to focus on scenes of pinup-pretty body-armored soldiers blasting away at hordes of gigantic, gruesome bugs. As usual, Verhoeven tries to have it both ways, pumping up the "kill 'em all!" action while tweaking audience expectations with stiff propaganda intervals whose style is taken straight from *Triumph of the Will*. While the sight of Neil Patrick Harris in a Wehrmacht-style uniform makes the filmmaker's intentions clear, the satire is buried so deep here it's practically ineffectual. For such a high-budget production, f/x are surprisingly chintzy. Calling the acting cardboard would be an insult to all tree-based materials. Followed by a couple straight-to-DVD sequels and a gruesomely cheap animated series.

STAR TREK

2009 (PG-13) 127m / **D:** J. J. Abrams / **W:** Roberto Orci, Alex Kurtzman / **C:** Chris Pine, Zachary Quinto, Simon Pegg, Eric Bana, Bruce Greenwood, Karl Urban, Zoe Saldana, John Cho, Anton Yelchin, Leonard Nimoy

The sound of relief heard when J. J. Abrams's series reboot hit theaters was just about as loud as the many explosions that ripple through this action-

Zachary Quinto took over the role of Spock and Chris Pine was Captain James T. Kirk in the revamped *Star Trek* based on the original 1960s TV series.

packed adventure that did its best to return to the *Star Trek* mystique while trying to rope in broader audiences unfamiliar with the mythology (the latter having been something the *Next Generation* entries never tried too hard to do). It's a *Starship Enterprise* origin story, with a cocky young Captain Kirk (Chris Pine), first spotted racing a car toward a cliff edge while Beastie Boys blasts on the soundtrack, angling to get his first command and to fill the void left by his father, who dies in the opening scenes to save his family. Eventually, Kirk and a ship's worth of fresh-faced young cadets will have to face down time-traveling villain Nero (Eric Bana). While there's not much dramatic shading to keep things interesting (a common problem with the mechanistic Abrams), the film wins out not just for its eagerness to entertain and bright sparkling design revamp but for the spot-on new casting of the old crew members. From Simon Pegg's Scotty to Zachary Quinto's Spock, their characters all mesh with the kind of chemistry most franchise filmmakers can only dream of. Even so, bringing back Leonard Nimoy to meet his younger self certainly doesn't hurt. As with most blockbuster event pictures in the 2000s, the script doesn't give the story anywhere to go in its last third except to continually up the chase/explosion stakes. Four Oscar nominations; won for makeup.

STAR TREK II: THE WRATH OF KHAN

1982 (PG) 113m / D: Nicholas Meyer / **W:** Jack Sowards / **C:** William Shatner, Leonard Nimoy, Ricardo Montalbán, DeForest Kelley, Nichelle Nichols, James Doohan, George Takei, Walter Koenig, Kirstie Alley, Merritt Butrick, Paul Winfield, Bibi Besch

The second and by all likelihood still the greatest of the *Star Trek* films goes back to one of the show's better episodes (1967's "Space Seed") for its inspiration. A volcanic, over-the-top Ricardo Montalbán plays Khan, the genetically engineered supervillain whom Kirk marooned at the end of that episode but who now has captured a ship of his own and is looking for a big cold plate of revenge. It's been noted by many that next to Khan's Melville-quoting theatricality ("from hell's heart I stab at thee!"), William Shatner's fecklessly impetuous Kirk hardly seems worth the effort. But Shatner ably makes up some of the distance between the two, first in the opening "Kobayashi Maru" segment that's become something of a nerd philosophy exercise and later in the big tear-jerker of a climax. None of the following original-cast films could match this one in full-blooded melodrama, though the later J. J. Abrams films were clearly looking here for inspiration. Supposedly, Leonard Nimoy had to be enticed back, and his one requirement was that they kill off Spock.

Star Trek III: The Search for Spock

1984 (PG) 105m / D: Leonard Nimoy / **W:** Harve Bennett / **C:** William Shatner, Leonard Nimoy, DeForest Kelley, James Doohan, George Takei, Walter Koenig, Mark Lenard, Robin Curtis, Merritt Butrick, Christopher Lloyd, Judith Anderson, John Larroquette

Being the undisciplined scamp that he is, Captain Kirk hijacks the USS *Enterprise* and commands the somewhat weary-looking crew on a mission

Not as strong as *Wrath of Khan, The Search for Spock* still was a crowd pleaser for many "Star Trek" fans.

to the Genesis Planet, whose environment has been given a jump-start by a mysterious scientific device. Kirk is determined to find out whether Mr. Spock has somehow survived his death in *The Wrath of Khan*. As usual, there are plenty of Klingons to provide danger. Definitely slower than *Khan* (from which it seems to be simply tying up loose ends), but still fun for fans. Christopher Lloyd is wonderful as a Klingon commander.

STAR TREK IV: THE VOYAGE HOME

1986 (PG) 119m / **D:** Leonard Nimoy / **W:** Steve Meerson, Peter Krikes, Nicholas Meyer, Harve Bennett / **C:** William Shatner, DeForest Kelley, Catherine Hicks, James Doohan, Nichelle Nichols, George Takei, Walter Koenig, Mark Lenard, Leonard Nimoy

The *Star Trek* film with the broadest non-fan appeal is also, not surprisingly, the cast's most determinedly comedic outing since the "Trouble with Tribbles" episode. This time, the crew of the *Bounty* (remember, the *Enterprise* was destroyed in *The Search for Spock*) time travels back to 1980s San Francisco to retrieve two humpback whales and bring them back to the 23rd Century to save the Earth from a space probe unwittingly wreaking havoc while trying to communicate with the extinct species (it's complicated). Director Leonard Nimoy proves to be a dab hand at comedy, particularly his character's own deadpan delivery and fish-out-of-water status in contemporary America. Its Earth-bound nature will disappoint more serious sci-fi fans. Four Oscar nominations: cinematography, music, sound, sound editing.

STAR TREK V: THE FINAL FRONTIER

1989 (PG) 107m / **D:** William Shatner / **W:** David Loughery / **C:** William Shatner, Leonard Nimoy, DeForest Kelley, James Doohan, Laurence Luckinbill, Walter Koenig, George Takei, Nichelle Nichols, David Warner

A renegade Vulcan kidnaps the *Enterprise* and takes it on a journey to the mythic center of the universe. William Shatner's big-action directorial debut (he also co-wrote the original story) is a poor follow-up to the Nimoy-directed fourth *Trek* film. The series was getting pretty tired by this time anyway, but this heavy-handed and pretentiously pseudo-theological entry certainly didn't help matters any. Long-time fans, though, will delight in yet another example of Shatner's obsessive bravado.

STAR TREK VI: THE UNDISCOVERED COUNTRY

1991 (PG) 110m / **D:** Nicholas Meyer / **W:** Nicholas Meyer, Denny Martin Flinn / **C:** William Shatner, Leonard Nimoy, DeForest Kelley, James Doohan, George Takei, Walter Koenig, Nichelle Nichols, Christopher Plummer, Kim Cattrall, Iman, David Warner, Mark Lenard, Grace Lee Whitney, Brock Peters, Kurtwood Smith

The original crew of the *Enterprise* exits in grand style in the sixth *Star Trek* film. Mirroring the fall of the iron curtain, a disaster in the Klingon Empire leads to negotiation of a peace treaty between the Klingons and the Federation. At the request of Spock, and over Kirk's reservations, the intrepid crew of the *Enterprise* is sent to escort the Klingon Chancellor to the talks. When the Klingon ship is attacked, Kirk and his crew are accused of the crime. The search for the real perpetrators leads the *Enterprise* on another galaxy-saving adventure. A great cast accompanies the regulars, particularly Christopher Plummer as a Klingon general fond of throwing around out-of-context Shakespeare quotes (apparently you can't *really* appreciate the Bard until you've heard him in the original Klingon). Terrific f/x, typical Trekkie humor, and action-packed direction from *Khan*'s Nicholas Meyer make this a fitting conclusion to the original-cast films. Look for cameos from Christian Slater and Michael Dorn (Worf of *Star Trek: The Next Generation*). Two Oscar nominations.

STAR TREK: FIRST CONTACT

1996 (PG-13) 111m / **D:** Jonathan Frakes / **W:** Brannon Braga, Ronald D. Moore / **C:** Patrick Stewart, Jonathan Frakes, Brent Spiner, LeVar Burton, Michael Dorn, Gates McFadden, Marina Sirtis, Alfre Woodard, James Cromwell, Alice Krige

The second of four films in the *Next Generation* series is an amiable effort from director Jonathan Frakes, who also stars as Picard's broad-shouldered number two, Riker. The *Enterprise* gets stuck in some kind of time-distortion field and discovers that Earth has been taken over by the series' popular villains the Borg—a race of part-machine creatures all plugged into the same consciousness who obsessively fight to "assimilate" every race they come across into their collective. So to stop the Borg, the crew follows a wormhole back to 2063, just before humans discovered warp speed and made first contact with the Vulcans. Heavy on Borg-Federation combat, further complicated by Picard's memories of having been partially assimilated years before. James Cromwell brings some pep as the daffy inventor of the warp drive and Alice Krige stands out as the creepy/seductive Borg queen. Worf gets to deliver either the best or worst line of the entire *Star Trek* franchise: "Assimilate *this*!" Oscar nomination for makeup.

STAR TREK: GENERATIONS

1994 (PG) 117m / **D:** David Carson / **W:** Ronald D. Moore, Brannon Braga / **C:** William Shatner, Patrick Stewart, Malcolm McDowell, Whoopi Goldberg, Jonathan Frakes, Brent Spiner, LeVar Burton, Michael Dorn, Gates McFadden, Marina Sirtis, James Doohan, Walter Koenig, Alan Ruck

A rousingly good space adventure, the seventh *Star Trek* film bridges the gap between the *Next Generations* cast and the earlier series in the ob-

"Great f/x and a heroic ending for Captain Kirk are mixed with the traditional *Star Trek* morality lesson."

Star Trek: Generations

vious way: Captain James Tiberius Kirk. Following an explosion aboard the newly christened *Enterprise B*, Kirk is trapped in a space anomaly known as the Nexus; everyone who enters thinks they're in a Nirvana, forever reliving their happiest moments. Years later, Kirk is rescued by his successor and current captain of the *Enterprise*, Jean-Luc Picard (Patrick Stewart). The captains join forces to save the galaxy from the evil Dr. Soren (played with villainous glee by Malcolm McDowell), who longs to return to the Nexus at all costs, even if it means destroying a solar system. Meanwhile, the *Enterprise* battles renegade Klingons who have joined Soren's quest. Android Data (Brent Spiner) provides comic relief after he receives an emotion chip. Great f/x and a heroic ending for Captain Kirk are mixed with the traditional *Star Trek* morality lesson.

STAR TREK: INSURRECTION

1998 (PG) 103m / **D:** Jonathan Frakes / **W:** Michael Piller / **C:** Patrick Stewart, Jonathan Frakes, Brent Spiner, LeVar Burton, Michael Dorn, Gates McFadden, Marina Sirtis, F. Murray Abraham, Donna Murphy

What becomes more clear in the third *Next Generation* film is that while the original *Star Trek* cast might not have had the acting chops to really deliver on the small screen, this generally more dramatically astute cast can't play up enough to the big, hammy moments that Jonathan Frakes's TV-ish direction would demand. The crisis this time is a conspiracy between a Starfleet admiral and a dying race called the Son'a to forcibly eject the few hundred members of the placidly hippieish Ba'ku race from a planet whose radiation fields appear to provide eternal youth. The needs of the many, after all. Picard disagrees, particularly after falling in love with one of the Ba'ku (Donna Murphy). Considering the advances in technology seen elsewhere in big-budget films, by this point the generic settings and plasticky f/x were showing their age, as was the indifferent scripting.

STAR TREK INTO DARKNESS

2013 (PG-13) 132m / **D:** J. J. Abrams / **W:** Roberto Orci, Alex Kurtzman, Damon Lindelof / **C:** Chris Pine, Zachary Quinto, Zoe Saldana, Karl Urban, Simon Pegg, John Cho, Anton Yelchin, Benedict Cumberbatch, Bruce Greenwood, Peter Weller, Alice Eve

The in-jokes land with a steady thud in J. J. Abrams's second *Trek* adventure, which finds Kirk still breakin' rules and sleepin' with alien chicks (two at a time!) and Bones experimenting on a sick Tribble. It's bang-bang action most of the way, as Kirk and Company do battle with an unfrozen superhuman (Benedict Cumberbatch, playing a certain beloved nemesis of Kirk's from the 1980s) who wishes death and destruction on all of humanity … or at least the *Enterprise*. With a brief appearance by some Klingons, more of a token effort is put into exploring the non-human races than in Abrams's previous film. But this remains a primarily Earth-centric and mainstream film, with little of the deep-space adventuring that more dedicated *Trek* fans will be wanting. F/x are effortlessly dazzling and the action is sleekly handled. But while the crackling humor of the intra-crew camaraderie again gives the picture a lot of juice, that can't totally compensate for stale villainy and rehashed storylines from earlier films. Oscar nomination for f/x.

STAR TREK: THE MOTION PICTURE

1980 (G) 143m / **D:** Robert Wise / **W:** Alan Dean Foster, Harold Livingston / **C:** William Shatner, Leonard Nimoy, DeForest Kelley, James Doohan, Stephen Collins, Persis Khambatta, Nichelle Nichols, Walter Koenig, George Takei

The first of the original show's many film adaptations is a ponderous and slow-moving thing that reflects the many years of second-guessing and start-stop production problems. The old crew of the *Enterprise* reassembles under the command of now-Admiral James Tiberius Kirk (William Shatner) to search out and fight a strange alien vessel speeding towards them. Director Robert Wise gives it his all, and the f/x from a star team that included John Dykstra (*Star Wars*) and Douglas Trumbull (*Blade Runner*) are top-shelf in their glittery and wondrous appeal. But this is ultimately something of a disappointing effort that gets crushed under the weight of competing interests (honor the original series or bring in new audiences). Twelve additional minutes was later added for home video. Three Oscar nominations: art direction, f/x, music.

STAR TREK: NEMESIS

2002 (PG-13) 116m / **D:** Stuart Baird / **W:** John Logan / **C:** Patrick Stewart, Jonathan Frakes, Brent Spiner, LeVar Burton, Michael Dorn, Gates McFadden, Marina Sirtis, Tom Hardy, Ron Perlman

The fourth and final *Next Generation* film tries to bring some juice back to the series but it's too little, too late. John Logan's script has a rogue Romulan (technically a Reman, but it's all very complicated) leader (a very young-looking Tom Hardy) agitating for war against the Federation. The story is heavy with space battles and mythological allusions, layered with more realistic and dramatic f/x, but the overall sensation is that of a franchise that had outrun its last interesting storylines.

STAR WARS: THE CLONE WARS

2008 (PG) 98m / **D:** Dave Filoni / **W:** Henry Gilroy, Steven Melching, Scott Murphy

A feature-length version of the second *Star Wars* cash-cow animated series set in the chaotic battles that marked the end of the Republic and the ascendency of the Empire. (Between the action in *Episodes II* and *III*, for those keeping track.) In order to keep a fragile peace, Anakin Skywalker has to rescue Jabba the Hutt's kidnapped child. It all gets tiresome pretty quick, with endless zap-zapping battles between droid and clone troopers, with the Jedis zipping in and out of the action at will. Lacking both the angular grace of Genndy Tartakovsky's first *Clone Wars* microseries and the epic grandeur of the feature films.

STAR WARS: EPISODE I—THE PHANTOM MENACE

1999 (PG) 136m / **D:** George Lucas / **W:** George Lucas / **C:** Ewan McGregor, Liam Neeson, Natalie Portman, Jake Lloyd, Ian McDiarmid, Terence Stamp, Ray Park

George Lucas's original vision was a landmark event in sci-fi movie history. The second "Star Wars" trilogy was less inspiring.

When George Lucas came back to his landmark series for this powerfully disappointing prequel trilogy, he forgot one big thing: the importance of collaborators. The lack of any strong creative voices besides Lucas's becomes apparent not long after this dramatically sludgy story opens. It's set decades prior to *Episode IV*, before the Republic has fallen. Two Jedis—young Obi-Wan Kenobi (Ewan McGregor) and his superior, Qui-Gon Jinn (Liam Neeson)—are trying to negotiate peace as the sleazy Trade Federation's drone army threatens to assault the peaceful planet of Naboo. They fail and war begins, setting in motion the complex web of plots that will bring about the rise of the Empire. The rest of the film follows the Jedis' fight to save the Naboo's Queen Amidala (Natalie Portman) and a young Anakin Skywalker from devil-faced assassin Darth Maul (Ray Park). The all-CGI backgrounds are frequently gorgeous but the humans move stiffly through them, mouthing some of the clunkiest dialogue heard outside of a 1950s B-movie. The lack of any human chemistry showed just how important characters like Han Solo were to the original trilogy's success. Heavy criticism was leveled at Lucas not just for the existence of the painfully "comic" and widely loathed sidekick Jar Jar Binks (though Lucas did wryly point out to the series' adult fans that these are meant to be *children's* movies) but also for his Steppin' Fetchit-like locutions, not to mention the Trade Federation characters who come off like cartoonish Japanese villains from a World War II propaganda film. Maybe if Lucas had brought on collaborators to direct and write, somebody could have pointed that out to him. Three Oscar nominations.

STAR WARS: EPISODE II—ATTACK OF THE CLONES

2002 (PG) 142m / D: George Lucas / **W:** Jonathan Hales, George Lucas / **C:** Ewan Mc-Gregor, Natalie Portman, Hayden Christensen, Christopher Lee, Samuel L. Jackson, Ian Mc-Diarmid, Temuera Morrison, Daniel Logan, Jimmy Smits

The middle point in George Lucas's second trilogy still has its flaws, but being the fulcrum of this universe's entropic decay from sclerotic Republic to the fascistic Empire delivers by far the most dramatically engaging prequel film. Danger lurks around every corner this time, as an older and wildly immature Anakin Skywalker (the perpetually pained Hayden Christensen) starts his Jedi training under a perpetually annoyed Obi-Wan Kenobi. Anakin's also pursuing a highly unromantic romance with Amidala, now a member of a Senate that is so highly dysfunctional that a less democratic government might be needed. Lucas has a decent enough historical understanding to show the tragedy of such slides towards authoritarianism; too bad he still shows an inability to understand how people actually talk. The sense of looming danger is palpable and the increasing tempo of action makes this one move a bit speedier than *Episode I*. But what's still lacking is the first trilogy's pulp giddiness. One exception is the lightsaber duel between a spry, leaping Yoda and looming Count Dooku (Christopher Lee), which has the true showman's disregard for common sense. Oscar nomination for f/x.

STAR WARS: EPISODE III—REVENGE OF THE SITH

2005 (PG-13) 140m / D: George Lucas / **W:** George Lucas / **C:** Hayden Christensen, Natalie Portman, Ewan McGregor, Christopher Lee, Samuel L. Jackson, Ian McDiarmid, Jimmy Smits, Temuera Morrison

The prequel cycle comes to an overdone conclusion in this faux-operatic tying-up of loose ends. The Jedis and their clone army wage war on the Separatists who want to overthrow the Republic. Meanwhile, Anakin (now married to Amidala) continues his slide toward the dark side, as shown by the increasingly dark circles around his eyes. Efforts to contain Senator/Emperor Palpatine's treacherous powergrab come just too late to do any good and the forces mobilized to purportedly save the Republic now prove to be the tools used to complete its downfall. The final lightsaber battle between Obi-Won and Anakin through a mining facility surrounded by volcanoes and lava is both too little and far too much, like the prequels as a whole. Exhausting, and not in a good way. Oscar nomination for makeup.

STAR WARS: EPISODE IV—A NEW HOPE

1977 (PG) 121m / **D:** George Lucas / **W:** George Lucas / **C:** Mark Hamill, Carrie Fisher, Harrison Ford, Alec Guinness, Peter Cushing, Kenny Baker, Peter Mayhew, David Prowse, Anthony Daniels

The film that changed everything. George Lucas's exuberant space opera opened in the summer of 1977, at a time when Hollywood was going through one of its occasional identity crises. This rousing adventure provocatively set "a long time ago in a galaxy far, far away ..." follows a farm boy on a desert planet who joins an intergalactic rebellion against an evil Empire. Lightsaber duels, swings across deep chasms, smartass quips, last-minute escapes, and scads of evil henchmen give it all the feel of an old movie serial compressed into a breathless two hours. The characters—a young hero, a captured princess, a hot-shot pilot, cute robots, a vile villain, and a heroic and mysterious Jedi knight—are more archetypes than individuals but that's intentional on Lucas's part; he acknowledged a heavy debt to Joseph Campbell's writings on myth and storytelling. Lucas's other influences (John Ford, Akira Kurosawa, David Lean) are all quite obvious, but in a good way. One of the most popular films ever made. Followed by two sequels, three prequels, animated series, and billions of dollars' worth of merchandise that made Lucas, the one-time insurgent filmmaker, a multibillionaire (though notably not his actors, who signed over licensing rights). Ten Oscar nominations, won six, plus special award for sound effects. AKA: *Star Wars*; once the prequel trilogy was produced, Lucas renamed all films in chronological order.

STAR WARS: EPISODE V—THE EMPIRE STRIKES BACK

1980 (PG) 124m / **D:** Irvin Kershner / **W:** Leigh Brackett, Lawrence Kasdan / **C:** Mark Hamill, Carrie Fisher, Harrison Ford, Billy Dee Williams, Alec Guinness, David Prowse, Kenny Baker, Frank Oz, Anthony Daniels, Peter Mayhew, Clive Revill, Julian Glover

In the second and most dramatically satisfying film of George Lucas's first *Star Wars* trilogy, the characters become more firmly set. Luke continues his Jedi training—now with the Zen master figure of Yoda showing him the way; Han and Leia begin to sort things out; Lando Calrissian enters the story as a reminder of Han's smuggler roots; Darth Vader becomes an even darker and more complex figure. The stop-motion and creature f/x are terrific (particularly in the slam-bang opening battle on the ice planet of Hoth), but the real key is the never-a-dull-moment script from veterans Leigh Brackett (her last work) and Lawrence Kasdan that actually manages a few moments of

Han Solo and Chewbacca rescue Princess Leia and her droid friends from the ice planet Hoth in the second installment of the "Star Wars" saga, *The Empire Strikes Back.*

humor. In handing off the directing duties to TV pro Irvin Kershner, Lucas ensures a steady pace and dramatic build that doesn't get bogged down in the mythology as much as the second trilogy, when Lucas returned to the director's chair. Despite the fact that the film is a second act, it stands on its own and has a terrific twist at the end kept so secret even the cast didn't know about it until the movie premiered. Lucas's changes to this film in his later reissues are mostly minor tweaks to the sound and design. Three Oscar nominations; won for best sound and also a special achievement award for f/x. AKA: *The Empire Strikes Back.*

STAR WARS: EPISODE VI—RETURN OF THE JEDI

1983 (PG) 132m / D: Richard Marquand / **W:** George Lucas, Lawrence Kasdan / **C:** Mark Hamill, Carrie Fisher, Harrison Ford, Billy Dee Williams, David Prowse, James Earl Jones, Alec Guinness, Kenny Baker, Denis Lawson, Anthony Daniels, Peter Mayhew, Ian McDiarmid

The third volume in George Lucas's first trilogy does everything right. Two memorable villains—Jabba the Hut and the Emperor—are introduced, and the almost-too-cute Ewoks (like roly-poly miniature Wookies crossed with koala bears) join our heroes as they fight against the forces of the Empire on three fronts. Brighter and cheerier throughout than the previous two films. One surprisingly meaningful scene has translator android C-3PO telling a crowd of rapt Ewoks gathered around a campfire the story up until then in their own language; it's a beautiful evocation of the power of mythology. The stunning effects somehow manage to outdo the first two, with the whole story wrapping up neatly but perhaps a little too much so. The appearance of a second, larger Death Star shows that Lucas's story well may have been running dry at this point. Small improvements on sound design and digital effects added here and there in Lucas's rereleases. Four Oscar nominations, won special achievement award for f/x. AKA: *Return of the Jedi*.

STEALTH

2005 (PG-13) 121m / **D:** Rob Cohen / **W:** W. D. Richter / **C:** Josh Lucas, Jessica Biel, Jamie Foxx, Sam Shepard, Richard Roxburgh, Joe Morton

Steampunk and anime fans will at least appreciate Katsuhiro Otomo's gorgeous but repetitive *Steamboy.*

A poor man's sci-fi *Top Gun* that pits man and machine vs. just machine. A trio of hotshot Navy test pilots (Jamie Foxx, Jessica Biel, Josh Lucas) are given cool new experimental jets called Talons to test out. They're also provided with a fourth wingman: an unpiloted drone-like device called Extreme Deep Invader (EDI), which they resent as being a potential replacement for human pilots. When EDI goes medium compu-rogue (less destructive than Skynet but more belligerent than HAL 9000), the three have to chase it down and blow up many things. Big in budget, poor in imagination. Hard to believe that *Buckaroo Banzai*'s W. D. Richter wrote what passes for a screenplay.

STEAMBOY

2004 (PG-13) 126m / **D:** Katsuhiro Otomo / **W:** Sadayuki Murai, Katsuhiro Otomo

Superbly drawn steampunk anime eschews the standard near-future template of crime-ridden megalopolises and street-fighting mecha, preferring a setting of Industrial Age England, 1866. James Steam, a spunky young boy inventor, gets a mysterious package from his grandfather, working with his father in America. Inside the package is an invention that will revolutionize steam power, vaulting Western civilization decades into the future in one leap. The three generations of tinkerers are then wrapped up in a struggle between a rapacious corporation that wants to use this new power to develop profitable new lines of weaponry, and the British Crown, which wants the technology for itself. A good hour of initial exposition and the occasional chase scene is draggy In the extreme. The second half is an extended battle scene, inventively set on the grounds of the Crystal Palace, featuring steam-powered armored soldiers, tanks, submarines, and a flying vessel the size of a small mountain. Still, a good forty minutes could have been cut without losing a beat. As in Otomo's earlier *Akira*, the setting and destruction are all impeccably detailed; conflicts and characters aren't developed, they are simply established and repeated ad nauseam.

STEEL DAWN

1987 (R) 90m / **D:** Lance Hool / **W:** Doug Lefler / **C:** Patrick Swayze, Lisa Niemi, Christopher Neame, Brett Hool, Brion James, Anthony Zerbe

Another monosyllabic post-apocalypse samurai western; *Shane* with a *Mad Max* makeover. After war has turned the world into a desert (and evidently melted all the guns; everyone wields bladed weapons), leather-clad swordsman Patrick Swayze defends a frontier widow (his real-life wife Lisa Niemi) in a dispute over water and territory. Far from the worst of its overpopulated breed, but it loses points for the hero's ludicrous method of warrior meditation—he stands on his head (an unfortunate premonition of Swayze's bouncer-philosopher from *Road House*). Title was rumored to be an in-joke jab at Columbia Pictures president Dawn Steel.

THE STEPFORD WIVES (1975)

1975 (PG) 115m / **D:** Bryan Forbes **W:** William Goldman / **C:** Katharine Ross, Paula Prentiss, Nanette Newman, Tina Louise

Another Ira Levin (*Rosemary's Baby*) novel about women who start digging under society's seemingly placid surface and find a sinister cult controlling not the entire world but just *everybody around them*. Katharine Ross moves with her husband into the suburb of Stepford. Everybody seems happy, but in a creepy, too-wide smile way. The women busy themselves with chores and consumerism and making themselves look perfect for their contentedly sexist men. Ross and her husband think something is up at the town's spooky old castle of a men's club. Heavy on the gothic atmosphere, with a sci-fi reveal.

THE STEPFORD WIVES (2004)

2004 (PG-13) 97m / **D:** Frank Oz / **W:** Paul Rudnick / **C:** Nicole Kidman, Matthew Broderick, Bette Midler, Roger Bart, Christopher Walken

Frank Oz's cupcake-colored design and Paul Rudnick's quip-heavy screenplay dumps the original's 1970s paranoia for bright and sassy sheen. In this outing, Nicole Kidman plays a maniacally driven TV executive who gets fired and decamps with her family from Manhattan to Stepford, Connecticut, where all the lawns are gorgeous and the pastel-loving housewives act like some suspiciously perfect male fantasy of Playboy Bunny and Martha Stewart. Barely bothers aiming for any kind of real satire and the sci-fi secret is laughably chintzy. Breezy, at least, with decent comic support from Christopher Walken as a sinister figure (what else?) and *The Producers'* Roger Bart as Kidman's flamboyantly gay sidekick.

> "Heavy on the gothic atmosphere, with a sci-fi reveal."
>
> *The Stepford Wives (1975)*

STRANGE DAYS

1995 (R) 145m / **D:** Kathryn Bigelow / **W:** James Cameron, Jay Cocks / **C:** Ralph Fiennes, Angela Bassett, Juliette Lewis, Tom Sizemore, Michael Wincott, Vincent D'Onofrio

Earnestly edgy pre-millennial cyberpunk freakout from a between-things Kathryn Bigelow, who tries to marry her subtext-laden style with the more straightforward action stylings of her one-time husband James Cameron (who co-wrote and produced). Ralph Fiennes plays a stylishly skeevy ex-cop in 1999 Los Angeles who does a brisk business in digital memory recordings that customers can jack right into and experience as though they were their own. It's a decadently illicit business that nobody cares much about until Fiennes gets his hands on a memory that the city fathers want erased. Meanwhile, the clock is ticking towards the end of the century and the city's about to explode in a Rodney King-esque cataclysm of racially charged violence. At the time, Fiennes's liaison with security sidekick Angela Bassett was notable not just for being a rare Hollywood interracial relationship but for how Bigelow upended gender roles (Fiennes is something close to a coward, while Bassett is a bonafide warrior in the true Cameron mold). Not lacking for ambition, Bigelow and Cameron try to wrap up too much into this intriguing but overlong tech noir.

STRANGE INVADERS

1983 (PG) 94m / **D:** Michael Laughlin / **W:** Michael Laughlin, Bill Condon / **C:** Paul Le Mat, Nancy Allen, Diana Scarwid, Michael Lerner, Louise Fletcher, Wallace Shawn, Fiona Lewis, Kenneth Tobey, June Lockhart, Charles Lane, Dey Young, Mark Goddard

Rare attempt to recreate the attitude of 1950s alien flicks gets the deadpan tone just right, without tipping into camp. Apparently, grotesque space beings conquered the Midwest town of Centerville in the '50s and body-snatched the locals' appearance and attire. Twenty-five years later, Paul Le Mat's search for his disappeared ex-wife, a Centerville native, begins to unravel the conspiracy. Some details—notably the gimmick that supermarket tabloid tall tales about flying saucers turn out to be TRUE!—aren't so fresh anymore, but the f/x are still effective—except perhaps the spaceship interior that looks like a boiler room. Co-writer Bill Condon would later make *Gods and Monsters*, about *Frankenstein* director James Whale.

STRANGERS IN PARADISE

1986 (NR) 81m / D: Ulli Lommel / **W:** Ulli Lommel / **C:** Ulli Lommel, Ken Letner, Thom Jones

A scientist who had cryogenically frozen himself to escape the Nazis is thawed out in the present, and his powers are used by sociopathic uber-suburbanite parents determined to reprogram all of their delinquent, punk-rocker, gay offspring. Did we mention that it's a *musical*?

SUMMER WARS

2009 (PG) 114m / D: Mamoru Hosada / **W:** Satoko Okudera

Mamoru Hosada's sparkly anime posits a near-future world where all of civilization plugs into the same virtual-reality environment; named Oz, of course. To no viewers' surprise, Oz turns out to be a less-than-ideal place after a programmer accidentally releases a virus that threatens to destroy all of Oz and, by extension, the real world. The endgame scenario is just backdrop for Hosada's real tale, wherein the shy programmer suddenly notices a cute girl noticing him. Its genius is that it makes you believe the YA romantic subplot is more important than the virtual apocalypse threatening them all.

SUN RA & HIS INTERGALACTIC SOLAR ARKESTRA: SPACE IS THE PLACE

1974 (R) 63m / D: John Coney / **W:** Joshua Smith / **C:** Sun Ra, Barbara Deloney, Raymond Johnson

Long-unseen indie production showcasing the cosmology of jazz-improv innovator and self-styled space-age prophet Sun Ra, mythologized as a shaman who descends in a starship that looks like a pair of blazing eyeballs. Accompanied by an entourage of Egyptian gods, Sun Ra puts on a few concerts and informs Oakland's skeptical black youth that he can save them from oppression and self-destruction via relocation to a paradise planet. Uptight FBI types watch nervously, certain it's some scheme to launch an African space agency. Strange, surreal, politically simplistic, and more than a little self-indulgent, it's not for all tastes but certainly a trip. AKA: *Space Is the Place*.

SUNSHINE

2007 (R) 107m / **D:** Danny Boyle / **W:** Alex Garland / **C:** Cillian Murphy, Rose Byrne, Chris Evans, Michelle Yeoh, Troy Garity, Hiroyuki Sanada, Mark Strong

Decades hence, the Sun starts to cool down, and Earth is freezing into a dead ball of ice. In this thoughtful final-mission film, the massive *Icarus II* is rocketing towards the Sun with a Manhattan-sized payload and one mission: deliver bomb and kickstart the Sun's core without burning up the entire crew in the process. Problems? Whatever happened to *Icarus I*, for starters. Also, a malfunction that leaves the ship with vastly depleted oxygen doesn't help, or the hints of sabotage. Great ensemble work from a crew blessedly short of the usual clichés and some ravishing imagery of solar fires against the inky black of space. But director Danny Boyle and writer Alex Garland's second sci-fi collaboration after *28 Days Later ...* lazily devolves into little more than another killer-on-the-loose-in-space story.

SUPER 8

2011 (PG-13) 112m / **D:** J. J. Abrams / **W:** J. J. Abrams / **C:** Joel Courtney, Kyle Chandler, Elle Fanning, Riley Griffiths, Noah Emmerich, Ron Eldard

There's imitation and there's homages and then there's this big sloppy valentine from J. J. Abrams to Steve Spielberg, who perhaps not surprisingly also served as producer. Some kids trying to make a zombie movie with their Super-8 camera are almost killed by a runaway train with a top secret payload. Soon after, things start going bump in the night around town, and only the kids truly know what's going on. Then the military shows up to lock the whole place down in a manner straight out of the Area-51 coverup playbook. But while the 1970s setting, ragtag band of kid protagonists, lightly dysfunctional family issues, and carefully teased shock and awe reveal about the alien visitor would seem pure Spielberg from the *Close Encounters* era, Abrams can't maintain the mood. While the master would have crafted a conclusion both satisfyingly gooey and electrifyingly dramatic, the student can only offer up an exercise in pale, mechanical cynicism. Nice work from Elle Fanning as the incomparably cool neighborhood girl all the boys have a crush on but who only has eyes for the smart, sensitive protagonist.

SUPER FUZZ

1981 (PG) 97m / **D:** Sergio Corbucci / **W:** Sergio Corbucci / **C:** Terence Hill, Joanne Dru, Ernest Borgnine

In an homage to Steven Spielberg, four young people armed only with a camera discover the truth about a huge alien monster in *Super 8*.

Rookie policeman develops super powers after being exposed to radiation. Somewhat ineptly, he uses his abilities to combat crime. As inept as it gets. AKA: *Supersnooper*.

SUPERGIRL

1984 (PG) 114m / D: Jeannot Szwarc / **W:** David Odell / **C:** Faye Dunaway, Helen Slater, Peter O'Toole, Mia Farrow, Brenda Vaccaro, Marc McClure, Simon Ward, Peter Cook

Helen Slater made her debut in this big-budget bomb and nearly killed off her career in the process. Tells the story of a young woman with super powers—Superman's cousin or something—who's in pursuit of a magic doo-dad. Naturally evil sorceress Faye Dunaway wants it too. Dunaway makes a sharp villainess, and Peter O'Toole, as a good sorcerer, is the best thing in the film. F/x are decent, but nothing would be enough to rescue this tiresome turkey.

SUPERMAN: THE MOVIE

1978 (PG) 144m / D: Richard Donner / **W:** Leslie Newman, Mario Puzo, Robert Benton, David Newman / **C:** Christopher Reeve, Margot Kidder, Marlon Brando, Gene Hackman,

Christopher Reeve played the Man of Steel in 1978's *Superman: The Movie* and three sequels.

Glenn Ford, Susannah York, Ned Beatty, Valerie Perrine, Jackie Cooper, Marc McClure, Trevor Howard, Sarah Douglas, Terence Stamp

The DC Comics legend comes alive in this slightly overblown but still very rewarding saga that represents the first serious, mainstream, superhero film, and still one of the best. Epic script that neatly blends heroism and humanity follows Superman's life from infancy on the doomed planet Krypton to his adult career as Earth's Man of Steel. Gene Hackman and Ned Beatty pair marvelously as super criminal Lex Luthor and his bumbling sidekick. Marlon Brando is suitably imposing as Superman's Kryptonian father, and Margot Kidder makes a fine Lois Lane, while Christopher Reeve's humble, self-deprecating do-gooder is next to perfect. Award-winning f/x, a just-campy-enough script, and an instant-classic of a John Williams score help make sure that this film hits on all cylinders. Followed by three progressively less interesting sequels. Three Oscar nominations: sound, editing, music.

SUPERMAN II

1980 (PG) 127m / D: Richard Lester / **W:** Leslie Newman, Mario Puzo, David Newman / **C:** Christopher Reeve, Margot Kidder, Gene Hackman, Ned Beatty, Jackie Cooper, Sarah Douglas, Jack O'Halloran, Susannah York, Marc McClure, Terence Stamp, Valerie Perrine, E. G. Marshall

Cracking good sequel that ups the ante from a highly impressive first effort. This time, Superman has his hands full with three villains from his home planet Krypton (Terence Stamp standing out as the creepy General Zod), whose imprisonment ironically allowed them to escape its destruction. Inconveniently enough, they now have powers to match Superman's own. The romance between reporter Lois Lane and our superhero is made a tad more believable and the storyline is in many ways livelier than the original film. Now that the breathtaking responsibility of creating Superman's origin story was discharged, the actors could get down to telling an exciting story.

SUPERMAN III

1983 (PG) 123m / D: Richard Lester / **W:** Leslie Newman, David Newman / **C:** Christopher Reeve, Richard Pryor, Annette O'Toole, Jackie Cooper, Margot Kidder, Marc McClure, Annie Ross, Robert Vaughn, Pamela Stephenson

The *Superman* series started going seriously awry with this second sequel, which showed a franchise somehow already running out of decent ideas even with decades' worth of comics to pull from. Villainous businessman Robert Vaughn tries to defeat Superman via the expertise of bumbling computer expert Richard Pryor and the judicious use of artificial Kryptonite. The Man in the Cape explores his darker side after undergoing transformation into a sleaze-ball. Director Richard Lester tried to take this one in a different direction, utilizing satire and direct, physical comedy in place of the previous films' gentler humor. Unfortunately, that's not really what the Superman myth is about, and although Pryor does his best, this just can't measure up. The downplaying of the Superman/Lois Lane romance didn't help, either.

SUPERMAN IV: THE QUEST FOR PEACE

1987 (PG) 90m / D: Sidney J. Furie / **W:** Mark Rosenthal / **C:** Christopher Reeve, Gene Hackman, Jon Cryer, Marc McClure, Margot Kidder, Mariel Hemingway, Sam Wanamaker, Jackie Cooper

The third and quite unnecessary sequel, where the Man of Steel endeavors to rid the world of nuclear weapons. In the process, he again runs afoul of Lex Luthor, who is, of course, very interested in nuclear energy. So interested, in fact, that he uses it to create Nuclear Man, a sort of atomic anti-Superman who's cloned in record time from a few of the superhero's stray cells. F/x are dime-store quality and it appears that someone may have walked off with parts of the plot. Still, Christopher Reeve deserves credit for remaining true to character through four films of very uneven quality.

SUPERMAN RETURNS

2006 (PG-13) 154m / D: Bryan Singer / **W:** Michael Dougherty, Dan Harris / **C:** Brandon Routh, Kate Bosworth, Kevin Spacey, James Marsden, Parker Posey, Frank Langella, Sam Huntington, Eva Marie Saint, Kal Penn

After years of delays, frightening Nicolas Cage rumors, and bad memories of the one that co-starred Richard Pryor, it feels safe to say that Bryan Singer approached the first *Superman* film in almost two decades with an overabundance of reverence. As an attempted relaunch for the franchise, it has the appropriate sense of gravitas and nobility, not to mention a touchingly Boy Scout-ish Clark Kent/Superman in Brandon Routh. But the story that follows Superman's return to Earth after a bad trip back to Krypton never quite gels. While casting Kevin Spacey as Lex Luthor makes a ridiculous amount of sense, his plot to create a new continent embedded with Kryptonite just doesn't have the kind of evil pizzazz one has come to expect from the cackling bald villain. Oscar nomination for f/x.

SUPER MARIO BROS.

1993 (PG) 104m / **D:** Rocky Morton, Annabel Jankel / **W:** Edward Solomon, Parker Bennett, Terry Runte / **C:** Bob Hoskins, John Leguizamo, Samantha Mathis, Dennis Hopper, Fisher Stevens, Richard Edson, Dana Kaminski, Fiona Shaw, Lance Henriksen

Chaotic, mega-budgeted adventure fantasy perceived as something of a disaster at the time, but it seemed to point the way (for better or, likely, much worse) toward the junky, anything-goes blockbusters that would follow. Mario (Bob Hoskins) and Luigi (John Leguizamo) have to save Daisy (Samantha Mathis)—a paleontology student who's been abducted to an alternate Manhattan whose inhabitants are descended from dinosaurs—from the evil King Koopa (Dennis Hopper, basically doing a reptilian version of his Frank Booth from *Blue Velvet*). Alt-country bandleader Mojo Nixon has a cameo as a street musician named Toad. Second and last feature film from the creators of early cyberpunk series *Max Headroom*.

SUPERNOVA

2000 (R) 90m / **D:** Walter Hill / **W:** David Campbell Wilson / **C:** James Spader, Angela Bassett, Robert Forster, Lou Diamond Phillips, Peter Facinelli, Robin Tunney, Wilson Cruz

One of the more infamously tortured development-hell films of its time ended up being not much more than another creeper where things go horrendously wrong on an isolated spaceship. William Malone's original story was along the lines of *Hellraiser* in space. What's there now is not much different, with a medical ship rescuing a mysterious stranger who brings on board a dangerous artifact. A superb cast does their best with B-grade material and f/x that seem to be straining for something more than an outer-space horrorfest. It's all something of a muddle, not surprising after last-minute script-doctoring, spiraling budgets, and production turmoil. First director Geoffrey Wright (*Romper Stomper*) quit and then Walter Hill came on board, only to leave himself after an early cut tested poorly (he shows up in the credits as Walter Thomas). Expensively re-edited at the last minute by studio board member Francis Ford Coppola, who should have known better. None of this tortuous interference made any appreciable difference.

SURROGATES

2009 (PG-13) 89m / **D:** Jonathan Mostow / **W:** Michael Ferris, John Brancato / **C:** Bruce Willis, Radha Mitchell, Rosamund Pike, Boris Kodjoe, James Cromwell, Ving Rhames

What's to risk in a nearly crime-free future where everybody stays safely at home in virtual reality sets, experiencing their lives via android "surrogates" out in the world? Nothing, and that's the attraction. At least, until a man shows up with a weapon that not only fries surrogates' circuitry but also kills their stay-at-home "operators." Surrogate-suspicious FBI agent Bruce Willis digs into the case, alternating running down leads with trying to get his scared wife (Rosamund Pike) out of her surrogate and back into life. Rote crime story takes back seat to the film's playful take on a world where fantasy has overtaken reality: everyone's surrogates either look like idealized versions of themselves (younger, sleeker, sexier) or somebody else entirely. James Cromwell plays essentially the same conflicted inventor role he had in the similarly themed but inferior *I, Robot*.

SURVIVOR

1987 (NR) 92m / **D:** Michael Shackleton / **W:** Bima Stagg / **C:** Chip Mayer, Richard Moll, Sue Kiel

Alone astronaut returns to Earth to find it a sterile, post-nuclear holocaust wasteland where he must battle the usual megalomaniac ruler. Richard Moll as the philosophy-spouting villain is watchable, but overall the film remains a wasteland, too, albeit an impressively photographed one. Made in South Africa.

Bruce Willis plays an FBI agent trying to track down a killer who murders people by destroying their android copies in *Surrogates*.

SWAMP THING

1982 (PG) 91m / **D:** Wes Craven / **W:** Wes Craven / **C:** Adrienne Barbeau, Louis Jourdan, Ray Wise, Dick Durock

Overlooked camp drama and ecological parable about scientist accidentally turned into tragic half-vegetable, half-man swamp creature, with government agent Adrienne Barbeau caught in the middle, *occasionally* while topless. Wes Craven adapted this from the critically acclaimed comic just two years before he hit it big with *A Nightmare on Elm Street*.

THE SWARM

1978 (PG) 116m / **D:** Irwin Allen / **W:** Stirling Silliphant / **C:** Michael Caine, Katharine Ross, Richard Widmark, Lee Grant, Richard Chamberlain, Olivia de Havilland, Henry Fonda, Fred MacMurray, Patty Duke, Ben Johnson, Jose Ferrer, Slim Pickens, Bradford Dillman, Cameron Mitchell

Back in the late 1970s, in addition to demonic possession, Legionnaire's Disease, stagflation, and punk rock, everyone was worried about a rumored species of "killer bees" flying up from Latin America to sting everyone to death. Several bee-oriented cheapies were rushed into production to allow filmgoers to vicariously live out their newfound terror of murderous insects. *The Swarm* was the most ambitious of the lot, but despite the usual (for the time) roster of A-list actors looking for work, this is strictly D-list product from *The Towering Inferno* and *The Poseidon Adventure* producer Irwin Allen. Scientist Michael Caine fends off a swarm of the much-vaunted killer bees when they attack metro Houston. The bees everybody was so scared of are really just black spots painted on the film.

TANK GIRL

1995 (R) 104m / D: Rachel Talalay / **W:** Tedi Sarafian / **C:** Lori Petty, Ice-T, Malcolm Mc-Dowell, Naomi Watts

Ah, the 1990s. For a few minutes there, studios thought they needed to follow the changes convulsing the music industry and find themselves some real out-there "alternative" product to keep everybody coming to the multiplex. Nobody wanted to miss out on the next *Easy Rider*, after all. That's about all that can explain why United Artists tossed tens of millions of dollars at this freeform adaptation of the long-running punk comic by Jamie Hewlett and Alan Martin about a tank-driving riot girl in the year 2033 after a meteor turned the Earth into one big desert. She spends most of her time zipping around the place, getting into scrapes with the tyrannical water company (headed up by Malcolm McDowell), hanging out with her genetically modified kangaroo pal/boyfriend (he talks), and blowing stuff up. Lori Petty brings all the scruffy gutter-child sass she can to this sputtering calamity, which has producer interference stamped all over it. Ice-T plays the kangaroo-man and a young Naomi Watts shows up as Tank Girl's sidekick Jet Girl.

TARANTULA

1955 (NR) 81m / D: Jack Arnold / **W:** Robert M. Fresco, Martin Berkeley / **C:** Leo G. Carroll, John Agar, Mara Corday, Nestor Paiva, Ross Elliott, Clint Eastwood

The best of the giant-bug flicks that infested movie theaters after *Them*. Scientist Leo G. Carroll's growth formula literally gets away from him when the spider on which he is experimenting accidentally gets loose. This "crawling terror 100 feet high" wreaks havoc in the Arizona desert, until the Air Force (led by pilot Clint Eastwood) saves the day.

TEENAGE CAVEMAN

1958 (NR) 66m / D: Roger Corman / **W:** R. Wright Campbell / **C:** Robert Vaughn, Darrah Marshall, Leslie Bradley, Frank de Kova, Beach Dickerson, Jonathan Haze

After *I Was a Teenage Werewolf* and *I Was a Teenage Frankenstein*, intrepid American International Pictures further mined the youth market with—what else?—*Teenage Caveman*. Early starring role for Robert Vaughn, as the rebellious teen in question who defies his elders by venturing from his clan's desolate terrain into the forbidden land beyond, where he encounters the dreaded God That Gives Death with Its Touches. If you have seen *Planet of the Apes* (or even if you haven't), you can anticipate the surprise ending. Villain Frank de Kova is more fondly remembered as Chief Wild Eagle on TV's *F-Troop*. Look for Jonathan Haze (*Little Shop of Horrors*) as one of the tribespeople. Roger Corman directed this in ten days on a $70,000 budget. He certainly got his money's worth out of Beach Dickerson, who was utilized for four roles, including that of a bear. Dinosaur footage courtesy of *One Million B.C.* AKA: *Out of the Darkness*; *Prehistoric World*.

TEENAGE MUTANT NINJA TURTLES: THE MOVIE

1990 (PG) 95m / D: Steven Barron / **W:** Todd W. Langen, Bobby Herbeck / **C:** Judith Hoag, Elias Koteas, Michael Turney, James Sato

A very close, if more attitudinal, adaptation of Kevin Eastman and Peter Laird's surprise hit self-published comic books. Straightforward and hugely successful, kid-friendly action not surprisingly leaves out the series' tongue-in-cheek satire implicit in the title. Four sewer-dwelling turtles turned into warrior ninja mutants by radiation exposure take it upon themselves to rid the city of crime and pizza. Much head-kicking and rib-crunching action as Leonardo, Donatello, Raphael, and Michelangelo fight for the rights of pre-adolescents everywhere. Being produced by Hong Kong's Golden Harvest, the martial arts action is far superior to that of most American kung-fu features. Elias Koteas, looking like a young Robert De Niro, stands out as the Turtles' ally Casey Jones. Combines real actors with Jim Henson creatures.

TEENAGE MUTANT NINJA TURTLES II: THE SECRET OF THE OOZE

1991 (PG) 88m / D: Michael Pressman / **W:** Todd W. Langen / **C:** François Chau, David Warner, Paige Turco, Ernie Reyes Jr., Vanilla Ice

A mphibious animatronic pizza-devouring mutants search for the toxic waste that turned them into marketable martial-artist ecologically correct kid idols. Same formula as the first go-round with some new characters tossed in. Feels more manufactured this time, without the original's attention to character. Appearance by Vanilla Ice further cements film's status as

Based on comic book characters, the Teenage Mutant Ninja Turtles have appeared in several movies and television cartoon series.

left-behind 1990s' relic. From the director of the worst Dan Aykroyd movie of all time: *Doctor Detroit*.

TEENAGE MUTANT NINJA TURTLES 3

1993 (PG) 95m / D: Stuart Gillard / **W:** Stuart Gillard / **C:** Elias Koteas, Paige Turco, Stuart Wilson, Sab Shimono, Vivian Wu

The turtles hit 17th-century Japan to rescue loyal friend, reporter April O'Neil (Paige Turco). Plenty of smoothly executed, blood-free martial arts moves keep the pace rolling, while the turtles battle an evil lord and English pirates. Meanwhile, old pal Casey Jones (Elias Koteas) babysits the samurais sent to New York in exchange for the Turtles, teaching them the wonders of hockey and beer. Seeing the TMNT's use more of their reptilian grey matter, and less pizza, contributes to a (relatively) higher adult tolerance level (for the series, at least). More heart and a better story than the previous two combined, with nicely choreographed battle scenes and beautiful scenery (Washington's national forest areas stand in for Japan).

TEENAGERS FROM OUTER SPACE

1959 (NR) 86m / **D:** Tom Graeff / **W:** Tom Graeff / **C:** Dave Love, Dawn Anderson, Harvey B. Dunn, Bryant Grant, Tom Lockyear

"Thrill-crazed space kids blasting the flesh off humans!" So screamed the ads for this sadly neglected contender in the Golden Turkey sweepstakes. A flying saucer unloads a rowdy pack of aliens packing disintegrating ray guns (that look suspiciously like Buck Rogers cap pistols). They unleash on the unsuspecting populace a giant Gargon (or, as we call it on this planet, a lobster). An indication of writer-producer-director Tom Graeff's limited budget is the Gargon's suspicious tendency to be seen only in shadow. Chock-full of classically Ed Wood-esque touches as an unsteady command of day for night (and vice-versa). Picked up by Warner Brothers and released with *Gigantis*. Apparently, this was the only film that Graeff inflicted on the world. AKA: *The Gargon Terror*.

TEKNOLUST

2002 (R) 85m / **D:** Lynn Hershman-Leeson / **W:** Lynn Hershman-Leeson / **C:** Tilda Swinton, Jeremy Davies, James Urbaniak, Karen Black, Josh Kornbluth

Multimedia artist Lynn Hershman-Leeson wrote and directed this vaguely cyberpunk-ish film that comes across as a rambling essay about digital-era sexuality, feminism, and the loss of identity. More directly, it's about bio-geneticist Tilda Swinton deciding to replicate herself into three essentially identical automatons. They need continual infusions of the male Y chromosome to survive, so one of them starts going out at night to harvest sperm. An unfunny folly whose idea of wit is telling the Swintons apart by putting them in different color wigs.

THE 10TH VICTIM

1965 (NR) 92m / **D:** Elio Petri / **W:** Tonino Guerra / **C:** Ursula Andress, Marcello Mastroianni, Elsa Martinelli, Salvo Randone, Massimo Serato

A dyed-blonde Marcello Mastroianni and go-go babe Ursula Andress pursue one another in a 21st-century society where legalized murderous "hunts" are used as the means of population control. Famously insane sado-masochistic cult relic where Andress kills with a double-barreled bra, the characters hang out at the hyper-cool jet-set Club Masoch, and comic books are considered literature. Based on Robert Sheckley's *The Seventh Victim*.

THE TERMINAL MAN

1974 (R) 107m / **D:** Mike Hodges / **W:** Mike Hodges / **C:** George Segal, Joan Hackett, Jill Clayburgh, Richard Dysart, James B. Sikking, Norman Burton

A slick, visually compelling adaptation of the Michael Crichton novel in which a scientist plagued by violent mental disorders has a computer-controlled regulator implanted in his brain. The computer malfunctions and he starts a murdering spree. Director of classic Brit-noir *Get Carter* delivers a well-acted vision of man-machine symbiosis gone awry, but still falls short of the novel.

THE TERMINATOR

1984 (R) 108m / D: James Cameron / **W:** James Cameron, Gale Anne Hurd / **C:** Arnold Schwarzenegger, Michael Biehn, Linda Hamilton, Paul Winfield, Lance Henriksen, Bill Paxton, Rick Rossovich, Dick Miller

After military computer system Skynet achieves sentience, it decides to start a nuclear war and get rid of the humans. Years afterward, though, pesky mankind is still fighting a guerrilla war in the ruins. To stop the problem once and for all, a T-800 "Terminator" cyborg that looks and acts like a muscular and somewhat dull-witted human (Arnold Schwarzenegger) is sent back in time to kill Linda Hamilton, the mother of the human resistance's leader. Chiseled-jaw action stalwart Michael Biehn plays the resistance fighter who sneaks back through the time portal to stop the Terminator. James Cameron's surprise hit is a lean, economical sci-fi thriller that goes heavy on the firepower but keeps the pacing tight and the time-travel paradoxes knotty. The steely color scheme, functional hardware, new wave styling, and keenly felt sense of apocalyptic dread make it a key originator of the decade's Tech Noir subgenre. Bill Paxton makes a brief appearance as a blue-haired punk who gets brutally iced by the Terminator. Followed by sequels, a TV show, and uncounted lame knock-offs.

TERMINATOR 2: JUDGMENT DAY

1991 (R) 139m / D: James Cameron / **W:** James Cameron / **C:** Arnold Schwarzenegger, Linda Hamilton, Edward Furlong, Robert Patrick, Earl Boen, Joe Morton

James Cameron's mega-budgeted sequel (reportedly the first $100 million film) nearly ruined the studio, but pretty much every dollar is up there on the screen. In keeping with the sequel logic of Hollywood (do the same thing again, only bigger), the story is similar to the first, only now there's a newer and sleeker T-1000 Terminator (Robert Patrick) looking to take out Linda Hamilton's future-resistance leader son Edward Furlong. The twist this time is that the humans have sent back an older T-800 model (Arnold Schwarzenegger) to keep Furlong safe, setting the stage for cyborg-on-cyborg action. The shapeshifting T-1000's f/x were mind-blowing at the time, and retain a malevolent beauty. Some of Cameron's backstory elements are surprisingly effective—during the interregnum, Hamilton's character went insane, as would most anybody who thought the species' survival rested on their shoulders—and the re-creation of a nuclear blast remains one of the most terrifying scenes of devastation ever filmed. Impressive follow-up, but it began Cameron's descent from clever filmmaker to blockbuster engine. Six Oscar nominations; won for sound, makeup, visual and sound effects.

TERMINATOR 3: RISE OF THE MACHINES

2003 (R) 109m / **D:** Jonathan Mostow / **W:** John Brancato, Michael Ferris / **C:** Arnold Schwarzenegger, Nick Stahl, Claire Danes, Kristanna Loken, David Andrews

The first non-James Cameron *Terminator* film is a mostly dutiful exercise that lacks the epic sensibility or visual stylistics of the first two but slightly makes up for it with a genuinely twisty paradox of an ending. Plus: there's now a Terminatrix (dead-eyed Kristanna Loken) who's traveled back in time to hunt down the steadily aging John Connor (Nick Stahl), who's trying to live off the grid in preparation for the Skynet apocalypse to come. Claire Danes plays the hapless love interest stuck with Connor as he's being chased, and Arnold shows up as yet another Terminator 101 model here from the future to protect humanity's (eventual) savior.

Arnold Schwarzennegger is a robot from the future who is sometimes programmed for good, sometimes for evil, in the "Terminator" movies.

TERMINATOR SALVATION

2009 (PG-13) 115m / **D:** McG / **W:** John Brancato, Michael Ferris / **C:** Christian Bale, Sam Worthington, Moon Bloodgood, Helena Bonham Carter, Anton Yelchin, Bryce Dallas Howard, Common, Michael Ironside

After Arnold's swan song in the third *Terminator*, the series seemed to have reached a logical finale. The full backstory behind Skynet was revealed, and everything wrapped up into a satisfyingly tight time-travel paradox. Then came the fourth film, which decided to take most of James Cameron's ideas about fate and focus on expanding the tantalizingly glimpsed battle scene at the start of *Judgment Day*. It's a pretty straight war story, with Christian Bale joining the series as humanity's savior John Connor, who's got a lot on his hands. He's busy battling the forces of Skynet across a nuke-ravaged Western America circa 2018 while simultaneously trying to save the skin of the teenaged Kyle Reese (Anton Yelchin), who will be Connor's dad in the future/past. The visual inspiration here is clearly *Children of Men*'s sooty gun-metal aesthetic, but there's not quite as much thought going into the story itself. F/x are convincingly deployed and tend to be worked into the narrative instead of standing alone as ooh and ahh showpieces. Heightened, as all things are, by a campy Helena Bonham Carter and that old genre baddie Michael Ironside.

TERROR BENEATH THE SEA

1966 (NR) 85m / **D:** Hajime Sato / **W:** Koichi Otsu / **C:** Sonny Chiba, Peggy Neal, Franz Gruber, Gunther Braun, Andrew Hughes, Mike Daneen

A mad scientist wants to rule the world with his cyborgs. American and Japanese scientists unite to fight him. Fine f/x from this Japanese production, especially the transformation from human to monster. Stars a young Sonny Chiba several years before he hit his stride with the *Street Fighter* series. AKA: *Water Cyborgs*.

TERRORNAUTS

1967 (NR) 77m / **D:** Montgomery Tully / **W:** John Brunner / **C:** Simon Oates, Zena Marshall, Charles Hawtrey, Stanley Meadows

When man begins space exploration, Earth is attacked by aliens. The defenders are taken to an outdated fortress where they learn that their forebears were similarly attacked. Juvenile, lackluster, contrived, and really dumb. No help from screenplay by groundbreaking sci-fi novelist John Brunner.

TERROR OF MECHAGODZILLA

1978 (G) 79m / **D:** Ishiro Honda / **W:** Yukiko Takayama / **C:** Katsuhiko Sasaki, Tomoko Ai

It's monster vs. machine in the heavyweight battle of the universe as a huge mechanical Godzilla built by aliens is pitted against the real thing. The last Godzilla movie made until *Godzilla 1985*. AKA: *Monsters from the Unknown Planet*; *The Escape of Megagodzilla*.

TESTAMENT

1983 (PG) 90m / **D:** Lynne Littman / **W:** John Sacret Young / **C:** Jane Alexander, William Devane, Ross Harris, Roxana Zal, Lukas Haas, Philip Anglim

Matter-of-fact drama about what happens to a family in a small California town after a nuclear war. It's a smaller-scale piece than *The Day After*, which came out the same year; there are no outright scenes of destruction and little news about the exchange itself. But as time wears on, radiation sickness starts to creep in and the skies gradually darken from nuclear winter. Produced by PBS for *American Playhouse*, it received a short theatrical run. Cameo by Rebecca De Mornay. Oscar nomination for best actress.

TETSUO: THE IRON MAN

1989 (NR) 67m / D: Shinya Tsukamoto / **W:** Shinya Tsukamoto / **C:** Tomoroh Taguchi, Kei Fujiwara, Shinya Tsukamoto

> "Highly allegorical concept has been linked to everything from extreme technophobia to a metaphor for the repression of homosexuality in Japanese society."
>
> *Tetsuo: The Iron Man*

"Your future is metal!" 16mm live-action Japanese body-horror cult item about an office worker gradually and inexplicably transformed into a walking metal collection of cables, drills, wires, and gears. The mutant creature faces off with an equally bizarre metals fetishist (played by the director) whose rituals somehow spawned him. Graphic violence and mutilation mated with near-nonstop stop-motion f/x and nightmare/folklore imagery. Tough going if you're not in the mood for this kind of extreme cyberpunk Cronenbergian body horror. Or even if you are in the mood. Highly allegorical concept has been linked to everything from extreme technophobia to a metaphor for the repression of homosexuality in Japanese society. Followed by sequels *Tetuso II: Body Hammer* (1992) and *Tetsuo: The Bullet Man* (2009), which delivered more of the same.

THEM!

1954 (NR) 93m / D: Gordon Douglas / **W:** Ted Sherdeman / **C:** James Whitmore, Edmund Gwenn, Fess Parker, James Arness, Onslow Stevens, Jack Perrin, Joan Weldon, Leonard Nimoy, Sandy Descher, Olin Howlin

Inspired by the success of *The Beast from 20,000 Fathoms*, this was the first and the best of the postwar era's giant bug movies. What hath the atomic age wrought? Radiation-enhanced behemoths terrorize New Mexico before devastating a Navy ship and finally hiding out in the sewers of Los Angeles. Hoping to stomp them out are policeman James Whitmore, FBI agent Jame Arness, and scientist Edmund Gwenn (best-remembered as Santa Claus in the 1947 *Miracle on 34th Street*). According to Fess Parker, Walt Disney saw his brief bit here as a pilot and sought him out to audition for Davy Crockett. Olin Howlin, who appears as a drunk, was "The Blob's" first victim. Look quick for Leonard Nimoy. The ants were actual-sized models and were not stop-motion animated. This was Warner Brothers' highest-grossing film of the year. Oscar nomination for effects.

THERE'S NOTHING OUT THERE

1990 (NR) 91m / **D:** Rolfe Kanefsky / **W:** Rolfe Kanefsky / **C:** Craig Peck, Wendy Bednarz, Mark Collver, Bonnie Bowers, John Carhart III, Claudia Flores, Jeff Dachis

No-budget parody of screen schlock manages to be barely better than what it's skewering. Seven teenagers spend spring break at a secluded mountain cabin, anticipating sex and wild times. But one boy, who claims to have seen every horror movie on video, knows the signs of a horror plot just waiting to happen. He's the only one prepared when an alien frog monster attacks. There's one famous scene in which a potential victim swings out of the danger by grabbing the dangling microphone boom at the top of the frame.

THEY CAME FROM WITHIN

1975 (R) 87m / **D:** David Cronenberg / **W:** David Cronenberg / **C:** Paul Hampton, Joe Silver, Lynn Lowry, Barbara Steele

David Cronenberg's first *nearly* mainstream film is set in the sterile, clinical Starliner high-rise, the perfect contrast to the spread of a messy venereal disease crossed with an aphrodisiac. Look for 1960s horror queen Barbara Steele in the famous bathtub "entry" scene. Similar in attitude to many zombie films, this shocking, gory, and highly sleazy ride is also awash in symbolic critiques. AKA: *Shivers*; *The Parasite Murders*.

THEY LIVE

1988 (R) 88m / **D:** John Carpenter / **W:** John Carpenter / **C:** Roddy Piper, Keith David, Meg Foster, George Flower, Peter Jason, Raymond St. Jacques, John Lawrence, Sy Richardson, Jason Robards III, Larry Franco

John Carpenter's last seriously vital film is a semi-serious spoof about a drifter (ex-wrestler "Rowdy" Roddy Piper hamming it up brilliantly) who accidentally discovers a conspiracy by aliens to take over America under the guise of Reaganite yuppie consumerism. Piper and his down-and-out pals decide to do something about it once he realizes that the aliens-in-human-form can be spotted once he puts on the special sunglasses. Screenplay written by Carpenter under the pseudonym Frank Armitage. Piper delivers one of the decade's finest moments in cinema as he stands before an American flag, shotgun in hand and alien-spotting sunglasses on, and announces: "I have come here to chew bubblegum and kick ass ... and I'm *all out of bubblegum*."

THEY SAVED HITLER'S BRAIN

1964 (NR) 91m / **D:** David Bradley / **W:** Steve Bennett, Peter Miles / **C:** Walter Stocker, Audrey Caire, Nestor Paiva, Carlos Rivas, Dani Lynn nfamous golden turkey has little to offer except the ludicrous title and fleeting shots of Der Fuhrer's severed head in a jar and still giving orders. The years have not mellowed "Mr. H." (as he is now called). Even in his pickled state, he wants to take over the world by unleashing the deadly "Nerve Gas G." This film was assembled from footage from a 1950s espionage melodrama combined with new footage. Incredibly, director David Bradley started out filming Shakespeare stage plays and directed Charlton Heston in his debut in *Peer Gynt* before graduating to the glories of *Dragstrip Riot*, *12 to the Moon*, and of course, this. AKA: *Madmen of Mandoras*; *The Return of Mr. H.*

THE THING (1951)

1951 (NR) 87m / D: Christian Nyby, Howard Hawks / **W:** Charles Lederer / **C:** James Arness, Kenneth Tobey, Margaret Sheridan, Dewey Martin

One of the best of the Cold War film allegories and a potent lesson to those who won't eat their vegetables. Sci-fi classic begins with an alien spacecraft embedded in the Arctic ice and the creature (Arness as the killer carrot), discovered by a research team. The critter is accidentally thawed and then wreaks havoc, sucking the life from sled dog and scientist alike. It's a giant seed-dispersing vegetable run amuck, unaffected by missing body parts, bullets, or cold. In other words, Big Trouble. Excellent direction—assisted substantially by producer Howard Hawks—and supported by strong performances, sparkling dialogue, a machine-gun pace, and the potent atmosphere of frozen claustrophobia and isolation. Available colorized (don't do it). Twice remade and often copied. Loosely based on John Campbell's story "Who Goes There?" AKA: *The Thing from Another World*.

THE THING (1982)

1982 (R) 109m / D: John Carpenter / **W:** Bill Lancaster / **C:** Kurt Russell, Wilford Brimley, T. K. Carter, Richard Masur, Keith David, Richard Dysart, David Clennon, Donald Moffat, Thomas G. Waites, Charles Hallahan

Less a remake of the 1951 original than a more faithful version of the John Campbell story. Scientists at a remote Antarctic outpost discover a buried spaceship with an unwelcome alien survivor still alive. The suspense is expertly calibrated at first, emphasizing the setting's claustrophobic nature, though ultimately it and the superb cast (Carpenter standbys Keith David and Kurt Russell in particular) are overwhelmed by Rob Bottin's disgustingly bombastic creature f/x. The eerie score is by Ennio Morricone.

THE THING (2011)

2011 (R) 103m / D: Matthijs van Heijningen Jr. / **W:** Eric Heisserer / **C:** Mary Elizabeth Winstead, Joel Edgerton, Ulrich Thomsen, Eric Christian Olsen, Adewale Akinnuoye-Agbaje

In all three three versions of *The Thing*, an alien that can take the form of any living thing attacks an Antarctic outpost; this still is from the 1982 version.

Third and swiftly forgotten adaptation of the old John Campbell short story is itself set in Antarctica in the early 1980s. When some Norwegian researchers die after their vehicle plunges through the ice, an investigating team gets more than they bargained for when they discover and unfortunately awaken a strange alien organism that likes to infect and reanimate human hosts in a variety of grotesque ways.

THINGS TO COME

1936 (NR) 100m / D: William Cameron Menzies / **W:** Lajos Biro, H. G. Wells / **C:** Margaretta Scott, Edward Chapman, Raymond Massey, Ralph Richardson, Cedric Hardwicke, Derrick De Marney

Groundbreaking (and very loose) adaptation of H. G. Wells's utopian technocratic prophecies, best viewed today as taking place on an alternate world, an Earth that might have been. Narrative begins in 1940 and runs to 2036, chronicling the travails of Everytown, where the filmmakers show what would soon become tragically true: innocent civilians bombed, gassed, and infected in a global war that lasts until 1970. Politicians having made a mess of things, a group of scientific airmen take over running the world (a frequent, quasi-totalitarian fantasy of sci-fi writers in the earlier 20th century), and when the dust rolls away, behold Everytown of 2036 in its shining whiteness and glory. Every man is a superman, every woman a superwoman, wearing zoot-suit togas with huge shoulders (original script notes said our descendants will have so many items in their pockets that the shoulders must fortify and hold their clothing up). Scientists build a huge space gun to fire two astronauts to the moon, but a division between the sciences and humanities (shades of divisions at real-life universities in the 1960s and '70s) rears its ugly head, and a group of artists try to tear the space gun down with their bare hands. Final scene, with Raymond Massey pointing to the stars and declaring "It is this or nothingness. Which shall it be? Which shall it be?" is a triumphant declaration of man's destiny in space. Since it's gone into the public domain, *Things to Come* is available in many different versions, many of them lousy quality. Look for the U.S.-release prints that include a five-minute montage of titanic machines rebuilding civilization, a sequence designed by director William Cameron Menzies to surpass anything ever seen in *Buck Rogers* comics. Superb musical score by Arthur Bliss.

THE THIRTEENTH FLOOR

1999 (R) 100m / **D:** Josef Rusnak / **W:** Josef Rusnak, Ravel Centeno-Rodriguez / **C:** Craig Bierko, Armin Mueller-Stahl, Gretchen Mol, Vincent D'Onofrio, Dennis Haysbert

The decade's fascination with reality-distorting virtual spaces explored in everything from *Disclosure* to *Virtuality* took a more Philip K. Dickian turn in this pulpy redo of the Daniel F. Galouye novel *Simulacron-3* (shot a quarter-century earlier by Rainer Werner Fassbinder as *World on a Wire*). After billionaire computer innovator Armin Mueller-Stahl is stabbed to death following a trip into his company's secret new product—a lavishly imagined virtual Los Angeles, circa 1937—his right-hand guy (Craig Bierko) tries to solve the mystery before getting arrested for the killing. Most of the details here are straight from the thriller playbook, with the not-too-bright blonde (Gretchen Mol) and the intrusive detective (Dennis Haysbert) bracketing an increasingly paranoid Bierko, who's about two beats behind the audience figuring out what the *real* real secret is. The filmmakers went for a look that's third-rate *Blade Runner* without bothering to write a script to match. When the final reveal comes, it's less surprising than insulting for how little thought was put into exploring all of its ramifications.

THIS ISLAND EARTH

1955 (NR) 86m / **D:** Joseph M. Newman / **W:** Franklin Coen, Edward G. O'Callaghan / **C:** Jeff Morrow, Faith Domergue, Rex Reason, Russell Johnson

A dying planet seeks help from Earthling scientists in 1955's *This Island Earth*.

The planet Metaluna is in desperate need of uranium to power its defense against enemy invaders. A nuclear scientist and a nuclear fission expert from Earth are kidnapped to help out. Although the first serious movie about interplanetary escapades, remembered today mostly for the unintentional giggles it causes. So awful it was given pride of place in *Mystery Science Theater 3000: The Movie*.

THIS IS NOT A TEST

1962 (NR) 72m / **D:** Fredric Gadette / **W:** Peter Abenheim, Betty Lasky, Fredric Gadette / **C:** Seamon Glass, Mary Morlas, Thayer Roberts, Aubrey Martin

When news comes of an impending nuclear attack, a state trooper at a roadblock offers sanctuary to passing travelers. The effectiveness of the film's social commentary is hindered by its small budget.

THOR

2011 (PG-13) 115m / **D:** Kenneth Branagh / **W:** Ashley Miller, Zack Stentz, Don Payne / **C:** Chris Hemsworth, Natalie Portman, Tom Hiddleston, Anthony Hopkins, Stellan Skarsgard, Kat Dennings, Clark Gregg, Colm Feore, Idris Elba

Pan-dimensional, world-smashing, mythological action-drama with the sci-fi-ish elements standard to all the Marvel Avengers films (big robot with devastating laser-eyes in this one). Chris Hemsworth's Thor is appropriately broad-shouldered and prone to rash decision-making (he would have made a great Viking). Tossed out of Asgard by Odin (Anthony Hopkins), Thor ends up in a small desert town for some fish-out-of-water humor. He makes friends with a few scientists just in time for his trickster brother Loki (Tom Hiddle-

Anthony Hopkins played Odin, ruler of Asgard and father of Thor and Loki in the blockbuster *Thor*.

ston) to show up for one of them Ragnarök-like apocalypse brawls. Mostly just setup for the *Avengers* movie that followed the next year, but director Kenneth Branagh throws in a welcome dash of comedy amidst all the thunder-flashes and battle cries.

THOR: THE DARK WORLD

2013 (PG-13) 112m / **D:** Alan Taylor / **W:** Christopher Yost, Christopher Markus, Stephen McFeely / **C:** Chris Hemsworth, Natalie Portman, Tom Hiddleston, Stellan Skarsgård, Idris Elba, Anthony Hopkins, Christopher Eccleston, Kat Dennings

Back from having helped save the world (not *his* world, but Earth) in *The Avengers*, Thor still has his hands full with mythological contretemps. Loki has been given a life sentence (which for an Asgardian like him means several thousand years); some Dark Elves are causing problems back in Asgard; and his astrophysicist girlfriend Natalie Portman is in the eye of the storm after being infected with a McGuffin which the head Dark Elf needs to possess in order to conquer the universe. The many battle scenes are a fascinating mix of fantasy-world accoutrements and sci-fi weaponry, with the

Viking-esque Asgardians wielding golden armor and swords against white-masked Dark Elves with laser rifles and nasty antimatter hand grenades that create small devastating black holes. The high-tech Middle-earth mélange makes for some particularly gorgeous imagery; a mass Viking funeral in Asgard, with flaming long boats floating off into space, has the kind of poetic beauty that Peter Jackson always pushed for but never quite achieved.

THREADS

1984 (NR) 112m / D: Mick Jackson / **W:** Barry Hines / **C:** Karen Meagher, Reece Dinsdale, David Brierly, Rita May, Nicholas Lane

Another in a spate of unsparing 1980s films on the aftermath of a nuclear attack—which focused more on how ordinary civilians would suffer in such an attack rather than in more escapist mutant post-apocalyptic scenarios—this made-for-TV British film posits a U.S.-Soviet flashpoint in the Middle East leading to a quick escalation in tensions. The pseudo-documentary film follows what happens after a nuclear warhead hits the British city of Sheffield and the citizenry is forced to fend for itself amidst the destruction. The effect on the British populace after being broadcast in 1984 was reportedly almost as traumatic as after American television showed *The Day After*.

THE THREE STOOGES IN ORBIT

1962 (NR) 87m / D: Edward L. Bernds / **W:** Elwood Ullman / **C:** Moe Howard, Larry Fine, Joe DeRita, Emil Sitka, Carol Christensen, Edson Stroll

Another of the series of features the Stooges were signed up for to capitalize on the popularity resulting from the syndication of their classic two-reelers on TV, the trio battles a Martian army after a nutty inventor's flying submarine/tank/robot/something. For die-hard fans only.

THX 1138

1971 (PG) 88m / D: George Lucas / **W:** George Lucas, Walter Murch / **C:** Robert Duvall, Donald Pleasence, Maggie McOmie, Don Pedro Colley, Ian Wolfe, Marshall Efron

George Lucas's first film, inspired by a 20-minute student short he made at USC, is a virtuoso piece of minimalism. In the dehumanized world of the future, identically dressed and shaven-headed people live in computer-controlled underground cities, are force-fed drugs to keep them passive, emotions and sex are forbidden, and people no longer have names—just serial numbers. Robert Duvall is THX 1138. When the computer-matched couple THX 1138 and LUH 3417 discover true love, they attempt to escape their oppressive society to be together. With only sparse, catatonic dialogue, the story is told via a stunning sound design (created by master editor Walter Murch), Lalo Schifrin's eerie score, and a pristinely chilling and stark visual scheme that makes everything look like a laboratory. Lucas borrows his vision of society as consumerist drone-machine ("Buy … and be happy") and totalitarian control from *1984*, *Brave New World*, and particularly E. M. Forster's story "The Machine Stops." The 2004 re-release features the usual late-period Lucas tinkering, with jazzed-up f/x here and there that don't add much to, but at least don't detract from, what is still an impressive achievement.

TIME AFTER TIME

1979 (PG) 112m / **D:** Nicholas Meyer / **W:** Nicholas Meyer / **C:** Malcolm McDowell, David Warner, Mary Steenburgen, Patti D'Arbanville, Charles Cioffi, Kent Williams, Andonia Katsaros

In Victorian London, circa 1893, H. G. Wells (Malcolm McDowell, playing it nice for once) is experimenting with the time machine that apparently he invented

and didn't just write about. He discovers the machine has been used by an associate (who turns out to be Jack the Ripper) to travel to San Francisco and wreak havoc in 1979. Wells follows to stop any further murders and the ensuing battle of wits is both entertaining and imaginative. Mary Steenburgen does a fine job as Wells's modern American love interest. Impressive debut from *Star Trek II: The Wrath of Khan* writer/director Nicholas Meyer.

TIME BANDITS

1981 (PG) 110m / **D:** Terry Gilliam / **W:** Terry Gilliam, Michael Palin / **C:** John Cleese, Sean Connery, Shelley Duvall, Katherine Helmond, Ian Holm, Michael Palin, Ralph Richardson, Kenny Baker, Peter Vaughan, Craig Warnock, David Warner

Director Terry Gilliam's first non-Monty Python film features several Python alumni. A gang of mad, robbing dwarves, being pursued by the Supreme Being (Ralph Richardson), leads a young boy (Craig Warnock) on a journey through time and space with the likes of Robin Hood (John Cleese), Napoleon (Ian Holm), King Agamemnon (Sean Connery), and other time-warp pals. David

Former Monty Python member Terry Gilliam transitioned successfully to producing his own works with his debut *Time Bandits* in 1981.

Warner is a natural Evil Incarnate. As in Gilliam's *The Adventures of Baron Munchausen*, much of it plays like a cartoon, as reality shatters into one dreamworld after another. The rare fantasy epic that managed to be funny and imaginative while still succeeding at the box office.

TIMECOP

1994 (R) 98m / **D:** Peter Hyams / **W:** Mark Verheiden, Mike Richardson / **C:** Jean-Claude Van Damme, Ron Silver, Mia Sara, Bruce McGill, Scott Lawrence, Kenneth Welsh, Gabrielle Rose, Duncan Fraser

Improbably popular comic adaptation is set in 2004, when time travel has been perfected and a special Time Enforcement unit set up to deal with the inevitable abuse. Timecop Jean-Claude Van Damme travels back in time to present evil Senator Ron Silver from altering the past to ensure his election to the presidency. Van Damme also seizes the chance to alter his personal history and prevent the death of his wife. Sadly, the technology does not yet exist that would allow someone to travel back in time and prevent this film from being made.

TIMECRIMES

2007 (R) 92m / **D:** Nacho Vigalondo / **W:** Nacho Vigalondo / **C:** Karra Elejalde, Candela Fernández, Bárbara Goenaga, Nacho Vigalondo, Juan Inciarte

Spanish time-travel paradox film in which binocular-carrying regular guy Karra Elejalde goes into the woods to investigate a woman he sees removing her shirt, only to get attacked by a scissors-wielding psycho with a pink sack over his face. Elejalde tries to hide from the masked man at a neighbor's house and ends up jumping into his time travel machine. Time starts looping back in on itself and things get complicated.

THE TIME GUARDIAN

1987 (PG) 89m / **D:** Brian Hannant / **W:** Brian Hannant, John Baxter / **C:** Tom Burlinson, Carrie Fisher, Dean Stockwell, Nikki Coghill

Time-traveling city from the 40th century arrives in the Australian desert in 1988, pursued by killer cyborgs (looking a lot like *Star Trek*'s the Borg). Muddled and confusing mélange of borrowed sci-fi elements with no clear identity of its own. Some good f/x. Carrie Fisher and Dean Stockwell show up for a few minutes but depart quickly.

TIMELINE

2003 (PG-13) 116m / **D:** Richard Donner / **W:** Jeff Maguire, George Nolfi / **C:** Paul Walker, Frances O'Connor, Gerard Butler, Billy Connolly, David Thewlis, Ethan Embry, Anna Friel, Michael Sheen allid time-travel hooey based on Michael Crichton's best-selling novel about a company that has developed a way of traveling through time via wormholes. Instead of selling the discovery to the Pentagon or doing something world-changing with it, though, they decided to send an archaeologist back to 14th-century France. When he goes missing, the company convinces his (woefully unprepared) coworkers to go looking for him. Problem is, when they show up in France, the English and French are fighting the Hundred Years' War and don't care much who gets caught in the crossfire. Builds up to a big nighttime castle siege where plenty of cool-looking flaming arrows are used. Less fun than it should be.

THE TIME MACHINE (1960)

1960 (G) 103m / **D:** George Pal / **W:** David Duncan / **C:** Rod Taylor, Alan Young, Yvette Mimieux, Whit Bissell, Sebastian Cabot, Tom Helmore

H. G. Wells's classic novel *The Time Machine* has been adapted to film several times, including this 1960 version starring Rod Taylor.

Georg Pal's adaptation of H. G. Wells's allegorical novel about a time traveler to a futuristic Earth where humans have been divided into two species—the blonde, sprightly above-ground Eloi and the monstrous underground Morlocks—has aged poorly. It's a slow, talky thing in which Rod Taylor is actually not the most wooden performer on screen. Wells's ideas about the future have rarely seemed less prescient. Won an Oscar for f/x.

TIME MACHINE (1978)

1978 (G) 99m / **D:** Henning Schellerup / **W:** Wallace C. Bennett / **C:** John Beck, Priscilla Barnes, Andrew Duggan

Markedly inferior adaptation of the H. G. Wells novel from 1970s schlock-factory Sunn Classics. Setting is unwisely moved to the then-present time, keeping down costuming costs but also losing the charm of the original's Victorian milieu. John Beck is the Time Traveller, whose adventures in history incorporate a lot of economical stock footage.

THE TIME MACHINE (2002)

2002 (PG-13) 96m / **D:** Simon Wells / **W:** John Logan / **C:** Guy Pearce, Mark Addy, Sienna Guillory, Samantha Mumba, Phyllida Law, Orlando Jones, Omero Mumba, Jeremy Irons

The limitations of H. G. Wells's original novel are made a little too clear in this rickety adaptation by the normally more thoughtful John Logan (*Gladiator*), who moves the action to New York. Guy Pearce plays the late-19th-century inventor who shoots 800,000 years into the future to find humanity divided into two species: Eloi, the pacific surface dwellers, and Morlocks, the cannibalistic underground monsters who feed on them. Wells's utopian-socialistic critique of the dehumanization of industrial society gets jettisoned in favor of an added-on story about Pearce trying to change time in order to stop the murder of his fiancée. There's a new add-on about society being destroyed in the 2030s by its own techno-hubris after demolition on the Moon causes it to break up. But that's rushed past in order to get to Pearce running around caverns doing battle with beastly Morlocks and trying to save his pretty Eloi girlfriend. Orlando Jones delivers some humor as an AI that's incredibly still working after missing several hundred thousand years' worth of software and firewall updates. Director Simon Wells is the author's great-grandson. Oscar nomination for makeup; surprising given the pre-*Planet of the Apes* quality of the Morlocks' stone-like masks.

TIMEMASTER

1995 (PG-13) 100m / **D:** James Glickenhaus / **W:** James Glickenhaus / **C:** Jesse Cameron-Glickenhaus, Pat Morita, Joanna Pacula, Michael Dorn, Duncan Regehr, Michelle Williams

In this scrap-heap of pasted-together and semi-coherent genre clichés, orphaned 12-year-old Jesse Cameron-Glickenhaus (the director's son, to nobody's surprise) discovers his parents are still alive, fighting battles throughout history for the amusement of advanced aliens on a distant world. Kindly extraterrestrial Pat Morita sends the boy on a rescue mission bouncing around time and space. Shocking thing is it doesn't look cheap at all; someone armed with a real script could have made a decent movie with this budget. Your chance to see Michael Dorn out from under his Klingon forehead as the main villain.

TIME OF THE WOLF

2003 (R) 114m / D: Michael Haneke / **W:** Michael Haneke / **C:** Isabelle Huppert, Lucas Biscombe, Anaïs Demoustier, Béatrice Dalle, Patrice Chéreau

It takes admirable restraint to conjure up a post-apocalyptic story and to avoid *all* the usual standbys. No panicked evacuation, no moment where a character says "we're on our own," and so on. But it takes an altogether different kind of stubbornness to go into such a scenario with no story to tell. Michael Haneke's dry exercise follows a mother (Isabelle Huppert) and her two children after some unnamed disaster has driven them out of Paris to their summer cottage only to find it occupied by squatters who kill her husband and steal their car and supplies. Wandering the countryside, the three fall in with a ragtag group holding up at a depot hoping that a train will come through. As the days wear on without news and supplies run low, civilization's veneer skins away; religious fanaticism rears its head and the threat of pogrom is in the air. Haneke's wide-frame camerawork is immaculate and the gradations of desperation are carefully captured—the penultimate scene has a timeless, almost medieval quality to it. But the dry screenplay is just too schematic to let any air in.

> "Great Moments in Low-Budget Aliens: their devastating, incomprehensible battle machine turns out to be a bulldozer with fog lights."
>
> *Time Runner*

TIME RUNNER

1992 (R) 90m / D: Henning Schellerup / **W:** Chris Hyde, Greg Derochie, Ian Bray, Michael Mazo, John Curtis / **C:** Mark Hamill, Brion James, Rae Dawn Chong

Canadian sci-fi washout lacks logic, to say the least. It's 2022, and the Earth is being used as target practice by alien invaders. Space captain Mark Hamill (sporting an ill-advised 'stache) falls through an unexplained time warp back to 1992 where he can battle the secret alien vanguard of humanlike infiltrators and change the planet's destiny. Great Moments in Low-Budget Aliens: their devastating, incomprehensible battle machine turns out to be a bulldozer with fog lights.

THE TIME TRAVELERS

1964 (NR) 82m / D: Ib Melchior / **W:** Ib Melchior / **C:** Preston Foster, Phil Carey, Merry Anders, John Hoyt, Joan Woodbury, Delores Wells, Dennis Patrick, Forrest J. Ackerman, Carol White

Scientists discover a porthole leading to Earth's post-Armageddon future where they encounter tribes of nasty mutants. The last remnants of humanity use androids (who with their featureless, noseless faces look faintly menacing) as slave labor to build a spaceship to escape the dying planet. Sensing (correctly) that there's not much fun to be had in the future, the time travelers make a serious effort to return to their past. Fairly serious, thoughtful, and bleak sci-fi emphasizing ideas rather than just phony-looking monsters. Cinematography by a young Vilmos Zsigmond (then working as William). Remade three years later as *Journey to the Center of Time*. AKA: *Time Trap*.

TIME WALKER

1982 (PG) 86m / D: Tom Kennedy / **W:** Tom Friedman, Karen Levitt / **C:** Ben Murphy, Nina Axelrod, Kevin Brophy, Robert Random, Austin Stoker

An archaeologist unearths King Tut's coffin in California. An alien living inside is unleashed and terrorizes the public. Early appearance by Harry Belafonte's daughter Shari, who at the time had a busy schedule of *Love Boat* and *Diff'rent Strokes* roles.

TIMERIDER

1983 (PG) 93m / D: William Dear / **W:** Michael Nesmith, William Dear / **C:** Fred Ward, Belinda Bauer, Peter Coyote, Richard Masur, Ed Lauter, L. Q. Jones, Tracey Walter

Your basic dirt bike sci-fi western finds intellectually challenged motorcycle rider Fred Ward stuck in 1877 (he never quite figures out why he gets blank stares when he asks to use the phone). Ward plays the clueless time traveler to perfection, getting fine support from Belinda Bauer and bad guy Peter Coyote. Co-written and co-produced by one-time Monkee Michael Nesmith. Wry sense of humor has earned this one a solid cult status. AKA: *The Adventure of Lyle Swan*.

TITAN A.E.

2000 (PG) 94m / D: Don Bluth, Gary Goldman / **W:** Ben Edlund, John August, Joss Whedon

The film that essentially ended the career of the great animator Don Bluth (*The Secret of NIMH*) is actually something of an underappreciated gem. The vibrant, perhaps overbusy story is set in the 31st century, after Earth has been annihilated by an alien species, the Drej. Years later, humanity is scattered around the galaxy, scavenging to get by. Matt Damon voices the plucky and headstrong young guy who just happens to hold the secret to recreating Earth as it once was. Not surprisingly the Drej want him dead. Also not surprisingly (given Joss Whedon's handprint on the script), there's a *Serenity*'s worth of sarcasm-equipped oddballs and misfits willing to help him in his quest. The mix of hand-drawn and computer animation is frequently awe-inspiring, with a far-future space-traveling civilization that feels lived in and not just drawn to look cool. Still, since the plotting was too dense for a kids' animated film and the level of pessimism and violence more appropriate for a PG-13 live-action feature, audiences stayed away. (Not long after, 20th Century Fox shut down its animation division.) Worth seeking out.

TOBOR THE GREAT

1954 (NR) 77m / D: Lee Sholem / **W:** Philip MacDonald / **C:** Charles Drake, Billy Chapin, Karin Booth, Taylor Holmes, Joan Gerber, Steve Geray

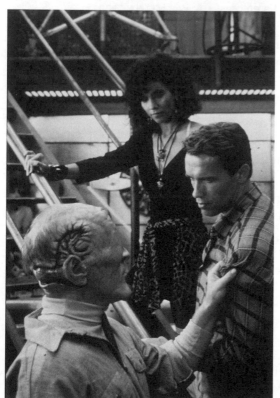

Another sci-fi flick based on a story by Philip K. Dick, *Total Recall* was filmed in 1990 with Arnold Schwarzenegger starring, and again in 2012.

Juvenile sci-fi nostalgia about a boy, his inventor grandfather, and their pride and joy, Tobor the Robot. Villainous commie spies try to misuse Tobor, only to be thwarted in the end.

TOTAL RECALL (1990)

1990 (R) 113m / D: Paul Verhoeven / **W:** Gary Goldman, Dan O'Bannon / **C:** Arnold Schwarzenegger, Rachel Ticotin, Sharon Stone, Michael Ironside, Ronny Cox, Roy Brocksmith, Marshall Bell, Mel Johnson Jr.

Initially interesting and ultimately bludgeon-like sci-fi action set in the 21st century, when Earth's citizens have fictionalized memories implanted to grant them adventures they couldn't afford to experience. Restless construction worker Arnold Schwarzenegger undergoes the procedure to exorcize his annoying fixation with the Mars mining colony, but something goes wrong. Turns out he really *was* a secret agent on Mars and had a false memory implant to wipe his true identity out. Or did he? Dodging assassins at every turn, Arnold heads for Mars for answers. Elaborate expansion of Philip K. Dick's short tale "We Can Remember It for You Wholesale" is an entertaining but problematic puzzler, rewritten to fit Schwarzenegger's Conan-scale persona; whenever the mazelike plot becomes too much, he can just punch his way out. This results in a progressively tortured storyline, until the hero can't even exist if everything is taken literally. Rarely one for subtlety, director Paul Verhoeven keeps the graphic violence rampant throughout. Grotesque mutant makeup by Rob Bottin. Two Oscar nominations: sound and sound f/x editing.

TOTAL RECALL (2012)

2012 (PG-13) 118m / **D:** Len Wiseman / **W:** Kurt Wimmer, Mark Bomback / **C:** Colin Farrell, Kate Beckinsale, Jessica Biel, Bryan Cranston, Bokeem Woodbine, Bill Nighy, John Cho

Coming at the tail end of a string of imagination-deprived remakes, Len Wiseman's redo of this early 1990s sci-fi actioner throws even the minimally psychological dimension of Paul Verhoeven's original out in exchange for wall-to-wall gunplay. In a future-set story nominally inspired by Philip K. Dick, depressed factory drone Colin Farrell goes for an implant of an exciting fake memory about being a secret agent. Turns out his memories were wiped, he actually already *is* an agent, and dutiful wife Kate Beckinsale is not who she seems to be. Lavishly detailed backgrounds of an overcrowded, vertically built futureworld are ripped straight from *Blade Runner* and *The Fifth Element* but still stun initially, as does the idea that there's just two habitable parts of Earth left, and they're connected via a tunnel through the planet's core. But a witless script and pallid leads leach any fun out of the nearly endless chase scenes, and that's *before* the movie comes to a logical end ... and then burns through yet another half-hour of pointless gunplay.

TOWARD THE TERRA

1980 (NR) 112m / **D:** Hideo Onchi / **W:** Hideo Onchi, Chigusa Shioda

Japanese anime set in a distant future where mankind has been forced to evacuate Earth for another planet. Society suppresses anything potentially destabilizing to prevent the mistakes that destroyed the Earth. Breaking the calm is the MU, a new race with incredible mental powers, who are ruthlessly hunted, but whose leader reaches out to a human with his own inexplicable powers to aid in establishing a new world.

TRANCERS

1984 (PG-13) 76m / **D:** Charles Band / **W:** Danny Bilson, Paul De Meo, Phil Davies / **C:** Tim Thomerson, Michael Stefani, Helen Hunt, Art LaFleur, Telma Hopkins, Richard Herd, Anne Seymour

Psycho zombie cult of the future known as Trancers goes back in time to 1985 to meddle with fate. Only veteran Trancer terminator Jack Deth (Tim

Thomerson) can save mankind. Low-budget *Blade Runner* imitation, with widely scattered clever touches. One is the gimmick of time-travel via a drug that injects one's consciousness down "the genetic bridge" to the bodies of distant ancestors (hence Deth's tough-talking superior officer shows up in the Reagan era as a tough-talking little girl). Followed by five straight-to-video sequels; too many. AKA: *Future Cop*.

TRANSATLANTIC TUNNEL

1935 (NR) 94m / D: Maurice Elvey / **W:** Kurt Siodmak, L. du Garde Peach, Clemence Dane / **C:** Richard Dix, Leslie Banks, Madge Evans, Helen Vinson, Sir C. Aubrey Smith, George Arliss, Walter Huston

Wishful 1930s prophecy, set after 1950, about engineer Richard Dix spearheading the construction of a giant undersea tunnel from England to America, which will apparently help guarantee world peace. Remake of a 1933 German epic *Der Tunnel* (from a 1913 novel by Bernhard Kellerman), which critics generally hold to be superior. The English film suffers distracting subplots about financial trickery and Dix's family problems that take the camera off the impressive futuristic designs and f/x. All versions of *The Tunnel* were banned among the Allies when WWII began. AKA: *The Tunnel*.

TRANSCENDENCE

2014 (PG-13) 119m / D: Wally Pfister / **W:** Jack Paglen / **C:** Johnny Depp, Rebecca Hall, Paul Bettany, Morgan Freeman, Cillian Murphy, Kate Mara, Clifton Collins Jr., Cole Hauser

Beware of scientists who come bearing messages of perfecting humanity with technology, or should you? That's the purportedly complex message of this intriguing and well-cast but simple-minded thriller from Christopher Nolan's longtime cinematographer that throws AI, nanotech, and every other buzzy technology into the mix for another man vs. machine showdown. Johnny Depp's sulky AI researcher is on the verge of a great discovery when he's mortally wounded by neo-Luddite terrorists. His frantic wife (Rebecca Hall) uploads Depp's consciousness to their quasi-sentient database, at which point his digital ghost achieves consciousness. In no time, digital Depp is playing Skynet games with humanity, building his own city-sized solar-powered datafarm in the desert, and apparently plotting world domination. The appearance of Nolan second-stringers like Morgan Freeman and Cillian Murphy make one hope for a more tech-heavy *Inception*. But like more obviously schlocky VR/AI flicks from *Colossus: The Forbin Project* to *The Lawnmower Man*, it loses the story in ooh-and-aah f/x that will seem laughable a few years hence.

TRANSFORMERS

2007 (PG-13) 144m / **D:** Michael Bay / **W:** Roberto Orci, Alex Kurtzman / **C:** Shia LaBeouf, Megan Fox, Josh Duhamel, Tyrese Gibson, Rachael Taylor, Anthony Anderson, Jon Voight, John Turturro, Kevin Dunn, Julie White

Once upon a time only Saturday morning cartoons were used for full-length product placement. Then producer Steven Spielberg and director Michael Bay figured that by resurrecting the old Hasbro toy line of cars and trucks that folded into supercool battling Transformer robots (Autobots are the good ones, Decepticons the bad), they could blow lots of stuff up in a PG-13 kind of way. That's what happens in this thunderous, deafening battle royale of a movie in which the building-sized Autobots and Decepticons wage war on Earth while humans like plucky hero Shia LaBeouf, racecar calendar pinup girl Megan Fox (a millennial Pamela Anderson type), and strong-chinned soldier Josh Duhamel try to look relevant to what's going on. There's a whole lot of doctored guff about something called an Allspark that the robots are battling over, but the emphasis is really on Bay's toilet humor and the overpowering Industrial Lights and Magic f/x, which detail the robots' transformations in a loving, granular way that the humans could only wish was getting lavished on them. Three Oscar nominations; sound mixing, sound editing, f/x.

TRANSFORMERS: DARK OF THE MOON

2011 (PG-13) 154m / **D:** Michael Bay / **W:** Ehren Kruger / **C:** Shia LaBeouf, Rosie Huntington-Whiteley, Tyrese Gibson, Josh Duhamel, John Turturro, Patrick Dempsey, Frances McDormand, John Malkovich, Kevin Dunn, Julie White, Buzz Aldrin

Giant, sentient, alien robots that can reorganize their parts to look like almost any mechanical object is the premise of the "Transformers" movies.

ooking for yet more reasons to keep blowing things up real good, the Transformers series this time imagines a neat Moon landing conspiracy twist: the *Apollo 11* mission was just an excuse for the U.S. government to investigate photos of a crashed spaceship on the dark side of the moon. Turns out there's another Autobot leader buried up there, Sentinel Prime (voiced with appropriately booming gravitas by Leonard Nimoy), and he's got a secret with him. Of course, that all gets jettisoned quickly for more lavishly choreographed Decepticon-on-human ultraviolence, including turning downtown Chicago into a war zone. John Malkovich and Frances McDormand are standout additions to the cast, but again the preadolescent gags, massacring of civilian bystanders, fawning product placement, and egregiously inflated running time add up to a wearying experience. Yes, that *is* Buzz Aldrin playing Buzz Aldrin. Three Oscar nominations: sound mixing, sound editing, f/x.

TRANSFORMERS: REVENGE OF THE FALLEN

2009 (PG-13) 150m / **D:** Michael Bay / **W:** Ehren Kruger, Roberto Orci, Alex Kurtzman / **C:** Shia LaBeouf, Megan Fox, Josh Duhamel, Tyrese Gibson, John Turturro, Ramon Rodriguez, Kevin Dunn, Julie White

The planet demolition derby continues with the Spielberg/Bay/Hasbro cash machine inventing new ways for Transformers and Decepticons to smash holy hell out of each other for two and a half hours. (After all, this was the year the franchise had to contend with a new toy tie-in rival in *G.I. Joe: The Rise of Cobra*.) The CGI showdown, which had at least the attraction of novelty in the first film, gets a lot more tiresome this time out. To nobody's surprise, the Decepticons refuse to stay defeated, so the Autobots run around Earth beating them up wherever they appear with the help of humans like Tyrese Gibson and Josh Duhamel, who the film patronizes by pretending they would be helpful in battling blindingly fast killer robots the size of an apartment complex. Nothing is helped by the addition of a couple comic-relief Autobots (Mudflap and Skids) whose curiously racial antics read as an offensive minstrel show. The exclamation mark-heavy screenplay is again from the imagination-starved team of Roberto Orci and Alex Kurtzman (*Star Trek into Darkness*, *Cowboys and Aliens*). Oscar nomination for sound mixing.

TREASURE PLANET

2002 (PG) 95m / **D:** Ron Clements, John Musker / **W:** Ron Clements, John Musker, Rob Edwards

Outer-space steampunk reimagining of Robert Louis Stevenson's *Treasure Island*. In this version, rocket-powered sailing ships ply interstellar space. The rebellious Jim Hawkins finds a treasure map and hops aboard a ship filled with aliens and cyborgs to go find riches and adventure. Beautiful animation with then somewhat groundbreaking 3-D backgrounds. Oscar nomination for best animated feature.

TREKKIES

1997 (PG) 86m / **D:** Roger Nygard

Affectionate documentary on the Trekkie subculture of costumes, fan fiction, collectibles, and generally taking things way, way too far. Nominal host is Denise Crosby (Tasha Yar on *Star Trek: Next Generation*) but for the most part this is awkwardly enthusiastic people holding the camera hostage. Interviewed about all the stunningly personal contact they have with fans, cast members from Leonard Nimoy to LeVar Burton (William Shatner is conspicuously absent, as is Patrick Stewart) try to provide some depth about the emotional context of fandom. But this is mostly an oddity clipshow for those who have never attended a convention, with some standouts like the woman who claims to actually be a Federation commander and the people writing erotic fan fiction about the show's characters. Followed by *Trekkies 2* in 2004.

TREMORS

1989 (PG-13) 96m / **D:** Ron Underwood / **W:** S. S. Wilson, Brent Maddock / **C:** Kevin Bacon, Fred Ward, Finn Carter, Michael Gross, Reba McEntire, Bibi Besch, Bobby Jacoby, Charlotte Stewart, Victor Wong, Tony Genaro

Comic sci-fi creature feature has a tiny desert town being attacked by giant man-eating worm-type "Graboids." Luckily, handymen Kevin Bacon and Fred Ward are on the scene to accidentally save the day with the help of guns-R-us couple Michael Gross and Reba McEntire. Not your average *Jaws*-on-dry-land ripoff. Just the right mixture of scares and the funny stuff as people and even entire cars are sucked under and devoured.

TREMORS II: AFTERSHOCKS

1996 (PG-13) 100m / **D:** S.S. Wilson / **W:** S.S. Wilson, Brent Maddock / **C:** Fred Ward, Michael Gross, Helen Shaver, Christopher Gartin, Marcelo Tubert

The Graboids have resurfaced and are eating their way through Mexican oil fields. Fred Ward is back in demand as the man who can put a stop to the toothy worms' carnage (good thing, too, because all his profits from even the Graboid video game have been eaten up by dumb decisions). Joined by my-gun-is-bigger-than-your-gun Michael Gross, he sets out to once again put an end to the wriggly rampage before the damn things vomit up (a new reproductive twist) too many more wormkids. More tongue-in-cheek humor, even messier f/x, and larger quantities of worm guts than the first film. *Almost* as much fun. Followed by yet more straight-to-disc sequels.

A TRIP TO THE MOON

1902 (G) 21m / **D:** Georges Méliès / **C:** Victor André, Bleuette Bernon, Georges Méliès

The first sci-fi film is a comically ramshackle silent affair that retains a fantastical fascination more than a century on. Up to this time, audiences had been thrilled by photographed events such as a train arriving at a station. French visual pioneer George Méliès, a professional magician, opened up a whole new world of imagination with stop-motion photography, multiple exposure, and other ingenious camera tricks that gave birth to the art of f/x. Achieved cinematic immortality with the scene in which a rocket is launched right into the eye of the Man in the Moon. Based in theory on Jules Verne's *From the Earth to the Moon* and H. G. Wells's *First Men in the Moon.*

Released in 1902, *A Trip to the Moon* achieved amazing visual effects for its time thanks to the groundbreaking work on director Georges Méliès whose ambition it was to bring magic to the silver screen.

Méliès' efforts to bring magic to the screen were later captured in Martin Scorsese's *Hugo*. AKA: *A Trip to Mars*.

TRON

1982 (PG) 96m / **D:** Steven Lisberger / **W:** Steven Lisberger / **C:** Jeff Bridges, Bruce Boxleitner, David Warner, Cindy Morgan, Barnard Hughes, Dan Shor

Computer programmer Jeff Bridges is sucked into the memory banks of a giant mainframe and exists as a warrior in a virtual-reality civilization running parallel to the outside world. Wielding never-defined superpowers, the bewildered hero fights video-game battles against a rogue artificial intelligence seeking to dominate mankind. The sketchy plot of this much-anticipated Disney effort sounds better than it plays, with more attention paid to ground-breaking computer f/x (which imagine the programs inside the AI as people) than the inane script. Some designs by famed sci-fi illustrator Jean "Moebius" Girard. Two Oscar nominations: sound, costume design.

TRON: LEGACY

2010 (PG) 125m / **D:** Joseph Kosinski / **W:** Edward Kitsis, Adam Horowitz / **C:** Jeff Bridges, Garrett Hedlund, Olivia Wilde, Bruce Boxleitner, James Frain, Beau Garrett, Michael Sheen

Unlike most of the remakes that plagued the 2000s, Disney's return to the old computer-animated experiment *TRON* was less a do-over than decades-delayed sequel that keeps much of the same plot elements but updates the f/x and tries to build something of a franchise. Trapped-in-the-computer programmer Jeff Bridges' son Garrett Hedlund ventures into his dad's virtual world, where all programs are visualized as humans, and has to defeat all sorts of evil data-spawn to save him and fetching New Wave-styled compu-siren Olivia Wilde. The spectacle is everything here, as in the original, with only the throbbing, otherworldy Daft Punk score and a clownish Michael Sheen standing out. Oscar nomination for sound editing.

TROUBLE IN MIND

1985 (R) 111m / **D:** Alan Rudolph / **W:** Alan Rudolph / **C:** Kris Kristofferson, Keith Carradine, Lori Singer, Geneviève Bujold, Joe Morton, Divine

Moody, romantic, post-noir pseudo-sci-fi from Robert Altman protégé Alan Rudolph that seems like Tom Waits should have done the soundtrack for. It's set in Rain City (really Seattle) in some alternate universe where culture seemed to jump straight from the 1940s of fedoras, suits, and gangster patter to the fractured New Wave 1980s. Kris Kristofferson plays an ex-con named Hawk trying to get his life straight, Keith Carradine is a thief, and Lori Singer is the blonde they both have eyes for. The story is straight noir, but the setting is highly dystopian, with a crumbling and depressed city closely watched by an overbearing militia breaking up protests and making pronouncements. That's John Waters star Divine as the local crime boss.

THE TROUBLE WITH DICK

1987 (R) 86m / **D:** Gary Walkow / **W:** Gary Walkow / **C:** Tom Villard, Susan Dey

Plenty of trouble with this adolescent would-be comedy. An ambitious young sci-fi writer's personal troubles (which include being involved with several over-sexed women) begin to appear in his writing. Basically a genre-movie reworking of *The Secret Life of Walter Mitty*, but nowhere near as charming as that description might suggest. The story (what there is of it) gets very tedious after the first five minutes. Former Partridge Family member Susan Dey appears as one of Dick's women.

THE TRUMAN SHOW

1998 (PG) 103m / **D:** Peter Weir / **W:** Andrew Niccol / **C:** Jim Carrey, Ed Harris, Laura Linney, Noah Emmerich, Natascha McElhone

In an example of voyeurism taken to extremes, a man is placed in an artificial world from the time of his birth so that his entire life can become a reality program in *The Truman Show*.

Andrew Niccol's second produced screenplay remains his most thoughtful and prescient; directed by Peter Weir with grace and speed, it avoids the rigidity of *Gattaca* and Niccol's other directing work. It's a quietly earth-shattering story about a happy-go-lucky guy (Jim Carrey, his first venture into drama) living a peaceful life in a peaceful small town who gets something of a shock: Turns out his entire life from childhood has been staged as a TV show watched by millions. Ed Harris plays the show's director as a sly jape on the pretensions of grand artists with dictatorial personalities while Carrey is touchingly blank, a genial guy who's never been allowed to live a single real moment. In the tradition of great sci-fi, it asks viewers to accept a few implausibilities (how would even a hit show be able to afford this kind of expense for decades on end?) in the service of exploring questions of reality, societal pressures, techno-narcissism, and the survival of the soul in pixellated modern times. Three Oscar nominations.

12 MONKEYS

1995 (R) 131m / **D:** Terry Gilliam / **W:** David Peoples, Janet Peoples / **C:** Bruce Willis, Madeleine Stowe, Brad Pitt, Christopher Plummer, David Morse, Frank Gorshin, Jon Seda

Forty years after a plague wipes out 99 percent of the human population and sends the survivors underground, scientists send prisoner James Cole (Bruce Willis) to the 1990s to investigate the connection between the virus and seriously deranged fanatic Brad Pitt, whose father happens to be a renowned virologist. Terry Gilliam's demented vision is tougher and less capricious than usual, and the convoluted plot and accumulated detail require a keen attention span, but as each piece of the puzzle falls into place the story becomes a fascinating sci-fi spectacle. Pitt aggressively combats his then-pretty boy image with a fully schizoid performance, while Willis brings the right amount of wounded, wistful gravitas to this ultimately rather tragic film. Inspired by Chris Marker's 1962 short *La Jetée*. Two Oscar nominations: supporting actor (Pitt), costume design.

28 DAYS LATER ...

2002 (R) 113m / **D:** Danny Boyle / **W:** Alex Garland / **C:** Cillian Murphy, Naomie Harris, Brendan Gleeson, Christopher Eccleston, Megan Burns

In one fell swoop, Danny Boyle recovered from the critical drumming his big-budget tourist-hell thriller *The Beach* received and relaunched the zombie film, a genre that had long been consigned to the bargain basement of George Romero ripoffs and *giallo* gorefests. The twist of an opener has a blood-borne virus released into the world by animal activists liberating infected chimpanzees from a laboratory. Four weeks later, Cillian Murphy wakes up from his pre-outbreak coma to find the hospital and all of London eerily emptied of the living. Run-ins with the red-eyed, blood-spewing infected are charged and terrifying; this was the start of the running-zombie phenomenon. He teams up with machete-wielding New Wave babe Naomie Harris and a resourceful father and daughter to find the source of a radio message promising a haven from the undead. Boyle shoots his post-apocalyptic story like an indie experimental film, with skewed angles and cheap-looking, overexposed video that makes everything look like it was captured by left-over security cameras. Like the better zombie stories, Boyle and Alex Garland's thoughtful story is less interested in fighting off walking corpses than it is in studying how people keep their humanity, and how they lose it.

28 WEEKS LATER

2007 (R) 100m / **D:** Juan Carlos Fresnadillo / **W:** Rowan Joffé, Juan Carlos Fresnadillo, E.L. Lavigne, Jesus Olmo / **C:** Robert Carlyle, Rose Byrne, Jeremy Renner, Harold Perrineau, Catherine McCormack, Idris Elba, Imogen Poots, Mackintosh Muggleton

There's a certain lack of drama that automatically comes with this kind of sci-fi horror. Set over half a year after the virus of the first film had blazed like wildfire across the United Kingdom, survivors are being resettled in a highly fortified corner of London and hoping for things to get back to normal. Of course, even though the experts in the film insist that the last infected are dead, everyone watching is just waiting for the next outbreak to come. That's the point at which the military commander in charge starts to get an itchy trigger finger. Features none of the creative team from the first film but a strong roster of UK performers and a loyal adherence to the original's gritty aesthetic.

20 MILLION MILES TO EARTH

1957 (NR) 82m / **D:** Nathan Juran / **W:** Bob Williams, Christopher Knopf / **C:** William Hopper, Joan Taylor, Frank Puglia, John Zaremba

Spaceship returning from expedition to Venus crashes on Earth, releasing a fast-growing reptilian beast that rampages throughout Athens. Another entertaining example of stop-motion animation master Ray Harryhausen's work, offering a classic battle between the monster and an elephant.

THE 27TH DAY

1957 (NR) 75m / **D:** William Asher / **W:** John Mantley / **C:** Gene Barry, Valerie French, George Voskovec, Arnold Moss, Stefan Schnabel, Ralph Clanton, Friedrich Ledebur, Mari Tsien, Azenath Jani

Surprisingly literary example of postwar sci-fi that stands the test of time, despite some outdated philosophy and all-too-obvious preaching about the good and bad guys of the Cold War. An alien, piloting one of the ships from *Earth vs. the Flying Saucers*, gives five mysterious capsules to five Earthlings from five different countries. Only the mind of each human can open his/her capsule. Once open, however, anyone can order the three contained radiation pellets to instantly vaporize all humans within 1,500 miles; anything not human will be totally unharmed. Twenty-seven days or the death of the holder will render the capsules harmless. All five, even the "English Bathing Beauty" (as Valerie French's character was called in the press kits), want to save the world, but of course some of the evil governments involved have other ideas. Despite flaws, an intelligent film adaptation of the John Mantley novel.

20,000 LEAGUES UNDER THE SEA

1954 (NR) 127m / D: Richard Fleischer / **W:** Earl Fenton / **C:** Kirk Douglas, James Mason, Peter Lorre, Paul Lukas, Robert J. Wilke, Carleton Young

James Mason played the brilliantly deranged Captain Nemo in the 1954 production of *20,000 Leagues under the Sea*.

Hugely successful and frequently revived definitive Disney adaptation of the frequently filmed Jules Verne novel firmly established it as a live-action studio. From his futuristic submarine, Captain Nemo (James Mason at his most crepuscular Mason-ness) wages war on a surface world he has deemed wholly corrupt. A shipwrecked scientist and sailor (Kirk Douglas and Peter Lorre, each playing to their muscular/comic strengths) do their best to thwart Nemo's seemingly evil but ultimately understandable schemes. Bright, buoyant, and packed with action and humor, Richard Fleischer's film also sports outstanding f/x and a lively cast. The showstopper of a battle with an animatronic squid had to be completely and expensively reshot at Walt Disney's demand. Three Oscar nominations, won for art direction and f/x.

TWILIGHT ZONE: THE MOVIE

1983 (PG) 101m / D: John Landis, Steven Spielberg, George Miller, Joe Dante / **W:** John Landis, George Clayton Johnson, Richard Matheson, Josh Rogan, Jerome Bixby / **C:** Dan Aykroyd, Albert Brooks, Vic Morrow, Kathleen Quinlan, John Lithgow, Scatman Crothers, Kevin McCarthy, Bill Quinn, Selma Diamond, Abbe Lane, John Larroquette, Jeremy Licht, Patricia Barry, William Schallert, Burgess Meredith, Cherie Currie

John Landis directed one of the segments in *Twilight Zone: The Movie*, an anthology film mostly based on episodes from the original TV series.

Uneven but energetically delivered four-part horror/fantasy anthology produced by Steven Spielberg and John Landis in tribute to Rod Serling's series. Three episodes are based on classic *Twilight Zone* scripts. "Nightmare at 20,000 Feet" is the most genuinely chilling, effectively reworking the original tale of a monster glimpsed on the wing of a plane. Joe Dante's "It's a Good Life," the story of a malevolent little boy gifted with supernatural powers, brings a cartoonish kick to its horrific premise. Spielberg's "Kick the Can" is an icky-sweet tale of senior citizens who briefly regain their lost childhoods. Most memorable of the four is "Time Out" (only loosely based on an earlier episode), a horrific parable about racism in which bigot Vic Morrow is subjected to a litany of prejudicial horrors, being chased by everyone from Klansman to the SS. (Morrow was killed when a helicopter crashed on him during filming of this episode.)

Two Lost Worlds

1950 (NR) 63m / **D:** Norman Dawn / **W:** Tom Hubbard / **C:** James Arness, Kasey Rogers, Laura Elliott, Bill Kennedy

A young hero battles monstrous dinosaurs, pirates, and more in this cheapie when he and his shipmates are shipwrecked on an uncharted island. Don't miss the footage from *Captain Fury*, *One Billion B.C.*, and *Captain Caution*, and James Arness long before his Sheriff Dillon fame and his role in *The Thing*.

2046

2004 (R) 129m / **D:** Wong Kar Wai / **W:** Wong Kar Wai / **C:** Tony Leung, Zhang Ziyi, Faye Wong, Carina Lau, Maggie Cheung

Lusciously filmed romantic epic set for the most part in 1960s Hong Kong, where gloomy journalist and occasional sci-fi hack Tony Leung spends his nights sinuously gliding through nightclubs and restaurants, occasionally bringing beautiful women (Zhang Ziyi, Gong Li, Faye Wong) back to his boarding-house room 2046. In between Wong Kar Wai's trademark langorous reveries of smoke and music, he intercuts dreamy scenes presumably taken from one of Leung's novels, where a man rides a bullet train in the year 2046 (the year that China's promise of sovereignty for Hong Kong expires) and makes eyes at android women. The realism is no less stringently deployed in the past scenes than they are in the future; it's all filtered through a smoke-tinged, symbol-twigged moodiness where a plot would feel just plain intrusive.

2001: A Space Odyssey

1968 (G) 139m / **D:** Stanley Kubrick / **W:** Stanley Kubrick, Arthur C. Clarke / **C:** Keir Dullea, Gary Lockwood, William Sylvester, Dan Richter, Leonard Rossiter

The biggest, strangest, most gorgeous film of the 1960s was this curious and unforgettable masterpiece of cinematic sci-fi that forever redefined what the genre could do. Stanley Kubrick and his co-writer Arthur C. Clarke (who pulled heavily from his novel *The Sentinel* for this film) told the centuries-spanning story in oblique segments, dispensing with conventional narrative and just about all dialogue. It's a story of evolution, following pre-human primates in Africa discovering an alien monolith to humans uncovering a similar monolith on the moon, to a spaceship crew journeying to Jupiter to find out who or what the monolith was signaling. Meanwhile, the ship's computer, HAL, seems to be gaining sentience in disturbing ways. While the tale is highly mystical, Kubrick makes all the technology resolutely realistic, slapping contemporary logos like PanAm on a

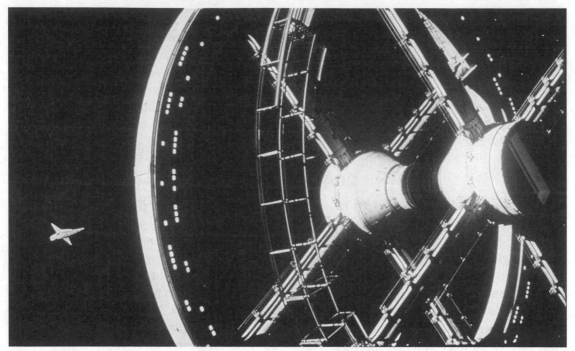

One of the great, mysterious works of sci-fi cinema, *2001: A Space Odyssey* is Stanley Kubrick's take on a story by Arthur C. Clarke about mankind's first contact with an alien intelligence.

space shuttle. The beautiful f/x, calibrated for depth and wonder instead of firecracker-wow, took decades to top and are still awesome today; particularly when paired with Kubrick's soundtrack that combines ghostly choirs with classical waltzes. The enigmatic ending will strike some as poetic, others as infuriating. Either way, unforgettable. Four Oscar nominations; won for f/x.

2010: THE YEAR WE MAKE CONTACT

1984 (PG) 116m / **D:** Peter Hyams / **W:** Peter Hyams / **C:** Roy Scheider, John Lithgow, Helen Mirren, Bob Balaban, Keir Dullea, Madolyn Smith, Mary Jo Deschanel

Peter Hyams' hard-working but resolutely unmagical sequel is best taken if viewed simply as a mystery. Americans and Russians unite to investigate the abandoned starship *Discovery*'s decaying orbit around Jupiter and try to determine why the HAL 9000 computer sabotaged its mission years before, while signs of cosmic change are detected on and around the giant planet. Plot rather inventively answers most of the questions left hanging by Kubrick and Clarke—to which one might ask: where's the fun in that? Five Oscar nominations.

2012

2009 (PG-13) 158m / **D:** Roland Emmerich / **W:** Roland Emmerich, Harald Kloser / **C:** John Cusack, Chiwetel Ejiofor, Oliver Platt, Thandie Newton, Danny Glover, Amanda Peet, Thomas McCarthy, Woody Harrelson, Zlatko Buric

Roland Emmerich solidified his role as the latter-day Irwin Allen with this massively campy, half tongue-in-cheek gargantuan disaster film based on the Mayan prophecy about the world ending in 2012. Chiwetel Ejiofor is the scientist who discovers solar radiation Is power-heating the Earth's core, which will destabilize the crust and End Life As We Know It. World leaders' secret plan to build modern-day arks to keep part of the species safe from the giant tsunamis to come is a welcome return to the grand tradition of big idea sci-fi mostly abandoned by Hollywood. (No matter how laughable it would seem to any scientist who's spent years waving actual predictions of catastrophic climate change at disbelieving politicians.) John Cusack is the hero, a divorced writer who rescues his family from one catastrophic scrape after another. The f/x demolitions here are impeccably delivered, from the tipping of Southern California into the Pacific to tidal waves cresting over the Himalayas; though Emmerich's need to demolish the White House yet again (before in *Independence Day* and later in 2013's *White House Down*) seems curious. Amidst all the ooh-aah devastation and repetitive melodrama, the script presents a dilemma of who will be saved, as the world's richest are able to buy a seat on an ark for one billion euros (*not* dollars, an official tells a disappointed oil sheik), though it's ultimately less a critique of the one percent than an excuse for the heroes to eventually act even more heroic. The film's positive portrayal of modern China (depicted here as the only country able to construct the arks in such a short amount of time) helped make it a huge hit there.

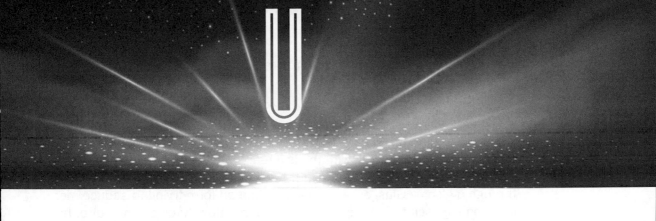

Uforia

1981 (PG) 92m / **D:** John Binder / **W:** John Binder / **C:** Cindy Williams, Harry Dean Stanton, Fred Ward, Hank Worden

Good ol' boy Fred Ward meets up with a UFO-obsessed girl played by Cindy Williams. Their budding romance is threatened by Ward's friend, a crooked evangelist (Harry Dean Stanton) who sees Williams's UFO-babble as a potential money-making scheme. Stanton intends to use Arlene's prophecies of impending extraterrestrial contact to bilk his revivalist audiences. The humor is sometimes clumsy but works often enough to make for fun viewing.

The Ultimate Warrior

1975 (R) 92m / **D:** Robert Clouse / **W:** Robert Clouse / **C:** Yul Brynner, Max von Sydow, Joanna Miles, Richard Kelton, Lane Bradbury, William Smith

Yul Brynner (the *ultimate warrior*, of course) must defend the plants and seeds of a pioneer scientist to help replenish the world's food supply in this mostly forgotten 2012-set thriller.

Ultraviolet

2006 (R) 88m / **D:** Kurt Wimmer / **W:** Kurt Wimmer / **C:** Milla Jovovich, Cameron Bright, Nick Chinlund, Sebastien Andrieu, Ida Martin, William Fichtner

Equilibrium's Kurt Wimmer distracted Milla Jovovich long enough from zombie-killing duties to stick her in another futuristic bulletfest. Jovovich plays some kind of "hemophage" (with some kind of allergic reaction to midriff-concealing clothing, it seems) genetically engineered to be a superproficient killing machine who uses said skills to keep from being killed by one of the hundreds of interchangeable extras who keep charging cluelessly at her. They just don't learn.

UNDER THE SKIN

2014 (PG-13) 108m / **D:** Jonathan Glazer / **W:** Walter Campbell, Jonathan Glazer / **C:** Scarlett Johansson, Jeremy McWilliams, Lynsey Taylor Mackay

Scarlett Johansson is an alien; this much we know. But what Jonathan Glazer's curiously creepy sci-fi stalker film engages with is something far more mysterious. Keeping with the is-it-real? trickery of Glazer's *Sexy Beast* and *Birth* (both of which flirted with the fantastic), here Johansson floats through a gloomy Glasgow as an alien in human form trying to seduce men into coming back to her cross-dimensional abattoir. After getting out of her predator van and following her inside for a hoped-for tryst, they're immersed in a sticky black goo and sucked right out of their skin. It all seems like a lot of work for a few pounds of raw meat, and Glazer's resistance to most of the requirements of drama frustrate quickly. But his knack for archetypal nightmare imagery is unmatched: There's an unnerving shot of a reddish slurry being fed into an hungry industrial maw; not to mention the unforgettable image of a victim's degloved skin floating like a ghost. Still, it's only in the haunting final stretches, where it seems like Johansson is finally gaining an interest in these humans she hunts, that the film really starts to engage with the questions of identity and the soul that it hints at throughout. Somehow David Bowie is nowhere to be found.

THE UNEARTHLY STRANGER

1964 (NR) 75m / **D:** John Krish / **W:** Rex Carlton / **C:** John Neville, Gabriella Licudi, Philip Stone, Patrick Newell, Jean Marsh, Warren Mitchell

Earth scientist John Neville marries woman and decides she's from another planet. Seems she's part of an invading alien force but really does love her Earth man. Surprisingly good low-budget sci-fi.

UNIVERSAL SOLDIER

1992 (R) 98m / **D:** Roland Emmerich / **W:** Dean Devlin / **C:** Jean-Claude Van Damme, Dolph Lundgren, Ally Walker, Ed O'Ross, Jerry Orbach

Reporter Ally Walker discovers a secret government project to design perfect robo-soldiers by reanimating dead, memory-wiped GIs, including tough guys Dolph Lundgren and Jean-Claude Van Damme, who were killed in Vietnam. But the knowledge is going to get her killed until Van Damme has flashbacks of his past and agrees to help her. Lundgren, not quite cured of the psychosis he had when alive (which included massacring South Vietnamese civilians), doesn't have the same compassion and goes after them both. Big-budget thriller with some good action sequences and lotsa gunplay. Lundgren is surprisingly good in a few over-the-top scenes. German director Emmerich's first big American hit was later followed by a surprising number of sequels and imitators.

UNIVERSAL SOLDIER: DAY OF RECKONING

2012 (R) 114m / D: John Hyams / **W:** John Hyams / **C:** Jean-Claude Van Damme, Dolph Lundgren, Scott Adkins, Andrei Arlovski

Regeneration's John Hyams keeps the series going with an even-more brutally violent sequel that starts with a now-legendary series of queasy POV shots in which journeyman kickboxer Scott Adkins watches masked men butcher his family at the command of a (now seemingly villainous) bald and vacant-eyed Jean-Claude Van Damme. Things get a might bit confusing after that, in a claustrophobically *Cyborg*-meets-David Lynch kind of day, as Adkins—who wakes up a few months after the murders—sets out for answers and vengeance. Belarussian mixed-martial arts fighter Andrei Arlovski, one of *Regeneration*'s evil UniSols, returns for more punishment, as does Lundgren, who's pushing 55 years old at this point, compared to the spring chicken-like Van Damme (a mere 52 or so).

Jean-Claude Van Damme (left) and Dolph Lundgren are dead-GIs-turned-robosoldiers in 1992's *Universal Soldier.*

UNIVERSAL SOLDIER: REGENERATION

2009 (R) 114m / D: John Hyams / **W:** Victor Ostrovsky / **C:** Jean-Claude Van Damme, Dolph Lundgren, Andrei Arlovski

The original *Universal Soldier*'s ear-slicing Vietnam War psychopath villain Dolph Lundgren is back to life in this gritty reboot of the genre-splicing sci-fi actioner whose third-generation dubs had been wearing out Third World VCRs for years (action always translates better than drama). Van Damme is also reanimated—proving that, as some have claimed, this series is less sci-fi or war film than zombie—to stop Lundgren's terrorist baddies from blowing up the Chernobyl reactor. The two meet up only near the end for the expected lunk-versus-lunk showdown.

UNIVERSAL SOLDIER: THE RETURN

1999 (R) 83m / **D:** Mic Rodgers / **W:** William Malone, John Fasano / **C:** Jean-Claude Van Damme, Michael Jai White, Bill Goldberg, Xander Berkeley

First official sequel to 1992's *Universal Soldier* features the Muscles from Brussels as the only survivor of the first film's team. He's forced to fight one of those pesky Pentagon-engineered cyborg super-soldiers (kick-boxin' Michael Jai White, of *Spawn* infamy), whose team of cyborgs, or "UniSols," takes it a little too personally when their would-be creators try and terminate them with extreme prejudice. Pro-wrestling brawler Bill Goldberg makes an appearance as a cyborg whose language skills are just a tad out-stripped by his ass-whupping abilities.

UNKNOWN WORLD

1951 (NR) 73m / **D:** Terrell O. Morse / **W:** Millard Kaufman / **C:** Bruce Kellogg, Marilyn Nash, Victor Kilian, Jim Bannon

Scientists tunnel to the center of the Earth to find a refuge from the dangers of an atomic bomb-armed world. Big start winds down fast.

UNNATURAL

1952 (NR) 90m / **D:** Arthur Maria Rabenalt / **W:** Kurt Heuser / **C:** Hildegarde Neff, Erich von Stroheim, Karl-Heinz Boehm, Harry Meyen, Harry Helm, Denise Vernac, Julia Koschka

Mad scientist (director-turned-actor Erich von Stroheim) creates a soulless child from the genes of a murderer and a prostitute. The child grows up to be the beautiful Hildegarde Neff, who makes a habit of seducing and destroying men. Dark, arresting film from a very popular and frequently filmed German novel.

UNTIL THE END OF THE WORLD

1991 (R) 158m / **D:** Wim Wenders / **W:** Wim Wenders, Peter Carey / **C:** William Hurt, Solveig Dommartin, Sam Neill, Max von Sydow, Rüdiger Vogler, Ernie Dingo, Jeanne Moreau

Confused but fascinating Wim Wenders road movie works best when viewed at least twice, and it's well worth the effort. It's 1999 and Sam Farber (William Hurt) needs to take some snapshots, and quick. His mom is blind, and dying. His dad (Max von Sydow) is one superbrain inventor and has come up with a camera capable of recording images that can then be played back in a device that will allow mom to view them. Beautiful jetsetter Solveig Dommartin, her lover Sam Neill, a bounty hunter, a private dick, and a couple of bank robbers are all on his trail after the camera, stolen money, Hurt, or one of the other trackers. The route covers 15 cities worldwide and ends up in the Australian outback at dad's secret lab. An about-to-explode nuclear satellite adds tension and leads to a dreamy aboriginal climax. Cinematically stunning. Wenders's humor and life philosophies are apparent throughout and every performance from the international cast is top notch. Use of high-definition video (HDTV) is a first and the soundtrack (a mix of Graeme Revell's spooky compositions and songs by everyone from Talking Heads to Lou Reed) is fantastic, though occasionally unrelated to what's happening on screen. The director's cut runs some 280 minutes and manages to clear some things up.

> **"An about-to-explode nuclear satellite adds tension and leads to a dreamy aboriginal climax."**
> *Until the End of the World*

Upside Down

2012 (PG-13) 100m / **D:** Juan Solanas / **W:** Juan Solanas / **C:** Jim Sturgess, Kirsten Dunst, Timothy Spall

Magical, heart-on-its-sleeve sci-fi fantasy romance positing twin worlds that exit in a synchronized orbit right on top of each other, with gravity fields that pull in opposite directions; people living in the one can look directly up at people in the other. Orphaned inventor Jim Sturgess lives in the lower, poorer world that's used for resource extraction by the richer upper world. Wouldn't you know, he falls for upper-world designer Kirsten Dunst and has to figure out how to reverse his gravity to get into her world. Frequently goes too far, calling its characters Adam and Eve, and giving one of its characters dramatically convenient amnesia. But the gorgeous effects are frequently breathtaking and verge on the poetic in the manner of Vincent Ward's *What Dreams May Come*. Both conceptually daring *and* full of heart, a sci-fi rarity.

Urusei Yatsura Movie 1: Only You

1983 (NR) 100m / **D:** Mamoru Oshii / **W:** Tomoku Konparu

Lum is a Princess of the Oni, an alien race come to repossess Earth. The planet's one chance is for an Earthling to beat Lum in the Oni's national sport—tag. When unlucky teenager Ataru Moroboshi is chosen, he actually beats Lum. Which means he has to marry her. First feature anime of the popular manga and TV series; followed by numerous sequels.

V

VARAN THE UNBELIEVABLE

1961 (NR) 70m / **D:** Ishiro Honda / **W:** Sid Harris / **C:** Myron Healey, Tsuruko Kobayashi

Chemical experiment near a small Japanese island disturbs a prehistoric monster beneath the water. (*When will humanity learn?*) The awakened monster spreads terror on the island. Most difficult part of this movie is deciding what the rubber monster model is supposed to represent. AKA: *The Monster Baran*.

V FOR VENDETTA

2005 (R) 132m / **D:** James McTeigue / **W:** Andy Wachowski, Lana Wachowski / **C:** Natalie Portman, Hugo Weaving, Rupert Graves, Stephen Fry, Stephen Rea, John Hurt, Tim Pigott-Smith

In this problem-plagued but notable adaptation of the Alan Moore graphic novel, a virus has wreaked havoc on England, leading its countrymen to do the usual thing: turn to dictatorship, xenophobia, and the stifling of dissent. Undesirables like Muslims, immigrants, and gays have been rounded up into detention camps. Meanwhile, the mysterious and jauntily poetic V (Hugo Weaving, behind the mask and cape) wages a sabotage campaign against the regime, recruiting street urchin Natalie Portman as his gal Friday. The Wachowskis-written story tries unsuccessfully to update the material; Moore's novel was too solidly rooted in its reaction to 1980s Thatcherite fascism to have the same power when it's broadened into a more general (and curiously watered down) populist call to arms. Also, they insert far too much in the martial-arts department. Even though the book was published in 1989, it wasn't until the film popularized the Fawkes mask that anarchists and members of the hacker collective Anonymous began adopting it for their real-life and online demonstrations.

David Cronenberg directed *Videodrome,* a surreal gross-out film that actually offers some intriguing speculative themes.

VIDEODROME

1983 (R) 87m / D: David Cronenberg / **W:** David Cronenberg / **C:** James Woods, Deborah Harry, Sonja Smits, Peter Dvorsky

David Cronenberg continues his exploration of both the evolution and the deterioration of the flesh in this queasy and surreal slice of satirical horror. Cable programmer James Woods becomes hooked on the pirate TV show *Videodrome*, which delivers loads of real sex, real torture, and real murder. Unfortunately for Woods, the show is having an effect on his love life (with Deborah "Blondie" Harry), genetically altering his body (turning him into a human VCR), and blurring his view of reality. With Woods's newly formed stomach orifice, he is easily programmed by organic videocassettes; the possibilities are endless. While another filmmaker would be using such off-putting imagery simply to shock, Cronenberg's fantasies are of a darker and more speculative nature that actually reward multiple viewings. F/x by Rick Baker. Stick around for the last scene, it may be one of the most perfect ever filmed. All hail the new flesh!

VILLAGE OF THE DAMNED (1960)

1960 (NR) 78m / D: Wolf Rilla / **W:** Wolf Rilla, Stirling Silliphant, George Barclay / **C:** George Sanders, Barbara Shelley, Martin Stephens, Laurence Naismith, Michael C. Goetz, Michael C. Gwynn

This adaptation of John Wyndham's novel *The Midwich Cuckoos* is both another take on the *Invasion of the Body Snatchers* theme—infiltration by aliens who are like us but not like us—and an early signaling of post-World War II generational conflicts. It's also very simply one of the best sci-fi thrillers ever made. When an English village is subjected to a mysterious event, several unusual children are conceived. Later, the children with the blond hair, glowing eyes, and eerie stares demonstrate remarkable, threatening powers. Casting the urbane George Sanders in the lead is a deft move by the filmmakers, as he brings a restrained emotional power to the story's conclusion. Pay no attention to the dated soundtrack. Followed by a sequel, *The Children of the Damned*, in 1964 and an atrocious 1995 remake.

VILLAGE OF THE DAMNED (1995)

1995 (R) 98m / D: John Carpenter / **W:** John Carpenter, David Himmelstein / **C:** Christopher Reeve, Kirstie Alley, Linda Kozlowski, Mark Hamill, Meredith Salenger, Michael Paré, Peter Jason, Constance Forslund

Pale remake of the British horror classic fails to capture the eeriness of its predecessor. The quiet town of Midwich, California, has been enveloped by a strange force that impregnates the local women. The albino children born of this incident have disturbing telepathic powers displayed through their bright orange and red eyes—supposedly precipitating a plot to take control. The characters have no personalities, the dialogue is sloppy and stilted, the plot comes to a slapdash conclusion, and the pedestrian f/x appear to have been tailored for the small screen. The children's glowing eyes make them look about as threatening as Nintendo addicts.

VILLAGE OF THE GIANTS

1965 (NR) 82m / D: Bert I. Gordon / **W:** Alan Caillou / **C:** Ronny Howard, Johnny Crawford, Tommy Kirk, Beau Bridges, Freddy Cannon, Robert Random

Youth in revolt! Beau Bridges and some teen delinquents looking for kicks steal some size-enhancing goop, get supersized, and proceed to take over the town, imposing curfew on the adults. Ronny (not yet Ron) Howard, a long way from Mayberry, costars as Genius, who invented the formula, with Johnny Crawford, son of "The Rifleman," as one of the good teens who try to cut Bridges down to size. With music by the Beau Brummels, who were more believable as animated characters on *The Flintstones*.

VIRTUOSITY

1995 (R) 105m / D: Brett Leonard / **W:** Eric Bernt / **C:** Denzel Washington, Russell Crowe, Kelly Lynch, Stephen Spinella, William Forsythe, Louise Fletcher, William Fichtner, Costas Mandylor, Kevin J. O'Connor

Sadistic and gimmicky sci-fi cop movie set in near-future L.A. has Denzel Washington playing another of his strong, silent types as an ex-cop with a tragic past who gets sprung from unjust imprisonment for agreeing to help capture computer-generated killer Russell Crowe (his first Hollywood starring role). Crowe plays a virtual reality program with a personality composed of some 200 serial killers and assorted criminals who have escaped from cyberspace, taken human form with the help of his mad-scientist creator (don't ask how), and gone on a killing spree. Conveniently, criminal-behavior psychologist Kelly Lynch is around to lend expert advice to Washington as Crowe plays the usual bloody movie-

> "Sadistic and gimmicky sci-fi cop movie set in near-future L.A.
>
> *Virtuosity*

serial killer cat-and-mouse games. Solid performances from the two leads do what they can here but it isn't enough to overcome the déjà vu.

VIRUS (1982)

1982 (PG) 102m / **D:** Kinji Fukasaku / **W:** Koji Takada, Kinji Fukasaku, Gregory Knapp / **D:** George Kennedy, Sonny Chiba, Glenn Ford, Robert Vaughn, Stuart Gillard, Stephanie Faulkner, Ken Ogata, Bo Svenson, Olivia Hussey, Chuck Connors, Edward James Olmos

After nuclear war and plague destroy civilization, an international group of survivors (a wildly eclectic grab-bag of American and Japanese performers) gathers in Antarctica and struggles to carry on the species, which ultimately involves a mission back into the virus-zone to stop a doomsday machine from wiping out what is left. A look at humankind's genius for self-destruction and its endless hope from the director of *Battle Royale*. AKA: *Day of Resurrection*.

VIRUS (1999)

1999 (R) 99m / **D:** John Bruno / **W:** Chuck Pfarrer, Dennis Feldman / **C:** Jamie Lee Curtis, William Baldwin, Donald Sutherland, Joanna Pacula, Marshall Bell, Sherman Augustus

Ever wanted to see a movie that has crusty, shotgun-wielding tugboat captain Donald Sutherland stalking onto a ship that is (unbeknowest to him) infested by an alien virus/thing that had been beamed down to it from the *Mir* space station (don't ask)? Now is your chance. Also on board are Jamie Lee Curtis and sundry crew people who won't stand much of a chance against the alien being once it starts learning. They *always* learn.

VOYAGE OF THE ROCK ALIENS

1987 (PG) 97m / **D:** James Fargo / **W:** S. James Guidotti, Edward Gold, Charles Hairston / **C:** Pia Zadora, Tom Nolan, Craig Sheffer, Rhema, Ruth Gordon, Michael Berryman, Jermaine Jackson

The extravagantly talentless Pia Zadora is Dee-Dee, a small-town girl who yearns to be a singer. Her town ("Speelburgh"—this is what passes for humor here) is visited by rock-musician aliens who provide her big break. This truly awful film wants to be a heartwarming musical fantasy but ends up falling on its face. Jermaine Jackson does a tiresome dance-number, Pia can't act, and the few decent actors (like Michael Berryman of *The Hills Have Eyes*) are wasted as stereotypical small-town "eccentrics." Avoid.

VOYAGE TO THE BOTTOM OF THE SEA

1961 (PG) 106m / **D:** Irwin Allen / **W:** Irwin Allen, Charles Bennett / **C:** Walter Pidgeon, Joan Fontaine, Barbara Eden, Peter Lorre, Robert Sterling, Michael Ansara, Frankie Avalon

Master of disaster Irwin Allen's best film, if that does it for you. Here, the crew of experimental atomic submarine *Seaview* is put to the test when Earth is threatened by a burning radiation belt (?). Among the crew are Walter Pidgeon, as a nuke-happy admiral of questionable sanity, Peter Lorre as a trustworthy marine biologist, Joan Fontaine as a not-so-trustworthy scientist, and Michael Ansara as a religious fanatic who believes the blazing sky is God's will. A fetchingly uniformed Barbara "Jeannie" Eden dances on the mess hall tabletops and Frankie Avalon is available to sing the title tune. Much better than the TV series that ran this movie's good name aground.

VOYAGE TO THE PLANET OF PREHISTORIC WOMEN

1968 (NR) 78m / **D:** Peter Bogdanovich / **W:** Henry Ney / **C:** Mamie Van Doren, Mary Mark, Paige Lee, Aldo Roman

Peter Bogdanovich's directorial debut (under the pseudonym Derek Thomas) is not, repeat, *not* any relation to the 1966 cheapie *Women of the Prehistoric Planet*, let's be clear about that. Rather it's the story of some astronauts who journey to Venus and discover a race of gorgeous, telepathic women led by Mamie Van Doren who wear sea-shell bikinis and worship a pterodactyl. The second film to incorporate footage from the much better *Planeta Burg* (*Planet of Storms*); 1965's *Voyage to the Prehistoric Planet* cannibalized the Russian movie as well. As you might expect, this cheap splice-job is pretty much incomprehensible. Also narrated by Bogdanovich. AKA: *Gill Woman*; *Gill Women of Venus*.

VOYAGE TO THE PREHISTORIC PLANET

1965 (NR) 80m / **D:** John Sebastian / **W:** John Sebastian / **C:** Basil Rathbone, Faith Domergue, Marc Shannon, Christopher Brand

In the year 2020, an expedition to Venus is forced to deal with dinosaurs and other perils. The first of two hatchet-job remakes of *Planeta Burg*. For this go-round, executive producer Roger Corman edited in some new scenes featuring Basil Rathbone and Faith Domergue, as well as a few from his own *Queen of Blood*, which coincidentally also starred Rathbone and also was based on an acquired Russian sci-fi film. AKA: *Voyage to a Prehistoric Planet*.

THE WALL

2013 (NR) 108m / D: Julian Pölsler **/ W:** Julian Pölsler **/ C:** Martina Gedeck, Ulrike Beimpold, Wolfgang M. Bauer

A cabin-fever experiment in pristinely gorgeous isolation. A woman (the astonishing Martina Gedeck) vacationing at a hunting lodge far up in the Austrian mountains finds herself cut off from the outside world by an invisible and impenetrable wall. Her one glimpse of life in the outside world is two farmers who appear frozen. Julian Pölsler's painstaking and psychologically brutal story is told mostly in flashback by a hollow-eyed Gedeck, writing a journal of her imprisonment in an idyllic world of lush meadows and fairytale forests. Her attempts to figure out the how and why of the wall are perfunctory and quickly overtaken by the basic necessities of food production and the staving off of madness. An austere, poetic realist counterpoint to Stephen King's more grandiose experiment in group isolation, *Under the Dome*.

WALL-E

2008 (G) 98m / D: Andrew Stanton **/ W:** Andrew Stanton, Jim Reardon

Many years from now, Earth has been abandoned by humanity, which is busy stuffing itself with processed foods on massive R&R ships. The mountain-sized trash heaps that the species left behind are busily tended by the rusted little WALL-E garbage bot. WALL-E doesn't really talk and that doesn't really matter. The first long stretch of Andrew Stanton's glorious masterpiece is a sad comedic riff on *Silent Running* that follows WALL-E trundling amidst the apocalyptic junk-mountains, picking out the occasional bit that he wants to save for himself, watching and singing along to his old tape of "Hello, Dolly!" A chance encounter with EVE, a sleeker and newer research

WALL-E

bot sent down to check out Earth, leads WALL-E to fall madly in love with her and get accidentally taken for a ride into space to one of those ships filled with the blob-like gelatinous masses that humans have devolved into. Sweetly romantic, but also a savagely anti-consumerist satirical sci-fi disguised as family comedy from the great consumer-glut factory itself. Six Oscar nominations; won for best animated feature.

THE WAR GAME

1965 (NR) 48m / **D:** Peter Watkins / **W:** Peter Watkins / **C:** Michael Aspel, Peter Graham, Kathy Staff

Another of Peter Watkins's politically barbed mockumentaries, and possibly his most furious. A British TV announcer calmly details the step-by-step buildup to a limited nuclear exchange and then the gruesome effects of the aftermath. The impact of Watkins's stark newsreel imagery and the just-the-facts reportage makes for an uncommonly powerful statement—particularly given that the horrifying details (firestorms, starvation, brutal triage) are mostly taken from reports of the attacks on Dresden and Hiroshima. The disassociated narration and bleak devastation make it seem like the less poetic cousin of *La Jetée*, another mournful study of the apocalypse. Necessary viewing. Considered too frightening for TV audiences at the time, Britain banned it from broadcast until 1985. Oscar for best documentary.

WarGames

1983 (PG) 110m / **D:** John Badham / **W:** Walter F. Parkes, Lawrence Lasker / **C:** Matthew Broderick, Dabney Coleman, John Wood, Ally Sheedy, Barry Corbin

Teen hacker Matthew Broderick, thinking he's sneaking an advance look at a new line of video games, accidentally breaks into the U.S. missile-defense system and challenges it to a game of Global Thermonuclear Warfare. The game might just turn out to be the real thing if the boy can't stop it. Though heavily grounded in the Reagan era, this remains one of the first and best of the cyberflicks; oft-imitated formula of high-tech whiz kids getting into trouble comes on like gangbusters, though the plot slackens near the end. One of the great Cold War films, with a haunting opening segment in which a missile silo crew almost accidentally launches a warhead at the Soviet Union, had surprisingly many real-life parallels. Directed with efficient thrills and humor by John Badham, who took over from Martin Brest after filming had already begun. The first film to deal with the then-unknown subculture of hackers, co-writer Walter F. Parkes would explore that world again with 1992's *Sneakers*. Three Oscar nominations: cinematography, sound, screenplay.

Matthew Broderick is a computer hacker who realizes that the U.S. military's war simulation program is about to start World War III in *WarGames.*

WAR IN SPACE

1977 (NR) 91m / **D:** Jun Fukuda / **W:** Shuichi Nagahara, Ryuzo Nakanishi / **C:** Kensaku Morita, Yuko Asano, Ryo Ikebe

Powerful U.N. Space Bureau starships and UFOs band together to battle alien invaders among the volcanoes and deserts of Venus. Rushed into theaters by Japanese studio Toho to cash in on *Star Wars* hoopla before George Lucas's film opened there in 1978. Dubbed.

WARLORDS OF THE 21ˢᵗ CENTURY

1982 (PG) 91m / **D:** Harley Cokeliss / **W:** Harley Cokeliss, Irving Austin, John Beech / **C:** Michael Beck, Annie McEnroe, James Wainwright, John Ratzenberger

The post-apocalyptic wasteland is ruled by a bandit gang who roll around the place in an indestructible battle truck that's really just a big rig with a lot of armor plating bolted on, *A-Team*-style. But wouldn't you know, a lone hero emerges to battle the battle truck. AKA: *Battletruck.*

WARLORDS 3000

1993 (R) 92m / **D:** Faruque Ahmed / **W:** Ron Herbst, Faruque Ahmed / **C:** Jay Roberts Jr., Denise Marie Duff, Steve Blanchard, Wayne Duvall

In the future, Earth is a barren wasteland ravaged by raging electrical storms. Deadly cancers are rampant and the few people who have survived take their comfort in a hallucinogenic drug that provides a temporary pleasure and a permanent madness. Drug lords control the planet but one man (*one* man!) is out to eliminate the scum and save the future. AKA: *Dark Vengeance*.

WARM BODIES

2012 (PG-13) 98m / **D:** Jonathan Levine / **W:** Jonathan Levine / **C:** Nicholas Hoult, Teresa Palmer, John Malkovich, Rob Corddry, Dave Franco, Analeigh Tipton

When it's funny, the zombies in this post-apocalyptic romantic action comedy can walk slow; when drama is needed they can run. Jonathan Levine's chuckle-worthy take on Isaac Marion's novel is told from the perspective of Nicholas Hoult, a zombie annoyed at everything about his kind: particularly their bad memories and inability to communicate. After eating the brains of a human girl's (Teresa Palmer) boyfriend, he decides to keep her safe instead of dining on her. Conflicted emotions arise. Some innovative wrinkles here include the Boners, a more vicious devolution of zombie, and the ability of not-so-far-gone zombies to (slowly) regain their humanity. Unlike almost all other undead dramas, this one tries to imagine what happens if there's an *after*, though it punts on the post-traumatic stress question. (How *would* rehumanized zombies deal with having eaten all those people?) Deadpan voiceover competes with cold-to-the-touch romance. A listless John Malkovich plays Palmer's dad, the zombie-killing leader of humanity's last redoubt.

Starfish aliens menace Japan in *Warning from Space.*

WARNING FROM SPACE

1956 (NR) 87m / **D:** Koji Shima / **W:** Hideo Oguni / **C:** Toyomi Karita, Keizo Kawasaki, Isao Yamagata, Shozo Nanbu, Buntaro Miake, Mieko Nagai, Kiyoko Hirai

Aliens visit Earth to warn of impending cosmic doom. When it becomes apparent that the one-eyed starfish look is off-putting, they assume human form. Not released in the U.S. until 1967. In Japanese, dubbed. AKA: *The Mysterious Satellite*; *The Cosmic Man Appears in Tokyo*; *Space Men Appear in Tokyo*; *Unknown Satellite over Tokyo*.

THE WAR OF THE COLOSSAL BEAST

1958 (NR) 68m / D: Bert I. Gordon / **W:** George Worthing Yates / **C:** Dean Parkin, Sally Fraser, Russ Bender, Roger Pace, Charles Stewart

Sequel to *The Amazing Colossal Man* finds the seventy-foot Colonel Manning even angrier than he was in the first film. So he wreaks more havoc until scolded by his sister into committing suicide for being such a troublemaker. Cheesy f/x but good for a laugh. AKA: *The Terror Strikes*.

THE WAR OF THE GARGANTUAS

1970 (G) 92m / D: Ishiro Honda / **W:** Ishiro Honda, Kaoru Mabuchi / **C:** Russ Tamblyn, Kumi Mizuno, Kenji Sahara, Jun Tazaki

Sequel to *Frankenstein Conquers the World* in which Tokyo is once again the boxing ring for giant monsters. This time, instead of pseudo-dinosaurs, we have a not-so-jolly green giant called the gargantuan that emerges from the ocean to save a ship from a rubbery giant octopus before eating the crew (and spitting out their clothes afterwards). Suave American scientist-type Russ Tamblyn speculates on whether the beast is the adult version of a young ape-like critter he and his colleagues had found and lost some years before. When a gentle "brown gargantua" appears, Tamblyn decides that it's his original subject, who "may have scraped off some flesh on a rock" during his escape from the lab and thus engendered a clone of itself (?!). When the green gargantua won't mend its people-eating ways, its brother engages it in an apocalyptic, building-busting battle. Fairly out-there even by the standards of the Japanese monster flick. One scene In a nightclub features an incredible, jaw-droppingly awful song called "The Words Get Stuck in My Throat," which is alone worth the rental price. AKA: *Duel of the Gargantuas*; *Frankenstein Monsters: Sanda vs. Gairath*.

THE WAR OF THE WORLDS (1953)

1953 (NR) 85m / D: Byron Haskin / **W:** Barré Lyndon / **C:** Gene Barry, Ann Robinson, Les Tremayne, Lewis Martin, Robert Cornthwaite, Sandro Giglio

H. G. Wells's most enduring novel, about the invasion of Earth by a death-dealing armada of Martians, received its perhaps definitive treatment with producer George Pal's action-oriented update from Victorian England to 1950s California. Fairly tense and frightening throughout, with spectacular f/x of destruction caused by the Martian war machines that wouldn't truly be equaled in scope until the 1990s' CGI sci-fi disaster boom. The scenes of the Martian tripods implacably annihilating everything and everyone in their path were pretty much unmatched by any other sci-fi of the period, which remained mostly low-budget and narrow in scope. Late scene of

The classic H. G. Wells novel about Martians attacking Earth was first adapted to the silver screen in 1953.

redemption set in a church would have infuriated the resolutely anti-clergy Wells. Pal makes a cameo. Three Oscar nominations; won for f/x.

WAR OF THE WORLDS (2005)

2005 (PG-13) 116m / **D:** Steven Spielberg / **W:** David Koepp / **C:** Tom Cruise, Dakota Fanning, Miranda Otto, Justin Chatwin, Tim Robbins

Steven Spielberg's other big sci-fi Tom Cruise film is a remake of the H. G. Wells story that rather incredibly hadn't already been redone a half-dozen times or more in the half-century since George Pal's original. David Koepp's screenplay takes some real liberties with the story, as almost everyone does (one day *somebody* will make a straight Wells adaptation), but he gets right more than he gets wrong. The first hour or so is a rigorously orchestrated descent into chaos, after Martian war machines erupt from the ground and start laying waste to everything around them. Cruise adeptly plays the single dad who has to try and get his son through a hauntingly transformed landscape. The implacable unknowability of the aliens helped inform many of the invasion films that were to follow; all of a sudden first contact became much less interesting than the idea of all-out war. The first major sci-fi film to so explicitly play off post-9/11 fears of sudden devastation coming from the skies, it terrifyingly shows how swiftly civilization melts away in the heat of sudden catastrophe. A predictably Spielbergian gloss to the conclusion notwithstanding, this is surprisingly bleak stuff for such a big-star, big-budget concoction. Three Oscar nominations.

THE WASP WOMAN

1959 (NR) 84m / **D:** Roger Corman / **W:** Leo Gordon / **C:** Susan Cabot, Anthony Eisley, Barboura Morris, Michael Marks, William Roerick, Frank Gerstle, Bruno VeSota, Frank Wolff

Roger Corman dishes up the tale of female cosmetics mogul Susan Cabot who unwisely tests a beauty-potion made of wasp enzymes on herself. As a result, she starts moonlighting as a hokey-looking wasp-headed fiend. That'll teach her! Anthony Eisley is her prospective boyfriend, who unfortunately seems to prefer her assistant Barboura Morris. Not what you'd call blindingly original, it's still decently schlocky fun. Interestingly, the monster in the film was a reversal of the one depicted on the movie's poster, which showed a sultry woman's face attached to a humongous wasp. Extant prints have added footage shot to fill television time slots. *Evil Spawn* (1987) was an unofficial remake.

THE WATCH

2012 (R) 102m / **D:** Akiva Schaffer / **W:** Jared Stern, Seth Rogen, Evan Goldberg / **C:** Ben Stiller, Vince Vaughn, Jonah Hill, Richard Ayoade, Rosemarie DeWitt, Will Forte, Mel Rodriguez, R. Lee Ermey, Billy Crudup

Uptight busybody Ben Stiller Is convinced that the murder of a security guard at his Costco is a sign of something dark and sinister threatening his bucolic suburban neighborhood. He forms history's worst neighborhood watch with comic supergroup Vince Vaughn (looking for drinking buddies), Jonah Hill (likes fighting), and Richard Ayoade (recently divorced, wants to meet ladies). In between bickering and boozing and bonding, they discover that murderous aliens are afoot. Mixes elements from other Seth Rogen and Evan Goldberg scripts like *Superbad* and *Pineapple Express* into a fairly raunchy sci-fi comedy that is no classic but far better than its chilly reception warranted. Worth watching almost for Billy Crudup's energetically creepy turn as Stiller's too-interested neighbor.

WATCHMEN

2009 (R) 162m / **D:** Zack Snyder/ **W:** Zack Snyder / **C:** Billy Crudup, Carla Gugino, Matthew Goode, Jackie Earle Haley, Jeffrey Dean Morgan, Patrick Wilson, Malin Akerman

The grim and cynical superhero world of Alan Moore is brought to life in 2009's *Watchmen*.

The most common complaint made about graphic novel adaptations is that they didn't follow the source material with enough fidelity. That can't be said about Zack Snyder's lovingly exact interpretation of Alan Moore's mid-1980s epic that dismantled both the psychology of superheroes and the American Cold War psychology of might making right in one long, carefully calibrated slide toward the apocalypse. In this alternate history, a band of masked vigilantes with appropriately goofy names and outfits but no superhuman powers starts fighting crime during World War II before falling prey to cynicism and madness. Action picks up in 1980s New York, where somebody is bumping off the old Watchmen. Rorschach (Jackie Earle Haley), one of the band's more schizophrenic antiheroes (there are no squeaky-clean good guys here), uncovers a plot that puts the lives of millions of people up against the survival of humanity itself. Snyder gets about as much of the book on screen as Robert Rodriguez did with *Sin City*. But while it's gratifying for fans to see characters like Dr. Manhattan and the Comedian brought to life by such an ardent admirer of the original, without Moore's running internal monologues and rueful moodiness, the story just never clicks together. Not surprisingly, Moore's commentary on American militarism and Reagan-era politics gets chucked by the wayside. Perhaps some graphic novels were just never meant to be filmed. The opening credits sequence, which sets a tabloid slideshow of the Watchmen's rise to and fall from glory to Bob Dylan's "The Times They Are A-Changin'," is one of the more perfect distillations of American postwar disillusionment ever put to film.

WATERWORLD

1995 (PG-13) 135m / **D:** Kevin Reynolds / **W:** Peter Rader, Marc Norman, David N. Twohy / **C:** Kevin Costner, Dennis Hopper, Jeanne Tripplehorn, Tina Majorino, Michael Jeter, R. D. Call, Robert Joy, Zakes Mokae

The Man from Atlantis meets *Mad Max* in this infamously overbudget Kevin Costner vanity project that had industry knives sharpening ("Fishtar," "Kevin's Gate," etc.) before anybody saw a single frame of it. Once all is said and done, much of the money does appear to have ended up on screen in this visually epic film, but it's rather needless as the story, about a water-covered world where melted polar ice caps have left humanity struggling to survive on the ocean, is strictly pumped-up straight-to-VHS mid-'80s postapocalyptic corn. Costner, who did just about everything but cater the meals, stars as Mariner, a gill-featuring mutant who reluctantly helps human survivors search for the mythical Dryland. The bad guys are the Smokers, a gang of ocean-roaming bandits who are led by an evil Dennis Hopper, who can do these roles in his sleep. Of course, Mariner grows fond of his human charges and ultimately must rescue them from the Smokers. The action, sets, and effects are stunning, particularly an awe-inspiring but wildly unnecessary floating city, but a patched-together script ultimately sinks it. Wouldn't have been quite so bad if they had found a way to lop about 45 minutes off the runtime. Supposedly, the script was originally pitched to Roger Corman's company as *Mad Max* on water; ironically the idea, projected to cost $5 million, was rejected for being too expensive. Costner's version would ultimately run about $150 million.

WAVELENGTH

1983 (PG) 87m / **D:** Mike Gray / **W:** Mike Gray / **C:** Robert Carradine, Cherie Currie, Keenan Wynn

Rocker Robert Carradine's psychic girlfriend picks up hypersonic distress signals—sounds like whales—from childlike aliens, recovered from a UFO crash site and kept on ice in a secret government base beneath the Hollywood hills (script takes pains to make that geographic novelty quite plausible). Fun, enthusiastically cheap sci-fi with an ending strikingly similar to that of *Starman*; writer/director Mike Gray would actually direct the short-lived TV series based on that John Carpenter film. Soundtrack by Tangerine Dream.

WAXWORK II: LOST IN TIME

1992 (R) 104m / **D:** Anthony Hickox / **W:** Anthony Hickox / **C:** Zach Galligan, Alexander Godunov, Bruce Campbell, Michael Des Barres, Monika Schnarre

Sequel to the ostensibly non-sci-fi *Waxwork*, in which monsters in an infamous waxworks museum turned out to be real. On trial for the fiends' crimes, a heroic young couple must travel through a bizarre time machine and enter other universes ("God's Nintendo game") where horror and sci-fi movie characters actually do exist. It's a pretext to recreate scenes from past genre efforts, from the gothic horror of *Frankenstein* to the high-tech gore of *Alien*, and it all hangs together like an explosion in a cliché factory. An end title boasts "Filmed entirely in the fourth dimension."

WEIRD SCIENCE

1985 (PG-13) 94m / **D:** John Hughes / **W:** John Hughes **C:** Matthew F. Leonetti / **C:** Kelly Le Brock, Anthony Michael Hall, Ilan Mitchell-Smith, Robert Downey Jr., Bill Paxton, Suzanne Snyder, Judie Aronson

The most hard-to-define of John Hughes's 1980s comedies energetically if unevenly mixes the era's fascination with both prurient teen boy humor (lots of eyes goggling at hot women) and the new wave of technology (plenty of wildly fantastical representations of personal computers' power). Anthony Michael Hall and his fellow nerd Ilan Mitchell-Smith use a very special kind of software to create the ideal woman, in the person of Kelly LeBrock. The leering implications of these two junior Frankensteins "making a woman" are mostly glossed over. Le Brock functions as a guide into maturity, proving to be less their object of lust than best friend. She solves all of their problems in a fairly zany way, turning Hall's bullying older brother (a fantastically oafish Bill Paxton) into a toadlike creature and such. Utter non sequitur of an ending features a superbly comic moment from *The Hills Have Eyes*'s Michael Berryman as a cross-dimensional mutant biker who is worried about losing his teaching job. The smart casting includes an early appearance by Robert Downey Jr. Typically for Hughes, the soundtrack features New Wave of the time like Oingo Boingo, OMD, and Wall of Voodoo. Rather puzzlingly, the film inspired a cable series that didn't get off the ground until the 1990s.

> "The most hard-to-define of John Hughes's 1980s comedies energetically if unevenly mixes the era's fascination with both prurient teen boy humor … and the new wave of technology…."
>
> *Weird Science*

WES CRAVEN PRESENTS MIND RIPPER

1995 (R) 90m / **D:** Joe Gayton / **W:** Jonathan Craven, Phil Mittleman / **C:** Lance Henriksen, John Diehl, Natasha Gregson Wagner, Dan Blom, Claire Stansfield

Secret government experiment to produce self-healing super soldiers goes awry, as it usually does. The mad scientists who created the beast become trapped in an abandoned nuclear site and get picked off one by one with the usual grotesque results. A slumming Lance Henriksen plays the good-hearted lead scientist who left the experiment when he discovered its violent purpose, but is forced to return now that the creature has run amok. Just barely adequate retread of very familiar ground. Executive producer Wes Craven's name is heavily featured here; the script was co-written by his son. AKA: *Mind Ripper*; *The Outpost*.

WESTWORLD

1973 (PG) 90m / **D:** Michael Crichton / **W:** Michael Crichton / **C:** Yul Brynner, Richard Benjamin, James Brolin, Dick Van Patten, Majel Barrett, Norman Bartold, Alan Oppenheimer

Novelist Michael Crichton wrote and directed this story of Delos, a futuristic adult vacation resort where guests' every need and fantasy are serviced by lifelike robots. James Brolin and Richard Benjamin play businessmen who choose the Wild West fantasy world. When an electrical malfunction occurs, the robots begin to go berserk, and the vacation turns deadly. Despite low-end f/x, the taut script and good performances make this a solid thriller. Yul Brynner is perfect as the menacing western gunslinger whose skills become all too real. Followed by sequel *Futureworld* in 1976. Never one to let a cash-generating idea gather dust, Crichton would return to the technology-run-amok theme again with *Runaway* and *Jurassic Park*.

WHAT PLANET ARE YOU FROM?

2000 (R) 105m / **D:** Mike Nichols / **W:** Garry Shandling, Michael Leeson, Ed Solomon, Peter Tolan / **C:** Garry Shandling, Annette Bening, John Goodman, Greg Kinnear, Ben Kingsley, Linda Fiorentino, Judy Greer

Just about the only time that darksome cynic Garry Shandling ever starred in a movie was for this poorly received sci-fi comedy where he plays an alien who has been sent to Earth to find a woman to impregnate so that he can bring the child back to his own planet. Needless to say, things don't go well, as his pickup lines are all delivered to him by his fellow emotionless aliens and are not well received by the human females.

WHEN WORLDS COLLIDE

1951 (G) 81m / **D:** Rudolph Maté / **W:** Sydney Boehm / **C:** Richard Derr, Barbara Rush, Larry Keating, Peter Hansen, John Hoyt, Judith Ames

Another planet is found to be rushing inevitably towards Earth. Luckily, a companion planet will likely arrive in time to take Earth's place. A select group of people attempts to escape in a spaceship; others try to maneuver their way onboard. Oscar-quality f/x and fascinating plot make up for some cheesy acting and bad writing. The only movie spaceship to be launched from a ramp rather than the traditional launch pad. The new planet is disappointingly represented only by a poor landscape painting—apparently an elaborate model of the scenery was planned, but time ran out on the production. A remake has been rumored/threatened for years. Two Oscar nominations; won for f/x.

WHERE TIME BEGAN

1977 (G) 87m / **D:** J. Piquer Simón / **W:** John Melson, Carlos Puerto / **C:** Kenneth More, Pep Munné, Jack Taylor

The discovery of a strange manuscript of a scientist's journey to the center of the Earth leads to the decision to recreate the dangerous mission.

THE SCI-FI MOVIE GUIDE: The Universe of Film from "Alien" to "Zardoz"

Like Noah's Ark, a spaceship to carry away a few lucky humans to a new planet is the only escape in *When Worlds Collide*.

Based on Jules Verne's *Journey to the Center of the Earth*, but not anywhere near its equal.

WHITE MAN'S BURDEN

1995 (R) 89m / D: Desmond Nakano / **W:** Desmond Nakano / **C:** John Travolta, Harry Belafonte, Kelly Lynch, Margaret Avery

Not precisely subtle racial allegory presents an alternate America, where whites are an oppressed underclass living in downtrodden neighborhoods, while blacks occupy the top rungs of society. John Travolta is a fired factory worker who kidnaps his wealthy one-time boss Harry Belafonte out of frustration. They eventually discover that they have more in common than they might have thought.

WHO?

1973 (PG) 93m / D: Jack Gold / **W:** John Gould / **C:** Elliott Gould, Trevor Howard, Joseph Bova

Adaptation of 1958 Algis Budrys's smart, John LeCarre-esque Cold War sci-fi novel about an American scientist (Joseph Bova) who's critically injured in East Germany but rehabilitated by commie scientists as an android metal man and sent back to the Free World, where he is promptly suspected of being a Soviet Bloc spy. Elliott Gould plays the FBI agent assigned to interrogate Bova. Less about techno-intrigue than the nature of identity. AKA: *Roboman*.

WICKED CITY (1987)

1987 (NR) 82m / D: Yoshiaki Kawajiri / **W:** Kisei Choo

Gruesome futuristic anime about secret police force the Black Guard that protects Earth from cross-dimensional demonic beasts. Some intriguing fantasy noir and cyberpunk elements are overshadowed, though, by a strain of hyperviolent misogyny that was all too prevalent in Japanese comics at the time.

WICKED CITY (1993)

1993 (NR) 92m / D: Peter Mak / **W:** Tsui Hark / **C:** Jacky Cheung, Leon Lai, Michelle Li

Based on the Japanese comic strip by Hideyuki Kikuchi, but looking more like a remake of the hyperviolent 1987 anime of the same name, *Wicked City* delivers the now-expected doses of over-the-top Hong Kong-style action and outrageous stunts. The atmospherics are memorable, the lush cinematography capturing a futuristic Hong Kong with both its neon-lit color and the dark *Blade Runner*-esque feel necessary to convey the uncomfortable feelings of the humans forced to co-exist with the sinister reptoids, shape-shifting disguised-as-human creatures intent on ruling the world. Luckily for humankind, the monster-police are more than happy to do a little reptoid-bashing. A little like John Carpenter's *They Live*, but without the glasses and a whole lot more intense. Produced and co-written by Tsui Hark, who has directed a few superb demon-kung-fu action movies himself.

> "A little like John Carpenter's *They Live*, but without the glasses and a whole lot more intense."
>
> *Wicked City (1993)*

WILD IN THE STREETS

1968 (R) 97m / D: Barry Shear / **W:** Robert Thom / **C:** Shelley Winters, Christopher Jones, Hal Holbrook, Richard Pryor, Diane Varsi, Millie Perkins, Ed Begley Sr.

"If you're over 30, you'd better forget it...." So goes the theme song to this half-chilling, half-hilarious black comedy that puts a paranoid spin on youthful rebellion. Christopher Jones stars as rock idol Max Frost, who uses his influence with the young (not to mention LSD dumped in Washington, D.C.'s water supply) to get the voting age lowered to 14 and himself elected president. His first act is to incarcerate all citizens over the age of 30 in "retirement homes." Richard Pryor co-stars as Stanley X, drummer and author of *The Aborigine Cookbook*. Shelley Winters goes over the top as Max's groovy-impaired mother ("Senator," she rebukes Hal Holbrook, "I'm sure my son has a very good reason for paralyzing the country"). Notable for how it satirizes the consequences-be-damned youths in revolt as much as it does the out-of-touch adult establishment. The soundtrack scored a hit, "Shape of Things to Come." The chilling last line is a knockout: "Everybody over 10 ought to be put out of business."

THE WILD WORLD OF BATWOMAN

1966 (NR) 70m / **D:** Jerry Warren / **W:** Jerry Warren / **C:** Katherine Victor, George Andre, Steve Brodie, Lloyd Nelson

Cult spectacle in which Batwoman (Katherine Victor, who earlier starred in director Jerry Warren's truly wretched *Teenage Zombies*) and a bevy of so-called Bat Girls are pitted against an evil doctor in order to find the prototype of an atomic hearing aid/nuclear bomb. Out-camps the *Batman* series Warren is explicitly trying to capitalize on. Most of the entertainment value comes from the fact that you can't believe you're actually watching this. Also released theatrically as *She Was a Hippy Vampire* due to legal pressure.

A WIND NAMED AMNESIA

1993 (NR) 80m / **D:** Kazuo Yamazaki / **W:** Hideyuki Kikuchi

In this anime, a strange amnesia-causing wind sweeps away all of mankind's knowledge and human civilization vanishes, leaving brutality in its wake. Then a mysterious young man is miraculously re-educated and searches for those who destroyed man's memories. Wandering the deserted landscape, he finds a woman who can speak, and a lethal robot that has it in for him. While that could be the basis for any number of B-movies, writer Hideyuki Kikuchi, animator Satoru Nakamura, and director Kazuo Yamazaki take time to speculate on the larger questions raised by the story: the philosophical implications of pure innocence, the nature of men and women, and the evolution of religion.

WING COMMANDER

1999 (PG-13) 100m / **D:** Chris Roberts / **W:** Kevin Droney / **C:** Freddie Prinze Jr., Saffron Burrows, Matthew Lillard, Tchéky Karyo, Jürgen Prochnow

27th-century space opera about a galaxy-wide war between the Terran Confederation and a race of cat-like aliens called the Kilrathi, who seem to be based on the Kzins from Larry Niven's Known Space novels. Starred a number of fresh-faced 1990s kids like Matthew Lillard and Freddie Prinze Jr., ordinarily seen in Miramax teen fare, as the *de rigeur* hot-shot pilots who are humanity's last hope. Based on a series of once-popular video games.

WINGS OF HONNEAMISE

1987 (NR) 121m / **D:** Hiroyuki Yamaga / **W:** Hiroyuki Yamaga

Epic anime that didn't receive a true American release until 1995. Alternate-world sci-fi about an Earth-like planet where a kingdom is half-heartedly developing a space program that might end up instigating a war. Writer/director Hiroyuki Yamaga's Utagawa Hiroshige-inspired animation style was more fully advanced than most of the factory-produced anime coming out of Japan at the time. AKA: *Royal Space Force: The Wings of Honneamise.*

WIRED TO KILL

1986 (R) 96m / **D:** Franky Schaeffer / **W:** Franky Schaeffer / **C:** Merritt Butrick, Emily Longstreth, Devin Hoelscher, Frank Collison

In a wrecked future world (yes, again), two whiz-kid teens seek justice for their parents' murder by building a remote-controlled erector set programmed for revenge. Shot in South Africa, this formula revenge story gains a few shreds of interest if you know writer/director Franky Schaeffer is a one-time evangelical activist and son of hugely influential apocalyptic Christian evangelical leader Francis Schaeffer. Schaeffer's involvement gives the film a stronger-than-usual sense of moral doom in its dystopian society where nothing seems to work except automated 800 numbers. Otherwise, no revelation.

WIZARDS

1977 (PG) 81m / **D:** Ralph Bakshi / **W:** Ralph Bakshi

A profane, crude, beautifully animated, and typically Bakshian fantasy in which post-apocalyptic Earth has turned into a medieval fantasy world full of fairies and monsters. The good but bumbling sorcerer Avatar teams up with a shell-shocked battle-android and a couple of elves to battle his evil brother Blackwolf, who seeks to take over the world from the ruined land of Scortch. In a rather startling touch, Blackwolf uses old Nazi propaganda films to inspire his army of bloodthirsty mutants. Alternately funny and bleak, comic and thought-provoking; all in all a perfect mix for 1970s midnight movie heads. Underground comics fans will note a similarity between Bakshi's character-designs and those of cartoonist Vaughn Bode.

THE WOLVERINE

2013 (PG-13) 126m / **D:** James Mangold / **W:** Mark Bomback, Scott Frank / **C:** Hugh Jackman, Tao Okamoto, Rila Fukushima, Hiroyuki Sanada, Svetlana Khodchenkova, Brian Tee, Hal Yamanouchi, Famke Janssen

Hugh Jackman has played the popular X-Men hero Wolverine in several Marvel films.

It might not be what the film's original team of Darren Aronofsky (*Requiem for a Dream*) and Christopher McQuarrie (*The Usual Suspects*) had planned (their idea was *Akira Kurosawa's Wolverine*), but James Mangold's follow-up to the underwhelming *X-Men Origins: Wolverine* is a swift superhero adventure with a strong emotional core. Trying to hide from his tragic memories in the Canadian woods, Wolverine (Hugh Jackman) is summoned to Japan by pixie-ish warrior girl Rila Fukushima to say goodbye to an old friend. Before you know it, Wolverine is mired in a bloody dynastic struggle that has him battling Yakuza thugs, a giant robot, *and* swarms of ninjas (in other words, no Japanese cliché left unused) while trying to exorcise his demons and deal with his own mortality—it seems the adamantine-clawed loner doesn't feel like being immortal anymore. Some gorgeous filming, particularly one battle on a dark, snowy street that leaves Wolverine pincushioned with arrows as a possible nod to Akira Kurosawa's *Throne of Blood*. But including the atom-bombing of Nagasaki for the film's prologue can't help but feel exploitative.

WOMAN IN THE MOON

1929 (NR) 115m / D: Fritz Lang / **W:** Fritz Lang / **C:** Klaus Pohl, Willy Fritsch, Gustav von Wagenheim, Gerda Maurus

Assorted characters embark on a trip to the moon and discover water, and an atmosphere, as well as gold. Fritz Lang's last silent outing is nothing next to *Metropolis*, with a rather predictable plot (greedy trip bashers seek gold), but interesting as a vision of the future. Lang's predictions about space travel often hit the mark. One of Lang's technical advisors on the film, Hermann Oberth, came up with the idea of showing a countdown to the rocket's launch, the first time such a thing was ever shown on film. After Lang fled Germany for Hollywood, Oberth stayed behind and joined the Nazis' rocket program under Wernher von Braun. AKA: *By Rocket to the Moon*; *Girl in the Moon*.

WOMEN OF THE PREHISTORIC PLANET

1966 (NR) 90m / **D:** Arthur C. Pierce / **W:** Arthur C. Pierce / **C:** Wendell Corey, Irene Tsu, Robert Ito, Stuart Margolin, Lyle Waggoner, Adam Roarke, Merry Anders, John Agar, Paul Gilbert

Members of a space rescue mission face the usual deadly perils on a strange planet, including a "giant" spider and lizards, and very unrealistic man-eating plants. During their stay, the astronauts manage to bring together a native couple, Linda and Tang. As far as the title is concerned, get this: Linda is the only woman, and she's not "of" the planet in question. See if you can last long enough to catch the "amazing" plot twist at the end.

WORLD GONE WILD

1988 (R) 95m / **D:** Lee H. Katzin / **W:** Jorge Zamacona / **C:** Bruce Dern, Michael Paré, Adam Ant, Catherine Mary Stewart, Rick Podell

Action yarn about a post-apocalyptic world of the future where an evil cult leader brainwashes his disciples. Together they battle a small band of eccentrics for the world's last water source. Stale rehash (with ineffective satiric elements) of the *Mad Max* genre, served with Adam Ant for campy appeal.

WORLD ON A WIRE

1973 (NR) 212m / **D:** Rainer Werner Fassbinder / **W:** Fritz Müller-Scherz, Rainer Werner Fassbinder / **C:** Klaus Löwitsch, Adrian Hoven, Ivan Desny, Barbara Valentin, Mascha Rabben

Two-part TV movie from prolific German filmmaker Rainer Werner Fassbinder that went mostly unseen until its 2011 restoration. Buries a forward-thinking story about virtual reality (in all likelihood, the first sci-fi film to have imagined it) inside a gruesomely lugubrious Godardian grab-bag of gangster-flick tropes and stilted, self-aware dialogue. Tricky but sluggish story follows computer engineer Klaus Löwtisch, whose boss dies in a suspicious accident just after revealing that he's discovered a deadly secret about their virtual reality experiments (themselves a refreshingly low-tech apparatus involving helmets and closed-circuit TV). There are femme fatales and meaningful stares aplenty but precious little warmth in this purposefully cold, modernistic story whose bleak spaces can be read as almost a textbook on soulless postwar European architecture. Based on the Daniel F. Galouye novel *Simulacron-3*, as was the 1999 film *The Thirteenth Floor*.

THE WORLD'S END

2013 (R) 119m / **D:** Edgar Wright / **W:** Simon Pegg, Nick Frost / **C:** Simon Pegg, Martin Freeman, Eddie Marsan, Nick Frost, Paddy Considine, Rosamund Pike, Pierce Brosnan

Another raucous genre tribute from the *Shaun of the Dead* team, this time paying homage to the British tradition of stories where the characters enter a small town whose placid surface hides strange goings-on. Co-writer Simon Pegg leads the cast as an aging tosser whose life apparently peaked one night in 1990 when he led his high school mates on an abortive but nevertheless epic twelve-pub crawl. Possessed of boundless energy and zero pride, he rounds up the old gang (a roll call of greats, from young Bilbo himself, Martin Freeman, to Paddy Considine, Eddie Marsan and Pegg's writing partner Nick Frost) and cajoles them into reenacting the crawl back in their home town. Things go cockeyed in a script that mixes camera-mugging humor and '90s cultural references with a story that might have made for a decent *Dr. Who* episode or tossed-off Hammer film. Fittingly, the world's fate will be decided at the last pub on the crawl: The World's End.

THE WORLD, THE FLESH AND THE DEVIL

1959 (NR) 95m / **D:** Ranald MacDougall / **W:** Ranald MacDougall / **C:** Harry Belafonte, Inger Stevens, Mel Ferrer

Curious post-apocalyptic allegory based on a novel by M. P. Shiel in which miner Harry Belafonte emerges from underground to find the world deserted. Drawn to New York he finds society blonde Inger Stevens in the city's emptiness. Eventually Mel Ferrer shows up to cause problems of a racial, sexual, and irritational nature. Ferrer points out to Belafonte what he sees as their one big dilemma: "There's two of us and one of her." Stevens asks, "Why don't you flip a coin?" Music by the great Miklós Rózsa when Belafonte (at the time one of the country's top recording artists) isn't strumming a guitar.

WORLD WAR Z

2013 (PG-13) 116m / **D:** Marc Forster / **W:** Matthew Michael Carnahan, Drew Goddard, Damon Lindelof / **C:** Brad Pitt, Mireille Enos, Matthew Fox, James Badge Dale, David Morse

Brad Pitt produced this humanity-vs.-zombies war movie through numerous budget-busting rewrites and reshoots so, not surprisingly, he gets to play the UN worker whose skills are apparently the only thing standing between the species and oblivion once the infestation occurs. No cause is given for the outbreak, It just seems that in no time at all, the undead are running amok, biting and eating at a breakneck pace that's like *28 Days Later* mixed with an insect swarm (one of their tactics is to pile up on each other by the thousands so as to swarm over human barriers). The story is a globetrotter, with Pitt looking in on the zombie fight around the world, from a beleaguered army outpost in South Korea to a besieged Jerusalem, while his family tries not to get tossed off the only truly safe place on earth: An aircraft carrier surrounded by nothing but water. Quick-paced and filled with potential but ultimately unsatisfying. Based on a best-selling novel by Max Brooks (Mel Brooks's nerdy son) that was more oral history than action story.

WORLD WITHOUT END

1956 (NR) 80m / **D:** Edward Bernds / **W:** Edward Bernds / **C:** Hugh Marlowe, Nancy Gates, Nelson Leigh, Rod Taylor

Lost-astronaut time-travel adventure (shot in glorious Cinemascope!) that finds our four intrepid explorers tossed through a time warp to the 26th century, where the aftereffects of a nuclear war have left the Earth crawling with giant spiders, one-eyed mutants, and underworld-dwellers whose menfolk are as craven as their women are attractive and scantily clad.

WRESTLING WOMEN VS. THE AZTEC APE

1962 (NR) 75m / **D:** René Cardona Sr. / **W:** Alfredo Salazar / **C:** Elizabeth Campbell, Lorena Velázquez, Armando Silvestre, Roberto Cañedo

An unclassifiable epic of brawny beauties versus a brawnier beast. The Golden Rubi and her sister Gloria Venus battle a mad doctor and his Aztec robot gorilla. Badly dubbed, of course, but are you going to let that bother you? The much anticipated follow-up to the classic *Wrestling Women vs. the Aztec Mummy*. AKA: *Doctor of Doom*.

THE X-FILES

1998 (PG-13) 121m / D: Rob Bowman / **W:** Chris Carter / **C:** David Duchovny, Gillian Anderson, John Neville, William B. Davis, Martin Landau, Mitch Pileggi, Terry O'Quinn

Just as the TV show was hitting its peak (or starting to spiral into irrelevance), Chris Carter generated this lavishly budgeted feature version of the show that again put Mulder (David Duchovny) and Scully (Gillian Anderson) at the center of a potentially world-ending threat. A kid falls into a cave in Texas, which unfortunately contains some alien beings from tens of thousands of years prior that turn his eyes black (proving again the rule that anybody seen in the opening of an *X-Files* episode doesn't stand much chance of surviving). What follows is glossily packaged pop conspiracy stuff about government covering up the impending alien invasion, played out against Mulder and Scully's smolder and bicker. More of interest to those well-versed in the show's dense plotting, but still has more the feel of a Very Special Two-Night Television Event than a standalone feature. The opening scene, in which a dedicated operative kills himself blowing up a government office building queasily evokes the Oklahoma City terrorist bombing just a few years prior.

THE X-FILES: I WANT TO BELIEVE

2008 (PG-13) 104m / D: Chris Carter / **W:** Chris Carter, Frank Spotnitz / **C:** David Duchovny, Gillian Anderson, Amanda Peet, Billy Connolly, Xzibit, Mitch Pileggi

Highly unnecessary add-on to the *X-Files* mythology coming six years after the show wheezed to an end. Both Scully and Mulder are done with alien-hunting, but they're brought back by the FBI to work with a priest (Billy Connolly) claiming to be a psychic who can help them find an agent who has

David Duchovney reprised his role as Fox Mulder from the TV series for *The X-Files* and *The X-Files: I Want to Believe.*

gone missing. Disposable plot that follows is as tiresome as the half-baked spiritual crises that Chris Carter concocts for Scully and Mulder to bicker about.

X-MEN

2000 (PG-13) 104m / **D:** Bryan Singer / **W:** David Hayter / **C:** Hugh Jackman, Patrick Stewart, Ian McKellan, Famke Janssen, James Marsden, Halle Berry, Anna Paquin, Tyler Mane, Ray Park, Rebecca Romijn-Stamos

The most dramatically engaging of the sci-fi comic-book franchises in the 2000s started with this clever, emotive origin story that married gee-whiz superhero whiff-bang-pow with angsty melodrama and stark allusions to genocide. Just as in the long-running Marvel series, the mutant heroes are a new breed of humans who've been popping up around the world with nifty powers that make people around them nervous. Prof. Xavier (a fatherly Patrick Stewart) gathers the young mutants together at his school for training and safekeeping. Anna Paquin's Rogue is typical of the smoldering teenage alienation the mutants are meant to symbolize: She absorbs energy from those she touches, putting her boyfriend into a coma after kissing him. Battle is joined when Magneto (Ian McKellan) demands that all mutants join his alliance to wipe out humans. Giving Magneto's villainy a dark complexity is the logic of his reasoning: mutants should destroy the humans before the reverse is done (Magneto, a Nazi concentration camp survivor, knows what humans are capable of). A dour, sardonic Hugh Jackman plays the claw-handed and near-indestructible Wolverine as the young mutants' protective older brother, while Halle Berry is the weather-controlling Storm and Rebecca Romijn-Stamos the blue-skinned shape-shifter Mystique.

X-MEN: FIRST CLASS

2011 (PG-13) 132m / **D:** Matthew Vaughn / **W:** Ashley Miller, Zack Stentz, Jane Goldman, Matthew Vaughn / **C:** James McAvoy, Michael Fassbender, Kevin Bacon, Rose Byrne, Jennifer Lawrence, Oliver Platt, Jason Flemyng, Zoë Kravitz, January Jones, Nicholas Hoult

Matthew Vaughn's trim, spirited relaunch of the *X-Men* franchise is a 1962-set prequel that provides the roots of Magneto (Michael Fassbender) and Xavier (James McAvoy)'s complicated friendship / rivalry and also cleverly threads the mutant story into an alternate historical take on the Cuban Missile Crisis. There's a crop of different performers here ranging from younger versions of older mutants (Jennifer Lawrence as a young and less-evil Mystique) to entirely new ones (Jason Flemyng as the red-skinned teleporting assassin Azazel). A revenge-obsessed Magneto hunts down Nazis in South America while Xavier is an Oxford scholar just learning about mutants; the time period and their different paths make the Malcolm X / Martin Luther King Jr. analogy even stronger than it was in earlier films. Kevin Bacon cackles wildly as a Nazi villain and head of a secret society trying to bring the world to the brink of nuclear war.

X-Men Origins: Wolverine

2009 (PG-13) 107m / **D:** Gavin Hood / **W:** David Benioff, Skip Woods / **C:** Hugh Jackman, Liev Schreiber, Danny Huston, Will.i.am, Lynn Collins, Kevin Durand, Dominic Monaghan, Taylor Kitsch, Daniel Henney, Ryan Reynolds

Judging that the biggest star from the *X-Men* series was Wolverine (correctly) and that any story all about him would be a sure-fire winner (incorrectly), Fox decided to spin him off with his own retread of an origin story. Anything of interest here to the non-completist was already covered in Bryan Singer's films and the only thing left with much dramatic worth is Wolverine's (Hugh Jackman) relationship with his also animalistic and nearly impossible to kill half-brother Victor Creed, aka Sabretooth (a superb Liev Schrieber). Once the film moves past the young brothers' career as eternal soldiers (Civil War to Vietnam), it turns into a Wolverine vs. Sabretooth snarl-off, with an extended version of the high-tech military experiments on Wolverine. Overly reliant on second-rate f/x, with director Gavin Hood's sloppy action scenes failing to overcome an indifferent script.

X-Men: The Last Stand

2006 (PG-13) 104m / **D:** Brett Ratner / **W:** Simon Kinberg, Zak Penn / **C:** Hugh Jackman, Patrick Stewart, Ian McKellen, Famke Janssen, James Marsden, Halle Berry, Anna Paquin, Rebecca Romijn, Vinnie Jones, Ellen Page, Ben Foster, Kelsey Grammer

The tortured-mutant series almost came to an end with this ignominiously generic effort from characterless blockbuster generator Brett Ratner (Bryan Singer would have returned but he went off to do *Superman Returns*). A new drug that "cures" mutants of their abilities leads to increased agitation by Magneto's mutants to take the fight to the humans. Notable new characters include Kelsey Grammar as the head of the government's Department of Mutant Affairs, who's also a hairy blue mutant called Beast, and Ben Foster as a teen mutant named Angel who sports a broad span of white wings

Patrick Stewart has played Dr. Charles Xavier, the leader of the X-Men, in several installments of the sprawling film series.

and a healthy sense of self-hatred. All somewhat repetitive, building up to a massive mutant-vs.-human-vs.-mutant battle on Alcatraz that's far less dramatic than it should have been.

X: THE MAN WITH THE X-RAY EYES

1963 (NR) 79m / D: Roger Corman / **W:** Robert Russell, Robert Dillon / **C:** Ray Milland, Diana Van Der Vlis, Harold J. Stone, John Hoyt, Don Rickles, Dick Miller, Jonathan Haze, Lorie Summers, Vicki Lee

One of Roger Corman's best sci-fi efforts, an existential horror story about a doctor (Ray Milland) who fools around with experimental eye-drops that give him X-ray vision. The idea of being able to see through solid objects like clothes was run into the ground in early nudie pictures, but Corman bypasses such sophomoric pleasures in favor of a slowly mounting feeling of unease. Although Milland has fun with his powers at first, things go awry when he accidentally offs a colleague. Now on the lam, he begins to realize his enhanced sight is slowly getting stronger. Finally he sees through eternity itself, going mad in the process. A powerful, disturbing story; too bad Corman didn't make more films like it. Don Rickles has a small part as a carny owner. AKA: *The Man with the X-Ray Eyes*; *X*.

XTRO

1983 (R) 80m / **D:** Harry Bromley Davenport / **W:** Iain Cassie, Robert Smith / **C:** Philip Sayer, Bernice Stegers, Danny Brainin, Simon Nash, Maryam D'Abo, David Cardy, Anna Wing, Peter Mandell, Robert Fyfe

English chap abducted by aliens returns to his family as a fast-metamorphosing mutant "bearing black magic from outer space" (that's how the original ads helpfully explained a pointless subplot about the man's nasty little son doing the *Carrie* routine with telekinesis). Emphasis on slime, sex, disease, and splatter, ranging from the inventively nightmarish to the truly offensive.

X2

2003 (PG-13) 133m / **D:** Bryan Singer / **W:** Michael Dougherty, Dan Harris, David Hayter / **C:** Hugh Jackman, Patrick Stewart, Ian McKellen, Famke Janssen, James Marsden, Halle Berry, Anna Paquin, Brian Cox, Alan Cumming, Rebecca Romljn-Stamos

Probably one of Roger Corman's best films, *The Man with the X-Ray Eyes* goes beyond shlock horror and sci-fi to create a powerful and disturbing story.

Powerful follow-up to Bryan Singer's first *X-Men* film provides some backstory for the series' most popular character: Wolverine. Hugh Jackman chomps his way through cigars and hard-bitten dialogue as he works through his tortured, amnesiac past and faces down Col. Stryker (Brian Cox), who's now busy trying to eliminate *all* mutants before Magneto goes too far. Angsty romance between Wolverine and Jean Grey (Famke Janssen) continues. Standout sequences include Magneto's escape from his all-plastic prison and a walloping battle scene when Xavier's mutant school is assaulted by Stryker's soldiers looking for mutants to kidnap. A fey Alan Cumming appears as the slithery invisible Nightcrawler, who infiltrates the White House in the opening scene to plant a message in the Oval Office: "Mutant freedom now."AKA: *X2: X-Men United*.

Yor, the Hunter from the Future

1983 (PG) 88m / **D:** Anthony Dawson / **W:** Anthony Dawson, Robert D. Bailey / **C:** Reb Brown, Corinne Cléry, Luciano Pigozzi, Carole André

Classic Italian grindhouse box-checking. Cavemen? Dinosaurs? Scantily clad damsels being distressed? Laser guns? Spaceships? Check to all! Crammed down from an Italian TV four-parter and released to surprising success in American theaters, this is straight caveman action as the muscled and mulleted Yor (Reb Brown) fights everything in sight, from vicious dinosaurs to other cavemen to androids (don't ask how this is all possible in the same film). Along the way, Yor even manages to swing across a chasm while avoiding the enemy's laser blasts, Luke Skywalker-style. The excruciating "Yor's World" theme song is justifiably beloved by fans of all things terrible.

Young Frankenstein

1974 (PG) 108m / **D:** Mel Brooks / **W:** Gene Wilder, Mel Brooks / **C:** Peter Boyle, Gene Wilder, Marty Feldman, Madeline Kahn, Cloris Leachman, Teri Garr, Kenneth Mars, Richard Haydn, Gene Hackman

In Mel Brooks's hilarious and affectionate parody, Gene Wilder plays Dr. Frankenstein ("Franken-*shteen*"), a brain surgeon who inherits the family castle back in Transylvania. He's skittish about the family business, but when he learns his grandfather's secrets, he becomes obsessed with making his own monster, aided by Marty Feldman as Igor ("*Eye*-gor"). Wilder and monster Peter Boyle make a memorable song-and-dance team to Irving Berlin's "Puttin' on the Ritz," and Gene Hackman's cameo as a blind man is inspired. Teri Garr is adorably clueless, while Cloris Leachman's Teutonic stereotype is old as the hills but still works. Brooks's vaudevillian, shtick-layered classic is as much homage to as it is satire of the Universal horror classic, to the extent of mimicking the classic cinematography and reusing part of James Whale's old sets. According to legend, Brooks first got the studio to sign off on the project and then told them he'd be shooting in black-and-white just before darting out of the room. Two Oscar nominations: sound, adapted screenplay.

ZARDOZ

1973 (R) 105m / D: John Boorman / **W:** John Boorman / **C:** Sean Connery, Charlotte Rampling, John Alderton, Sara Kestelman, Sally Anne Newton, Niall Buggy

In John Boorman's curious parable of the far future, it's 2293 and Earth society is broken into strict and segregated classes: a society of bored, detached intellectuals burdened with eternal life; a horde of primitives who have the privilege of breeding as long as they're slain regularly; and an elite unit of killers who do the job. Sean Connery (in a role first offered to Burt Reynolds) is one of the latter, a clever barbarian who destroys the old order of things by stowing away in the floating monolithic head of the god Zardoz (as in *Wizard of Oz*) to penetrate the immortals' stronghold. The pretentions may be overwhelming and the outfits ludicrous, but Boorman's impressive visuals and weighty metaphysical meditations make up much of the difference. Boorman turned to this curious project only after his attempt to film *The Lord of the Rings* fell through.

ZATHURA

2005 (PG) 113 / D: Jon Favreau / **W:** David Koepp, John Kamps / **C:** Josh Hutcherson, Jonah Bobo, Tim Robbins, Dax Shepard, Kristen Stewart

Summer fun-time adventure whose overheated family togetherness message was exploded out of Chris Van Allsburg's classically simple children's book, much like what was done with 1995's *Jumanji*. Two bickering brothers (the surlier one played by *The Hunger Games*' Josh Hutcherson) are left in the house by overworked dad Tim Robbins and kill time playing dusty old spaceship game "Zathura," which promptly comes to life and sends their tastefully retro yuppie bungalow zooming into space. The brothers spend most of the movie dodging everything from meteor showers to giant killer robots while still finding time to gripe at each other. Director Jon Favreau delivers a couple sly jokes amidst the repetitive battling-sibling narrative, mostly courtesy of Dax Shepard as the astronaut who pops by the space-sailing house to help out. Takes a casually old-fashioned approach to the impressive f/x, from the Jules Verne-esque spaceships and the reptilian Zorgons who could have sprung straight from the pages of an Edgar Rice Burroughs Mars adventure.

ZERO POPULATION GROWTH

1972 (PG) 95m / D: Michael Campus / **W:** Frank De Felitta, Max Ehrlich / **C:** Oliver Reed, Geraldine Chaplin, Diane Cilento, Don Gordon

In the 21st century the government has decreed that no babies may be born for a 30-year span in order to control the population. But Geraldine Chaplin and Oliver Reed (who aren't satisfied with the robot babies the government provides as a substitute for the real thing) secretly have a child. When discovered, they are sent to be executed. Can they escape? Maudlin and simplistic. AKA: *Z.P.G.*

ZOMBIELAND

2009 (R) 88m / D: Ruben Fleischer / **W:** Rhett Reese, Paul Wernick / **C:** Jesse Eisenberg, Woody Harrelson, Emma Stone, Abigail Breslin, Amber Heard, Bill Murray

The zombie apocalypse isn't that hard to make it through, you just need to have some rules. That's according to loner and survivor Jesse Eisenberg, whose long list of survival hints include "always look in the back seat," and the importance of cardio workouts. But things get lonely even for him, so he's happy to play uptight sidekick to wahoo zombie-killing machine Woody Harrelson (updating his grinning psychopath from *Natural Born Killers*). They team up with grifter girls Emma Stone and Abigail Breslin and head west to an amusement park rumored to be zombie-free. Horror show version of *National Lampoon's Vacation* takes a playful approach to the bloodletting, turning the end of the world into something of a stoner road-trip—with double-barreled shotguns and a pitch-perfect cameo from Bill Murray (as Bill Murray). Great soundtrack with Metallica, Velvet Underground, and Van Halen.

"Horror show version of *National Lampoon's Vacation* takes a playful approach to the bloodletting...."

Zombieland

ZOMBIES OF THE STRATOSPHERE

1952 (NR) 167m / D: Fred Brannon / **W:** Ronald Davidson / **C:** Judd Holdren, Aline Towne, Leonard Nimoy, John Crawford, Ray Boyle

Condensing of Republic's third Martian-invasion serial, which showed denizens of the red planet at their very worst. This time three Martians (i.e., "zombies") practice their skullduggery against Earth. The extraterrestrials hope to plant an H-bomb to blow Earth out of orbit and upgrade their dying world to being third from the sun. Luckily for humanity, opposing them is Judd Holdren. Six months after Republic finished this, the U.S. detonated its own H-bomb for the first time. One of the Martians is played by a very young Leonard Nimoy. AKA: *Satan's Satellites*.

ZONE TROOPERS

1985 (PG) 86m / **D:** Danny Bilson / **W:** Danny Bilson, Paul DeMeo / **C:** Timothy Van Patten, Tim Thomerson, Art LaFleur, Biff Manard

Five American GIs in WWII-ravaged Europe stumble upon a wrecked alien spacecraft. The pilot is dead, but the co-pilot manages to get away, and soon the boys find themselves confronted by an alien rescue party—an intergalactic posse known as the "Zone Troopers"—who have come to save their injured comrade. The historical setting gives this one an interesting twist.

ZONTAR: THE THING FROM VENUS

1966 (NR) 68m / **D:** Larry Buchanan / **W:** Larry Buchanan, Hillman Taylor / **C:** John Agar, Anthony Huston, Warren Hammack, Pat Delaney, Susan Bjorman

Scientist is contacted by alien intelligence from Venus and begins doing its bidding, convinced its intentions are benevolent. Surprise! "Zontar" turns out to be a giant batlike critter that takes over people's wills with smaller replicas of itself, which implant control-devices in their victims' necks. Hokey, fun remake of Roger Corman's 1956 epic *It Conquered the World*. Some might argue that a remake of Corman's rather routine monster film was hardly necessary; clearly, they are fools.

SCI-FI ON TV

BABYLON 5

Broadcast: 1994–98 / **Episodes:** 110

In the proliferation of new broadcast-TV channels during the 1980s and '90s, the WB network—with the vast entertainment resources of the Warner Bros. empire behind it—had a leg up on the more upstart UPN. Nevertheless, the WB didn't have a space opera show like all the *Star Trek* spinoffs that UPN kept turning out. And so, in 1994, it made good sense for the WB to come up with its own multi-character, outer-space show. Much like *Deep Space: Nine*, the 23rd century-set *Babylon 5* takes place aboard a space station, where the exigencies of trade and diplomacy bring numerous encounters between humanity and the various alien species in the galaxy. Veteran sci-fi writer J. Michael Straczynski's show was rife with metaphorical allusions to hot-button modern-day conflicts, one of the only sci-fi shows to do so in such a robust fashion before the revamp of *Battlestar Galactica*. It was also the first TV show to make such extensive use of solely computer-generated graphics, something it put to good use in the many massive battle scenes. Straczynski also produced several *Babylon 5* TV movies and the spinoff series *Crusade*, which lasted for one season in 1999. Six Emmy nominations; one win.

BATTLESTAR GALACTICA (ORIGINAL SERIES)

Broadcast: 1978–79 / **Episodes:** 24

American TV's brief flirtation with sci-fi in the late-1970s and '80s was mostly driven by one man: Glen Larson. He had a minor hit with *Buck Rogers in the 25th Century* (1979–81). Less successful at the time but more influential in the long term was the short-lived *Battlestar Galactica*. Like many shows of the time, it started out as a TV movie before morphing into a series. One of TV's few space operas, it began with the cataclysmic near-anni- hilation of a twelve-planet human civilization many light-years from Earth by the robotic Cylon race. The titular space battleship escapes, along with a rag- tag fleet of civilian vessels to protect against incredible odds as they set out on an epic voyage to find the mythical planet Earth. The highly dramatic prem- ise was quickly sabotaged by the many demands of contemporary TV: cute kids, robot sidekick, over-obvious dialogue, repetitive plots that reset to zero at the end of each episode, and disco-era décor; Larson was, after all, the man responsible for the likes of *Magnum, P.I.* and *Knight Rider*. An off- shoot series, *Galactica 1980*, which followed the adventures of the crew once they landed on Earth, thankfully lasted for just 10 episodes in 1980.

BATTLESTAR GALACTICA (REVISED SERIES)

Broadcast: 2004–09 / **Episodes:** 75

The re-launch of *Battlestar Galactica* was close to a seismic event for cable TV and contemporary sci-fi. Starting his series just three years after 9/11 and in the fiery midst of the Iraq War, show creator Ronald D. Moore stripped away most of the tacky frippery that had obscured the greatness of the show's original concept. The Cylon attack and the flight to the fabled thirteenth colony of Earth remained, but the execution was much more raw and modernistic, with a constant everything-is-at-stake intensity; a counter at the start of each episode showed the number of humans still alive. Actors like Edward James Ol- mos and Mary McDonnell brought a more steely-tempered drama to the show, whose mood was gun-metal-stark in a way that space opera rarely manages. Moore's grimmer, relevant vision also dealt with post-9/11 themes of terrorism, religious fanaticism, and paranoia more directly than any other TV show at the time. In the original series, characters could be heard saying "frack" and "feldergarb" instead of more recognizable English curses that would not have been allowed on network television. For the reboot, Moore amped up the usage of "frak" in dialogue, explaining that it was simply a reflection of the coarse lan- guage common to military cultures like the one which his show explored.

A prequel show, *Caprica*, had one season in 2010, and the Web-only prequel series, *Battlestar Galactica: Blood & Chrome*, ran in 2012. Eighteen Emmy nominations, four wins.

BLAKE'S 7

Broadcast: 1978–81 / **Episodes:** 52

Key writers behind *Doctor Who* concocted this leaner, meaner sci-fi ad- venture, which might accurately be called the anti-*Star Trek*; creator Terry Nation reportedly pitched it to the BBC as *"The Dirty Dozen* in space."

Instead of a touchy-feely crew of super-competent comrades, this has future freedom-fighter Blake in an alliance of convenience with a band of cut-throats and rogues (who threaten to murder one another at least once per episode), piloting the advanced spaceship *Liberator* on raids against an evil empire known as ... The Federation. Sure, it's got the impoverished production values of many a BBC serial, and the colossal cosmic clash at the climax of episode 26 looks like something out of *Hardware Wars*. But characters are well-conceived, with a surprisingly high mortality rate thanks to actors regularly exiting the series (Gareth Thomas himself departed after two seasons, leaving half of *Blake's 7* Blakeless).

BBC executives did not like the show, and its unforgettable finale is designed to leave no possibility for revival. Ever. A Vampire Lestat-ish cult following of female sci-fi fans developed a crush on co-star Paul Darrow, who plays the ambitious criminal antihero Avon with Richard III panache. For the guys there's Jacqueline Pearce's vulpine haute-couture villainess, Servalan.

BUBBLEGUM CRISIS

Broadcast: 1987–91 / **Episodes:** 8

One of the earliest of the many Japanese anime series set in a future Tokyo inspired by actual plans for city-wide renovation. The nefarious, ever-expanding GENOM corporation unleashes bio-mechanical soldiers called Boomers—originally designed for outer-space projects and foreign wars, but now causing havoc within the city as part of a plot for world domination. The AD Police, a special crimes unit assigned to deal with the Boomers, find their resources stretched to the limit as the Boomers become increasingly powerful. Only some hi-tech-armored young women called the Knight Sabres pose a threat to GENOM's evil plan. Heavily influenced by *Macross* and *Blade Runner* (one of the Knight Saber's names is Priss, and her band is The Replicants), this series was highly influential on other anime series for its MegaTokyo setting and cute girl heroes battling scary monsters, all set to rocking "J-pop" music. This popular eight-part series was followed by the sequel series *Bubblegum Crash* and *AD Police Files*.

DOCTOR WHO

Broadcast: 1963–89, 2005– / **Episodes:** over 800

In the late 1970s, American sci-fi fans began hearing a lot about a strange British television show called *Doctor Who*. Pictures in fan magazines showed a tall man with a mop of curly hair and an apparently endless scarf, usually standing beside what looked like a blue telephone booth.

This fellow was pretty far removed from the conventional American sci-fi hero, who, from Captain Video to Captain Kirk, has usually been military. But plenty of fans were intrigued and began tuning in when the show appeared on their local channels (often the graveyard slot on PBS). The man in the scarf was Tom Baker, and for many he was the first glimpse of a most unusual hero known only as the Doctor. The show's history had quite a bit more to it than Tom Baker, however. At that point, it was already the longest-running sci-fi show in the world, having started broadcasting in England in 1963 and ended, for the first time, in 1989, before starting up again in 2005.

Doctor Who was originally conceived by the BBC as an "adventure in time and space" and was long regarded in its native country as a children's show, though certainly a remarkable one. The Doctor, as originally played by British character actor William Hartnell, was an elderly, slightly crotchety scientific genius who traveled the cosmos in an enormous time-and-space machine that was somehow contained within an ordinary police call-box. This was the TARDIS ("Time and Relative Dimensions in Space"), probably the show's most recognizable icon, next to the comically unthreatening but extermination-happy Daleks. Doctor Who quickly became a beloved fixture of British culture. The TARDIS allowed the Doctor and his companions (and he had a total of 33 over the course of the series) to travel anywhere from Aztec Mexico to alien planets thousands of years in the future. The stories were always fast-moving and imaginative, and over time the show developed an internal mythology that was as far-ranging as it was colorful.

At first the Doctor's identity (and that of his "granddaughter" Susan) was left vague. But by the time the aging Hartnell was ready to leave the show in 1966, things had firmed up somewhat. The Doctor was not a human being at all, but a rebel "Time Lord," one of an immensely advanced race of beings from the planet Gallifrey. Time Lords have two hearts and also the enviable ability to "regenerate" their bodies when critically injured. Hartnell was thus able to relinquish the role of the Doctor to the younger Patrick Troughton, who gave the role a gentler, more humorous touch. In 1970, the tall, imposing Jon Pertwee took over, playing the Doctor as a theatrical dandy. Most of the shows in the Pertwee years were set on Earth, with the Doctor collaborating with a paramilitary organization called UNIT. In 1974 fans saw the advent of Tom Baker, who, with his slightly off-kilter humor, remains *the* Doctor to many fans. In 1982, Peter Davidson, the youngest man to play the Doctor, took the role. He was followed by the burlier, slightly more acerbic Colin Baker in 1984, and then in 1987 by Sylvester McCoy, who seemed to echo Troughton's whimsical approach.

The Doctors who came after the interregnum, like Christopher Eccleston and David Tennant, mostly followed the mold of whippet-thin hyperactive eccentrics so common in British fiction. As the years went on, though, it became harder for the show to justify his sidekick always being a sprightly and attractive young woman. After the series was started up again in 2005, its popularity rebounded, resulting in a slew of new novels, merchandise, and even spinoff series such as the *X Files*-like *Torchwood* and *The Sarah Jane Adventures*.

FIREFLY

Broadcast: 2002 / **Episodes:** 14

For American sci-fi shows set on a vessel, the preference was for them to be engaged in some official capacity: military, exploration, or other. One of the more remarkable things about Joss Whedon's sadly short-lived 26th-century space western was that it didn't send a team of soldiers and scientists out to the far reaches of the galaxy, it sent criminals. Nathan Fillion puts in a droll, Harrison Ford-ian turn as Captain Mal Reynolds. Once part of a failed rebellion against the system-spanning Alliance, Mal now captains the reconfigured Firefly-class cargo ship *Serenity* with various other ex-rebels and sundry misfits including a preacher, a rich-kid doctor, and a mysterious young woman on whom the Alliance had been experimenting and is now hunting for. The *Serenity*'s crew bumps around to various planets on the ragged edge of civilized space, trying to stay one step ahead of the Alliance and eke out a living with smuggling and the occasional light piracy. The anachronistic Americana-tinged theme music evoked a post-Civil War moral landscape familiar to fans of classic Westerns. *Firefly* managed a deft balancing act between action, suspense, and humor, most effectively the latter.

The back story is densely layered, and Whedon's characters are exactly the sort of three-dimensional people rarely seen in typically plot-heavy sci-fi television. In other words, it is the kind of show that could have easily found three or four seasons' worth of stories to explore. If it had premiered 10 years later on a cable channel, that may have happened. But this was Fox, and ratings weren't what they could be—possibly because the comedy was a little too dry and too much of its universe left unexplained. (For example, many characters occasionally expostulate in Mandarin Chinese; this is supposedly because centuries earlier America and China were the only two countries to expand into space, but nowhere in the first few episodes is this spelled out.) So the plug was pulled after 14 episodes. Strong DVD sales and a dedicated fan letter-writing campaign ultimately led to Whedon telling a feature-length story in the 2005 film *Serenity*. One Emmy for f/x.

FUTURAMA

Broadcast: 1999–2003, 2010–13 / **Episodes:** 140

*T*he *Simpsons* creator Matt Groening always had a soft spot for genre; thus, the series' perennial *Tales from the Crypt*-ish "Treehouse of Horror" episodes and constant references to classic sci-fi from *The Twilight Zone* to *The Village of the Damned*. In 1999, Groening got his chance for a fully sci-fi animated show and launched *Futurama*. Clueless pizza delivery guy Philip J. Fry is cryogenically frozen in the 20th century and reawakened in the 31st, whereupon he goes to work for an interstellar shipping company. The show dealt with more adventurous plots than the family comedy of Groening's first series. But in between the tangles with various alien species, and comic interplay between the dramatically misaligned characters, the show functioned as a fairly similar and even more biting satire on contemporary culture. The references came thick and fast throughout, covering everything from politics (Richard Nixon's reanimated head gets elected president of Earth) to the works of M.C. Escher, not to mention just about every notable work of film, TV, or written sci-fi ever created. The humor was a little too densely layered for a mass audience, so the show was canceled in 2003. However, after years of very popular reruns on Cartoon Network's Adult Swim (where it arguably inspired many of that network's more groundbreaking series), it was re-launched on Comedy Central for two more seasons.

THE HITCHHIKER'S GUIDE TO THE GALAXY

Broadcast: 1981 / **Episodes:** 6

*B*BC-TV adaptation of Douglas Adams' hilarious radio serial adaptation of his bestselling book series, it starred many of the original audio cast members, positing a riotous universe of adventure, absurdity, and philosophical quandaries. Thus, typical Englishman Arthur Dent survives the sudden demolition of his planet (by a hyperspace road crew) thanks to the hitchhiking skills of his best friend, who is secretly an alien travel writer updating the latest edition of the eminent *Hitchhiker's Guide* (Adams essentially invented the concept of the tablet device decades before it hit the market). Together, they ricochet through time and space, meeting characters like Marvin the Paranoid Android and mod master criminal/entrepreneur/galactic president Zaphod Beebelbrox. Dry, absurdist humor makes this worthy of watching, despite distracting cut-rate f/x (dig Zaphod's inanimate, superfluous second head). Adams' crafty intellect makes this not just first-rate comedy but splendidly imaginative sci-fi. David Prowse—the guy inside Darth Vader's suit—cameos as an intergalactic rock star's thug bodyguard.

LOST IN SPACE

Broadcast: 1965–67 / **Episodes:** 83

good story is a good story, no matter how the storyteller might change
or update it. For *Lost in Space*, producer Irwin Allen took *Swiss Family Robinson* to the space age, exploring the adventures of a futuristic but all-American family marooned on an alien planet.

Guy Williams and perpetual TV-mom June Lockhart were the perfect parents, Marta Kristen was their perfect teenage daughter, Judy, and Angela Cartwright and Billy Mumy played the perfectly mischievous kids Penny and Will. There was even a Nice Young Man for Judy in the person of Don West (Mark Goddard).

Things had a way of shifting around in the show. In *Lost in Space*'s 1965 pilot, "The Reluctant Stowaway," Dr. Zachary Smith (Jonathan Harris) was a villain, pure and simple. A spy representing an unnamed foreign power, Smith sabotages the Robinson family's spaceship, the *Jupiter 2*, but is unexpectedly trapped onboard. By the time the *Jupiter 2* settled on the planet where the better part of the series would take place, Smith had changed from a cold, heartless spy to a lazy and greedy, but lovable scoundrel. Likewise, the *Jupiter 2*'s robot (always known simply as "the Robot" in the series), originally a vaguely menacing machine with little personality, became Smith's chief flunky and foil. Although many episodes focused on the problems of growing up in outer space, or the constant problem of trying to get back to Earth, most fans fondly remember the show as a series of misadventures instigated by Dr. Smith and played out by him, the Robot, and Will.

The show's bright colors, cheesy f/x, and increasingly juvenile tone over its three-year run led many fans to regard the show as nothing more than a campy period piece. Still, the show had humor, occasional pathos, and an impressive menagerie of rubbery monsters (including a blob-like creature which for some reason screamed like a mountain-lion). A pointlessly high-budget and action-packed 1998 film adaptation tried to take the premise seriously (casting Gary Oldman as Dr. Smith being every kind of overkill) and failed miserably in the process.

MAX HEADROOM

Broadcast: 1987–88 / **Episodes:** 14

In 1984, Britain's Channel 4 wanted to create an innovative music video/interview program and came up with the idea of TV's first cyberpunk, with a computer-generated head-with-an-attitude as its host. The result was a fairly surreal goof, with heavily made-up actor Matt Frewer interviewing guests and playing music videos while spouting nonsense.

In 1987, Lorimar acquired the U.S. rights, redid the pilot, and got one season out of trying to turn this paper-thin concept into a real series. The series' tagline, "twenty minutes into the future," found a world where TV ruled (in fact, it was illegal to turn it off) and ratings and advertisers were in control. Frewer plays an intrepid TV reporter who is injured while investigating network secrets. His memories are downloaded into a special program that translates people into data, but they only had enough memory to translate his head. So Max (who took his name from the last thing Carter saw—a sign reading "Max Headroom") is born—complete with maniacal stutter and sarcasm to spare. He proceeds to wander through the giant network's computer system, popping up unexpectedly to insult advertisers, interrupt programming, and garner great ratings.

Unfortunately, the quirky and heavily stylized but story-thin series didn't do the same, lasting only 14 episodes—although Max at least managed a second career as a successful huckster for Coca-Cola.

MYSTERY SCIENCE THEATER 3000

Broadcast: 1988–99 / **Episodes:** 199

*M*ystery Science Theater 3000 stands today as still the funniest sci-fi show of all time; though granted the competition hasn't exactly been fierce. "MST3K," as abbreviated by fans, was created in 1988 at a small UHF station in Minneapolis by comedian Joel Hodgson and producer-writer-director Jim Mallon. The premise was that a worker (played first by Hodgson and later Michael Nelson) at someplace called the Gizmonic Institute ticks off his bosses, who send him into space inside the *Satellite of Love*, where he's forced to watch bad movies as part of an experiment. To ease his loneliness, Joel created robot companions Crow, Gypsy, and Tom Servo. In loving tribute to late-night gimmicky TV hosts who introduced the Z-grade horror and sci-fi flicks that smaller TV stations bought in blocks to fill up programming hours, Joel and the 'bots (whose low-tech origins range from a bowling pin to a gumball machine) do comic sketches in between commercials. Then they settle down to watch the movie (their figures, plus a row of movie theater seats, silhouetted at the bottom of the screen) and crack wise.

Movies like *Robot Monster* and *It Conquered the World* provoke rapid-fire references to everything from C.S. Lewis to Vidal Sassoon, free will, God, artist Mark Rothko, Bill Keene's "Family Circus" comic strip, playwright Tom Stoppard, Robert Ludlum novels, dumb fish puns, *The Wizard of Oz*, and *The Dirty Dozen*. When Joel remarks that a character on screen looks like a cross between Jerry Mathers and James Dean, one of the 'bots cracks, "Beaver without a Cause."

The series eventually moved to Comedy Central, where it became something of a standby for the fledgling network, which devoted entire Thanksgivings to *MST3K* marathons. The crew's high point of popularity probably came around 1996, when *Mystery Science Theater 3000: The Movie* actually played in theaters. A couple seasons at the Sci-Fi Channel followed, before the show ended in 1999. Some of the crew later regrouped as Riff-Trax, making comic audio commentary that can be played in-sync with bigger-budget flicks like *Star Trek II: The Wrath of Khan* and *The Hunger Games*.

THE PRISONER

Broadcast: 1967–68 / Episodes: 17

*T*he Prisoner was a very special kind of science-fiction show, with a persistently dedicated cult following decades after it ended. Although it took place in a strange, otherworldly, possibly futuristic place, it wasn't about aliens or spaceships or time machines. Owing more to Kafka than Heinlein, it was the story of a secret agent who resigns his post and is abducted to a strange place called the Village.

Actor Patrick McGoohan was both star and creator. He had already turned down the role of Ian Fleming's super-agent James Bond, having been offered it before Sean Connery. He had created and starred in *Danger Man* (also known as *Secret Agent Man*), an unorthodox mid-1960s "spy series" about an agent who relies on his intellect rather than gadgets and fists. The filming of one *Danger Man* episode took McGoohan to the grounds of strange, whimsical-looking hotel in Portmeirion, Wales that looked like it belonged in Lewis Carroll's Wonderland. This got McGoohan thinking. Two years later he sold networks on the idea for *The Prisoner*.

For *The Prisoner*, McGoohan also played a secret agent who disdains his profession. As "Number 6," McGoohan resigns against his superiors' wishes and is abducted to the surreal Village, which seems to have no other purpose than to crush Number 6's individuality. Escape is rendered difficult by "rovers," strange bouncing bubble-creatures that can envelope straying Villagers. The 17 episodes of *The Prisoner* took on questions of identity and authority with a characteristically British sense of humor. The final episode saw Number 6 finally uncover the identity of the mysterious "Number 1," with a typically unexpected twist. Although a poorly regarded six-episode remake was broadcast by AMC in 2009, there's never been a show quite like *The Prisoner*, and it's possible there never will again.

QUANTUM LEAP

Broadcast: 1989–93 / Episodes: 97

*C*onsidering what a perfect format time travel is for television—hero goes to a different time period in each episode but can return home at the end, thus keeping the show self-contained—it's surprising that more shows haven't used the idea. In any case, it would be difficult for anybody to find a more broadly popular take than Donald Bellisario's *Quantum Leap*. A hit with both sci-fi fans and mainstream audiences, this five-season show had an appealingly everyday hero in Scott Bakula, playing a physicist who enters a time-travel machine accidentally and is thrown into another person's body in the past. In each episode, Bakula jumps from one time period to the next, assisted by the voice of a disembodied artificial intelligence and Dean Stockwell's snarky comic-relief hologram. His only way home is to set right something that went wrong in each time period. The comedy and drama in each episode usually resulted from Bakula's discomfort at the person he was then inhabiting, including everyone from a part-time Santa Claus to Lee Harvey Oswald. Bellisario's knack for genial, character-centered comedy, which made his later cop procedurals like *NCIS* such a success, was on full display here. Nominated for 32 Emmys; won five.

RED DWARF

Broadcast: 1988–93, 1997–2012 (intermittently) / **Episodes:** 61

As a rare-to-nonexistent breed like TV sci-fi sitcoms go, *Red Dwarf* is the one to beat. On the BBC since 1988, this British spoof started off with "The End," in which a ne'er-do-well crewman on the miles-long interstellar mining craft *Red Dwarf* awoke from cryogenic detention to learn that his shipmates succumbed to a radiation leak and three million years have gone by. Mankind is extinct, and his only companions are a sentient hologram of a much-disliked officer, the ship's sarcastic computer, and a natty-dressing humanoid evolved from a pet cat; later, a robot joined the ensemble. Coasting through a hostile universe, these pitiful remnants of humanity are constantly threatened by alien interlopers, bizarre phenomena, and their own incompatible personalities. Rob Grant and Doug Naylor scripts are riotously funny sci-fi in the best mind-expanding sense.

The show's cult fandom has dedicated 'zines, Web pages, and even destructive computer viruses to the glories of *Red Dwarf*. Attempts at an American remake of were, to put it mildly, unsuccessful. Or, in the words of show's far-future slang, all smegged up.

STAR BLAZERS

Broadcast: 1979–82 / **Episodes:** 77

In 1979, U.S. sci-fi fans were introduced to a new animated series of unusual depth and complexity. *Star Blazers*, called *Space Cruiser Yamato* in its native Japan, was set in the year 2199, when Earth has been rendered a radioactive wasteland and humanity has fled to underground cities. Just as things look hopeless, a message is received from Queen Starsha of the distant planet Iscandar, offering aid to the beleaguered planet. The World War II battleship *Yamato*, recently rediscovered on the now-dry ocean floor (a not-too-subtle bit of Japanese imperialist wish fulfillment), is refitted for space travel, and a group of intrepid heroes, the "Star Force," is assembled to make the dangerous journey to Iscandar.

Star Blazers was a surprise in several ways. Most obviously, its anime style was a strikingly different one than any American audiences had seen since *Speed Racer*. Also, each of the show's three seasons formed one long story, divided into consecutive episodes that had to be seen in order to be understood. This old film serial approach was practically revolutionary in late-1970s American TV, where producers always insisted that shows wrap everything up by the end of an episode. Finally, *Starblazers* aimed for full-blooded stories, with dramatic confrontations and a mortality rate among its characters that would be unknown in American animation for years to come. All of these factors made for classic space-opera adventure that is rightly still regarded today as a classic.

STAR TREK

Broadcast: 1966–69 / **Episodes:** 79

The classic, original *Star Trek* series of the late-1960s is just about the only enduring sci-fi of the post-JFK era to declare that tomorrow will be better than today, that mankind can become a force for good in the universe instead of spawning technological nightmares or backsliding into savagery. In a future where a United Nations-like Federation has brought peace to Earth and other planets, the giant, interstellar, science-military exploration vessel USS *Enterprise* spends its time not fighting aliens (though that certainly happened) but exploring the far reaches of a strange universe. Its multicultural, multispecies crew, led by Captain James Tiberius Kirk (William Shatner, who never had enough ham), Dr. "Bones" McCoy (DeForest Kelley), the emotionless Vulcan Mr. Spock (Leonard Nimoy, ice wouldn't melt in that wryly pursued mouth), and all those expendable guys in red shirts, found themselves matched against galaxies' worth of danger, foes, riddles, and rewards. And anytime that Paramount wanted to use one of their back lots, they could just invent a time travel story. It had adventure, humor, constant oddities, a strongly bonded ensemble cast, and resonant themes of cultural openness, not to mention the possibility of inter-species romance, thanks to Kirk's polyamorous inclinations.

With its well-drawn characters, sophisticated-for-the-time f/x, and prominent sci-fi writers like Harlan Ellison and Theodore Sturgeon assisting, the program won two Hugo Awards before chronically low ratings forced it off the air. Practically before cancellation, a subculture of so-called Trekkie fans began to organize. By the mid '70s, with the show in heavy syndication rotation across the world, thousands were attending *Star Trek* conventions, where they traded merchandise, argued over marginalia, and became a frequently mocked subculture meme.

Trek authorities squabble over the contributions and near-messianic status of executive producer Gene Roddenberry, as compared to barely remembered original producer Gene L. Coon, who died early on. There's no doubt, though, that Roddenberry's love of inserting progressive messages into his stories was central to the show's spirit. Also, Roddenberry's campaigns among the faithful certainly helped revive the *Star Trek* franchise, with the first motion picture in 1979 and the outstandingly successful *Next Generation* series in the late-'80s. Now it's virtually impossible to imagine broadcast sci-fi (or American popular culture) without the original *Star Trek*. There are those who profess greater love for offshoots like the more Shakespearean *Next Generation* or the angst-ridden *Deep Space Nine*, and even some who note the supposed greatness of the short-lived, mid-'70s NBC Saturday-morning cartoon continuation, but it's hard to argue against the greatness of the original.

Reviving an old television series and updating for a new audience is not such a new idea. Sometimes a series would disappear from the airwaves for a few years, only to return, even on another network. Personalities such as Jack Benny, Bob Newhart, Jackie Gleason, and Lassie would return again and again with different titles, formats, or networks.

But no television show had ever returned as a reincarnation of itself. Of course, *Star Trek* is a unique entity in the entertainment world. It was known as "the show that would not die." If it hadn't continued in movies and television, surely somewhere there would be a packed house enjoying it as community theater. By 1987, there was a demand for *Star Trek* that could not be satisfied by a theatrical motion picture every other year. There was a growing void—an unknown entertainment anomaly—that needed to be filled on a weekly basis.

STAR TREK: DEEP SPACE NINE

Broadcast: 1993–99 / **Episodes:** 176

Starting in 1993 as *Next Generation* was winding down, and just before *Babylon 5* would give *Star Trek* its first serious tele-sci-fi competition, *Deep Space Nine* was a completely different type of offshoot. Instead of sending its characters zipping around the universe at warp speed, *DS9* kept them ensconced for the most part inside its namesake space station, which was nominally under Starfleet command. In keeping with the United Nations-like sensibility of Gene Roddenberry's universe, *DS9* was generally about conflict resolution. In this case, an uneasy truce has to be maintained over the station, which is conveniently situated right next to an interdimensional wormhole and frequented by numerous alien races with divergent interests. This was in contrast to *Next Generation*, which sometimes overemphasized the interpersonal drama of the crew instead of exploring new alien frontiers. Keeping *Deep Space Nine* physically centered allowed for a greater emphasis on recurring characters and melodrama that could make it more soap opera than space opera. Still, the show has its adherents, who strongly prefer it to any of the other '90s *Trek* spinoffs. There were several crossovers with other shows: *Next Generation*'s Worf was a recurring character, and the *Voyager* launched its fateful journey from the station. Thirty-two Emmy nominations; won four.

STAR TREK: ENTERPRISE

Broadcast: 2001–2005 / **Episodes:** 98

When in doubt, go back to the past. At least, that was the idea behind *Star Trek: Enterprise*, the fifth live-action franchise series. In this one, *Quantum Leap*'s Scott Bakula plays the captain of an experimental Starfleet ship that's the first one capable of warp 5 drive, 100 years before space had seen the likes of Kirk and Spock. The universe of 2151 is a little different than that of the later series, and much more fraught with unknown challenges. Launched into action years after a Vulcan ship crash lands on Earth, and the Vulcan people help human recover from a devastating war, the early *Enterprise* was thrown from one crisis to the next. The show was never quite embraced by a larger audience, and was canceled after plans for season five had already commenced. Six Emmy nominations; won two.

STAR TREK: THE NEXT GENERATION

Broadcast: 1987–94 / **Episodes:** 178

The first season of *Star Trek*'s first live-action spinoff, *The Next Generation,* was a shake-down cruise. Under the command of Captain Jean-Luc Picard (accomplished stage actor Patrick Stewart), the crew of the *Enterprise* faced down many of the similar problems as Kirk and Company. Many episodes were simply retreads from the old series, with the new crew stepping through familiar paces. Maybe they didn't go so far as to have the ship overrun with Tribbles, but it wouldn't have been much of a surprise. Picard and his crew were often accused of being wimps, tossing daisies at their weekly nemesis when they should have been blasting away with hand-held phasers or photon torpedoes like the more impetuous Shatner would have done. Wry and graced with gravitas, Stewart couldn't help but feel like the ego to Shatner's id, particularly when faced with the likes of the Borg, an assimilationist alien presence that proved to be the new *Enterprise*'s most baffling and philosophically complex foe.

Luckily, sometime during the second season, the show began to hit its stride. No longer trying to be a kinder, gentler version of the original crew, the characters and story arcs began to take on a life of their own. The question was no longer "What new menace will the *Enterprise* have to face this week?" but "How will Worf deal with the issues of his Klingon heritage as a Starfleet officer?" or "What changes will take place in the political affairs of the Romulan empire?" What was synthetic became organic. Awkward children grew up to become adults. An emotionless android was given the gift of laughter by a cynical god. Themes that would have played false in the first season took on meaning because the characters became three dimensional.

Gaining speed during the following seasons, it became apparent that *The Next Generation* was no longer merely an outgrowth of a phenomenon. It could stand on its own—surely it would have been a great show, even if there'd never been a previous generation. While the two-part episodes were probably considered a bit of a gamble, they soon proved that not only could the series keep its audience interested for more than an hour's worth per story, but those episodes were very often overwhelming favorites. And so, after 178 episodes and a run over twice as long as the original, *Star Trek: The Next Generation* left the once-daring, now-cozy nest of syndication for bigger, wider, more expensive adventures on the silver multiplex screen. Fifty-eight Emmy nominations; won 19.

STAR TREK: VOYAGER

Broadcast: 1995–2001 / **Episodes:** 172

The 1990s were a high time for the Roddenberry universe, flush with awards and ratings after the successful *Next Generation* reboot. Even if the Picard-era films were generally seen as lacking, there seemed to be a real hunger for new Federation adventures on the small screen. The first series in the franchise launched after Roddenberry's death, *Voyager*, for all its strengths, may have been the series too far. A spinoff of sorts from *Deep Space Nine* and a centerpiece show of the short-lived United Paramount Network, *Voyager* follows the adventures of the titular Starfleet vessel, which is stranded tens of thousands of light years from Earth and forced to make peace with an unruly band of Maquis rebels in order to get home; a journey that will supposedly take 75 years. The standout of *Voyager* was always the presence of Captain Kathryn Janeway, played by the tougher-than-nails Kate Mulgrew, who more than capably led her crew on their impossibly long voyage home. Thirty-five Emmy nominations; won seven.

STAR WARS: CLONE WARS

Broadcast: 2003–05 / **Episodes:** 25

Abstract and mournful, with loads of action but a running subtext on the horrors of war, the offshoot series *Star Wars: Clone Wars* was structured as short episodes (some only three-minutes long) set during the battles that marked the end of the Old Republic. The episodes follow the tragic arc of Anakin's conversion to the dark side in the same way as the second trilogy of films did, only without George Lucas's concrete-stiff directing. Show creator and animator Genndy Tartakovsky's style, honed on hyperactive series like *Dexter's Laboratory*, was kinetic and strange, with an eerie, epic sensibility that recalls Russian Constructivism at times and Ralph Bakshi's *Wizards* at others. *Not* to be confused with the more cookie-cutter series *Star Wars: The Clone Wars* (note the ever-important extra "the") that ran from 2008 to 2013, its less distinctive animation and generic plots serving as mere filler in comparison.

THE TWILIGHT ZONE

Broadcast: 1959–64 / **Episodes:** 156

The Twilight Zone was created by Rod Serling, a distinguished playwright who in the golden age of live television set the standard of excellence with such scripts as "Patterns," "Requiem for a Heavyweight," and "The Comedian." One of television's last great anthology shows, Serling's weekly cornucopia of fantasy, terror, and sci-fi served up a series of thoughtful, fantastical morality plays on everything from racism to the follies of war and the wages of sin. The series attracted many of the best writers (Richard Matheson, Charles Beaumont, Serling himself) and a roster of stars (Burgess Meredith, Agnes Moorhead, Lee Marvin) and future stars (Robert Redford, Jack Klugman, William Shatner), who helped spin these dark tales that embodied the creepy aesthetic mood set by Serling's monotone opening and the eerie theme music.

Everyone has his or her favorite episode; sometimes more than one. Generally, the most popular are the ones with the jolting O. Henry twist, such as "Time Enough at Last," in which bookworm Burgess Meredith chooses the wrong time to break his glasses; "Nightmare at 20,000 Ft.," starring William Shatner as a mentally unstable plane passenger who doesn't really see a monster on the wing, or does he?; and "To Serve Man," about the unappetizing double meaning of a visiting extraterrestrial's book. One of the most extraordinary is "An Occurrence at Owl Creek Bridge," a French short based on the Ambrose Bierce story that went on to win an Academy Award. Like many of the greatest episodes, its twist wasn't just a shock, it cut you to the quick. Four Emmy nominations; won two.

The franchise was renewed twice in later years: once in 1985 and the second time in 2002. While both efforts were praiseworthy attempts at reviving the revered sci-fi anthology show, neither could ultimately hold a guttering candle to Serling's magnificent masterpiece.

V

Broadcast: 1984–85 / **Episodes:** 19

Advanced aliens known as Visitors land their saucers on Earth in the spirit of friendship, *or so they claim*. Their attractively human-like appearance is a facade; hiding their reptilian faces behind fake skin masks, the Visitors want to consume Earth's resources, including fillet of *Homo sapiens*. Started as a miniseries in 1983, *V* is sci-fi in the best *Twilight Zone* tradition, drawing parallels between the alien invasion and both U.S. foreign policy in Central America and the Holocaust, and also savaging the nation's media brainwash and pop-culture attitudes (a high-school band welcomes the Visitors with the *Star Wars* theme). Once hero newsman Marc Singer learns the Visitors' true intentions, a resistance movement is born, and the saga turns into a disappointingly standard blow-up-the-bad-guys action/adventure. Robert Englund (*Nightmare on Elm Street*'s Freddy), is a cast standout as a benign Visitor. Creepy and smart, though somewhat dated. Sequelled by miniseries conclusion *V: The Final Battle*. Revived in 2009 with the same basic idea but better f/x.

THE X-FILES

Broadcast: 1993–2002 / **Episodes:** 202

The X-Files surprised everyone when it premiered in 1993 by becoming first a cult hit for the still-fledgling Fox TV, and then growing into a solid ratings winner with a broad mainstream audience. The network known for comedies like *The Simpsons* and *Married: With Children* suddenly had on its hands the only televised sci-fi hit in years that had nothing to do with the starship *Enterprise*. The show also helped mainstream a particularly paranoid style of American discourse during a decade when conspiracy theories about nefarious government agencies and black helicopters proliferated like mushrooms. In the years between the end of the Cold War and 9/11, there was talk of many Americans becoming hypochondriacs of fear; *The X-Files* plugged right into those free-floating anxieties.

The show's premise was simple but inventive, and loose enough to give writers a broad range of subjects. Fox Mulder (David Duchovny) is an FBI agent who never met a conspiracy theory he didn't like, believing that his sister was abducted by aliens as a child. His partner, pathologist Dana Scully (Gillian Anderson), is a level-headed skeptic who demands hard evidence for everything. Their logic/passion dichotomy made for particularly smoldering sexual/intellectual repartee. Surrounding them, as they cover cases that nobody else in the agency wants to touch, is a supporting cast that ranges from shadowy bureaucrats to circus freaks and the usual supernatural suspects—vampires, werewolves, zombies, and, of course, aliens.

Show creator Chris Carter carefully balanced his nine seasons of episodes between standalone supernatural mysteries that frequently paid homage to old monster shows like 1974's *Kolchak: The Night Stalker*, and stories that linked back to a shadowy network of conspirators who have infiltrated the federal government and just might be connected to an imminent alien invasion. Not only did the show feature surprisingly mature direction and writing for early-1990s TV, it was also one of the first shows that didn't look like TV. Every episode was artfully shot, frequently in rainy and noirish shadows, like a miniature feature film. That said, like most successful series, it went on a couple seasons past its expiration date, and the feature films it sprouted off were less than necessary. Twenty-one Emmy nominations; three wins.

INDEX

Note: (ill.) indicates photos and illustrations.

Burton, Richard, 267
Burton, Tim, 56, 118, 235–36, 266–67, 284–85, 308
Buscemi, Steve, 21, 122, 203
Busey, Gary, 51, 288, 335
Busey, Jake, 349
Bush, Billy Green, 86
Bush, Grand, 149
Butler, Gerard, 301, 387
Butler, Robert, 78
Butrick, Merritt, 350–51, 435
Butterfield, Asa, 120–21
Byars, Floyd, 233
Byrne, Eddie, 204
Byrne, Rose, 217, 364, 402, 442
Byrne, Stuart J., 123
Byron, Jean, 199
Byron, Jeffrey, 243
Byron, Lord, 149
Byun, Hee-bong, 182

C

Caan, James, 12, 316
Caan, Scott, 239
Cabot, Sebastian, 388
Cabot, Susan, 427
Cage, Nicolas, 129, 217, 264, 367
Cahill, Mike, 19
Cahn, Edward L., 198–99, 207
Caillou, Alan, 417
Caine, Michael, 66, 190, 369–370
Caire, Audrey, 379
Calegory, Jade, 231
Calhoun, Rory, 175
Call, John, 320
Call, R. D., 428
Callaham, Dave, 110
Callan, Michael, 258
Camargo, Christian, 126
Cambridge, Godfrey, 335
Cameron, James, 3, 3 (ill.), 12–13, 27–28, 101, 362, 375–76
Cameron, Kirk, 224
Cameron, Rod, 119
Cameron-Glickenhaus, Jesse, 389–390
Cammell, Donald, 103
Camp, Colleen, 93
Camp, Hamilton, 26
Campanella, Joseph, 244
Campbell, Bill, 275, 314
Campbell, Bruce, 122, 246–47, 255, 429
Campbell, Chuck, 209

Campbell, Elizabeth, 439
Campbell, John, 380–81
Campbell, Joseph, 358
Campbell, Martin, 168, 267
Campbell, Nell, 211
Campbell, R. Wright, 372
Campbell, Walter, 410
Campos, Rafael, 23
Campus, Michael, 449
Candy, John, 174, 339
Canedo, Roberto, 439
Cannon, Danny, 211
Cannon, Freddy, 417
Canterbury, Chandler, 217
Caplan, Lizzy, 75, 182
Capra, Frank, 287
Capshaw, Kate, 112
Carbone, Antony, 222
Card, Orson Scott, 4, 120
Cardona Sr., Rene, 439
Cardoza, Anthony, 40
Cardy, David, 445
Carell, Steve, 324
Carey, Peter, 412
Carey, Phil, 391
Carey Jr., Harry, 66
Carhart III, John, 379
Carlin, George, 44–45
Carlino, Lewis John, 323
Carlisle, Anne, 226
Carlos, Walter (Wendy), 72
Carlson, Joel, 77
Carlson, Richard, 84, 205, 205 (ill.)
Carlton, Rex, 410
Carlyle, Robert, 402
Carmine, Michael, 35, 225
Carnahan, Matthew Michael, 438
Caro, Marc, 70, 102
Caron, Jean-Luc, 102
Carpenter, John
  Dark Star, 93
  District 13, 107
  Escape from L.A., 122
  Escape from New York, 123
  Ghosts of Mars, 159
  Memoirs of an Invisible Man, 241
  The Philadelphia Experiment, 281
  Planet Terror, 286
  Starman, 347–48
  They Live, 379
  The Thing (1982), 380
  Village of the Damned (1995), 417
  Wavelength, 429
  Wicked City (1993), 433

Carpenter, Paul, 136
Carr, Camilla, 227
Carradine, David, 99–100, 100 (ill.)
Carradine, John, 23–24, 188, 199
Carradine, Keith, 82, 188, 399
Carradine, Robert, 429
Carrera, Barbara, 120, 203
Carrey, Jim, 117, 125, 400–401
Carrillo, Elpidia, 288
Carrivick, Gareth, 150
Carroll, Lane, 83
Carroll, Leo G., 371
Carroll, Lewis, 304
Carruth, Shane, 289–290
Carson, David, 353
Carson, Hunter, 196
Carson, John David, 120
Carter, Chris, 441–42
Carter, Finn, 397
Carter, Helena Bonham, 146, 195, 284–85, 376–77
Carter, Jack, 14, 173, 305
Carter, Nell, 249
Carter, T. K., 380
Cartwright, Lynn, 297
Cartwright, Veronica, 8, 45, 141, 196–97
Caruso, D. J., 187–88
Carver, Brent, 246
Case, Caroline, 189
Case, Tom, 255
Casey, Bernie, 44, 234
Cash, Rosalind, 4, 272
Caspary, Katrina, 231
Cassavetes, Nick, 23, 129
Cassidy, Joanna, 46
Cassie, Iain, 445
Cassini, Nadia, 347
Castillo, Gloria, 198, 244
Castle, John, 310
Castle, Nick, 123, 221
Castle, Peggie, 41, 42 (ill.)
Castle, Roy, 108
Castle, William, 59
Cates, Phoebe, 169
Catlin, Victoria, 256
Cattrall, Kim, 69, 346, 352
Caulfield, Maxwell, 118
Caviezel, Jim, 102, 135, 149, 274–75, 275 (ill.)
Cavill, Henry, 234
Celi, Adolfo, 90
Cellier, Frank, 268
Centeno-Rodriguez, Ravel, 382

Cera, Michael, 322
Cervi, Gino, 249
Chabert, Lacey, 229
Chabon, Michael, 209–10, 344
Chabot, Gregg, 301
Chabrol, Claude, 75
Chadwell, John, 245
Chadwick, June, 299
Chaiken, Ilene, 35
Chalmers, Kitty, 87
Chamberlain, Richard, 369
Chambers, John, 284
Chambers, Phil, 250
Chancellor, Anna, 183
Chandler, Chick, 229
Chandler, Kyle, 97, 364
Chaneac, Delphine, 345
Chaney, Tom, 255
Chaney Jr., Lon, 25
Chao, Rosalind, 241
Chapin, Billy, 392
Chaplin, Charlie, 17
Chaplin, Geraldine, 449
Chaplin, Paul, 258
Chapman, Ben, 84
Chapman, Edward, 381
Chapman, Marguerite, 16, 141–42
Chappelle, Dave, 269
Chapple, Geoff, 261
Charbonneau, Patricia, 309
Charles, Rebecca, 262
Charleson, Ian, 211
Chase, Chevy, 183, 241, 249
Chase, Daveigh, 109
Chatelain, Helene, 209
Chatto, Tom, 296
Chatwin, Justin, 426
Chau, Francois, 372
Chaves, Richard, 288
Chayefsky, Paddy, 15
Chaykin, Maury, 47, 101, 246
Cheadle, Don, 201–2, 248
Chebotaryov, Vladimir, 16
Chen, Joan, 49, 211
Chereau, Patrice, 390
Chester, Vanessa Lee, 230
Chetwynd, Lionel, 297
Cheung, Jacky, 433
Cheung, Maggie, 405
Cheyney, Peter, 14
Chiaki, Minoru, 163
Chiba, Sonny, 377, 418
Chien-lung, Huang, 193
Chiklis, Michael, 131–32

Chiles, Lois, 254, 254 (ill.)
Chin, Tsai, 57, 64, 129, 196
Chin, Yao, 110
Chinlund, Nick, 409
Chitty, Erik, 137
Cho, John, 349, 354, 393
Cho, Margaret, 129
Choate, Tim, 101
Chong, Rae Dawn, 51, 69–70, 390
Choo, Kisei, 433
Christ, Jesus, 238–39
Christensen, Carol, 385
Christensen, Hayden, 212, 357
Christian, Claudia, 177
Christian, Paul, 40
Christian, Roger, 37, 349
Christie, Julie, 103, 130
Christie, Warren, 20
Christmas, Eric, 26, 281
Christopher, Dennis, 69, 286
Chubby Checker, 293
Chung, Peter, 19
Church, Thomas Haden, 209, 345
Ciannelli, Eduardo, 108
Cilento, Diane, 449
Cimino, Michael, 328
Cinciripini, Tony, 223
Cioffi, Charles, 386
Clair, Jany, 176
Clanton, Ralph, 402
Clark, B. D., 153
Clark, Candy, 48–49, 234
Clark, Devin, 287
Clark, Eugene, 219
Clark, Fred, 112
Clark, Greydon, 305
Clark, Louise Caire, 290
Clark, Susan, 77
Clarke, Arthur C., 37, 405–6
Clarke, Gary, 248
Clarke, Jason, 99
Clarke, Mae, 146, 216
Clarke, Robert, 23, 43, 177, 245
Clarke, Robin, 181
Clarke, Warren, 71
Clavell, James, 142
Clayburgh, Jill, 374
Cleese, John, 5, 97, 146, 386
Clement, Jemaine, 242
Clements, Ron, 396
Clennon, David, 380
Clery, Corinne, 254, 447
Clive, Colin, 56, 146
Clive, E. E., 56, 199

Clive, John, 71
Clooney, George, 27, 131, 167, 334
Close, Del, 48–49
Close, Glenn, 226, 235
Clouse, Robert, 409
Cluzel, Raphael, 226
Coates, Kim, 37, 304
Coates, Lewis, 347
Coatman, Cindy, 156
Cobbs, Bill, 275
Coburn, James, 228, 269
Cochrane, Rory, 321
Cocks, Jay, 362
Coen, Franklin, 382
Coffey, Charlie, 117
Coffin, Tristram, 216
Coghill, Nikki, 387
Cohen, Etan, 188, 242
Cohen, J. J., 33
Cohen, Jon, 247
Cohen, Larry, 161, 207
Cohen, Rob, 360
Cohn, Roy, 295
Cokeliss, Harley, 423
Colantoni, Enrico, 154
Colbert, Bob, 173
Colbert, Nicholas, 36
Coldeway, Michael, 174
Cole, Lester, 199
Cole, Royal, 216, 293
Coleman, Dabney, 249, 422
Coles, Michael, 108
Coley, Thomas, 111
Colleary, Michael, 129
Collector, Robert, 241, 264
Collet, Christopher, 233, 287
Colley, Don Pedro, 385
Collins, Bootsie, 189
Collins, Joan, 120
Collins, Lynn, 209–10, 443
Collins, Roberta, 99–100
Collins, Stephen, 355
Collins, Suzanne, 184
Collins Jr., Clifton, 276, 394
Collison, Frank, 435
Collver, Mark, 379
Colosimo, Vince, 94
Colpaert, Carl, 194
Colton, John, 199
Coltrane, Robbie, 332
Columbus, Chris, 43, 169
Combs, Jeffrey, 150, 170, 299
Common, 376
Comport, Brian, 22

THE SCI-FI MOVIE GUIDE: The Universe of Film from "Alien" to "Zardoz"

H

THE SCI-FI MOVIE GUIDE: The Universe of Film from "Alien" to "Zardoz"

THE SCI-FI MOVIE GUIDE: The Universe of Film from "Alien" to "Zardoz"

THE SCI-FI MOVIE GUIDE: The Universe of Film from "Alien" to "Zardoz"

THE SCI-FI MOVIE GUIDE: The Universe of Film from "Alien" to "Zardoz"

THE SCI-FI MOVIE GUIDE: The Universe of Film from "Alien" to "Zardoz"

Wheeler-Nicholson, Dana, 69
Whigham, Shea, 298
Whishaw, Ben, 74
Whitaker, Forest, 37, 49, 281, 302, 342
White, Carol, 391
White, Julie, 395–96
White, Michael Jai, 412
White, Stiles, 217
Whitford, Bradley, 43, 61
Whitford, Peter, 98
Whitlock Jr., Isiah, 126
Whitlow, Jill, 265
Whitmore, James, 284, 378
Whitney, Grace Lee, 352
Whiton, James, 2
Whitta, Gary, 6, 50
Whittaker, James, 240
Whittaker, Jodie, 27
Wibberley, Cormac, 329
Wibberley, Marianne, 329
Wicking, Christopher, 323
Widen, Gregory, 178
Widmark, Richard, 369
Wiest, Dianne, 118
Wiggins, Wiley, 78
Wiig, Kristen, 277
Wilbur, Crane, 258
Wilcox, Fred M., 143
Wilcox, Ralph, 240
Wilcox, Robert, 108
Wilcox, Toyah, 211
Wilcoxon, Henry, 123
Wild, Katy, 127
Wildaker, Poul, 303
Wilde, Andrew, 267
Wilde, Olivia, 82–83, 176, 194, 399
Wilder, Billy, 216, 333
Wilder, Gene, 447
Wilder, Myles, 333
Wilder, W. Lee, 215–16, 333
Wildman, Valerie, 262
Wilhoite, Kathleen, 136
Wilke, Robert J., 403
Wilkinson, Charles, 295
Wilkinson, Tom, 125
Willcock, Dave, 297
Willes, Jean, 197
Will.i.am, 443
Williams, Billy Dee, 358–59
Williams, Bob, 402
Williams, Cindy, 158, 341, 409
Williams, Dick Anthony, 118
Williams, Douglas, 275

Williams, Grant, 123, 191–92, 251
Williams, Jesse, 61
Williams, JoBeth, 93
Williams, John, 125, 366
Williams, Kent, 386
Williams, Michael K., 308, 310
Williams, Michelle, 389
Williams, Olivia, 220, 287
Williams, Paul, 37–38, 333
Williams, Peter, 104
Williams, Robert, 306
Williams, Robin, 3, 43, 135, 312
Williams, Wade, 245
Williamson, Chase, 210
Williamson, David, 273
Williamson, Kevin, 130
Willingham, Noble, 136
Willis, Bruce, 21, 133, 229, 285–86, 368–69, 369 (ill.), 401
Wilmer, Douglas, 57
Wilson, Brian Anthony, 287
Wilson, David Campbell, 368
Wilson, Elizabeth, 192
Wilson, George, 26
Wilson, Ian, 95
Wilson, Joi, 86
Wilson, Lambert, 31
Wilson, Luke, 188–89
Wilson, Michael G., 284
Wilson, Owen, 21
Wilson, Patrick, 427
Wilson, Peta, 224
Wilson, S. S., 35, 327, 397
Wilson, Stuart, 267, 373
Wilson, Thomas F., 31–33
Wimmer, Kurt, 122, 343, 393, 409
Wincer, Simon, 93
Wincott, Michael, 12, 362
Windom, William, 26, 124
Windsor, Marie, 64–65
Winfield, Paul, 90, 350, 375
Wing, Anna, 445
Winger, Debra, 125
Winkless, Terence H., 263
Winnick, Katheryn, 298
Winnicka, Lucyna, 138
Winningham, Mare, 195
Winslet, Kate, 81, 107, 125
Winslow, Michael, 339
Winstead, Mary Elizabeth, 322, 380
Winston, Stan, 196, 225
Winter, Alex, 44–45
Winter, Vincent, 167
Winterbottom, Michael, 76–77

Winters, Jonathan, 325–26
Winters, Shelley, 293, 433–34
Wirth, Billy, 49
Wisdom, Robert, 129
Wise, Ray, 308, 369
Wise, Robert, 17–18, 96, 355
Wiseman, Joseph, 58
Wiseman, Len, 393
Wisher, William, 211
Withrow, Glenn, 264
Witney, William, 108, 237
Witt, Alexander, 304
Wittenbauer, John, 123
Wolfe, Ian, 385
Wolff, Frank, 427
Wollter, Sven, 319
Wong, B. D., 212
Wong, David, 210
Wong, Ellen, 322
Wong, Faye, 405
Wong, James, 272–73
Wong, Victor, 397
Woo, John, 103, 129, 262, 278
Wood, Christopher, 254
Wood, Ed, 206, 227, 236, 374
Wood, Elijah, 101, 125, 130, 144
Wood, Evan Rachel, 319
Wood, John, 422
Wood, Natalie, 54, 244
Wood, Sam, 248
Wood Jr., Edward D., 41, 56–57, 286
Woodard, Alfre, 145, 218, 353
Woodbine, Bokeem, 307, 393
Woodbury, Joan, 391
Woodley, Shailene, 107
Woods, Barbara Alyn, 69
Woods, Donald, 40
Woods, Jack, 335
Woods, James, 80, 136, 416
Woods, Ren, 57
Woods, Skip, 443
Woodthorpe, Peter, 127
Wooley, Sheb, 293
Woolf, Edgar Allan, 236
Wootton, Marc, 150
Worden, Hank, 409
Wordsworth, Richard, 296
Woronov, Mary, 68, 99–100, 265
Worth, Nicholas, 286
Worthington, Sam, 27–28, 28 (ill.), 376
Wray, Fay, 108–9
Wren, Doug, 33